European Intellectual Property Law

European Intellectual Property Law

TEXT, CASES AND MATERIALS

Annette Kur

Max Planck Institute for Intellectual Property and Competition Law, Munich, Germany

Thomas Dreier

Karlsruhe Institute of Technology, Karlsruhe, Germany

Edward Elgar
Cheltenham, UK • Northampton, MA, USA

Published by
Edward Elgar Publishing Limited
The Lypiatts
15 Lansdown Road
Cheltenham
Glos GL50 2JA
UK

Edward Elgar Publishing, Inc.
William Pratt House
9 Dewey Court
Northampton
Massachusetts 01060
USA

A catalogue record for this book
is available from the British Library

Library of Congress Control Number: 2012946662

MIX
Paper from
responsible sources
FSC
www.fsc.org   FSC® C013056

ISBN 978 1 84844 879 7 (cased)
     978 1 84844 880 3 (paperback)

Typeset by Servis Filmsetting Ltd, Stockport, Cheshire
Printed and bound in Great Britain by T. J. International Ltd, Padstow

Overview

Contents

Foreword

In the information society, the economic importance of intellectual property (IP) has grown tremendously in the last year, as has the complexity of its legal structure. This is particularly true for the European Union. Even specialists in one IP area often get lost or cannot manage to keep up with new developments in another IP area. Understanding European IP law is particularly difficult for non-EU citizens who are not familiar with the internal mechanisms of the European Union, its different legal traditions and the often complex overlay and interplay of EU and national norms. The same is true for EU and non-EU students, who want to obtain both an overview and gain a fundamental understanding of the subject matter which goes beyond a simple outline.

This book has been written in order to answer these needs. It is a handbook aimed primarily at students, but also at lawyers – Europeans as well as non-Europeans – who want to familiarise themselves with the fundamental structure and current state of the subject matter. Fundamental knowledge in IP law is useful, but not strictly required.

The book is not a Treatise in a classical sense, since in addition to the explanatory and summarising text it also contains a fair amount of original, verbatim text of original documents. However, because of the density of accompanying text written by the authors and the proportional distribution between text and materials, it differs from a traditional 'Cases and Materials' format: hence its subtitle 'Text, Cases and Materials'. This somewhat new and unusual form of presentation has to do with the sheer volume into which the subject matter of European IP law has grown in the past years, which would indeed have turned a true 'Cases and Materials' book into a rather heavy 'brick' difficult to carry around.

Having to make a selection from among the original documents to be included in the book, in most chapters the main focus was laid on excerpts from decisions by the Court of Justice of the European Union. That choice is owed to the authors' conviction that legal reality in the EU is starkly shaped by the Court's jurisprudence, most visibly in trade mark law, but with growing intensity also in other areas of IP law (with the current exception of patent law). Further sources cited in the original – apart from decisions by other judicial or quasi-judicial bodies such as the General Court and the Appeal Boards of the OHIM and EPO – primarily consist of official reports, comments and background papers that are available on the websites of the EU Commission or other European or international institutions. With few exceptions, the text does not quote from books or articles, and it also as a rule does not include references to literature in the footnotes. Instead, a list of books is provided in the bibliography, to which the interested reader is referred for further information and in-depth study.

Each chapter and subchapter of the book begins with an introductory text, makes references to legislative documents and relevant case law. At the end of each subchapter there are a number of questions. The purpose of these questions is twofold: first, they encourage the students to actively think about and discuss the issues presented. Second, they may serve as guidelines for the teacher to give some homework for students. In general, the questions may be answered by reflecting on the preceding text. But a more in-depth analysis might often require additional research by way of consulting preparatory materials, studies, scholarly articles and, as the case may be, European and/or national case law.

There is no need to study the book from beginning to end, although the first two chapters should be read first by people who are unacquainted with neither IP and/or the EU and its legal mechanism. The book can thus be used in whole or in part. Also, it can be used as the basis for studying the subject matter at various levels of detail.

Covering an area as wide as European IP law is an almost impossible task for only two authors. Hence, the authors first of all would like to express their deep gratitude to Dr. Stefan Luginbühl from the European Patent Office and author of *European Patent Law – Towards a Uniform Interpretation*, who was of great help in drafting the chapter on European patent law. Warm thanks also go to Rochelle Dreyfuss, who reviewed an early version of the book when its nucleus was first formed at the New York University/National University of Singapore joined NYU@NUS Dual Master's Program for Global Business Lawyers under the direction of Simon Chesterman. Of course, however, all errors and omissions inevitably contained in the book remain the authors' own responsibility. Furthermore, special thanks are owed to Susanna Licht from the Munich Max Planck Institute for preparing the tables and for bringing the manuscript in line with Elgar's author's guidelines. At Elgar, the editorial staff has to be thanked for their thorough work of turning the manuscript into the final book, as well as Luke Adams and Tim Williams for their patience with the authors.

Legislative developments were taken into account up to September 2012. The websites referred to in the book were all last accessed on 6 November 2012. After that date, new developments such as Directive 2012/28/EU on orphan works were only taken into account to the extent compatible with the advanced process of publication.

Finally, the authors would be grateful to their readers for any comment and suggestions for a – hopefully – future edition of the book.

Abbreviations

ACTA	Anti-Counterfeiting Trade Agreement
ALI	American Law Institute
ARIPO	African Regional Intellectual Property Organization
B2C, B2B	Business-to-consumer, Business-to-business
BASCAP	Business Action to Stop Counterfeiting and Piracy
BC	Berne Convention
BIEM	Bureau International des Sociétés Gérant les Droits d'Enregistrement et de Reproduction Mécanique
Biotech	biotechnological
BIRPI	Bureaux Réunis Internationales pour la Protection de la Propriété Intellectuelle
BIT	Bilateral Investment Treaty
BoA	Boards of Appeal (OHIM)
BOIP	Benelux Office for Intellectual Property
CBD	Convention on Biological Diversity
CD	Community Design
CDPA	Copyright, Designs and Patents Act
CELAS	Joint venture of the German GEMA and the UK MCPS-PRS
CFI	Court of First Instance (EU; now referred to as 'General Court')
CII	Computer-implemented inventions
CLIP	European Max Planck Group on Conflict of Laws in Intellectual Property
CoE	Council of Europe
CPC	Community Patent Convention
CPR	Community Patent Regulation
CPV	Community Plant Variety
CPVO	Community Plant Variety Office
CPVR Reg.	Community Plant Variety Rights Regulation
CPVR	Community Plant Variety Right
CTM	Community Trade Mark
CTMIR	Implementing Regulation to the CTMR
CTMR	Community Trade Mark Regulation
DCMA	U.S. Digital Copyright Millennium Act

DD	Design Directive
DG	Directorates-General
DPMA	German Patent and Trade Mark Office
DSD	Duales System Deutschland
dUPCA	draft Agreement on a Unitary Patent Court (not yet reported)
dUPR	draft Unitary Patent Regulation
DUS criteria	Art. 6 CPVR Regulation: distinct; uniform and stable
EC	European Community
ECHR	European Convention on Human Rights
ECJ	European Court of Justice
ECR	European Court Reports
ECSC	European Coal and Steel Community
ECtHR	European Court of Human Rights
EDL Foundation	Educate, develop, learn Foundation
EEA	European Economic Area
EEC	European Economic Community
EEUPC, PC	European and EU Patents Court Agreement
EFTA	European Free Trade Agreement
EP	European Parliament
EPA	Economic Partnership Agreement
EPC	European Patent Convention
EPJ	European Patent Judiciary
EPLA	European Patent Litigation Agreement
EPO	European Patent Office
EPOrg	European Patent Organisation
EU	European Union
EUR	Euro (€)
EURATOM	European Atomic Energy Community
FEIA	Spanish Foundation for the Progress of Arts
FLOSS	Free and open source software
FRAND	Fair, reasonable and non-discriminatory (terms)
FSS	Farm-saved seeds
FTA	Free Trade Agreement
GATS	General Agreement on Trade in Services
GATT	General Agreement on Tariffs and Trade
GDP	Gross domestic product
GEMA	Society for musical performing and mechanical reproduction rights
GI	Geographical Indication
HADOPI	Haute Autorité pour la diffusion des oeuvres et la protection des droits sur Internet

ICANN	Internet Corporation for Assigned Names and Numbers
ICC	International Chamber of Commerce
ICT	Information and communication technology
ILC	International Law Commission
InfoSoc	Information Society
INPADOC	International Patent Documentation Center
IP, IPR	Intellectual Property, Intellectual Property Right
IP5	The Five IP Offices
IPEA	International Preliminary Examination Authority
IR	Internationally registered
ISA	International Searching Authority
ISP	Internet service provider
IVIR	Institute for Information Law
JPO	Japan Patent Office
KIPO	Korean Intellectual Property Office
MA	Madrid Agreement
MCPS-PRS	Mechanical-Copyright Protection Society *and* Performing Right Society
MFN	Most Favoured Nation Treatment
MP	Madrid Protocol
MPI	Max Planck Institute
NGO	Non-governmental Organisation
OECD	Organization for Economic Co-operation and Development
OEM	Original Equipment Manufacturer
Ofcom	Office of Communications
OHIM	Office for Harmonization in the Internal Market (Trade Marks and Design)
OJ (C or L)	Official Journal of the EU (series C or L)
P2P	Peer-to-peer
PC	Paris Convention
PCT	Patent Cooperation Treaty
PDO	Protected Designation of Origin
PGI	Protected Geographical Indication
PLT	Patent Law Treaty
PVR	Plant Variety Right
R&DBER	Block Exemption on R&D Agreements
SACEM	Société des auteurs, compositeurs et éditeurs de musique
SCPA	Semiconductor Chip Protection Act
SCT	WIPO Standing Committee on the Law of Trademarks, Industrial Designs, and Geographical Indications
Sec.	Section

SIPO	State Intellectual Property Office of the People's Republic of China
SME	Small and medium enterprise
SPC	Supplementary Protection Certificate
SPLT	Substantive Patent Law Treaty
SQS	Supply Quota System
TCE	Treaty establishing a Constitution for Europe
TEC	Treaty establishing the European Community
TEEC	Treaty establishing the European Economic Community
TEU	Treaty on European Union
TFEU	Treaty on the Functioning of the European Union
TK	Traditional Knowledge
TLT	Trade Mark Law Treaty
TMD	Trade Mark Directive
TPM	Technological Protection Measures
TRIPS	Trade Related Aspects of Intellectual Property Rights
TRT	Trademark Registration Treaty
TTBER	Technology Transfer Block Exemption Regulation
UCC	Universal Copyright Convention
UCD	Unregistered Community Design
UCP	Unfair Commercial Practices
UDHR	Universal Declaration of Human Rights
UDRP	Uniform Dispute Resolution Policy
UK	United Kingdom
UN	United Nations
UNESCO	United Nations Educational, Scientific and Cultural Organization
UNFCC	UN Framework Convention on Climate Change
UPCA, UPC	(Agreement on a) Unified Patent Court
UPOV	International Convention for the Protection of New Varieties of Plants
UPR	Unitary Patent Regulation
USPTO	United States Patent and Trademark Office
VCLT	Vienna Convention on the Law of Treaties
WCT	World Intellectual Property Organization Copyright Treaty
WIPO	World Intellectual Property Organization
WPL	Working Party on Litigation
WPPT	WIPO Performances and Phonograms Treaty
WTO	World Trade Organization

Table of cases

EU Commission decisions

European Court of Human Rights

1

IP, IPRs and the international context

1.1 Introduction

European intellectual property (IP) law and the intellectual property rights (IPRs) granted within the European Union (EU) do not exist in a legal void. Rather, apart from being regulated by European law in the form of Regulations, Directives and Recommendations, they are shaped by the rationale which underlies the grant of exclusive rights to holders of IPRs with regard to 'their' IP as well as by the international legal framework. The latter binds the national and the European legislature alike and thus defines their room for political and legal manoeuvre. Also, it contains the fundamental principles which enable a legal system which is still based on the principle of territoriality as developed in the 19th century to function in the increasingly globalised world of the 21st century.

Before the functioning of institutional mechanisms of the EU and the place of IP law within the system of both primary and secondary EU law is presented in Chapter 2, this introductory chapter shall therefore briefly recall the nature of intellectual property and of intellectual property rights, outline the principles of international IP Law and give an overview of the current framework of international IP Conventions. This first chapter may thus refresh the memory of those who are already familiar with IP law, and it also lays the ground for those who for the first time encounter the subject matter of IP law in general and of European IP law in particular. Of course, within the framework of the present book and its focus on European IP law, this introductory chapter cannot provide an in depth analysis of either IP or international IP law. Rather, it can only briefly highlight some of IP's key characteristics and key elements of IPRs and the international legal IPR framework.

1.2 The nature of IP and IPRs

Concept and definition

'Immaterial' character of IP

Whereas material goods are composed of their physical substance, *immaterial* goods are characterised by their intangible or non-physical form. The immaterial goods which are protected by IPRs are mostly the product of a creative mental human activity in the industrial, scientific, literary and artistic fields. As their main examples they comprise – but are not limited to – intellectual creations (text, music, image), technical inventions, and signs used in commerce.[1] Of course, these intellectual creations are in most cases fixed in some tangible form, but the object which embodies the intellectual creation may not be confused with the intellectual creation itself. For example, a copy of a book is a material object as far as paper, binding and printing ink is concerned, but at the same time, the physical book embodies the non-physical literary work expressed by the letters fixed by the ink. Similarly, a washing machine is a tradable physical object, whereas the invention describing the way in which, for example, the drum is operated, is the immaterial good. The same is true with regard to the abstract sign and its physical imprint on the product.

The *property* aspect of immaterial goods that are protected by IPRs results from the fact that IPR legislation grants to the holders of IPRs the legal power to use and to exclude others from using the immaterial good in question in any way as defined by IPR legislation. In this way, IPRs in intangible objects are modelled after property rights in tangible objects. However, it should already be noted at this point that in spite of the similarities between property in tangible objects and IPRs protecting intangible objects, there are also differences, the most marked one of them being the limited time for which protection by IPRs is granted.[2] Moreover, as described later,[3] IPRs are much more concerned with balancing proprietary (exclusionary) and non-proprietary (non-exclusionary or access) interests than is traditional for property rights attached to physical objects. Hence, the property 'metaphor', although it has its justification in the exclusivity as the right's most distinguishing feature, is also somewhat limited and is even considered misleading by some commentators.

---

1 For additional immaterial goods which are protected by IPRs see Chapter 6.

2 Trade marks provide the main exception from that rule: Whereas registration is usually limited in time, it may be renewed infinitely, and the trade mark remains valid as long as it is (registered and) used on the market.

3 See in this chapter, section 1.2.2.1.

Types of rights and protection requirements

The following categories of intellectual property rights are usually distinguished:

- *copyright* pertaining to literary, artistic and scientific works;
- '*related rights*', (i.e., rights related to copyright) accorded to performing artists, producers of phonograms and broadcasting organisations; also known as *neighbouring rights;*
- *patents* granted for inventions;
- *industrial designs* protecting the 'eye appeal' of products;
- *trade marks* as well as other signs used in the course of trade to identify the commercial source of goods or services.

Other kinds of IPRs concern e.g. utility models (for 'petty patents'), new plant varieties, geographical indications as well as certain areas of unfair competition,[4] protection of undisclosed information (trade secrets), and protection for compilation of data (*sui generis* database protection). The number of IPRs is not finite; as new developments occur and markets react, new kinds of rights emerge and may eventually be added to the catalogue.

Although the details of legal regulation are a matter for national legislature, the fundamental features of protection requirements posed for the individual IPRs are largely the same in all countries. For example,

- in order to be patented, inventions must be *novel, inventive*, and *industrially applicable;*
- works must own some degree of *creativity* (or: *originality*) in order to attract copyright protection;
- trade marks must be *distinctive* in the sense that they identify and distinguish goods or services originating from one commercial source from those originating from another.

In addition to the substantive requirements listed above, some rights also need to be *registered* in order to obtain protection. This concerns in particular patents and trade marks, with the reservation having to be made with regard to the latter that the extent to which registration is required partly depends

---

4 In the meaning of Article 10 *bis* Paris Convention; see Chapter 7, 7.1 and 7.3.1.

on national legislation,[5] and is subject to certain international obligations.[6] The registration requirement also applies to most other industrial property rights such as industrial designs,[7] utility models, and plant variety protection. In contrast to that, no registration is required for copyright; on the contrary, it is even prohibited under the Berne Convention to make copyright protection dependent on formalities.

The distinction between registered and unregistered rights has several consequences: firstly, from the viewpoint of the individual applicant, registration rights require an additional activity and hence strategic planning in addition to the mere intellectual activity of, e.g., inventing. Secondly, the distinction has its bearings on both the internal structure of national as well as European IP laws and on the international IP treaty system. Regarding registered rights:

- *national* (or, in case of the EU: regional) law must provide for the necessary infrastructure (usually: by establishing and maintaining patent offices) – as well as for rules on how to apply for and register an IPR (i.e., provisions regarding the application itself as well as the examination and registration process, including appeals);
- on the *international* level, a demand exists to alleviate the burden to file in each individual state for which protection is sought by way of a separate application, e.g. by creating centralised or otherwise facilitated registration procedures, and by harmonising or streamlining the formal requirements posed by different national legislatures.

Regarding terminology, it should be noted that the use of 'intellectual property' as an all-encompassing term for all types of rights is not a self-evident matter. Historically, deriving from French parlance, 'intellectual property' (propriété intellectuelle) was often understood as relating to non-functional creations in the area of literature and the arts (copyright), whereas the term 'industrial property' was used to denote functional creations and IP used in industry (patents, trade marks, industrial designs, etc.). Traces of that nomenclature can still be found in official documents on the international or

---

5 For instance, under US law, trade mark rights are regularly acquired through use. In Europe, on the contrary, acquisition through registration is the rule, but Member States may additionally allow acquisition of rights through use.

6 On mandatory protection of unregistered, well-known marks under Article 6 *bis* Paris Convention see Chapter 4, 4.3.3.3.

7 In addition, the Community Design Regulation has introduced short-term protection for unregistered designs; see Chapter 6, 6.4.2.2.2

European level.[8] Finally, the term(s) used in non-English languages some-times lead to a slight shift of focus of the characteristics of IP and IPRs. For instance in Switzerland as well as in the Nordic countries, IPRs are addressed as "rights in immaterial goods" (Immaterialgüterrechte) or immaterial rights (immaterialrettigheder) thereby emphasising the aspect of the intangibility common to all objects protected by IPRs at the expense of the property aspect of the rights.

[?] QUESTIONS

1 Can you think of other immaterial human 'creations' which are not pro-tected by an IPR? What would be the reasons for the absence of IPRs in such cases?
2 What are the advantages and disadvantages of registration for IP rights?
3 What might be the reason for not making copyright protection depend-ent upon registration? Historically, has this always been the case? Also, in the current debate, it is sometimes suggested that copyright protection should also be made dependent on some form of registration, either right from the outset, or with regard to a second term after a (short) initial term of protection. What might be the reason for this idea and how can it be justified?
4 What is the name for IPRs in your country? Can you name reasons for the linguistic choice made by your national legislature?

Rationales and economic importance

Rationales for protection

There is more than one explanation for, or underlying rationale of, the exist-ence of IPRs. As briefly summarised in the WIPO Handbook on intellectual property:[9]

1.1 . . . Countries have laws to protect intellectual property for two main reasons. One is to give statutory expression to the moral and economic rights of creators in their creations and the rights of the public in access to those creations. The second is to promote, as a deliberate act of Government policy, creativity and the dis-semination and application of its results and to encourage fair trading which would contribute to economic and social development.

---

8 See ec.europa.eu/internal_market/indprop/index_en.htm and ec.europa.eu/internal_market/copyright/index_en.htm; see also www.wipo.int/about-ip/en.
9 WIPO Intellectual Property Handbook: *Policy, law and use*, 2nd ed. Geneva 2004, pp. 3–4, www.wipo.int/about-ip/en/iprm.

Moral and economic rights of creators can be justified on several grounds. Apart from the economic aspect to secure a dependable income to creators and their families, natural rights ideas also play a certain role. According to this view, the rights associated with IP are attributed to the inventor/creator because they 'belong' to him in some metaphysical justice-oriented sense, either because they are regarded – mainly with regard to copyright – as emanating from the creator's inalienable personality, or – more generally – as the fruit of his intellectual labour.

In contrast, the promotion of creativity and innovation, and as a consequence, of social welfare and consumer satisfaction, is largely economically motivated. From this perspective, the aim is to incentivise and reward investment made into creation and innovation. This is achieved by guaranteeing the first-mover a legally secured lead-time to recoup his investment made in order to come up with and market the invention or creation (including cost for unsuccessful research and cross-subsidies of the production of other less profitable, yet desirable goods). In achieving this, two important characteristics play a role which distinguish intangible from tangible goods. The first of these characteristics is their 'ubiquity'. In other words, an IP good is not confined to one particular place in time. Rather, it can be used and consumed at several places at the same time. The second of these characteristics is their 'non-rivalry'. In other words, use or consumption of an IP good does not exclude other users and consumers from using and consuming the same IP good at the same time, nor does it diminish its existence. This is markedly different from the rivalling consumption of – let's say – a non-ubiquitous apple.

In economic terms, the resulting lack of exclusivity with regard to the use and consumption of IP goods characterises them as 'public goods'. The problem with public goods – the classical example being the common pasture ground of a village – is that because of the lack of exclusivity, there tends to be under-investment in the creation and production together with over-use of the limited number of existing public goods (so-called 'tragedy of the commons').

As a consequence, according to economic theory, this tragedy can be avoided by creating an 'artificial' exclusivity for immaterial goods. Structurally, the exclusive rights thus granted to the holders of IPRs much resemble the rights granted as 'property' to material goods. They entitle the holder of an IPR to make use of the protected IP good and, at the same time, to exclude others from such use. However, the exclusivity thus granted comes with a cost. The problem is that in certain cases it may secure the IPR holder economically inefficient monopoly rents while at the same time excluding others, who might make good use of the IPR holder's protected IP. This, however, is equally inefficient. In addition, in certain cases protected IP might not be used at all if the IPR holder does not take steps to exploit his IP himself and if the initiative is not taken by third parties either, because the transaction costs of licensing (i.e., the cost of searching for the respective IPR holder, contacting him and negotiating a license agreement) are too high thus preventing the conclusion of a licensing agreement. Hence, a mirror-image to public goods with no exclusive rights attached (under-production and over-use), the exclusivity granted by IPRs bears the risk of over-production and under-use. In other words, too many people tend to invest into the creation of basically the same IP good, and the price to be asked for the IP goods produced and offered on the market excludes certain people who might be willing to use the particular IP good (so-called 'tragedy of the anti-commons').

From this it can easily be recognised that if in economic terms no protection on the one hand, and too much protection on the other hand are equally inefficient, what imports is the correct balance between exclusive rights and the freedom to use and consume IP goods. In sum, from an economic perspective, IPRs are a trade-off between too little and too much protection. Therefore, it is the task of both the legislature and the judges to strike the proper balance. Of course, this is not always easy in view of limited statistical data and the fact that it is not possible to repeat a certain economic development under exactly the same conditions but for a differently tailored IPR regime. A growing number of economists try to use a variety of economic models (mainly game theory, new institutional economics, behavioural economics) in the hope to obtain a better understanding of the complicated mechanisms of incentives, production, consumption, innovation and competition in the field of IP goods.

It adds to the complexity and urgency of the task that the concept of 'property' could be misguiding in certain ways. First, in many jurisdictions, the notion of (traditional) 'property' is based not on utilitarian (economic) concerns, but on natural law which as such does not need much further justification, if there is a need for justification at all. Second, and more importantly, the notion of 'property' generally insinuates a complete and total exclusive control rather than the result of a balance between conflicting proprietary interests on the one hand, and access and use interests on the other hand. In both cases, this has the grave consequence that exceptions to the exclusive rights, rather than the grant, are in need of justification. Moreover, in all likelihood 'property' receives stronger legal protection under constitutional law and fundamental rights than is the case with regard to the freedom to act on the grounds of limitations and exceptions to the exclusive rights. In view of this, the concept of 'property' – which perfectly suits the interests of IP-producing or mediating firms as well as of states which are net-exporters of IP – has been criticised by some scholars as an ideologically motivated metaphor which one-sidedly focuses on the interests of IPR holders. Without going into detail, two lines of arguments have been brought forward. One line of arguments points out that if it is true that the role of IPRs is to over-come a market failure which results from the public goods aspect of IP, then IPRs should only be granted up to the point to correct that particular market failure. Moreover, the focus on merely correcting market failure and main-taining competition where otherwise there would be no, or only distorted, competition therefore reverses the burden of justification. According to this view, the granting of the exclusive right would be in need of justification, and the exception would have to be regarded as the rule. However, for the time being both at the international and, in particular, the EU level, the 'property' metaphor and the logic resulting therefrom largely prevails, which is due not least to the economic importance of IP and IPRs in industrialised countries.

In sum, somewhat generalising, it can be said that there are both idealistic rationales for granting IPRs on the one hand, and utilitarian rationales on the other hand. Whereas the idealistic (or non-utilitarian) foundations of IPRs generally emphasise the link between the creator and his intellectual creation as the reason for granting IPRs, utilitarian theories focus on the effects which the use of IPRs has for society, such as regards innovation, competition and consumer satisfaction. Of course, in most jurisdictions the different ration-ales overlap. In spite of this, two distinctions can be noted in this respect: firstly, whereas non-utilitarian ideas are mostly to be found supporting the existing of authors' rights, utilitarian ideas prevail in the area of industrial property rights. Secondly, whereas in most continental European countries (in particular France, Germany, Italy, Spain and all other countries which in colonial times based their system on the laws of one of these states) authors' rights are largely based on idealistic theory, the rationale for Anglo-American copyright (UK, USA and all other countries which based their system on the laws of one of these states) is utilitarian.[10] This difference with regard to the rationale of protection has its effects on all aspects of legal protection, from conditions of protection to scope and remedies.

---

10 As best expressed in Sec. 8 (8) of the US-Constitution: 'The Congress shall have the Power . . . To promote the Progress of Science and useful Arts, by securing for limited Times to Authors and Inventors the exclusive Right to their respective Writings and Discoveries'.

Economic importance

The economic importance of IPRs already mentioned above, can be ascertained on both the macro and the micro level.

At the *macro* level they foster innovation and competition which in turn – so it is believed in view of some evidence – leads to employment, improves the gross national product and results in a higher per-capita-income. Already in the late 1970s and early 1980s of the 20th century, first statistical evaluations showed a 2–3 per cent of industrialised nations' gross domestic product (GDP) being generated by IP-related industries. The boost of the media sector and, in particular, the development of the software industries (computer programs have enjoyed copyright protection since the early 1990s) have led to a tremendous increase of this percentage (some 12 or more than 12 per cent of some countries' GDP). Today, intellectual innovative creations and the IPRs which protect them are the number one 'raw material' in the information and knowledge economy. It comes as no surprise that their legal protection is of paramount importance, in particular for all countries with a strong IP production. This is the main reason why IP and IPRs were 'discovered' in the 1990s as items of international trade, a development that culminated in the adoption of the WTO/TRIPS Agreement[11] and which still dominates the international debate today.

On the *micro* level, whereas in earlier years, the IP owned by a company often lay dormant, in particular if the company in question did not have a tradition of licensing, the role of IPRs as valuable company assets is by now generally recognised. For instance, it is said that the most valuable single item of the Coca Cola company is its trade mark, which surpasses in value the combined value of the production and distribution facilities. Not only can IPRs be used as generators of income and be valuable as such. Increasingly, they are regarded as an indicator for the innovative and creative strength and potential of a given company, thus determining the companies' market value.

? QUESTIONS

1 In your country, how could the prevailing rationale for IPRs best be described? Is there a difference with regard to intellectual and industrial property legislation?

2 In spite of the fundamental difference between the continental-European rationale for granting IP rights, which is largely natural rights-based, on

---

11 See in this chapter, section 1.4.3.

the one hand, and the Anglo-American rationale, which follows a marked utilitarian approach, how can it be explained that at the international level, there is not much disagreement between Europe and the USA with regard to the effort to achieve a rather high-level IP protection?

3 The debate about 'incentives' often obscures the fact that 'incentives' might be rather different with regard to individual inventors/creators and firms which employ inventors/creators or which commission works in order to market them. Can you elaborate on this distinction?

4 Proponents of open contents often make the argument that where there is no need to provide for additional incentives to create (e.g., with regard to poems, scientific literature, but also parts of fictional writing and news reporting) there would be no need for exclusive copyright. Is this a convincing argument? What interests might be infringed if such proposals were implemented? What alternative means of financing creativity can you think of?

1.3 Principles of international IP law

Preliminary remarks: sources of international law and treaty interpretation

It is obvious that international norms are not based on legislation in the usual sense; there is no such thing as an 'international lawmaker'. What is usually referred to as '(public) international law' is derived from two main sources:

- *international treaties and conventions*, including codes enacted by legislative bodies designated as such by the members of the treaty system within which they shall apply;
- *customary international law* (e.g. freedom of the high seas, immunity of foreign envoys, and legal principles common to mankind such as the protection of basic human rights).

In addition to that, binding consequences can ensue from decisions handed down by international courts within the framework of their competence.

Of those sources, the accent of international IP law lies on treaties and conventions. In that regard, IP law shares basic rules and principles with other fields that are also regulated in their international aspects by agreements concluded between sovereign nations. Most of those rules form part of customary law in the sense that they have been developed in long-standing practice and are generally accepted as providing a fair and solid framework for treaty-based cooperation among nations. In the 1960s, a thorough inventory of such rules was drawn up by the International Law Commission (ILC) of the United Nations (UN), and finally took the form of a draft treaty. As a result, the Vienna Convention on the Law of Treaties (VCLT)[12] was concluded in 1969 and went into force in 1980. Today, the VCLT counts 111 members, among them all EU Member States. In addition, countries which have not adhered to the VCLT basically acknowledge that it expresses rules which are part of customary international law, and which are therefore binding even in the absence of written obligations.

A centrepiece of the VCLT is the rule on treaty interpretation (Article 31 VCLT). In the first paragraph it is stipulated that:

> A treaty shall be interpreted in good faith in accordance with the ordinary meaning to be given to the terms of the treaty in their context and in the light of its object and purpose.

'Context' in the meaning of Article 31 VCLT comprises primarily the text of the treaty including the preamble and annexes, as well as agreements reached (or later-on accepted) by all the parties, or subsequent unanimous practices (Article 31 (2) and (3) VCLT). So-called supplementary means of interpretation, including the preparatory work of the treaty and the circumstances of its conclusion, can only be taken into account for the interpretation in order to confirm the meaning resulting from application of Article 31 VCLT, or, exceptionally, if the interpretation under Article 31 remains obscure or ambiguous, or would lead to manifestly absurd or unreasonable results (Article 32 VCLT).

The relevance of the VCLT in general and Article 31 in particular in the area of IP have risen considerably since the WTO Panels, in their assessment of alleged violations of the WTO/TRIPS Agreement, regularly point to the VCLT for their interpretation of the obligations incurred by the Member States.

 QUESTIONS

1 As pointed out above, it is basically universally acknowledged that the rules embedded in the VCLT apply even to states that have not adhered to the Convention. Does that appear plausible to you?

2 In their decisions interpreting provisions of the TRIPS Agreement, the WTO Panels often start by referring to the meaning of particular notions

---

12 See www.untreaty.un.org/ilc/texts/instruments/english/conventions/1_1_1969.pdf.

according to the Oxford dictionary. This was often criticised as too rigid and inflexible. In the light of Article 31 VCLT, would you say that the criticism is justified or unjustified?

3 Which other methods of treaty interpretation than the approach enshrined in Article 31 VCLT could you think of?

Specific features of IP conventions

Territoriality: the defining element of international protection

Probably the most important element of IP law defining the need and the structure of international protection is the principle of territoriality. According to this principle, IP rights are not universal, but are limited in their effect to the territory of the state under the laws of which they have been granted.

The principle has most likely been taken over from privileges which, although construed differently, can in many ways be seen as the precursors of modern IPRs. Since the first known record of a printing privilege granted by a European government in Venice in 1469, privileges were granted on an individual basis by the royal, ducal or other state authority entitling an individual person to perform certain acts within the territory of the respective state at the exclusion of anybody else. Today's principle of territoriality dates back to the 18th and certainly the 19th century, when territories and emerging nation states began drafting their first IP statutes. As far as registered rights are concerned, it follows from the Act of State Doctrine[13] that the effects of acts by national administrative authorities are limited to the territory of the respective state where the administrative authority is endowed with prescriptive power. The same is true regarding national IP legislation, which – like all national legislation – in general does not have extra-territorial effect.

However, this does not *per se* preclude nation states from recognising the effects which foreign legislation or foreign administrative authorities create within the boundaries of a particular foreign country. Such mutual recognition is the rule with regard to ownership titles to physical property, or the validity of passports issued by the competent foreign administrative authority. But in the area of IP law, such examples are rare. The closest parallel to

---

13 According to the Act of State Doctrine a nation is sovereign in the sense that it alone is competent to regulate within its own borders. From this it follows that domestic actions have no effect abroad unless the foreign state decides otherwise.

the mutual recognition of ownership in physical property can be found in the theory of 'universality' in copyright, which has motivated some countries to apply the law of the country of origin when determining first ownership in a work protected under copyright.[14]

The reason for the still prevailing emphasis of the principle of territoriality may be explained by political reasons. In the beginning, when only a small number of states granted legal protection for IP, states that didn't care or that explicitly decided against this option, did not want the effects of foreign IP laws to be extended to their own territory. Today, when most states are under an obligation to recognise at least some sort of IP protection,[15] the issue has become one of fine-tuning a state's national legislation to that state's particular economic, innovative, creative and consumptive needs. In other words, the principle of territoriality enables nation states to exercise an – albeit limited – freedom to adjust their IP policies and following their national IP laws to their particular national needs. These needs greatly differ between industrialised, newly industrialised or threshold countries and developing countries, between net exporters and net importers of IP-related goods and services.

As such, the principle of territoriality has the following consequences:

- All IPRs are of a national character, unless rights are created which take effect throughout a particular region, such as the EU;
- A right granted in one country, e.g., a patent granted by the patent office in country A, only has effect in country A, whereas the grant in country A does not confer any rights with regard to the patented invention in country B. Consequently, if the inventor wants to be protected in country A *and* B, he/she will, besides applying for a patent in country A, have to apply for a patent in country B as well. Moreover, absent a patent in country B, any third party is free to use the invention in country B, although it has been patented in country A. However, on the basis of his/ her patent in country A, even if the patentee has not taken out a patent in country B, he/she can nevertheless prevent the importation into country A of goods that have been legally produced by a third person in country B. This is so because exporting goods legitimately manufactured in country B to country A is, at the same time an act of importation into country A and hence – if done without authorisation by the holder of

---

14 For discussion see Chapter 9, section 9.3.2.2.

15 In particular the minimum rights which a state must grant according to the TRIPS Agreement in order to become a member of the WTO, see in this chapter, 1.4.1.2 and 1.4.1.3.

the patent in country A – infringes the distribution right granted to the patentee by the laws of country A.

Moreover, although this does not follow directly from the principle of territoriality, historically, it went hand in hand with it that with regard to granting IP rights, states made use of their general power to exempt foreign nationals from the application of their domestic laws. Consequently, in many cases absent an international Treaty or Convention to the contrary, foreigners are not protected or cannot obtain protection in another State, unless a state provides otherwise under its own national law.

Typical elements of international IP treaties

From what has just been said regarding the principle of territoriality and the general possibility to exclude foreigners from the benefits bestowed upon a state's own nationals by that state's national legislation, it also follows what sorts of issues are typically addressed by an international treaty with regard to a particular IPR:

- Member States have to declare under what conditions and to what extent they *promise to protect foreigners* who are nationals of another contracting State. In general, the principle which is most favourable to foreigners is the one of 'national treatment'. According to this principle, a state promises to protect foreigners in the same way it protects its own nationals.[16] However, international agreements may also be based on the principle of 'reciprocity'. According to that principle, protection is only extended to foreigners if the foreign state grants a similar or identical protection to the promising state's own nationals. The reciprocity may be 'formal' (i.e., based on the mutuality of the promise alone), or 'substantial' (i.e., be granted only if the substantive law of the other state is essentially similar or identical to the granting state's own national law).
- In order for the principle of national treatment to be not devoid of any practical effects with regard to the substantive level of protection, the treaty regularly contains certain *minimum rights* to be granted to the beneficiaries of the Conventions (regularly: foreigners) since otherwise they would have to rely on an eventually low level of protection for nationals.

---

16 Another principle, which originated in the area of tariffs is the principle of 'most-favoured nation', according to which 'any advantage, favour, privilege or immunity granted by a member to the nationals of any other country shall be accorded immediately and unconditionally to the nationals of all other members' (Article 4 TRIPS). Whereas the principle of national treatment aims at non-discrimination between individuals, the principle of most-favoured nation aims at non-discrimination between trading partners.

- Moreover, treaties must define the individual *beneficiaries* of the protection granted under the respective treaty. As a rule, these are all nationals of other Member States of the Treaty. However, other factors are also, or instead, defined, such as, e.g., the existence of a genuine and permanent business establishment in a Member State in the case of patents, trade marks and industrial designs, publication of a work within a member country in the case of copyright, or the place of a performance or fixation of a phonogram in the case of protection for neighbouring rights.
- In addition most, if not all, treaties contain *organisational provisions* and provisions on how to *change* them, as well as *transition rules* regulating how to treat IP created in newly acceding Member States before the date of accession.
- Some treaties also contain rules on *enforcement* of the treaty provisions vis-à-vis the Member States of the Treaty.

? **QUESTIONS**

1 In your opinion, what are the advantages and disadvantages of the principle of territoriality in IP law?
2 In the text, it is stated that the principle of territoriality enables nation states 'to adjust their IP policies and following their national IP laws to their particular national needs'. Could you elaborate on this statement? What about the policies of your home country in this respect?
3 In addition to 'national treatment' and 'formal'/'substantive reciprocity', some international treaties, in particular concerning international trade, encompass the principle of 'most-favoured nation'. Do you know what it means? Can you name examples? (See also below, 1.4.3.2.2)

Different types of treaties

Differentiation by membership (bilateral, multilateral and plurilateral treaties)

Whereas what has just been outlined in general applies to all transnational treaties in the area of IP, a distinction should be made between *bilateral, multilateral* and *plurilateral* treaties.

International IP law started with bilateral treaties. This, of course, had the disadvantage that each of these bilateral treaties had to be negotiated individually, that no two of them looked alike, and that their number threatened to explode if more states adhered to the system. Hence, as early as 1883 and 1886 with the Paris Convention and the Berne Convention two multilateral IP treaties were concluded which, together with a number of 'special agreements' concluded on that basis, have furnished the fundament on which the development of international IPR protection has thrived throughout most of the 20th century.

A shift of forum occurred when IPRs became an object for regulation in the context of international trade agreements, most notably by their inclusion in the WTO/TRIPS Agreement.[17] While the WTO system itself is multilateral, the move away from traditional fora has initiated a number of subsequent trade agreements, most of which are concluded in a bilateral form, such as Free Trade Agreements (FTAs), Economic Partnership Agreements (EPAs), or Bilateral Investment Treaties (BITs).[18]

A third type of international treaty system is characterised by the fact that it is only conceived for being established among a limited number of countries. Most frequently, such *plurilateral* treaties are concluded among countries within a particular geographic region, such as Europe, South America (e.g. Mercosur, Andean Pact) or Africa (e.g. ARIPO). Others are limited by the common interests and policies pursued by the countries participating in the negotiations. This was the case in particular with regard to the recently concluded Anti-Counterfeiting Trade Agreement (ACTA).

Differentiation by legal objectives

International IP agreements are further distinguished by their legal objective. WIPO's index of international treaties[19] lists the following categories:

- *Intellectual Property Protection Treaties* define internationally agreed basic standards of intellectual property protection in each country;
- *Global Protection System Treaties* ensure that one international registration or filing will have effect in any of the relevant signatory states; and
- *Classification Treaties* create classification systems that organise information concerning inventions, trade marks and industrial designs into indexed, manageable structures for easy retrieval.

Important examples of such treaties are presented below.

---

17 See in this chapter, section 1.4.3.
18 See in this chapter, section 1.5.3.2.
19 See www.wipo.int/treaties/en.

Administration of IP treaties

Most international treaties in the field of IP are administered by the World Intellectual Property Organization (WIPO). WIPO was founded in 1967[20] and became operative in 1970 as a specialised agency of the United Nations Organization[21] with the task of promoting the protection of intellectual property throughout the world. *Inter alia*, WIPO provides a forum for the negotiation of new, and amendments of existing intellectual property agreements and it carries out studies in preparation of such endeavours. Also, WIPO fulfils a number of administrative tasks in the framework of the current treaty system, in particular regarding international registration of patents, trade marks and industrial designs. The Organisation has its main seat in Geneva.

WIPO's dominance as the institution negotiating and administering intellectual property treaties was challenged by the conclusion of the Agreement on Trade Related Aspects of Intellectual Property Rights (TRIPS) as an annex to the World Trade Organization (WTO) Agreement. Amendments and other changes to be introduced in the WTO treaty and its annexes are negotiated in the framework of so-called ministerial rounds. The administration of TRIPS proper, in particular the monitoring of the operation of the agreement, lies in the hands of the Council for TRIPS (or TRIPS Council). *Inter alia*, the TRIPS Council can be consulted by WTO Members in all TRIPS-related matters. Furthermore, the Council shall entertain cooperation agreements with WIPO. Indeed, in view of the limited resources of the WTO regarding IP-related matters, the cooperation with WIPO is very close in practice.[22] Like WIPO, the WTO and its constituencies are located in Geneva.

In addition to the two major institutional actors just mentioned, a number of other institutions are also involved in the administration of international intellectual property agreements. This concerns *inter alia* the United Nations Educational, Scientific and Cultural Organization (UNESCO) in its role as the administrator of conventions in the field of copyright[23] and neighbouring

---

20 Before the establishment of WIPO, the tasks resulting from administration of international agreements in the field of intellectual property were handled by the United International Bureaux for the Protection of Intellectual Property (Bureaux Réunis Internationales pour la Protection de la Propriété Intellectuelle, BIRPI), with headquarters in Berne.

21 Convention Establishing the World Intellectual Property Organization, signed at Stockholm on 14 July 1967 and as amended on 28 September 1979, http://www.wipo.int/export/sites/www/treaties/en/convention/pdf/trtdocs_wo029.pdf.

22 See the Agreement between WIPO and the WTO (22 December 1995), www.wipo.int/treaties/en/agreement/trtdocs_wo030.html.

23 Universal Copyright Convention, concluded in Geneva (6 September 1952), with annexes. The UCC was concluded as an alternative to the Berne Convention, with minimum requirements that were less strict than

rights.[24] In the field of industrial property, the International Union for the Protection of New Varieties of Plants (UPOV) was established in 1961 with the aim to provide and promote an effective system of plant variety protection.[25] While formally independent, UPOV's administrative tasks are *de facto* handled by WIPO.

A number of institutions and agencies are active in the field on a regional level, e.g. the European Patent Organisation.[26] For practical purposes, the Office of Harmonization for the Internal Market (OHIM)[27] which grants Community Trademarks and Community Designs is of importance, but it is an administrative body of the EU and not an organisation on the basis of an international or regional agreement.

? QUESTIONS

1 Whereas WIPO's mission is 'to promote innovation and creativity for the economic, social and cultural development of all countries, through a balanced and effective international intellectual property system', WTO is 'dealing with the rules of trade between nations'. To what extent are these missions different? What is meant in the text above where it says that the cooperation of WIPO and WTO has been described as 'very close'?

2 Although its focus on culture and hence on copyright and neighbouring rights protection to creators and performing artists, the role of UNESCO in the area of IP has never been very strong. What could be the reasons for this?

1.4 Major IP conventions

The Paris and Berne Conventions

Coverage and structural commonalities

Historically, the universe of intellectual property was strictly divided into the hemispheres of industrial property – patents, trade marks, unfair com-

those contained in the latter. For instance, in contrast to the Berne Convention, it is not prohibited under the UCC to require registration as a prerequisite for copyright protection.

24 Convention for the Protection of Producers of Phonograms against Unauthorized Duplication of their Phonograms, concluded in Geneva, 29 October 1971; International Convention for the Protection of Performers, Producers of Phonograms and Broadcasting Organizations, concluded in Rome (26 October 1961).

25 International Convention for the Protection of New Varieties of Plants, adopted in Paris, 1961. For the protection of plant varieties in Europe, see Chapter 6, section 6.2.

26 See www.epo.org/about-us/organisation.html.

27 See www.oami.europa.eu.

petition – on one side and copyright on the other. Accordingly, the Paris Convention (1883)[28] and the Berne Convention (1886)[29] are distinguished by the subject matter covered – the Paris Convention encompasses industrial property, whereas the Berne Convention covers copyright in a strict sense, i.e. the right of authors to their literary or artistic creations ('works').

In spite of the differences in coverage, both Conventions are characterised by a number of structural commonalities. In particular, both rely on the principle of *national treatment* (see above), which is enshrined in Article 2 (1) Paris Convention and Article 5 (1) Berne Convention respectively:

Article 2 (1) Paris Convention:

> Nationals of any country of the Union[30] shall, as regards the protection of industrial property, enjoy in all the other countries of the Union the advantages that their respective laws now grant, or may hereafter grant, to nationals; all without prejudice to the rights specially provided for by this Convention. Consequently, they shall have the same protection as the latter, and the same legal remedy against any infringement of their rights, provided that the conditions and formalities imposed upon nationals are complied with.

Article 5 (1) Berne Convention:

> Authors shall enjoy, in respect of works for which they are protected under this Convention, in countries of the Union[31] other than the country of origin, the rights which their respective laws do now or may hereafter grant to their nationals . . .

In addition to that, both Conventions provide for certain *minimum rights* that Member States are obliged to grant to the beneficiaries.[32]

Minimum rights in the Paris Convention

Of primary importance among the minimum rights granted in the Paris Convention is the fundamental principle of *priority*, which is set forth in Article 4 of the Paris Convention. It operates as follows: once an application

---

28 See www.wipo.int/treaties/en/ip/paris.

29 See www.wipo.int/treaties/en/ip/berne.

30 The term 'Union' designates the community of members of the (Paris) Convention.

31 See the previous footnote: in the context of the Berne Convention, 'Union' stands for the members of the Berne Convention.

32 For a definition of the beneficiaries, see (also) Articles 3 of the Berne Convention and 3 of the Paris Convention.

has been filed with the competent authorities in one country within the Paris Union, the date of that initial filing is taken, within a certain time period,[33] as the relevant filing date for the purpose of filing the same application in any of the other Member States. Consequently, any subsequent filing in any other country party to the Paris Convention will not be invalidated by reason of any acts accomplished in the interval (in particular another filing or the publication or exploitation of an invention or an industrial design). Moreover, such acts cannot give rise to any third-party rights.[34]

Whereas the priority principle applies to all industrial property rights, other minimum rights guaranteed by the Paris Convention are specific for particular IP categories. Only a few of those minimum rights are listed here:

- Regarding *patents*, Article 4 *ter* of the Paris Convention stipulates that the inventor is entitled to be named as such in the patent application. Furthermore, Article 5 A ensures that a patent which is only imported into the country of protection without being worked locally may not be cancelled ('forfeited') for that reason, but may solely, under certain conditions, become the object of compulsory licences that Member States are generally entitled to grant for reasons of public policy, Article (5 B of the Paris Convention);
- With regard to *trade marks*, Article 6 *bis* of the Paris Convention enshrines an obligation for courts and authorities in other Member States to protect marks without registration against appropriation or use by others, if it is already *well-known* in the country concerned that the mark belongs to a person who is entitled to the benefits of the Paris Convention. Article 6 *quinquies* A of the Paris Convention stipulates that a trade mark which is validly registered in the country where the owner has its seat or an establishment must be accepted for registration in the same form (French: *'telle quelle'* = 'as is') in other Member States, unless it falls short of particular protection requirements that Paris Convention Members are entitled to impose pursuant to Part B of the provision.

Minimum rights and limitations in the Berne Convention

The Berne Convention contains a rather comprehensive range of minimum rights, such as translation (Article 8), reproduction (Article 9), adaptation (Article 12), and many more. As a corollary to that rather detailed kind of

---

33 For patents and utility models, the period within which priority can be claimed is 12 months; for trade marks and industrial designs, it is six months.

34 See Article 4 (A) (I) of the Paris Convention.

norm-setting, the Berne Convention also sets forth the conditions under which the rights may (or must) be limited. The most prominent examples for such limitations and exceptions are the quotation right (Article 10 (1)), which is one of the rare cases of internationally mandatory limitations, and the three-step test[35] detailing the conditions under which the reproduction right may be restricted (Article 9 (2) of the Berne Convention). Contrary to the Paris Convention, which does not undertake to define the subject matter which must be protected, the Berne Convention demarcates its scope of application by providing in Article 2 of the Berne Convention a catalogue of work categories for which copyright must be granted in all Member States.

The structure and contents of the Berne Convention are deeply influenced by the concept of copyright as a natural right of the personal creator of literary or artistic works. Several provisions reflect this author-centred way of thinking. Thus, the minimum term of protection for works is measured according to the author's lifetime (50 years after the death of the author). As it is the act of creation itself that is considered to give rise to protection, the Berne Convention bans any formal protection requirements such as registration (Article 5 (2)). Lastly, and most importantly, Article 6 *bis* establishes the obligation for all Member States to protect the *moral rights* of authors to claim ownership and to object to mutilation or distortion, or to other modifications of their works which are detrimental to the author's honour or reputation.

? QUESTIONS

1 The Berne Convention is much more concerned with minimum rights than the Paris Convention. What might be the explanation for this?
2 Also, the Paris Convention contains the so-called 'right of priority' (Article 4 A-I of the Paris Convention). Why is no such right to be found in the Berne Convention?

Special agreements based on the Paris and Berne Conventions

Both the Paris and the Berne Convention provide for the possibility of Member States to conclude special agreements *inter se* (Article 19 of the Paris Convention; Article 20 of the Berne Convention). In the framework of such agreements, Members remain bound to the rules set out in the basic Conventions. In Article 20 of the Berne Convention, it is even expressly stipulated that to conclude special agreements is only permissible in so far as

---

35 For the three-step test under TRIPS see also in this chapter, section 1.4.3.2.4.

such agreements grant to authors more extensive rights than those granted by the Berne Convention or contain other provisions not contrary to it.

Special agreements in copyright

As the Berne Convention only accords protection to authors, i.e. persons who have created a work of art or literature, the particular needs of those who 'bring a work to life' by performing it or otherwise enabling its communication to the public are not encompassed thereby. For the protection of such intermediaries, a separate treaty was established in 1960 – the *Rome Convention* for the Protection of Performing Artists, Producers of Phonograms and Broadcasting Organizations.[36] Performing artists are protected against the unauthorised fixation of their performances, the unauthorised broadcasting of live performances and the reproduction of recordings of their performances that were made without consent or for different purposes; phonogram producers are primarily protected against unauthorised reproduction of phonograms, and broadcasters can prohibit the rebroadcasting or fixation of content as well as the reproduction of unauthorised fixations.

Of particular relevance in the area of copyright and neighbouring rights are the special agreements concluded in 1996 about the rights of authors, performers and phonogram producers in the digital environment, the WIPO Copyright Treaty (WCT) and the WIPO Performances and Phonograms Treaty (WPPT) as well as the *Beijing Treaty on Audiovisual Performances* of 2012.[37] Those treaties are addressed below, section 1.5.2.1.

Special agreements on industrial property rights

In the field of industrial property, a number of special agreements were concluded with the aim to establish *centralised international registration proceedings* and/or to *facilitate certain administrative* aspects with regard to those proceedings.

Centralised registration is typically carried out via the *International Bureau* established at WIPO. The conditions and effects of international registration are regulated in the relevant Conventions:

---

36 See www.wipo.int/treaties/en/ip/rome.
37 See www.wipo.int/treaties/en/ip/wct and www.wipo.int/treaties/en/ip/wppt; www.wipo.int/treaties/en/ip/beijing.

- the *Madrid system* for the international registration of trade marks, consisting of the Madrid Agreement (1891) and the Madrid Protocol (1989);[38]
- the *Patent Cooperation Treaty* (PCT, 1970),[39] which – in addition to providing a central application for patent protection – also entrusts certain authorities with the issuance of an international search report and, upon request, a preliminary examination, and
- the *Hague Agreement*[40] on the international registration of industrial designs.

While the details vary, all systems have in common that registration on the international level has the same effect as if the application had been filed nationally. The operation of international registration of patents and trade marks with effect in Europe is addressed in Chapters 3 and 4.

Without prejudice to international registration, Paris Convention Member States are basically free to regulate their own domestic registration procedures, and to impose specific procedural requirements on foreign or non-resident applicants. It lies therefore in the interest of entrepreneurs engaging in international business activities to harmonise and streamline those procedures, for instance by promulgating an exhaustive list of formalities (such as evidentiary documents) that Member States may require, but cannot go beyond. Examples of such treaties are the Trade Mark Law Treaty (TLT, 1994), and its successor, the Singapore Treaty (2006) as well as the Patent Law Treaty (PLT, 2000).

Finally, some treaties serve to harmonise classification and its terminology, i.e. they provide schemes according to which applications and registrations of IP rights can be divided in specific sub-groups ('classes') for purposes of administration[41] and search. Such schemes are established by the Nice, Locarno and Strasbourg Classification Agreements for trade marks, industrial designs and patents respectively.[42]

---

38 See www.wipo.int/treaties/en/registration/madrid and www.wipo.int/treaties/en/registration/madrid_protocol.

39 See www.wipo.int/treaties/en/registration/pct.

40 See www.wipo.int/treaties/en/registration/hague.

41 For instance, classes usually serve for the calculation of fees: the more classes are comprised in an application, the higher the fees that must be paid.

42 See, respectively, www.wipo.int/treaties/en/classification/nice, www.wipo.int/treaties/en/classification/locarno and www.wipo.int/treaties/en/classification/strasbourg.

1 Why have the issues dealt with in special agreements not been integrated into the general agreements?
2 Can you imagine why it was considered worthwhile to streamline the formal requirements for registration in the Patent Law Treaty (PLT) and the Trademark Law Treaty (TLT)/Singapore Treaty?
3 What is the practical impact of harmonising classification by way of international treaties?

TRIPS

Background

Originating from the early years of industrialisation, the Paris and Berne Conventions had to be adapted several times to the economic and technical developments in order to remain compatible with the relevant legal challenges. Throughout the first half of the 20th century, a number of such revision conferences were summoned and mostly led to positive results. However, in the 1960s and early 1970s, the end of this period was reached: the last successful revision conferences were concluded, in the case of the Paris Convention, in 1967 (Stockholm), and – in the case of the Berne Convention – in 1971 (Paris). During the period of the Cold War and, in particular, during the block-building following the process of decolonisation at the beginning of the second half of the 20th century, as well as the ensuing radicalisation in the 1970s, and the emergence of China as yet another player on the global scene (which all resulted in markedly differing opinions as to how development and trade should be regulated), it proved increasingly difficult, and ultimately impossible, to reach consensus on any substantial amendment to either convention. This led to growing discontent and increasing frustration of industrialised countries and IPR holders. In reaction to this, the USA began to negotiate IP issues within a trade environment and concluded a number of free trade agreements (FTAs) with some East-Asian and later on also eastern European States which were considered as having largely benefitted from free riding on foreign IP. In these agreements, the bilateral partners were made to subscribe to a rather high level of IP protection in exchange for certain trade advantages. Subsequently, at the initiative of both the US and European as well as Japanese industries, the issue of effective international protection of IP was introduced as part of the Uruguay Round of GATT[43] negotiations. The main argument for this move was that

---

43 General Agreement on Tariffs and Trade.

a response was urgently needed to the rising surge of pirated and counterfeit goods distorting international trade flows.

The forum shift from WIPO to GATT led to the desired result: when the WTO Agreement was concluded in Marrakesh in 1994, the Agreement on Trade-Related aspects of Intellectual Property Rights (TRIPS) became an integral part of the Treaty.[44]

Structure and contents

Overview

From a negotiation point of view, the advantage of integrating IP into a broader framework is that it opens up a much greater room for concessions than is the case in negotiations which are confined to IP alone. Within the WTO-negotiations, this led to a trade-off between the promise by industrial-ised countries to lower import restrictions on agricultural goods on the one hand, and the promise by developing countries to provide for high-level IP protection on the other.[45] As a result, the standards of internationally man-datory protection for IPR were elevated to a much higher level than what had been prescribed by the Paris and Berne Conventions. This is usually described as the 'Paris-' and 'Berne-Plus' approach of TRIPS: in Articles 2 (1) and 9 (1) respectively, the substantive provisions of both Conventions are explicitly encompassed in their most recent versions so as to form an integral part of TRIPS (except for the protection of moral rights). In addition to that, the minimum rights prescribed in the Paris Convention and Berne Convention are enhanced, and new obligations are imposed, in a manner reflecting by and large what has emerged over the years as the accepted standard in industrialised countries. Developing countries and in particu-lar threshold countries such as Brazil, Chile, Argentina and India tended to object, arguing that a general upgrade of protection levels was not needed in order for TRIPS to fulfil its declared aim of bolstering the fight against counterfeiting and piracy. However, the coalition of industrialised countries stood firm, and the counterarguments did not get through.

---

44 TRIPS is Annex 1 C to the WTO Agreement.

45 It is, of course, another matter that developing countries, especially if they have made serious attempts to bring their national IP laws in line with the TRIPS standard, feel 'cheated' in view of the continued state sub-ventions of agricultural production both in the USA and in Europe.

Part I of TRIPS: general provisions; principles and objectives

Part I of TRIPS lays down certain general rules and principles. The national treatment principle, which is set out in Article 3, is complemented by the Most Favoured Nation Treatment (MFN) according to which Member States must extend trade benefits that were granted to certain trading partners also to other members of the Agreement.

The objectives and principles are set out in the preamble as well as in Articles 7 and 8 TRIPS. Regarding the *objectives* on which TRIPS is based, Article 7 sets out that:

> The protection and enforcement of intellectual property rights should contribute to the promotion of technological innovation and to the transfer and dissemination of technology, to the mutual advantage of producers and users of technological knowledge and in a manner conducive to social and economic welfare, and to a balance of rights and obligations.

Article 8 defines the *principles* which must be observed for the application of the Agreement:

> 1. Members may, in formulating or amending their laws and regulations, adopt measures necessary to protect public health and nutrition, and to promote the public interest in sectors of vital importance to their socio-economic and technological development, provided that such measures are consistent with the provisions of this Agreement.
> 2. Appropriate measures, provided that they are consistent with the provisions of this Agreement, may be needed to prevent the abuse of intellectual property rights by right-holders or the resort to practices which unreasonably restrain trade or adversely affect the international transfer of technology.

Although it is conditioned by the requirement of compatibility with 'the provisions of this Agreement', Article 8 is not without its proper weight, as became evident in the Doha process (see below, section 1.5.3.1).

Substantive minimum requirements

Part II of TRIPS contains minimum standards concerning the availability, scope and use of individual IPRs. *Inter alia*:

- regarding *copyright*, computer programs and databases are added to the catalogue of works eligible for protection under the Berne Convention (Article 10);
- regarding *trade marks*, a definition of protectable subject matter is added (Article 15); the rights to be granted to well-known marks are enhanced (Article 16 (2), (3)), and TRIPS members are prohibited from unreasonably encumbering the use of trade marks (Article 20);
- *patents* must be granted in all fields of technology, including pharmaceutical products, and the right must be enjoyable without discrimination as to the field of technology or the place of production (Article 27); compulsory licenses are made subject to detailed conditions (Article 31);
- *geographical indications* must be protected against any misleading use; for wines and spirits, absolute protection must be granted irrespective of the risk of the public being misled.

Apart from further details regarding the above-mentioned rights, *Part II* of TRIPS also addresses industrial designs, layout-designs (topographies) of integrated circuits as well as undisclosed information. Furthermore, by way of granting Member States an option rather than imposing minimum rights, it also details the conditions under which license contracts may be considered as anti-competitive.

The three-step test

Of particular importance among the substantive provisions in *Part II* of TRIPS is the so-called three-step test (set out in Article 13, 17, 26 (2), and 30 TRIPS), which addresses and confines the possibilities for Member States to legislate on limitations and exceptions to IPRs. The test originates from Article 9 (2) of the Berne Convention, where it demarcates the limits of admissible derogations from the reproduction right accorded to authors in Article 9 (1) of the Berne Convention. In TRIPS, the test applies – with slight variations, as outlined in the following chart – to all kinds of IPRs, and, in copyright, to all kinds of rights accorded not only to an author, but to all right-holders.

The structure and wording of the test in the different areas of IP are shown in Table 1.1, below.

Although the test might only have been intended as a safeguard against an erosion of exclusive rights against all too far-reaching limitations and exceptions (developing countries may even have regarded the test as a clause 'enabling' them to maintain existing, and introduce certain new exceptions), IPR

Table 1.1 Different formulations of the three-step test in TRIPS

Patents (+ industrial designs)	Trade marks	Copyright
Members may provide *limited exceptions* to the exclusive rights conferred. . .	Members may provide *limited exceptions* to the rights conferred by a trade mark	Members shall confine limitations or exceptions to exclusive rights to *certain special cases*
provided that such exceptions do not *unreasonably conflict with a normal exploitation* and do not *unreasonably prejudice* the legitimate interests of the [right-holder], taking account of the legitimate interests of *third parties*	(such as fair use of descriptive terms) provided that such exceptions *take account of the legitimate interests* of the owner of the trade mark *and of third parties*	which do not *conflict with a normal exploitation* of the work and do not *unreasonably prejudice* the legitimate interests of the right-holder

holders have subsequently tried to give it a rather strict interpretation. The restrictive attitude was basically confirmed by two WTO-Panel decisions addressing Article 30 (patents) and Article 13 (copyright) respectively.[46] In particular, it was held as a basic axiom by both panels that all three steps must be passed separately and cumulatively, meaning that if one single step is missed, the test is failed in its entirety. As the panels have also held that on the first step, the notion of 'limited exceptions' or 'certain special cases' must be interpreted as allowing only for 'small diminutions' of the IPR in an absolute sense, without normative aspects being taken into account, it may occur that limitations are 'sorted out' without any consideration of the importance and weight of the policy objectives underlying the provision at stake. Furthermore, the copyright panel has argued with regard to the guarantee of 'normal exploitation' (second step) that it does not matter whether or not a right is actually exploited in the relevant manner, thereby creating the impression that all possible (future) modes of use are to be taken into account for the determination of what is considered as 'normal'.

Procedural measures and sanctions; registration proceedings

As said above, the declared aim of introducing IPR protection as a topic for trade negotiations was to enhance the efficiency of measures taken against

---

46 See also the two WTO panel decisions *Canada-Patent* (WT/DS114/R of 17 March 2000) and *US-Music* (WT/DS160/R of 15 June 2000), which both gave the test a somewhat narrow reading, limiting Member States' room for national legislation. For discussion of the three-step test as transposed by the EU in Article 5 (5) of Directive 2001/29/EC, [2001] OJ L 167/10, see Chapter 5, sections 5.3.2.5.3.

counterfeiting and piracy, which have thrived ever since the growing sophistication and falling costs of copying techniques. Since those problems cannot be addressed by elevating the protection standards under substantive law alone, *Part III* of TRIPS contains a detailed description of obligations of WTO Member States to provide for effective enforcement rules, regarding civil and administrative procedures, provisional measures, border measures, and criminal proceedings. In particular:

- enforcement procedures must be efficient and shall not be unnecessarily costly or complicated; judicial review of administrative decisions must be granted; sanctions in civil and administrative proceedings must include, in addition to permanent injunctions and damages, also other remedies such as disposal of infringing goods outside the channels of commerce, without compensation being paid to the infringer;
- preliminary measures must be available for the purpose of preventing infringements or securing evidence; in urgent cases, this must be possible without the other party being heard;
- criminal procedures and penalties must be available at least in cases of wilful trade mark counterfeiting or copyright piracy on a commercial scale.

Procedural issues of a different kind are addressed in *Part IV* of TRIPS, which deals with the acquisition and maintenance of IPRs. Consisting only of one provision (Article 62), *Part IV* lays down some mandatory rules in order to make sure that the application and registration of rights is not unduly burdensome, costly or time-consuming.

Dispute prevention and settlement; transitional arrangements; final provisions

The implementation and application of the Rules laid down in the TRIPS Agreement is regulated in *Part V* (Articles 63 and 64) as follows:

- Firstly, Member States meet in regular intervals in the so-called Council for TRIPS; here, Member States report on their domestic implementation of the TRIPS provisions, and they may also ask other Members about the process and degree of TRIPS-compliance.
- Secondly, alleged violations of the TRIPS Agreement are subject to the WTO Dispute Settlement procedure. Here, a major change from the old to the new GATT rules comes into play: whereas before 1995, a dispute settlement report only became binding, if all parties agreed to it, it now only will *not* be binding, if the parties agree to that. In other words, whereas in former times the infringing party could always block the

adoption of a report, it is now in the hands of the infringed party which has initiated the dispute settlement proceedings to decide whether it will go ahead with a favourable report. Moreover, the dispute settlement rules set a rather tight time frame. Most important, however, under the new GATT cross-retaliation is now allowed if a party does not abide to the terms of a binding dispute settlement (meaning that certain privileges can be suspended vis-à-vis the infringing Member in areas other than the one in which the infringement occurred). In practice, this often increases the pressure on the infringing state's legislature, to bring its national law in line with the WTO TRIPS standard.[47]

In *Part VI*, the transitional periods are set forth. Developing countries and countries in transition from regulated economy to market economy had to abide by the TRIPS rules until 2000; the transition period for least developed countries was first set at ten years, but was subsequently prolonged until 2013. Moreover, least developed countries can make a duly motivated request for a further extension. Furthermore, regarding the obligation to grant patent protection for pharmaceutical products, the 2001 Doha Declaration on TRIPS and Public Health had already extended the period for least developed countries to comply with the relevant provisions on to 2016.

? QUESTIONS

1 Criticism has been made that TRIPS provides for a minimum level of protection which reflects the protection standard of industrialised countries, but which would not be appropriate for developing and even less for least-developed countries. In response to this, TRIPS provides for transition periods for both developing and least-developed countries (Articles 65 and 66 TRIPS), complemented by technical assistance (Article 67 TRIPS). Does that criticism make sense to you?

2 The obligation of Member States not to 'unreasonably encumber' the use of trade marks (Article 20 TRIPS) has become topical in connection with 'plain packaging' legislation that would prohibit displaying any figurative elements on cigarette packages. Would you consider such legislation to be TRIPS-compliant?

3 Under the Paris Convention Member States were free to subject patents to a so-called local working requirement, meaning that compulsory

---

47 Although it be noted that this doesn't always work out as the non-compliance of the US with the Panel Report in *US-Music* (WT/DS160/R of 15 June 2000) has demonstrated, where the US, rather than changing Sec. 110 (5) of their domestic Copyright Law, pays the compensation fixed, although paying a compensation for non-compliance should only be a temporary solution.

licenses could be issued for domestic firms if the patent holder did not produce the invented technology in the country of protection. Do you think such a rule would be compatible with Article 27 TRIPS? What would be the reasons for abolishing/maintaining the possibility to introduce a local working requirement into national patent law?

4 With regard to copyright, upon insistence of the US and against the proposal made by the EU, authors' moral rights do not form part of the minimum standard to be granted under TRIPS. Can you imagine why?

1.5 Post-TRIPS developments

Appraisal of results; ensuing policies

Nearly 20 years after the conclusion of TRIPS, one would expect that an appraisal of the results would yield a clear and objective answer to the question whether the Agreement has entailed positive results; in particular, whether the prospects of (relative) economic growth and increased technical innovation have actually materialised. However, the answer largely depends on the perspective of the person(s) consulted. From a right-holder's point of view, which largely also determines the position taken by industrialised countries, it is argued that raising the standard of substantive law due to TRIPS obligations has been beneficial for a major number of countries, and that even better results could be achieved if more protection were granted, and if enforcement became more efficient and deterrent. That position is also reflected in a range of bilateral or plurilateral trade agreements that were concluded in the post-TRIPS era.

Contrary to that, for those taking sides with the majority of developing and least developed countries TRIPS has failed its promises, and the situation is getting worse due to repeated pressure in the framework of bilateral negotiations to accept even stronger protection standards. Similar discontent is articulated by growing parts of the civil society in industrialised countries. In addition to pointing out that the constant upgrading of protection standards hampers the poorer countries' legitimate attempts to adapt the level of domestic IP protection to their own state of development, it is argued that too strong protection encumbers contemporary forms of creativity and information exchange, and stifles innovation where it is not primarily market-driven, but rather aims to generate optimal social benefits.[48]

---

48 See in particular the 'Washington Declaration on Intellectual Property and the Public Interest', infojustice. org/washington-declaration, where the current concerns are expressed in a comprehensive manner, leading to the conclusion that 'public interest advocates (must) make a coordinated, evidence-based case for a critical re-

While the coalition between developing countries and civil society groups is less homogeneous, and its influence on law-making is generally inferior to that of established industries and their political allies, there are signs indeed that the era of intellectual property maximisation may eventually come to an end. Such signals can be found e.g. in the fact that most efforts undertaken under the auspices of WIPO to conclude major 'TRIPS-Plus' Agreements have failed. Furthermore, both WIPO and the WTO have expressed their commitments to the special needs of developing countries by adopting development-oriented agendas, which – in the case of TRIPS – have led to a first amendment of the Agreement in order to encompass the demand of developing and least developed countries for access to medicines.

In the following, a brief account is given of the relevant activities and policies.

Follow-up activities at WIPO

Treaties and recommendations

When the final TRIPS text was conceived in its final version (1992), digital communication was still unknown or at least its full potential was not understood. TRIPS, therefore, does not include any provisions addressing the pertinent issues. This is of particular concern for copyright, where the possibility of worldwide dissemination of content by the simple click of a button poses an existential threat to right-holders. The matter was considered as urgent, and thus, as early as the end of 1996, two new treaties were adopted under the auspices of WIPO, the WIPO Copyright Treaty (WCT)[49] and the WIPO Performances and Phonograms Treaty (WPPT).[50]

The common aim of both treaties is to bring copyright and neighbouring rights into line with demands of digitisation and the internet. As their core elements, the treaties include:

- an exclusive right of authorising any communication of protected content to the public, including the making available to the public in such a way that members of the public may access the protected content from a place and at a time individually chosen by them ('making available right');

---

examination of intellectual property maximalism at every level of government, and in every appropriate institutional setting, as well as to pursue alternatives that may blunt the force of intellectual property expansionism'.

49 See www.wipo.int/export/sites/www/treaties/en/ip/wct/pdf/trtdocs_wo033.pdf.

50 See www.wipo.int/export/sites/www/treaties/en/ip/wppt/pdf/trtdocs_wo034.pdf.

- an obligation for Member States to prohibit circumvention of technical protection measures or removal of digital rights management information.

WCT and WPPT are 'special agreements' in the meaning of Article 20 of the Berne Convention and are open to all Members of the Berne Convention, but have, of course, not been adhered to by all of them.

A third, parallel treaty proposal on *sui generis* protection for databases, which was modelled after the European protection scheme adopted by Directive 9/96/EC,[51] however, fell through in the same year, mainly due to the resistance of natural scientists. Adoption of yet another proposal concerning the protection of audiovisual performances, which was designed to complement the legal protection of performers with regard to phonograms as granted under the WPPT, had initially failed at a Diplomatic Conference at the end of the year 2000, because Europe and the US could not agree on what happens with the rights of performers once a performer has agreed to the inclusion of his performance in an audiovisual fixation. However, after the negotiations had resumed, the treaty was finally concluded at a Diplomatic Conference in June 2012. The resulting Beijing Treaty on Audiovisual Performances[52] brings audiovisual performers for the first time into the fold of the international copyright framework in a comprehensive way which comprises both analog and digital uses made of their performances. Besides economic rights and rules on how to share the proceeds between producers and performers, the Beijing Treaty also grants performers moral rights to prevent lack of attribution or distortion of their performances.

Regarding broadcasting organisations, it is equally intended to arrive at an international instrument regarding their legal protection in the digital age. However, the work has been complicated by the fact that the legal status which internet broadcasters should obtain is still rather unclear.[53]

Also, no success was achieved with regard to proposals for a new Substantive Patent Law Treaty (SPLT), which would have constituted a major step towards further worldwide harmonisation of patent law. *Inter alia*, no agreement could be reached on the issue of whether Member States should be

---

51 See Chapter 5, section 5.2.2.5. The USA did not have – and still does not provide for – comparable *sui generis* protection to databases.
52 See www.wipo.int/treaties/en/ip/beijing.
53 See www.wipo.int/copyright/en/activities/broadcast.html and www.wipo.int/copyright/en/limitations/index.html.

able to, or even be obliged to, require that the geographical origin of genetic material on which an invention is based must be indicated in the patent application, by failure of which the application is rejected (or the patent is invalid). However, consent was achieved at least with regards to streamlining and harmonising the formalities of application and registration procedures, leading to the adoption of the Patent Law Treaty (PLT) in 2006.[54]

A treaty with similar objectives was concluded in the area of trade mark law in 1994 (TLT).[55] A new version of the Treaty was adopted in 2006 (Singapore Treaty).[56] Several Joint Recommendations addressing trade mark issues were also negotiated in the framework of the WIPO Standing Committee on the Law of Trademarks, Industrial Designs, and Geographical Indications (SCT) and were adopted by the WIPO Assemblies.[57] These Recommendations concern the protection of famous and well-known marks, protection of signs in case of internet uses, and the recordal of licenses.[58] While they are only soft law, the Joint Recommendations are of considerable political relevance, because they often form a point of reference in bilateral trade agreements.

Finally, to be mentioned in this context is the fact that WIPO has become a major venue for regulation of domain name disputes under the Uniform Dispute Resolution Policy (UDRP), which was adopted by ICANN[59] in 1999.

The WIPO Development Agenda

As a reaction to the growing criticism against a – perceived – rights-holder biased approach by WIPO and other international organisations, WIPO launched its 'Development Agenda' in 2007, with the aim of enhancing the development dimension of the Organisation's activities. Based on a number of proposals received from Member States and interested NGOs, 45 recommendations were formulated and grouped into six clusters,[60] one of which

---

54 See www.wipo.int/treaties/en/ip/plt.
55 See www.wipo.int/treaties/en/ip/tlt.
56 See www.wipo.int/treaties/en/ip/singapore.
57 See www.wipo.int/about-ip/en/development_iplaw.
58 See www.wipo.int/export/sites/www/about-ip/en/development_iplaw/pdf/pub833.pdf (Recommendation on the protection of well-known marks) and www.wipo.int/about-ip/en/development_iplaw/pdf/pub845.pdf (protection of signs on the internet). The Joint Recommendation on recordal of licences was subsequently included in the Singapore Treaty (2006).
59 Internet Corporation for Assigned Names and Numbers, www.icann.org.
60 See www.wipo.int/ip-development/en/agenda/recommendations.html.

is geared towards norm-setting, flexibilities, public policy and the public domain.

A number of initiatives within WIPO are linked to that cluster. In particular, limitations and exceptions, which were hardly ever in the focus of previous work undertaken by WIPO, have become an important target of attention. *Inter alia*, detailed studies in all fields of IPR are conducted with the aim to add transparency in the field and possibly provide for regulation models or even for internationally mandatory 'ceilings' (i.e., rules limiting IPR protection worldwide). In the copyright context, mandatory limitations are currently debated with regard to securing participation and access to protected content by the blind and visually impaired.[61]

Another issue ranking high on the Development Agenda concerns the effort to craft adequate protection for traditional knowledge, genetic resources and traditional cultural expressions/folklore.[62] A considerable amount of energy has been devoted to the issue, without, however, leading to tangible results as yet.

Post-TRIPS developments in the arena of international trade law

The Doha Round

Negative reactions against the allegedly one-sided approach favouring the interests of developed countries were also strongly felt in the WTO context. In order to soothe the concerns, the Doha Round of WTO negotiations (since 2001) adopted as its declared aim the so-called Doha Development Agenda. The objectives pursued were set out in a Ministerial Declaration adopted at the Fourth Ministerial Conference at Doha, in November 2001.[63] Regarding intellectual property rights, it was stated that the development dimension should be taken into full account for the implementation of the agreement in the light of its objectives and principles.[64]

The topic most prominently featuring in public debates about intellectual property at the time concerned the impact of the patent system on access to essential medicines in developing and least developed countries stricken by pandemics such as HIV/AIDs, malaria and tuberculosis. Pursuant to Article

---

61 See www.wipo.int/copyright/en/limitations/index.html and www.visionip.org/portal/en/index.html.
62 For details see www.wipo.int/tk/en.
63 'Ministerial Declaration' (20 November 2001), WT/MIN(01)/DEC/1, adopted on 14 November 2001.
64 Paragraph 2 of the Doha Ministerial Declaration.

27 in conjunction with Article 31 (f) TRIPS, it was no longer possible for countries like India to fulfil its previous role as the 'pharmacy of the Third World' by supplying (relatively) cheap pharmaceuticals to countries without their own manufacturing capabilities. Recognising that the situation posed a serious problem with regard to the devastating health crisis that had befallen some of the poorest countries in the world, in particular in Sub-Saharan Africa, and that a solution had to be worked out urgently, the Ministerial Conference issued its 'Doha Declaration',[65] by which the Council for TRIPS was instructed to find an expeditious solution to the problem. In August 2003, the mandate led to a waiver declared by industrialised countries to exercise their relevant rights under TRIPS, and, in December 2005, to the inclusion of a new Article 31 *bis* TRIPS by which the waiver shall become permanent.[66]

Bilateral trade agreements; ACTA

Apart from the success achieved with regard to the specific aspect addressed above, the Doha Round has basically stalled. Realising the difficulties encountered at the ministerial conferences in Seattle, Cancun and Hong Kong, the USA again resorted to including IP issues in a new round of Free Trade Agreements (FTAs) concluded with several developing countries but also with major trading partners such as Australia. The rules on IP contained in these bilateral agreements may well become the point of reference for a future multilateral agreement.

The EU has also concluded a number of Economic Partnership Agreements (EPAs), which envisage progressive regulatory approximation of the partner countries' legislation and practices to the EU *Acquis* in the most important trade-related areas, amongst them IP.[67] Most often, this is done by way of 'transplantation' of domestic (European) rules into the legal systems of trading partners, with special emphasis being placed on enforcement legislation modelled on the European Enforcement Directive (2004/48/EC).

Enforcement issues were also at stake when Europe, the USA, Japan and several other – mostly industrialised – nations began to secretly negotiate an Anti-Counterfeiting Trade Agreement (ACTA). Initially limited to improve

---

65 WT/MIN(01)/DEC/2 (14 November 2001).

66 Until now, the necessary number of ratifications has not been reached, and thus Article 31 *bis* TRIPS has not entered into force. However, as the waiver remains in force, this does not change the situation in practice.

67 For further information regarding bilateral trade relations of the EU, see http://ec.europa.eu/trade/creating-opportunities/bilateral-relations.

the fight against counterfeit trade mark goods, the proposed text was subsequently enlarged to cover other IP rights as well. In view of the mounting pressure of both some individuals and NGOs, the plans finally had to be made public. Since the main focus of this Agreement is on enforcement of IP rights, it shall further be discussed in Chapter 8, section 8.5.

IPRs in other fora

Long gone is the time when IPRs were largely considered as a 'niche issue' known and debated only by specialists, being remote from, and of little interest to, the rest of the world. Nowadays, IPRs are at the centre of – mostly controversial – discussions in all kinds of fora. Accordingly, other international instruments than those dealing with IP proper make reference to, or have effects upon IPRs. This is notably the case for the Convention on Biological Diversity (CBD), adopted in Rio de Janeiro in June 1992.[68] Pursuant to Article 16 (5) CBD, IP 'should be used to support, and not to run counter to, the objectives of the Convention'. Furthermore, Article 8 (j) CBD proclaims that utilisation of biodiversity, for instance by patents, should require involvement and approval of those who provided the genetic material or traditional knowledge on which the achievement was based, and that equitable benefit sharing should be encouraged. The issue was further addressed in the Nagoya Protocol adopted in 2011.[69]

IP has also raised attention in the context of the UN Framework Convention on Climate Change (UNFCC).[70] Concerns are voiced in particular by developing countries that 'green technology' should remain available at low price, to foster greater dissemination. The role of patents and possible instruments securing access in particular situations are examined in that context, without leading to any clear and uncontested suggestions.

Finally, IPRs have become an object of debates – and most often a target for criticism – in connection with human rights in all their different aspects, concerning access to medicines, nutrition, education and information. Vice versa, political debates also emphasise that IPRs have 'property' value and therefore also enjoy protection as a fundamental right. Resulting from this juxtaposition of rights is the permanent need to find the right balance as a primary task for legislatures and authorities.

---

68 For the text of the Convention see www.cbd.int/convention/text, and for background information and details www.cbd.int.
69 See www.cbd.int/abs/text.
70 For information, see unfccc.int/2860.php.

? **QUESTIONS**

1 What subject matter not yet dealt with either by the Paris and the Berne Convention nor by TRIPS might be covered by post-TRIPS international or bilateral activities?

2 What are the advantages and disadvantages of a multilateral international treaty as opposed to bilateral treaties? What are the main reasons for concern about the current trends towards bilateralism?

3 To what extent can the Convention on Biological Diversity (CBD) serve as the basis of, or least be a justification of, the fight against so-called 'bio piracy'?

4 What is your opinion about the proposition to include 'ceilings' in the international conventions so as to prevent any further expansion of international or even national IP protection? What are the possible benefits and drawbacks? Which type of ceilings could be imagined?

5 Why is it so difficult to integrate traditional knowledge, genetic resources and traditional cultural expressions (TK) into the framework of international protection of IP rights? What elements would a TK Convention have to contain?

2

IP in the European legal framework

2.1 Introduction: treaties, aims and institutions

From Rome to Lisbon

The European Economic Community (EEC) was established in 1957, when the Founding Treaty was signed together with the EURATOM Treaty. As the signature ceremony took place in Rome, both treaties are also referred to as the 'Rome Treaties'. Already in 1951, the European Coal and Steel Community (ECSC) had been created as the first of the three basic European treaty systems. Being concluded shortly after World War II, the goal of the ECSC was to reconstruct the economies of the European continent, prevent war in Europe and ensure a lasting peace. Similarly, the preamble to the EEC Treaty (TEEC) sets out that it aims to 'preserve peace and liberty and to lay the foundations of an ever closer union among the peoples of Europe'.

More specifically, the founding members of the EEC sought to tighten the economic links between them and to foster prosperity by establishing a common market. Initial steps towards that goal were the creation of a customs union with a common external tariff, and the formulation and implementation of common policies with regard to agriculture, transport and trade. Market integration was subsequently enhanced on the basis of the Single European Act (1986) which required that the Common Market became a Single Market by the end of 1992. In 1993, with the Treaty of Maastricht, the European Economic Community changed its name to 'European Community', and, together with the ECSC and EURATOM,[1] formed the three pillars of the European Communities (EC).

---

1 The executive organs of the three treaty system had been combined already in 1967 on the basis of the 'Merger Treaty' so as to form a common institutional structure.

In the 1990s, it became obvious that the structure of the system had to be modified in order to become more efficient and to comply with democratic decision procedures. Steps in that direction were taken in the Treaties of Amsterdam (1997) and Nice (2001). Parallel to that, a new Constitutional Treaty was promulgated (Treaty establishing a Constitution for Europe, TCE) which would have replaced the EC Treaties with a single text addressing fundamental rights, voting rules, and other basic structural elements of the system. However, the TCE was abandoned after it had been rejected by plebiscites held in the Netherlands and in France. In spite of the failure, the aim to arrive at substantial reforms was not given up, and renewed efforts resulted in the Treaty of Lisbon, which was signed in 2007 and entered into force on 1 December 2009.

According to the preamble to the Lisbon Treaty the primary motivation for concluding the reform project lay in the wish:

> to complete the process started by the Treaty of Amsterdam and by the Treaty of Nice with a view to enhancing the efficiency and democratic legitimacy of the Union and to improving the coherence of its action.

As important elements serving those aims, the Lisbon Treaty:

- switches from required unanimity to majority vote in the Council with regard to several policy areas;
- strengthens the role of the European Parliament in the legislative process; and
- institutes a long-term President of the European Council and a High Representative of the Union for Foreign Affairs and Security Policy.

The Lisbon Treaty contains many of the elements originally set out in the TCE. However, instead of setting forth a single text, the Lisbon Treaty consists of three separate instruments:

- the EU Treaty,[2]
- the Treaty on the Functioning of the European Union (TFEU),[3] complemented by a number of protocols and annexes, and
- the Charter of Fundamental Rights of the European Union.[4]

---

2 Consolidated version of the Treaty on [the] European Union, [2010] OJ C 83/13.
3 Consolidated version of the Treaty on the Functioning of the European Union, [2010] OJ C 83/47.
4 Charter of Fundamental Rights of the European Union, [2010] OJ C 83/389.

Both the EU Treaty and the TFEU set out rules concerning the aims, institutions, competences and procedures applying in the EU, while they are different in their contents and structure. While the EU Treaty addresses the fundamental norms and principles governing the EU policies and activities, thereby setting the general framework, the TFEU contains the provisions implementing that framework and is therefore more detailed and practice-oriented.

A number of changes brought about by the EU Treaty and the TFEU also have an impact on intellectual property matters, as will be pointed out at the relevant instances in this book. Least important – but nevertheless confusing – among them is that the provisions of the previous Treaties have been renumbered, and that the Treaties themselves as well as some institutions – in particular the Court of Justice – have changed their names. Those changes are addressed in the following where they become relevant. Regarding the Treaties, the term 'Treaties' or 'Basic Treaties' is used when reference is made to issues occurring under the EEC, EC and EU/TFEU Treaties. Otherwise, the acronym for the respective Treaty (TEEC, TEC or TEU respectively TFEU) is employed.

Institutions

The institutional framework set out in the Basic Treaties comprises three key players:[5]

- the *Council* represents the governments of the Member States;
- the *Commission* represents the Community; and
- the *Parliament* represents the citizens.

The tasks of those institutions have remained essentially the same, although the division of competences has been rearranged quite substantially in the course of the shift of powers from the Council to the European Parliament. The Commission, the Parliament and the Council act together when new legislation is passed (see in this Chapter, 2.3.1.2). Quite importantly, the Commission also has a watchdog function regarding violations of the Basic Treaties and other (secondary) Community legislation. It is therefore competent *inter alia* for the monitoring and injunction of conduct violating the competition provisions of the Treaties, thus acting as a Community competition authority.

---

5 More institutions have been joined to the system, in particular the European Central Bank and the Court of Auditors.

As a fourth player of seminal importance, the Court of Justice (ECJ; since 2009: Court of Justice of the European Union[6]), exercises judicial control. The Court has its seat in Luxembourg.[7] Its structure, tasks and competences are set out in Articles 251 *et seq.* TFEU. In summarised form, the tasks can be described as follows:[8]

The ECJ:

- reviews the legality of the acts of the institutions of the European Union;
- ensures that the Member States comply with obligations under the Treaties; and
- interprets European Union law at the request of the national courts and tribunals.

Since 1989, the institution of the Court of Justice has been complemented by the Court of First Instance (CFI; now: General Court[9]).[10] The General Court is competent *inter alia* for reviewing the legality of acts of bodies, offices or agencies of the Union intended to produce legal effects *vis-à-vis* third parties, which includes review of decisions taken by the Office for Harmonization in the Internal Market (OHIM) regarding Community Trade Marks and Community Designs, decisions by the Community Plant Variety Office (CPVO), and injunctions and other measures issued by the Commission against private parties. Judgements of the General Court can be appealed in points of law to the Court of Justice.

Two types of decisions by the Court of Justice are particularly important for the development and understanding of European intellectual property law:

- First, preliminary rulings in case that a national court or tribunal in proceedings pending before it has doubts as to the interpretation of EU law: in such a situation the court or tribunal may (and a court of last instance must) refer that question to the ECJ. The answer given by the Court to those questions is binding with regard to the interpretation; however, the competence to decide the case on its merits rests with the national instances.[11]

---

6 For convenience and consistency, the acronym ECJ is used throughout the text as a designation for the Court of Justice.

7 For information see www.curia.europa.eu.

8 See curia.europa.eu/jcms/jcms/Jo2_6999.

9 In the following, the term 'General Court' is used throughout the text.

10 The system was further extended in 2004, when the Civil Service Tribunal was created as a specialised department within the Court of Justice.

11 Article 177 EEC; Article 234 TEC; Article 267 TFEU. The conditions under which national courts of last

- Second, appeals against orders issued by the Commission against conduct by private parties by which the competition provisions of the Basic Treaties are violated,[12] as well as, since enactment of the respective Community rights, appeals against decisions of the General Court concerning Community trade marks or Community designs.

The actual relevance and impact of ECJ jurisprudence varies between the different fields of IP law. For now, its relevance is highest in trade mark law, but other areas are also increasingly shaped by case law, as will be pointed out in the individual chapters.

Membership; relationship with EFTA and EEA

Treaty membership and successive enlargements

The founding members of the EEC Treaty were the three Benelux countries, France, Italy and Germany, also referred to as the 'inner six'. Denmark, the United Kingdom and Ireland were the first to join in 1973, followed by Greece (1981), Portugal and Spain (1986). Another wave of accessions brought the former EFTA States Austria, Finland and Sweden into the Communities (1995). Ten new Members, mostly from central and Eastern Europe, acceded in 2004: Cyprus, the Czech Republic, Estonia, Hungary, Latvia, Lithuania, Malta, Poland, Slovakia, and Slovenia. With the accession of Bulgaria and Romania in 2007, membership has risen to 27 States. Croatia is the next state to join (2013). Further applications for membership are pending from Macedonia, Montenegro and Iceland.

EFTA and EEA

When the EEC was concluded by the 'inner six', the European Free Trade Agreement (EFTA) was established in 1960 by the 'outer seven': Austria, Denmark, Norway, Portugal, Switzerland, Sweden and the UK, being joined later on by Finland and Iceland. The aim of EFTA was to create an alternative to the EEC in the form of a free trade zone, but without a uniform external tariff and without establishing common policies with regard to agricultural or maritime products.

---

instance must refer the case to the ECJ are specified in case C-283/81, *CILFIT and Lanificio di Gavardo SpA* v. *Ministry of Health*, [1982] ECR 3415.

12 Decisions by the ECJ and, after 1989, by the General Court regarding appeals against Commission orders based on the competition provisions of the EEC/EC Treaties are primarily considered in Chapter 7, section 7.2.3.

After Denmark and the UK as well as Portugal adhered to the EC and Austria, Finland and Sweden were preparing their accession in the mid-1990s, three of the remaining EFTA Members – Iceland, Liechtenstein and Norway – entered into an agreement with the EEC to establish the European Economic Area (EEA). Together with the EU, the EEA forms an enlarged free trade zone. EEA Member States are obliged to implement the EU *acquis*, that is they must bring their legislation in accordance with Community Directives, and must apply the same fundamental principles as are enshrined in the Basic Treaties. Jurisdiction regarding violations of the EEA Treaty is vested in the EFTA Court, which also has its seat in Luxembourg.

2.2 Intellectual property rights and the Basic Treaties

Free movement of goods and services

Issue and legal basis

As cornerstones for establishing a common market, the Basic Treaties have enshrined what is commonly referred to as the 'Four Freedoms', that is the free movement of :

- goods,
- services,
- persons, and
- capital.

The principle of free movement of goods was (and is) expressed in Article 30 TEEC (Article 34 TFEU)[13] as follows:

> Quantitative restrictions on exports, and all measures having equivalent effect, shall be prohibited between Member States.

However, Article 36 TEEC (Article 36 TFEU)[14] allows derogating from that rule under certain conditions:

> [The principle of free movement of goods] shall not preclude prohibitions or restrictions on imports . . . justified on grounds of [*inter alia*] the protection of industrial or commercial property. Such prohibitions or restrictions shall not,

---

13 Likewise: Article 28 TEC.
14 Likewise: Article 30 TEC.

however, constitute a means of arbitrary discrimination or a disguised restriction of trade between Member States.

Inevitably, the goal to ensure free movement of goods over national borders within the common market is liable to clash with the principle of territoriality governing intellectual property law. The fact that patents, trade marks, and also rights protected under copyright law are basically valid and enforceable separately within the boundaries of individual states implies the possibility for a right-owner to oppose the importation and marketing of goods to which the right pertains. Intellectual property rights have indeed made their appearance on the European scene first in the context of what is usually referred to as the parallel import cases:[15] proprietors of trade marks or other intellectual property rights tried to enjoin independent traders from buying goods, at a low price, in one Member State in order to market them in another state where the price level maintained by the proprietor and/or the dealers authorised by him was much higher.

In reaction to those practices, the ECJ has addressed fundamental issues in the relationship between the property rights concerned and the freedom to compete by marketing the same or similar goods within Europe. Although mostly dating from an early phase of European integration, those decisions have retained their importance.

Early case law: from Grundig to Deutsche Grammophon

The first dispute in which the conflict between intellectual property and free movement of goods became topical concerned a rather atypical constellation. An agreement had been concluded between the German firm Grundig and its French representative Consten, by which Consten was granted the right to register in its own name the trade mark GINT (Grundig International) to be used for radio receivers, TV sets and other similar devices on the French market. The goods were manufactured by Grundig in Germany. Part of the production was sold on the German market; another part was exported to France, being sold exclusively through Consten. Although German retailers had been prohibited by contract to deliver the goods to France, a company unrelated with Grundig or Consten nevertheless managed to buy products under the trade mark GINT from German traders and offered them for sale in France. Consten filed a claim for infringement and succeeded in the first instance. Having been alerted of the case, the Commission intervened,

---

15 ECJ Case 15/74, *Centrafarm v. Sterling Drug*, [1974] ECR 1147; Case 16/74, *Centrafarm v. Winthrop*, [1974] ECR 1183; Case 51/75, *EMI Records v. CBS*, [1976] ECR 811.

holding that the agreement between Grundig and Consten affected the trade between Member States and hence infringed Article 85 TEEC (now: Article 101 TFEU). Grundig and Consten appealed, arguing *inter alia* that the Commission's decision violated Article 36 TEEC, which must be read in the light of Article 222 TEEC, pursuant to which the rules of property ownership existing in the Member States shall not be encroached upon. The ECJ found, however, that:

> Article 36 . . . cannot limit the field of application of Article 85. Article 222 confines itself to stating that the 'Treaty shall in no way prejudice the rules in the Member States governing the system of property ownership'. The injunction [issued by the Commission] to refrain from using rights under national trademark law in order to set an obstacle in the way of parallel imports does not *affect the grant* of those rights but *only limits their exercise* to the extent necessary to give effect to the prohibition under Article 85 (1). (Emphasis added)[16]

In subsequent cases, the reasoning employed in *Grundig* was tested again, without leading to satisfactory results. Both in *Parke Davis*[17] and *Sirena*,[18] the right-holders themselves objected to the parallel importation of goods that were protected by patent and trade mark law respectively. As no agreement between a right-holder and his representative was involved, Article 85 TEEC could not be applied. The ECJ considered instead the application of Article 86 TEEC (Article 102 TFEU), pursuant to which measures affecting intra-Community trade can be enjoined if they constitute an abuse of a dominant position. However, the Court shunned away from qualifying mere ownership of an intellectual property right as a 'dominant position', and thus did not find a basis for qualifying the obstruction of parallel imports as abusive.

The route to a solution of the pertinent problems was finally paved in *Deutsche Grammophon*.[19] The dispute concerned unauthorised imports into Germany of records released by the right-holder, Deutsche Grammophon, on the French market. Infringement proceedings had been brought by Deutsche Grammophon against the German retailer of the re-imported

---

16 ECJ Joined Cases 56/64 and 58/64, *Établissements Consten* and *Grundig v. Commission*, [1968] ECR 299, 344.

17 ECJ Case 24/67, *Parke Davis v. Centrafarm*, [1968] ECR 55.

18 ECJ Case 40/70, *Sirena v. Eda*, [1971] ECR 69. In this case, the trade marks in the countries of export (Germany) and of import (Italy) were originally owned by the same American enterprise. However, the mark had been split by transferring the 'Italian part' to the firm acting as the plaintiff in the underlying dispute, whereas the imported products originated from a German firm acting under a license granted by the American proprietor.

19 ECJ Case 78/70, *Deutsche Grammophon v. Metro SB*, [1971] ECR 487.

records. The appeal court in Hamburg referred to the ECJ the question whether by opposing the sales in Germany, Deutsche Grammophon violated the competition provisions – Article 85 or 86 – of the EEC Treaty. The ECJ answered that, if the obstacle against importation resulted from an agreement between two parties, Article 85 TEEC was applicable. However, where:

> (7) . . . the exercise of the right does not exhibit those elements of concerted practice referred to in Article 85 (1), it is necessary . . . further to consider whether the exercise of the right . . . is compatible with other provisions of the treaty, in particular those relating to the free movement of goods. . . . (11) . . . it is . . . clear from [Article 36] that, although the Treaty does not affect the existence of rights recognised by the legislation of a Member State with regard to industrial and commercial property, the exercise of such rights may nevertheless fall within the prohibitions laid down by the Treaty . . . Article 36 only admits derogations from [free movement of goods] to the extent to which they are justified for the purpose of safeguarding rights which constitute the *specific subject matter* of such property. (12) If a right related to copyright is relied upon to prevent the marketing in a Member State of products *distributed by the holder of the right or with his consent* on the territory of another Member State on the sole ground that such distribution did not take place on the national territory, such a prohibition, which would legitimise the isolation of national markets, would be repugnant to the essential purpose of the Treaty, which is to unite national markets into a single market. (Emphasis added)

From that decision, the principle of 'regional exhaustion' became an established part of European jurisdiction. In essence, it means that the justification enshrined in Article 36 TEEC can only be invoked to safeguard the *specific subject matter* of intellectual property rights, and that the possibility of opposing importation of goods which were distributed *by the proprietor or with his consent* on other territories within the common market does, in principle, *not* form part of that specific subject matter.

Further development of case law

Whereas the basic rule remained unchanged since *Deutsche Grammophon*,[20] subsequent decisions have specified further aspects of relevance for the different intellectual property rights.

---

20 In the meantime, regional exhaustion is enshrined in practically all legal instruments harmonising IP law, not only as a minimum, but also as a maximum rule, meaning that Member States are prohibited from applying a principle of global exhaustion. See in particular Chapter 4, section 4.4.2.2.1.

Trade mark law

Trade marks having the same origin

The first decision in the aftermath of *Deutsche Grammophon* addressing trade mark law concerned importation into Belgium of coffee produced in Germany under the trade mark 'HAG' (*HAG I*).[21] Objections were raised by the Belgian owner of the trade mark, who had acquired the mark subsequent to expropriation of the previous German owner as a reparation measure after World War II. The ECJ found that the prohibition of import was not justified under Article 36 for safeguarding the specific subject matter of the trade mark right:

> (12) . . . one cannot allow the holder of a trade mark to rely upon the exclusiveness of a trade mark right . . . with a view to prohibiting the marketing in a Member State of goods legally produced in a Member State under an identical trade mark having the same origin.

Concerning the role played by trade marks in a common market consisting of several territories, the ECJ appeared rather dismissive. It was held that:

> (14) [w]hilst in such a market the indication of origin of a product covered by a trade mark is useful, information to consumers on this point may be ensured by measures other than such as would affect the free movement of goods.

Fears that this reasoning might lead to a serious erosion of trade mark rights were alleviated by the *Terranova* judgment[22] which clarified that *HAG I* was only meant to apply in the rare cases when trade marks, although currently belonging to different owners, have the same origin, whereas measures prohibiting import of goods under the same or a confusingly similar mark are justified where the marks were acquired by different and independent proprietors under different national laws.[23]

In 1990, the ECJ revisited its *HAG I* decision.[24] This time, the dispute concerned coffee imported into Germany under the trade mark HAG by the successor in title of the Belgian company which lost the first HAG case. Reconsidering the issue, the ECJ pointed out that:

---

21 ECJ Case 192/73, *Van Zuylen Frères v. HAG AG*, (HAG I), [1974] ECR 731.
22 ECJ Case C-119/75, *Terrapin v. Terranova*, [1976] ECR 1039.
23 Ibid., Paragraph 7.
24 ECJ Case C-10/89, *Cnl-Sucal NV SA v. HAG GF AG* (HAG II), [1990] ECR I-3711.

(13) Trade mark rights are . . . an essential element in the system of undistorted competition that the Treaty seeks to establish. Under such a system, an undertaking must be in a position to keep its customers by virtue of the quality of its products and services, something which is possible only if there are distinctive marks which enable customers to identify those products or services. For the trade mark to be able to fulfil this role, it must offer a guarantee that *all goods bearing it have been produced under the control of a single undertaking* which is accountable for their quality. (Emphasis added)

After defining that the essential function of a trade mark is:

(14) . . . to guarantee the identity of the origin of the marked product to the consumer . . . by enabling him without any possibility of confusion to distinguish that product from other products which have another origin

and that this function would be jeopardised if the proprietor of a trade mark could not oppose the importation of goods bearing a confusingly similar mark,[25] the ECJ concludes that this is not altered by the fact that, as in the underlying dispute, the two marks originally belonged to the same proprietor, because:

(18) [f]rom the date of expropriation and notwithstanding their common origin, each of the marks independently fulfilled its function, within its own territorial field of application, of guaranteeing that the marked products originated from one single source.

The final step away from *HAG I* was taken when the ECJ found in *Ideal Standard*[26] that the protection of the specific subject matter of trade mark law justified to prohibit importations even if the trade marks concerned were of the same origin, and had been separated through voluntary transfer by the proprietor.

Repacking, rebranding, relabeling
A long line of cases have addressed the implications of trade mark law on parallel importation of pharmaceuticals, in particular where the products have been repackaged, relabelled or rebranded. Those cases will be addressed in more detail in Chapter 4, section 4.4.2.2).

---

25 Ibid., Paragraph 16.
26 ECJ Case C-9/93, *IHT Internationale Heiztechnik v. Ideal Standard*, [1994] ECR I-2789.

Copyright

The notion of 'industrial or commercial property'

Applying the principle of regional exhaustion to copyright and related rights presented an issue because Article 36 TEEC, which provided the basis for the doctrine, only refers to 'commercial and industrial property'. The issue was briefly addressed, but not finally decided in *Deutsche Grammophon*;[27] the Court merely declared that it acted 'on the assumption' that Article 36 may be relevant to a right related to copyright.[28] The point was clarified in *Musik-Vertrieb Membran v. GEMA*.[29] Considering the argument brought forward by the French government that copyright was not comparable to other industrial and commercial property rights, and that the case law developed with regard to patents and trade marks could therefore not be applied, the ECJ held that although copyright differs from other intellectual property rights because it comprises the moral rights of the author, it also 'comprises other rights, notably the right to exploit commercially the marketing of the protected work', and that this right 'constitutes a form of market control exercisable by the owner', which raises the same issues as the commercial exploitation of any other industrial or commercial property right.[30] As a result, it was found that a collective rights management organisation in a Member State could not demand remuneration being paid for the importation of records, for which remuneration had already been paid to another collective society in the Member State where the records had been released on the market. The fact that differences existed with regard to the level of remuneration did not change that result.

Distribution of copies v. other forms of exploitation

Another line of cases distinguished the distribution of copies, which are subject to exhaustion, from other forms of exploitation where the principle does not apply. The dispute in the leading case *Coditel*[31] concerned the unauthorised diffusion on cable television in Belgium of a film which had already been shown on television in Germany, where it had been picked up by the cable company Coditel. The right to show the film in Belgium had previously been acquired, on the basis of a license obtained from the right-holder, by Ciné Vog. The ECJ notes, first, that:

---

27 ECJ Case 78/70, *Deutsche Grammophon v. Metro*, [1971] ECR 487.
28 Ibid., Paragraph 11.
29 ECJ Joined Cases C-55/80 and C-57/80, *Musik-Vertrieb Membran* and *K-tel Int. v. GEMA*, [1981] ECR 147.
30 Ibid., Paragraphs 12, 13.
31 ECJ Case 62/79, *Coditel v. Ciné Vog Films* (Coditel I), [1980] ECR 881.

(12) [a] cinematographic film belongs to the category of . . . works made available to the public by performances which may be infinitely repeated. In this respect the problems involved in the observance of copyright in relation to the requirements of the Treaty are not the same as those which arise in connection with literary or artistic works the placing of which at the disposal of the public is inseparable from the circulation of the material form of the works, as in the case of books or records. (13) In these circumstances the owner of the copyright in a film and his assigns have a legitimate interest in calculating the fees due in respect of the authorisation to exhibit on the basis of the actual or probable number of performances [and according to the observation of certain time schemes]. (14) [In view of those facts] the right of a copyright owner and his assigns to require fees for any showing of the film *is part of the essential function of copyright* in this type of . . . work. (Emphasis added)

A further notable detail about this case is the fact that it turned upon Article 59 TEEC – free movement of services – and not on Article 36, as no physical goods were transported over borders. However, this made no difference to the legal evaluation. The Court emphasised that, very similar to the interplay between Articles 30 and 36 TEEC, the fact that Article 59:

(13) . . . prohibits restrictions upon freedom to provide services, . . . does not thereby encompass limits upon the exercise of . . . activities which have their origin in the application of national legislation for the protection of intellectual property, save where such application constitutes a means of arbitrary discrimination or a disguised restriction on trade between the Member State.

As was pointed out above, in the actual case the restrictions imposed by enjoining diffusion of the film in Belgium without authorisation was considered as justified. Those principles were confirmed in *Coditel II*,[32] where the same parties met in the reverse constellation.

Disparities of substantive law
A third type of copyright cases resulted from disparities in the substantive law applying in the Member States. In *Warner Brothers v. Christiansen*,[33] the defendant had bought video cassettes in the UK and brought them to Denmark for the purpose of hiring them out. At the relevant time, no legislation existed in the UK which made the hiring out of legally acquired films subject to authorisation by the right-holder; in Denmark, however, such authorisation was required by law. The ECJ agreed to the proposition that

---

32 ECJ Case 262/81, *Coditel v. Ciné Vog Films* (Coditel II), [1982] ECR 3381.
33 ECJ Case 158/86, *Warner Brothers v. Christiansen*, [1988] ECR 2605.

the Danish legislation resulted in a measure having equivalent effect to quantitative restrictions of import, and therefore had to be justifiable in the light of Article 36 TEEC. For the assessment, the grounds on which the legislation was founded were examined, thereby taking account of the fact that the hiring-out of video cassettes offered a strong and growing form of commercial exploitation of cinematographic works. This led to the conclusion that:

> (15) . . . by authorizing the collection of royalties only on sales to private individuals and to persons hiring out video-cassettes, it is impossible to guarantee to makers of films a remuneration which reflects the number of occasions on which the video-cassettes are actually hired out and which secures for them a satisfactory share of the rental market. That explains why . . . certain national laws have recently provided specific protection of the right to hire out video-cassettes. (16) Laws of that kind are therefore clearly justified on grounds of the protection of industrial and commercial property pursuant to Article 36 of the Treaty.

The second important example of a dispute triggered by diversity of substantive copyright laws, *EMI* v. *Patricia*,[34] concerned the different terms of protection for related rights. In the underlying conflict, sound recordings had been produced by a German firm, on commission by a Danish undertaking, for sales in Denmark and the Netherlands. Some of those records were re-imported into Germany. According to the Danish copyright act, the rights in the sound recordings had expired at the relevant date, whereas they were still valid in Germany at the time of re-importation. Considering, in the light of Article 36 TEEC, whether the right-holder's claim to prohibit such imports amounted to an abusive exercise of rights, the ECJ found that this was not the case:

> (11) [I]t should be noted that in the present state of Community law, which is characterized by a lack of harmonization or approximation of legislation governing the protection of literary and artistic property, it is for the national legislatures to determine on the condition and detailed rules for such protection. (12) In so far as the disparity between national laws may give rise to restrictions on intra-Community trade in sound recordings, such restrictions are justified under Article 36 of the Treaty if they are the result of differences governing the period of protection and this is inseparably linked to the very existence of the exclusive rights.

Both *Warner Brothers* v. *Christiansen* and *EMI* v. *Patricia* provided strong incentives for the Community legislature to enact harmonising legislation in

---

34 ECJ Case C-341/87, *EMI Electrola v. Patricia*, [1989] ECR 79.

the respective fields.[35] Similarly, the need for harmonisation within industrial design protection was highlighted in *Keurkoop v. Nancy Kean Gifts*,[36] where impediments for intra-Community trade resulted from the different notions of novelty applying in the TEEC Member States at the relevant time.

Patent law

In patent law, the validity of the approach established in *Deutsche Grammophon* was first tested and confirmed in *Centrafarm v. Sterling Drug*,[37] where the patent holder had tried to intervene against parallel import from the UK and Germany into the Netherlands of patented drugs that were manufactured under a contractual licence. The ECJ held that:

> (9) [i]n relation to patents, the specific subject matter of the industrial property is the guarantee that the patentee, to reward the creative effort of the inventor, has the exclusive right to use an invention with a view to manufacture industrial products and putting them into circulation for the first time, either directly or by the grant of licenses to third parties, as well as the right to oppose infringements.

The consequences of that approach were tested in two subsequent cases. The first of these, *Merck v. Stephar*,[38] concerned a situation where drugs were released on the Italian market by the manufacturer. At the relevant priority date Italian law did not provide for protection of patents for pharmaceutical products. When the drugs were imported by the defendant from Italy into the Netherlands, Merck claimed infringement of its Dutch patent, and the question was referred to the ECJ whether that was justified under Article 36 TEEC. Referring to its decision in *Centrafarm*, the ECJ pointed out that:

> (10) [The] right of first placing a product on the market enables an inventor, by allowing him a monopoly in exploiting his product, to obtain a reward for his creative effort, without, however, guaranteeing that he will obtain such a reward in all circumstances. (11) It is for the proprietor of the right to decide . . . under what conditions he will market his product, including the possibility of marketing it in a Member State where the law does not provide patent protection for the product in question. If he decides so he must then bear the consequences of his choice with regard to the free movement of the product within the Common Market . . .

---

35 For Directives 92/100/EEC on rental and lending rights and 93/98/EEC on the term of copyright and related rights see below, Chapter 5, 5.2.2.2 and 5.2.2.4.

36 ECJ Case 144/81, *Keurkoop v. Nancy Kean Gifts*, [1982] ECR 2853.

37 ECJ Case 15/74, *Centrafarm v. Sterling Drug*, [1974] ECR 1147.

38 ECJ Case 187/80, *Merck & Co v. Stephar*, [1981] ECR 2063.

The second case to be mentioned in this context, *Pharmon* v. *Hoechst*,[39] concerned a drug which had been manufactured in the UK under a compulsory licence. Although export was prohibited under the terms of that licence, the UK company had sold, shortly before expiry of the compulsory licence, a large consignment of the drug to a Dutch company which marketed them in the Netherlands. The ECJ found that contrary to *Merck* v. *Stephar*, the holder of the Dutch patent was entitled under Article 36 TEEC to oppose those sales:

> (26) As the court held [in *Merck* v. *Stephar*], the substance of a patent right lies essentially in according the inventor an exclusive right of first placing on the market so as to allow him to obtain a reward for his creative effort. It is therefore necessary to allow the patent proprietor to prevent the importation and marketing of products under a compulsory licence in order to protect the substance of his exclusive rights under his patent.

Finally, in *Generics* v. *Smith Kline*[40] the ECJ had to consider whether a rule of national law, which prohibits the making and submission of samples of medicinal products to the competent authority for issuing of marketing authorisations during the term of patent protection, amounts to a measure having equivalent effect in the meaning of Article 30 TEEC, and if so, whether it is justified under Article 36. Both questions were answered in the affirmative. Although no actual imports were involved in the underlying dispute, it was found that the contested legislation had the potential to prevent the importation of medicinal products from Member States where they have been lawfully produced after expiry of the patent into another Member State where, due to the prohibition to submit the required samples during the patent term, the authorisation needed for marketing the drugs will be delayed. Nevertheless, it was found that the right to prohibit the production and use of samples for purposes of obtaining marketing authorisation falls within the specific subject matter of the patent right, and that its exercise is therefore justified under Article 36 TEEC.

Non-discrimination

Apart from free movement of goods and services (as well as regarding the relationship with the competition provisions: see Chapter 6), the impact of Treaty provisions on the exercise of intellectual property rights was tested with regard to the principle of non-discrimination.

---

39 ECJ Case 19/84, *Pharmon BV* v. *Hoechst AG*, [1985] ECR 2281.
40 ECJ Case C-316/95, *Generics* v. *Smith Kline & French Laboratories*, [1997] ECR I-3929.

The first of those decisions concerned two cases brought by the singers Phil Collins and Cliff Richard, both British, regarding sales in Germany of recorded music performed by the artists.[41] In the case of Phil Collins, the recordings had been made, without authorisation, at a live concert in the USA. The German court seized with the case had pointed out that, if the artist were German, he would be protected under the German copyright act. However, regarding foreign nationals, German copyright was only applicable to the extent protection could be claimed under the international conventions of which Germany was a member. In this case, the claims concerned the right of performing artists. This meant that the Berne Convention, according to which national treatment must be granted to nationals of other Berne Member States, did not apply (as the Berne Convention only applies to authors, see Chapter 1, section 1.4.1). Instead, the case had to be considered under the Rome Convention on the Protection of Performing Artists, Phonogram Producers and Broadcasting Organizations ('Rome Convention'). Under the Rome Convention, no protection could be claimed against unauthorised recording of performances which had taken place in a non-Member State – in this case the USA. Also in the case of Cliff Richard, protection was to be denied under the Rome Convention, as the recordings had taken place in the UK at a time which was not covered by the Rome Convention. Being aware of the prohibition of discrimination among nationals of EEC Member States, which at the relevant time was set out in Article 7 (1) of the EEC Treaty, the German court referred to the ECJ the question whether copyright and related rights were subject to that principle, and if so, whether it must be applied directly by the courts and authorities in the Member States. The ECJ confirmed that this was indeed the case:

> (31) . . . [N]either the disparities between the national laws relating to copyright and related rights nor the fact that not all Member States have yet acceded to the Rome Convention can justify a breach of the principle of non-discrimination . . .
> (32) In prohibiting 'any discrimination on the grounds of nationality', Article 7 of the Treaty requires . . . that persons in a situation governed by Community law be placed on a completely equal footing with nationals of the Member State concerned [citation omitted]. In so far as that principle is applicable, it therefore precludes a Member State from making the grant of an exclusive right subject to the requirement that the person concerned be a national of that State.

---

41 ECJ Joined Cases C-92/92 and C-326/92, *Phil Collins v. Imtrat* and *Kraul v. EMI Electrola*, [1993] ECR I-5145.

Following, in *Ricordi*[42] the ECJ applied the principle of non-discrimination also to the protection of copyright in cases where the author had already died when the EEC Treaty entered into force in the Member State of which he was a national. Consequently, this precludes the term of protection granted by the legislation of a Member State to the works of an author who is a national of another Member State being shorter than the term granted to the works of its own nationals.

A third case, *Tod's and Tod's France*,[43] concerned the protection of a shoe design under copyright law. The shoe had been designed and manufactured in Italy, where at the relevant time copyright was not available for such products. Unauthorised copies of the shoe were sold in France, where copyright is readily available for such items under the French rule of 'unité de l'art'. As the copyright claim raised in this case fell under the Berne Convention, national treatment had to be granted, as a general rule, under Article 5 (1) Berne Convention. However, Article 2 (7) Berne Convention allows to derogate from that rule: if works are protected in their country of origin solely as designs or models, they are not entitled to claim full copyright protection in other Berne member countries, even if such protection is available under the national law of that other State; instead, like in their country of origin, they are only entitled to the protection granted to industrial designs. Hence, the argument was made by the alleged infringer that, as the shoe could only be protected on the basis of design legislation in its country of origin – Italy – protection could only claimed under design legislation in France, which would have required registration of the shoe. The situation differed from *Phil Collins* and *Ricordi* insofar as the discrimination did not resolve from the different nationality of the right-holder, but from the fact that the shoe originated from another Member State. The question was therefore referred to the ECJ whether the non-discrimination principle applied also in such a constellation. Again, the question was answered in the affirmative:

> (24) The existence of a link between the country of origin of a work within the meaning of the Berne Convention, on the one hand, and the nationality of the author of that work, on the other, cannot be denied . . . (26) As regards published works, the country of origin is essentially . . . the country where the work was first published. The author of a work first published in a Member State will, in the majority of cases, be a national of that State, whereas the author of a work published in another Member State will generally be a person who is not a national of the first Member State. (27) It follows that the application of rules such as those at

42 ECJ Case C-360/00, *Land Hessen v. G. Ricordi & Co. Bühnen- und Musikverlag GmbH*, [2002] ECR I-5089.
43 ECJ Case C-28/04, *Tod's SpA and Tod's France SARL v. Heyraud*, [2005] ECR I-5781.

issue in the main proceedings is liable to operate mainly to the detriment of nationals of other Member States and thus give rise to indirect discrimination on grounds of nationality. (Citations omitted)

As the ECJ did not find any reasons under which, exceptionally, such discrimination could be justified, the denial of protection under French copyright law was found to be incompatible with the EC Treaty.

? QUESTIONS

1 The ECJ has pointed out in HAG I that although trade marks are 'useful' as indications of commercial origin, the relevant information could also be obtained by 'measures other than such as would affect the free movement of goods'. What could be meant thereby? What, in your opinion, made the ECJ change its position in later decisions?

2 For the application of Article 36 with its reference to 'industrial and commercial property' to copyright and related rights the ECJ distinguishes between the moral rights of an author and the exploitation rights. Apart from the fact that according to the 'monist' theory applying e.g. in Germany such a split cannot be made for systematic reasons – do you agree that the approach is feasible in practice?

3 In *Merck v. Stephar*, the ECJ applied the doctrine of regional exhaustion even though the products could not be protected in Italy, where they had been released on the market. Do you agree with the reasoning? How would you argue against it, if you were counsel for Merck?

2.3 Secondary legislation on intellectual property

Legal instruments

Primary and secondary Community law

ECJ case law based on the provisions of the Basic Treaties demonstrates the strength, but also the confines of application of the Treaty provisions. While misuse of IP rights resulting in an artificial partitioning of markets can be enjoined if the proprietor of the right is the same in the countries of import and export, or if she has given consent to the goods being released in the country of export by a third party, the common market will remain to be territorially divided if the proprietors are separate and independent from each other, as is frequently the case in trade mark law. Furthermore, distortions of intra-Community trade are inevitable as long as the substantive laws applying in the Member States are conspicuously different. Both aspects can only be addressed by legislative measures: to overcome the territorial split between Member States, unitary rights extending over the Community must be created, and in order to straighten out the differences between Member States' substantive laws, harmonising legislation must be enacted. In contrast to the legal principles and obligations resulting directly from the basic Treaties – the so-called *primary (Community) law* – such legislative acts which are passed on the basis of primary law are referred to as *secondary (Community) law*.

The legal instruments of secondary law which are of primary importance in intellectual property are Regulations and Directives. The nature and effect of both instruments are set out in Article 288 TFEU as follows:[44]

> A regulation shall have general application. It shall be binding in its entirety and directly applicable in all Member States.
> A directive shall be binding, as to the result to be achieved, upon each Member State to which it is addressed, but shall leave to the national authorities the choice of form and methods.

Although the legal bases for such measures existed since the conclusion of the EEC Treaty, it took several decades before actual use was made of them in the field of intellectual property. The most active phase of European legislation on intellectual property fell into the 1990s, when the urge to complete the Single Market as well as the dynamic developments on the international level resulted in a strong drive towards unification and harmonisation.

Directives

Directives are aimed at ensuring the approximation of legal provisions where and to the extent that this appears necessary for the establishment and functioning of the internal market. This objective has not changed since the EEC Treaty.[45] It is now enshrined in Article 114 2nd sentence TFEU:

> The European Parliament and the Council shall, acting in accordance with the ordinary legislative procedure and after consulting the Economic and Social Committee, adopt the measures for the approximation of the provisions laid down by law, regulation or administrative action in Member States which have as their object the establishment and functioning of the internal market.

---

44 Article 288 TFEU also lists decisions, opinions and recommendations as further legal acts through which the EU's legal competences are exercised. Whereas decisions also have binding effects, opinions and recommendations are not binding.

45 It was enshrined in Articles 100, 100a TEEC and later in Article 95 TEC.

Since the Treaty of Maastricht (1993), Directives are subject to the so-called co-decision procedure, which warrants the right of the European Parliament not only to be heard, but also to vote on legislative measures. Under the TFEU, the voting rights of the Parliament were further enhanced. The rules orchestrating the ordinary legislative procedure are set out in Article 294 TFEU. Legislation is regularly initiated by the Commission which submits its proposal to the European Parliament (EP) and the Council. The EP commences the process by a First Reading, the results of which are submitted to the Council. If the Council doesn't agree with the EP but makes its own proposals, these have to be considered by the EP in a Second Reading, the results of which are then communicated to the Commission and the Council. If, again, no consensus is reached, the proposal is referred to conciliation proceedings. A schematic overview is represented below.

Regulations

Other than Directives, Regulations establishing unitary intellectual property rights could only be created under the EEC and EC Treaties on the basis of an unspecified 'default clause' (Article 235 TEEC; Article 308 TEC), which allowed the Council to act, unanimously on a proposal by the Commission, to attain one of the objectives set out in the treaties where the treaties did not provide the necessary powers. As the ECJ noted in its opinion 1/94 on the competence to conclude the WTO Agreement, this meant that the European Parliament only had consultation rights with regard to such legislation, and was not competent to co-decide on the matter.[46] This has changed fundamentally under the TFEU. A specific legislative basis for the creation of unitary intellectual property rights is provided in Article 118 (1) TFEU:

> In the context of the establishment and functioning of the internal market, the European Parliament and the Council, acting in accordance with the ordinary legislative procedure, shall establish measures for the creation of European intellectual property rights to provide uniform protection of intellectual property rights throughout the Union and for the setting up of centralised Union-wide authorisation, coordination and supervision arrangements.

It follows that the creation of such rights is subject to the ordinary legislative procedure and thereby also to co-decision by the European Parliament. However, that does not apply to the language regime of such acts, as resolves from Article 118 (2) TFEU:

---

46 ECJ Opinion 1/94, Competence of the Community to conclude international agreements concerning services and the protection of intellectual property, [1994] ECR I- 5267, Paragraph 56.

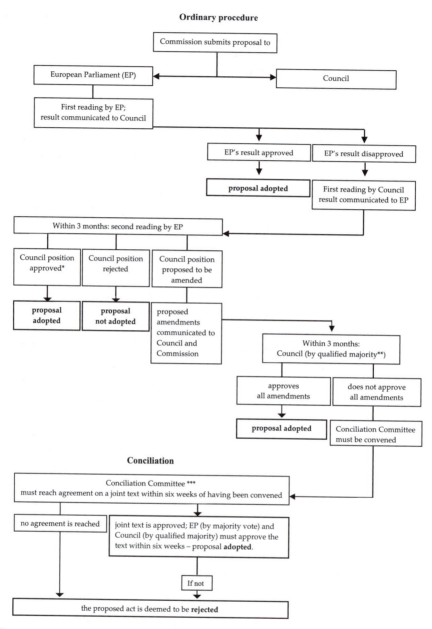

Ordinary procedure

Commission submits proposal to

European Parliament (EP) — Council

First reading by EP;
result communicated to Council

EP's result approved — EP's result disapproved

proposal adopted — First reading by Council
result communicated to EP

Within 3 months: second reading by EP

Council position approved* | Council position rejected | Council position proposed to be amended

proposal adopted | **proposal not adopted** | proposed amendments communicated to Council and Commission

Within 3 months:
Council (by qualified majority**)

approves all amendments | does not approve all amendments

proposal adopted | Conciliation Committee must be convened

Conciliation

Conciliation Committee ***
must reach agreement on a joint text within six weeks of having been convened

no agreement is reached | joint text is approved; EP (by majority vote) and Council (by qualified majority) must approve the text within six weeks – proposal **adopted**.

If not

the proposed act is deemed to be **rejected**

Notes:
* The same ensues if the EP does not a take a decision within 3 months, Article 294 (7) (a) TFEU.

** The Council must act unanimously on the amendments on which the Commission has delivered a negative opinion, Article 294 (9) TFEU.

*** The Conciliation Committee is composed of the members of the Council or their representatives and an equal number of EP members. The Commission shall take part in the Conciliation Committee's proceedings.

Figure 2.1 Co-decision procedure (Art. 294 TFEU)

The Council, acting in accordance with a special legislative procedure, shall by means of regulations establish language arrangements for the European intellectual property rights. The Council shall act unanimously after consulting the European Parliament.

Enhanced cooperation

As European integration progressed and reached a stage where the development of common policies in the areas of foreign and security policy as well as police and judicial cooperation became a declared goal of the EC, it was also realised that it might be necessary to provide for the possibility of advancing at differentiated speeds, to give those Member States that were willing to progress the option to move ahead, with others following once they found themselves ready ('Europe à deux vitesses'). The topic was prominently addressed in the preparatory consultations for the Amsterdam Treaty, in which the mechanism for so-called 'enhanced cooperation' between groups of EC Members was first established. The option is now addressed in Article 20 TEU:

> Member States which wish to establish enhanced cooperation between themselves within the framework of the Union's non-exclusive competences may make use of its institutions and exercise those competences by applying the relevant provisions of the Treaties, subject to the limits and in accordance with the detailed arrangements laid down in this Article and in Articles 326 to 334 of the Treaty on the Functioning of the European Union.

Furthermore, it is set out that:

> [e]nhanced cooperation shall aim to further the objectives of the Union, protect its interests and reinforce its integration process. Such cooperation shall be open at any time to all Member States, in accordance with Article 328 of the Treaty on the Functioning of the European Union.

Requests for enhanced cooperation must be addressed by one or more Member States to the Commission, who then refers the proposal to the European Parliament and the Council. Permission to proceed with the enhanced cooperation can only be granted by unanimous decision of the Council, after obtaining consent by the Parliament. Before that, the Commission and the Council must try to invite the participation of as many Member States as possible, so as to avoid fragmentation wherever that is possible. When the process of enhanced cooperation has been authorised, unanimity requirements are replaced by the votes of the participating Member States. Otherwise, all the requirements for Community legislation must be fulfilled. In particular, it is crucial to observe that the enhanced cooperation must not lead to discrimination between the Member States or to distortions on the internal market.

In the field of IP, enhanced cooperation has become topical in the context of patent law, where the envisaged 'unitary patent' shall be established on that basis.[47]

Current state of EU legislation on intellectual property: overview

In the following, a bird's eye view is given on the current state of secondary legislation on IP and adjacent fields in the EU. More detailed information is found in the individual chapters of this book.

Trade mark law

Trade mark law was the first area where the visions of creating a unitary Community right were pursued in an ultimately successful manner. However, the road to success was not quick and easy. From the first studies and memoranda, which date back to the early 1960s, it took until 1994 for the Community Trade Mark Regulation (CTMR) to be enacted.[48] For the first time, the CTMR made it possible to acquire one single right, by filing a application with a single authority, that extends throughout the territory of the European Communities. For administration of the system, a specialised agency was established – the Office for Harmonization in the Internal Market (OHIM) with a seat in Alicante (Spain). The OHIM has operated since April 1, 1996.

In addition to creating a unitary title, national trade mark law was harmonised to the extent this was necessary with a view to the proper functioning of the internal market. In their contents, the substantive rules set out in the Harmonization Directive (TMD) are congruent with the core provisions in the CTMR. The TMD was enacted in 1990[49] and the implementation process was completed in 1996.

---

47 See Chapter 3, section 3.6.

48 Council Regulation (EC) No 40/94 of 20 December 1993 on the Community trade mark, [1994] OJ L 11/1, now enacted as Council Regulation (EC) No 207/2009 of 26 February 2009 on the Community trade mark (Codified version), [2009] OJ L 78/1.

49 First Council Directive 89/104/EEC of 21 December 1988 to approximate the laws of the Member States relating to trade marks, [1989] OJ L 159/60, now enacted as Directive 2008/95/EC of the European Parliament and of the Council of 22 October 2008 to approximate the laws of the Member States relating to trade marks (Codified version), [2008] OJ L 299/25.

Industrial designs

The two-tier coexistence model represented by trade mark law was also implemented in the area of industrial design legislation. The Design Directive (DD) dates from October 1998[50] whereas the Community Design Regulation (CDR)[51] entered into force on March 6, 2002. Regarding registered Community designs, the system is also administrated by OHIM. As a novel feature, the CDR includes a design right which comes into existence without the formal act of registration, the Unregistered Community Design (UCD).

Copyright

Harmonisation in copyright law has taken a cautious, pragmatic step-by-step approach. The Copyright Directives, eight of which exist at present, have mostly dealt with specific, limited issues, typically where technical or economic developments have created an obvious and urgent need for uniform regulation in the Member States. The first of these Directives concerned the protection of computer programs under copyright law[52] – certainly not a very central issue, particularly from a continental *droit d'auteur* perspective, but nevertheless quite real and without doubt of considerable practical relevance. The subsequent four Directives have dealt with rental and lending rights,[53] satellite broadcasting and cable transmission,[54] duration of copyright[55] and protection for databases.[56] In particular the harmonisation of rental and lending rights as well as of the copyright term were motivated by

---

50 Directive 98/71/EC of 13 October 1998 of the European Parliament and of the Council on the legal protection of designs, [1998] OJ L 289/28.

51 Council Regulation (EC) No 6/2002 of 12 December 2001 on Community designs, [2002] OJ L 3/1.

52 Council Directive 91/250/EEC of 14 May 1991 on the legal protection of computer programs, [1991] OJ L 122/42, republished as Directive 2009/24/EC of the European Parliament and of the Council of 23 April 2009 on the legal protection of computer programs (Codified version), [2009] OJ L 111/16.

53 Council Directive 92/100/EEC of 19 November 1992 on rental right and lending right and on certain rights related to copyright in the field of intellectual property, [1992] OJ L 346/61, republished as Directive 2006/115/EC of the European Parliament and of the Council of 12 December 2006 on rental right and lending right and on certain rights related to copyright in the field of intellectual property (codified version), [2006] OJ L 376/28.

54 Council Directive 93/83/EEC of 27 September 1993 on the coordination of certain rules concerning copyright and rights related to copyright applicable to satellite broadcasting and cable retransmission, [1993] OJ L 248/15.

55 Council Directive 93/98/EEC of 29 October 1993 harmonising the term of protection of copyright and certain related rights, [1993] OJ L 290/9, republished as Directive 2006/116/EC of the European Parliament and of the Council of 12 December 2006 on the term of protection of copyright and certain related rights (codified version), [2006] OJ L 372/12, and amended by Directive 2011/77/EU of the European Parliament and of the Council of 27 September 2011, [2011] OJ L 265/1.

56 Directive 96/9/EC of the European Parliament and of the Council of 11 March 1996 on the legal protection of databases, [1996] OJ L 77/20.

the obstacles for intra-Community trade resolving from the legal differences of substantive law which had become visible in the previous ECJ decisions *Warner Brothers v. Christiansen*[57] and *EMI v. Patricia.*[58]

Number six in the range of European Copyright Directives, the so-called Information Society Directive (InfoSoc),[59] is more comprehensive in its contents than its predecessors. Being motivated by the need to provide a common European basis for the implementation of the obligations set out in the WIPO Internet Treaties of 1996, WCT[60] and WPPT,[61] the Infosoc Directive contains a rather comprehensive regulation of the rights granted to authors and owners of related rights as well as a conclusive, although non-binding, catalogue of limitations. The area of traditional copyright protection rules is further expanded by the introduction of provisions concerning circumvention of technical protection measures and the collection of data for administrative purposes.

The seventh piece of Community legislation in the field of copyright, the Resale Right Directive,[62] is again quite specific in its content. The driving force in this case was not so much the need to cope with new technical developments and/or economic phenomena, but rather motives of social fairness and support *vis-à-vis* a frequently underprivileged group of artists. In addition, the disparities in national art markets created by different legal standards with regard to the resale of art works have played a decisive role.

The most recent Directive, enacted in October 2012, concerns 'orphan works', i.e. works of which the author is unknown or cannot be traced through reasonably diligent searches. The Directive determines the standards to be met by such a search, and establishes the principle that if it does not lead to the author being found, the work will have orphan status throughout the EU, with the result that Member States may allow, on the basis of legal mechanisms available under national law, the use of such works for certain privileged purposes. Also, in the summer of 2012, the Commission published its long-awaited proposal for a directive on collective rights management, which will enhance transparency and facilitate cross-border licensing.

---

57 ECJ Case 158/86, *Warner Brothers v. Christiansen*, [1988] ECR 2605.

58 ECJ Case C-341/87, *EMI Electrola v. Patricia*, [1989] ECR 79.

59 Directive 2001/29/EC of the European Parliament and of the Council of 22 May 2001 on the harmonisation of certain aspects of copyright and related rights in the information society, [2001] OJ L 167/10.

60 WIPO Copyright Treaty, www.wipo.int/treaties/eu/ip/wct; see Chapter 1, 1.5.1.1

61 WIPO Performances and Phonograms Treaty, www.wipo.int/treatises/eu/ip/wpp; see Chapter 1, 1.5.1.1

62 Directive 2001/84/EC of the European Parliament and of the Council of 27 September 2001 on the resale right for the benefit of the author of an original work of art, [2001] OJ L 272/32.

Patent law

Patent law is certainly one of the key areas of intellectual property. It is also the area among all fields of intellectual property where European structures have been dominating for the longest time, in the form of European patents being granted by the European Patent Office (EPO) with its main branches in Munich and The Hague. However, the existing European patent system is not based on an act of Community legislation, but it is founded on an international convention, the European Patent Convention (EPC), which was concluded as early as 1973.[63]

The substantive provisions in the national patent law systems have not been subject to one comprehensive harmonisation Directive. However, harmonisation of some central notions of patent law has been achieved by another international convention preceding the EPC, the so-called Strasbourg Convention.[64] Furthermore, although the first attempt to create a unitary patent system through the Community Patent Convention (CPC) of 1975 resulted in failure, it created a strong incentive for Member States to adapt their national laws to the envisaged European standards, even without being legally obliged to do so.

Finally, in some sensitive and economically important areas, it was found necessary to introduce specific, complementary EU legislation. Two Regulations have been enacted concerning the grant of a so-called supplementary protection certificate for inventions in the pharmaceutical[65] and the agro-chemical[66] sector. Legislation was founded on the consideration that, as a major part of the normal term of patent protection actually passes before marketing permission is obtained, an extension of the term is needed so that the right-owner is able to reap the commercial benefit of her innovative activities.

Furthermore, harmonisation of national patent laws in the EU has been achieved, with some difficulties, in the sensitive and controversial field of biotechnological inventions.[67] Concerning the likewise controversial field

---

63 Convention on the Grant of European Patents (EPC) signed in Munich 1973, www.epo.org/law-practice/legal-texts/epc.html.

64 Strasbourg Convention on the Unification of Certain Points of Substantive Law on Patents for Inventions, of 27 November 1963.

65 Regulation (EC) No 469/2009 of the European Parliament and of the Council of May 6, 2009 concerning the creation of a supplementary protection certificate for medicinal products, [2009] OJ L 152/1.

66 Regulation (EC) No 1610/96 of the European Parliament and of the Council of 23 July 1996 concerning the creation of a supplementary protection certificate for plant protection products, [1996] OJ L 198/30.

67 Directive 98/44/EC of the European Parliament and of the Council of July 6, 1998 on the legal protection of biotechnological inventions, [1998] OJ L 213/13.

of patents for computer programs, the resistance organised by interested groups from the civil society against a directive proposal[68] proved to be so strong that the plans for harmonisation were ultimately discarded.

Lastly, the long-standing plans to create a unitary patent system on the Community level finally seem to be maturing. If the current proposals are implemented as intended, the system will operate on the basis of enhanced cooperation[69] between 25 Member States, who agree that among them, patents granted under the EPC will be treated as having unitary effects.

Further legislation in IP and adjacent areas

Further unitary Community rights

Community Regulations creating unitary titles on the Community level were also enacted with regard to geographical indications for foodstuff and agricultural products[70] as well as plant variety protection.[71]

Competition law

Competition law in the sense of antitrust law is still largely based on primary law as enshrined in Articles 101 and 102 TFEU. In addition, several Regulations have been enacted which illuminate the scope of application of Article 101 paragraph 3.

Unfair competition legislation has been harmonised by several Directives, most importantly by the Directive on Comparative and Misleading Advertising[72] and the Unfair Commercial Practices (UCP) Directive.[73] Of particular interest in this field is also the E-Commerce Directive,[74] which

---

68 Proposal for a Directive of the European Parliament and Council on the patentability of computer implemented inventions, COM(2002) 92 final.

69 See this Chapter, section 1.3.1.4.

70 Council Regulation (EC) No 2006/510 of 20 March 2006 on the Protection of Geographical Indications and Designations of Origin for Agricultural Products and Foodstuffs, [2006] OJ L 93/12.

71 Council Regulation (EC) No 2100/94 of 27 July 1994 on Community plant variety rights, [1994] OJ L 227/1.

72 Directive 2006/114/EC of the European Parliament and of the Council 12 December 2006 concerning misleading and comparative advertising (codified version), [2006] OJ L 376/21.

73 Directive 2005/29/EC of the European Parliament and of the Council of 11 May 2005 concerning unfair business-to-consumer commercial practices in the internal market and amending Council Directive 84/450/ EEC, Directives 97/7/EC, 98/27/EC and 2002/65/EC of the European Parliament and of the Council and Regulation (EC) No 2006/2004 of the European Parliament and of the Council, [2005] OJ L 149/22.

74 Directive 2000/31/EC of the European Parliament and of the Council 8 June 2000 on certain legal aspects of information society services, in particular electronic commerce, in the Internal Market ('Directive on Electronic Commerce'), [2000] OJ L 178/1.

harmonises certain practices and prescribes the application of the country of origin principle to information services.

Enforcement

The Enforcement Directive (Directive 2004/48/EC[75]) is a centrepiece of intellectual property protection in the EU. It regulates in a horizontal manner the civil and administrative sanctions and procedures that are available in the Member States for infringement of intellectual property rights. This is of particular importance not least for unitary rights like the CTM and the CD, where a comprehensive regulation of such aspects is missing, so that a mosaic approach may have to be applied on the basis of the national laws where the infringement takes place.

Apart from the Enforcement Directive, the E-Commerce Directive[76] is also relevant for enforcement insofar as it regulates the conditions under which ISPs of different kinds are to be held liable for content which is made available with the help of their services. Furthermore, regarding protection against import of infringing merchandise, the Border Measures Regulation provides for the possibility to seize and, where applicable, order the destruction of counterfeits and pirated goods.[77]

Jurisdiction and applicable law

Uniform rules applying to matters involving *inter alia* intellectual property rights were created by Regulation No 44/2001 (Brussels I Regulation)[78] with regard to jurisdiction and enforcement of foreign judgments in civil and commercial matters, and, with regard to applicable law, by Regulation No 864/2007 (Rome II Regulation)[79] on the law applicable to non-contractual obligations and Regulation No 593/2008 (Rome I Regulation)[80] on the law applicable to contracts. Predecessors of the Brussels I and Rome I

---

75 Directive 2004/48/EC of the European Parliament and of the Council of 29 April 2004 on the enforcement of intellectual property rights, [2004] OJ L 157/45, corrected version in [2004] OJ L 195/16.

76 Above, footnote 74.

77 Council Regulation (EC) No 1383/2003 of 22 July 2003 concerning customs action against goods suspected of infringing certain intellectual property rights and the measures to be taken against goods found to have infringed such rights, [2003] OJ L 196/7.

78 Council Regulation 44/2001 of 22 December 2000 on the Recognition and Enforcement of Foreign Judgments in Civil and Commercial Matters ('Brussels I'), [2001] OJ L 12/1.

79 Regulation 864/2007 of the European Parliament and of the Council of 11 July 2007 on the Law Applicable to Non-Contractual Obligations ('Rome II'), [2007] OJ L 199/40.

80 Regulation 593/2008 of the European Parliament and of the Council of 17 June 2008 on the Law Applicable to Contractual Obligations ('Rome I'), [2008] OJ L 177/6.

Regulations had already existed since 1968 and 1980 respectively in the form of international Conventions between EEC Member States.

Primacy of EU law

Where Community legislation has been enacted, it must be applied faithfully and cannot be overridden or set aside by national law. This principle has been confirmed by the ECJ in several decisions.[81] In *Simmenthal* II,[82] the ECJ went so far as to say that national provisions that are in violation of obligations resulting from Community law must be disregarded.[83] In *Marleasing*,[84] it was emphasised that national courts applying national provisions must, as far as possible, apply an interpretation which avoids a conflict with a Community rule.[85] Furthermore, it was set out in *Francovich*[86] that if a Member State has neglected its duties under Community law, for instance by not implementing a directive in due time into national law, the state is liable to pay compensation for damage resulting from such omissions in the vertical relationship between citizens and public authorities.[87]

The envisaged European Constitution enshrined the principle of primacy in an explicit form. Pursuant to Article 1-6 of the Constitution, the

> Constitution as well as law adopted by the institutions of the European Union in exercising competences conferred on it shall have primacy over the law of the Member States.

However, the Constitution was never ratified, and no provision correspond-

---

81 For an early case addressing the principle of supremacy see ECJ Case C-6/64, *Costa* v. *E.N.E.L.*, [1964] ECR, 585, 594.

82 ECJ Case 106/77, *Amministrazione delle Finanze* v. *Simmenthal* (Simmenthal II), [1978] ECR 629

83 Ibid., Paragraph 17: '. . . in accordance with the principle of the precedence of Community law, the relationship between provisions of the Treaty and directly applicable measures of the institutions on the one hand and the national law of the Member States on the other is such that those provisions and measures not only by their entry into force render automatically inapplicable any conflicting provision of current national law but – in so far as they are an integral part of, and take precedence in, the legal order applicable in the territory of each of the Member States – also preclude the valid adoption of new national legislative measures to the extent to which they would be incompatible with Community provisions.'

84 ECJ Case C-106/89, *Marleasing* v. *La Comercial*, [1991] ECR I-7321.

85 Ibid., Paragraph 8: '. . . in applying national law, whether the provisions in question were adopted before or after [a] directive, the national court called upon to interpret it is required to do so, as far as possible, in the light of the wording and the purpose of the directive in order to achieve the result pursued by the latter.'

86 ECJ Joined Cases 6/90 and 9/90, *Andrea Francovich, Danilo Bonifaci and others* v. *Republic of Italy*, [1991] ECR I-5404.

87 Ibid., Paragraph 35: '. . . the principle whereby a State must be liable for loss and damage caused to individuals as a result of breaches of Community law for which the State can be held responsible is inherent in the system of the Treaty.'

ing to the envisaged Article 1-6 was inserted into the TEU. Instead, in the context of the Lisbon Treaty, the following declaration[88] was issued:

> 17. Declaration concerning primacy
> The Conference recalls that, in accordance with well settled case law of the Court of Justice of the European Union, the Treaties and the law adopted by the Union on the basis of the Treaties have primacy over the law of Member States, under the conditions laid down by the said case law.
> The Conference has also decided to attach as an Annex to this Final Act the Opinion of the Council Legal Service on the primacy of EC law as set out in 11197/07 (JUR 260):
> *'Opinion of the Council Legal Service of 22 June 2007*
> It results from the case-law of the Court of Justice that primacy of EC law is a cornerstone principle of Community law. According to the Court, this principle is inherent to the specific nature of the European Community. At the time of the first judgment of this established case law (Costa/ENEL, 15 July 1964, Case 6/641[(1)]) there was no mention of primacy in the treaty. It is still the case today. The fact that the principle of primacy will not be included in the future treaty shall not in any way change the existence of the principle and the existing case-law of the Court of Justice.
> (1) It follows . . . that the law stemming from the treaty, an independent source of law, could not, because of its special and original nature, be overridden by domestic legal provisions, however framed, without being deprived of its character as Community law and without the legal basis of the Community itself being called into question.'

 QUESTIONS

1 The TFEU has subjected the creation of new Community-wide intellectual property rights to the ordinary legislative process and thereby to majority vote. Do you consider that appropriate?

2 Pursuant to Article 118 (2) TFEU, language issues have been singled out and are still subject to a unanimity requirement. What could be the reason for that?

3 Secondary Community legislation in the area of IP is rather far advanced. In your opinion, is there any major loophole left (apart from the fact that the unitary patent is not yet operative)?

---

88 See eur-lex.europa.eu/en/treaties/dat/12007L/htm/C2007306EN.01025602.htm.

2.4 International conventions and EU intellectual property law

Membership in international agreements

Until recently, international conventions on the protection of intellectual property did not provide for the possibility of accession by supra-national organisations such as the EU. This has changed in the 1990s, when the EU (at that time: the EC) – after realising the outstanding importance of intellectual property matters for internal as well as external trade flows – began to take a stand as a powerful player in the pertinent international negotiations. In the first place, this concerned the WTO Agreement with its annexes including TRIPS. The EU became a member of those agreements and is therefore bound to comply with the norms and standards set out therein as well as to observe the substantive obligations under the Paris and Berne Conventions by virtue of Article 2 and 9 TRIPS. Thereafter, the EU has acceded to a number of other international agreements, such as the WCT and the WPPT as well as the Madrid Protocol on the international registration of trade marks. Furthermore, the EU has adopted a proactive policy with regard to concluding bilateral agreements with its trading partners in the form of so-called Economic Partnership Agreements (EPAs), which usually include a chapter on intellectual property protection.[89]

Competence

Previous situation: joint competence

In the context of accession to the WTO Agreement, the division of competence between the EC and its Member States had been contentious, and the ECJ was therefore requested to render an Opinion on the issue (Opinion 1/94).[90] The Commission had argued *inter alia* that the Community's exclusive competence to conclude GATS[91] and TRIPS flowed implicitly from the provisions of the Treaty establishing its *internal* competence. The ECJ accepted the argument in principle, but found that, with the sole exception of the release of counterfeit goods on the Common Market which was

---

89 See Chapter 1, section 1.5.3.2.

90 ECJ Opinion 1/94, Competence of the Community to conclude international agreements concerning services and the protection of intellectual property – Article 228 (6) of the EC Treaty, [1994] ECR I-5267.

91 General Agreement on Trade in Services, Annex 1B to the WTO Treaty, wto.org/english/docs_e/legal_e/26-gats.pdf.

addressed at the time by Regulation No 3842/86,[92] it did not warrant exclusivity of the competence established on that basis. Based on previous case law,[93] the ECJ first pointed out with regard to GATS that the EC acquires exclusive competence where it has achieved complete harmonisation of the relevant rules, because the common rules thus adopted could be affected if the Member States retained freedom to negotiate with non-member countries. Applying those rules to TRIPS, it was emphasised that:

> (103) . . . the harmonization achieved within the Community in certain areas covered by TRIPS is only partial and . . . in other areas, no harmonization has been envisaged. There has been only partial harmonization as regards trade marks, for example . . . In other areas covered by TRIPS, no Community harmonization measures have been adopted.

Whereas no exclusive competence of the Community could therefore be established in the areas where harmonisation was still lacking, the ECJ also did not accept either the argument made by some Member States that at least some measures falling under TRIPS were within their sole competence:

> (104) Some of the Governments which have submitted observations have argued that the provisions of TRIPs relating to the measures to be adopted to secure the effective protection of intellectual property rights, such as those ensuring a fair and just procedure, the rules regarding the submission of evidence, the right to be heard, the giving of reasons for decisions, the right of appeal, interim measures and the award of damages, fall within the competence of the Member States. If that argument is to be understood as meaning that all those matters are within some sort of domain reserved to the Member States, it cannot be accepted. The Community is certainly competent to harmonise national rules on those matters, in so far as . . . they 'directly affect the establishment or functioning of the common market'. But the fact remains that the Community institutions have not hitherto exercised their powers in the field of the 'enforcement of intellectual property rights . . .'. (105) It follows that the Community and its Member States are jointly competent to conclude TRIPS.

It followed from the systematic approach taken by the ECJ that the scope of the Community's exclusive competence increases in accordance with the

---

92 Council Regulation (EEC) No 3842/86 of 1 December 1986 laying down measures to prohibit the release for free circulation of counterfeit goods, [1986] OJ L 357/1; now replaced by Council Regulation (EC) No 1383/2003 of 22 July 2003 concerning customs action against goods suspected of infringing certain intellectual property rights and the measures to be taken against goods found to have infringed such rights, [2003] OJ L 196/7.

93 ECJ Case 22/70, *Commission v. Council* (AETR judgment), [1971] ECR 263.

progress of harmonisation and unification measures in all areas of intellectual property.

Changes under the TFEU

Pursuant to Article 3 lit e TFEU, the EU has exclusive competence in the area of common commercial policy. The ambit of Union competence deriving therefrom is further specified in Article 207 (1) TFEU:

1. The common commercial policy shall be based on uniform principles, particularly with regard to changes in tariff rates, the conclusion of tariff and trade agreements relating to trade in goods and services, *and the commercial aspects of intellectual property,* foreign direct investment, the achievement of uniformity in measures of liberalisation, export policy and measures to protect trade such as those to be taken in the event of dumping or subsidies. The common commercial policy shall be conducted in the context of the principles and objectives of the Union's external action. (Emphasis added)

2. The European Parliament and the Council, acting by means of Regulations in accordance with the ordinary legislative procedure, shall adopt the measures defining the framework for implementing the common commercial policy.

3. Where agreements with one or more third countries or international organisations need to be negotiated and concluded, Article 218 shall apply, subject to the special provisions of this Article.

The Commission shall make recommendations to the Council, which shall authorise it to open the necessary negotiations. The Council and the Commission shall be responsible for ensuring that the agreements negotiated are compatible with internal Union policies and rules.

The Commission shall conduct these negotiations in consultation with a special committee appointed by the Council to assist the Commission in this task and within the framework of such Directives as the Council may issue to it. The Commission shall report regularly to the special committee and to the European Parliament on the progress of negotiations.

4. For the negotiation and conclusion of the agreements referred to in paragraph 3, the Council shall act by a qualified majority.

For the negotiation and conclusion of agreements in the fields of trade in services and the commercial aspects of intellectual property, as well as foreign direct investment, the Council shall act unanimously where such agreements include provisions for which unanimity is required for the adoption of internal rules.

. . .

6. The exercise of the competences conferred by this Article in the field of the common commercial policy shall not affect the delimitation of competences between the Union and the Member States, and shall not lead to harmonisation of

legislative or regulatory provisions of the Member States in so far as the Treaties exclude such harmonisation.

Without prejudice to the division of competences set out in Article 207, the procedures to be followed in the negotiation and conclusion of international agreements are regulated by Article 218 TFEU. As a matter of principle:

- the *Council* authorises the opening of negotiations, adopts negotiating Directives, authorises the signing of agreements and concludes them;
- the *Commission* submits recommendations to the Council; and
- the *European Parliament* must, in most cases, give consent to the conclusion of an agreement; otherwise, it must be consulted.

ECJ case law addressing international obligations

Compatibility of EU legislation with TRIPS

Where the EC had gained exclusive competence, national provisions addressing issues falling into the ambit of TRIPS and, by implication, of the Paris and Berne Conventions, could be examined with regard to their TRIPS-compliance by the ECJ. Thus, in *Hermès International*[94] the ECJ had been asked for a preliminary decision concerning the compliance with Article 50 TRIPS of a provision on preliminary injunctions anchored in Dutch procedural law. The underlying case concerned an alleged infringement of copyright and trade mark law. The ECJ affirmed that Community competence existed due to the fact that the CTMR, which went into force briefly before TRIPS had been signed, includes an obligation in Article 99 (now Article 102) to provide for injunctive relief in case of Community trade mark infringement:

> (28) It is true that the measures envisaged by Article 99 and the relevant procedural rules are those provided for by the domestic law of the Member State concerned for the purposes of the national trade mark. However, since the Community is a party to the TRIPS Agreement and since that agreement applies to the Community trade mark, the courts referred to in Article 99 [CTMR], called upon to apply national rules with a view to ordering provisional measures for the protection of rights arising under a Community trade mark, are required to do so, as far as possible, in the light of the wording and purpose of Article 50 of the

---

94 ECJ Case C-53/96, *Hermès International* v. *FHT Marketing Choice*, [1998] ECR I-3603; confirmed in Joined Cases C-300/98 and C-392/98, *Dior* v. *Tuk* and *Assco* v. *Layher*, [2000] ECR I-11307.

TRIPS Agreement [citations omitted]. (29) It follows that the Court has, in any event, jurisdiction to interpret Article 50 of the TRIPS Agreement.

Furthermore, regarding the aspect that the measure did not only relate to the alleged infringement of trade mark law, but also to copyright, the ECJ held that:

> (32) [w]here a provision can apply both to situations falling within the scope of national law and to situations falling within the scope of Community law, it is clearly in the Community interest that, in order to forestall future differences of interpretation, that provision should be interpreted uniformly, whatever the circumstances in which it is to apply.

Compatibility of national law with TRIPS and – by implication – with the Paris Convention also played a role in case C-245/02 *Anheuser-Busch*,[95] where the ECJ had been asked *inter alia* whether Article 8 of the Paris Convention, pursuant to which trade names 'shall be protected . . . without the obligation for filing a registration' was violated by a rule of Finnish law which accorded protection to unregistered trade names only under the condition that they have achieved a certain level of recognition among the interested circles. Having confirmed its competence, the ECJ ruled that neither Article 16 (1) TRIPS nor Article 8 of the Paris Convention preclude such conditions as are posed under Finnish law.[96]

Different from that, in *Merck v. Merck Genéricos*[97] the ECJ denied jurisdiction with regard to the question whether a rule anchored in Portuguese patent law contravened Article 33 TRIPS (minimum term of protection), as enjoyment of the full term was denied to patents which were already in force at the time when TRIPS was implemented. Considering whether Community legislation existed in the field of patents, the ECJ concluded that there was none:

> (41) . . . [O]nly [the Biotech Directive] concerns the field of patents itself. However, it is only a specific isolated case in that field which is regulated by the directive, namely, the patentability of biotechnological inventions which is, moreover, quite distinct from the object of Article 33 of the TRIPs Agreement. (42) Regulation No 2100/94 sets up a system for the Community protection of plant varieties which . . . cannot be placed on the same footing as the system of patents

---

95 ECJ Case C-245/02, *Anheuser-Busch v. Budějovický Budvar*, [2004] ECR I-10989.
96 Ibid., Paragraph 97.
97 ECJ Case C-431/05, *Merck Genéricos v. Merck & Co*, [2007] ECR I-7001.

... (43) Lastly, [the Regulations on a supplementary protection certificate for pharmaceuticals and] plant protection products ... [have another purpose that patent law and do not] (44) ... affect the domestic, and therefore perhaps different, extent of the protection conferred by the patent or, more specifically, the term as such of the patent, which is still governed by the domestic law under which it was obtained.

Also, in *British American Tobacco*[98] the ECJ made it clear that even where its competence basically exists, it is not willing to exercise jurisdiction for purposes of making a general assessment of the compatibility of Community legislation with TRIPS. The actual dispute concerned Directive 2001/37/EC on the manufacture, presentation and sale of tobacco products. The legality of the obligation of the UK government to transpose the Directive into national law had been challenged in court by tobacco firms, and the deciding court had referred the questions on to the ECJ, *inter alia* concerning the compatibility of the prescribed labelling measures with Article 20 TRIPS. Citing previous case law, the ECJ declared that:

> (154) ... the lawfulness of a Community measure cannot be assessed in the light of instruments of international law which, like the ... TRIPS Agreement ... are not in principle ... among the rules in the light of which the Court is to review the lawfulness of measures adopted by the Community institutions [*citations omitted*] ... (155) [O]nly where the Community intended to implement a particular obligation assumed in the context of the WTO, or where the Community measure refers expressly to the precise provisions of the WTO agreements, ... it is for the Court to review the legality of the Community measure in question in the light of the WTO rules. (Citations omitted)

Direct effect of international norms

One crucial distinction between national systems concerns the issue of whether and to what extent they provide for direct application of norms enshrined in international agreements. The key to the issue lies, firstly, in the constitutional elements of national legal systems, i.e. in whether they apply a 'monist' approach which basically treats international instruments as part of the law that must also be applied internally, or whether they adhere to a strictly 'dualist' theory which accepts as binding national law only legal acts which have been passed as such through the ordinary legislative procedures. Secondly, the question of whether a provision of international law can be

---

98 ECJ Case C-491/01, *The Queen v. Secretary of State for Health, ex parte British American Tobacco (Investments) and Imperial Tobacco*, [2002] ECR I-11453.

applied directly also depends on the nature of that provision, i.e. whether it is clear, precise and unconditional. And finally, it is of relevance whether direct application is appropriate in the light of the purpose, structure and context of the relevant international agreement.

The legal systems in the EU Member States follow different schemes in that regard. At least in some Member States – e.g. Germany, France – some provisions of the Paris Convention were found capable of direct application. This concerns in particular Article 6 *bis* (protection of non-registered, well-known marks) and 6 *quinquies* (so-called *telle quelle* protection of marks that are validly registered in the proprietor's country of origin) Paris Convention.[99]

Regarding the EU itself, the ECJ has repeatedly ruled that the law does *not* provide for direct application of international norms, at least insofar as TRIPS is concerned. The issue was first addressed in the context of intellectual property law in the *Dior* judgment.[100] Similar to the *Hermès* case addressed above, the dispute concerned *inter alia* the question of whether provisions on preliminary injunctions set out in Dutch procedural law complied with TRIPS, as they did not provide for an obligatory review clause as prescribed in Article 50 (6) TRIPS. The referring court requested an answer to the question whether, upon default of national law in the relevant regard, Article 50 (6) can, or must be, applied directly. The ECJ referred to its previous judgment in *Portugal* v. *Council*,[101] where it had been set out that the mechanisms ensuring compliance with the agreement were such that they demanded action or relied on negotiations between the contracting parties involved in the dispute about reasonable compensation, and that those mechanisms would be disrupted if the judicial organs of Member States were required to refrain, by way of direct application of international norms, from applying the rules of domestic law which are inconsistent with the WTO agreements.[102] Accordingly, like in *Portugal* v. *Council*, it was found that:

> (44) . . . the provisions of TRIPS . . . are not such as to create rights upon which individuals may rely directly before the courts by virtue of Community law.

In accordance with that ruling, the ECJ denied the request to consider the compatibility of OHIM's examination standards with Article 6 *quinquies* of the Paris Convention in the context of an appeal filed against a judgment by

---

99 See Chapter 1, section 1.4.1.2.
100 ECJ Joined Cases C-300/98 and C-392/98, *Dior* v. *Tuk* and *Assco* v. *Layher*, [2000] ECR I-11307.
101 ECJ Case C-149/96, *Portuguese Republic* v. *Council of the European Union* (*Portugal* v. *Council*), [1999] ECR I-8395.
102 Ibid., Paragraphs 37–40.

the General Court confirming the decision of OHIM to reject the application for registration of the relevant sign (shape of plastic bottle for *Develey* mustard) as a Community trade mark. As the Court pointed out, the Paris Convention could not be applied directly already on the ground that the EU is not a member, and TRIPS – which implies the obligations under the Paris Convention – is not directly applicable for the reasons set out in the *Portugal* v. *Council* and *Dior* judgments.[103]

? QUESTIONS

1 Do you consider the ECJ's arguments regarding direct application of the TRIPS Agreement as convincing?

2 Please compare Develey (when the ECJ denied jurisdiction with regard to the interpretation of Article 6 *quinquies* of the Paris Convention) with Anheuser-Busch (when the ECJ commented on the interpretation of *inter alia* Article 8 Paris Convention). Do you find a reason for the different reactions?

3 Likewise, is the broad affirmation of ECJ competence in Hermès and Dior compatible with the refusal to adjudicate on issues of patent law in Merck Genéricos?

2.5 Human rights and European intellectual property law

The European Human Rights Convention

As the EEC and EC Treaties were primarily focused on economic integration, human rights were not directly addressed therein. Instead, the leading role in this matter was played by another Europe-based treaty organisation, the Council of Europe (CoE). The CoE – not to be confused with the European Council – was founded in 1949 as a pan-European political organisation. Today it counts 47 Member States including all 27 EU Member States, as well as Switzerland, the EEA Member States and most other States on the European continent (with the exception of Belarus), including Russia and Turkey.[104] The CoE describes its primary goal as:

---

103 ECJ Case C-238/06 P, *Develey v. OHIM,* [2007] ECR I-9375, Paragraphs 39–44. See also ECJ Case 428/08, *Monsanto* v *Cefetra,* [2010] ECR I-6765, Paragraphs 70–77, concerning the compatibility of the Biotech Directive with Article 27 and 30 of the TRIPS Agreement: while direct applicability of TRIPS is denied in accordance with the pre-cited decisions, it is also emphasised that when applying the relevant provisions, Member States must try, as far as may be possible, to 'supply an interpretation in keeping with the TRIPS Agreement'. In the actual case, the relevant TRIPS provisions were considered to be met; for details see Chapter 3, section 3.3.1.3.2.3.

104 For information see hub.coe.int.

creat[ing] a common democratic and legal area throughout the whole of the continent [and] ensuring respect for its fundamental values: human rights, democracy and the rule of law.[105]

Several conventions have been promulgated in the framework of the CoE, the most recent one being the Medicrime Convention which aims at raising public awareness and bolstering the fight against fake medicaments.[106] Of primary importance among those texts is the European Convention on Human Rights (ECHR) of 1950 with its five protocols.[107] Similar to the Universal Declaration of Human Rights (UDHR),[108] the ECHR guarantees the rights to life, freedom from servitude, and personal integrity as well as freedom of expression and the right to privacy. The first protocol to the ECHR also protects in Article 1 the peaceful enjoyment of one's possessions, with a reservation being made for the right of a State to enforce laws which are deemed necessary to control the use of property in accordance with, *inter alia*, the general interest.

Violations of the ECHR are brought before the European Court of Human Rights in Strasbourg (ECtHR). The history, role and competence of the ECtHR are briefly described as follows:[109]

> The European Court of Human Rights is an international court set up in 1959. It rules on individual or State applications alleging violations of the civil and political rights set out in the European Convention on Human Rights. Since 1998 it has sat as a full-time court and individuals can apply to it directly.
>
> In almost fifty years the Court has delivered more than 10,000 judgments. These are binding on the countries concerned and have led governments to alter their legislation and administrative practice in a wide range of areas. The Court's case-law makes the Convention a powerful living instrument for meeting new challenges and consolidating the rule of law and democracy in Europe.

Judgments by the ECtHR addressing intellectual property matters are presented in this Chapter, section 2.5.3.1.

---

105 See www.coe.int/aboutcoe/index.asp?page=nosObjectifs&l=en.
106 See www.coe.int/t/DGHL/StandardSetting/MediCrime/Medicrime-version%20bilingue.pdf.
107 See www.hri.org/docs/ECHR50.html.
108 See www.hri.org/docs/UDHR48.html.
109 See www.echr.coe.int/NR/rdonlyres/DF074FE4-96C2-4384-BFF6-404AAF5BC585/0/Brochure_en_bref_EN.pdf.

Human Rights and Community law

The European Communities and the ECHR

Unlike the Member States, the European Communities did not adhere to the ECHR. This was due to the fact that, according to the ECJ, the Basic Treaties did not provide a sufficient legal basis for such a step being taken. In an opinion on the issue which had been requested by several Member States, the ECJ had pointed out that:[110]

> (32) It should first be noted that the importance of respect for human rights has been emphasised in various declarations of the Member States and of the Community institutions. . . . (33) Furthermore, it is well settled that fundamental rights form an integral part of the general principles of law whose observance the Court ensures. For that purpose, the Court draws inspiration from the constitutional traditions common to the Member States and from the guidelines supplied by international treaties for the protection of human rights on which the Member States have collaborated or of which they arc signatories. In that regard, the Court has stated that the [ECHR] has special significance. (34) Respect for human rights is therefore a condition of the lawfulness of Community acts. Accession to the [ECHR] would, however, entail a substantial change in the present Community system for the protection of human rights in that it would entail the entry of the Community into a distinct international institutional system as well as integration of all the provisions of the [ECHR] into the Community legal order. (35) Such a modification of the system for the protection of human rights in the Community, with equally fundamental institutional implications for the Community and for the Member States, would be of constitutional significance and . . . could be brought about only by way of Treaty amendment.

The required Treaty amendment was effected by the Treaty of Lisbon. Pursuant to Article 6 (2) of the EU Treaty:

> The Union shall accede to the European Convention for the Protection of Human Rights and Fundamental Freedoms. Such accession shall not affect the Union's competences as defined in the Treaties.

However, before the obligation implied in Article 6 (2) EU can be implemented, it is necessary also that the ECHR is changed, which until now does not provide for accession of supranational organisations.

---

110 ECJ Opinion 2/94 , *Accession by the Community to the European Convention for the Protection of Human Rights and Fundamental Freedoms* (28 March 1996), [1996] ECR I-1759.

The Charter of Fundamental Rights

In a more direct manner than through accession to the ECHR, human rights are now protected under EU law on the basis of the Charter of Fundamental Rights, which forms part of the Lisbon Treaty. The Charter had been promulgated already in 2000; it was intended to form part of the Treaty establishing a Constitution for Europe (TCE), which failed after having been rejected in referendums by the French and Dutch voters. Other than originally foreseen, the Charter has not been integrated into the EU Treaty. However, Article 6 (1) EU makes reference to the Charter and sets forth that it is of equal legal value.

In its contents, the Charter basically reflects the same fundamental values and principles as other instruments dealing with protection of human rights. Protection of property is addressed in Article 17 (1):

> Everyone has the right to own, use, dispose of and bequeath his or her lawfully acquired possessions. No one may be deprived of his or her possessions, except in the public interest and in the cases and under the conditions provided for by law, subject to fair compensation being paid in good time for their loss. The use of property may be regulated by law in so far as is necessary for the general interest.

Quite remarkably, the second paragraph makes express reference to intellectual property rights:

> Intellectual property rights shall be protected.

It has been questioned whether that clause is merely of a declaratory character or whether it has a reinforcing effect weighing in favour of proprietary interests in case of conflicts. At least until now, nothing in the case law of the ECJ indicates that such a reinforcing effect has actually occurred.

Case law

ECtHR

The ECtHR has adjudicated several times on the 'property' aspects of intellectual property. The most important of those decisions concerned the question whether such protection already had to be granted to applications for registered intellectual property rights. In the actual dispute, the American firm Anheuser-Busch had applied in Portugal for registration of the trade mark 'Budweiser' for beer. Subsequent to the filing of the application, Portugal concluded a bilateral treaty with the Czech Republic by which protection for 'Budweiser' was reserved for indicating the geographic origin of beer brewed by the Czech firm Budějovický Budvar, thereby precluding Anheuser-Busch's application from maturing into a trade mark registration. One chamber of the ECtHR ruled that although trade mark registrations were to be considered as 'property' in the sense of Article 1 first protocol to the ECHR, protection did not extend to mere applications. That finding was however overruled on appeal by the Grand Chamber:[111] although the application, unlike the final registration, does not grant a proprietary right, it nevertheless gives rise to the legitimate expectation that the registration will be effected if no obstacles are found under the legislation in force. If registration is denied due to intervention of legislation with retroactive effect, this may therefore amount to depriving the applicant of a position which is protected under the property rights clause of the ECHR.

Further decisions by the ECtHR have dealt with freedom of speech in the context of Advertising Regulations. Importantly, it was found that the right to free speech does not only apply to political statements and similar types of comments,[112] but also to commercial expressions.[113]

Finally, a remarkable decision by the ECtHR addressed the conflict between freedom of expression and the right to privacy. The case concerned photos taken at various occasions of the former princess of Monaco, Caroline (whose married name was 'von Hannover'), and the publication of those photos in the German yellow press. The German courts had applied a doctrine developed in case law, which allowed publishing photos being taken of a figure of contemporary society *par excellence* ('absolute Person der Zeitgeschichte') when she appeared in a public place, unless her personal interests were ostensibly violated thereby. That approach had been expressly endorsed by the German constitutional court as striking a fair balance between the public and private interests involved. The ECtHR arrived at a different conclusion,[114] holding that the interest of the public to know where

---

111 ECtHR, *Anheuser-Busch v. Portugal*, Application No. 73049/01, (2007) 45 EHRR 36 [830].

112 See ECtHR, *X and Church of Scientology v. Sweden*, Application No. 7805/77, [1979] DR 16, p. 68; *Ingemar Liljenberg v. Sweden*, Application No. 9664/82; *Hertel v. Switzerland*, Application No. (53440/99) 59/1997/843/1049, Reports 1998-VI, 2298.

113 See ECtHR, *Markt Intern and Beermann v. Germany*, (1990) 12 EHRR 161, Paragraph 34; *Hertel v. Switzerland*, (1999) 38 EHRR 534, Paragraph 47, and, in particular, *Krone Verlag v. Austria (No. 3)*, (2006) 42 EHRR 28, Paragraph 30 *et seq.* (holding that the former ban on price comparisons in Austrian law violated Article 10 ECHR).

114 ECtHR, *Von Hannover v. Germany*, Application No. 59320/00, (2005) 40 EHRR 1. In a second case between the same parties decided on 7 February 2012, the Court came to a different conclusion, based on a somewhat more nuanced reasoning; see *Von Hannover v. Germany (2)*, Application Nos. 40660/08 and

a well-known person like the applicant is and how she behaves in her private life is generally inferior to her right to privacy, meaning that an overriding interest of the public must only be acknowledged where the person appears in the context of performing her official functions.

ECJ

Although Community law until recently did not contain an express reference to human rights, the ECJ has confirmed several times that it considers itself bound to the observation of the principles enshrined in the UDHR and the ECHR.[115] It is indeed a matter of general understanding that the core principles of human rights protection form part of international customary law in the sense of *jus cogens*, meaning that they apply with binding effect irrespective of whether or not they have been cast in the form of express codifications.

In the context of intellectual property rights, the issue became relevant when the Directive on Biotechnological Inventions (98/44/EC) was attacked by the government of the Netherlands as unconstitutional.[116] The claim was founded on several grounds, *inter alia* concerning the fundamental right to respect for human dignity. It was argued that:

> the patentability of isolated parts of the human body provided for by Article 5 (2) of the directive reduce living human matter to a means to an end, undermining human dignity [and that] the absence of a provision requiring verification of the consent of the donor or recipient of products obtained by biotechnological means undermines the right to self-determination.[117]

In its response, the ECJ pointed to various elements in the Directive (Recital nos 20 and 21, Articles 5 (1), (3) and (6)), which, according to the ECJ, showed:

> (77) . . . that the Directive frames the law on patents in a manner sufficiently rigorous to ensure that the human body effectively remains unavailable and inalienable and that human dignity is thus safeguarded.

60641/08.

115 This was emphasised in the ECJ's Opinion 2/94, *Accession by the Community to the European Convention for the Protection of Human Rights and Fundamental Freedoms* (28 March 1996), [1996] ECR I-1759.

116 ECJ Case C-377/98, *Netherlands v. European Parliament and Council of the European Union*, [2001] ECR I-7079.

117 Ibid., Paragraph 69.

Furthermore, with regard to the right to self-determination, it was held that:

> (79) . . . reliance on this fundamental right is . . . clearly misplaced as against a directive which concerns only the grant of patents and whose scope does not therefore extend to activities before and after that grant, whether they involve research or the use of the patented products.

Similar issues were raised in the *Brüstle* judgment[118] regarding uses of human embryos for industrial or commercial purposes. The background and implications of that decision are considered in Chapter 3, section 3.4.1.1.2.2.

Another topic of strong and growing concern where fundamental rights are poised against each other regards the tension between efficient enforcement of intellectual property rights on the one hand and the protection of personal data and privacy on the other. The issue has been addressed by the ECJ in several decisions concerning claims for information against internet service providers (ISPs) which are presented in Chapter 5, section 5.3.2.10 and Chapter 8, section 8.2.2.2.

 QUESTIONS

1 In recent years, the interface between intellectual property and human rights has been the subject of much debate. What are the reasons? Why has the topic become so controversial?
2 After enactment of the Charter of Fundamental Rights, the ECJ is competent to adjudicate on alleged violations of human rights in parallel with the ECtHR. What would happen if the two courts arrive at different conclusions? (Potential conflicts of that kind are addressed in the ECtHR's decision of 30 June 2005, *Bosphorus Airways* v. *Ireland*, Application No. 45036/98).
3 In your opinion, why was intellectual property mentioned expressly in Article 17 (2) of the Charter on Fundamental Rights? Does it make a difference? In what way?
4 With regard to copyright in the digital environment, several commentators have suggested that the fundamental property right should be balance with the equally fundamental human right to information. What could be meant by this?

---

118 ECJ Case C-34/10, *Brüstle v. Greenpeace*, [2011] ECR I-0000.

3

Patents

3.1 Introduction

Objectives and developments

The core objective pursued by the grant of patents is to spur innovative activities so as to promote technical progress. In earlier times, such rights were granted in the form of privileges issued by the sovereign to artisans or merchants in particular sectors of trade, in order to secure their sole right of manufacturing, or sometimes importing, highly valued articles. In the industrial age, patents became the preferred tool for boosting a country's competitiveness in the production of new technology, by rewarding inventors with an exclusive market position for a limited number of years. By making disclosure of the invention a mandatory condition for protection,[1] it was ensured that the technical knowledge embodied in the invention became publicly available, thus enhancing the general level of technical expertise in the field concerned.

As with the other major IP rights, the basic tenets of patent law are still the same as they were more than a century ago. However, due to the fundamental changes in the kind and pace of technological development, the role and impact of patents in the current socio-economic environment have little in common with the original concepts. Most conspicuously, this concerns the number of patents that may apply to a single product. Whereas in the early days, new machines or tools were basically covered by a single patent, nowadays more than a thousand patents may apply to a single product. This is true in particular for information and communication technology (ICT) such as cell phones and personal computers etc. Whoever engages in activities within that sector therefore has to secure the necessary multitude of rights, usually by acquiring licenses, which typically entails high transaction costs. It has been questioned therefore whether patent law, at least in crowded industry sectors such as ICT, is still capable of fulfilling its original func-

---

1 Indeed the term 'patent' derives from the Latin word 'patere' – lying open.

tion, or whether it has become a tool for obstructing rather than promoting innovation.

On the other hand, clear evidence is lacking that the pace of innovation is actually slowed down by the sheer mass of patents. In practice, ways have been developed to deal with the problem. As most firms find themselves on the demand side as well as in the position of holding rights, they usually contract out of potential infringements by offering cross-licenses to other firms that are possibly affected. Such arrangements can also be made in more firmly structured forms, by building so-called patent pools. Here, companies assemble complementary patents that are needed as building blocks for development of new products and offer them – in particular in the process of standardisation – for licensing under fair, reasonable and non-discriminatory terms (FRAND licenses). However, the smooth functioning of such licensing arrangements depends on the willingness of all actors to cooperate, and it will fail if an outsider – most frequently a right-holder who does not produce anything, and therefore does not have an interest in cross-licensing – is in possession of a patent covering a key element of the technology needed, which cannot be substituted by others. Patent holders using such bottleneck positions to demand exorbitant sums as license fees and/or filing excessive damage claims for infringement – so-called 'patent trolls' – have become a nuisance haunting patentees in particular in the USA, but to some extent also in Europe. As a reaction to that phenomenon, it has been questioned whether prohibitive injunctions with their high potential of making competitors vulnerable to 'hold-up' situations should actually remain to be the regular consequence for every kind of patent infringement, or whether companies acting as 'patent trolls' should rather be referred to claiming (modest) damages.[2]

The problem is exacerbated by the fact that the quality of patents is sometimes rather poor. This is due to a number of factors: first, applications in general have become more voluminous and complex to examine for patent offices. This has an impact on the workload of the office and may consequently compromise the quality of the patents granted. Second, in particular in new sectors of technology, the documentation of prior art may be inconclusive and does not yield a solid basis for a comprehensive scrutiny of the innovative character of an invention. Third, smaller patent offices often only have a limited number of patent examiners who have to cover a too broad variety

---

2 As far as can be seen, there is no (published) European jurisprudence on this issue. The exemplary case to which reference is regularly made in the context of discussions about patent trolls is a US Supreme Court decision, *eBay Inc. v. MercExchange*, 547 US 388 (2006).

of technological fields when examining the patent applications. Fourth, the budget of patent offices usually depends on the number of patents granted, hence providing an incentive for granting rather than rejecting patent applications. Furthermore, it is true that in many technological sectors, even incremental progress has become a matter of high investment. If it is assumed that such investments will only be made under the expectancy that the findings are eventually rewarded by an exclusive right, it appears logical to lower the threshold accordingly. On the other hand, as mentioned before, the proliferation of patents ensuing from such policies is liable to create obstacles for others engaging in innovative activities in the same field. This is particularly problematic where so-called patent thickets are created: patents covering different variations and modes of use of a certain technology, making it impossible for others to find a proper space for their own research efforts, and blocking activities on downstream (or upstream) markets.

Another crucial difference distinguishing contemporary patent law from its beginnings concerns the technologies covered. Whereas patents were originally granted for new machines and other mechanical inventions, their ambit has been expanded to cover also chemical processes and products, and lately also biotechnological inventions. The latter has given rise to a number of very sensitive issues, in particular regarding the possibilities and restrictions of 'patenting life'. Furthermore, obtaining patents for isolated genes or strands of DNA triggers the question of where to draw the borderline between (patentable) inventions and (non-patentable) discoveries. Also, chemical products as well as biotechnological inventions are often relevant in the medical sector, as pharmaceuticals or diagnostic tools, hence forming the background for the political clash between IP protection and the right to get access to (affordable) medicines.[3]

Patent law in Europe

In view of the importance of patents as a major instrument in shaping national industrial innovation policies, it is rather surprising that up until now the EU has not produced much European patent law in the strict sense.[4]

Harmonisation of EU patent law consists of only one sectorial harmonising measure, the Directive on biotechnological inventions of 1998.[5] A second Directive that had been proposed with the aim of harmonising the practice of

---

3 On some of those issues see Chapter 1, section 1.5.3.1.
4 See the overview in Chapter 2, section 2.3.2.4.
5 Directive 98/44/EC of the European Parliament and of the Council of 6 July 1998 on the legal protection of biotechnological inventions, [1998] OJ L 213/13 (Biotech Directive).

granting patents for computer-related inventions met with fierce resistance mainly from the open source community and was ultimately withdrawn.[6] Likewise, efforts begun in the mid 1990s to approximate the legal arrangements for the protection of inventions by utility models[7] were subsequently no longer pursued.

On the Community level, with the exception of the so-called supplementary protection certificates for medicinal and agrochemical products,[8] the long-standing plans to establish a Community patent have not until now led to tangible results. A first attempt at establishing the necessary legal structures was undertaken in 1975, when the Community Patent Convention (CPC) was concluded between the (then) nine EEC Members.[9] However, the CPC never went into force – *inter alia*, ratification of the convention proved to be impossible in Denmark, where a 5/6 majority of votes would have had to be secured in parliament. Only in the last decade have the plans to establish a unitary patent right for the territory of the European Union been revived and may ultimately lead to success.[10]

In spite of the failure until now to establish a unitary right within the Community, patent law has attained a rather high level of Europeanisation. This results primarily from the fact that since 1973, with the European Patent Convention (EPC), there exists a highly efficient system for obtaining patent protection in Europe albeit outside of the EU institutions, and with a membership comprising a considerable number of non-EU states.[11] And although the common granting procedures established under the EPC leave the national patent laws basically unaffected, the joint effect of the EPC and

---

6 See ec.europa.eu/internal_market/indprop/comp/index_en.htm and the Proposal for a Directive of the European Parliament and of the Council 20 February 2002 on the patentability of computer-implemented inventions, COM(2002) 92 final.

7 See ec.europa.eu/internal_market/indprop/model/index_en.htm. As explained in the Commission's initial Proposal for a European Parliament and Council Directive approximating the legal arrangements for the protection of inventions by utility model, COM(97) 691 final, a utility model is a 'registered right which confers exclusive protection for a technical invention. It resembles a patent in that the invention must be new it must possess "novelty" and must display a measure of inventive achievement it must involve an "inventive step", though generally the level of inventiveness required is not as great as it is in the case of patents. Unlike patents, utility models are granted as a rule without a preliminary examination to establish novelty and inventive step. This means that protection can be obtained more rapidly and cheaply, but that the protection conferred is less secure.'

8 Regulation (EC) 469/2009 of 6 May 2009 concerning the creation of a supplementary protection certificate for medicinal products (codified version), [2009] OJ L 152/1, and Regulation (EC) 1610/96 of 23 July 1996 concerning the creation of a supplementary certificate for plant protection products, [1996] OJ L 198/30. For discussion see in this Chapter, section 3.5.

9 Convention for the European patent for the common market (Community Patent Convention), [1976] OJ L 17/1.

10 For details, see in this Chapter, section 3.6.

11 See in this Chapter, section 3.2.1.

the (failed) CPC has been that the substantive patent laws of the Member States were approximated to a fairly large extent – without being subject to a formal obligation to harmonise, legislatures were eager to bring their laws in accordance with the European model provided by the two Conventions (so-called cold harmonisation).[12]

Unlike the unitary patent for the European Union still to be established, the 'European Patent' granted by the European Patent Office (EPO) upon one single application, examination and registration procedure is not a unitary right, but a bundle of national patents. Moreover, this bundle doesn't necessarily cover all EU Member States, but only comprises the countries designated by the patent holder. In certain states the patent holder has to validate the European bundle patent once it has been granted. For this purpose he has to fulfil certain formal requirements, in particular the filing of a translation of the entire patent or parts of it in the official language of that state.[13] Depending on the number of Member States for which the validation is requested, this can lead to high additional costs. Also, the bundle structure of European patents has the disadvantage that infringement and/or invalidation procedures must be conducted separately in the individual Member States.[14]

However, from an industry point of view, these disadvantages are not always as great as they may appear at first sight. The European Patent system allows applicants to limit their patent protection to those Member States for which they think exclusive protection will be necessary. Under strategic and economic aspects, it is often not necessary to obtain patent protection in all EU Member States. Rather, protection needs only to be obtained in those states in which the invention in question can be manufactured and in which there is a sufficient market for the invention to be sold or used. Moreover, even if there exists a market for the invention in question it could be appropriate not to extend the patent protection to a certain state, for instance if the number of products sold in this state does not generate enough turnover to recoup the investment that third parties would have to make in order to produce for this patent-free market alone. In sum, selecting only some countries allows applicants to implement flexible patenting strategies and, most importantly,

---

12 Adding to this was the fact that some central notions of patent law had been harmonised by the Strasbourg Convention on the Unification of Certain Points of Substantive Law on Patents for Inventions, of 27 November 1963.

13 For additional details, see in this chapter, section 3.2.2.

14 It should be noted in this regard that the problems resulting therefrom are somewhat mitigated by the fact that European judges dealing with patent cases meet annually to discuss upcoming issues and further align the application of patent law in practice.

to save cost by doing so. Hence, obtaining patent protection for the major EU countries such as the UK, France, Germany and perhaps Italy or Spain, may be sufficient to secure *de facto* EU-wide protection.

In this situation it has been questioned by industry whether the establishment of an EU patent is actually necessary or even desirable. This seems to be the case only if it facilitates the life of the industries by being cheaper, more efficient and providing for greater legal certainty than the existing European patent. Whether that will be the case depends on a range of factors such as the need for (costly) translations and their legal effect, the level of renewal fees, and the quality of the centralised judicial system to be established for hearing invalidation and infringement claims. Another issue to be solved resides in the fact that the EPC and the EPO are not part of the institutional structure of the EU, and currently count amongst their members 11 non-EU Member States. In other words, although all EU Members have by now become EPC members, a Community patent cannot as such be identical with the 'European Patent'. Since creating a totally new EU patent structure with a separate registration, examining and granting procedure parallel to the existing EPC and EPO does not make sense either in economic or in organisational terms, the issue of how to 'graft' the EU Community patent on to the existing EPC structure had to be solved.

All of this has caused long delays and much frustration in the process of creating the unitary patent for the European Union. However, the European legislature remained firmly determined to accomplish the work. At the time of printing, under the latest proposals for unitary patent protection based on enhanced cooperation among 25 participating EU Member States (draft Unitary Patent Regulation [dUPR] and draft Agreement on a Unitary Patent Court [dUPCA]) a 'unitary patent' would be a European patent granted on the basis of the EPC to which unitary effect is provided after grant, in accordance with Article 142 EPC. Complementary with this, a unified Patent Court shall be established for adjudicating infringement and invalidity claims filed with regard to unitary patents as well as European bundle patents effective in the participating EU Member States.[15]

Lastly, regarding the international context, it should be noted that inventors who want to protect their invention in multiple countries may benefit from the centralised search and preliminary examination under the Patent Cooperation Treaty (PCT).[16] Under this Treaty, applications are filed with

---

15 For details, see in this chapter, section 3.6.
16 See Chapter 1, section 1.4.2.2; for details see in this chapter, section 3.2.2.10.

WIPO – either directly at WIPO's International Bureau in Geneva, or via a national patent office or the EPO (the 'Receiving Office'); after that, a central search as well as, if requested, a preliminary examination are performed by patent offices which – such as the EPO – are operating as International Searching Authority (ISA) and/or International Preliminary Examination Authority (IPEA). However, other than the EPC, the PCT does not lead to centralised grant of the patent, but is forwarded by the International Bureau to the offices of the countries designated in the application ('Designated Offices'),[17] where the application is subsequently examined according to each patent office's own rules.[18]

3.2   European patents: structure and proceedings

Overview

Legal basis and structure

Before the EPC and the PCT entered into force, an applicant seeking to obtain patent protection in more than one European country was required to file a separate patent application in each country for which he was seeking patent protection. For applicants, this meant a distinct grant procedure in each country which not only required the costly translation of all the application documents into the languages of all the countries where an application was filed, but which also entailed the cost for multiple representations by patent attorneys. Moreover, national patent laws were only harmonised up to the point as required by the rather unspecific framework of the Paris Convention, and therefore showed a great number of differences regarding both substantive patent law and the rules governing the granting procedure.

In order to overcome these hindrances and to create a framework for a European patent administration and policy, first the Strasbourg Convention was concluded in 1963,[19] unifying certain points of substantive patent law,

---

17 It should be noted, however, that by now 11 EPC Contracting States (Belgium, Cyprus, France, Greece, Ireland, Italy, Latvia, Malta, Monaco, the Netherlands and Slovenia) have excluded to obtain a national patent directly via the international (PCT) phase without entering into the regional European phase and obtaining a European patent ('closing of the national route').

18 While the substantive laws remain to be different, the formal procedures in the national or regional offices were harmonised and streamlined by the Patent Law Treaty (PLT) negotiated in 2000, thus making such procedures more user-friendly; see Chapter 1, section 1.4.2.2; for further details see www.wipo.int/treaties/en/ip/plt.

19 Strasbourg Convention on the Unification of Certain Points of Substantive Law on Patents for Inventions, of 27 November 1963.

followed by the adoption of the EPC in Munich in 1973. As laid down in the Preamble of the EPC, its goal was:

> to strengthen co-operation between the States of Europe in respect of the protection of inventions, [and] that such protection may be obtained in those States by a single procedure for the grant of patents and by the establishment of certain standard rules governing patents so granted.

The EPC constitutes a special agreement within the meaning of Article 19 of the Paris Convention, and a regional patent treaty within the meaning of Article 45 (1) of the PCT.[20] In its centralising effect, the EPC goes beyond the PCT system. Whereas the PCT only provides for a centralisation of patent applications, an international search report, and, on request of the applicant, a preliminary examination, the EPC unifies the entire examination process and results in the grant of one common title, the 'European Patent', on the basis of a body of unified substantive patent law.

However, in spite of those and other common features such as the unitary term of twenty years from the date of application, the European Patent is *not* a unitary legal title valid throughout the EPC Member States. Rather, after the grant, the patent will only become valid in the Member States that are designated by the patent holder according to his marketing needs. After entering in the 'national stage', the European Patent therefore turns into a bundle of national rights which continue to live their own lives in the respective Member States. Consequently, the annual renewal fees for maintaining the patent have to be paid in each of those countries separately. Also, in each of the Member States for which it is granted, the European Patent is basically subject to the same conditions, and has the same effects, as a national patent, including the rules governing infringement and/or invalidation procedures concerning national and European bundle patents.

Without changing the basic structure, the EPC was revised in 2000, with the revised version entering into force on 13 December 2007.[21] The aim of the revision[22] was to take account of developments in international law, in particular the TRIPS Agreement and the Patent Law Treaty.[23] Furthermore it

---

20 For the relationship between the EPC and the PCT see also in this chapter, section 3.2.2.10.

21 European Patent Convention as revised by the Act revising the EPC (29 November 2000). According to Article 3 (1) of the Revision Act, EPO's Administrative Council was authorised to draw up and adopt the new text.

22 See the explanations offered on the EPO website, www.epo.org/law-practice/legal-texts/archive/documentation/diplomatic-conference.html.

23 See Chapter 1, sections 1.4.3 and 1.5.2.

served to streamline and facilitate the proceedings in the EPO as well as the administration and adaptability of the EPC itself. Most importantly, articles of the EPC addressing details of a procedural or administrative character were transferred to the Implementing Regulations. In consequence, those details can be changed by way of decisions taken by the Administrative Council (the legislation body of the European Patent Organisation, see below), instead of being submitted to the cumbersome procedure of a Diplomatic Conference to be convened in case of an EPC revision.

The European Patent Organisation

The European Patent system is administered by the European Patent Organisation (EPOrg). The EPOrg consists of two organs: the European Patent Office (EPO)[24] which acts as the executive body of the organisation, and the Administrative Council, which consists of representatives of the 38 EPC Member States. The Administrative Council supervises the activities of the EPO and, to the extent allowed by Article 33 EPC, acts as a legislative body, concerning in particular changes and amendments in the Implementing Regulations.[25] Legislative changes and amendments of the EPC going beyond those addressed in Article 33 EPC can only be determined by the Contracting States themselves, at a Diplomatic Conference convened for that purpose.

Examination and grant of European patents are carried out by the EPO. The Office has its main seat in Munich and a branch in The Hague (Netherlands), sub-offices in Berlin (Germany) and Vienna (Austria) and a 'liaison bureau' in Brussels (Belgium). The official languages of the EPO are English, French and German.[26]

According to the tasks assigned to it, the EPO has the following departments (Art. 15 EPC):[27]

- a Receiving Section (responsible for the examination on filing and the examination as to formal requirements of European patent applications);
- Examining Divisions (responsible for prior art searches and the examination of European patent applications);

---

24 See www.epo.org.

25 See www.epo.org/law-practice/legal-texts/html/epc/2010/e/ma2.html.

26 Concerning the language regime and translation requirements see in this Chapter, section 3.2.2.3.

27 The corresponding internal organisation consists of five Directorates-General (DG), each being directed by a Vice-President: DG 1 Operations, DG 2 Operational Support, DG 3 Appeals, DG 4 Administration, and DG 5 Legal/International Affairs.

- Opposition Divisions, responsible for the examination of oppositions against any granted European patent;
- a Legal Division;
- Boards Of Appeal (responsible for the examination of appeals); and
- an Enlarged Board Of Appeal (dealing with issues of particular legal importance and ensuring uniform application of the law).

Although the boards of appeal are integrated in the organisational structure of the EPO, they are independent from the Office in their decisions and are bound only by the European Patent Convention. It is therefore held that this is sufficient to guarantee in the framework of the EPC that the requirement under Article 62 TRIPS is fulfilled in that 'final administrative decisions in ... procedures [for acquisition of an IP right] shall be subject to review by a judicial or quasi-judicial authority'.

Member States

The European Patent Convention currently has 38 Contracting States (October 2012).[28] All EU members are members of the EPC, but the EPC is also open to non-EU members. In fact, 11 EPC Member States are currently not members of the EU (in the order of their accession date: Switzerland [1977], Liechtenstein [1980], Monaco [1991], Turkey [2000], Iceland [2004], Croatia [2008], Norway [2008], Former Yugoslav Republic of Macedonia [2009], San Marino [2009], Albania [2010] and Serbia [2010]). In addition, as of spring 2011, there are two so-called extension states (Bosnia and Herzegovina and Montenegro). This means that patents granted by the EPO may be extended to those countries by the payment of additional fees and completion of certain formalities. Former extension states later often became full EPC Member States.

Workload, quality and international cooperation

Although the EPC did not create a fully harmonised, unitary right, it subsequently proved extremely successful. The first applications were received on 1 June 1978. Already in that year, the Office in Munich expanded to include a site in Berlin and the former International Patent Institute in The Hague. In the early 1990s, the EPO bought the patent documentation centre INPADOC in Vienna and established another site, and a small EPO liaison office was opened in Brussels to build up relations with the EU institutions.

---

28 See www.epo.org/about-us/epo/member-states.html.

Source: EPO.[29]

Figure 3.1 Member States of the European Patent Organisation

---

29 See documents.epo.org/projects/babylon/eponet.nsf/0/E65E85FAF2F200F4C125744A00294866/$File/epo_member_states_10_10.gif.

The filing figures reflect the EPO's rapid development: the 100,000th application was filed in 1983 and eight years later the total was 500,000. 1997 saw filing figures reach the million mark. In the last decade, the annual European patent filing figures (direct filings under the EPC and international filings under the PCT filings) increased until 2007, but slowed down in 2008 and decreased in 2009 due to the economic crisis; however, 2010 saw again a clear increase in filing figures which continued in 2011.[30]

Though principally welcome as a sign of success, the great number of applications also has its drawbacks. One pertinent risk concerns the fact that the task cannot be tackled efficiently by the examiners, in particular as the complexity of technology is on the rise and the volume of technical literature to be consulted for the examination is growing rapidly. Also, the quality of applications appears to deteriorate – the EPO remarks that it receives fewer patent applications drafted in accordance with the EPC standard, which makes the applications substantially more difficult for examiners to process.[31] Those factors may result in the accumulation of a backlog of pending applications and hence to the procrastination of the granting procedure. In addition, they may entail a deterioration of patent quality, not least in terms of clarity and conciseness, thereby causing obstacles for competition and subsequent innovations or giving rise to activities of 'patent trolls'.[32]

In response to those risks, the EPO announced in 2007 an initiative under the heading of 'raising the bar'.[33] Apart from improving the quality management system at the EPO, the initiative also seeks to re-structure the working routines and the classification of the technical literature so as to improve the access of examiners to the information needed for a thorough and targeted examination. In addition, the EPO incites users to be more quality-oriented already when the applications are drafted, so that they fulfil the criteria of the EPC in terms of clarity, precision, and completeness.[34]

---

30 The relevant figures are: 210.800 (2006), 222.600 (2007), 226.000 (2008), 211.300 (2009), 235.000 (2010) and 244.437 (2011); see www.epo.org/about-us/statistics/filings.html.

31 See www.epo.org/about-us/office/annual-report/2007/focus.html.

32 On the phenomenon of patent trolls see above in this Chapter, section 3.1.1. The risks are addressed by the EPO at www.epo.org/about-us/office/annual-report/2007/focus.html.

33 See annual report of 2007, at www.epo.org/about-us/office/annual-report/2007/focus.html.

34 As steps undertaken in the framework of the initiative, the EPC Implementing Regulations were amended in several regards: for example, applicants may already be required to limit the number of independent claims when filing their application; patents cannot be granted with claims relating to non-searched subject matter; improvement of the processing of applications for which no meaningful search can be performed or which make substantive examination difficult because the claims are not supported, clear and concise; streamlining

Another element seeking to improve the quality of patent applications concerns the so-called utilisation scheme introduced by the EPO: since 1 January 2011 an applicant claiming priority of a previous application has to file with the EPO a copy of the results of any search carried out by or on behalf of the authority with which the previous application(s) was/were filed. As a consequence the EPO examiner may use the work of the national patent office of first filing for his own search. However, there is no automatic recognition of the search results. A key principle of the utilisation scheme is that the use of work of the patent office of first filing is always at the discretion of the EPO examiner.[35]

Further to such measures, the EPO has teamed together with the Japan Patent Office (JPO), the Korean Intellectual Property Office (KIPO), the State Intellectual Property Office of the People's Republic of China (SIPO), and the United States Patent and Trademark Office (USTPO) in order 'to improve the efficiency of the examination process for patents worldwide' (the five IP offices: IP5).[36] Together, the IP5 account for 90 per cent of all patent applications filed worldwide and for 93 per cent of all work carried out under the PCT. As stated on their common website:

> [t]he vision of the IP5 Offices is global co-operation, which has been defined as 'the elimination of unnecessary duplication of work among the IP5 Offices, the enhancement of patent examination efficiency and quality and guarantee of the stability of patent right'. The objective is to address the ever-increasing backlog at the world's five biggest intellectual property offices. As the world sees economic barriers between nations fade away, innovators want their intellectual creations protected concurrently in multiple major markets. Hence, applications for the same technology are filed at more than one patent office. The solution to the backlog problem is to reduce, to the maximum extent possible, the duplication of work which takes place at each office for a family of patent applications.[37]

---

of certain deadlines; improvements of the communication between applicant and examining body, imposing certain requirements the details of which cannot be discussed here. See the Notice from the EPO concerning amendments to the Implementing Regulations to the EPC (15 October 2009), [2009] OJEPO 533, archive. epo.org/epo/pubs/oj009/11_09/11_5339.pdf.

35 Notice from the European Patent Office dated 23 July 2010 concerning amended Rule 141 EPC and new Rule 70b EPC – utilization scheme, [2010] OJ EPO 410.

36 See www.fiveipoffices.org/index.html.

37 To achieve this aim, ten founding projects have been set up: common documentation, hybrid classification, access to search and examination results, application format, training policy, mutual machine translation, common examination practice rules and quality management, common statistical parameter system for examination, a common approach to sharing and documenting search engines and, finally, search and common examination support tools.

? QUESTIONS

1 Like the EPC, the envisaged CPC would have been created in the form of an international convention rather than a Community Regulation. Can you imagine the reason for that?
2 Why, in your opinion, was the EPC opened for non-EU Members?
3 What is done within the IP5 to tackle the workload problem?
4 Would it be a solution for the big patent offices to outsource search and/ or examination work to other patent offices or private companies in order to deal with the workload problem?

Granting procedure

Overview

The granting procedure for a European patent is completely regulated by the EPC and its Implementing Regulations. It is an *ex parte* administrative procedure which begins with the filing of a European patent application and which ends with the grant of a patent or the refusal of the application, unless the application is withdrawn or deemed withdrawn.[38]

Applications are filed either directly with the EPO, or by a filing via the PCT with the EPO as one of the designated offices ('Euro-PCT application').[39] Direct applications to the EPO can be made in Munich or at its branch at The Hague or its sub-office in Berlin.

The application process can be divided into two stages: the first stage comprises a formalities examination, preparation of the European search report and a preliminary opinion on patentability; it ends with the publication of the European patent application and the search report in general after 18 months from the date of filing. At the applicant's request this is followed by the second stage, which comprises substantive examination and grant or refusal of the application.

After the patent has been granted, any third party may file an opposition with the EPO against a granted patent within nine months. Oppositions may be filed by any party, but it is usually done by competitors of the patentee. The

---

38 For additional detail, see the information provided by the EPO in its information brochure 'How to get a European patent – Guide for applicants, Part 1', 13th edition, May 2010, documents.epo.org/ projects/babylon/eponet.nsf/0/8266ED0366190630C12575E10051F40E/$File/guide_for_applicants_part1_05_10_en.pdf, from which the following description is drawn.
39 See also in this chapter, section 3.2.2.10.

opposition is under the responsibility of Opposition Divisions. Also, at any time after the grant of the patent, there may also be, upon request of the patentee, limitation or revocation proceedings. Decisions on the revocation or limitation of European patents are taken by the Examining Divisions.

Appeals against the decisions taken during the granting procedure can be filed with the boards of appeal. A decision which does not terminate proceedings with regard to one of the parties can only be appealed together with the final decision, unless the decision allows separate appeal. In certain exceptional cases it may be possible to file a petition for review by the Enlarged Board of Appeal.

Application requirements

European patent applications can be filed by any natural or legal person, or anybody equivalent to a legal person, irrespective of nationality and place of residence or business. There is no obligation to be represented by a professional representative at this stage. However, apart from filing the application, a person not having either their residence or place of business within the territory of one of the EPC Contracting States must be represented by a professional representative (a European Patent Attorney) and act through him in all proceedings (Article 133 EPC).

The application for a European patent must contain as a minimum:

(a) a request for the grant of a European patent;
(b) a description of the invention;
(c) one or more claims;
(d) any drawings referred to in the description or the claims;
(e) an abstract.

Furthermore, the application must satisfy the formal requirements laid down in the Implementing Regulations. The inventor must be designated in the application.

The most important elements in the application are the *claims*. Their purpose is to define the subject matter for which protection is sought in terms of the technical features of the invention; they must therefore be clear and concise and be supported by the description. Unlike trade mark and copyright law where the protected subject matter is determined objectively, the invention is protected by a patent only in the way and to the extent as it is claimed. Drafting the claims is therefore a kind of art: they must be broad enough to cover the invention to its fullest; on the other hand, if they are too broad, the patent is likely to evoke objections and will have to be limited or eventually even fail for lack of novelty or inventive step.[40]

The information contained in the application must *disclose* the invention (i.e. indicate the technical problem that the invention is designed to solve and describe its proposed technical solution) in a manner sufficiently clear and complete for it to be carried out by a person skilled in the art. Once a European patent application has been filed, no amendments extending beyond its content as filed may be made to the description, the claims or the drawings. European patent applications must relate to a single invention only, or to a group of inventions so linked as to form a single general inventive concept (so-called unity of the invention). In the latter case there usually will be multiple independent claims in different categories (although multiple independent claims in the same category are allowed as long as they are in the same category (product, process, apparatus or use) and the subject matter of the application involves either a plurality of interrelated products, different uses of a product or apparatus, or alternative solutions to a particular problem, where it is inappropriate to cover these alternatives by a single claim (Rule 43 (2) of the Implementing Regulations).

Languages and translations

European patent applications can be filed in one of the three official languages of the EPO (English, French or German). Filing in another language is possible, but a translation has then to be filed into one of the official languages of EPO within two months of filing the application.[41] In written proceedings, any party may use any of the EPO's official languages. The official language in which the application is filed or translated into is generally used as the language of proceedings in all proceedings before the EPO.

Translations may be required when, after the grant, the European patent is to be validated in (a) given EPC Contracting State(s) whose language differs from those of the proceedings before the EPO (Article 65 EPC). Although the EPC with its centralised procedure therefore results in a substantial reduction of costs compared to the filing of separate national applications, translations in many states and the ensuing expenses remain to be an issue.

---

40 For the substantive requirements, see in this chapter, section 3.3.4.
41 Failing to do so, the applicant is invited to file a translation within two months of the notification of the invitation, and if the translation is then not filed within the time limit set in the invitation, the application is deemed to be withdrawn.

Relief was heralded by the optional Agreement on the application of Article 65 EPC (the 'London Agreement'), which entered into force on 1 May 2008 as the fruit of long-standing efforts to provide for a cost-attractive post-grant translation regime. The Agreement results in the signatories[42] waiving, entirely or largely, the requirement for translations of European patents.[43] Under Article 1 (1), (2) and (3) of the London Agreement, a state which has an official language in common with one of the official languages of the EPO dispenses entirely with the translation requirements. A state which does not have an official language in common with one of the official languages of the EPO dispenses with the translation requirements if the European patent is available in the official language of the EPO prescribed by that State and supplied under the conditions provided for in Article 65 (1) EPC. These states may however require that a translation of the claims (as opposed to the entire documentation including the description) into one of their official languages be supplied.[44]

While translations and the issues connected therewith continue to account for a substantial part of the problems encumbering the European patent system, it is hoped – and increasingly appears realistic – that they will be eased considerably with the assistance of automatic translation programs that are currently in their test phase.[45]

Examination of formal requirements and search report

When an application has been received, the Receiving Section at the EPO checks whether certain minimum requirements set out in the implementing regulations have been fulfilled, so that a filing date can be accorded. The filing date is crucial for the subsequent procedure, inter alia for establishing

---

42 The London Agreement was ratified by Denmark, France, Germany, Liechtenstein, Luxembourg, Monaco, Netherlands, Sweden, Switzerland and the United Kingdom, and until now acceded to by Croatia, Finland, Hungary, Iceland, Latvia, Lithuania, Slovenia and the Former Yugoslav Republic of Macedonia. See www.epo. org/law-practice/legal-texts/london-agreement/status.html.

43 For additional details see www.epo.org/law-practice/legal-texts/london-agreement.html; the London Agreement itself can be found at documents.epo.org/projects/babylon/eponet.nsf/0/7FD20618D28E9FBF C125743900678657/$File/London_Agreement.pdf. The resulting translation requirements in the validation phase of a European patent can be found at www.epo.org/applying/european/validation.html.

44 The current status is as follows: seven EPC contracting states do not require a translation (France, Germany, Liechtenstein, Luxembourg, Monaco and Switzerland), three contracting states only require translation of the claims (Latvia, Lithuania and Slovenia) and eight contracting states require a translation of the claims if the patent is available in English (Croatia, Denmark, Finland, Hungary, Iceland, Netherlands, Sweden, and the Former Yugoslav Republic of Macedonia) and a complete translation is required in the remaining 20 EPC contracting states.

45 Agreements concerning mutual recognition of machine translated documents have been signed between the EPO and the Patent Offices of Japan, South Korea, and most recently also Russia.

the date as of which the relevant state of the art has to be ascertained. After that, the Receiving Section continues to check whether the application is in compliance with formal requirements, including the translations, if required.

Parallel to the formalities examination, the European search is performed by the search division on the basis of the claims, taking into consideration the description and drawings where necessary, in order to find the documents available to the EPO which may be taken into consideration in assessing novelty and inventive step. The search report is accompanied by a preliminary, non-binding opinion on whether the application and the invention to which it relates meet the requirements of the EPC. This enables the applicant to reconsider his application and either pursue the grant procedure, amend the application to reflect the results of the search, or withdraw the application, if he comes to the conclusion that it has no chance of success.

Publication of the patent application

The first phase ends with the publication of the European patent application (in online-form on the EPO's publication server)[46] 18 months after the date of filing or the earliest priority date. The applicant may, however, request that his application be published earlier. The European search report is usually published together with the application.

It should be noted that a European patent application will not be published if it has been finally refused or withdrawn or deemed withdrawn before completion of the technical preparations for publication. This enables the applicant to keep his innovation secret even after having it initially filed. Of course, the problem is that if the search report is not available before the end of the 18-month period, the applicant generally lacks the basis for making an informed decision to withdraw the application.

Examination procedure and grant

After the publication of the European search report, the applicant has six months to decide whether to file a request for a substantive examination (Request for Grant), pay the examination fee and thus start the second phase. If no request for examination has been filed by the end of this period, the application is deemed to be withdrawn.

---

46 Accessible via the EPO website, www.epo.org.

The European Patent Office then examines, in the light of the search report and applicant's response to it, whether the invention meets the requirements of the EPC, i.e. whether the invention concerns patentable subject matter and fulfils the patentability requirement of novelty, inventive step and of industrial applicability.

If the Examining Division is of the opinion that a European patent cannot be granted, it will refuse the application. The grounds of refusal must be stated and a refusal may be based only on grounds on which the applicant has had an opportunity to comment.

If, however, the application and the invention to which it relates meet the requirements of the EPC, the Examining Division will grant a European patent provided that the requisite fees have been paid in due time and a translation of the claims into the other two official languages of the EPO than the language of proceedings has been filed in due time.

The second phase ends with the mention of the decision of grant in the European Patent Bulletin. At the same time, a European patent specification is published containing the description, the claims and any drawings.

Opposition and limitation procedure

During nine months after the grant of the patent,[47] third parties can file an opposition on the grounds that (a) the patent's subject matter is not patentable, (b) the patent does not disclose the invention clearly and completely enough for it to be carried out by a person skilled in the art, or (c) the patent's subject matter extends beyond the content of the application as filed.

Since the revision of the EPC in 2000 the patent holder may also himself request the revocation or limitation of his own patent (Art. 105a (1) EPC). 'Limitation' means a reduction in the scope of protection of the claims. Clarifications or changes made simply to protect different subject matter are not considered to be limitations. As explained in a preparatory document:

> Limitation proceedings . . . enable patentees to narrow down the protection conferred by a patent post-grant by means of a simple, quick and inexpensive administrative procedure. For example, it may be necessary to limit a granted patent if,

---

47 The EPC does not provide for pre-grant opposition. However, third parties always have the opportunity to file observations during the proceedings (Article 115 EPC).

because of prior art which was not known during the examination proceedings or prior national rights not taken into account in these proceedings, the extent of the protection conferred is too great. Using the limitation procedure, patent proprietors may themselves reduce the extent of the protection claimed in a manner which is binding, and thus generally preclude disputes over the validity of a patent. Post-grant limitation is also in the public interest, because it limits the protection claimed by the patentee with effect for the general public. This creates legal certainty and facilitates access by competitors to the freely available prior art.[48]

A limitation and revocation procedure is possible at any time after – not, however, before the end of – opposition proceedings or even after expiry of the patent.

Appeals; petition for review; referrals in order to ensure a harmonised case law

The decisions of the Receiving Section, Examining Divisions, Opposition Divisions and the Legal Division of the EPO are subject to appeal. The appeal, which must be filed in writing within two months from the date of notification of such decisions, has a suspensive effect. This means that the contested decisions do not yet become final and their effects are suspended. In case the appellant is opposed by another party to the proceedings the appeal is referred to the department whose decision is contested and, if that department considers it to be admissible and well founded, it rectifies its decision within three months. Otherwise the appeal is remitted to the EPO's independent boards of appeal.

The technical boards of appeal, which generally consist of three members, are responsible for appeals against decisions of the Examining Divisions concerning the refusal of European patent applications or the granting of European patents and for appeals against decisions of the Opposition Divisions. Where the technical boards of appeal are not competent – particularly in the case of appeals against decisions of the Receiving Section or the Legal Division – a legal Board of Appeal consisting of three legally qualified members deals with such procedures. The decisions of the boards of appeal are final and can only be petitioned for review by the Enlarged Board of Appeal on the grounds either that the composition of the board was not correct, or that a fundamental violation or any other fundamental procedural defect of the right to be heard had occurred, or that a criminal act may have had an impact on the decision. If the boards of appeal uphold a patent it is

---

48 Doc. CA/PL 29/99 (8 November 1999), documents.epo.org/projects/babylon/eponet.nsf/0/17CCA14 4861F7BC0C12572800038E805/$File/capl_99029_en.pdf.

still possible to file a revocation action with the responsible courts of the contracting states in which the European patent takes effect.

Finally, to ensure uniform application of the law or if an important point of law arises, referrals may be submitted to the Enlarged Board of Appeal, if a Board of Appeal considers this as necessary. Decisions by the Enlarged Board of Appeal are binding on the referring board. In addition, the President of the EPO may refer a point of law to the Enlarged Board of Appeal if two boards of appeal have given different decisions on the issue.[49]

National validation

As already indicated above, as a bundle patent, the European Patent once granted will subsequently enter into its national phase and live on in the form of one or several separate national patent(s). This requires the validation of the European patent in the different Contracting States for which the applicant seeks patent protection. Validation means national registration and – in certain cases – also requires the filing of a translation.[50]

Relationship with the PCT system

Euro-PCT applications

Apart from filing direct European patent applications, the applicant can also file international applications under the Patent Cooperation Treaty (PCT) as described above.[51] That is to say that in making a PCT filing, the European Patent Office may be designated as one of the designated Offices ('Euro-PCT application'). After having completed the international phase, the application enters the 'European regional phase', which in general follows the usual procedure before the EPO.[52]

In other words, an applicant who wants to obtain a European patent has the choice between the direct European route and the Euro-PCT route.

---

49 For a recent instructive example see the opinion of the Enlarged Board of Appeal (12 May 2010) in Case G 3/08, regarding EPO's practice of granting patents for software-related inventions and the relevant decisions by the different technical boards of appeal, documents.epo.org/projects/babylon/eponet.nsf/0/DC6171F182D 8B65AC125772100426656/$File/G3_08_opinion_en.pdf.
50 For translation requirements see above in this chapter, section 3.2.2.3.
51 See above in this chapter, section 3.1.2 at the end.
52 See EPC Part X (Articles 150–153). For additional detail in this respect, see 'How to get a European patent – Guide for applicants, Part 2: PCT procedure before the EPO – Euro-PCT', 4th edition, April 2008, documents.epo.org/projects/babylon/eponet.nsf/0/7c5ef05581e3aac0c12572580035c1ce/$FILE/applicants_guide_part2_en.pdf.

Whereas with the direct European route, the entire European patent grant procedure is governed by the EPC alone, with the Euro-PCT route, the first phase of the grant procedure (the international phase) is subject to the PCT, while the second phase (the regional phase) before the EPC as *designated office* is primarily governed by the EPC.[53]

Moreover, since applicants can choose whether they want to file an international application either directly with the International Bureau established at WIPO, or with the national office of the PCT contracting state of which the applicant is a resident or national ('receiving office'), natural and legal persons who are nationals or residents of an EPC contracting state may also file international applications with the EPO acting as the *receiving office*.

EPO acting as International Searching Authority (ISA)

According to Article 152 EPC, the EPO also works as an International Searching Authority (ISA) and an International Preliminary Examining Authority (IPEA) within the meaning of Articles 16 and 32 PCT for any international application on condition that the relevant receiving Office has specified the EPO as ISA. Acting as ISA, the EPO establishes the documentary search reports on prior art with respect to inventions which are the subject of international applications.[54]

 QUESTIONS

1 It has been stated in the text that 'it is not necessary to obtain patent protection in all EU Member States'. Could you elaborate on the explanation given in the text? Can you name practical examples, if possible from your professional background, of inventions which have been patented only in a select number of EU Member States?

2 As part of international patent law, the Patent Cooperation Treaty (PCT) is not a subject discussed in the book on European IP law. However, since the international filing procedure established by the PCT can also be used to obtain patent protection in Europe, it is important that you have an understanding of the workings of this mechanism. How does the PCT work? Where can international applications be filed?

3 Find out about and compare the fees for a patent application which covers

---

53 More precisely, for international applications which are the subject of proceedings before the EPO, the provisions of the PCT and its Regulations ('the PCT Rules') apply, supplemented by the provisions of the EPC. In case of conflict between the provisions of the EPC and those of the PCT or the PCT Rules, however, the PCT prevails, unless the PCT explicitly allows a reservation with regard to such conflicting PCT provision.

54 For details, see the 'Guidelines – Part 2', C.

the United Kingdom, France, Germany and Sweden if these States are named (a) in a European Patent Application, (b) in a PCT-application, and (c) if the inventor files a separate application in each of the countries named.

3.3 Substantive patent law

Overview

Although the EPC deals primarily with organisational and administrative matters, Part II (Articles 52 to 74) of the Convention is devoted to substantive patent law. Of particular importance are Articles 52 to 57 setting forth the prerequisites for protection, and Article 69, in which the scope of protection is defined. Of relevance in that context is also the Protocol on the interpretation of Article 69.[55]

As the prospective unitary patents to be created on the basis of enhanced cooperation[56] will be granted as European patents, they will likewise be governed by the EPC provisions. In addition, it has been envisaged that the final text of the Regulation implementing the unitary patent protection (in the following: draft Unitary Patent Regulation, dUPR) should contain in Articles 6 to 8 further provisions of substantive law, in particular on prohibited acts as well as on limitations and exceptions to patent protection. At the time of publication, it is unclear whether those provisions are to remain within the dUPR, or whether they will be removed, following a recommendation by the Council expressed in the Council Conclusions of 28–29 June 2012.[57]

Quite remarkably, the Council's misgivings against Article 6 to 8 do not concern the content of the provisions as such. Very similar rules were already found in the (failed) CPC of 1975, and like many of the other substantive provisions in the EPC and CPC, they have largely impacted the national laws of EU Member States and beyond; hence they are broadly accepted and time-tested. The concerns rather relate to the fact that those provisions would be embedded in a legal instrument which, in case of doubt, is subject to interpretation by the ECJ upon referral of questions for preliminary decision under Article 267 TFEU, and would therefore extend the ECJ's competence to adjudicate on matters of substantive patent law. On the other hand,

---

55 Protocol on the interpretation of Article 69 EPC of 5 October 1973, as revised by the Act revising the EPC of 29 November 2000, www.epo.org/law-practice/legal-texts/html/epc/2010/e/ma2a.html.

56 See in this chapter, section 3.6.2.1.

57 Council Conclusions, 28–29 June 2012, CO EUR 4, CONCL 2, www.consilium.europa.eu/uedocs/cms_data/docs/pressdata/en/ec/131388.pdf.

it needs to be asked whether eliminating the provisions would risk being incompatible with Art. 118 TFEU, as it would render the dUPR void of any substantive content.[58]

While no secure prospects exist at this time with regard to the future of the dUPR – with or without Articles 6 to 8 – the provisions continue to be relevant. Apart from the fact that they already exist in various national laws, the recommendation in the Council Conclusions to remove Articles 6 to 8 from the dUPR do not affect the envisaged Agreement on a Unified Patent Court (UPCA) with its chapter on substantive law containing largely the same rules.[59]

In spite of all the question marks existing in this regard, the following will give an overview of the substantive rules that currently are, or may in future become, part of European patent law, irrespective of the instrument(s) of implementation.

Patentable subject matter

Art. 52 (1) EPC describes patentable subject matter as 'any inventions, in all fields of technology, provided that they are new, involve an inventive step and are susceptible of industrial application'. This language of the revised EPC reflects both the language of Article 27 (1) TRIPS and the established practice of the EPO to examine applications for their 'technical character' or for the 'technical solution' they provide for 'technical problems'.

In doing so, the EPC, however, does not define the meaning of 'invention', but rather goes on to provide a non-exhaustive list of subject matter and activities that may not be regarded as inventions but are expressly excluded from patentability.

First, Article 52 (2) EPC exempts certain subject matter which, in particular, is not to be regarded as patentable inventions within the meaning of Article 52 (1) EPC. These exclusions concern:

---

58 Opposite legal opinions on the issue were endorsed by two leading experts on German and European patent law, namely Rudolf Krasser (www.ipeg.eu/wp-content/uploads/Prof-Krasser-opinion-on-EU-Patent. pdf), arguing against an inclusion of Articles 8-6 into the dUPR, and Winfried Tilmann, (www.publications. parliament.uk/pa/cm201012/cmselect/cmeuleg/1799/1799vw06.htm) arguing that the dUPR cannot be enacted without also determining on the substance of the right. As a manifestation of protest against the emasculation of the proposal that would be entailed by the Council's recommendation to delete Article 6-8, the European Parliament has postponed its decision on the dUPR, which was originally scheduled for the end of June 2012.

59 This is based on the expectation that those rules – which would apply to both European and unitary patents – would not fall into the ECJ's competence. For more details regarding the draft UPCA see below, section 3.6.2.2.2. and Chapter 9, section 9.2.3.7.2.2.

(a) discoveries, scientific theories and mathematical methods;
(b) aesthetic creations;
(c) schemes, rules and methods for performing mental acts, playing games or doing business, and programs for computers;
(d) presentations of information.

The reasons for the exclusion of this subject matter have to do with the fact that for innovative and economic reasons monopolisation does not seem desirable in a particular field of innovative activity, partly because in solving a technical problem, an activity only addresses the human brain and describes mere mental acts, but does not involve the use of forces of nature. It should be noted, however, that according to Article 52 (3) EPC, patentability is only excluded to the extent to which a European patent application relates to such subject matter or activities *as such*. The qualification is of particular importance in the area of software protection: although no patent protection is available for an invention which *claims* a computer program, patent protection can be granted for an invention which *contains* a computer program. The line is difficult to draw and has triggered a rich body of decisions by the EPO boards of appeal, which is addressed below (section 3.3.3).

Second, Article 53 excludes from patentability:

(a) inventions the commercial exploitation of which is contrary to ordre public or morality;

(b) plant or animal varieties or essentially biological processes for the production of plants or animals, with the exception of microbiological processes and the products thereof;

(c) methods for treatment of the human or animal body by surgery or therapy and diagnostic methods practised on the human or animal body, with the exception of products, in particular substances or compositions, for use in any of these methods.

Most contentious among those grounds is the exclusion of inventions that are liable to clash with *ordre public* and morality. The issue has become topical in particular with regard to biotechnological inventions, where an ethical dilemma arises between the wish to incentivise cutting edge research for new cures or other important goals,[60] and the risk that this amounts to a commodification of the very bases of life. Some of those problems are addressed in this chapter, see section 3.4.1.

---

60 Such as e.g. methods for optimising food supply, etc.

Regarding the exclusion of plant varieties, the purpose of the exclusion is to separate the ambit of patent protection from protection under specific legislation on plant varieties (in the EU: Regulation No 2100/94; see Chapter 6, section 6.2). However, the exclusion only regards patents which are claimed for one *specific variety* of plants (or animals); the exclusion does not apply when inventions are claimed which concern overarching traits to be found in more than one variety.

Finally, the exclusion of therapeutic or diagnostic methods derives from the consideration that the application of such methods in the activities of the medical or veterinary profession cannot be considered as 'industrial' and should not be interfered with on the basis of exclusive commercial rights. However, this does not exclude patenting of products to be used for such treatments, such as the first and second indication of pharmaceuticals; see this chapter, section 3.3.3.

 QUESTIONS

1   Why, in your opinion, are discoveries not protected by IPRs? Can the line between discoveries and inventions be clearly drawn?
2   What is the reason for the exclusion from patentability of scientific theories and mathematical methods? And what is the reason for the exclusion of 'aesthetic creations'?
3   How can the exclusion from patentability of inventions the commercial exploitation of which is contrary to morality be justified?

Types of patents

Before considering in more detail the substantive requirements for protection, it is of interest to note that patentable inventions can take different forms: patents can be granted for products, processes, or for particular uses of a (known) substance. Product patents protect an item embodying the invention – such as a machine – either in its entirety or in view of specific features for which protection is claimed. Process patents only protect the way in which a technical result is obtained, and not the result as such.[61] Use patents are granted for specific effects obtained by the use of a given substrate.

The requirements for protection as well as the basic principles governing scope apply uniformly to all types of patents. However, the practical effects

---

61 However, if a product is achieved by using the patent process, it is equally covered by the patent; see Article 64(2) EPC.

differ widely. This becomes most relevant in the case of chemical compounds, in particular pharmaceuticals. In former times, many countries only granted patent protection for the process of manufacturing drugs instead of protecting the substance itself. This left the possibility for others to isolate and re-manufacture the active ingredients without infringing the patent. However, since the 1980s it has gradually become the norm that chemicals, including pharmaceuticals, can be covered by a product patent which secures a sole right for the patentee to produce the substance. This rule is now enshrined in Article 27 TRIPS, pursuant to which patents must be granted in all fields of technology, for processes as well as for products.

When patents are filed for pharmaceutical products the claims and description must disclose specific therapeutic effects, so as to sustain the requirement of industrial application. However, it is quite possible that such substances, once they are thoroughly tested and/or used in practice, turn out to have more and different effects from what was anticipated. A well-known example of such a case is *Viagra*, which was developed first as a medicament to cure angina pectoris, but turned out to be effective against male erectile dysfunction as well. As it is deemed useful to encourage investment into research for novel fields of application, separate patents can be obtained for the new-found use, if it fulfils the criteria of novelty and inventive step (second medical use). The patentability of such claims is secured by Article 53 (c) EPC, which exempts 'products, in particular substances or compositions, for use in any of these methods' from the general exclusion from patentability of methods for therapeutic or diagnostic treatment. Although the economic rationale for granting such patents is generally considered as well founded it is sometimes criticised that – at least when the substantive requirements for protectability of the second medical indication are applied in a rather lax manner – it will lead to an unjustified prolongation of the product patent obtained for the substance (so-called evergreening of patents).

Biotechnological inventions pose specific problems. Other than pharmaceuticals, the potential uses (or 'functions') of isolated strands of DNA are countless. If absolute protection were granted for the product as such, its scope could become extremely broad. This has motivated requests to grant only 'purpose-bound' protection, that is, to limit the scope of the patent to the function disclosed in the application. The topic was addressed in an ECJ decision which is considered in this chapter, section 3.4.1.3.2.3.

? | **QUESTIONS**

1 Before TRIPS, developing countries heavily opposed product patents for chemical substances. What may have been their reasons? What happened in these countries after TRIPS?
2 Do you know about any other patent granted for second medical use of a pharmaceutical product for which a patent had already been granted?

Conditions for protection

The conditions for patent protection are defined in Articles 54, 55 (novelty), 56 (inventive step) and 57 EPC (industrial application).

Novelty

An invention is considered new if it does not form part of the worldwide *state of the art* (so called 'absolute novelty'). The state of the art in turn comprises, according to Article 54 (2) EPC:

> everything made available to the public by means of a written or oral description, by use, or in any other way, before the date of filing of the European patent application.

In addition, the content of all European patent applications with filing dates prior to the filing date of the application in question are detrimental to novelty, even if they are only published on or after the filing date (Article 54 (3) EPC). With regard to (second) medical uses in the meaning of Article 53 (c) EPC the requirement of absolute novelty does not exclude the patentability of any substance or composition if its use for a method of medical treatment (or, if certain use is comprised in the state of the art, its *specific use*) is not comprised in the state of the art (Article 54 (4) and (5) EPC).

The novelty requirement applies quite strictly. The criterion of the invention having been 'publicly available' does not mean that the public must actually have been aware of the disclosure, or that the invention was made known to a larger audience. For example, an oral presentation before a selected audience (which was not subject to a secrecy agreement) will be considered as novelty-destructive.[62] The harshness of the test is mitigated to some extent by Article 55 EPC: if the disclosure constitutes 'evident abuse' in relation to

---

62 See for instance Technical Board of Appeal, T 877/90, *Hooper Trading/T-CELL GROWTH FACTOR*, [1993] EPOR 6.

the applicant or his legal predecessor, it will be disregarded if the application is filed within six months following the publication. The same applies if the invention has been displayed at an official or officially recognised international exhibition within the terms of the Convention on international exhibitions of 1928[63] in conformity with the relevant formal requirements (Art. 55 (1) (a) and (b), (2) EPC).

Inventive step

An invention is considered as involving an inventive step if, having regard to the state of the art, it is *not obvious to a person skilled in the art*. Contrary to novelty, the content of European patent applications with filing dates prior to the filing date of the application in question and which were published on or after that date is not taken into account in deciding whether there has been an inventive step (Article 56 EPC).

In the Examination Guidelines of the EPO, the assessment of whether an invention was 'obvious' is described as follows:

> [T]he question to consider, in relation to any claim defining the invention, is whether before the filing or priority date valid for that claim, having regard to the art known at the time, it would have been obvious to the person skilled in the art to arrive at something falling within the terms of the claim. If so, the claim is not allowable for lack of inventive step. The term 'obvious' means that which does not go beyond the normal progress of technology but merely follows plainly or logically from the prior art, i.e. something which does not involve the exercise of any skill or ability beyond that to be expected of the person skilled in the art. In considering inventive step, as distinct from novelty . . . it is fair to construe any published document in the light of knowledge up to and including the day before the filing or priority date valid for the claimed invention and to have regard to all the knowledge generally available to the person skilled in the art up to and including that day.[64]

Regarding the 'person skilled in the art', the Examination Guidelines contend that:

> [t]he 'person skilled in the art' should be presumed to be a skilled practitioner in the relevant field of technology, who is possessed of average knowledge and ability

---

63 For the text of this Convention see www.bie-paris.org/site/en/component/docman/doc_download/3-bie-convention.html.

64 Guidelines for Examination at the EPO, Part G – Chapter VII.4; www.epo.org/law-practice/legal-texts/html/guidelines/e/g_vii_4.htm.

and is aware of what was common general knowledge in the art at the relevant date. He should also be presumed to have had access to everything in the 'state of the art', in particular the documents cited in the search report, and to have had at his disposal the means and capacity for routine work and experimentation which are normal for the field of technology in question. If the problem prompts the person skilled in the art to seek its solution in another technical field, the specialist in that field is the person qualified to solve the problem. The skilled person is involved in constant development in his technical field. He may be expected to look for suggestions in neighbouring and general technical fields or even in remote technical fields, if prompted to do so. Assessment of whether the solution involves an inventive step must therefore be based on that specialist's knowledge and ability. There may be instances where it is more appropriate to think in terms of a group of persons, e.g. a research or production team, rather than a single person. It should be borne in mind that the skilled person has the same level of skill for assessing inventive step and sufficient disclosure. (References to EPO case law omitted.)[65]

Contrary to novelty where the claimed invention is compared in its entirety with the previous state of the art, a mosaic approach is applied to assessing inventive step, that is, it is examined whether it would be obvious to the person skilled in the art to combine various elements of pre-existing technique in order to arrive at the result for which the patent is claimed.

The examination of inventive step by the EPO is usually carried out in three steps (problem/solution approach):

1. identification of the closest field of prior art and comparison between the field and the invention claimed;
2. definition of the technical problem purported to be solved;
3. assessment of whether on that basis, the invention would have been obvious to a person skilled in the art, in the sense that under consideration of the closest prior art in its entirety, the skilled person would have arrived at a solution which lies within the claims and achieves the same effects which are ascribed to the invention.

Industrial application

The notion of industrial applicability is defined as being 'susceptible of industrial application if it can be made or used in any kind of industry, including

---

65 Ibid., Part G – Chapter VII.3.

agriculture'. It is basically sufficient that an invention owns a potential for industrial application; it does not already have to be so used. On the other hand, mere speculation about potential uses would not satisfy the protection criteria. This aspect is of particular relevance for biotechnological inventions, as it prohibits the claiming of isolated biological material as such, without disclosing its function(s) (this chapter, section 3.3.2.3). The requirement of industrial application has furnished the reason inter alia for excluding therapeutic and diagnostic methods from patentability, as such uses are not considered to be of an industrial character. Otherwise, the term 'industrial' is understood in a very broad sense which includes all possible fields of modern technology and only exempts uses and purposes that are strictly private.

? QUESTIONS

1 What is the justification for the three protection requirements (novelty, inventive step and industrial applicability)?

2 In particular, why has the 'person skilled in the art' been chosen as the reference to ascertain whether or not an application contains an inventive step? And why is the '(non)-obviousness', defined as what goes/or doesn't go 'beyond the normal progress', the decisive measure?

3 In practice, which of the three requirements often proves to be the most difficult hurdle to be overcome for a person applying for a patent to be granted? Which one is usually the least problematic?

4 Why is the content of European patent applications with filing dates prior to the filing date of the application in question and which were published on or after that date taken into account in deciding about novelty, but not for assessing the inventive step?

Scope of protection

Interpretation of claims (Article 69 EPC)

The rights conferred on the holder of a European Patent in each state for which it has been granted are the same as those conferred on holders of a national patent granted in each of those states (Article 64 (1) EPC).[66] Consequently, the same is true with regard to limitations and exceptions to the exclusive rights of the patent holder. Like infringements of patents which

---

66 Protection under Article 64 (1) EPC commences on the date on which the mention of the grant is published in the European Patent Bulletin. Provisional protection in the Member States is already granted under Article 67 (1) EPC from the date of the publication of the application, unless the respective Member State derogates from that rule.

have been filed nationally, the 'national parts' of bundle patents granted under the EPC are under the jurisdictional authority of the national courts.

However, the EPC does contain certain rules determining the scope of protection which are binding also in the post-grant phase. Thus, Article 64 (2) EPC makes it mandatory that patent protection conferred to a process shall extend to the products directly obtained by such process. More importantly, Article 69 (1) EPC stipulates that the extent of the protection conferred by a European Patent is determined by the claims, and that the description and drawings are used to interpret the claims. For the period up to grant of the European patent, the extent of the protection conferred by the European patent application is determined by the claims contained in the application as published; however, once the European patent has been granted, its scope is measured retroactively by the way in which it has been granted or was amended in opposition, limitation or revocation proceedings, in so far as such protection is not thereby extended (Article 69 (2) EPC).

In consideration of the fact that Article 69 is of crucial importance for the scope of the exclusive right conferred and hence for the economic impact of patent protection, and realising that Member States had different traditions in measuring the scope of patents, guidelines for the interpretation of Article 69 were set out in a Protocol to the EPC.[67] Article 1 of the Protocol declares that:

> Article 69 should not be interpreted in the sense that the extent of protection conferred by a European patent is to be understood as that defined by a strict, literal meaning of the wording used in the claims, the description and drawings being employed only for the purpose of resolving an ambiguity found in the claims. Neither should it be interpreted in the sense that the claims serve only as a guideline and that the actual protection conferred may extend to what, from a consideration of the description and drawings by a person skilled in the art, the patentee has contemplated. On the contrary, it is to be interpreted as defining a position between theses extremes which combines a fair protection for the patentee with a reasonable degree of certainty for third parties.

The 'extremes' banned by the Protocol concern, on the one hand, previous British practice where it had been held in a landmark case that 'the forbidden field must be found in the language of the claims and nowhere else',[68] and, on the other hand, countries where the scope of protection was considered

---

67 Protocol on the interpretation of Article 69 EPC of 5 October 1973, as amended by the Act revising the EPC of 29 November 2000, www.epo.org/law-practice/legal-texts/html/epc/2010/e/ma2a.html.

68 *Electrical and Musical Industries and Boonton Research Corporation v. Lissen*, [1939] 56 RPC, HL.

to derive from the essential elements defining the invention, without being necessarily identified precisely in the claims. The latter approach, usually referred to as 'doctrine of equivalents' is followed in particular in American law, but some continental European jurisdictions, such as Germany, also had a tendency to 'look beyond' the claims.

Having been advised under the Protocol to take a middle route, it is still somewhat unclear to what extent court practice in Europe has actually converged. For instance, it was held in decisions by the German Federal Supreme Court that whereas the claims are determinative for the scope of protection, infringement can be found if the contested embodiment made use of the semantic content ('Sinngehalt') of the invention protected by the claims.[69] By somewhat different reasoning, but similar in the result, Lord Hoffmann expanded on the meaning of Article 69 and the Protocol in the *Kirin Amgen* decision by the House of Lords.[70] After thoroughly considering the history of Article 69 and comparing it with the doctrine of equivalents as employed in American practice, he concluded that the correct way of interpreting Article 69 was to engage in a 'purposive construction' of the claims – that is, to identify what, in view of the wording and syntax of the claims, the applicant intended to express – without thereby extending the scope of protection in a way which would be possible under the doctrine of equivalents (as applied in American law).

In the same decision, Lord Hoffmann also remarks that under the revised EPC, a new Article 2 has been added to the Protocol which holds that:

> [f]or the purpose of determining the extent of protection conferred by a European patent, due account shall be taken of any element which is equivalent to an element specified in the claims.

However, this is not considered to compel any changes in the practice of British (or other European) courts. It is simply regarded as confirming the common sense-induced practice already observed, meaning that:

> [A]lthough Article 69 prevents equivalents from extending protection outside the claims, there is no reason why it cannot form an important part of the background of facts known to the skilled man which would affect what he understood the claims to mean.[71]

---

69 German Federal Supreme Court, Case X ZR 43/01 of 2 March 2002, Kunststoffrohrteil, partial translation in [2003] IIC, 302.

70 House of Lords, *Kirin Amgen v. Hoechst Marion Roussel,* [2004] UKHL 46.

71 Ibid., Paragraph 49.

Prohibited acts

Further to Article 69 – which will remain unaffected by the unitary patent system – the dUPR and dUPCA also contain provisions defining the scope of protection with regard to the acts which can be prohibited by the patent owner (Article 6 dUPR; Article 14f dUPCA). Similar to most patent legislations currently in force, and in accordance with Article 29 TRIPS, these are:

- *for product patents*: 'making, offering, placing on the market or using a product which is the subject matter of the patent, or importing or storing the product for those purposes';
- *for process patents*: 'using a process which is the subject matter of the patent or, where the third party knows, or should have known, that the use of the process is prohibited without the consent of the proprietor of the patent, from offering the process for use within the territory of the participating Member States in which that patent has unitary effect';
- *furthermore, for products resulting from a protected process*: 'offering, placing on the market, using, importing or storing for those purposes a product obtained directly by a process which is the subject matter of the patent'.

In addition, a provision on *indirect patent infringement* has been added in Article 7 dUPR and Article 14g dUPCA. A corresponding provision was already contained in the CPC and is therefore found in a number of national legislations. It concerns the situation where someone makes a substantial contribution to patent infringement, without committing the complete act. For example, if the parts of an infringing machine are delivered into a patent-free state in order to be assembled there, this would, strictly speaking, not amount to an infringement of the patented invention in the country from which the parts were exported, even if the person making the contribution was aware that the infringing machine would be re-imported later. *Inter alia* with a view to those situations,[72] it is provided that third parties also commit an infringement if they supply or offer to supply to any other person means relating to an essential element of the invention so as to put it into effect, if the third party knows or should have known that those means are suitable and intended for putting that invention into effect and will eventually be

---

72 In more sophisticated cases, determining indirect infringement can be very complicated. See Rudolf Krasser, Effects of an inclusion of regulations concerning the content and limits of the patent holder's rights to prohibit in an EU regulation for the creation of unitary patent protection, at www.ipeg.eu/wp-content/uploads/Prof-Krasser-opinion-on-EU-Patent.pdf (arguing that inter alia for that reason, substantive patent law should not be adjudicated upon by the ECJ).

used to cause an infringement in the territory where the patent is protected. In order to avoid conflicts with free trade and competition, the provision is qualified by stipulating that no infringement shall be found if the means delivered are standard goods capable of multiple uses ('staple commercial products'), except where the third party induces the person supplied to perform any of the acts prohibited by Article 6 dUPR.

Limitations and exceptions

Limitations and exceptions are not addressed in the EPC. However, a catalogue of limitations and exceptions is contained in Article 8 dUPR and Article 14h dUPCA.[73] Most of those provisions were already included in the CPC[74] and have thus served as models for national legislation due to the phenomenon of 'cold harmonisation'.

Pursuant to the current proposals, the following modes of use shall in particular be exempted from the exclusive right conferred by a patent:

- acts done privately and for non-commercial purposes;
- acts done for experimental purposes relating to the subject matter of the invention (experimental use);
- acts for conducting the tests necessary for obtaining marketing permission for medicaments or other substances for which such permission is required (regulatory exception);
- the extemporaneous preparation of medicines in a pharmacy upon medical prescription;
- use which is necessary to allow repair for a vessel or aircraft which are on transit in the country of protection;[75]
- use of an invention by farmers on their own holdings for propagating purposes (farmers' privilege);[76]

---

73 See this chapter, section 3.3.1.

74 See Articles 29–31 CPC 1975 and Articles 25–27 CPC 1989. However, a remarkable difference lies in the fact that contrary to the CPC in its 1975 and 1989 versions the current draft text of the UPR does not include a provision addressing prior users' rights, that is, the right of a person who has taken an invention into use, or has made substantial preparations for that, before the date of filing may continue to use the invention even after the patenting (provided of course that he has acted in good faith). In order to preserve at least the current level of protection of prior users, Article 14i dUPCA stipulates that whoever would have enjoyed a prior user's right in one of the contracting states will continue to do so under the newly established judicial regime at least vis-à-vis European (bundle) patents.

75 These rules derive from Article 5 *ter* Paris Convention; see also Article 27 of the Convention on International Civil Aviation of 7 December 1944.

76 This rule is intended to solve potential conflicts between patent law and plant variety protection; see Chapter 6, section 6.2.3.

- acts and use of information as allowed under Articles 5 and 6 of Directive 24/2009/EC (Software Directive);[77]
- acts allowed under Article 10 of Directive 44/1998/EC (biotechnological inventions).[78]

Among those provisions, the exception for experimental use and the regulatory exception are of specific interest in the pharmaceutical field. With regard to the regulatory exception, most EU Member States already provide for the possibility of testing substances covered by a patent prior to the expiry of protection, in order to instigate the necessary procedures to obtain marketing permission after the patent has lapsed.[79] Hence the time period between the expiry of protection[80] and the market entry of generic manufacturers offering an equivalent substance can be shortened, thus serving the interest of the public at large.[81]

Experimental use is frequently also relevant in the context of regulatory approval: generic companies use experimentation in order to deconstruct the protected substances and to test the medical equivalence of substitutes. However, apart from that, experimental use may also occur for purposes of finding novel applications or improvements of the protected substance. Considering that the objective of patent law is to spur innovative activities, it appears consequent to declare such experiments permissible. A provision to that effect was already set out in the CPC (Article 31(b)), and corresponding rules were subsequently included in the national patent laws of most Member States.[82] In Belgium, legislation goes even further than that, by allowing not only experimentation *on*, but also *with* the invention, meaning that inventions functioning as research tools may be used as such by others without requiring permission from the right-holder.[83]

---

77 Technically necessary copying; backup copies and decompilation of computer programs; see Chapter 5, section 5.2.2.1.2.

78 See in this chapter, section 3.4.1.2.

79 This exception was also contained in Article 31 (b) CPC. For a similar rule developed in US case law see *Roche Products v. Bolar Pharmaceutical*, 733 F.2d 858 (Fed. Cir. 1984): the so-called Bolar exemption.

80 Under EU law, the expiry of protection for medicaments is regularly prolonged by the possibility for patent holders to apply for a Supplementary Protection Certificate (SPC), see in this chapter, section 3.5.

81 Similarly, a provision in the Canadian Patent Act which permitted potential competitors to use the patented invention without authorisation by the patent holder during the term of protection for the purposes of obtaining government marketing approval (so-called regulatory review exception) was held compatible with Article 30 TRIPS was confirmed in the WTO Panel Report *Canada – Patents*; however, national law which allowed to manufacture and stockpile patented goods during a certain period before the patent expires (so-called stockpiling exception) was held not to be covered by Art. 30 TRIPS (WT/DS114/R of 17 March 2000).

82 The only EU Member State which does not appear to have such a rule is Austria.

83 Article 28(1) (b) of the Belgian Patents Act (2005).

In a series of cases decided by the German Federal Supreme Court, the scope and meaning of the experimental use exception were laid out. Regarding the qualification of uses which are permitted under the clause, the Court defined the term 'experiment' as meaning:

> any planned procedure for obtaining information, irrespective of the purpose which the information gained is eventually intended to serve. To limit this intrinsically broad concept of the experiment, the provision requires as further factual characteristic determining the scope of exemption that the experiments must relate to the subject matter of the patented invention.[84]

In a subsequent decision, the Court further emphasised that the exception clause does not distinguish between commercial and non-commercial uses, as long as the ultimate goal is to promote the technical or scientific progress. However:

> this does not mean that research activities of any and every sort are exempted. Should the research have no relation whatsoever to technological theory or should the experiments be undertaken in such proportions as to no longer allow for justification on research grounds, then the activities are not considered to be permissible research activities within the meaning of the [experimental use exception].[85]

Whether those findings are a valid interpretation of the experimental use exception will only become clear after – and if – the unitary patent is finally enacted and the provision is adjudicated in proceedings before the common judiciary that will be established in due course.[86]

Finally, Article 9 dUPR[87] sets out the principle of regional exhaustion, meaning that the right conferred by a patent with unitary effect does not extend to acts concerning a product covered by the patent carried out in the participating Member States if the product was put on the market in the European Union by the proprietor or with his consent, unless the proprietor has legitimate reasons to oppose further commercialisation of the product.

---

84 German Federal Supreme Court, X ZR 99/92 of 11 July 1995, Clinical Trials I, [1996] GRUR, 109; English translation in [1997] RPC 623.

85 German Federal Supreme Court, X ZR 68/94 of 17 April 1997, Clinical Trials II, [1997] NJW, 3092; English translation in [1998] RPC 423.

86 See in this chapter, section 3.6.2.2.

87 In contrast to Articles 6–8 it is not contested that Article 9 shall remain part of the UPR.

? QUESTIONS

1 A relatively new type of patent infringement regards the situation that different elements of a patented process are located in different countries, in the sense that only if they are operated together, a complete infringement can be established. How can patent law deal with the matter? How would the situation change if the unitary patent system were actually established?

2 How do you evaluate the decision by the Belgian legislature to allow experimenting not only on but also with the invention (limitation of protection for research tools)? What are the arguments for and against such a rule?

3 In general, copyright law contains a far greater number of limitations and exceptions to the exclusive rights granted to the right-holder than patent law. What might be the explanation?

4 What could be 'legitimate reasons' for a patent holder to oppose the further commercialisation of a patented product that was put on the market with his consent?

Patents and patent applications as object of property; duration of patents

Regulations in the EPC

Patents are acknowledged in all EU Member States as forming parts of the owner's property rights and are protected as such on the basis of the national laws as well as, on the Community level, under Article 17 (2) of the Charter of Fundamental Rights. At present, explicit provisions dealing with patents as objects of property are only found in the EPC insofar as European patent applications are concerned (Articles 71 to 74). Article 71 sets out that a European patent application is a legal object of its own, and can be transferred for one or more of the designated Contracting States. Contracts concerning the assignment of a European patent application shall be made in writing and signed by the contracting parties (Article 72 EPC). Also, a European patent application may be licensed in whole or in part for the whole or part of the territories of the designated Contracting States (Art. 73 EPC). Finally, for all other questions, the European patent application as an object of property shall, in each designated Contracting State and with effect for such State, be subject to the law applicable in that State to national patent applications (Article 74 EPC).

Unitary patents

Regarding unitary patents, it is set out in Article 3 (2) dUPR that, in accordance with their unitary nature, they can only be transferred in their entirety, i.e. with effect for all the participating Member States. However, licenses may still be granted for individual Member States separately.

Additional rules concerning unitary patents as objects of property are set out in Article 10 dUPR. As a matter of principle, it is stipulated that unitary patents shall be treated in all the participating Member States as national patents in the Member State where the patent holder has his seat or establishment or, where the proprietor is not established in the EU, as national patents in the country where the central patent authority has its seat (i.e., Germany).

Furthermore, Article 11 dUPR addresses so-called licenses of right. The proprietor of a European patent with unitary effect may file a statement with the European Patent Office that he/she is prepared to allow any person to use the invention as a licensee in return for appropriate compensation. Licenses granted on that basis are treated as contractual licenses. Until now, such schemes have been applied under the national laws of several Member States, as a tool intended to encourage more widespread use of patented technology. Indeed, it is a common observation that for various reasons a high percentage of patented inventions are never used on the market, but will nevertheless block the use by others. By signaling the patent holder's readiness to license on reasonable terms, transaction costs are lowered in the interest of both parties. As an additional incentive for patent holders to embark on that scheme, Member States usually offer a reduction in renewal fees. The same is envisaged for the unitary patent.

While previous drafts of the Community patent regulation also contained provisions on compulsory licenses, the pertinent rules have been taken out, in order to avoid controversies during the legislative process. Instead of stipulating common rules, the conditions under which compulsory licenses can be issued therefore remain a matter of national legislation.

Duration

The term of the European patent is 20 years from the date of filing of the application (Article 63 (1) EPC). However, a *de facto* prolongation of the regular term can result from the granting of supplementary protection certificates in cases in which the subject matter of the European patent is a product or a process for manufacturing a product or a use of a product which has to undergo an administrative authorisation procedure required by law before it can be put on the market in that particular State (Article 63 (2) (b) EPC). The opportunity to obtain such a supplementary protection certificates has been created by EU Council Regulations No. 469/2009 and 1610/96.[88]

? QUESTIONS

1 Why is it possible to grant licences with regard to a unitary patent for individual States separately, whereas the unitary patent as such can only be transferred in its entirety? Does this not undermine the freedom of movement of goods?

2 In what ways does a 'licence of right' under Article 11 dUPR lower transaction costs, as stated above? Why would a 'licence of right' appeal to patent holders who usually shun any form of compulsory licensing?

3 Does the 'one size fits all' term of protection in patent law make sense in view of individual characteristics of inventions in different fields of technology and the different competitive market situations which these characteristics entail? What other special rules besides the Supplementary Protection Certificates (SPCs), discussed below (section 3.5), could come to mind?

4 Why is there such a big difference between the patent and the copyright term of protection?

3.4 Patents relating to specific fields of technology

The Biotechnology Directive

History and purpose

In view of the fact that biotechnology and genetic engineering play an increasingly important role in a broad range of industries and the corresponding importance of the protection of biotechnological inventions, the EU has enacted Directive 98/44/EC harmonising the legal protection of biotechnological inventions (Biotech Directive).[89] As stated in Recitals 2 and 3, the Commission followed the opinion that:

---

88 For discussion see in this chapter, section 3.5.

89 Directive 98/44/EC of the European Parliament and of the Council of 6 July 1998 on the legal protection of biotechnological inventions, [1998] OJ L 213/13 (Biotech Directive). The information by the Commission is provided at ec.europa.eu/internal_market/indprop/invent/index_en.htm.

in particular in the field of genetic engineering, research and development require a considerable amount of high-risk investment and therefore only adequate legal protection can make them profitable [and therefore] effective and harmonized protection throughout the Member States is essential in order to maintain and encourage investment in the field of biotechnology.

A first effort to achieve harmonisation in this field had already been undertaken in 1988.[90] However, controversies about the appropriateness of 'patenting life' proved to be so strong that the process was slowed down and the proposal was finally rejected in 1995 by the European Parliament, even after the text had been approved in conciliation proceedings. The main point of criticism was that access should remain free to the human genome data and possible restrictions on the research and applications for which this data could be used should be avoided.

In the same year, the Commission tabled another proposal, which was adopted in 1998 after several changes had been made in the text. As in other harmonising directives, the legal basis was primarily found in the risk that the existing differences in the law and practice of Member States might create barriers to trade and hence impede the proper functioning of the internal market.[91] Following the adoption, that legal basis was challenged by the Netherlands, claiming that the Directive could not be justified by invoking the creation of the Single Market. Furthermore the Dutch government pleaded that there was a breach of the principle of legal certainty, of obligations in international law, of the fundamental right to respect for human dignity and of procedural rules in the adoption of the Commission's proposal. However, all of these pleas were rejected by the ECJ, so that the Directive could enter into force as approved.[92]

The aim of the Biotech Directive is to regulate and harmonise the conditions under which patents can be granted in Europe. Like other directives, it is addressed to the Member States and obliges them to bring their national laws in accordance with the provisions set out therein. However, many patents in the relevant field are not granted by the national offices, but by the EPO, which is not subject to EU legislation. In order to attain the necessary degree of harmonisation, the systems therefore had to be synchronised with regard to the subject matter to be excluded from protection. This was achieved on

---

90 Proposal for a Council Directive on the legal protection of biotechnological inventions, COM(1988) 496 final.

91 See recitals 5–7 of the Biotech Directive 98/44/EC.

92 ECJ Case C-377/98, *Netherlands* v. *European Parliament and Council of the European Union*, [2001] ECR I-7079. On the Human Rights aspects of the case see Chapter 2, section 2.5.3.2.

the one hand by reiterating the exclusions anchored in Article 53 (a) and (b) EPC (ordre public, exclusion of plant and animal varieties) in the Biotech Directive, and on the other hand by incorporating the core provisions of the Biotech Directive into the Implementing Regulations of the EPC (Rules 23b–e; complemented by Rules 27a–28a; now Rules 26–29, complemented by Rules 30–34).

Contents

Patentability

Rather than creating a separate body of law in place of the rules of national patent law (Recital 8), the objective of the Biotech Directive is to clarify the distinction between what is patentable in this area and what is not.

In that regard, challenges are posed by the fact that biotechnological inventions relate to living matter. This not only raises ethical concerns, but also makes it necessary to demarcate the borderline between patentable inventions and mere discoveries, which are excluded from protection for lack of inventive activity. The issue is addressed in Article 3, where it is pointed out that:

> inventions which are new, which involve an inventive step and which are susceptible of industrial application shall be patentable even if they concern a product consisting of or containing biological material or a process by means of which biological material is produced, processed or used (Article 3 (1))

and that:

> [b]iological material which is isolated from its natural environment or produced by means of a technical process may be the subject of an invention even if it previously occurred in nature. (Article 3 (2))

As under the EPC, plant and animal varieties as well as essentially biological processes for the production of plants or animals are not patentable. This is without prejudice to the patentability of inventions which concern a microbiological or other technical process or a product obtained by means of such a process (Articles 4 (1) and (3)). Likewise, inventions which concern plants or animals are patentable if the technical feasibility of the invention is not confined to a particular plant or animal variety (Article 4 (2)).

A categorical exclusion from patentability applies to the human body at the various stages of its formation and development, as well as to the simple discovery of one of its elements, including the sequence or partial sequence of a gene (Article 5 (1)).[93] However, material that is isolated from the human body, including gene sequences, can be patented even if they occur in nature, subject to the requirement that the function making them liable to industrial application is disclosed in the application documents (Article 5 (2) and (3)).

The reason given for this in Recital 17 of the Biotech Directive 98/44/EC is that since:

> significant progress in the treatment of diseases has already been made thanks to the existence of medicinal products derived from elements isolated from the human body and/or otherwise produced, such medicinal products resulting from technical processes aimed at obtaining elements similar in structure to those existing naturally in the human body and whereas, consequently, research aimed at obtaining and isolating such elements valuable to medicinal production should be encouraged by means of the patent system.

The ethical concerns raised by opponents of any propertisation of living matter are addressed by Article 6. First, Article 6 (1) reiterates the principle also enshrined in Article 53 (a) EPC that patents shall not be available for inventions the exploitation of which would be contrary to ordre public. More specifically, Article 6 (2) declares unpatentable:

(a) processes for cloning human beings;
(b) processes for modifying the germ line genetic identity of human beings;
(c) uses of human embryos for industrial or commercial purposes;[94]
(d) processes for modifying the genetic identity of animals which are likely to cause them suffering without any substantial medical benefit to man or animal, and also animals resulting from such processes.

Scope of protection

Regarding the scope of protection of patents concerning biological material, Article 8 stipulates that:

> [t]he scope of protection conferred by a patent on a biological material possessing specific characteristics as a result of the invention extends to any biological mate-

---

93 See also Recital 16 of the Biotech Directive 98/44/EC.
94 With regard to this provision, the qualification is made in Recital 42 of the Biotech Directive 98/44/EC that the exclusion 'does not affect inventions for therapeutic or diagnostic purposes which are applied to the human embryo and are useful to it.'

rial derived from that biological material through propagation or multiplication in an identical or divergent form and possessing those same characteristics.

Similarly, regarding the scope of protection for *process patents*, it is stipulated that:

> a patent on a process that enables a biological material to be produced possessing specific characteristics as a result of the invention shall extend to biological material directly obtained through that process and to any other biological material derived from the directly obtained biological material through propagation or multiplication in an identical or divergent form and possessing those same characteristics. (Article 8 (1) and (2))

Likewise:

> [t]he protection conferred by a patent on a product containing or consisting of genetic information shall extend to all material . . . in which the product is incorporated and in which the genetic information is contained and performs its function. (Article 9)

However, the exclusive protection does not extend:

> to biological material where the multiplication or propagation necessarily results from the application for which the biological material was marketed and the material obtained is not subsequently used for other propagation or multiplication. (Article 10)

Finally, Article 11 is intended to benefit farmers and breeders by stating that consent to the sale or any other form of commercialisation of patented plant propagating material and breeding stock or other animal reproductive material implies consent to use the harvested product for propagation or multiplication by him on his own farm, or, respectively, to use the protected livestock for an agricultural purpose, including the making available of animal or other animal reproductive material for the purposes of pursuing his agricultural activity, except sale within the framework or for the purpose of a commercial reproduction activity.

The remaining articles of the Directive contain provisions on compulsory cross-licensing in cases in which a plant breeder cannot acquire or exploit a plant variety right without infringing a prior patent, or in which the holder of a patent concerning a biotechnological invention cannot exploit it without infringing a prior plant variety right (Article 12), as well as rules on deposit, access and re-deposit of biological material, e.g. in cases in which an invention involves the use of or concerns biological material which is not available to the public and which cannot be described in a patent application in such a manner as to enable the invention to be reproduced by a person skilled in the art (Articles 13 and 14).

Contentious issues and ethical concerns

Regular assessment

From the inception of the Biotech Directive, concerns were raised about the ethical hazards possibly connected with it. To some, the notion that patents can be obtained for isolating or manipulating genes is repulsive *per se*. And although it is widely accepted that research is conducted in the area, certain borderlines should not be crossed, and by matching scientific ambition with the rent-seeking behaviour typically associated with patenting, erosion of those borderlines may appear more likely. Also, it is feared that monopolisation of biological material could result in serious impediments for the access to cures or medical testing, and that it could have detrimental side effects on the world's ecosystem as well as on the traditional production of food, particularly in developing countries.

Article 16 of the Biotech Directive therefore submits the pertinent developments to regular assessment. An important task in that framework has been assigned to the Commission's European Group on Ethics in Science and New Technologies,[95] which is charged with the evaluation of all ethical aspects of biotechnology. So far, it has issued an opinion on ethical aspects of patenting inventions involving human stem cells (2002), on ethical aspects of animal cloning for food supply (2008), on ethics of modern developments in agricultural technologies (2008) and on ethics of synthetic biology (2009).[96]

The EU Commission itself is obliged pursuant to Article 16(c) to inform the European Parliament annually on the development and implications of patent law in the field of biotechnology and genetic engineering. However, so far only two such reports have been issued, the last one in in 2005.[97]

---

95 See ec.europa.eu/bepa/european-group-ethics/index_en.htm.

96 See the list of opinions at ec.europa.eu/european_group_ethics/avis/index_en.htm.

97 Reports pursuant to Article 16c of the Directive 98/44/EC: 'Development and implications of patent law in the field of biotechnology and genetic engineering', Report from the Commission to the European Parliament and Council, COM(2005) 312 final, and Report from the Commission to the European Parliament and the Council, COM(2002) 545 final, both available at ec.europa.eu/internal_market/indprop/

Apart from the assessment duties inscribed in the legal text, the ethical aspects and contentious issues involved in the Biotech Directive were also addressed by jurisprudence. Apart from decisions rendered by the EPO Appeal Boards or its Enlarged Board of Appeal, the Court of Justice has also adjudicated on the matter, as the – so far – only area of substantive patent law for which the ECJ can claim competence.

Case law

Animal suffering; animal varieties: the Oncomouse case

Broad and heated discussions about the ethical implications of protection for biotechnological inventions were triggered already in the 1990s by the Oncomouse[98] case. The claimed invention concerned a transgenic (laboratory) mouse carrying a specifically modified gene which made it susceptible to developing cancer, and thus suitable for cancer research. Patents for the invention were claimed worldwide. The claims filed at the EPO related to a 'transgenic non-human mammalian animal (in particular a mouse)'. The patentability of the invention depended *inter alia* on the question whether the exclusion in Article 53 (b) EPC must be read as a general ban against patenting animals, or whether it must be construed more narrowly. Based on the wording of Article 53 (b) which relates to 'animal varieties', the technical Board of Appeal concluded that the exclusion did not apply to the higher taxonomic unit of 'non-human mammalian animals', so that the patent could be granted.[99]

The issue was raised again (with the same result) in opposition proceedings against an amended version of the patent, this time under consideration also of the Biotech Directive which in the meantime had been incorporated into the Implementing Regulations of the EPO.[100] In addition to Article 53 (b), the decision considered whether the patenting of animals clashed with *ordre public* in the meaning of Article 53 (a) EPC. However, as set out by the technical Board of Appeal, the law did not sustain such categorical exclusions:

---

invent/index_en.htm. The European Parliament has criticised the Commission for not fulfilling its obligation to deliver annual reports since 2005, see European Parliament resolution of 10 May 2012 on the patenting of essential biological processes, available at www.europarl.europa.eu/sides/getDoc.do?pubRef=-//EP//TEXT+TA+P7-TA-2012-0202+0+DOC+XML+V0//EN#def_1_5.

98 Also known as 'Harvard mouse'. The modifications of the gene carried by the mouse had been developed by two researchers at Harvard, Philip Leder and Timothy A. Stewart.

99 T 19/09, *Harvard v. OncoMouse*, [1990] OJ EPO 476.

100 T 315/03, *Harvard v. OncoMouse*, [2006] OJ EPO 15.

(4.4) The categories of exclusions and exceptions may, depending on one's moral, social or other point of view, appear acceptable or unacceptable, quixotic or outdated, liberal or conservative. There may certainly be scope within the express wording of certain of those categories for interpretation in order to establish the exact boundaries of the categories but, subject to such interpretative scope, the law is clear: there is no excluded or excepted category of 'animals in general'.

Furthermore it was examined whether the patent was contrary to Rule 28 (d) (at that time: Rule 23d (d)) of the Implementing Regulations, which corresponds to Article 6 (d) of the Biotech Directive (suffering of animals). The board concluded that application of the rule compelled a balancing exercise between animal suffering and medical benefit:

9.7. To summarise, the Rule 23d (d) EPC test requires three matters to be established: likely animal suffering, likely substantial medical benefit, and the necessary correspondence between the two in terms of the animals in question. The level of proof is the same for both animal suffering and substantial medical benefit, namely a likelihood. Since only a likelihood of suffering need be shown, other matters such as the degree of suffering or the availability of non-animal alternatives need not be considered.

Stem cell patenting
EPO: <u>WARF (the Edinburgh patent)</u>
Even more sensitive issues than in the Oncomouse case are raised by patenting of human stem cells, in particular where that leads to 'consumption' of human embryos. The leading case decided in EPO practice, *WARF*, concerned the so-called 'Edinburgh patent' regarding a cell culture comprising primate embryonic stem cells capable of in vitro fertilisation. The patent had been refused by the Examining Division. The Board of Appeal considered the question of patentability of human stem cells and the relevant conditions as an outstandingly important point of law and referred a number of questions to the Enlarged Board of Appeal (Article 112 (1) (a) EPC),[101] regarding *inter alia* the interpretation of Rule 28 (c) (formerly Rule 23d (c)) of the Implementing Regulation, which corresponds to Article 6 (2) (c) of the Biotech Directive (use of human embryos for industrial or commercial purposes). The main argument put forward by the applicant had been that the use of human embryos to make the claimed human embryonic stem cell cultures is not a use 'for industrial or commercial purposes'. However, the Enlarged Board of Appeal responded that:

---

101 T 1374/04, *Stem cells v.WARF*, [2007] OJ EPO 13.

(25) A claimed new and inventive product must first be made before it can be used. Such making is the ordinary way commercially to exploit the claimed invention and falls within the monopoly granted, as someone having a patent application with a claim directed to this product has on the grant of the patent the right to exclude others from making or using such product. Making the claimed product remains commercial or industrial exploitation of the invention even where there is an intention to use that product for further research. On the facts which this Board must assume in answering the referred question . . ., making the claimed product involves the destruction of human embryos. This use involving destruction is thus an integral and essential part of the industrial or commercial exploitation of the claimed invention, and thus violates the prohibition of Rule 28 (c) . . . EPC.[102]

ECJ: The *Brüstle* judgement

In *WARF*, the applicant had requested the Enlarged Board of Appeal to refer the relevant questions to the ECJ, in order to secure harmonised practice within the EU. However, the request was denied as inapplicable due to the fact that the EPO is not subject to EU law. The Enlarged Board of Appeals held that neither the EPC nor the Implementing Regulations thereto make any provision for a referral by any instance of the EPO of questions of law to the ECJ. Furthermore, it concluded that whereas boards of appeal have been recognised as being courts or tribunals, they are not courts or tribunals of an EU Member State but of an international organisation whose contracting states are not all members of the EU. Therefore, the boards of appeal would not be eligible under the EU Treaties to request a preliminary ruling from the ECJ.[103]

It took more time therefore before the ECJ had an opportunity to address Article 6 (2) (c) of the Biotech Directive in a preliminary ruling (*Brüstle*).[104] Different from the Edinburgh patent case decided by the Enlarged Board of Appeal, the claimed patent did not concern the cell cultures as such, but only their use for medical purposes, in particular for treating Parkinson's disease. Another difference lay in the fact that the production of the cell cultures did not require primary embryonic stem cells, but only the use of so-called neural precursor cells, that is, pluripotent stem cells of human origin which are removed in an early stage of the development of the result of the fertilisation of an ovum by a sperm. Highlighting those differences, the German Federal Supreme Court requested clarification from the ECJ regarding the

---

102 G 2/06, *Stem cells* v. *WARF*, [2009] OJ EPO 306. For further case law of the Enlarged Board of Appeal regarding biotechnological inventions see G 3/95, G 1/98, G 1/03, G 2/03 and G 1/04, Annex I).
103 G 2/06, *Stem cells* v. *WARF*, [2009] OJ EPO 318.
104 ECJ Case C-34/10, *Brüstle* v. *Greenpeace*, [2011] ECR I-0000.

concept of 'human embryo' and the meaning of the phrase 'uses of human embryos for industrial or commercial purposes' with regard to the specific constellation at stake in this case.

Concerning the first of these issues, the ECJ took a broad approach by holding that:

> (34) [t]he context and aim of the Directive . . . show that the European Union legislature intended to exclude any possibility of patentability where respect for human dignity could thereby be affected. It follows that the concept of 'human embryo' within the meaning of Article 6 (2) (c) of the Directive must be understood in a wide sense. (35) Accordingly, any human ovum must, as soon as fertilised, be regarded as a 'human embryo' within the meaning and for the purposes of the application of Article 6 (2) (c) of the Directive, since that fertilisation is such as to commence the process of development of a human being. (36) That classification must also apply to a non-fertilised human ovum into which the cell nucleus from a mature human cell has been transplanted and a non-fertilised human ovum whose division and further development have been stimulated by parthenogenesis. Although those organisms have not, strictly speaking, been the object of fertilisation, due to the effect of the technique used to obtain them they are . . . capable of commencing the process of development of a human being just as an embryo created by fertilisation of an ovum can do so.

However, it remains for the national courts in an individual case, in the light of scientific developments, to ascertain whether the cell cultures concerned are actually capable of such a development.

Regarding the second issue (exclusion from patentability concerning the use of human embryos for industrial or commercial purposes), the ECJ observed that the exclusion also covers the use of human embryos for purposes of scientific research, with the sole exception of use for therapeutic or diagnostic purposes which is applied to the human embryo and is useful to it (as mentioned in Recital 42). In accordance with the stem cells decision by the EPO Enlarged Board of Appeal it is therefore concluded that Article 6 (2) (c) of Directive 98/44 excludes an invention from patentability where:

> (53) the technical teaching which is the subject matter of the patent application requires the prior destruction of human embryos or their use as base material, whatever the stage at which that takes place and even if the description of the technical teaching claimed does not refer to the use of human embryos.

Purpose-bound protection: Monsanto
Further issues are presented by the potential breadth of patent protection for biotechnological inventions. The problem derives from the fact that whereas in case of traditional product and process innovation the scope of applicability of the invention is fairly clear-cut and foreseeable, the application of biological material is rarely apparent at the time of sequencing. If absolute protection were granted for the isolated material, this would arguably fall short of the key objectives of patent law. The reward obtained would be disproportional to the inventive activity, as it would cover also 'windfall profits' ensuing from functions of the subject matter which were not anticipated when the relevant investments took place. In this context, it must also be considered that the sequencing of DNA as such nowadays hardly ever represents an inventive step in the sense that it exceeds the ordinary capacity of a person skilled in the art. The sole achievement meriting protection and encouragement is the identification of a specific function, which makes it seem consequent to limit the protection accordingly.

Furthermore, the concept that the inventor, in exchange for obtaining an exclusive right, discloses the technical teaching embedded therein would have no basis if the functions possibly performed by the biological material are not disclosed. This consideration is reflected at various instances in the Biotech Directive and its Preamble. Thus, Article 5(3) specifies that:

> The industrial application of a sequence or a partial sequence of a gene must be disclosed in the patent application.

Furthermore, according to Recitals 23 and 24:

> a mere DNA sequence without *indication of a function* does not contain any technical information and is therefore not a patentable invention . . .

and:

> in order to comply with the industrial application criterion it is necessary in cases where a sequence or partial sequence of a gene is used to produce a protein or part of a protein, to specify which protein or part of a protein is produced or *what function it performs.* (Emphases added)

While this leaves no doubt about the necessity of specifying at least one function in the patent application, it is unclear whether it also entails a corresponding limitation of the scope of protection.

The issue was considered by the ECJ in the *Monsanto* case.[105] The European patent at stake concerned modified genes making plants resistant against the use of certain herbicides, thereby solving the problem that whereas herbicides are destined to kill weeds, they are also often dangerous for the crop they are supposed to protect. The dispute arose when soy meal produced from genetically engineered plants was imported into the EU from Argentina, where Monsanto did not hold a patent. It was undisputed that the plants contained the protected DNA sequence; however, it was also obvious that in the actual form of the soy meal commercialised on the EU market, the gene did not perform its function of protecting the living plant against the use of herbicides. Being uncertain about whether in spite of that, the presence of the DNA alone was sufficient to constitute infringement in the meaning of Article 9 Biotech Directive, the national court referred the issue to the ECJ for a preliminary ruling.

The ECJ first pointed towards Article 5 (3) and Recitals 23 and 24 of the Biotech Directive, pursuant to which a DNA sequence does not enjoy protection under patent law when the function performed by that sequence is not specified.[106] Thus:

> (45) [s]ince the Directive thus makes the patentability of a DNA sequence subject to indication of the function it performs, it must be regarded as not according any protection to a patented DNA sequence which is not able to perform the specific function for which it was patented. . . . (47) An interpretation to the effect that, under the Directive, a patented DNA sequence could enjoy absolute protection as such, irrespective of whether or not the sequence was performing its function, would deprive that provision of its effectiveness. . . . (50) Accordingly, the answer to the first question is that Article 9 of the Directive must be interpreted as not conferring patent right protection in circumstances such as those of the case in the main proceedings . . .

According to the ECJ, the same result must obtain also under national law, because Article 9 of the Biotech Directive:

> (63) . . . effects an exhaustive harmonisation of the protection it confers, with the result that it precludes the national patent legislation from offering absolute pro-

---

105 ECJ Case C-428/08, *Monsanto Technology v. Cefetra*, [2010] ECR I-6765. The questions referred to the ECJ also concerned the compatibility of the restrictions eventually following from Article 9 of the Biotech Directive with Article 27 (prohibition of discrimination) and 30 TRIPS (three-step test). The ECJ responded that TRIPS was not directly applicable, but that Member States were obliged to follow as much as possible the obligations resulting from TRIPS. However, in the concrete case, no violations of Article 27 or 30 TRIPS were considered to result (Monsanto, Paragraphs 70–71).
106 Ibid., Paragraph 44.

tection to the patented product as such, regardless of whether it performs its function in the material containing it.

The ECJ has thus somewhat mitigated fears that patent protection for genetically modified processes might have an all too far-reaching monopolising effect. However, it is still unclear what the result will be if a conflict does not concern the commercialisation of products for which the protected function is irrelevant, such as the soy meal in *Monsanto*, but if it is about the use by third parties of a function performed by the protected gene sequence which is different from the function disclosed in the application.

Essentially biological methods: tomatoes and broccoli
Finally, of high practical importance in this context is the distinction between the ambit of patent law and *sui generis* protection for plant varieties. The latter is generally considered as leaving more room for independent and self-supporting farming, whereas patent law is said to increase the dependency of plant breeders on the bioengineering industry. The borderline is highlighted in Article 53 (b) EPC, pursuant to which protection of plant or animal varieties or 'essentially biological processes' for the production of plants or animals are excluded from patent protection.[107]

The latter issue was addressed in decisions by the EPO Enlarged Board of Appeal concerning patent applications for genetically engineered vegetable varieties (tomatoes and broccoli).[108] In the broccoli case, the claimed invention concerned a method for selectively increasing the level of a potentially anti-carcinogenic substance in the plants, by locating the relevant genes on the broccoli genome and identifying them with genetic markers. According to the previous practice of the EPO, marker-assisted selection had been considered to be a technical process and therefore patentable. However, the Enlarged Board of Appeals considered that to be insufficient: while genetic markers themselves may be patentable, their use alone does not confer patentability on an essentially biological process. If the invention concerns a process for the production of plants involving sexually crossing whole plant genomes, and the subsequent selection of plants, it is 'essentially biological' and thus not patentable, even where a genetic marker is used for the selection.

Although less remarkable in terms of the subject treated than the Oncomouse case or stem cell patenting, the broccoli and tomato cases were closely

---

107 See also Chapter 6, section 6.2.3.
108 EPO Enlarged Board of Appeals, G 2/07 Broccoli/PLANT BIOSCIENCE, [2012] OJ EPO 230 and G 1/08, Tomatoes/STATE OF ISRAEL, OJ EPO 206.

observed by the interested public and by policy-makers. The European Parliament took the opportunity to issue a resolution on the patenting of essential biological processes,[109] in which it:

1. Acknowledges the important role of the EPO in supporting innovation competitiveness and economic growth in Europe;

2. Recognises that patents promote the dissemination of valuable technical information and are an important tool for the transfer of technology;

3. Welcomes the decisions of the Enlarged Board of Appeal of the EPO in the so-called 'broccoli' (G 2/07) and 'tomato' (G 1/08) cases . . . ;

4. Calls on the EPO also to exclude from patenting products derived from conventional breeding and all conventional breeding methods, including SMART breeding (precision breeding) and breeding material used for conventional breeding;

5. Calls on the Commission to address in its forthcoming report the 'broccoli and tomato decisions' of the Enlarged Board of Appeal of the EPO;

6. Welcomes the recent decision of the European Patent Office in the WARF case and of the European Court of Justice in the Brüstle case, as they appropriately interpret Directive 98/44/EC and give important indications on the so-called whole content approach; calls on the European Commission to draw the appropriate consequences from these decisions also in other relevant policy areas in order to bring EU policy in line with these decisions;

7. Calls on the Commission to address in its forthcoming report the potential implications of the patenting of breeding methods for plants and their impact on the breeding industry, agriculture, the food industry and food security;

8. Calls on the Commission and the Member States to ensure that the EU will continue to apply a comprehensive breeders' exemption in its patent law for plant and animal breeding;

9. Instructs its President to forward this resolution to the Council, the Commission, the governments of the Member States and the EPO.

? QUESTIONS

1 Patents for biotechnological inventions are highly controversial. What is your opinion? How far should patentability extend? And what ethical, economic and health reasons should be taken into account?

2 What is the relationship between a – national or European – patent granted for a biotechnological invention and national law provisions which regulate or even prohibit the use of the patented invention (see Recital 14 of the Biotechnology Directive and Article 54 (1) EPC)?

---

109 European Parliament resolution of 10 May 2012 on the patenting of essential biological processes, available at www.europarl.europa.eu/sides/getDoc.do?pubRef=-//EP//TEXT+TA+P7-TA-2012-0202+0+DOC+XML+V0//EN#def_1_5.

3 Article 54 (2) and (3) EPC exclude from patentability both 'plant or animal varieties or essentially biological processes for the production of plants or animals', and 'methods for treatment of the human or animal body by surgery or therapy and diagnostic methods practised on the human or animal body', with the exception of 'products, in particular substances or compositions, for use in any of these methods'. To what extent does this differ from the Biotechnology Directive (see also Recital 15 of the Biotechnology Directive)? And what could be the results of any discrepancy?

4 In the popular press it has often been concluded that the ECJ-decision in case C-34/10 – Brüstle puts a ban on biotechnology research in Europe and that all scientists would most likely emigrate to the US and other countries, where research with stem-cell is allowed. Is this statement true, and if so, for what reason?

5 What should the EPO do with regard to the implementation of the Brüstle decision, as 11 Member States of the European Patent Organisation are not bound to the decisions of the ECJ? Should the EPO consider itself bound to Brüstle even though in view of the differences between that case and the previous WARF decision the ECJ's conclusions are not free from doubt and were heavily criticised by experts?

Computer-implemented inventions

The issue

Computer programs, the first digital objects to appear, are cost-intensive to write and, at the same time, easy to copy at low cost. In view of this, it was undisputed that computer programs should enjoy some form of exclusive protection. However, in the beginning, it was not quite clear which of the existing protection regimes would be most appropriate to satisfy the protection needs. True, computer programs are written in a special language, but contrary to works protected by copyright law they lack the aesthetic appeal. Rather, they are functional in nature, but as mere instructions directed at a machine they do not as such fulfil the criteria for patentability. Hence, attempts were made at the international level to devise a *sui generis* scheme of protection, but already in the middle of the 1980s, those plans were given up, because by then software industries had successfully lobbied for the inclusion of computer programs as objects of copyright protection.[110] Because

---

110 Article 10 (1) TRIPS. For detail in Europe see Council Directive 91/250/EEC of 14 May 1991 on the legal protection of computer programs, [1991] OJ L 122/42 (Computer Program Directive), discussed in Chapter 5, section 5.2.2.1.

of the lack of formalities and the principle of national treatment, copyright provides an easy to obtain, low cost international protection scheme. Also, because copyright provides protection to the code of a program against literal copying, partial copying and certain adaptations, it mainly satisfies the needs of creators of application programs against illegal copying by re-sellers and end-users as well as against adaptations by competitors.

But copyright does not protect the ideas which underlie a particular program, nor a program's particular functionalities. In other words, although the code of a computer program can be protected by copyright, there is still additional need for protection with regard to the functional properties of a program which can be implemented in different forms of code. In particular, this is true regarding inventions which contain and make use of a computer program without specifying only one implementation in a particular code. Patent law might well fill this gap. As expressed in a text by the EU Commission:

> A *patent* protects an invention as delimited by the patent claims which determine the extent of the protection conferred. Thus, the holder of a patent for a computer-implemented invention has the right to prevent third parties from using any software which implements his invention (as defined by the patent claims). This principle holds even though various ways might be found to achieve this using programs whose source or object code is different from each other and which might be protected in parallel by independent copyrights which would not mutually infringe each other.[111]

Of course, on the one hand, with regard to inventions which are computer (or hardware)-related, no particular problem arises. Any invention which innovates on hardware is eligible for patent protection, provided it is new, includes an inventive step and is capable of industrial application. On the other hand, since the 1970s, according to Article 52 (2) (c) and (3) EPC, computer programs as such were expressly excluded from patent protection. But does this mean that inventions which incorporate a computer program (so-called software-related or computer-implemented inventions) are likewise excluded from patent protection? Or does the exclusion not apply, because inventions which do not relate to a computer program alone, but which incorporate a computer program are not inventions concerning a computer program as such?

---

111 Proposal for a Directive of the European Parliament and of the Council 20 February 2002 on the patentability of computer-implemented inventions, COM(2002) 92 final, eur-lex.europa.eu/LexUriServ/LexUriServ.do?uri=COM:2002:0092:FIN:EN:PDF.

According to Article 27 TRIPS, 'patents shall be available for any inventions, whether products or processes, in all fields of technology'. But then the exclusion of computer programs as such from patent protection in Article 52 (2) (c) and (3) EPC was justified on the assumption that a computer program is to be considered as a non-technical process. This, however, creates a dilemma: whereas it may perhaps be justified to exclude computer programs as such from patentability, it may likewise be economically unwise to refuse patent protection in traditional technical areas just because certain tasks can today be performed by computer programs. Moreover, today, there are many inventions in all sorts of technological fields which make, *inter alia*, use of a computer program. Most important, refusing patent protection for computer-implemented inventions would exclude from patentability almost the whole area of information and communications technology (ICT), and with it one of the most dynamic and innovative industries.

The issue to what extent patent protection shall be available to computer-implemented inventions is still controversial. If one doesn't want to opt for either extreme, the problem becomes one of distinguishing between inventions which claim nothing more than a program *per se*, and inventions which contain a computer program, but are otherwise patentable. Of course, no problem exists with regard to computerised control systems of technical machines. Rather, the problem is those inventions which in essence consist of no more than a computer program used to make the hardware perform a certain task or to carry out certain methods of operation. The history of both the granting practice and of court decisions regarding such inventions cannot be retraced here in detail. Suffice it to say that it followed a course meandering between a more restrictive and a more liberal attitude. Whereas the patent offices' granting practice was driven, at least in part, by the concern to attract customers, the decisions handed down by the courts often reflected the prevailing general attitude towards patents as either a stimulus for innovation or an unjustified and dangerous monopoly hindering competition and innovation. For instance, whereas in the 1970s the Courts in the US were rather reluctant to uphold patent protection, in subsequent years the formula prevailed that 'everything under the sun',[112] including computer programs and even computerised business methods can be patented.[113] Recently, however, the pendulum seems to have begun to swing back in the

---

112 *Diamond v. Chakrabarty*, US Supreme Court, 447 US 303 (1980). The decision concerned the patenting of a bacterium capable of breaking down crude oil, being the first spectacular case of patenting biotechnological inventions.

113 *State Street Bank v. Signature Financial Group*, US Supreme Court, 149 F. 3d 1368 (1998).

US.[114] In Europe, the development has followed a similar, but somewhat less accentuated path.

Granting practice and figures

Both the EPO and national European patent offices grant patents for inventions which make use of a computer program. Whereas patent protection is still not available for mere computer programs, computer-implemented inventions (CII) are patentable in Europe (as well as in the US, Japan and other industrialised countries), provided the invention as a whole either makes a non-obvious 'technical contribution' or solves a 'technical problem' in a non-obvious way, even if that technical problem is solved by running a computer program.

This raises two issues, namely how to distinguish a patentable CII from unpatentable computer programs 'as such' within the meaning of Articles 52 (1), (2) (c) and (3) EPC on the one hand, and when does a new invention involve an inventive step.

Discussing existing case law of the boards of appeal, the Enlarged Board of Appeal of the EPO has given some answers to these questions in his opinion G 3/08 of 12 May 2010.[115] It first stated that:

> a claim utilising a synonym for 'computer program', such as 'a sequence of computer-executable instructions' or 'an executable software module' . . . would clearly not avoid exclusion from patentability if the equivalent claim to a computer program did not.

Moreover, the Enlarged Board of Appeal summarised the present position of the case law by the boards of appeal as follows:

> [A] claim in the area of computer programs can avoid exclusion under Articles 52 (2) (c) and (3) EPC merely by explicitly mentioning the use of a computer or a computer-readable storage medium.

However:

> it is also quite clear from the case law of the Boards of Appeal . . . that if a claim to program X falls under the exclusion of Articles 52 (2) and (3) EPC, a claim which

---

114 *Bilski v. Kappos*, US Supreme Court, 130 S. Ct. 3218 (2010); for the previous instance see *In re Bilski*, CAFC, 545 F.3d 943 (2008).

115 See www.epo.org/news-issues/issues/computers/eba.html. Quotations are from Paragraphs 10.1, 10.13 and 10.13.1.

specifies no more than 'Program X on a computer-readable storage medium,' or 'A method of operating a computer according to program X', will always still fail to be patentable for lack of an inventive step under Articles 52 (1) and 56 EPC. Merely the EPC article applied is different . . . [I]f the Boards continue to follow the precepts of [previous case law] it follows that a claim to a computer implemented method or a computer program on a computer-readable storage medium will never fall within the exclusion of claimed subject matter under Articles 52 (2) and (3) EPC . . . However, this does not mean that the list of subject matters in Article 52 (2) EPC (including in particular 'programs for computers') has no effect on such claims. An elaborate system for taking that effect into account in the assessment of whether there is an inventive step has been developed, as laid out in T 154/04, *Duns*. . . . [I]t is evident . . . that the list of 'non-inventions' in Article 52 (2) EPC can play a very important role in determining whether claimed subject matter is inventive.

In other words, in view of the modified problem/solution approach,[116] under which the closest prior art is identified and the problem to be solved deduced from the difference between the claims as drafted and the prior art, in practice the main issue is not whether what is claimed by an applicant as the invention merely is a computer program as such, nor is it novelty, but rather whether there is an inventive step. Although the problem to be solved must be of a technical nature, the invention may also contain non-technical aspects as constraints to be met. However, with regard to the examination for non-obviousness of the solution as claimed, only the features which contribute to the solution of a technical problem or which imply non-trivial technical considerations when being implemented will be considered, whereas features which do not contribute to the solution of a technical problem, i.e. which do not make a technical contribution to the prior art, will not.

Details regarding the dividing line between patentable and non-patentable computer-implemented inventions and issues of non-obviousness cannot be discussed here, since they require an in-depth analysis of each individual application involved.[117] Moreover, as also stated in the opinion G 3/08 of the Enlarged Board of Appeal:[118]

---

116 See, e.g., T 641/00 (3.5.1.), *SIM card/COMVIC*, OJ 2003, 352.

117 See, e.g., the following cases: for search, retrieval and evaluation of images T 643/00 (3.5.1), *Searching image data/CANON*; for a particular display T 928/03 (3.5.1), *Guide display device/KONAMI*; as regards designing diagrams T 125/04 (3.5.1), *Assessment system/COMPARATIVE VISUAL ASSESSMENTS*; T 49/04 (3.4.3), *Text processor/WALKER*, and T 740/05 (3.5.1), *Attention Management/ACCENTURE*; for information modelling T 49/99 (3.5.1.), *Information modeling/INT. COMPUTERS*; T 354/07 (3.5.1.), *Funktionspläne/SIEMENS*, all to be found at http://www.epo.org/law-practice/case-law-appeals.html.

118 Paragraph 7.3.3, www.epo.org/news-issues/issues/computers/eba.html.

. . . in the field of new technologies, the Technical Boards often have to subject their established case law to critical review, applying accepted judicial procedure and general legal principles to decide whether the often broadly formulated undefined legal terms in the EPC are applicable to the specific nature of the new field, i.e. in particular whether the existing widely accepted case law also yields acceptable solutions in the new field. It is entirely conceivable that the interpretation of undefined legal terms in the light of the EPC's purpose and principles will necessitate drawing further distinctions which, depending on what they include or exclude, may determine whether a patent is granted or refused in a specific case.

Nevertheless, it has to be noted that contrary to the United States Patent and Trademark Office, USPTO, the EPO does not grant patents to computerised business methods, i.e. to inventions which merely solve a business problem with the help of a computer rather than a technical problem, for lack of an inventive step. Again, however, the fact that an invention is useful in business does not mean that it is not patentable if it also solves a technical problem.

Whereas the USPTO is said to have granted some 30,000 software patents in 2004 and 2005, and 40,000 in 2006,[119] the exact number for the EPO is difficult to ascertain because computer-implemented inventions are made in many areas of technology and are therefore to be found in many classes of patents. Yet, the number of an estimated 30,000 software-related patents granted so far, with an additional number of several tens of thousands of applications, is also quite impressive. This demonstrates that granting software-related patents is by now a well established practice.

The failed Commission proposal for a Directive and the rejected proposal for the EPC 2000

In view of this, after consultation with the interested parties, the Commission tabled a proposal for a directive on the patentability of computer-implemented inventions in 2002.[120] Its aim simply was to harmonise the way in which national patent laws of the EU Member States deal with inventions using software. The distinction between patentable inventions whose

---

119 For 2004 see *Bessen/Hunt*, An Empirical Look at Software Patents Working Paper No. 03-17/R, www.researchoninnovation.org/swpat.pdf.

120 Proposal for a Directive of the European Parliament and of the Council 20 February 2002 on the patentability of computer-implemented inventions, COM(2002) 92 final, eur-lex.europa.eu/LexUriServ/LexUriServ.do?uri=COM:2002:0092:FIN:EN:PDF. For activities of the Commission in this area see ec.europa.eu/internal_market/indprop/comp/index_en.htm.

operation involves the use of a computer program and which make a 'technical contribution' and unpatentable computer programs as such as well as unpatentable business methods that simply employ existing technological ideas and apply them to, for example, e-commerce, was to be maintained. In addition, the system should be made more transparent for SMEs. Similarly, the inclusion of corresponding clarifications had been proposed in the EPC 2000 revision.

However, both the Commission's proposal of a directive clarifying the issue of patenting of software-related inventions and the corresponding proposal to amend the EPC 1973 accordingly in the course of the process of drafting the EPC 2000 met with fierce criticism by the opponents of patentability in the field of software, in particular from the open source communities. The main argument was that patents granted in the software and internet fields might lead to a patent 'thicket' which would make innovation either impossible or at least only feasible for big enterprises, which dispose of the resources to research prior patents and negotiate licensing agreements, but not for SMEs. In addition, it was feared that those firms which market their products on a proprietary basis might use patents in order to block free and open source software (FLOSS). The counter-argument raised by proponents of patentability that patents are often the only weapon of defence for small software producing companies against hostile actions and takeover bids by bigger corporations, was generally discarded by the critics of an all too far-reaching patentability. Also, the critics pointed out that many of the patents granted should probably not have been, mainly due to the fact that prior art is not very well documented in the area of software-related inventions and that, in particular in the US, the examination regarding the inventive step isn't very strict. It should be noted, however, that the problem seems to be less acute with the EPO, when it comes to ascertaining the non-obviousness of a claimed invention.

Ultimately, the intensive protests and lobbying activities by the critics[121] with the European Parliament, which rejected the Commission's proposal, and with EPC members' governments were successful and both initiatives to clarify the EPC and to adopt a harmonising directive, were ultimately abandoned.

However, this in no way altered the practice of granting patents for computer-implemented inventions neither by the EU Member States'

---

121 See, e.g., the special site of the Electronic Frontier Foundation, eff.org/patent-busting.

national patent offices nor by the EPO. Moreover, because no EU law exists, there is no judicial control regarding the standard for patenting software-related inventions by the ECJ and consequently different interpretations as to what is patentable or not continue amongst the Member States.

? QUESTIONS

1 In your opinion, will it ever be possible to formulate a legal definition which, when applied in practice, will unambiguously indicate whether a particular computer-implemented invention is patentable or not?

2 Both proponents and opponents of plans to harmonise the rules for granting computer-implemented inventions wanted to strengthen the position of the small and medium enterprises (SMEs). In its proposal for a Directive, the Commission stated that 'SMEs however often have little or no experience with the patent system. Therefore, they have frequently preferred to rely solely on copyright, which provides protection for the expression of computer programs as literary works. In order for SMEs to be able to make full use of the different possibilities offered by the patent system, they must have easy access to information about the means of obtaining patent protection, the benefits which this protection can provide, and the conditions for obtaining patents for their own inventions, for licensing them and for securing patent licenses from other patent holders'.[122] Do you agree with this argument? What would be the counter-argument?

3 In what ways can the patenting of computer-implemented inventions interfere with the fundamental principles of FLOSS?

4 Computer-implemented inventions cover a broad spectrum in between inventions which innovate on the working of hardware devices on the one hand, and mere computer programs 'as such' on the other hand. What groups of computer-implemented inventions can be distinguished?

3.5 Supplementary protection certificates

History and purpose

Council Regulation (EC) No. 469/2009[123] – which codifies the initial Council Regulation (EEC) No. 1768/92 and its subsequent amendments

---

122 Proposal for a Directive of the European Parliament and of the Council 20 February 2002 on the patentability of computer-implemented inventions, COM(2002) 92 final, Explanatory Memorandum, p. 12.

123 Council Regulation (EC) No. 469/2009 of the European Parliament and of the Council 6 May 2009 concerning the supplementary protection certificate for medicinal products, [2009] OJ L 152/1. For Regulation

– defines the EU-wide rules on granting supplementary protection certificates (SPCs) for medicinal products. It addresses a particular problem of the medicinal sector, namely that before obtaining authorisation to place a medicinal product on the market, applicants generally have to undergo a rather regulated and lengthy procedure of testing and admission. A comparable problem arises with regard to plant protection products, which also require authorisation before they are allowed to be placed on the market and where, therefore, a parallel kind of regulation was found necessary.[124] In cases in which the medicinal substance, the medicinal product or its application contains an invention (as it does in most cases), the period that elapses between the filing of the patent application and the granting of the authorisation to place the medicinal product on the market shortens the period in which the applicant and subsequent patent holder can exclusively exploit his new medicinal product. This in turn might render the remaining period of effective patent protection insufficient to recover the investment put into the research, and hence deter pharmaceutical companies from putting up the investment necessary for the development of new drugs in the first place. Moreover, this shortening of the period of effective patent protection penalises pharmaceutical research vis-à-vis other innovative industries.

The problem was first remedied by the United States in 1984 by introducing patent term restoration for pharmaceuticals. The model was subsequently copied by Japan (1987) and, at the beginning of the 1990s, similar solutions were also provided for by the EU Member States France and Italy. Since it was feared that these discrepancies might incite research to relocate to countries that offered greater protection, the EU followed suit in 1992, thus helping EU industries to compete internationally and preventing distortion of competition. Refuting the Spanish challenge of the competency of the EU in this matter, the ECJ concluded that the creation of the SPC 'to prevent the heterogeneous development of national laws, which would be

---

(EEC) No 1768/92 of 18 June 1992 concerning the creation of a supplementary protection certificate for medicinal products see [1992] OJ L 182/1, as subsequently amended at the occasion of the adhesion of new Member States, as well as by Regulation (EC) No 1901/2006 of the European Parliament and of the Council of 12 December 2006 on medicinal products for paediatric use and amending Regulation (EEC) No 1768/92, Directive 2001/20/EC, Directive 2001/83/EC and Regulation (EC) No 726/2004, [2006] OJ L 378/1.

124 See Regulation (EC) No 1610/96 of the European Parliament and of the Council of 23 July 1996 concerning the creation of a supplementary protection certificate for plant protection products, [1996] OJ L 198/30, defining 'plant protection products' as active substances and preparations containing one or more active substances, intended to protect plants or plant products against harmful organisms, influence the life process of plants, preserve plant products, destroy undesirable plants or parts thereof, including to check or prevent undesirable growth of plants. Since the conditions and the mechanism for obtaining an SPC for a plant protection product are almost identical to the conditions and mechanisms for obtaining an SPC for medicinal products, SPCs for plant protection products will not be discussed here in further detail.

likely to create obstacles to the free movement of medicinal products within the Community and thus directly affect the establishment and the functioning of the internal market . . . came within the scope of Article 100a [now Article 114 TFEU]'.[125]

Mechanism

In order for an SPC to be granted, two conditions must be fulfilled. First, the applicant must hold a patent in force in an EU Member State (i.e. either a European patent designating an EU Member State or a national patent) to a medicinal 'product', which is defined as 'the active ingredient or combination of active ingredients of a medicinal product',[126] or to a process to obtain such a product or an application of such a product (so-called 'basic patent'). Second, he must have obtained a valid first authorisation to place the product on the market as a medicinal product. This first marketing authorisation must be one according to relevant EU Directives,[127] not one of national law only.[128]

The SPC is granted upon application by the holder of the basic patent or his successor in title to the national patent office which has granted the basic patent or on whose behalf it was granted and in which the authorisation to place the product on the market was obtained. Since an SPC relates to a national patent or a European patent and is granted by a national patent office, it has effect only in the state in which it has been granted. The application has to be made within six months after the grant of the authorisation to place the medicinal product on the market, or, if the authorisation to

---

125 ECJ Case C-350/92, *Spain* v. *Council*, [1995] ECR I-1985.

126 Article 1 (b) of the Regulation. For interpretation see ECJ Case C-431/04, *MIT*, [2006] ECR I-4089 (holding that the concept of 'combination of active ingredients of a medicinal product does not include a combination of two substances, only one of which has therapeutic effects of its own for a specific indication, the other rendering possible a pharmaceutical form of the medicinal product which is necessary for the therapeutic efficacy of the first substance for that indication').

127 Administrative authorisation procedure in accordance with Directive 2001/83/EC of the European Parliament and of the Council of 6 November 2001 on the Community code relating to medicinal products for human use, [2001] OJ L 311/67, or Directive 2001/82/EC of the European Parliament and of the Council of 6 November 2001on the Community code relating to veterinary medicinal products, [2001] OJ L 311/1.

128 Art. 2 and 3 (b) of the Regulation. It should be noted that initially, an authorisation to market in Switzerland was also considered as being a first authorisation to market for the calculation of the SPC duration, even though Switzerland is not part of the European Economic Area (EEA). The reason was that such a Swiss authorisation was automatically effective in Liechtenstein, which is a member of the EEA; see ECJ Joined Cases C-207/03 and C-252/03, *Novartis and others* v. *Comptroller-General of Patents, Designs and Trade Marks* and *Ministre de l'Économie* v. *Millennium Pharmaceuticals*, [2005] ECR I-3209. However, following this decision, the contract between Switzerland and Liechtenstein was amended and the automatic effect of a Swiss authorisation to put to market in Liechtenstein abolished. The recognition is now delayed by a time period, which is normally 12 months.

place the product on the market is granted before the basic patent is granted, within six months of the date on which the patent is granted.

The additional protection granted by an SPC takes effect at the end of the lawful term of the basic patent. Ideally, the extra duration should exactly compensate for the effective exploitation time lost in each particular Member State due to the fact that authorisation to market was only granted after application or even after the patent had been issued. However, in order not to have different terms running in different Member States (which would indeed have been contrary to the principle of the single market), the EU legislature based the calculation of the term in all Member States on the date of the first authorisation to place the product on the market in the EU. Hence, the term is equal to the period which elapsed between the filing of the patent and the date of the first authorisation in the EU reduced by five years. However, the maximum term of an SPC is five years (also, the term comes to an end if the holder of the SPC fails to pay the annual renewal fees).[129] Consequently, all additional terms granted come to an end in all Member States at the same time. Finally, it should be noted that where an application for an SPC includes the results of all studies conducted in compliance with an agreed Paediatric Investigation Plan (PIP) as set out in Article 36 of Regulation (EC) No 1901/2006, an extension of an additional 6 months can be applied for.[130]

Technically speaking, the SPC does not extend the term of protection of the basic patent. Rather, it is a *sui generis* regime which 'confer[s] the same rights as conferred by the basic patent and shall be subject to the same limitations and the same obligations'.[131] However, these rights are only granted with respect to the 'product covered by the authorisation to place the corresponding medicinal product on the market and for any use of the product as a medicinal product that has been authorised before the expiry of the certificate.'[132] In other words, the additional protection granted by an SPC does not have effect for the basic invention in its entirety. Rather, it only covers the product as it has received authorisation to be placed on the market as a medicinal product. However, in this respect, the certificate reserves the right-holder the full rights of the basic patent which enables the right-holders, after the basic patent has expired and while the term of the

---

129 Article 13 of the Regulation.
130 Article 13 (3) of the Regulation, as amended by Article 52 (7) of Regulation (EC) No. 1901/2006. It should be noted that other than in the case of SPCs for medicinal products, EU law does not foresee for the possibility of an additional six-month extension for an SPC that relates to a plant protection product.
131 Article 5 of the Regulation.
132 Article 4 of the Regulation.

SPC is still running, to prevent both identical products and products with therapeutically equivalent effects from being marketed.

Case law

Finally, it should be noted that although the mechanism of the SPC seems relatively straightforward and simple, in practice, the Regulation in the past has given and still gives rise to a surprising number of questions referred to the ECJ by national courts as to the conditions, scope and exact calculation of the SPCs.

To cite just some recent examples, with regard to the conditions for granting an SPC, in *Medeva*[133] the ECJ held that an SPC may not be granted relating to active ingredients which are not specified in the wording of the claims of the basic patent relied on in support of the application for the certificate. However, an SPC may be granted for a combination of two active ingredients, corresponding to that specified in the wording of the claims of the basic patent relied on, where the medicinal product for which the marketing authorisation is submitted in support of the application for a special protection certificate contains not only that combination of the two active ingredients but also other active ingredients.

With regard to the exact scope of the protection conferred upon the holder of an SPC, in particular in relation to the scope of the protection granted by the basic patent, e.g., in *Novartis*[134] the issue was whether in a case in which the SPC held by Novartis was for a basic patent which only had one substance as an active ingredient, therefore, the marketing of a medicinal product containing that active ingredient in combination with another active ingredient – after the basic patent had expired – would amount to the marketing of a different product from the product protected by the SPC. The ECJ's answer to this question was to the negative, provided the basic patent would have allowed its holder to oppose the marketing of a medicinal product containing that active ingredient in combination with one or more other active ingredients.

Other cases, such as *Merck, Sharp & Dohme*[135] deal with the exact calculation of the term of the SPC and the paediatric extension.

---

133 ECJ Case C-322/10, *Medeva v. Comptroller-General of Patents, Designs and Trade Marks*, [2011] ECR I-0000. See also ECJ Case C-6/11, *Daiichi Sankyo v. Comptroller-General of Patents, Designs and Trade Marks*, [2011] ECR I-0000; Case C-630/10, *University of Queensland and CSL v. Comptroller-General of Patents, Designs and Trade Marks*, [2011] ECR I-0000; Case C-422/10, *Georgetown University and Others v. Comptroller-General of Patents, Designs and Trade Marks*, [2011] ECR I-0000.
134 ECJ Case C-442/11, *Novartis v. Actavis*, [2012] ECR I-0000.
135 ECJ Case C-125/10, *Merck Sharp & Dohme v. Deutsches Patent- und Markenamt*, [2011] ECR I-0000.

1 Why are SPCs of EU Member States granted by national patent offices rather than by the EPO? Could or should this change once a unitary patent[136] has come into force?

2 How does it affect the working of the internal market that SPCs are granted by individual Member States with effect for the granting Member State only, rather than for the EU as a whole?

3 Calculate the different durations of SPCs applied for if:
   - fewer than five years have elapsed between the date of filing of the corresponding patent and the date of issuance of the first authorisation to market;
   - more than five years but less than ten years after the filing date of the corresponding patent have expired at the date of issuance of the first authorisation to market;
   - more than 10 years after the filing date of the corresponding patent have elapsed before the first authorisation to market has been issued.

3.6 Towards a unitary patent

First phase of developments (2000–2009)

The EPC and European Patent Litigation Agreement (EPLA)

As stated in the introduction, the efforts undertaken in the 1970s to establish a Community patent system on the basis of an international Convention (CPC) ended in a failure, since it was not ratified by all Member States.[137] A revised version of the CPC, the Agreement relating to Community patents (Second Community Patent Convention),[138] was tabled in 1989, but likewise remained unsuccessful.

Contrary to that, the EPC thrived and grew in terms of membership and applications received. As a matter of principle, its most significant (or: only) drawback concerned the fact that litigation concerning infringement or invalidity of European patents had to be conducted separately in the individual Member States, which typically entails legal uncertainty and multiple

---

136 See in this chapter, section 3.6.2.1.

137 A collection of documents can be found at the website of the EU Commission at ec.europa.eu/internal_market/indprop/patent/index_en.htm.

138 Agreement relating to Community patents – Done at Luxembourg on 15 December 1989, [1989] OJ L 401/1.

costs, (although strategically, it can be advantageous not to place 'all eggs in one basket').

Considering that the plans for establishing a patent system at the Community level could not be expected to mature any time soon, the Contracting States of the EPC decided to embark on an effort to solve the problems resulting from the lack of a common judiciary within the framework of the EPC. For that aim, a Working Party on Litigation (WPL) was formed at the Paris Intergovernmental Conference on 25 June 1999. The mandate given to the WPL included the tasks:

- to present 'a draft text for an optional protocol to the European Patent Convention which . . . would commit its signatory states to an integrated judicial system, including uniform rules of procedure and a common appeal court'
- to define 'the terms under which a common entity can be established and financed to which national jurisdictions can refer, with a view to obtaining advice, that part of any litigation relating to validity and infringement'.[139]

The efforts finally led to the promulgation of the text for a European Patent Litigation Agreement (EPLA)[140] aimed at establishing a common legal system for the settlement of litigation concerning the infringement and validity of European patents, and at creating a new international organisation, the so-called European Patent Judiciary (EPJ).[141]

Renewed efforts regarding the Community patent

In parallel with the efforts undertaken in the framework of the European Patent Organisation, a new proposal for a Community Patent Regulation (CPR) was submitted to the Commission in 2000.[142] The basic idea was to create a link between the EPC and the Community patent system by way of accession of the EU to the EPC. Patents should be granted by the EPO, with special provisions regarding Community patents being inserted into the EPC. In order to achieve a substantial reduction of the translation costs (thereby

---

139 Already in 1999, the Commission had issued a Green Paper, outlining the situation in the EU and examining whether new measures would be necessary, what they might involve, and which form they might take.
140 Text available at documents.epo.org/projects/babylon/eponet.nsf/0/B3884BE403F0CD8FC125723 D004ADD0A/$File/agreement_draft_en.pdf.
141 Articles 2 and 3(1) draft EPLA.
142 'Proposal for a Council Regulation on the Community patent' COM(2000) 412 final, eur-lex.europa.eu/LexUriServ/LexUriServ.do?uri=COM:2000:0412:FIN:EN:PDF.

making the Community patent system more attractive than the EPC), it was envisaged to require that a Community patent be granted and published by the EPO only in one of its procedural languages (English, German or French) with a translation of only the claims into the two other procedural languages. Only in the case of litigation should the translation of the patent into the official language of the Member State where the infringer is based be mandatory. Regarding the judicial arrangements, it was proposed to create a two-instance 'Community IP Court', the basis for which was established by inserting Articles 225a and 229a into the Treaty of Nice (now: Articles 257 and 262 TFEU), which allow establishing specialised courts attached to the Court of First Instance (now: General Court).

The reactions by the EU Member States and to a certain extent industry to the CPR proposal were rather sceptical; the language issues as well as the jurisdictional arrangements were not considered as having been adequately solved. In particular, a strong disadvantage vis-à-vis the proposed EPLA was seen in the fact that the proposal would have led, even in the first instance, to centralised litigation before one single court (though hearings could be conducted in other Member States). By contrast, EPLA had foreseen that the EPJ in the first instance consists of regional divisions to be established in the Member States. Furthermore, only EPLA offered a litigation system under which European patents as well as, optionally, the prospective Community patent could both be adjudicated, whereas the CPR proposal only foresaw the creation of a Community patent judiciary, meaning that the large number of existing European patents would have been left without centralised jurisdiction.

Faced with the resistance in the patent community against certain elements of the proposed CPR, and after thorough consultations with the stakeholders, a compromise proposal for a patent judiciary within the legal framework of the EU was finally elaborated by the Commission which adopted some of the elements represented by EPLA, inter alia the possibility for establishing regional court divisions for first instance litigation. At the same time, it was clarified by the Commission and the Council that a common Community patent judiciary will not be established in Europe without a Community patent. The EPLA project was consequently put on ice.

Post-2009 developments

Unitary patents

With the entry into force of the Lisbon Treaty at the end of 2009, the legislative procedures in the EU have changed: whereas regulations, just as directives, are adopted by majority vote, unanimity is still required for adopting the language regime (see Article 118 (2) TFEU). Legislation creating a patent extending throughout the EU therefore had to be split up into two separate regulations: one dealing mainly with post grant issues, such as the transfer, licensing, lapse, etc. of the EU patent and the other dealing with the translation arrangements related to the EU patent.

The language regime stipulated by the latter proposal was basically congruent with the EPO's three-language regime (English, French and German being the official working languages). Italy and Spain raised objections against that approach,[143] and due to their resistance, it was not possible to reach the unanimous agreement on the translation arrangements in the Council that is required under Article 118 (2) TFEU. Therefore, again, it became clear by the end of 2010 that no progress would be possible in the foreseeable future.

In order to overcome the deadlock, the Commission, on the request of several Member States, proposed to continue the unification process on the basis of enhanced cooperation (Article 20 TEU; Article 326 et seq. TFEU), [144] which allows, under certain circumstances, Member States that are willing to advance towards a higher stage of integration to go ahead and take the necessary steps, without having to involve those that prefer to move at a slower pace. Hence, a decision authorising enhanced cooperation in the area of the creation of unitary patent protection[145] was approved by the Council in March 2011 after the European Parliament gave its earlier clear consent. It forms the basis for the current legislative efforts. Spain and Italy protested against this decision of the Council, arguing inter alia that enhanced cooperation was not created for 'overruling' the objections of certain Member States against legislative proposals, but that it can only apply if general agreement exists about the legality of legislative measures, with the sole reason for abstention of some Member States being that they consider it too early for them to go along. Based on those and other grounds, Spain and Italy have filed complaints with the ECJ that are currently pending.[146]

---

143 Italy and Spain were of the opinion that the same language regime should apply as with Community trade marks, where Spanish and Italian are accepted in addition to the three EPO languages.

144 'Enhanced cooperation' is a procedure where a minimum of nine EU Member States are allowed to establish advanced integration or cooperation in an area within EU structures but without the other members being involved; see Articles 326 et seq. TFEU, and Chapter 2, section 2.3.1.4.

145 Proposal for a Council Decision authorising enhanced cooperation in the area of the creation of unitary patent protection of 14 December 2010, COM(2010) 790 final, ec.europa.eu/internal_market/indprop/docs/patent/COM(2010)790-final_en.pdf.

146 Joined Cases C-274/11 and 295/11, *Spain and Italy v. Council.*

Nevertheless, in April 2011 the European Commission re-introduced the two draft regulations on the unitary patent for Europe,[147] the first concerning enhanced cooperation on unitary patent protection which establishes a unitary patent regime (dUPR), and the second setting out the translation arrangements for the unitary patent. Both regulations were endorsed by the EU Council at the end of June 2011 and are currently pending consideration in the European Parliament.[148]

Unlike the EU patent originally envisaged in the 2009 proposal, the unitary patent shall not be 'granted' as such by the EPO. Instead, in accordance with an option already enshrined in Article 142 EPC, European patents granted with the same set of claims in respect of all the participating Member States will obtain unitary effect in those Member States, provided that an entry to that effect is made in a special register kept by the EPO (Register for unitary patent protection; see Article 3 dUPR).

The common judiciary

The EEUPC and the ECJ opinion 1/09

Following a recommendation by the Commission to the Council to open negotiations for the adoption of an agreement between the Community, its Member States and other Contracting States of the EPC with the aim of creating a Unified Patent Litigation System,[149] in 2009 the Council agreed to set up an integrated specialised and unified jurisdiction by way of an international agreement for patent-related disputes, the so-called European and EU Patents Court Agreement (EEUPC Agreement). As in previous proposals, the EEUPC would have been competent to hear infringement as well as invalidity claims. It should be composed of a court of first instance,

---

147 Proposal for a Regulation of the European Parliament and of the Council implementing enhanced cooperation in the area of the creation of unitary patent protection of 13 April 2011, COM(2011) 215 final, ec.europa.eu/internal_market/indprop/docs/patent/com2011-215-final_en.pdf (see also Council Document 10629/11 of 26 May 2011), and Proposal for a Council Regulation implementing enhanced cooperation in the area of the creation of unitary patent protection with regard to the applicable translation arrangements of 13 April 2011, COM(2011) 216 final, eur-lex.europa.eu/LexUriServ/LexUriServ.do?uri=COM:2011:0216:FIN:en:PDF. See also Council Decision (2011/167/EU) of 10 March 2011 authorising enhanced cooperation in the area of the creation of unitary patent protection, [2011] OJ L 76/53.

148 At the time of finalising this manuscript, the European Parliament has postponed its voting – originally scheduled for the end of June 2012 – as a manifestation of protest against the Council's recommendation to delete Article 6 to 8 dUPR; see this chapter, section 3.3.5.3.

149 Recommendation from the Commission to the Council of 20 March 2009 to authorise the Commission to open negotiations for the adoption of an Agreement creating a Unified Patent Litigation System, SEC 2009/330 final, ec.europa.eu/internal_market/indprop/docs/patent/recommendation_sec09-330_en.pdf.

comprising a central division and local and regional divisions, and a court of appeal, with competence to hear appeals brought against decisions delivered by the court of first instance.

As misgivings were raised in certain Member States against the legal construction of the EEUPC, the Council requested a legal opinion from the ECJ pursuant to Article 218 (11) TFEU. In its opinion 1/09 rendered on 8 March 2011,[150] the ECJ indeed concluded that the Agreement establishing the EEUPC was not compatible with the provisions of the EU Treaty and the TFEU.

The main point of criticism by the ECJ concerned the fact that the Patent Court to be established would be an authority created by way of an international agreement including EU and non-EU Member States, and would therefore not be fully integrated into the legal structures of the EU. According to the ECJ, the linkage between the unitary patent system with its restriction to EU members and the EPC system with its larger membership proved to be fatal for the proposal:

> (78) . . . the international court envisaged in this draft agreement is to be called upon to interpret and apply not only the provisions of that agreement [i.e., the EEUPC] but also the future regulation on the Community patent and other instruments of European Union law, in particular Regulations and Directives in conjunction with which that regulation would, when necessary, have to be read, namely provisions relating to other bodies of rules on intellectual property, and rules of the FEU Treaty concerning the internal market and competition law. Likewise, the[EEU] PC may be called upon to determine a dispute pending before it in the light of the fundamental rights and general principles of European Union law, or even to examine the validity of an act of the European Union. (79) As regards the draft agreement submitted for the Court's consideration, it must be observed that the [EEU]PC:
> - takes the place of national courts and tribunals, in the field of its exclusive jurisdiction described in Article 15 of that draft agreement,
> - deprives, therefore, those courts and tribunals of the power to request preliminary rulings from the Court in that field,
> - becomes, in the field of its exclusive jurisdiction, the sole court able to communicate with the Court by means of a reference for a preliminary ruling concerning the interpretation and application of European Union law and
> - has the duty, within that jurisdiction, in accordance with Article 14a of that

---

150 Opinion 1/09 of the Court (Full Court), [2011] ECJ I-00000.

draft agreement, to interpret and apply European Union law. (80) While it is true that the Court has no jurisdiction to rule on direct actions between individuals in the field of patents, since that jurisdiction is held by the courts of the Member States, nonetheless the Member States cannot confer the jurisdiction to resolve such disputes on a court created by an international agreement which would deprive those courts of their task, as 'ordinary' courts within the European Union legal order, to implement European Union law and, thereby, of the power provided for in Article 267 TFEU, or, as the case may be, the obligation, to refer questions for a preliminary ruling in the field concerned.

The Unified Patent Court

As a result of the Opinion 1/09 the EU Council presented a revised version for a common judiciary, now called the 'Unified Patent Court' (UPC).[151] In the revised version (draft Agreement on a Unitary Patent Court (dUPCA)) it is made clear that the UPC agreement is only open to EU Member States. Furthermore, it is clarified that the UPC is an international court common to the participating EU Member States which is part of their judicial order and that it must apply the entire body of Community law and respect its primacy. In addition, the UPC will have to cooperate in the same way with the ECJ as national courts. This means that in order to ensure the supremacy of the ECJ regarding EU law it is suggested that the Court of First Instance of the UPC may, if it considers this necessary to enable it to give a decision, request the ECJ to give a binding decision on a question of interpretation of the EC treaties or the validity and interpretation of acts of EU institutions. Where such a question is raised before the Court of Appeal of the UPC, the referral to the ECJ becomes mandatory. The decisions of the ECJ will be binding on the Court. Finally, provisions were included in the draft agreement which provide that the Contracting States to the UPC Agreement will be liable for infringements of Union law by the UPC. Furthermore, as pointed out before, the dUPCA contains a chapter on substantive law which would harmonise the law of European patents that are effective in the participating Member States.[152] It is still unclear at present how it is ensured that the same rules are also applied to unitary patents.

Although it appears to be less contentious than the dUPR, it is still uncertain at this time whether and when the dUPCA will actually become operative.

---

151 A consolidated version dated 12 October 2012 has been published as Council Document 14750/12 PI 127 Cour 67, at register.consilium.europa.eu/pdf/en/12/st14/st14750.en12.pdf.
152 For the contents of those provisions, see this chapter, section 3.5.3; for the provisions regulating jurisdiction see Chapter 9, section 9.2.4.2.2.

Progress was made in the Council session of 28–29 June 2012, when it was decided that the seat of the Central Chamber of the first instance court shall be Paris, with certain functions being delegated to branches in London and Munich.[153] Nevertheless, a substantial number of details still need to be resolved. This will in all likelihood prolong the procedure, and it may even freeze the process in its entirety.

QUESTIONS

1 What, in essence, are the reasons that make it so difficult for a unitary patent system to be established?

2 What is your opinion about the option for enhanced cooperation being used as a basis for the creation of the unitary patent system?

3 At present, the inclusion of provisions on scope, including limitations and exceptions, is contested, due to misgivings regarding the potential involvement of the ECJ in the interpretation of patent law. However, both the definition of rights conferred and the limitations and exceptions are subject to Member States' and the EU's obligation to comply with the TRIPS Agreement. Reflecting on what was said about that in Chapter 2 and in view of the ECJ's opinion 1/09, how do you evaluate the current attempts by the Member States to empty the dUPR of all provisions dealing with rights conferred and limitations (see above in this chapter, section 3.3.5.3), so as not to involve the ECJ in the interpretation of substantive patent law?

---

153 Council Conclusions, 28–29 June 2012, CO EUR 4, CONCL 2, www.consilium.europa.eu/uedocs/cms_data/docs/pressdata/en/ec/131388.pdf.

4

Trade marks

4.1 Introduction

Objectives and developments

Throughout the history of commerce, distinctive signs have served to indicate the origin of products, by way of identifying and distinguishing goods stemming from one source from those of a different origin. In the pre-industrial era, such identity markers were of importance not least for the purpose of quality control by the authorities, and for policing the hermetic regime of the guilds. The picture changed profoundly after the liberalisation of markets: as production and consumption of goods became detached from each other, being separated by an increasingly complex chain of intermediate commerce, the use of trade marks acquired a different function – rather than enabling control and supervision by the authorities, they became a communication tool *par excellence* which allowed producers to address their customers without direct physical contact, and permitted consumers to repeat purchases that were satisfactory, and avoid those that were not.

It is undisputed that trade marks occupy a special place within the spectrum of IP. Unlike inventions or original works, distinctive signs are not considered to be achievements that are worthy of protection as such; the ground for protection rather lies in their capacity to convey information enabling consumers to make informed choices. This in turn provides an incentive for entrepreneurs to invest in the quality of goods and services offered, and to develop a larger variety of commodities so as to comply with the preferences of specific target groups. For those reasons, the conflict between the exclusive right and free competition is less acute in trade mark law than in other areas of IP: rather than restraining competition, trade marks are an enabling tool without which meaningful competition would hardly be possible.

However, the positive picture needs to be qualified in several regards. First, economic reality will only function as indicated if the acquisition of trade marks remains competition-neutral, in the sense that appropriation of the mark as such does not confer on its holder a competitive advantage from which others are excluded. It complies indeed with conventional wisdom that new trade marks are in infinite supply, so that new market entrants are not hindered from choosing a suitable sign for themselves. However, while that assumption is based on long-standing experience with traditional forms of marks such as word marks or picture marks, it is less obvious for forms of signs which were included into the catalogue of protectable marks in more recent times, such as colours *per se* or the shape of products. Where such signs are only available in limited stock, their protection entails (more or less aggravating) obstacles for competition, to which the law must respond.

Second, it is common knowledge that trade marks can be much more than just tools for conveying information about the origin of goods and services. Supported by sophisticated marketing efforts, marks can turn into much-coveted symbols of lifestyle, prestige or attitude. Once a mark has attained that force of attraction, it becomes a business asset whose value is basically independent from the goods or services for which it is, or was originally, used. Trade mark law has adapted to these developments by offering protection, under certain conditions, for the value of marks as such against abuse or detriment.

From the perspective of competition and consumer policy, the phenomenon is not without risks. Due to their capacity to symbolise and communicate extra-objective qualities such as status or lifestyle, the psychological dimension of trade marks and hence their market power can be enormous. This may impair market transparency and can lead to high entry barriers, as well as, in their wake, to high consumer prices. Although that is a psycho-sociological phenomenon rather than resulting from legal dispositions, such considerations tend to support a critical view of those elements of trade mark law by which protection is extended beyond the core aspect of indicating origin, without completely denying the appropriateness of protecting the specific 'aura' of trade marks against deterioration or misappropriation. In particular, care must be taken to avoid that the communication channel provided by trade marks is fully 'monopolised' in the sense that it is foreclosed for competitors or other market actors who want to convey messages of commercial relevance, such as comparative advertisement, or otherwise engage in activities covered by the right to free speech.

The risk for such undesirable effects increases where the use of marks for purposes other than to identify and distinguish the commercial origin of goods and services is included into the purview of protection. The extent to which such uses are deemed to be legally relevant has therefore become a key issue in European trade mark law, not least in the context of trade mark use on the internet.

Trade mark law in Europe

Legal bases and fundamental principles

Unitary character of Community trade marks

European trade mark law rests on two structures: the Trade Mark Directive (TMD)[1] and the Community Trade Mark Regulation (CTMR).[2] The TMD dates from 1989, but it wasn't implemented in all (then) 15 Member States until 1996. At the same time, the Community trade mark system became operational: after enactment of the CTMR in 1994, it had been necessary first to establish the administrative infrastructure provided by the Office for Harmonization established in Alicante (OHIM, Spain).

From the very beginning, the Community trade mark system proved to be a tremendous success. Applications received in its first year of existence out-numbered by far any previous expectations, and the trend has been fairly stable over the years.[3] In the framework of an overall evaluation of the func-tioning of the European trade mark system undertaken in 2010/2011, the results were therefore largely positive, both with regard to the level of user satisfaction and the smooth functioning of the legal mechanisms. Although no major changes or amendments of the system are therefore needed, sug-gestions for certain clarifications and amendments were submitted to the European Commission as a result of a study conducted by the Max-Planck Institute as an element of the evaluation efforts.[4] It is unclear at the time of publication whether and to what extent those suggestions will be taken up in legislative proposals to be put forward by the Commission.

Although being largely congruent in their substantive contents, the legal structures of the TMD and the CTMR are markedly different. Whereas the

1 Directive 95/2008/EC of the European Parliament and of the Council to approximate the laws of the Member States relating to trade marks (codified version), [2008] OJ L 299/25, originally enacted as Directive 104/89/EEC, [1989] OJ L 40/1.

2 Council Regulation 207/2009 on the Community trade mark (codified version), [2009] OJ L 78/1; origi-nally enacted as Council Regulation 40/1994, [1994] OJ L 11/1.

3 For current statistics see oami.europa.eu/ows/rw/pages/OHIM/statistics.en.do. Annual reports showing relevant figures for previous years (since 1999) are accessible at oami.europa.eu/ows/rw/pages/OHIM/OHIMPublications/annualReport.en.do.

4 Study on the Overall Functioning of the European Trade Mark System (Trade Mark Study), see www.ip.mpg.de/files/pdf2/mpi_final_report.pdf.

Trade Mark Directive only purports to approximate the law of the Member States to the extent that the disparities between them would otherwise impede the free movement of goods and services, the CTMR undertakes to establish a unitary right extending throughout the entire Community, thereby creating an IP right that defies territoriality by transgressing over national borderline. The concept is expressed in the Preamble of the CTMR (Recitals 2 and 3) as follows:

> 2. It is desirable to promote throughout the Community a harmonious development of economic activities and a continuous and balanced expansion by completing an internal market which functions properly and offers conditions which are similar to those obtaining in a national market. In order to create a market of this kind and make it increasingly a single market, not only must barriers to free movement of goods and services be removed and arrangements be instituted which ensure that competition is not distorted, but, in addition, legal conditions must be created which enable undertakings to adapt their activities to the scale of the Community, whether in manufacturing and distributing goods or in providing services. For those purposes, trade marks enabling the products and services of undertakings to be distinguished by identical means throughout the entire Community, regardless of frontiers, should feature amongst the legal instruments which undertakings have at their disposal.
>
> 3. For the purpose of pursuing the Community's said objectives it would appear necessary to provide for Community arrangements for trade marks whereby undertakings can by means of one procedural system obtain Community trade marks to which uniform protection is given and which produce their effects throughout the entire area of the Community. The principle of the unitary character of the Community trade mark thus stated should apply unless otherwise provided for in this Regulation.

The unitary right principle is reiterated in Article 1 (2) CTMR:

> 2. A Community trade mark shall have a unitary character. It shall have equal effect throughout the Community: it shall not be registered, transferred or surrendered or be the subject of a decision revoking the rights of the proprietor or declaring it invalid, nor shall its use be prohibited, save in respect of the whole Community. This principle shall apply unless otherwise provided in this Regulation.

Whereas the unitary character of CTMs is a fundamental rule governing without exception the registration, transfer, surrender or other ways of cancellation, it is subject to certain exceptions insofar as *enforcement* is concerned. Under certain circumstances, it may therefore occur that the power of a CTM holder to enjoin use of other signs is territorially restricted. For instance, if for linguistic reasons a likelihood of confusion does not arise in certain Member States, prohibitive measures must be limited so as not to impede the use of the other sign in the territories where such use appears admissible.[5] Furthermore, use of a conflicting sign in a Member State cannot be prohibited on the basis of a CTM if the proprietor of the CTM has not objected to that use, despite having known about it for five consecutive years (acquiescence, Article 9 TMD).[6]

While in the cases mentioned above the CTM proprietor remains free to use the mark in the Member State(s) where it cannot be enforced, a territorial restriction of use may ensue from Article 165 CTMR, the provision regulating the consequences of the accession of new Member States to the EU in 2004 and 2007. Pursuant to the general rule, registered CTMs or applications pending at the time of accession are extended to the territory of the new Member(s). However, if an earlier trade mark or other earlier right was registered, applied for or acquired in good faith prior to the date of accession of that state, use of the CTM in the relevant territory can be prohibited (Article 165 (5) CTMR).[7]

Coexistence

The European trade mark system was not built with the intention that the CTMR should replace the national trade mark systems. Instead, both systems are meant to coexist. This is expressed in Recital 6 of the Preamble to the CTMR:

(6) The Community law relating to trade marks . . . does not replace the laws of the Member States on trade marks. It would not in fact appear to be justified to require undertakings to apply for registration of their trade marks as Community trade marks. National trade marks continue to be necessary for those undertakings which do not want protection of their trade marks at Community level.

Due to the principle of coexistence, a number of interfaces exist between the CTM system and national trade mark regimes:

---

5 ECJ Case C-235/09, *DHL* v. *Chronopost*, [2011] ECR I-00000, Paragraph 48. The case concerned the trade mark 'WEBSHIPPING' and its alleged infringement by a competitor using the term 'web shipping' in this and other spellings to announce his internet-accessible mailing services. Without that being addressed expressly by the ECJ, it appears plausible that in English-speaking countries, 'web shipping' is understood as describing the kind of services offered, meaning that it is covered by the limitation set out in Article 12 CTMR and thus does not infringe.

6 Further on acquiescence see this chapter, section 4.4.2.3.

7 A locally confined prohibition of use may also ensue if a CTM conflicts with a prior right of merely local significance, see Article 8 (4) CTMR in conjunction with Article 111 (1); this chapter, section 4.3.3.2.

- *Equality of rights*: National marks and CTMs are equal in the sense that they are mutually exclusive. If a CTM conflicts with a prior national right,[8] registration must be refused, or, if already registered, the CTM will be declared invalid. Vice versa, CTMs are to be regarded as prior rights in all Member States and will therefore bar any subsequent signs from protection under national as well as under Community law.
- *'Double protection'*: Nothing in the TMD or CTMR prohibits registration of the same sign for the same proprietor (or another person having the consent of the first proprietor) as a national mark and a CTM. However, Article 109 CTMR imposes certain restrictions against proprietors bringing double actions for infringement based on a CTM and an identical national mark in different fora.
- *Conversion and seniority*: If an application for registration of a CTM is refused, or the registration is cancelled, the proprietor can apply for conversion of the CTM into a national trade mark in those Member States where no obstacle for protection exists. The trade mark will then keep the same priority date as the CTM application or registration (Articles 112 *et seq*. CTMR). Furthermore, the CTMR has introduced the possibility of claiming seniority for a prior national mark (Article 34 *et seq*.). This has the effect that a person who has surrendered an earlier national registration after having registered an identical sign as a CTM, may still invoke the priority of that national mark vis-à-vis signs which have been acquired in the same national territory at a date preceding the priority date of the CTM, but subsequent to the priority date of the earlier national registration.

Recently, many Member States have experienced a significant drop in applications received, whereas applications for CTMs are increasing constantly. This has raised concerns that the principle of coexistence might be jeopardised, and the national systems might 'die out' in the longer run. As a reaction to those concerns, it was decided that an amount equivalent to 50 per cent of the annual renewal fees collected at OHIM is distributed to the national systems, so as to improve their services and infrastructure and thus maintain their competitiveness.

? QUESTIONS

1 In your opinion, what would have been the alternatives to supplementing the CTM system by a harmonised and coexisting national system? For instance, when the common Benelux trade mark system was created in

---

8 With the exception of signs having merely local significance; this chapter, section 4.3.3.2.

the 1970s, it was decided to transform all national marks existing at the time in the three countries into Benelux marks which are valid throughout the entire territory. Would that have been feasible in the EU as well?

2 OHIM was originally intended to be self-supporting, i.e. it should not take in more fees than necessary for maintaining its own infrastructure. However, as the fees were calculated on the basis of estimations that were exceeded by far by the actual number of applications received, a substantial surplus was accumulated over the years. A normal reaction to that would have been to lower the fees so that surplus is no longer generated. Instead, it was decided that (in addition to a modest lowering of the fees which became effective in 2009), part of the surplus should be distributed to the national offices (see above). Can you imagine why the decision was made? What reasons (apart from political bargaining) could be given for this decision?

4.2 Administration of the CTM system: procedural issues

OHIM: mission and structure

Administration of the Community Trade Mark system is carried out by the Office for Harmonization in the Internal Market (Trade Marks and Designs) (OHIM).

On its website, the mission and institutional structure of OHIM are described as follows:

Mission
The mission of the Office is to manage the Community Trade Mark and Community Design registration systems. In order to do so, the Office carries out examination, registration, opposition and cancellation procedures for Community Trade Marks and examination, registration and invalidity procedures for registered Community Designs. All decisions adversely affecting a party to proceedings can be appealed before the Boards of Appeal of the Office. The Office keeps public registers of these rights and procedures. It shares the task of issuing decisions on requests for invalidity or revocation of registered rights with the Courts of the EU Member States. . . .

Organisation
As a European agency, OHIM is supervised by the European Commission, but has legal, administrative and financial autonomy. The Council of Ministers decides on the appointment of the President, the Vice President, and the President and Chairs

of the Boards of Appeal. The President is responsible for the running for the office and there is also an Administrative Board and a Budget Committee each composed of one representative from each member state and one representative from the European Commission.[9]

The language regime

As a European agency, OHIM must be able to operate in a number of languages. The language regime is addressed in Article 119 CTMR:

Languages
1. The application for a Community trade mark shall be filed in one of the official languages of the European Community.
2. The languages of the Office shall be English, French, German, Italian and Spanish.
3. The applicant must indicate a second language which shall be a language of the Office the use of which he accepts as a possible language of proceedings for opposition, revocation or invalidity proceedings.
. . .
7. Parties to opposition, revocation, invalidity or appeal proceedings may agree that a different official language of the European Community is to be the language of the proceedings.

The compliance of the language regime with primary EU law was tested and approved by the ECJ in the *Kik* judgment.[10]

Registration proceedings

Regular proceedings at OHIM

Most CTM applications are filed directly with OHIM[11] or, under the Madrid Protocol, through the International Bureau of WIPO (see below). In addition, CTM applications can be filed with the national intellectual property offices (Article 25 (1) (b) CTMR), who must forward the applications to OHIM within two weeks (Article 25 (2) CTMR). If the application complies with certain minimum requirements – identification of the applicant

---

9 See oami.europa.eu/ows/rw/pages/OHIM/institutional/institutional.en.do.
10 See ECJ Case C-361/01 P, *Kik* v. *OHIM*, [2003] ECR I-8283, Paragraphs 92–94.
11 Applications can be filed by fax or letter or electronically. OHIM prefers the latter form of filing and provides an incentive for that by requiring a lower fee for electronic filing (currently: 900 EUR as compared to 1,050 EUR for traditional forms of filing).

as well as the sign to be registered and the goods and services to be designated by it – a filing date is accorded (Articles 26 (1), 27 CTMR).[12] If all filing requirements including payment of the fee[13] are fulfilled, OHIM embarks on an examination of the absolute grounds for refusal (Article 7 CTMR).[14] Furthermore, once a filing date has been established, an automated search is carried out in the CTM register with a view to potentially conflicting registrations or applications with an earlier priority date. A search report listing the results is communicated to the applicant as well as to the proprietors of CTMs that were found in the search. It is then left to the parties themselves to evaluate the search results and eventually draw consequences therefrom. Other than that, the search report has no impact on the proceedings at OHIM. Upon request by the applicant and against payment of a special fee, an optional search is also performed in the national trade mark registers by the Member States participating in the system. However, as major Member States such as France, Italy and Germany did not join the system, the usefulness of the optional search remains doubtful, and it is not frequently requested by the applicants.

If no obstacles for protection are found in the examination of absolute grounds, the CTM application is published in the Official Gazette of OHIM. Within three months from publication, oppositions can be filed against the application by the proprietors of prior rights such as CTMs or national trade marks,[15] other signs with more than local significance used in the course of trade, or well-known trade marks in the meaning of Article 6 *bis* Paris Convention (relative grounds for refusal, Article 8 CTMR). If no oppositions are filed, or if the opposition is rejected, the trade mark is registered as a CTM and is published as such in the Official Gazette. The registration lasts for 10 years and can be renewed regularly, against payment of a fee.[16]

Subsequent to registration, a CTM may be cancelled on the basis of claims that it is invalid for absolute or relative grounds (Article 52, 53 CTMR) or that it must be revoked, in particular if it has remained unused throughout

---

12 The basic fee covering the application and registration of a CTM must be paid within 30 days from the filing date.
13 Article 26 (2) CTMR. Currently, the basic fee covering three classes of goods and services under the classification of the Nice Agreement is 1,050 EUR (900 EUR if the application is filed electronically), and 150 EUR for each additional class. For details see Commission Regulation (EC) No 2869/95 of 13 December 1995 on the fees payable to the Office for Harmonization in the Internal Market (Trade Marks and Designs), available at oami.europa.eu/ows/rw/resource/documents/CTM/regulations/286995_cv_en.pdf.
14 On absolute grounds for refusal see section 4.2.2.
15 The same applies to pending applications for CTMs or national trade marks with an earlier priority date.
16 Articles 46, 47 CTMR. The renewal fee for a CTM covering up to the classes is currently 1,500 EUR.

five subsequent years (Article 52 CTMR). Claims for invalidity or revocation can be filed either at OHIM or, by way of counterclaim, in infringement proceedings before the (national) Community trade mark courts (for details see in this chapter, section 4.6).

International registration

The Madrid system: agreement and protocol

Similar to the relationship between the EPC and PCT described in Chapter 3, CTMs can also be obtained on the basis of an international registration. As early as 1891, the Madrid Agreement concerning the international registration of marks (Madrid Agreement: MA)[17] was established for that purpose as a special agreement under the Paris Convention. Although a number of features were changed since then, the basic elements have remained the same: The owner of a trade mark for which a registration has been obtained in his country of origin[18] applies, against payment of a uniform fee per designated country, for international registration of the mark. The application is forwarded to the International Bureau of WIPO[19] which, after a formal exam and entry into the register of internationally registered (IR) marks, notifies the offices in the designated Madrid Member States of the date of international registration. IR registrations produce the same effect as registration of marks which have been filed nationally. However, Madrid Member States retain the right to carry out a substantive examination of the IR mark and can refuse protection by communicating the refusal to the International Bureau within the prescribed time.

While the original MA system appeared most appropriate and attractive for non-examining countries, it did have serious drawbacks from the perspective of examining countries. In order to mitigate those concerns the MA was amended several times, however, without substantially increasing the membership.[20]

The issue became urgent at the end of the 1980s, when the CTM system was about to materialise. It was a declared aim of European legislature to create a link between the CTM and the system of international registration,

17 Text available at www.wipo.int/treaties/en/registration/madrid.
18 That is, the country where the owner of the mark has its seat or a permanent business establishment.
19 Now: WIPO; prior to 1971, this was the BIRPI (Bureaux Réunis pour la Protection de la Propriété Intellectuelle) in Berne.
20 In 1973, the Trademark Registration Treaty (TRT), was concluded in order to provide for an alternative to the Madrid system. Modelled on the PCT, the agreement went into force in 1980 after accession by the Soviet Union and four African States, but it never gained practical importance.

Table 4.1 Differences between the Madrid Agreement and the Madrid Protocol

Madrid Agreement	Madrid Protocol
Registration in country of origin (basis mark) is necessary	Application in country of origin suffices
IR mark depends on registration of basis mark for five years, i.e. IR mark lapses if basis mark is cancelled due to a 'central attack'	If basis mark is not registered or is cancelled within 5 years, IR mark becomes invalid, but can be transformed into national registrations with the same priority date
Notice of refusal by the offices of designated countries must be communicated within 12 months	Notice of refusal must be given within 18 months, with further extension possible in case of opposition
Uniform fees	'Individual' fees, which must however be somewhat lower than for national applications
Language: French only	Languages: French, English and Spanish
Only states can become members	Agreement is open to accession by intergovernmental organisations
Regular duration of registration: 20 years	Regular duration of registration: 10 years

but this meant that all European Member States and the Community had to join the Madrid system first, and that proved impossible under the pertinent rules. A breakthrough was finally achieved in 1989 when the Protocol to the Madrid Agreement (Madrid Protocol: MP) was established.[21] This provided the basis for adherence to the Madrid system not only of formerly abstinent European countries such as the UK and the Nordic States but also of Japan and the USA and finally the Community itself. Today, the Madrid system counts 85 members, most of which have adhered to either the MP or both the MA and the MP.

The main differences between MA and MP are summarised in Table 4.1:

As a matter of principle, MA and MP are separate treaties, though they are linked by common implementing regulations. Initially, their relationship was also regulated by Article 9 *sexies* MP, stipulating that the MA would continue to apply between States being members of both treaties ('safeguard clause'). However, according to an inbuilt review agenda, the safeguard clause was repealed in 2007, and since 1 October 2008, only the MP applies between countries that are members of both the MA and the MP, which was more apt to encompass the interests of examining states. As very few countries

---

21 Text available on the WIPO website at www.wipo.int/treaties/en/registration/madrid_protocol.

are members of the MA only, the practical relevance of the MA has been reduced quite drastically by the repeal.

Provisions in the CTMR

International registrations are addressed in Title XIII (Article 145 *et seq.*) CTMR. Pursuant to Articles 146 and 147, applications for international registrations based on a CTM or a CTM application must be filed with OHIM, using a form which is provided by the Office, and under payment of a fee. The application must use one of the official languages of the European Union; where necessary, it must indicate as a second language one of the three languages allowed under the MP. OHIM examines whether the application for international registration fulfills the necessary requirements, in particular whether it is identical in terms of the sign and the goods or services covered with the trade mark registered or filed as a CTM.[22] Thereafter, the application is forwarded to the International Bureau which, after examining its compliance with the relevant provisions, registers the trade mark, publishes it in the International Gazette and notifies the designated Member States thereof.

Article 149 CTMR states that if the owner of an international registration wishes to make use of the option granted in Article 3 *ter* (2) MP for subsequent territorial extension of the IR mark, the application must also be filed with OHIM and is handled accordingly.

The legal effects in the CTM system of IR marks that are based on a registration or an application in another Madrid Union country are regulated in Article 151 *et seq.* CTMR. In particular, it is set out that IR marks have, from the date of an international registration designating the EU, the same effect as an application for registration of a CTM, meaning that they are examined and may be opposed just as other applications (under consideration of the time limits set for communicating a refusal of protection under the MP).

Finally, Articles 159 and 161 address transformation issues: if the designation of the EU in an international application fails, it can be transformed either into (a) national application(s) in one or several Member States, or in a designation of those Member States in the international registration (instead of designating the EU); also, if the basic registration of application for a registration designating the EU fails, it can be transformed into an application for a CTM, without changing the priority date.

---

22 A certification of those aspects by the national office in the country of origin is requested by Article 3 (1) MP.

Administrative and judicial control

Appeals against decisions taken by OHIM are directed, first, to the Appeal Boards established at OHIM, and further to the General Court. On points of law, appeals against decisions by the General Court can be filed with the ECJ.[23] In that context, the General Court and the ECJ act as courts of superior instance within one common judicial system, meaning that they can decide the case for good, unless it is more appropriately referred back to the lower instances for further investigation. In contrast to that, proceedings for infringement of CTMs as well as, eventually, counterclaims for invalidity are filed with national courts that are designated by the respective Member States as Community trade mark courts.[24] The ECJ can be involved in such cases (only) if questions are referred to it by way of request for a preliminary ruling under Article 267 TFEU, that is, if the court has doubts about the correct interpretation of primary or secondary law provisions which are decisive for the outcome of the litigation pending before it. In that case, the ECJ can only answer the questions posed to it, while the competence to decide the case as such remains within the national court hierarchy.

In other words, the current system of judicial control is marked by its binary structure: whereas decisions concerning the registration and cancellation of CTMs are appealed and eventually reversed within a genuine Community system, civil remedies for infringement and similar claims are pursued in the framework of structures forming part of the national judiciary. In this situation, decisions by the ECJ constitute the sole unifying factor linking the procedural routes which otherwise remain strictly separate.

Due to its unique position within the system, decisions of the ECJ are of seminal importance not only for the CTMR, but also for the national trade mark systems to the extent that the substantive provisions of both systems coincide. As some of the central notions of trade mark law proved to be rather unclear and contentious, the number of ECJ decisions handed down since the European trade mark system became operative is rather high. Only the most important cases can therefore be presented in this book. This regards even more the jurisprudence of the General Court, which by now amounts to more than a thousand decisions and is constantly growing.

---

23 See Article 58 of the Statute of the Court of Justice. The CTMR – Article 65 – refers to the 'Court of Justice' in a general form and does not distinguish between the two instances.
24 See Article 95 *et seq.* CTMR; for details see Chapter 9, section 9.3.2.2.5.3.

1 The fact that administrative and judicial proceedings regarding CTMs are separated can lead to the same conflict being adjudicated differently in opposition and in infringement proceedings (for example: opposition filed on the basis of German mark Xy against CTM application Xx is rejected and the mark is registered as a CTM, whereas the CTM court in Germany rules that CTM Xx infringes Xy).What would be the consequences? How could the problem (submitting there is one) be solved?

2 What could have been the reasons for including a 'safeguard clause' (Article 9 *sexies*) into the MP?

4.3 Requirements for protection

Signs of which a trade mark may consist

A definition of protectable subject matter ('signs of which a [Community] trade mark may consist') is enshrined in Article 4 CTM and Article 2 TMD. Such signs must be capable of being represented graphically, and they must be capable of distinguishing the goods or services of one undertaking from those of other undertakings. In addition to those requirements, the provisions contain an exemplary, non-conclusive catalogue of protectable forms of signs.

Sign v. abstract concept

There is hardly any form of sign which is *per se* incapable of distinguishing goods and services as to their commercial origin. Accordingly, the reference to a sign's 'capability to distinguish' in Article 4 CTMR and Article 2 TMD is to be understood as an obligation to keep the system open for all conceivable types of signs rather than as a substantial restriction of access to protection.[25] The ECJ has also clarified that Article 2 TMD does not give Member States any leeway to exclude certain forms of signs from protection irrespective of whether they own a basic capability to distinguish, given that the nature of a sign of which a trade mark may consist cannot be assessed differently from one country to another.[26]

Until now, the basic capability of a sign to become a trade mark in the sense of Article 2 TMD was only denied for an application designating the 'trans-

---

25 More relevant in practice is the exclusion from protection of shape of product marks which results from Article 3 (1) (e) (i)–(iii) TMD or Article 7 (1) (e) (i)–(iii) CTMR; this chapter, section 4.3.2.2.5.3.

26 ECJ Case C-283/01, *Shield Mark v. Kist*, [2003] ECR I-14313, Paragraph 40.

parency' of a dust collector bin as the sign to be registered for vacuum cleaners (*Dyson*).[27] The ECJ considered the sign as a mere concept incapable of protection, declaring that:

> (40) Article 2 [TMD] . . . is to be interpreted as meaning that the subject-matter of an application . . . which relates to all the conceivable shapes of a transparent bin . . . forming part of the external surface of a vacuum cleaner, is not a 'sign' within the meaning of that provision and therefore is not capable of constituting a trade mark.

Other than that, no forms of signs were ever considered by the ECJ as precluded from trade mark protection *per se* under Article 2 TMD or 4 CTMR.

Graphical representation

More relevant in practice than the capability to distinguish is the second requirement in Article 4 CTMR and Article 2 TMD, that the sign must be capable of graphical representation. That requirement was first addressed by the ECJ in a case concerning a trade mark application in Germany for a scent which was described as 'balsamically fruity with a slight hint of cinnamon' (*Sieckmann*).[28] As means of representation, the applicant had offered the description of the smell and the chemical formula of the substance, $C6H5-CH = CHCOOCH3$; in addition, he had indicated where samples of the substance could be obtained. The application was rejected by the German Patent and Trade Mark Office (DPMA), and the decision appealed. The Federal Patent Court thereupon referred *inter alia* the following question to the ECJ:

> Is Article 2 of the [TMD] to be interpreted as meaning that the expression 'signs capable of being represented graphically' covers only those signs which can be reproduced directly in their visible form or is it also to be construed as meaning signs – such as odours or sounds – which cannot be perceived visually *per se* but can be reproduced indirectly using certain aids?

The ECJ answered, first, that signs are not excluded from protection for lack of visual perceptibility.[29] However, in order to meet the legal standards under Article 2 TMD and 4 CTMR, signs must be capable of being represented in a manner that is:

---

27 ECJ Case C-321/03, *Dyson v. Registrar of Trade Marks*, [2007] ECR I-00687.
28 ECJ Case C-273/00, *Sieckmann v. DPMA*, [2002] ECR I-11737.
29 Ibid., Paragraph 45.

(55) . . . clear, precise, self-contained, easily accessible, intelligible, durable and objective.

Pursuant to the ECJ, this is necessary for the competent authorities to know:

(50) with clarity and precision the nature of the signs of which a mark consists in order to be able to fulfil their obligations in relation to the prior examination of registration applications and to the publication and maintenance of an appropriate and precise register of trade marks . . .

as well as for competitors ('economic operators') who must be able:

(51) with clarity and precision . . . to find out about registrations or applications for registration made by their current or potential competitors and thus to receive relevant information about the rights of third parties.

In the actual case, it was found that the requirements of graphic represent-ability were *not* satisfied by a chemical formula, by a description in written words, by the deposit of an odour sample or by a combination of those elements.[30]

In a number of subsequent decisions, the ECJ ruled on the interpretation of 'graphical representation' with regard to other non-traditional forms of signs:

- *Colours per se*: for single colours, the legal conditions cannot be satis-fied merely by reproducing on paper the colour in question, but may be satisfied by designating that colour using an internationally recognised identification code (*Libertel*: colour 'orange').[31]
- *Colour combinations* must be systematically arranged by associating the colours concerned in a predetermined and uniform way (*Heidelberger Bauchemie*: colour combination 'blue and yellow').[32]
- For *musical tunes*, the requirements are satisfied where the sign is rep-resented by a stave divided into measures and showing, in particular, a clef, musical notes and rests whose form indicates the relative value and, where necessary, accidentals (*Shield mark* v. *Kist*: first nine notes of Beethoven's 'Für Elise'; cry of a rooster).[33]

---

30 Ibid., Paragraph 73; see also General Court Case T-305/04, *Eden SARL* v. *OHIM*, [2005] ECR II-4705 ('the smell of ripe strawberries').

31 ECJ Case C-104/01, *Libertel* v. *Benelux Merkenbureau*, [2003] ECR I-3793, Paragraph 37.

32 ECJ Case C-49/02, *Heidelberger Bauchemie* v. *DPMA*, [2004] ECR I-6129, Paragraph 33.

33 ECJ Case C-283/01, *Shield Mark* v. *Kist*, [2003] ECR I-14313, Paragraph 64.

? **QUESTIONS**

1 No ECJ decision so far has dealt with sonograms as a means of graphical representation of sounds. However, sonograms of sounds not represented by musical notes are accepted by OHIM in accordance with Rule 3 of the Implementing Regulation to the CTMR (CTMIR). Do you consider that justified in the light of the 'Sieckmann' criteria?

2 After Sieckmann, scents ('olfactory signs') are generally held to be excluded from trade mark protection. Do you consider that a practical problem? Which sectors of industry could have an interest in the protection of scents? Can you think of any other means for protection of olfactory substances?

3 The ECJ has ruled that 'transparency' of certain product features does not constitute a 'sign' in the meaning of Article 2 TMD and is therefore excluded from protection irrespective of its graphical representability. On the other hand, colours *per se* have been accepted as 'signs', and are registered accordingly, if they are represented graphically in the manner prescribed. Do you agree with the distinction made by the ECJ between the two forms of signs?

Absolute grounds for refusal

Distinctiveness and descriptive character: overview

The absolute grounds for refusal are listed in Articles 3 TMD and 7 CTMR.

As the CTM is a unitary right with effect throughout the Community, registration has to be refused even if the grounds for refusal obtain only in part of the Community (Article 7 (2) CTMR). In particular, examination of absolute grounds must take account of the *linguistic diversity* in the 27 Member States, and must therefore investigate the potential meaning of word marks or marks with word elements in all official languages spoken. Thus, for instance, registration of the Swedish wordmark 'ELLOS' for (men's) clothing was denied because in Spanish it means 'they' or 'them' in the masculine form and can therefore be understood as designating the target group for the products offered under the mark.[34] Contrary to that, in the context of national trade mark registrations national offices do not have to take account of the descriptive connotation trade marks may have in other official languages spoken in the EU. Therefore, a valid registration could be obtained in

---

34 General Court Case T-219/00, *Ellos v. OHIM*, [2002] ECR II-735.

Spain for the trade mark 'Matratzen' (meaning 'mattresses' in German) for exactly those products.[35]

Of foremost practical importance among the absolute grounds for refusal are the obstacles listed in Article 3 (1) (b)–(d) TMD and 7 (1) (b)–(d) CTMR. Trade marks are excluded from protection on the basis of those provisions if they:

- are devoid of any *distinctive character* (lit. (b));
- consist exclusively of signs or indications which may serve, in trade, to designate the kind, quality, quantity, intended purpose, value, geographical origin or the time of production of the goods or of rendering the service, or other characteristics of the goods or service (*descriptive* marks, lit. (c)); or
- consist exclusively of signs or indications that have become *customary* in the current language or in the bona fide and established practices of the trade (lit. (d)).

Those requirements were literally adapted from the Paris Convention (Article 6 *quinquies* B No. 2), so as to make sure that European trade mark legislation complies with international law.

According to ECJ jurisprudence, all three requirements must be assessed separately, although a broad area of overlap exists between them.[36] Regarding in particular the requirements addressed in lit. (b) and (c) – distinctiveness and descriptive character – they are distinguished according to the ECJ by the specific kind of general interest that underlies each one of them:[37]

- The general objective underlying the *distinctiveness* requirement, Article 7 (1) (b) CTMR and 3 (1) (b) TMD, concerns the *interest of consumers* to identify, in accordance with the mark's origin function, the products they want to buy.[38]

---

35 ECJ Case C-421/04, *Matratzen Concord* v. *Hukla*, [2006] ECR I-2303. The case had been referred to the ECJ for a preliminary ruling on the argument that by registering 'Matratzen' in Spain, the owner of that mark could hinder the import of such products from Germany. However, the ECJ found that the principle of free movement of goods did not oblige Member States to consider for purposes of national trade mark registration the possibly descriptive character in other Community languages of terms which, in view of their own population, did not have any connotative meaning.

36 ECJ Case C-191/01 P, *OHIM* v. *Wm. Wrigley* ('Doublemint'), [2003] ECR I-12447, emphasised again in C-37/03 P, *BioID* v. *OHIM*, [2005] ECR I-7975.

37 ECJ Joined Cases C-456/01 P and 547/01 P, *Henkel* v. *OHIM*, [2004] ECR I-1725, Paragraphs 45, 46; ECJ Case C-329/02, *SAT.1* v. *OHIM*, [2004] ECR I-8317; ECJ Case C-37/03 P, *BioID* v. *OHIM*, [2005] ECR I-7975.

38 ECJ Case C-329/02, *SAT.1* v. *OHIM*, [2004] ECR I-8317, Paragraph 55.

- In contrast, the public interest in free competition, i.e. the *interest of competitors* to keep a sign available for general use, is an aspect to be considered in the appraisal of *descriptive character*, i.e. in the context of Article 7 (1) (c).[39]

With regard to the ground for refusal listed under lit. (d), it has been held that the customary character of a wordmark must be assessed in relation to the goods or services it is intended to cover, meaning that it is not sufficient that the word is a laudatory term as such.[40]

If a trade mark application is found to fall short of the grounds for refusal listed in Article 7 (1) (b)–(d) CTMR and Article 3 (1) (b)–(d) TMD, it can only be registered if it is established that the mark has acquired distinctiveness through use (Article 7 (3) CTMR and Article 3 (3) TMD; see below).

Particular forms of signs

Compound marks

Word marks frequently consist of two or more elements combined with each other. While the elements as such may be non-distinctive or descriptive with regard to the goods or services they designate, their combination may be protected, depending on the circumstances. The issue was addressed in a number of ECJ cases.

The first of these cases concerned the word mark 'BABY DRY' for babies' diapers (or nappies).[41] The decision seemed to herald a very generous approach vis-à-vis compound marks. *Inter alia*, it was held that:

(40) any perceptible difference between the combination of words submitted for registration and the terms used in the common parlance of the relevant class of consumers to designate the goods or services or their essential characteristics is apt to confer distinctive character on the word combination enabling it to be registered as a trade mark.

In the case at hand, the necessary degree of distinctiveness was considered to be conferred to the mark by the 'syntactically unusual juxtaposition' of noun ('baby') and adjective ('dry').

---

39 ECJ Joined Cases C-108/97 and C-109/97, *Windsurfing Chiemsee* v. *Huber & Attenberger*, [1999] ECR I-2779, Paragraph 25.
40 ECJ Case C-517/99, *Merz & Krell* v. *DPMA* ('Bravo'), [2001] ECR I-04187.
41 ECJ Case C-383/99 P, *Procter & Gamble* v. *OHIM* ('BABY DRY'), [2001] ECR I-625.

A more cautious approach was taken in two subsequent decisions regarding protection of the compound marks 'Postkantoor'[42] for postal services and 'Biomild' for yoghurt.[43] The ECJ stated that:

> Article 3 (1) (c) [TMD] . . . must be interpreted as meaning that a trade mark consisting of a neologism composed of elements, each of which is descriptive of characteristics of the goods or services in respect of which registration is sought, *is itself descriptive* of the characteristics of those goods or services for the purposes of that provision, *unless there is a perceptible difference* between the neologism and the mere sum of its parts. (*Postkantoor*, Paragraph 100; *Biomild*, Paragraph 41; emphases added)

Again somewhat differently, a middle position was assumed by the ECJ regarding the distinctiveness of the trade mark 'SAT.2' for *inter alia* telecommunication services:[44]

> (40) the mere fact that each of [the elements of which the mark consists], considered separately, is devoid of distinctive character does not mean that their combination cannot present a distinctive character. . . Although the way in which the term 'SAT.2' is made up . . . does not reflect a particularly high degree of inventiveness, those facts are not sufficient to establish that such a word is devoid of distinctive character. (Emphasis added)

It follows that if a compound mark consists of descriptive or non-distinctive elements, it will frequently not quality for protection. However, its rejection must be motivated specifically and cannot simply be derived from lacking protectability of the individual parts as such.

Colours per se

Colours and combinations of colours which are represented graphically in the manner prescribed (see above) can be protected and registered as trade marks under the same terms as other categories of signs. However, the ECJ pointed out in *Libertel*[45] (regarding protection of the colour orange for telecommunication services) that:

> (65) [t]he perception of the relevant public is not necessarily the same in the case of a sign consisting of a colour *per se* as it is in the case of a word or figurative mark

42 ECJ Case C-363/99, *KPN&PTT v. Benelux Merkenbureau* ('Postkantoor'), [2004] ECR I-1619.
43 ECJ Case C-265/00, *Campina melkunie v. Benelux Merkenbureau* ('Biomild'), [2004] ECR I-1699.
44 ECJ Case C-329/02, *SAT.1 v. OHIM*, [2004] ECR I-8317.
45 ECJ Case C-104/01, *Libertel v. Benelux Merkenbureau*,[2003] ECR I-3793.

consisting of a sign that bears no relation to the appearance of the goods it denotes. While the public is accustomed to perceiving word or figurative marks instantly as signs identifying the commercial origin of the goods, the same is not necessarily true where the sign forms part of the look of the goods in respect of which registration of the sign as a trade mark is sought. Consumers are not in the habit of making assumptions about the origin of goods based on their colour or the colour of their packaging, in the absence of any graphic or word element, because as a rule a colour *per se* is not, in current commercial practice, used as a means of identification. A colour *per se* is not normally inherently capable of distinguishing the goods of a particular undertaking.

In addition the interests of competitors to keep the colour available for general use must also be considered for assessing its distinctive character:

(54) As regards the registration of trade marks consisting of a colour *per se*, not spatially limited, the fact that the number of colours actually available is limited means that a small number of registrations . . . could exhaust the entire range of colours available. Such an extensive monopoly would be incompatible with the system of undistorted competition, in particular because it could have the effect of creating an unjustified competitive advantage for a single trader . . .
(60) Accordingly . . . in assessing the potential distinctiveness of a given colour . . .regard must be had to the public interest in not unduly restricting the availability of trade marks for the other traders . . .

Slogans

Similar to colours *per se*, the ECJ has established with regard to slogans that although all categories of trade marks are assessed according to the same standards, the perception of such signs by the public may make it more difficult for them to establish that they are capable of distinguishing goods or services. In particular, distinctive character may be lacking if the slogan serves a promotional function, in order to recommend the quality of the product in question and if the importance of that function is not manifestly secondary to its purported function as a trade mark.[46]

On the other hand, this does not justify imposing specific criteria supplementing or derogating from the criterion of distinctiveness, such as to require a certain 'imaginativeness' of the slogan. In a more recent decision concerning the slogan 'Vorsprung durch Technik' (meaning, *inter alia,* advance or

---

46 ECJ Case C-64/02 P, *Erpo Möbelwerke* v. *OHIM* ('Das Prinzip der Bequemlichkeit'), [2004] ECR I-10031, Paragraph 35.

advantage through technology) for cars, it was considered as sufficient that the slogan was not a plain advertising message but required a measure of interpretation on the part of the public, and that it exhibits a certain originality and resonance which make it easy to remember.[47]

Surnames

Surnames can also be protected as trade marks if they meet the general criteria for protection. In a case concerning the family name 'Nichols', which was frequently listed in telephone directory of London and was therefore refused protection by the registrar of trade marks,[48] the ECJ declared that:

> (25) The criteria for assessment of the distinctive character of trade marks constituted by a personal name are. . . the same as those applicable to the other categories of trade mark. (26) Stricter general criteria for assessment based, for example on predetermined number of persons with the same name, above which that name may be regarded as devoid of distinctive character, cannot be applied to such trade marks.

Trade marks consisting of the appearance of the product (shape of product marks)

Overview

Trade mark protection for the shape of products constitutes a systemic irregularity in so far as it appears to clash with the general rule that protection for marks does not restrict competition in goods or services as such. The potential risk for free competition ensuing therefrom has motivated a special provision which excludes certain shapes from trade mark protection with absolute and permanent effect ('functional shapes', see below) Apart from that, shape of product marks are subject to the same protection criteria as other forms of signs.

Distinctiveness and descriptive character

As was pointed out with regard to advertising slogans and colours, it is an established principle of ECJ jurisprudence that in the perception of the buying public, unusual forms of marks are less likely to convey a message about commercial origin than other, more traditional forms of marks. In the same vein, it was set forth in joined cases *Linde, Winward* and *Rado*[49] (concerning the shapes of a truck lift, a torchlight and a wristwatch)

---

47 ECJ Case C-398/08, *Audi* v. *OHIM*, [2010] ECR I-535, Paragraph 59.
48 ECJ Case C-404/02, *Nichols* v. *Registrar of Trade Mark*, [2004] ECR I-8499.
49 ECJ Joined Cases C-53/01 to C-55/01, *Linde* and *Winward* and *Rado* v. *DPMA*, [2003] ECR I-03161.

that it may be more difficult in practice to establish distinctiveness with regard to shapes of products than for a word mark or a figurative trade mark.[50] As a matter of principle, the more closely the shape for which registration is sought resembles the shape most likely to be taken by the product in question, the greater will be the likelihood of the shape being devoid of any distinctive character. Only a mark which departs significantly from the norm or customs of the sector and thereby fulfils its essential function of indicating origin will not be found devoid of distinctive character for the purposes of that provision.[51]

Apart from lacking distinctiveness, protection of shape of product marks may also be refused on account of their descriptive character.[52] In that context, it must also be examined whether the shape should be freely available to all and not be registrable.[53]

Functional signs
Pursuant to Article 7 (1) (e) CTMR and Article 3 (1) (e) TMD, signs are excluded from protection if they exclusively consist of a shape which:

(i) results from the nature of the goods themselves
(ii) is necessary to obtain a technical result or
(iii) gives substantial value to the goods.

In the *Philips* judgment[54] (concerning a picture mark representing a triple-headed shaver), the ECJ defined the rationale underlying the exclusion of functional signs. The provision shall:

(78) prevent trade mark protection from granting its proprietor a monopoly on technical solutions or functional characteristics of a product which a user is likely to seek in the products of competitors.

Regarding in particular Article 3 (1) (e) (ii) TMD – exclusion of technically necessary shapes – the Court points out that the provision is intended to:

---

50 Ibid., Paragraphs 40, 41 and 48.
51 ECJ Case C-136/02 P, *Mag Instruments* v. OHIM, [2004] ECR I-9165, Paragraph 31; see also Joined Cases C-456/01 P and 457/01 P, *Henkel* v. OHIM, [2004] ECR I-1725, Paragraph 39.
52 ECJ Joined Cases C-53/01 to C-55/01, *Linde* and *Winward* and *Rado* v. DPMA, [2003] ECR I-03161, Paragraph 6.
53 Ibid., Paragraph 74.
54 ECJ Case C-299/99, *Philips* v. *Remington*, [2002] ECR I-5475.

(79) preclude the registration of shapes whose essential characteristics perform a technical function, with the result that the exclusivity inherent in the trade mark right would limit the possibility of competitors supplying a product incorporating such a function or at least limit their freedom of choice in regard to the technical solution they wish to adopt in order to incorporate such a function in their product.

Finally, concerning the question whether application of Article 3 (1) (e) (ii) is excluded if the same technical result could be obtained by other forms, the ECJ states that:

(81) there is nothing in the wording of that provision to allow such a conclusion ... (82) In refusing registration of such signs, Article 3 (1) (e) [ii] [TMD] reflects the legitimate aim of not allowing individuals to use registration of a mark in order to *acquire or perpetuate exclusive rights relating to technical solutions* ...
(84) ... [T]he ground for refusal or invalidity of registration imposed by that provision cannot be overcome by establishing that there are other shapes which allow the same technical result to be obtained.[55]

Based on similar reasoning, the ECJ (Grand Chamber) confirmed the decision by the Grand Board of Appeal at OHIM and the General Court to cancel the CTM registration of the basic LEGO building block.[56]

Regarding the third ground for refusal ('shapes which give substantial value to the goods'), the question was referred to the ECJ in *Benetton* v. *G-Star*[57] whether a shape mark could obtain protection in case that the appearance of the product (arrangement of stitches on a pair of jeans) had originally given substantial value to the goods in the meaning of Article 3 (1) (e) (iii) TMD, but had later on, by virtue of intense advertising campaigns, acquired distinctive character, so that, at the time of filing the application, the reputation enjoyed by the goods was largely attributable not to the aesthetic attractiveness of the shape but to the attractiveness resulting from recognition of the trade mark. The ECJ referred to the fact that the obstacles listed in Article 3 (1) (e) TMD are not mentioned in Article 3 (3) TMD, with the consequence that those obstacles cannot be overcome by establishing that the sign has acquired distinctiveness through use.[58]

---

55 See also ECJ Case C-48/09, *Lego Juris* v. *OHIM and Mega Brands*, [2010] ETMR 1121, with more explicit reasoning in Paragraph 54 *et seq.*
56 Ibid.
57 ECJ Case C-371/06, *Benetton* v. *G-Star*, [2007] ECR I-07975.
58 Ibid., Paragraphs 25, 27.

The repercussions of the *Benetton* judgment became visible in the *Bang & Olufsen* case, regarding the shape of a loudspeaker. The design of the product is quite unusual; it is shaped like a pencil or organ-pipe: its unusually tall and narrow tube-shaped body joins to an inverted cone, and the apex of the cone is attached to a square base. When the trade mark application was rejected by OHIM for lack of distinctiveness, the Court of First Instance reversed the decision, holding that the shape was so unusual that it could not be regarded as indistinctive.[59] Renewed assessment by the 1st Board of Appeals at OHIM led to the result that the design features of the loudspeaker are so dominant that they give substantial value to the product, meaning that – unlike under the first decision – there is not even a chance for the applicant to establish acquired distinctiveness.[60] The decision was confirmed by the General Court.[61]

? QUESTIONS

1 In Libertel, the ECJ has accepted that the interests of competitors to keep the sign free for general use are considered for the assessment of distinctiveness of colour marks (colours *per se*), whereas this is regularly rejected with regard to other forms of marks, where such considerations are confined to the assessment of descriptive character. Do you see any convincing reasons for the distinction?

2 The ECJ has ruled that surnames must be adjudicated according to the same standards as other trade marks, i.e. they can be indistinctive or descriptive. On the other hand, the 'commonness' of the name is not an aspect to be taken into account. On the basis of which criteria could it then be assessed whether a family name is 'indistinctive'?

3 As the ECJ pointed out in the Philips and Lego judgements, the exclusion of shapes which are necessary to perform a technical function (also) serves to prevent the perpetuation of protection for technical solutions (the technical features of the Philips razor as well as the Lego building block had been protected by patents which were meanwhile expired). Does the same reasoning also make sense with regard to shapes which were initially protected by an industrial design or by copyright?

4 As the Bang & Olufson case shows, ambitious product design may face a dilemma – although inherent distinctiveness is more easily found in products that are clearly distinct in their shapes from shapes usually found on the market, they will for the same reason be barred from trade mark

---

59 CFI Case T-460/05, *Bang & Olufsen v. OHIM* ('Shape of a loudspeaker'), [2007] ECR II-4207.
60 BoA Decision R 497/2005-1, *Bang & Olufsen AS.*
61 General Court Case T-508/08, *Bang & Olufsen v. OHIM*, [2011] ECR II-0000.

protection in permanence if the shape gives essential value to the product, that is if it attracts customers. In view of the problem, which strategy would you recommend as a lawyer to clients considering the filing of a trade mark application for product shapes?

Acquired distinctiveness

Pursuant to Article 7 (3) CTMR and Article 3 (3) TMD, the grounds for refusal set out in Articles 7 (1) (b)–(d) CTMR and 3 (1) (b)–(d) TMD can be overcome, if the mark has acquired distinctiveness through use.

The relevant criteria

In the leading decision, *Windsurfing Chiemsee*,[62] the question had been posed *inter alia* under which circumstances it could be assumed that the word 'Chiemsee', which denotes a lake in upper Bavaria, has acquired distinctiveness. The ECJ gave the following guidelines for the assessment:

> (49) In determining whether a mark has acquired distinctive character following the use made of it, the competent authority must make an overall assessment of the evidence that the mark has come to identify the product concerned as originating from a particular undertaking, and thus to distinguish that product from goods of other undertakings.

The following elements may be taken into account for that purpose:

> (51) the market share held by the mark; how intensive, geographically widespread and long-standing use of the mark has been; the amount invested by the undertaking in promoting the mark; the proportion of the relevant class of persons who, because of the mark, identify goods as originating from a particular undertaking; and statements from chambers of commerce and industry or other trade and professional associations.

In any case, acquired distinctiveness:

> (52) . . . cannot be shown to exist solely by reference to general, abstract data such as specific percentages.

In direct response to a question posed by the referring court, it was further set out that Article 3 (3) TMD:

---

62 ECJ Joined Cases C-108/97 and 109/97, *Windsurfing Chiemsee v. Huber & Attenberger*, [1999] ECR I-2779.

(49) does not permit any differentiation as regards distinctiveness by reference to the perceived importance of keeping the geographical name available for use by other undertakings.

This does not mean, however, that the same standards apply to all kinds of marks. With a view to the case at stake, the ECJ stated that:

(50) . . . where a geographical name is very well known, it can acquire distinctive character under Article 3(3) of the Directive only if there has been long-standing and intensive use of the mark by the undertaking applying for registration. A fortiori, where a name is already familiar as an indication of geographical origin in relation to a certain category of goods, an undertaking applying for registration of the name in respect of goods in that category must show that the use of the mark – both long-standing and intensive – is particularly well established.

Obstacles obtaining only in part of the Community

Linguistic diversity within the Community must be taken into account for examining the absolute grounds for refusal,[63] and it is also of relevance for showing acquired distinctiveness. For instance, in the example cited above of the trade mark 'ELLOS' for men's clothing, acquired distinctiveness would have to be established for those parts of the EU where the mark is understood as a personal pronoun relating to the persons targeted by the products (i.e. in this case Spain). In accordance with those principles, registration was denied for the word mark 'OPTIONS' for *inter alia* insurance, warranty and financial services. The mark was considered to be non-distinctive in English and in French, and as it had not been used in France in a manner satisfying the *Chiemsee* criteria, distinctiveness acquired through use could not be established.[64] Similar principles apply under the TMD, when different languages are spoken in particular countries or regions. This was confirmed by the ECJ in the *EUROPOLIS* judgment: in the underlying dispute, the applicant had sought to register the word mark 'EUROPOLIS' as a Benelux trade mark *inter alia* for insurance services.[65] The application had been rejected because 'polis' in Dutch refers to an insurance agreement. The applicant tried to establish that distinctiveness had been acquired through use of the mark in the Netherlands. However, as Dutch is also understood and spoken in other areas of the Benelux countries, this is not sufficient; instead, it must be

---

63 See already this chapter, section 4.3.2.1.
64 CFI Case T-91/99, *Ford Motor Company* v. *OHIM* ('Options'), [2000] ECR II-01925, Paragraphs 27, 28.
65 ECJ Case C-108/05, *Bovemij Verzekeringen NV* v. *Benelux Merkenbureau* ('Europolis'), [2006] ECR I-07605, Paragraph 28.

established that the mark has acquired distinctive character throughout the relevant linguistic area, that is, including Flanders, which is a part of Belgium.

Trade marks which are not distinctive anywhere in the Community

The situation is even more difficult for signs which consist of the shape of products, or of colours *per se*, and which typically lack distinctiveness throughout the Community. Decisions by the General Court that have addressed the issue so far appeared to signal that distinctiveness must be established for all Member States separately. In *Glaverbel* (concerning the surface design of glass panels used for building) it was held that:[66]

> (40) [u]nder Article 7 (1) (b) [CTMR], read in conjunction with Article 7 (2) thereof, a mark must be refused registration if it is devoid of any distinctive charac-ter in part of the Community and the part of the Community referred to in Article 7 (2) may be comprised of a single Member State . . . The Board of Appeal thus rightly examined the evidence concerning distinctive character acquired through *use for each Member State separately.* (Emphasis added)

In the same vein, the General Court decided in *Mars* (concerning the shape of a candy bar),[67] that if it was found that a mark is non-distinctive in the entire Community – which at the relevant date consisted of 15 Member States – it is no error in law to require that the mark must have acquired distinctive character through use in the entire Community, i.e. in those 15 Member States.[68]

If this is understood to mean that acquiring distinctiveness must be fully established in all 27 Member States, this would result in a practically insur-mountable obstacle for protection. The ECJ has therefore clarified in *Lindt & Sprüngli*[69] (concerning registrability of the shape of a sitting 'Easter bunny' wrapped in gold paper, with a red bow and a bell around its neck) that:

> (62) . . . even if it is true . . . that the acquisition by a mark of distinctive character through use must be proved for the part of the European Union in which that mark

---

66 General Court Case T-141/06, *Glaverbel v. OHIM*, [2007] ECR II-00114; see also ECJ Case C-25/05, *Storck* v. OHIM, [2006] ECR I-5719.
67 General Court Case T-28/08, *Mars* v. OHIM, [2009] ECR II-00106, Paragraph 46, with reference to ECJ Case C-25/05, *Storck* v. OHIM, Paragraphs 81–86 where the ECJ had confirmed that acquired distinctiveness of a trade mark consisting of the shape of a sweet in a golden wrapper with twisted ends cannot be established in a situation when the applicant had not run any advertising campaigns in certain Member States.
68 General Court Case T-28/08, *Mars* v. OHIM, [2009] ECR II-00106.
69 ECJ case C-98/11 P, *Chocoladefabriken Lindt & Sprüngli AG v OHIM*, [2012] ECR I-0000.

did not, ab initio, have such character, it would be unreasonable to require proof of such acquisition for each individual Member State.

1 Article 3 (3) 2nd sentence TMD gives Member States the option to accept signs for registration if distinctiveness has been acquired after the date of application, but before registration. How do you evaluate that option – would you recommend making use of it? What would be the consequences?

2 According to the ECJ, the strength of the 'need to keep free' cannot be taken into account for assessing acquired distinctiveness. Do you agree? What does that mean for instance with regard to trade mark protection of a colour which – like the colour magenta – does not only have certain signalling force, but is also one of the primary printing colours and may therefore save costs with regard to mass printing of advertising material?

3 Contrary to what seemed to be indicated by the General Court's jurisprudence, the ECJ has indicated in *Lindt & Sprüngli* that it would be 'unreasonable' to require evidence of distinctiveness acquired in each Member State separately (see above). However, the ECJ has not specified the standard to be applied instead. In your opinion, how should the territorial aspects of distinctiveness acquired 'in the Community' be measured?

Other absolute grounds for refusal

Overview

The CTMR and the TMD list further grounds for refusal, which are less important in practice than those presented above. Like the absolute and permanent grounds for refusal of functional shapes (Article 7 (1) (e) CTMR and 3 (1) (e) TMD), those further grounds for refusal cannot be overcome through use.

Signs are excluded from protection as CTMs:

- if they are contrary to public policy or accepted standards of morality (7 (1) (f));
- if they are deceptive (7 (1) (g));
- if their registration does not comply with the rules set out in Article 6 *ter* of the Paris Convention (7 (1) (h)) (protection for flags and other state symbols);
- if they concern other badges, emblems or escutcheons than those

mentioned in the Paris Convention, if the protection of those signs lies in the public interest (7 (1) (i));

- if they contain or consist of protected geographical indications for wines and spirits for products not having that origin (7 (1) (j));
- if they are in conflict with geographical indications which are protected on the basis of EU Regulation 510/2006 (7 (1) (k)).

Regarding the national trade mark systems, the TMD lists deceptive and immoral marks as well as marks conflicting with Article 6 *ter* Paris Convention in the catalogue of mandatory absolute grounds for refusal (Article 3 (1) (f) – (h) TMD). In addition, Member States are entitled to refuse registration of trade marks if their use can be prohibited due to legal provisions other than those in the trade mark act, or if the sign has a high symbolic value, in particular if it is a religious symbol, or if it includes badges, escutcheons etc. that are in the public interest, and, finally, if the application was made in bad faith (Article 3 (2) TMD).

Those options have been implemented to a varying degree. Most Member States have promulgated their own list of badges and escutcheons etc., which are barred from protection in the public interest. Most countries also list bad faith in the national catalogue of grounds for refusal, whereas in others – as in the CTM system – bad faith only figures as a ground for cancellation (Article 52 (1) (b) CTMR; see this chapter, section 4.5.3.3). Very few have implemented the option to exclude registration of signs with particular symbolic value; most legislatures consider such concerns as sufficiently covered by the exclusion from protection of marks which are contrary to public order and morality.

Examples

'Immoral' and offensive marks
Not many marks are found to be so grossly offensive or 'immoral' that registration is rejected. In a decision concerning the trade mark *Screw You* for a range of different products, including condoms, garments, and alcoholic beverages, the OHIM Grand Board of Appeal pointed out that:[70]

> (21) ... The office should not refuse to register a trade mark which is only likely to offend a small minority of exceptionally puritanical citizens. Similarly, it should not allow a trade mark on the register simply because it would not offend the equally small minority at the other end of the spectrum who find even gross obscenity

---

70 BoA Decision R 495/2005-G, *Kenneth Jebaraj trading as Screw You.*

acceptable. . . . The Office must assess the mark by reference to the standards and values of ordinary citizens who fall between those two extremes.[71]

A different kind of offensive character was at stake in a decision by the General Court regarding the State emblem of the former Soviet Union for fashion products.[72] The mark had been rejected at OHIM, *inter alia* because it clashed with a provision in Hungarian criminal law which prohibits the public use of 'symbols of despotism', thereunder the hammer and sickle and the five point red star which form part of the emblem. Accordingly, the emblem is not registrable under the guidelines applied by the Hungarian patent office. The appellant argued that rather than founding the decision on the specific situation in one Member State, CTMs should only be rejected as offensive or contrary to public order for grounds that are 'common' to all Member States.[73] The General Court refuted those arguments, holding that:

> (33) the perception of whether or not a mark is contrary to public policy . . . are influenced by the specific circumstances of the Member State in which the consumers who form part of the relevant public are found. (34) [Therefore] it is necessary to take account of not only the circumstances common to all Member States . . . but also of the particular circumstances of the Member States which are likely to influence the perception of the relevant public within those States.

Language may therefore also play an important role in the context. Thus, the German trade mark *PAKI* for logistics and packing services was denied registration as a CTM, as the term 'Paki' is understood in the English language as an invective designating foreigners of middle-Asian origin.[74]

Deceptive marks
Article 7 (1) (g) CTMR (deceptive marks) is sometimes addressed as a side issue in decisions by OHIM Boards of appeal dealing with (applications for) CTMs which have been rejected for being geographically or otherwise descriptive. When the applicant tries to establish that the goods or services do not match the descriptive implications of the sign, this could

---

71 Furthermore it was pointed out that the circumstances of the case, in particular the goods and services for which the mark shall be used, must be taken into account. In the actual case, the mark was considered acceptable with regard to condoms and other articles usually sold in sex shops, while it was refused for sports equipment, apparel and beverages.

72 General Court Case T-232/10, *Couture Tech* v. *OHIM*, [2011] ECR II-0000.

73 Furthermore, it was contended that to ban the registration of former state emblems would violate the right to free speech under Article 10 ECHR. However, the General Court concluded that the applicant had not put forward sufficient evidence to motivate his contention T-323/10, *Couture Tech* v. *OHIM*, [2011] ECR II-0000, Paragraph 71.

74 General Court Case T-526/09, *Paki Logistics* v. *OHIM* ('Paki'), [2011] ECR II-0000.

mean that the mark is deceptive (e.g. because it has a different geographical origin from what the mark appears to suggest). In most cases, however, the issue becomes moot – either because the mark is refused anyhow because of its descriptive character, or because it is rather considered as a fantasy sign which does not give rise to concrete associations by the public.[75]

In the context of the TMD, the issue of deceptive marks (Article 3 (1) (g) TMD) was addressed by the ECJ in *Elizabeth Emanuel*.[76] The dispute concerned the question whether a trade mark consisting of the name of a natural person becomes deceptive after having been transferred to an enterprise with which the person identified by that name has no relations. In the actual case, the trade mark at stake – Elizabeth Emanuel – corresponded to the name of a famous designer of wedding dresses, who was no longer involved in the activities of the firm to whom the mark had been transferred. The ECJ agreed that in such a situation, a risk of confusion in the mind of the average consumer may ensue:

> (46) especially where the person to whose name the trade mark corresponds originally personified the goods bearing that mark.

However, the ECJ then emphasised that Article 3 (1) (g) TMD presupposes the existence of actual deceit or a sufficiently serious risk that the consumer will be deceived. This was not found to be the case in the actual conflict, because:

> (48) even if an average consumer might be influenced in his[!] act of purchasing the garment . . . imagining that [Elizabeth Emanuel] was still involved in the design of that garment, the characteristics and the qualities of that garment remain guaranteed by the undertaking which owns the trade mark.

It is for the national court to determine whether the (new) proprietor of the mark was acting fraudulently by making consumers believe that the well-known designer was still involved in the production; however, even in that case, the practices:

---

75 For instance, the device mark 'Alaska' for *inter alia* mineral water, consisting of the word Alaska and a picture of a polar bear on a sheet of ice, was not considered to evoke the notion of freshness, and not the assumption that the water actually originated from there; BoA Decision R0877/2004-4, *Mineralbrunnen Rhön-Sprudel Egon Schindel GmbH,* Paragraphs 35, 36; deceptiveness is not addressed in the decision by the General Court in the same matter, General Court Case T-225/08, *Mineralbrunnen Rhön-Sprudel Egon Schindel v. OHIM,* [2009] ECR II-00111 (summary publication).
76 ECJ Case C-259/04, *Emanuel v. Continental Shelf,* [2006] ECR I-3089.

(50) could not be analysed as deception for the purposes of Article 3 [TMD] and
. . . would not affect the trade mark itself and, consequently, its prospects of being
registered.

Flags, official symbols, badges, escutcheons etc.
Article 6 *ter* (1) (a) Paris Convention stipulates that armorial bearings, flags,
and other state emblems of Member States as well as official signs and hallmarks 'and any imitation *from a heraldic point of view*' must be protected
against unauthorised registration or use by third parties (emphasis added).[77]
The provision became topical in *American Clothing Associates*.[78] The contested trade mark consisted of a maple leaf (forming part of the Canadian
flag), with the letters 'RW' reproduced below. Regarding the interpretation
of Article 6 *ter*, the ECJ expanded as follows:

> (48) . . . [T]he prohibition of the imitation of a [state] emblem[79] applies only to
> imitations of it from a heraldic perspective . . . (51) . . . [A] difference detected
> by a specialist in heraldic art between the trade mark applied for and the State
> emblem will not necessarily be perceived by the average consumer who, in spite of
> differences at the level of certain heraldic details, can see in the trade mark an imi-
> tation of the emblem in question.

? QUESTIONS

1 In recent times, protection of folklore and indigenous knowledge have
become important issues in the global debate on IP. Part of that debate
also concerns protection of indigenous names and symbols, such as tribal
names, or words and images used in connection with particular ceremo-
nies, etc. Do you find any provision in the catalogue of absolute grounds
for refusal by which such concerns might be encompassed?

2 Which, if any, absolute ground for refusal could be invoked against trade
mark protection claimed for famous works of art that form part of the
public domain, such as the 'Mona Lisa', or for the names of famous
deceased persons (e.g. Johann Sebastian Bach)?

---

77 This does not concern emblems of states that have ceased to exist, such as the Soviet Union; see General
Court Case T-232/10, *Couture Tech* v. *OHIM*, [2011] ECR II-0000 (above, footnote 72 and accompanying
text).
78 ECJ Joined Cases C-202/08 P and C-208/08 P, *American Clothing Associates* v. *OHIM*, [2009] ECR
I-06933.
79 In addition to State emblems and hallmarks, Article 6 *ter* (1) (b) Paris Convention also yields protection
for emblems and other insignia of international organisations. However, pursuant to Article 6 *ter* (1)(c), the
obligation of Member States to grant protection in such cases depends on there being a risk that the public is
misled as to a connection between the user of the mark and the organisation, whereas no such risk must be
established under Article 6 *ter* (1) (a).

3 Do you agree with the ECJ that even though consumers might be influenced in their purchasing decisions by the fact that a trade mark corresponds to the name of a natural person who has a particular reputation regarding the relevant goods and services, the mark does not become deceptive when the person is no longer involved in the business?

Relative grounds for refusal

Overview

Registration of a trade mark is also refused if it conflicts with a prior right in a trade mark or other distinctive sign. The relevant provisions are found in Article 8 CTMR and 4 TMD. In the CTM system, the proprietors of such rights may file an opposition against a CTM application which has been published subsequent to examination of the absolute grounds for refusal. Regarding the national systems, it is left to Member States to decide whether prior rights are examined *ex officio*, or only by way of opposition, which may take place either before or after registration of the trade mark.

Due to the unitary character of the CTM, registration is refused in case of all prior rights, irrespective of whether they exist on the Community level or on the national level. Vice versa, all prior CTMs form grounds for refusal in relation to younger national marks.

In addition to CTMs and national marks as well as trade marks which have been registered internationally with effect for a Member State or the Community (Article 8 (2) CTMR), Article 8 (4) CTMR also allows to file an opposition against a CTM on the basis of unregistered trade marks or other signs used in the course of trade which are of more than merely local significance. Furthermore, unregistered trade marks are considered as prior rights in the meaning of Article 8 (2) CTM if they are well-known in a Member State in the meaning of Article 6 *bis* Paris Convention (Article 6 (2) (c) CTMR).

The TMD basically contains the same catalogue of relative grounds for refusal as the CTMR. In addition, the option is granted to refuse registration also on the basis of other prior rights such as personality rights, industrial design rights, or copyright; furthermore, registration may also be refused of trade marks which are identical or similar with marks, in particular collective marks and certification marks, for a fixed period after the expiry of those older marks. Again, differences prevail as to the manner in which these options have been implemented in the various Member States.

Prior trade marks figuring as relative grounds for refusal enjoy the same substantive scope of protection as in infringement proceedings. Those issues are treated in section 4.4.1.3 of this chapter.

Unregistered rights of more than local significance

It is primarily a matter for national law to determine whether and how unregistered trade marks and other business identifiers are protected. Indeed, the manner in which protection is granted to such signs in the Member States varies widely. Some States (Denmark; to some extent also Italy) grant protection for non-registered marks on the basis of simple prior use; others – Germany, Sweden, Finland – require qualified use in the sense that the mark must have acquired a certain recognition on the market (Verkehrsgeltung, inarbetning). Protection under the aspect of 'passing off' in the UK and Ireland also requires a certain degree of market recognition ('goodwill'), but is distinguished from trade mark law by its non-proprietary structure. In the majority of Member States, registration is mandatory for obtaining protection under trade mark law; however, some degree of *de facto* protection for prior unregistered signs might be available on the basis of regulations against unfair competition.

For business names, the situation is different again. Article 8 Paris Convention stipulates that a trade name shall be protected in all countries of the Union without registration. Therefore, even Member States requiring registration as a precondition for trade mark protection regularly apply more relaxed regimes with regard to business names (e.g. France, Spain). In Germany, trade names are protected after first use, without additional requirements such as registration or market recognition (provided that the sign owns an inherent capacity to distinguish). Other Member States basically apply the same rules for trade names as for non-registered marks. Thus, the common law rules on passing off do not distinguish between both categories, and also the Italian and Danish rules are valid for both trade marks and trade names. Likewise, the protection requirements are the same in Finland and Sweden, meaning that protection for trade names is granted either on the basis of registration or upon showing of a certain degree of market recognition.

Whereas it is for national law to determine whether a trade name or other sign used in the course of trade enjoys protection in the relevant territory, European law governs the assessment of whether it is of more than local significance. The ECJ has elaborated on the relevant criteria in one of the numerous conflicts between the American firm Anheuser-Busch and the Czech brewery Budějovický Budvar concerning the designation 'Budweiser' or 'BUD' for beer.[80] In the actual dispute, the Czech brewery had filed an opposition against registration of BUD as a CTM, claiming *inter alia* a prior right based on the registration of BUD under the Lisbon Agreement on the Protection of Appellations of Origin, which had resulted in protection of the sign in France, Italy and Portugal, as well as protection under a bilateral treaty in Austria. One crucial aspect in the conflict concerned the question of whether the notion of more than local significance relates solely to the territorial extent of the protection obtained under national law, or also to the *significance of the use* which is made of the sign within the territory to which the protection pertains. The ECJ endorsed the latter position, pointing out that:

> (157) [t]he . . . purpose of the . . . conditions laid down in Article 8 (4) of Regulation No 40/94 is to limit conflicts between signs by preventing an earlier right which is not . . . important and significant in the course of trade . . . from preventing registration of a new Community trade mark. . . . (159) It follows that, in order to be capable of preventing registration of a new sign, the sign relied on in opposition must actually be used in a sufficiently significant manner in the course of trade and its geographical extent must not be merely local, which implies, where the territory in which that sign is protected may be regarded as other than local, that *the sign must be used in a substantial part of that territory*. (Emphasis added)

In the actual case, this meant that in spite of the fact that protection of the sign as an appellation of origin protected under the Lisbon Agreement was not geographically limited to a specific part of the territory where it was claimed to be protected, it could not be invoked as a relative ground for refusal under Article 8 (4) CTMR due to the fact that the extent of use had not been substantial enough.

Unregistered, well-known marks

Trade marks which are not registered in a country where protection is sought against registration or use of a conflicting sign are afforded a certain degree of minimum protection under Article 6 *bis* Paris Convention:[81]

> (1) The countries of the Union undertake, ex officio if their legislation so permits, or at the request of an interested party, to refuse or to cancel the registration, and to prohibit the use, of a trade mark which constitutes a reproduction, an imitation, or a translation, liable to create confusion, of a mark considered by the competent authority of the country of registration or use to be well known in that country

---

80 ECJ Case C-96/09, *Anheuser Busch v. Budějovický Budvar*, [2011] ECR I-0000.
81 See Chapter 1, section 1.4.1.2.

as being already the mark of a person entitled to the benefits of this Convention and used for identical or similar goods. These provisions shall also apply when the essential part of the mark constitutes a reproduction of any such well-known mark or an imitation liable to create confusion therewith . . .

Until now, the provision has been of little practical relevance for European case law. Where it is invoked in the framework of CTM registration proceedings in order to support an opposition filed by an unregistered right, the criteria for establishing that the sign is indeed well-known in the meaning of international law are hardly ever fulfilled. As a guideline for the assessment, the OHIM Boards of Appeal and the General Court rely on the catalogue of criteria spelled out in Article 2 of the WIPO Joint Recommendations Concerning Provisions on the Protection of Well-Known Marks.[82]

In a case concerning the alleged infringement of a Spanish unregistered trade mark by a subsequent registration of the same sign (*Nieto Nuño* v. *Franquet*),[83] the ECJ was asked for guidance on the interpretation of the requirement that a mark must be well-known 'in a Member State', in particular whether the earlier trade mark must be well known throughout the territory of the Member State of registration or in a substantial part of it. The ECJ responded that:

(17) . . . a trade mark certainly cannot be required to be well known 'throughout' the territory of the Member State and it is sufficient for it to be well known in a substantial part of it . . . (18) However, the customary meaning of the words used in the expression 'in a Member State' preclude the application of that expression to a situation where the fact of being well known is limited to a city and to its surrounding area which, together, do not constitute a substantial part of the Member State.

 QUESTIONS

1 Due to lack of harmonisation, the possibilities for right-holders in the individual Member States to file an opposition or request the cancellation of a CTM on the basis of an unregistered right vary in their conditions and extent. Do you consider that as an element which could potentially lead to distortion of competition within the common market? If yes, what could be the reason why the area has not been harmonised as yet?

---

82 See www.wipo.int/about-ip/en/development_iplaw/pub833.htm, see for instance General Court Case T-420/03, *El Corte Ingles* v. *OHIM*, [2008] ETMR 71 Paragraph 80, where the WIPO criteria are reiterated.
83 ECJ Case C-328/06, *Nieto Nuño* v. *Franquet*, [2007] ECR I-10093.

2 Article 8 Paris Convention (protection of trade names) requires that trade names must be protected irrespective of registration, whereas according to Article 6 *bis* Paris Convention, unregistered trade marks must only be protected if they are 'well known' in the country where protection is claimed. In your opinion, what could be the reason for treating trade marks and trade names differently in that regard? Is the differentiation justified?

Collective marks

In addition to marks that are used by individual commercial actors (individual marks), trade marks can also be registered for an association or similar collective body in order to be used by the members (collective marks). In the TMD, an option is left for the Member States to introduce specific regulations for collective marks as well as for certification or guarantee marks (Article 15 TMD), without going into further details.

In the CTMR, the conditions for application and registration of collective marks are set out in Title VIII (Articles 66–74). Acquisition and protection of collective marks largely follow the same rules as individual marks. However, contrary to what is stipulated in Article 7 (1) (c) CTMR, collective CTMs may consist of descriptive terms or designations (Article 66 (2) CTMR). In practice, this primarily concerns geographical indications, which are frequently registered as collective marks (possibly in addition to special protection which can be obtained on the basis of EU Regulation No. 510/2006; see Chapter 6). Furthermore, other than in the case of individual marks, applicants must submit to OHIM the regulations governing use of the collective marks, such as the statutes of the association, stipulating for which purposes and under what conditions the mark may be used by the members (Article 67 CTMR). In case of a collective mark consisting of a geographical indication, it must be specified in the regulations that any person whose goods or services originate in the same area must be entitled to become a member of the association (Article 67 (2) CTMR). If the regulations are not observed by the members using the collective marks, and if the association does not undertake steps to ensure compliance, the collective mark is liable to cancellation (Article 73 (a) CTMR).

? QUESTION

1 As mentioned above, collective marks are of some relevance with regard to geographical indications. Which other areas could you imagine to be particularly suitable for the use of collective marks? Do you know examples from your own experience?

4.4 Scope of rights

Conflicts and infringement

Overview: structure of provisions

The scope of rights conferred by a (Community) trade mark is defined in Articles 8 (1) CTMR and 4 (1) (3), (4) (a) TMD (concerning trade marks as relative grounds for refusal) and in Articles 9 (1) CTMR and 5 (1) and (2) TMD (concerning infringement). Further types of infringement are regulated in Articles 9 (2), (3) CTMR and 5 (3)–(5) TMD; in case of the TMD, those provisions, as well as Article 5 (2), are optional.

As a matter of principle, the registration of a trade mark under the CTMR and/or the TMD confers on the proprietor the right to enjoin unauthorised (registration or) use in the course of trade:

- of an *identical* mark for *identical* products or services; Article 9 (1) (a) CTMR; Article 5 (1) (a) TMD ('double identity');
- of an identical *or similar* mark for identical *or similar* products, if this entails *likelihood of confusion* (including association); Article 9 (1) (b) CTMR; Article 5 (1) (b) TMD;
- of an identical or similar mark for goods or services which are *not similar* to those for which the mark is protected, if the mark has a *reputation* and if the use made of it takes *unfair advantage* of or is *detrimental* to the reputation or the distinctive character of the mark; Article 9 (1) (c) CTMR; Article 5 (2) TMD.

Apart from criteria directly emerging from the provisions, such as identity or similarity of signs, identity or similarity of goods or services, and unfair advantage taken or detriment inflicted on the distinctive character or the reputation of a mark, infringement will only be found under the relevant provisions if the allegedly infringing conduct fulfils a number of implied preconditions, namely:

- the alleged infringer must have made *active use* of the sign;
- the use must be made *in the course of trade*;
- the use must have been made *in relation to goods or services*;
- the use must be such as to jeopardise the protected *trade mark functions*, in particular the essential function of guaranteeing commercial origin.

These preconditions have proved to be highly important and quite problematic. Though being primarily discussed in disputes under Article 9 (1)

(a) CTMR and Article 5 (1) (a) TMD (double identity cases), they are of general relevance for all types of infringement. In the legal discussion, the preconditions for infringement are often addressed in a summary form as relating to 'use as a mark'. The following remarks are also grouped under that term.

Use as a mark

Active use by the alleged infringer

Infringement cannot be found if the alleged infringer has not made active use of the sign. While that appears obvious, the question whether or not such use was actually made can give rise to doubts. The issue became relevant in the context of keyword advertisement. In brief, this means that a search engine such as Google offers the possibility against payment to appear with one's advertisement when a keyword – in the relevant cases: another person's trade mark – is typed into the browser. The technique involves two actors whose conduct may be adjudicated differently: the person 'buying' the keyword and making use of it for its own commercial purposes and the search engine providing the technical infrastructure ('reference service provider').

In the first decision dealing with those practices under the aspect of trade mark infringement (*Google*),[84] the ECJ declared that:

> (56) . . . use, by a third party, of a sign identical with, or similar to, the proprietor's trade mark implies, at the very least, that that third party uses the sign *in its own commercial communication*. A referencing service provider allows its clients to use signs which are identical with, or similar to, trade marks, *without itself using those signs*.

Active use of the sign was therefore only found to have been made by the competitor using the technique for positioning its own advertisements, but not by the search engine.[85]

Use in the course of trade

Private use v. commercial use
According to the formula established in ECJ case law, use in the course of trade is regularly found where it occurs in the context of commercial activ-

---

84 ECJ Joined Cases C-236/08 to C-238/08, *Google France and Google* v. *Vuitton*, [2010] ECR I-0000.

85 See also ECJ Case C-119/10, *Red Bull* v. *Frisdranken*, [2011] ECR I-0000: on commission of a third party which was not involved in the proceedings, the defendant had filled containers bearing the trade mark of the plaintiff with beverages of other origin. Also in that case, the ECJ found that the defendant had not made use of the mark in a manner which was relevant under Article 5(1)(a) TMD.

ity with a view to economic advantage and not as a private matter.[86] Most conflicts do not pose a problem in that regard. However, the boundaries between commercial and private activities become blurred for instance when privately owned goods are offered for sale to a large audience, such as on internet auction platforms. Until now, the question whether such sales, where they concern non-genuine goods, or goods which were or were not released on the market in the Community by the right-holder, must be regarded as infringing irrespective of the fact that the seller may be a private party, has not been addressed on the Community level. The positions taken under national law appear to be different. For instance in Germany, one-time sales or auctioning of (used) fake products are generally considered as non-infringing; however, a *prima facie* presumption of infringement applies if privately owned replicas of well-known brands are offered for internet sales or auctions in a manner which, with regard to volume and frequency, creates the impression that the sale forms part of regular, gain-oriented activities.

Furthermore, the exemption of private activities from trade mark infringement only concerns civil liability. In some Member States, private purchase and possession of counterfeit goods are treated as offences under criminal (France) or administrative law (Italy).

Use in transit
The requirement of use in the course of trade also has certain territorial implications. This is of particular relevance for goods which are on transit through the European Union or a Member State. As a matter of principle, infringement will be denied in such cases unless a pertinent risk of diversion of those goods to the European Union consumers can be established.[87] As the ECJ clarified in *Nokia* and *Philips*[88] the establishment of such a risk is also a necessary prerequisite for the detention and eventual destruction of such goods under the Border Measures Regulation (see Chapter 8).[89]

---

86 ECJ Case C-206/01, *Arsenal Football Club* v. *Matthew Reed,* [2002] ECR I-10273, Paragraph 40; regularly repeated in subsequent decisions.
87 See ECJ Case C-115/02, *Administration des douanes et droits indirects* v. *Rioglass and Transremar,* [2003] ECR I-12705, Paragraph 27; ECJ Case C-281/05, *Montex* v. *Diesel,* [2006] ECR I-10881, Paragraph 34.
88 ECJ Joined Cases C-446/09 and 495/09, *Koninklijke Philips Electronics* v. *Lucheng Meijing Industrial* and *Nokia Corporation* v. *Her Majesty's Commissioners of Revenue and Customs,* [2011] ECR I-0000.
89 Regulation 1383/2003. Somewhat different from *Philips* and *Nokia,* previous ECJ decisions (ECJ Case C-383/98, *The Polo/Lauren Company* v. *PT. Dwidua Langgeng Pratama International Freight Forwarders,* [2000] ECR I-2519 and ECJ Case C-60/02, *Rolex and Others* v. *X,* [2004] ECR I-665) seemed to confirm the position endorsed by some Member States that customs measures were justified if the goods would have to be regarded as infringing in case that they had been manufactured in the transit country ('manufacturing fiction'); see ECJ Case C-383/98, *The Polo/Lauren Company* v. *PT. Dwidua Langgeng Pratama International Freight Forwarders,* [2000] ECR I-2519 and ECJ Case C-60/02, *Rolex and Others* v. *X,* 2004] ECR I-665.

Use in relation to goods and services

Use in relation to a business

Use in relation to goods and services is denied if a sign is (solely) used to identify a business rather than the goods or services produced or offered by it. The principle has been expounded in a number of decisions.

In *Robeco*,[90] the ECJ had been asked whether use of a similar sign in order to identify a business could be considered as use taking unfair advantage of, or being detrimental to, a trade mark's reputation or distinctive character. The Court responded that protection of a trade mark's distinctive character or reputation against use for other purposes than to distinguish goods or services is not covered by the Directive, i.e. that the conflict does not fall under the provisions of Article 5 (1) or (2) TMD.[91] Similarly, it was held in *Anheuser-Busch*[92] that an infringement under Article 5 (1) TMD will only ensue if the sign is perceived as being used 'in relation to goods', whereas if the targeted consumers consider the use of the sign as being the use of a company or trade name, the case must be judged under (other provisions of) national law.[93]

The issue was treated in more detail in *Céline*.[94] The signs in conflict were the trade mark 'Céline' registered by Céline SARL in particular for clothes and shoes, and the trade name Céline registered in relation to the operation of a menswear and womenswear business. The defendant had argued that it did not use the trade name in relation to 'goods' and was therefore not liable for trade mark infringement. The ECJ took the opportunity to clarify its position as follows:

> (20) It is clear from the scheme of Article 5 [TMD] that the use of a sign in relation to goods or services within the meaning of Article 5 (1) and (2) is use for the purpose of distinguishing the goods or services in question . . . (21) The purpose of a company, trade or shop name is not, of itself, to distinguish goods or services . . . Accordingly, where the use of a company name, trade name or shop name is limited to identifying a company or designating a business which is being carried on, such use cannot be considered as being 'in relation to goods or services' within the meaning of Article 5 (1) [TMD]. (22) Conversely, there is use 'in relation to goods' within the meaning of Article 5 (1) [TMD] where a third party affixes the

---

90 ECJ Case C-23/01, *Robeco v. Robelco*, [2002] ECR I-10913.
91 Ibid., Paragraph 31.
92 ECJ Case C-245/02, *Anheuser-Busch v. Budějovický Budvar*, [2004] ECR I-10989.
93 Ibid., Paragraphs 62, 64.
94 ECJ Case C-17/06, *Céline SARL v. Céline SA*, [2007] ECR I-7041.

sign constituting his company name, trade name or shop name to the goods which he markets . . . (23) In addition, even where the sign is not affixed, there is use 'in relation to goods or services' within the meaning of that provision where the third party uses that sign in such a way that a link is established between the sign which constitutes the company, trade or shop name of the third party and the goods marketed or the services provided by the third party.

Use in relation to the infringer's goods or services only?
No doubt about a mark being used in a potentially infringing manner arises if it is affixed on, or otherwise used in close connection with, the goods or services offered by the alleged infringer so as to (incorrectly) indicate that those goods or services originate from him. More difficult issues are posed if the mark is used so as to identify and distinguish goods as originating from the proprietor of the mark (referential use).

In an early case concerning the offering of repair services for BMW cars by a person who was not part of the authorised dealers' net established by BMW (*BMW* v. *Deenik*[95]), the ECJ found that the mark had been used by the defendant 'as a mark', namely to identify and distinguish BMW from other car brands as the object of those services. The decision therefore seemed to indicate that the relevant precondition was satisfied by using the mark in relation to the brand owner's (i.e. BMW's) products. In a similar vein, it was held in a case when the mark 'Gillette' was used by a competitor on stickers affixed on his own, differently branded shavers in order to indicate that the exchange blades of the two brands were compatible that the prerequisites for application of Article 5 (1) (a) TMD were fulfilled.[96]

By contrast, it was established in *Opel* v. *Autec*[97] (concerning the use of Opel's trade mark on scale models) that the preconditions for finding of infringement are only met if the mark is used in respect of the goods or services offered by the competitor himself, and *not* as a reference to the goods and services of the brand owner:

> (28) Article 5 (1) (a) [TMD] must be interpreted as covering the use of a sign identical to the trade mark in respect of *goods marketed or services supplied by the third party* which are identical to those in respect of which the trade mark is registered. (Emphasis added)

---

95 ECJ Case C-63/97, *BMW* v. *Deenik*, [1999] ECR I-905.
96 ECJ Case 228/03, *Gillette* v *L.A. Laboratories*, [2005] ECR I-2337.
97 ECJ Case C-48/05, *Opel* v. *Autec*, [2007] ECR I-1017; further on this case see this chapter, section 4.4.1.2.4.2.

However, the expectation that consequently, use of a mark for the purpose of referring to the goods or services of the proprietor would no longer fall under Article 5 TMD (or Article 9 CTMR) proved wrong when it was decided in *O2 v. Hutchinson*[98] that use of another person's mark for the purpose of *comparative advertising* is to be considered as use in relation to the advertiser's own goods and services and therefore falls into the ambit of the trade mark provisions:

> (36) [t]he use by an advertiser, in a comparative advertisement, of a sign identical with, or similar to, the mark of a competitor for the purposes of identifying the goods and services offered by the latter can be regarded as use for the advertiser's own goods and services for the purposes of Article 5 (1) and (2) [TMD].

The same was held to apply in cases when a competitor books another party's trade mark as keyword triggering the display of his own advertisements, even when the mark is not even mentioned in those adverts. Thus, the ECJ stated in *Google*[99] that:

> (68) [w]hen advertising links to sites offering goods or services of competitors of the proprietor of that mark are displayed beside or above the natural results of the search, the internet user may . . . perceive those advertising links as offering an alternative to the goods or services of the trade mark proprietor. (69) In that situation . . . there is a use of that sign in relation to the goods or services of that competitor.

In conclusion, it can therefore be held that contrary to what seemed to have transpired from *Opel v. Autec*, 'use in relation to (the third party's) goods and services' simply means that the purpose of the use made must be to *promote* the marketing of the goods and services offered by the alleged infringer.

Use affecting the trade mark functions

Trade mark functions

It is a well-established fact in jurisprudence as well as, in particular, in marketing literature that the objectives and effects of trade marks and their use in commerce – the 'trade mark functions' – are manifold. Trade marks identify the source of goods and services, thus making them retraceable for consumers so as to repeat purchases of commodities they liked and avoid those they didn't. This provides an incentive for entrepreneurs to invest into achieving and maintaining a certain quality level. As market success not only requires

---

98 ECJ Case C-533/06, *O2 v. Hutchinson*, [2008] ECR I- 4231.
99 ECJ Joined Cases C-236/08 to C-238/08, *Google France and Google v. Vuitton*, [2010] ECR I-0000.

consumer awareness and a certain level of objective quality, but depends to a large extent on emotional factors, trade marks are also immensely important as vehicles for transporting advertising messages forming the brand image.

All those effects form an important part of economic reality. However, under legal aspects only one of them – the function of indicating commercial origin – is *indispensable* in the sense that trade mark law would not operate as such if no protection were granted against disruptions of that function by third parties. The other functions, which may be labelled as quality, investment, advertising and communication functions, are *accessory* in a double sense. First, while highlighting different aspects, they are to a large part comprised in the essential function of indicating origin. The incentive to invest in and to maintain quality as well as the possibility to establish a communication channel through which advertising messages forming a mark's 'personality' are conveyed already find a solid legal basis if the core function of trade marks is protected against unauthorised, illicit use. Second, where the accessory functions are not already covered by protection safeguarding the essential function, the legislature is free to decide whether and to what extent protection under trade mark law shall capture those additional needs. Other than with regard to the essential function, the operability of the trade mark system as such is not compromised if protection is denied.

ECJ case law
In recital 11 of the preamble to the TMD, trade mark functions are addressed as follows:

> The protection afforded by the registered trade mark, the function of which is *in particular to guarantee the trade mark as an indication of origin*, should be absolute in the case of identity between the mark and the sign and the goods or services . . .

The phrase became the focal point of a number of ECJ decisions expanding on the scope of protection under the double identity clause. The issue arises when, in case of an identical mark being used in relation to identical products, this does not lead to any confusion of the public as to the commercial origin of the goods or services involved. In such cases, the consequence regularly deriving from Article 5 (1) (a) TMD that the use falls under the infringement provision (protection under Article 5 (1) (a) is 'absolute'!) typically appears as inappropriate and unjustified. To some extent, the issue can be solved on the basis of the limitations and exceptions contained in Article 6 TMD and Article 12 CTMR. For instance, in the case of the mark 'BMW' being used by an independent dealer to announce his repair services, the defendant could invoke Article 6 (1) (c) TMD, which allows using another person's trade mark in order to indicate the purpose of one's goods or services. However, Article 6 TMD and Article 12 CTMR only contain a limited catalogue of exceptions that cannot be expanded by case law. Also, the ECJ seems to prefer solving the problem on a higher structural level, with the help of the trade mark functions, instead of venturing into a discussion of the limitations and exceptions. For instance, in a case concerning use of another person's mark in oral negotiations between a jeweller and the defendant, a dealer in precious stones, in order to describe the cut of the stones, the ECJ simply contended that 'the use of the trade mark does not infringe any of the interests which Article 5 (1) [TMD] is intended to protect', thereby denying the application of Article 5 in its entirety, instead of assessing whether the use was 'descriptive' and therefore justified under Article 6 (1) (b) TMD (*Hölterhoff* v. *Freiesleben*).[100]

The issue was further elaborated in a case concerning unauthorised marketing of products aimed at football supporters showing the word marks and emblems protected for the London football club Arsenal.[101] According to the national judge, the signs affixed to the goods were perceived rather as 'badges of support, loyalty or affiliation' than as signs indicating origin. The question was therefore referred to the ECJ whether this was a valid defence against the infringement claim raised by Arsenal, or whether, in view of the absolute character of the protection granted under Article 5 (1) (a) TMD, infringement must be found, even though there was no risk for the buying public to be misled. The ECJ pointed out that:

> (48) the essential function of a trade mark is to guarantee the identity of origin of the marked goods or services to the consumer or end user . . . For the trade mark to be able to fulfil its essential role . . . it must offer a guarantee that all the goods or services bearing it have been manufactured or supplied under the control of a single undertaking which is responsible for their quality . . . (51) . . . The exercise of [the exclusive right under Article 5 (1) (a) TMD] was conferred in order to enable the trade mark proprietor to *protect his specific interests as proprietor*, that is, to ensure that the trade mark can fulfil its functions. The exercise of that right must therefore be reserved to cases in which a third party's use of the sign *affects or is liable to affect the functions* of the trade mark, in particular its essential function of guaranteeing to consumers the origin of the goods. . . . (56) Having regard to the presentation of the word 'Arsenal' on the goods at issue in the main proceedings and the other secondary markings on them . . . the use of that sign is such as

---

100 ECJ Case C-2/00, *Hölterhoff* v. *Freiesleben*, [2002] ECR I-4187.
101 ECJ Case C-206/01, *Arsenal Football Club* v. *Matthew Reed*, [2002] ECR I-10273.

to create the impression that there is a material link in the course of trade between the goods concerned and the trade mark proprietor . . . In those circumstances, the use of a sign which is identical to the trade mark at issue in the main proceedings is liable to jeopardise the guarantee of origin which constitutes the essential function of the mark. . . . (Emphases added)

The ECJ has been criticised in this case for replacing the assessment of the national court as regards the public's perception of the signs by its own judgment, and thereby acted *ultra vires*. Indeed, the referring judge refused to follow the ECJ's ruling, and found for the defendant instead of granting Arsenal's infringement claim (however, the decision was reversed in the appeal stage).

A different outcome was reached in the Opel case already addressed above, concerning the figurative mark ('Opel-Blitz') protected for Adam Opel AG, which was affixed on toy models of the Opel car made by the defendant (Autec).[102] Opel had registered the mark not only for cars, but also for toys, and the case therefore arguably fell into the ambit of Article 5 (1) (a) TMD. Somewhat similar to *Arsenal*, the national court had come to the conclusion that the relevant public did not assume any commercial link between the toy firm and Opel. On the other hand, as the protection under Article 5 (1) (a) is absolute and does not require a likelihood of confusion, the issue was referred to the ECJ, who contended that:

(23) the referring court has explained that, in Germany, the average consumer of the products of the toy industry, normally informed and reasonably attentive and circumspect, is used to scale models being based on real examples and even accords great importance to absolute fidelity to the original, so that that consumer will understand that the Opel logo appearing on Autec's products indicates that this is a reduced-scale reproduction of an Opel car. (24) If by those explanations, the referring court intended to emphasise that the relevant public does not perceive the sign identical to the Opel logo appearing on the scale models marketed by Autec as an indication that those products come from Adam Opel or an undertaking economically linked to it, it would have to conclude that the use at issue in the main proceedings does not affect the essential function of the Opel logo as a trade mark registered for toys.

Opel thus appeared to send a clear signal that protection under Article 5 (1) (a) TMD requires that the essential function of indicating origin function is likely to be negatively affected. However, that seemingly clear rule

---

102 ECJ Case C-48/05, *Opel* v. *Autec*, [2007] ECR I-1017.

was disrupted by *L'Oréal* v. *Bellure*.[103] The case concerned the marketing of 'smell-alikes' – fragrances emulating the smell of famous brands. *Inter alia*, the defendants had provided comparison lists to their retailers which indicate the word mark of the fine fragrances to which their perfumes corresponded. It was undisputed that this did not give rise to any likelihood of confusion, or to the belief that the makers of the cheap brands were somehow commercially linked to the prestigious brand owners. Being asked whether the use nevertheless fell under Article 5 (1) (a) TMD, the ECJ responded that:

> (58) [t]he Court has already held that the exclusive right under Article 5 (1) (a) [TMD] . . . must be reserved to cases in which a third party's use of the sign affects or is liable to affect the functions of the trade mark [citations omitted]. These functions include *not only the essential function* of the trade mark . . . *but also its other functions*, in particular that of guaranteeing the quality of the goods or services in question and those of communication, investment or advertising. (Emphasis added)

The decision did not expand any further on the way in which those additional functions must be 'affected' so as to trigger the application of Article 5 (1) (a) TMD; it was left for the national court to decide on the matter.

More clarification was offered in *Google*, the first ECJ decision addressing keyword advertising.[104] Considering whether the use of another person's trade mark for triggering one's own advertisements was likely to have an adverse effect on the functions of the trade mark the ECJ started by reiterating the statement in *L'Oréal*, that the trade mark functions comprise not only the origin function, but also the advertising, communication and investment functions. Regarding the origin function, it is left to the national court to examine, on a case-by-case basis, whether the facts of the dispute before it indicate adverse effects, or a risk thereof, on the function of indicating origin, in particular if the existence of a link between the proprietor of the trade mark and the competitor is evoked. According to the ECJ, this will already be the case if:

> (86) . . . the ad, while not suggesting the existence of an economic link, is vague to such an extent on the origin of the goods or services at issue that normally informed and reasonably attentive internet users are unable to determine, on the basis of the advertising link and the commercial message attached thereto, whether the advertiser is a third party vis-à-vis the proprietor of the trade mark or, on the contrary, economically linked to that proprietor . . .

---

103 ECJ Case C-487/07, *L'Oréal* v. *Bellure*, [2009] ECR I-05185.
104 See in this chapter, section 4.4.1.2.1.

Turning then to the advertising function, the ECJ first points out that it would be negatively affected if:

> (95) . . . [the] use adversely affects the proprietor's use of its mark as a factor in sales promotion or as an instrument of commercial strategy.

However, although it is found that the possibility for competitors to use the mark for keyword advertising certainly has repercussions on the proprietor's own advertising strategies, those repercussions do not of themselves constitute an adverse effect on the advertising function of the trade mark. Even if the trade mark owner has to pay if he himself wants to be visible among the sponsored links, and must pay even more than his competitors if he wants to be on top of the list, this does not change the crucial fact that:

> (97) when internet users enter the name of a trade mark as a search term, the home and advertising page of the proprietor of that mark will appear in the list of the natural results, usually in one of the highest positions on that list. That display, which is, moreover, free of charge, means that the visibility to internet users of the goods or services of the proprietor of the trade mark is guaranteed, irrespective of whether or not that proprietor is successful in also securing the display, in one of the highest positions, of an ad under the heading 'sponsored links'.

The findings in Google were basically repeated in other cases dealing with keyword advertisements.[105]

Additional aspects arising in such cases were treated in *Interflora* v. *Marks & Spencer*,[106] which so far marks the last in a row of keyword advertisement cases referred to the ECJ. The constellation in the underlying dispute was special, *inter alia* because the claims were based not only on Article 5 (1) (a), but also on Article 5 (2) TMD. The ECJ therefore had the opportunity to comment on the relationship between the two provisions regarding the extent to which protection was granted under each one of the different trade mark functions. A brief addressing the issue had been submitted by the EU Commission, urging the ECJ to reconsider the *L'Oréal* decision and restrict the protection under Article 5 (1) (a) to use affecting the origin function, while allocating protection for the additional functions solely to Article 5 (2) TMD. The ECJ denied, however, pointing out that:

---

105 Those findings were basically repeated in other cases dealing with ad words; see ECJ Case C-278/08, *BergSpechte* v. *Guni*; [2010] ECR I-2517; ECJ Case C-91/09, *Eis.de* v. *BBY Vertriebsgesellschaft*, [2009] OJ C 129/06 (by way of order); C-558/08, *Portakabin* v. *Primakabin*, [2010] ECR I-06963.
106 ECJ Case C-323/09, *Interflora* v. *Marks & Spencer*, [2011] ECR I-0000.

(39) . . . both the European Union legislature – by using the words 'in particular' in the tenth recital to Directive 89/104 and in the seventh recital to Regulation No 40/94 – and the Court . . . have indicated that a trade mark's function of indicating origin is not the only function of the mark that is worthy of protection against injury by third parties. They have thus taken into account the fact that a trade mark is often, in addition to an indication of the origin of the goods or services, an instrument of commercial strategy used, *inter alia*, for advertising purposes or to acquire a reputation in order to develop consumer loyalty.

The ECJ then addresses, like in *Google*, the origin function and advertising function. In addition, the Court also expands on the investment function:

(62) When the use by a third party, such as a competitor of the trade mark proprietor, of a sign identical with the trade mark in relation to goods or services identical with those for which the mark is registered substantially interferes with the proprietor's use of its trade mark to acquire or preserve a reputation capable of attracting consumers and retaining their loyalty, the third party's use must be regarded as adversely affecting the trade mark's investment function. (63) In a situation in which the trade mark already enjoys such a reputation, the investment function is adversely affected where use by a third party of a sign identical with that mark in relation to identical goods or services affects that reputation and thereby jeopardises its maintenance. (64) However, it cannot be accepted that the proprietor of a trade mark may – in conditions of fair competition that respect the trade mark's function as an indication of origin – prevent a competitor from using a sign identical with that trade mark in relation to goods or services identical with those for which the mark is registered, if the only consequence of that use is to oblige the proprietor of that trade mark to adapt its efforts to acquire or preserve a reputation capable of attracting consumers and retaining their loyalty. Likewise, the fact that that use may prompt some consumers to switch from goods or services bearing that trade mark cannot be successfully relied on by the proprietor of the mark.

Further aspects of the decision deal more specifically with the protection available under Article 5 (2); they are addressed below.

? QUESTIONS

1 Do you agree with the ECJ that search engines do not 'use' other persons' trade marks by allowing their use as keywords and by operating the business model based on such choices? Before the Google decision, many national courts had decided otherwise. Try to find arguments for both sides!

2 In the final decision of the national court in *L'Oréal*, the judge held that by

extending protection under Article 5(1)(a) TMD to the advertising and investment functions, the ECJ had made it impossible for him to find for the defendant. Do you agree with the judge? Please consider that shortly before *L'Oréal* was decided by the national court, the ECJ had published its Google decision.

3 In the light of the ECJ's holdings in the keyword advertisement cases, how would you evaluate 'use as a mark' if a trade mark is used as a metatag, i.e. as an element of a website's 'metatext' which is invisible to the normal user?

4 How do you evaluate the ECJ's reaction to the Commission's plea to restrict the protection under Article 5 (1) (a) to the essential trade mark function?

Double identity and likelihood of confusion

While the preconditions for finding of trade mark infringement have become a prime topic of ECJ jurisprudence and a challenging issue intellectually, they only become relevant in practice for a small fraction of cases. Otherwise, trade mark practice is dominated by assessment of the criteria expressly mentioned in Article 5 (1) (a) and (b) TMD as well as in Article 9 (1) (a), (b) CTMR – the identity and similarity of goods and services, and how they result in a likelihood of confusion or produce other detrimental effects. Also those criteria have been addressed in numerous ECJ decisions, of which only the few leading cases are presented in the following.

Identity of trade marks

Regarding the criterion of 'identity' which must exist for the application of Article 5 (1) (a) TMD (or Article 9 (1) (a) CTMR) between the signs as well as between the respective goods or services, the ECJ has made clear that a strict interpretation must apply. In a case concerning a conflict between the trade marks 'Arthur' and 'Arthur et Félicie' (*LTJ* v. *Vertbaudet*)[107] it was held that:

> (50) [t]he very definition of identity implies that the two elements compared should be the same in all respects. (51) Indeed, the absolute protection in the case of a sign which is identical with the trade mark in relation to goods or services which are identical with those for which the trade mark is registered, which is guaranteed by Article 5 (1) (a) of the Directive, cannot be extended beyond the

---

107 ECJ Case C-291/00, *LTJ Diffusion v. Sadas Vertbaudet* ('Arthur/Arthur et Félicie'), [2003] ECR I-2799.

situations for which it was envisaged . . . (52) There is therefore identity between the sign and the trade mark where the former reproduces, without any modification or addition, all the elements constituting the latter. . . . (54) [A] sign is therefore identical with a protected trade mark if it reproduces, without any modification or addition, all the elements constituting the trade mark or where, viewed as a whole, it contains differences so insignificant that they may go unnoticed by an average consumer.

Standards for assessing likelihood of confusion

Similarity of marks; overall appreciation; impact of a mark's distinctiveness
In cases where either the marks or the goods or services (or both) are not identical with those protected on the basis of the trade mark right, it must be shown that a likelihood of confusion is caused thereby. This requires an assessment of the (degree of) similarity of the marks and the goods and services, and an overall evaluation of the impression created thereby on the relevant public.

The leading case establishing the standards for the assessment, *Sabèl* v. *Puma*,[108] concerned a conflict between a trade mark consisting of the image of a leaping cat of prey and a combination mark consisting of a word element and an image showing an animal slightly resembling the one shown in the older mark. The ECJ referred to the preamble of the TMD[109] where it is pointed out that:

> the appreciation of the likelihood of confusion depends on numerous elements and, in particular, on the recognition of the trade mark on the market, of the association which can be made with the used or registered sign, of the degree of similarity between the trade mark and the sign and between the goods or services identified.

The Court concluded that this meant that:

> (22) . . . [t]he likelihood of confusion must therefore be *appreciated globally*, taking into account all factors relevant to the circumstances of the case. (23) That global appreciation of the *visual, aural or conceptual* similarity of the marks in question, must be based on the overall impression given by the marks, bearing in mind, in particular, their *distinctive and dominant components*. . . . [T]he perception of marks in the mind of the average consumer of the type of goods or services in ques-

---

108 ECJ Case C-251/95, *Sabèl* v. *Puma*, [1997] ECR I-6191.
109 Recital 10 of TMD 104/89/EEC; Recital 11 of the codified version, 95/2008/EC.

tion plays a decisive role in the global appreciation of the likelihood of confusion. The average consumer normally perceives a mark as a whole and does not proceed to analyse its various details. . . . (24) . . . *[T]he more distinctive the earlier mark, the greater will be the likelihood of confusion.* It is therefore not impossible that the conceptual similarity resulting from the fact that two marks use images with analogous semantic content may give rise to a likelihood of confusion where the earlier mark has a particularly distinctive character, either *per se* or because of the reputation it enjoys with the public. (Emphases added)

Those standards have remained the same ever since, and are invariably quoted in decisions dealing with likelihood of confusion.

Similarity of goods and services

In addition to similarity between the sign and the mark, the similarity of goods and services for which the signs are or shall be used must also be taken into consideration for assessing likelihood of confusion. The issue was first addressed in *Canon* v. *MGM*.[110] The conflict concerned the application (in Germany) by MGM for the trade mark 'CANNON', to be used in respect of 'films recorded on video tape cassettes, production, distribution and projection of films for cinemas and television organisations'. Opposition had been filed on the basis of the earlier trade mark 'Canon', which was protected *inter alia* for 'still and motion picture cameras and projectors; television filming and recording devices, television retransmission devices, television receiving and reproduction devices, including tape and disc devices for television recording and reproduction'. According to usual German practice, the goods and services covered by the two signs were not regarded as similar; on the other hand, it was found unclear whether a different view should prevail in this case, given the strong distinctive character and reputation of the earlier mark. The German Federal Supreme Court therefore referred to the ECJ the question whether for assessing the similarity of goods or services account may be taken of the distinctive character, in particular the reputation, of the mark with earlier priority.

In its answer, the ECJ repeated that likelihood of confusion must be assessed globally, taking all relevant factors into account, and that such a global assessment:

> (17) . . . implies some interdependence between the relevant factors, and in particular a similarity between the trade marks and between these goods or services. Accordingly, a lesser degree of similarity between these goods or services may be offset by a greater degree of similarity between the marks, and vice versa. . . .

---

110 ECJ Case C-39/97, *Canon Kabushiki Kaisha* v. *MGM*, [1998] ECR 1-5507.

(18) Furthermore, according to the case-law of the Court, the more distinctive the earlier mark, the greater the risk of confusion. Since protection of a trade mark depends, in accordance with Article 4 (1) (b) of the Directive, on there being a likelihood of confusion, marks with a highly distinctive character, either *per se* or because of the reputation they possess on the market, enjoy broader protection than marks with a less distinctive character. . . . (23) . . . [I]n assessing the similarity of the goods or services concerned, all the relevant factors relating to those goods or services themselves should be taken into account. Those factors include, *inter alia, their nature, their end users [should read 'intended purpose'] and their method of use and whether they are in competition with each other or are complementary.* (Emphasis added; text in square brackets in the original)

The relevant public (notion of the 'average consumer')

With regard to the standard to be applied in the assessment, the ECJ has held that the concept of the 'average circumspect consumer', which was originally developed in unfair competition law should also apply in trade mark law. Furthermore, attention must be paid to the category of goods and services, which may impact the degree of sophistication determining the perception of the signs by the public. The leading case in that regard concerned the conflict between the trade marks 'Loints' and 'Lloyd', both used for shoes (*Meyer* v. *Klijsen*):[111]

(26) For the purposes of [the required] global appreciation, the average consumer of the category of products concerned is deemed to be reasonably well-informed and reasonably observant and circumspect. However, account should be taken of the fact that the average consumer only rarely has the chance to make a direct comparison between the different marks but must place his trust in the imperfect picture of them that he has kept in his mind. It should also be borne in mind that the average consumer's level of attention is likely to vary according to the category of goods or services in question.[112]

Likelihood of confusion in cases of composite marks

Special issues arise in cases of marks consisting of several different elements, such as words and pictorial elements or several (separate) word elements. In a dispute involving the prior trade mark 'LIFE' and the younger composite mark 'Thomson LIFE', the referring court had asked whether it was correct in such a case to appreciate the similarity of the signs by considering the overall impression conveyed by each of the two signs and to ascertain

---

111 ECJ Case C-342/97, *Lloyd Schuhfabrik Meyer* v. *Klijsen Handel*, [1999] ECR I-3819.
112 See, to that effect, ECJ Case C-210/96, *Gut Springenheide und Rudolf Tusky* v. *Amt für Lebensmittelüberwachung*, [1998] ECR I-4657, Paragraph 31.

whether the common component characterises the composite mark to the extent that the other components (in this case, the word 'Thomson') are largely secondary to the overall impression (*Medion* v. *Thomson*).[113] The ECJ responded that it was not possible to formulate such a general rule, but that:

> (30) . . . beyond the usual case where the average consumer perceives a mark as a whole, and notwithstanding that the overall impression may be dominated by one or more components of a composite mark, it is quite possible that in a particular case an earlier mark used by a third party in a composite sign including the name of the company of the third party still has an independent distinctive role in the composite sign, *without necessarily constituting the dominant element* (31) In such a case the overall impression produced by the composite sign may lead the public to believe that the goods or services at issue derive, at the very least, from companies which are linked economically, in which case the likelihood of confusion must be held to be established. (Emphasis added)

? QUESTIONS

1 Article 16 (1) 2nd sentence TRIPS stipulates that 'in case of the use of an identical sign for identical goods or services, a likelihood of confusion shall be presumed'. By not requiring any showing of likelihood of confusion, European trade mark law goes further than that. What could be the reason for that regulation (apart from the fact that TMD and CTMR were promulgated prior to TRIPS)? Can you imagine constellations, when no likelihood of confusion exists in cases of 'double identity'?

2 On the basis of the evaluation criteria listed by the ECJ, how would you assess the:
   a) Likelihood of confusion between 'Picasso' and 'Picaro' (both used for cars)?[114]
   b) Similarity of goods between handbags and shoes?[115]

Extended protection of marks having a reputation

General concept, economic rationale

It is common knowledge nowadays that the traditional paradigm of trade marks as tools providing information about the commercial origin of goods or services does not convey a full picture of economic reality. In addition to indicating origin, marks can acquire intrinsic value as business assets due to

---

113 ECJ Case C-120/04, *Medion v. Thomson Multimedia*, [2005] ECR I-8565, Paragraph 12.
114 ECJ Case C-361/04 P, *Ruiz-Picasso and others v. OHIM*, [2006] ECR I-00643.
115 General Court Case T-169/03, *Sergio Rossi v. OHIM*, [2005] ECR II-685, Paragraphs 53 *et seq*.

their capacity to symbolise prestige or lifestyle. In response to that, protection of trade marks which enjoy a reputation in the territory where protection is sought is not confined to conflicts giving rise to a likelihood of confusion, but may extend to situations when others take unfair advantage of, or act in a manner detrimental to, the reputation or distinctive character of the mark. An economic justification for that is found in the fact that reputation enjoyed by a mark is regularly the fruit of intense investment, for which further incentives are provided by the additional protection granted.

While extended protection is a mandatory element of the scope of rights conferred to CTMs, Member States were free to implement the corresponding provision in the TMD. All EU Members have chosen to make use of that option, which is also due to the fact that extended protection for well-known marks forms part of the canon of international obligations ensuing from the TRIPS Agreement (Article 16 (3) TRIPS).

The relevant aspects determining the grant and scope of extended protection are addressed in the following:

- Whether the mark can claim reputation in a qualitative and quantitative sense;
- Whether the reputation exists in the relevant territory;
- Whether the allegedly infringing sign evokes the reputed mark;
- Whether it is detrimental to the distinctive character or the reputation of the mark;
- Whether it takes unfair advantage of the distinctive character or the reputation of the mark;
- Whether the use is made "without due cause", or whether it can be justified for certain reasons.

Requirements for claiming reputation

As a precondition for extended protection, it is necessary to show that the mark has a reputation, which exists within the territory where protection is sought.

The relevant criteria

A list of aspects which must be taken into account for the assessment of reputation was set out by the ECJ in *General Motors* v. *Yplon*.[116] In the actual case, General Motors had raised infringement claims based on its

---

116 ECJ Case 375/97, *General Motors v. Yplon S.A* ('Chevy'), [1999] ECR I-05421.

Benelux trade mark 'Chevy' (which is registered for, *inter alia*, motor vehicles), against the registration and use of an identical mark for, *inter alia*, detergents. The national court seized with the matter asked the ECJ *inter alia* to explain the meaning of the expression 'has a reputation'. In response to that, the ECJ held that the term involves a certain 'knowledge threshold':

> (23) . . . Article 5 (2) TMD . . . implies a *certain degree of knowledge* of the earlier trade mark among the public . . . [which consists of] *either the public at large or a more specialised public*, for example traders in a specific sector. . . . The degree of knowledge required must be considered to be reached *when the earlier mark is known by a significant part of the public concerned* by the products or services covered by that trade mark. In examining whether this condition is fulfilled, the national court must take into consideration all the relevant facts of the case, in particular the *market share* held by the trade mark, the *intensity, geographical extent and duration of its use*, and the *size of the investment* made by the undertaking in promoting it. (Emphases added)

Territorial elements

The referring court in *General Motors* v. *Yplon* had also posed the question whether the earlier mark had to establish reputation throughout the territory of the Benelux countries, or only in a part thereof. The ECJ declared that:

> (28) [i]n the absence of any definition of the Community provision in this respect, a trade mark cannot be required to have a reputation 'throughout' the territory of the Member State. It is sufficient for it to exist *in a substantial part* of it. (Emphasis added)

The issue came up again with regard to CTMs in *PAGO International* v. *Tirolmilch*.[117] Pago is the owner of a figurative CTM for fruit drinks, representing a green glass bottle with a distinct label and lid. A competitor, Tirolmilch, sold fruit drinks in Austria under the trade mark 'Lattella', in glass bottles which in several aspects resemble those of Pago. The national court found that there was no likelihood of confusion, but considered that unfair advantage was taken by Tirolmilch of the reputation which Pago enjoyed in Austria. However, in view of the fact that such reputation had only been established for Austria, whereas an injunction was sought for the entire Community, the question was referred to the ECJ whether a mark having a 'reputation' only in one Member State is nevertheless protected in the whole Community as a 'trade mark with a reputation' for the purposes of

---

117 ECJ Case C-301/07, *PAGO International v. Tirolmilch*, [2009] ECR I-9429.

Article 9 (1) (c) CTMR. Referring to its decision in the Chevy case,[118] the ECJ responded that:

> (29) [a]s the present case concerns a Community trade mark with a reputation throughout the territory of a Member State, namely Austria, the view may be taken, regard being had to the circumstances of the main proceedings, that the territorial requirement imposed by Article 9 (1) (c) [CTMR] is satisfied.

Conditions and scope of protection

According to the pertinent provisions, protection is granted against use of the reputed mark for dissimilar goods, if, without due cause, it takes unfair advantage of, or is detrimental to, the repute or distinctive character of the trade mark.

Protection against use for similar goods

Article 5 (1) (2) TMD and Article 9 (1) (c) CTMR expressly refer to use of a sign 'in relation to goods or services which are *not similar* to those for which the (Community) trade mark is registered' (emphasis added). It therefore appeared questionable whether the provision could also be applied directly or by analogy if the reputation of a mark is abused or deteriorated by use for *identical or similar* products. The ECJ considered the issue in a case concerning the conflict between the marks 'Davidoff' and 'Durffee'.[119] Although the allegedly infringing mark was clearly different in spelling from the protected sign, it arguably tried to take commercial advantage of the latter's reputation by using similar graphical elements. The ECJ explained that the wording of Article 5(2) TMD did not pose an obstacle:

> (24) The Court observes that Article 5 (2) of the Directive must not be interpreted solely on the basis of its wording, but also in the light of the overall scheme and objectives of the system of which it is a part. (25) Having regard to the latter aspects, that article cannot be given an interpretation which would lead to marks with a reputation having less protection where a sign is used for identical or similar goods or services than where a sign is used for non-similar goods or services.

The result was confirmed in *Adidas* v. *Fitnessworld*.[120] The dispute concerned alleged infringement of Adidas' three stripes mark by articles of clothing bearing a motif of two parallel stripes. In so far as the outcome depended on

---

118 ECJ Case 375/97, *General Motors* v. *Yplon S.A* ('Chevy'), [1999] ECR I-05421.
119 ECJ Case C-292/00, *Davidoff* v. *Gofkid*, [2003] ECR I-389.
120 ECJ Case C-408/01, *Adidas* v. *Fitnessworld*, [2003] ECR I-12537.

the applicability of Article 5 (2), the ECJ even stated that a Member State would not comply with the Directive if it chose to implement the optional provision of Article 5 (2) without granting extended protection against use for similar goods.[121]

Necessity of a 'link'
In *Intel Corporation* v. *CPM*,[122] the ECJ was asked to comment on the conditions for finding detriment to the distinctive character of a mark with a huge reputation (see below, section 4.4.1.4.3.3). In that context, it was stated (again[123]) that the establishment of a link is a necessary condition for granting extended protection:

> (30) The types of injury referred to in Article 4 (4) (a) [or 5 (2)] TMD . . . are the consequence of a certain degree of similarity between the earlier and later marks, by virtue of which the relevant section of the public *makes a connection between those two marks, that is to say, establishes a link* between them even though it does not confuse them . . . (31) In the absence of such a link in the mind of the public, the use of the later mark is not likely to take unfair advantage of, or be detrimental to, the distinctive character or the repute of the earlier mark. (Emphasis added)

The following factors are listed as influencing the establishment of a link:

- the degree of similarity between the conflicting marks;
- the nature of the goods or services for which the conflicting marks were registered, including the degree of closeness or dissimilarity between those goods or services, and the relevant section of the public;
- the strength of the earlier mark's reputation;
- the degree of the earlier mark's distinctive character, whether inherent or acquired through use;
- the existence of the likelihood of confusion on the part of the public.[124]

Detriment to distinctive character
The concept that under certain circumstances the use of identical or closely similar signs in totally unrelated fields can lead to the 'whittling away' or 'dilution' of a famous mark's distinctive character, and thereby destroy its unique market position, was first described in a famous Harvard Law Review

---

121 Ibid., Paragraph 20.
122 ECJ Case C-252/07, *Intel Corporation* v. *CPM*, [2008] ECR 1-8823.
123 On the necessity of a link see already ECJ Case C-408/01, *Adidas* v. *Fitnessworld*, [2003] ECR I-12537, Paragraph 41.
124 ECJ Case C-252/07, *Intel Corporation* v. *CPM*, [2008] ECR 1-8823, Paragraph 42.

article by *Frank Schechter*.[125] There is no doubt that such a risk exists if the use of the mark by a third party is liable to create the impression among the interested circles that the mark is a generic term for the goods or services offered. This was confirmed by the ECJ regarding use of the mark *Interflora* as a keyword for advertising flower delivery services. However, the ECJ also emphasised in that context that the selection and use of another person's sign as a keyword does not necessarily contribute to such a development.[126]

A different constellation was at stake in *Intel Corporation* v. *CPM*.[127] In the actual conflict, the defendant had registered the sign INTELMARK for marketing and telemarketing services. According to Intel Corporation, this constituted an infringement of its own sign INTEL, which was claimed to have a huge reputation in the UK for microprocessor products and multimedia and business software. The Court of Appeal (England and Wales) found that the two signs were similar, so that consumers might be reminded of 'INTEL' when they saw 'INTELMARK', but that there was no suggestion of a business relationship between the two companies. The question was therefore posed whether that was sufficient for granting protection. The ECJ first points out that it is indeed a necessary condition for protection that a link is established between the two signs in the minds of the public (see above, section 4.4.1.4.3.2). However, with a view to the actual case, it is said that:

> (64) [t]he fact that:
> - the earlier mark has a huge reputation for certain specific types of goods or services, and
> - those goods or services and the goods or services for which the later mark is registered are dissimilar or dissimilar to a substantial degree, and
> - the earlier mark is unique in respect of any goods or services, does not necessarily imply that there is [such] a link.

Moreover:

> (32) the existence of such a link is not sufficient, in itself, to establish that there is one of the types of injury referred to in Article 4 (4) (a) of the Directive.[128]

---

125 *Frank Schechter*, The Rational Basis of Trademark Law, 40 Harv. L Rev. 813 (1926–27).
126 ECJ Case C-323/09, *Interflora* v. *Marks & Spencer*, [2011] ECR I-0000, Paragraphs 79, 80.
127 ECJ Case C-252/07, *Intel Corporation* v. *CPM*, [2008] ECR 1-8823.
128 Article 4 (4) (a) TMD concerns extended protection for marks having a reputation in the registration process. In its contents, it corresponds exactly to Article 5 (2) TMD.

In addition, it must be established that, with reference to the relevant public, a serious risk for injury exists or is imminent, meaning that:

(38) [t]he proprietor of the earlier trade mark is not required . . . to demonstrate *actual and present injury* to its mark. . . [he] must, however, prove that there is a *serious risk* that such an injury will occur in the future. (Emphases added)

More specifically, keeping in mind that:

(76) . . . detriment to the distinctive character of the earlier mark is caused when that mark's ability to identify the goods or services for which it is registered and used as coming from the proprietor of that mark is weakened, since use of the later mark leads to dispersion of the identity and hold upon the public mind of the earlier mark (77) [i]t follows that proof that the use of the later mark is or would be detrimental to the distinctive character of the earlier mark requires *evidence of a change in the economic behaviour* of the average consumer of the goods or services for which the earlier mark was registered consequent on the use of the later mark, or a serious likelihood that such a change will occur in the future. (Emphasis added)

Detriment to reputation

Another type of injury would occur when a mark is used in a manner which would destroy or jeopardise its positive perception by the public. For instance, this might be the case when a perfume mark is displayed on sewage trucks. Until now, such cases have not been decided by the ECJ. However, in *Intel* it is held as a dictum that:

(40) As regards detriment to the repute of the mark, also referred to as 'tarnishment' or 'degradation', such detriment is caused when the goods or services for which the identical or similar sign is used by the third party may be perceived by the public in such a way that the trade mark's power of attraction is reduced. The likelihood of such detriment may arise in particular from the fact that the goods or services offered by the third party possess a characteristic or a quality which is liable to have a negative impact on the image of the mark.

Taking unfair advantage

'Free-riding' on the commercial value and attractiveness of reputed signs takes advantage of reputation or distinctive character of a mark. As the ECJ already indicated in *Intel*, there is no need for injury to occur.[129]

---

129 ECJ Case C-252/07, *Intel Corporation v. CPM*, [2008] ECR 1-8823, Paragraph 41.

The concept was further elaborated in *L'Oréal* v. *Bellure*.[130] In addition to distributing comparison lists to retailers (see above, section 4.4.1.4.2), 'smell-alike' replicas of prestigious perfume brands had been sold in packages and bottles evoking the originals, without getting close enough to cause a likelihood of confusion. According to the referring court, there was no detriment to the prestige and market value of the famous brands. The question remained whether, nevertheless, unfair advantage was taken of the perfume marks' reputation. The response given by the ECJ was in the affirmative:

> (49) [W]here a third party attempts, through the use of a sign similar to a mark with a reputation, to *ride on the coat-tails* of that mark in order to benefit from its power of attraction, its reputation and its prestige, and to exploit, without paying any financial compensation and without being required to make efforts of his own in that regard, the marketing effort expended by the proprietor of that mark in order to create and maintain the image of that mark, the advantage resulting from such use must be considered to be an advantage that has been unfairly taken of the distinctive character or the repute of that mark.

In a previous decision concerning the alleged advantage taken of Adidas' three-stripes marks by a competitor selling garments adorned with two parallel stripes,[131] the ECJ had held that the interest of competitors in the availability of the protected sign for decorative purposes did not impact the assessment of unfair advantage being taken:

> (43) . . . the requirement of availability is extraneous both to the assessment of the degree of similarity between the mark with a reputation and the sign used by the third party and to the link which may be made by the relevant public between that mark and the sign. It cannot therefore constitute a relevant factor for determining whether the use of the sign takes unfair advantage of, or is detrimental to, the distinctive character or the repute of the trade mark.

Lack of due cause

A person taking advantage of, or inflicting detriment on, a mark's reputation or distinctive character will not be held liable for infringement if the relevant actions are taken with due cause. The reservation is not frequently addressed in ECJ case law. However, it has been clarified in *Interflora*[132] that it applies where use of the mark serves legitimate purposes, like allowing consumers to make a comparison between one's own products and those of a competitor:

---

130 ECJ Case C-487/07, *L'Oréal* v. *Bellure*, [2009] ECR I-05185.
131 ECJ Case C-102/07, *Adidas* v. *Marca Mode*, [2008] ECR I-02439.
132 ECJ Case C-323/09, *Interflora* v. *Marks & Spencer*, [2011] ECR I-0000.

(91) . . . where the advertisement displayed on the internet on the basis of a keyword corresponding to a trade mark with a reputation puts forward – without offering a mere imitation of the goods or services of the proprietor of that trade mark, without causing dilution or tarnishment and without, moreover, adversely affecting the functions of the trade mark concerned – an alternative to the goods or services of the proprietor of the trade mark with a reputation, it must be concluded that such use falls, as a rule, within the ambit of fair competition in the sector for the goods or services concerned and is thus not without 'due cause' for the purposes of Article 5 (2) [TMD] and Article 9 (1) (c) [CTMR].

? QUESTIONS

1 According to the ECJ's findings, it is much easier to establish unfair advantage being taken of reputation than detriment done to distinctive character. Do you find the differentiation convincing?
2 'Dilution', i.e. the detrimental effect of a trade mark's distinctive character by use of the same or closely similar sign for different products has also been described more drastically as 'death by a thousand cuts' – whereas the first cut won't kill or even inflict serious harm, it would open a possibility for others to act in the same way, and the summary effect would be destructive. Do you agree with that reasoning?
3 Try to make a complete list of arguments pro and contra infringement in the following cases:
   a) 'Microsoft' for Software v. 'Micro-Soft' for ladies' underwear (fictitious hypothetical);
   b) 'Baywatch' for video and music cassettes v. 'Babewatch' for a film production with 'explicit sexual content'?[133]

Limitations of protection

'Fair use'

Overview

Articles 6 (1) TMD and Article 12 CTMR allow for certain actions being performed by third parties in the course of trade, even if they involve use of a protected sign. The limitations concern:

- use of one's own name or address;
- use of signs or indications in a descriptive meaning;
- the use of a sign where this is necessary to indicate the intended purpose

---

133 *Baywatch Production Co. Inc.* v. *The Home Video Channel*, [1997] F.S.R. 22.

provided this is done in accordance with honest practice in industrial or commercial manners.

As a kind of unwritten limitation, the ECJ has further acknowledged that use of another person's trade mark in comparative advertisement cannot be considered as infringing, if the use complies with the conditions for lawful comparisons, as are set out in Directive 2006/114/EC.[134]

Use of one's name or address

It was an accepted principle in all Member States prior to harmonisation that no one should be prohibited from using her own personal name (and/or address) to identify her business. This principle was also meant to be expressed in Articles 6 (1) (a) TMD and 12 (a) CTMR. In order to clarify the legislative intent, a Joint Statement was issued by the Commission and the Council at the occasion of enactment of the TMD, to the effect that the provision should only cover the names of natural persons. The issue became relevant in *Anheuser-Busch* v. *Budějovický Budvar*,[135] regarding the question whether a trade name conflicting with a prior trade mark could nevertheless be used in commerce. Having been alerted of the position expressed by the Commission and the Council in the Joint Statement, the ECJ declared that such statements are not legally binding, and that the wording of Article 6 (1) (a) TMD does not reflect any restriction in the meaning of 'name'.[136] Therefore:

> (80) [a] third party may . . . rely on the exception provided for in Article 6 (1) (a) [TMD] in order to be entitled to use a sign which is identical or similar to a trade mark for the purpose of indicating his trade name, even if that constitutes a use falling within the scope of Article 5 (1) [TMD] which the trade mark proprietor may prohibit by virtue of the exclusive rights conferred on him by that provision.

However, it follows from the last sentence of Article 6 (1) TMD that such use is only permissible where it complies with honest business practices. In that regard, it was added that:

> (83) [i]n assessing whether the condition of honest practice is satisfied, account must be taken first of the extent to which the use of the third party's trade name is understood by the relevant public . . . as *indicating a link* between the third party's

---

134 For more details see Chapter 7, section 7.3.3.2.4.1.
135 ECJ Case C-245/02, *Anheuser-Busch* v. *Budějovický Budvar*, [2004] ECR I-10989.
136 Ibid., Paragraph 79.

goods and the trade-mark proprietor . . ., and secondly of the extent to which the third party *ought to have been aware* of that. Another factor to be taken into account when making the assessment is whether the trade mark concerned enjoys a certain *reputation* in the Member State in which it is registered and its protection is sought, from which the third party might profit in selling his goods. (Emphases added)

Use as an indication concerning certain properties of the goods

Article 6 (1) (b) TMD was addressed in a case concerning the conflict between the owner of the trade mark 'GERRI' for mineral water and a person marketing soft drinks bearing labels including the words 'KERRY Springs' (*Gerolsteiner v. Putsch*).[137] According to the defendant, the drinks were made with water from a source in county Kerry, Ireland. For the ECJ, this was sufficient reason to trigger the applicability of Article 6 (1) (b) TMD:

(18) Article 6 (1) (b) [TMD] provides that the proprietor of the trade mark may not prohibit a third party from using, in the course of trade, indications concerning, *inter alia*, the geographical origin of goods provided the third party uses them in accordance with honest practices in industrial or commercial matters. (19) . . . [T]hat provision draws no distinction between the possible uses of the indications referred to [therein]. For such an indication to fall within the scope of that Article, it suffices that it is an indication concerning one of the characteristics set out therein, like geographical origin.

As to the question of whether the use made was in compliance with honest business practices, the ECJ declared that:

(25) The mere fact that there exists a likelihood of aural confusion between a word mark registered in one Member State and an indication of geographical origin from another Member State is . . . insufficient to conclude that the use of that indication in the course of trade is not in accordance with honest practices. . . .
(26) . . . [I]t is for the national court to carry out an overall assessment of all the relevant circumstances . . . [which] would include in particular the shape and labelling of the bottle in order to assess, more particularly, whether the producer of the drink bearing the indication of geographical origin might be regarded as unfairly competing with the proprietor of the trade mark.

The possibility of invoking Article 6 (1) (b) TMD was also of relevance in *Opel v. Autec*,[138] concerning the affixing of the 'Opel-Blitz' on the

---

137 ECJ Case C-100/02, *Gerolsteiner Brunnen v. Putsch* ('Gerri/Kerry Springs'), [2004] ECR I-691.
138 ECJ Case C-48/05, *Opel v. Autec*, [2007] ECR I-1017.

miniature toy car. The Advocate General had argued in his opinion[139] that:

> (51) since the activity of creating models consists basically in making an accurate and detailed copy of reality, it may be considered that the emblem of the trade mark is an inherent part of the original which, in order for the consumer to be better informed and for all operators in the sector to compete on the same terms, is one of those *other characteristics* to which Article 6 (1) (b) [TMD] refers. (Emphasis added)

Contrary to that, the ECJ found that:

> (44) . . . the affixing of a sign which is identical to a trade mark registered, *inter alia*, in respect of motor vehicles to scale models of that make of vehicle in order to reproduce those vehicles faithfully is not intended to provide an indication as to a characteristic of those scale models, but is merely an element in the faithful reproduction of the original vehicles.

Use to indicate purpose

Article 6 (1) (c) specifies that a sign may be used where that is 'necessary' to indicate the intended use or purpose of goods or services, 'in particular as accessories or spare parts'. In *BMW* v. *Deenik*, the ECJ clarified that this includes use of a sign in order to advertise repair services by an independent trader.[140] The issue was treated more extensively in *Gillette* v. *LA Laboratories*,[141] concerning the marketing of razor blades by emphasising their compatibility with the leading brand. It was undisputed in this case that under economic aspects, the blades constituted the 'main article', as they were more valuable, and more important for business purposes, than the complete article (blades and shaft). The ECJ was therefore asked whether Article 6 (1) (c) TMD only applied to spare parts and accessories in a strict (economic) sense. Furthermore, the question was posed whether the express reference to Gillette blades was to be considered as 'necessary'. To the first question, the ECJ answered that:

> (32) . . . since the intended purpose of the products as accessories or spare parts is cited only by way of example . . . the application of Article 6 (1) (c) [TMD] is . . . not limited to those situations.

---

139 Ibid., opinion of Advocate General Ruiz Jarabo Colomer, delivered on 7 March 2006.
140 ECJ Case C-63/97, *BMW* v. *Deenik*, [1999] ECR I-905, Paragraph 60.
141 ECJ Case 228/03, *Gillette* v *L.A. Laboratories*, [2005] ECR I-2337.

And concerning the necessity of an express reference to the protected trade mark, it was held that:

> (35) . . . use of a trade mark is necessary in cases where that information cannot in practice be communicated to the public by a third party without use being made of the trade mark of which the latter is not the owner . . . [T]hat use must in practice be the only means of providing such information. (36) . . . [I]n order to determine whether other means of providing such information may be used, it is necessary to take into consideration, for example, the possible existence of technical standards or norms generally used for the type of product marketed by the third party and known to the public for which that type of product is intended. Those norms, or other characteristics, must be capable of providing that public with comprehensible and full information on the intended purpose of the product marketed by that third party in order to preserve the system of undistorted competition on the market for that product.

? QUESTIONS

1 Do you agree with the ECJ's reasoning regarding the use of names, or should the Joint Statement (i.e. that the limitation should only apply to personal names) be reinstalled?
2 Do you agree with the ECJ's statement that an element which forms part of a reproduction cannot, at the same time, be intended to give an indication of the product's characteristics? For your answer, please also consider that according to the ECJ, three-dimensional shapes of products can be descriptive of the goods designated by them.
3 It is argued by some that trade mark law should also include an express limitation with regard to parodies. Do you agree, or do you think that trade mark parodies enjoy a sufficient leeway under the law already in its current form?

Exhaustion

Basic principles: regional exhaustion

Pursuant to Articles 13 CTMR and 7 TMD, the proprietor of a trade mark cannot prohibit the use of the mark in relation to goods which have been put on the market in the Community (or within the EEA[142]) by the proprietor

---

142 By virtue of the EEA Treaty, the principle of free movement of goods extends to the entire territory of the European Economic Area. Although the current wording of the TMD and CTMR do not reflect that situation, its legal validity is uncontested.

or with his consent. The rule is meant to implement the jurisprudence of the ECJ which was developed in application of the principle of free movement of goods (now: Articles 34, 36 TFEU).[143] In contrast to the legal situation before enactment of the TMD, however, Member States are no longer free to apply the principle of 'global' exhaustion. This was clarified in *Silhouette*:[144]

> (26) . . . the [TMD] cannot be interpreted as leaving it open to the Member States to provide in their domestic law for exhaustion of the rights conferred by a trade mark in respect of products put on the market in non-member countries. (27) This . . . is the only interpretation which is fully capable of ensuring that the purpose of the [TMD] is achieved, namely to safeguard the functioning of the internal market. A situation in which some Member States could provide for international exhaustion while others provided for Community exhaustion only would inevitably give rise to barriers to the free movement of goods and the freedom to provide services.

Acts conferring exhaustion

Exhaustion will only occur when goods are actually sold, or ownership is otherwise transferred, within the EU; import as such is not sufficient. This was clarified in *Peak Holding*:[145]

> (40) [Only a] sale which allows the proprietor to realise the economic value of his trade mark exhausts the exclusive rights conferred by the [TMD] . . . (41) On the other hand, where the proprietor imports his goods with a view to selling them in the EEA or offers them for sale in the EEA, he does not put them on the market . . . (42) Such acts do not transfer to third parties the right to dispose of the goods bearing the trade mark. They do not allow the proprietor to realise the economic value of the trade mark. Even after such acts, the proprietor retains his interest in maintaining complete control over the goods bearing his trade mark, in order in particular to ensure their quality . . . (44) [Therefore], goods bearing a trade mark cannot be regarded as having been put on the market in the European Economic Area where the proprietor of the trade mark has imported them . . . without actually selling them.

In the same vein, it was held in another case that making available 'perfume testers' to dealers while prohibiting the sales of these testers does not amount to a disposition leading to exhaustion of rights.[146]

---

143 See Chapter 2, section 2.2.1.
144 ECJ Case C-355/96, *Silhouette International v. Hartlauer*, [1998] ECR I-4799.
145 ECJ Case C-16/03, *Peak Holding AB v. Axolin-Elinor AB*, [2004] I-11313.
146 ECJ Case C-127/09, *Coty v. Simex*, [2010] ECR I-4965.

Furthermore, it is important to note that exhaustion only relates to the individual items which have been placed on the market by the right-owner or with his consent. Therefore, it was held in *Sebago* v. *Unic*[147] that exhaustion did not ensue if the proprietor had released *other* products of the same quality on the market in the Community under the same brand.

Consent

The notion of 'consent' in Article 7 TMD must be given a uniform interpretation throughout the Community, and does not depend on particular doctrines developed under national law. The issue became topical in *Zino Davidoff* v. *Tesco*,[148] concerning *inter alia* the import into the UK of aftershave which had been released on the market in Hong Kong. According to the national judge, application of UK law would lead to the result that implied consent must be presumed, as the bottles had not been marked with an import ban, and retailers had not been under an obligation to bind their customers to a duty not to import into the EU. However, the ECJ found that consent:

> (53) . . . must be expressed positively and . . . the factors taken into consideration in finding implied consent must unequivocally demonstrate that the trade mark proprietor has renounced any intention to enforce his exclusive rights . . .
> (55) [Implied consent] cannot be inferred from the mere silence of the trade mark proprietor. (56) Likewise, implied consent cannot be inferred from the fact that . . . the goods do not carry any warning that it is prohibited to place them on the market within the EEA. (57) Finally, such consent cannot be inferred from the fact that the trade mark proprietor transferred ownership of the goods bearing the mark without imposing contractual reservations. . . . (58) A rule of national law which proceeded upon the mere silence of the trade mark proprietor would not recognise implied consent but rather deemed consent. This would not meet the need for consent positively expressed required by Community law.

Burden of proof

For the practical impact of the exhaustion principle on trade, the burden of proving whether the trade mark owner's consent is highly relevant. To impose that burden on traders would comply with the general rule that defences must be proven by the party raising them. On the other hand, this

---

147 ECJ Case C-173/98, *Sebago* v. *Unic*, [1999] ECR I-4103, Paragraph 19.
148 ECJ Joined Cases C-414/99 to C-416/99, *Zino Davidoff* v. *A & G Imports* and *Levi Strauss* v. *Tesco Stores*, [2001] ECR I-8691.

might force traders to lay open their sources of supply, thus giving the trade mark owner a chance to dry out the distribution channels and making parallel imports and other kinds of grey market trade impossible in the long run. The issue was brought to the ECJ in a case concerning sales of garments allegedly imported through 'grey channels' from the US.[149] The ECJ first remarked that the procedural rule invoked by the referring court, namely that the conditions for exhaustion must be proved by the party raising the plea in his defence, complies with Community law.[150] The Court continued:

> (37) However, the requirements deriving from the protection of the free movement of goods . . . may mean that that rule of evidence needs to be qualified. (38) This must be so where that rule would allow the proprietor of the trade mark to partition national markets and thus assist the maintenance of price differences which may exist between Member States . . . (39) . . . [T]here is a real risk of partitioning of markets . . . where . . . the trade mark proprietor markets his products in the EEA using an exclusive distribution system (40) [I]f the third party were required to adduce evidence of the place where the goods were first put on the market . . . the trade mark proprietor could obstruct the marketing of the goods purchased and prevent the third party from obtaining supplies in future from a member of the exclusive distribution network of the proprietor in the EEA . . . (41) Accordingly, where a third party against whom proceedings have been brought succeeds in establishing that there is a real risk of partitioning of national markets if he himself bears the burden of proving that the goods were placed on the market in the EEA by the proprietor of the trade mark or with his consent, it is for the proprietor of the trade mark to establish that the products were initially placed on the market outside the EEA by him or with his consent. If such evidence is adduced, it is for the third party to prove the consent of the trade mark proprietor to subsequent marketing of the products in the EEA.

Right to oppose further commercialisation

Even if the goods have been released on the market in the EU or the EEA with the proprietor's consent, he may oppose further commercialisation, in particular where the condition of the goods is changed or impaired after they have been put on the market (Articles 7 (2) TMD and 13 (2) CTMR).

Repackaging, relabeling, rebranding
The issue of goods being commercialised under changed conditions is particularly virulent with regard to pharmaceutical products which have been

---

149 ECJ Case C-244/00, *van Doren v. lifestyle sportwear* ('Stüssy'), [2003] ECR I-3051.
150 Ibid., Paragraphs 35, 36.

repackaged (and sometimes relabelled) so as to match the marketing conditions for such products in the importing country. In the leading decisions,[151] detailed guidelines were given as to the way in which such repackaging must proceed so as not to give rise to infringement claims by the trade mark proprietor. Pursuant to those principles, the trade mark proprietor is entitled to prevent the marketing of a product released on the market in another Member State which has been repackaged, and the trade mark reaffixed, by the importer, unless:

- it is established that the use of the trade mark right by the owner, having regard to the marketing system which he has adopted, will contribute to the artificial partitioning of the markets between Member States;
- it is shown that the repackaging cannot adversely affect the original condition of the product;
- the new packaging clearly states who repackaged the product and the name of the manufacturer;
- the presentation of the repackaged product is not such as to be liable to damage the reputation of the trade mark and of its owner; thus, the packaging must not be defective, of poor quality, or untidy; and
- the importer gives notice to the trade mark owner before the repackaged product is put on sale, and, on demand, supplies him with a specimen of the repackaged product.

Basically the same principles must be observed when a product is relabeled or rebranded for importation purposes.[152] The latter situation – rebranding – may occur when the same substance is sold under (slightly) different trade marks in diverse Member States, so that in order to be compatible, the imported products must also be branded accordingly. As the situation is not addressed by Article 7 (2) TMD – the provision requires that the goods must have been released on the market in the Community under 'that' trade mark – the permissibility of such acts is directly grounded on the provisions in the TFEU.

---

151 ECJ Case C-102/77, *Hoffman-La Roche* v. *Centrafarm*, [1978] ECR 1139; ECJ Joined Cases C-427/93, C-429/93 and C-436/93, *Bristol-Myers Squibb* v. *Paranova* and *Boehringer Sohn, Boehringer Ingelheim and Boehringer Ingelheim* v. *Paranova* and Bayer Aktiengesellschaft and *Bayer Danmark* v. *Paranova*, [1996] ECR I-3457, Paragraph 79; reaffirmed in ECJ Case C-348/04, *Boehringer Ingelheim* v. *Swingward and Dowelhurst*, [2007] ECR I-3391, Paragraph 21.

152 ECJ Cases C-349/95, *Loendersloot* v. *Ballantines* ('relabelling'), [1997] ECR 1-6227 and C-379/97, *Pharmacia & Upjohn SA* v. *Paranova A/S* ('rebranding'), [1999] ECR I-6927; Case C-588/08, *Portakabin* v. *Primakabin*, [2010] ECR I-06963.

Damage to reputation

As a matter of principle, exhaustion also means that legitimate resellers are free to use the mark in order to bring to the public's attention the further commercialisation of those goods.[153] An exception from that rule is made where use in advertising or selling announcements is such that it would seriously damage the reputation of the sign. The issue was addressed in *Dior* v. *Evora*.[154] The defendant in that case operates a chain of chemist stores which are not authorised dealers of Dior products. Nevertheless, the defendant offered in its stores a range of such products which had been obtained on the 'grey market'. The products were advertised in a manner customary to dealers in that market sector, i.e. on leaflets and billboards. There was no doubt in the proceedings that the products were genuine and the sales were legal as such; however, it was claimed by Dior that the advertisement did not suit the luxurious image of the products. The ECJ first stated that legitimate resellers must be free also to advertise the products. However:

> (43) The damage done to the reputation of a trade mark may, in principle, be a legitimate reason . . . allowing the proprietor to oppose further commercialization of goods which have been put on the market in the Community by him or with his consent . . . (45) As . . . concerns prestigious, luxury goods, the reseller must . . . endeavour to prevent his advertising from affecting the value of the trade mark by detracting from the allure and prestigious image of the goods in question and from their aura of luxury. (46) However, the fact that a reseller . . . uses for trade-marked goods the modes of advertising which are customary in his trade sector . . . does not constitute a legitimate reason . . . allowing the owner to oppose that advertising, unless it is established that . . . the use of the trade mark in the reseller's advertising seriously damages the reputation of the trade mark.

QUESTIONS

1 The principle of exhaustion and its exceptions are of particular relevance in the field of pharmaceutical products. Can you explain the economic background for that phenomenon?

2 The rule that a trade mark holder may oppose commercialisation of genuine goods under the trade mark in case of damage done to the mark's reputation was developed with a view to ensure that repackaged medicaments are not sold in untidy or 'sloppy' packages. Was it correct for the ECJ to equate that situation with the one at stake in *Dior* v. *Evora*, i.e.

---

153 ECJ Cases C-337/95, *Christian Dior* v. *Evora*, [1997] ECR I-6013, para 38; Case C-63/97, *BMW* v. *Deenik*, [1999] ECR I-905, Paragraph 48 and C-558/08, *Portakabin* v. *Primakabin*, [2010] ECR I-06963, Paragraph 77.
154 ECJ Case C-337/95, *Christian Dior* v. *Evora*, [1997] ECR I-6013, para 38.

when not the products or packages as such, but only the advertising is such that the reputation of the mark might be damaged? Can you think of examples when the damage inflicted, or threatened, to the reputation of a trade mark by way of advertising is actually so serious that it could be prohibited?

Acquiescence

Articles 9 TMD and 54 (1) CTMR encompass the principle that if a trade mark owner knowingly has tolerated the use of a registered, infringing mark for a period of five years, he may no longer oppose its use or apply for a declaration of invalidity of the other mark, unless the application of the younger mark was done in bad faith. This rule follows from general considerations of equity and fairness. Corresponding rules applied already before harmonisation as an element of substantive or procedural law in most EU countries.

Article 9 was addressed in the context of a lawsuit brought in the UK by Anheuser-Busch against Budějovický Budvar. The long-lasting conflict between the two breweries concerning the trade mark 'Budweiser' for beer had been settled in the UK by previous court decisions in the sense that both firms were concurrently entitled to use the trade mark, and accordingly, both had obtained a registration in 2000. One day before expiry of the five-year period prescribed in Article 9 TMD, Anheuser-Busch filed a claim for declaration of invalidity, arguing that because of the identity of the marks and the products they designated, protection must be absolute for the prior one of the two rights, and that in this case, Anheuser-Busch had the prior right because its application for registration had been filed earlier.[155] The Court of Appeal (England and Wales) referred to the ECJ *inter alia* the question whether acquiescence may occur in a situation when the holder of the prior right is not legally entitled to oppose the use of the younger sign, and whether the five-year period only commences after the younger sign has been registered. Both questions were denied by the ECJ:

> (45) [The] concept of 'acquiescence' must . . . be interpreted as meaning that the proprietor of an earlier trade mark cannot be held to have acquiesced in the . . . use, of which he has long been aware, by a third party of a later trade mark . . . if that proprietor was not in any position to oppose that use.

And:

---

155 ECJ Case C-482/09, *Anheuser-Busch v. Budějovický Budvar,* [2011] ECR I-0000.

(62) [r]egistration of the earlier trade mark in the Member State concerned does not constitute a prerequisite for the running of the period of limitation in consequence of acquiescence prescribed in Article 9 (1) of Directive 89/104.

Concerning the dispute at stake between the two breweries over the trade mark 'Budweiser', however, it was held that exceptionally, in spite of the absolute protection basically available in the case of identical marks being applied to identical products, this did not apply in this case, because consumers are well aware of the difference between the two beers, meaning that the essential function of guaranteeing origin is not affected by the concurrent use.

? QUESTIONS

1 Do you agree to the statement made above that acquiescence follows from general concepts of equity and fairness? Does that mean that it applies to other IP rights as well?
2 The CTMR and TMD set a maximum term in the sense that acquiescence must be assumed if the right-holder has remained passive for (more than) five years. Does it also follow that acquiescence cannot be assumed at an earlier point in time? Try to find arguments for and against that proposition!

The use requirement

Overview

The Preamble to the CTMR sets out in Recital (10) that:

> There is no justification for protecting Community trade marks or, as against them, any trade mark which has been registered before them, except where the trade marks are actually used.

The policy principle reflected in that statement forms the basis of the use requirement which is enshrined in Articles 10, 11 TMD and Article 15 CTMR. Pursuant to those provisions, trade marks lose their legal validity and may no longer be enforced vis-à-vis infringing signs, if no genuine use has been made of them during a consecutive period of 5 years (any time) after registration. It is sufficient for the requirement of use if the mark is used by a licensee (Articles 10 (3) TMD and 15 (3) CTMR), or for export purposes only (Articles 10 (2) (b) TMD, 15 (2) (b) CTMR). Furthermore, the use requirement may be satisfied by use of the mark in a different form from that which has been registered, provided that such changes do not alter the distinctive character of the mark.

'Genuineness' of use

In the leading case decided by the ECJ (*Ansul*),[156] the owner of the Benelux trade mark 'Minimax' had stopped selling the fire extinguishers for which the mark had been registered, and had used the mark only in connection with repair services and sales of spare parts for those products. A German company using the same mark in Germany and wanting to expand its business to the Benelux countries claimed for revocation on the ground of non-use (Article 12 (1) TMD). In response to the question whether the use made of 'Minimax' could possibly be genuine, the ECJ pointed out that:

> (38) . . . there is 'genuine use' of a trade mark where the mark is used in accordance with its essential function . . . When assessing whether use of the trade mark is genuine, regard must be had to all the facts and circumstances relevant to establishing whether the commercial exploitation of the mark is real, particularly whether such use is viewed as warranted in the economic sector concerned to maintain or create a share in the market for the goods or services protected by the mark, the nature of the goods or services at issue, the characteristics of the market and the scale and frequency of use of the mark. The fact that a mark that is not used for goods newly available on the market but for goods that were sold in the past does not mean that its use is not genuine, if the proprietor makes actual use of the same mark for component parts that are integral to the make-up or structure of such goods, or for goods or services directly connected with the goods previously sold and intended to meet the needs of customers of those goods.

The judgment was confirmed in subsequent case law.[157]

In *Silberquelle* v. *Maselli*,[158] the ECJ held that the use of a mark on goods distributed 'free', as promotional items, with other, unrelated goods does not amount to genuine use, because:

> (21) those items are not distributed in any way with the aim of penetrating the market for goods in the same class. In those circumstances, affixing the mark to

---

156 ECJ Case C-40/01, *Ansul BV* v. *Ajax Brandbeveiliging BV*, [2003] ECR I-2439.

157 ECJ Case C-259/02, *La Mer Technology Inc.* v. *Laboratoires Goemar SA*, [2004] ECR I-1159, Paragraph 27; for genuine use of CTMs (apart from the territorial aspect addressed below) see *e.g.* ECJ Case C-416/04 P, *The Sunrider Corp* v. *OHIM*, [2006] ECR I-04237.

158 ECJ Case C-495/07, *Silberquelle GmbH* v. *Maselli-Strickmode GmbH*, [2009] ECR I-137.

those items does not contribute to creating an outlet for those items or to distinguishing, in the interest of the customer, those items from the goods of other undertakings.

On the other hand, the ECJ declared in *Verein Radetzky-Orden*[159] that services provided for free by charitable institutions may satisfy the use requirement, because those associations:

(21) cannot be accused of not making actual use of those marks when in fact they use them for those goods or services.

However, it remains for the national court to verify whether the requirements for genuine use are actually fulfilled.

Genuine use of CTMs: territorial extent

Simultaneously with the enactment of the CTMR, the Council and the Commission issued a Joint Statement:

The Council and the Commission consider that use which is genuine within the meaning of Article 15 *in one country* constitutes genuine use in the Community. (Joint Statement of 20 December 1993; emphasis added)

The validity of the Joint Statement was evaluated critically e.g. in a decision by the Benelux Intellectual Property Office (BOIP). *Inter alia*, it is pointed out that:

[s]ince the establishment of the Community Trade Mark Regulation the Community has grown steadily to 27 Member States and further expansion is imminent. The actual and economic context has changed dramatically as a result. In a territory (currently) covering more than four million square kilometres and a (current) population of almost 500 million people, use in one member state only may essentially boil down to local use only. In the Office's opinion, such use is not acceptable in order to justify such an extensive exclusive right . . . [160]

Protection was therefore denied in opposition proceedings against registration of a Benelux trade mark based on a CTM which had only been used in

159 ECJ Case C-442/07, *Verein Radetzky-Orden v. Bundesvereinigung Kameradschaft Feldmarschall Radetzky*, [2008] ECR I-09223.
160 BOIP Decision of 15 January 2010, No. 2004448, *Leno Merken B.V. v. ONEL Trademarks*; [unofficial translation], Paragraph 34.

the Netherlands. Appeal was filed against the decision, and the issue was referred by the appeal court to the ECJ.[161]

Reasons for non-use

Non-use of a mark does not lead to invalidation where the owner can invoke proper reasons. The issue was raised in a conflict concerning a trade mark ('Chef de cuisine') intended for ready-made meals to be sold in the proprietor's supermarkets. As justification for non-use, the proprietor referred to the bureaucratic obstacles he had to face in connection with the permission to establish his supermarkets in the country of intended use. As a guideline for interpretation the ECJ points to Article 19 (1) TRIPS according to which 'circumstances arising independently of the will of the owner of the trade mark which constitute an obstacle to the use of the trade mark are to be recognised as valid reasons for non-use' (Paragraph 49). With regard to the actual case, it is then concluded that:

> (52) . . . [I]t does not suffice that 'bureaucratic obstacles' . . . are beyond the control the trade mark proprietor, since those obstacles must, moreover, have a direct relationship with the mark . . . (53) [H]owever, . . . the obstacle concerned need not necessarily make the use of the trade mark impossible in order to be regarded as having a sufficiently direct relationship with the trade mark, since that may also be the case where it makes its use unreasonable. If an obstacle is such as to jeopardise seriously the appropriate use of the mark, its proprietor cannot reasonably be required to use it none the less. Thus, for example, the proprietor of a trade mark cannot reasonably be required to sell its goods in the sales outlets of its competitors . . . (54) It follows that only obstacles having a sufficiently direct relationship with a trade mark making its use impossible or unreasonable, and which arise independently of the will of the proprietor of that mark, may be described as 'proper reasons for non-use' of that mark.

 · QUESTIONS

1 Do you think that the way in which the use requirement is regulated in EU trade mark law actually lives up to the policy objective reflected in Recital 10 of the CTMR (cited above)?
2 How do you evaluate the BOIP's position regarding genuine use of CTMs vis-à-vis the Joint Statement? In view of previous case law of the ECJ, what would you expect its position to be?

---

161 ECJ Case C-149/10, *Leno Merken v. BOIP* (pending).

3 It has been suggested that the current regulation of the use requirement should be complemented by an obligation for trade mark holders to file a 'statement of use' either after five years following registration, or at the time when a request for renewal is filed. On the other hand, it has been questioned whether such a regulation would make sense under a cost/benefit perspective. What is your opinion? What does the result depend on?

4.5 Loss of rights

Overview

Where trade mark rights are acquired through registration, they usually cease when the mark is surrendered by way of declaration vis-à-vis the trade mark office (for CTMs, cf. Article 50 CTMR) or due to non-prolongation of the right when the registration term has lapsed (usually after 10 years from registration, cf. Article 46 CTMR). In addition, trade marks may also be cancelled subsequent to having been declared invalid or revoked.

The grounds for revocation and invalidation are the same under the CTMR and the TMD; however, this only relates to the substantive scope and contents of those grounds, and not to the proceedings for invoking those grounds.

Revocation

Trade marks are liable to revocation if they:

- have not been put to genuine use in the Community or in the Member State where the mark is protected (Articles 12 (1) TMD, 51 (1) (a) CTMR);
- if the trade mark, in consequence of acts or activities of the proprietor, has become generic, (Articles 12 (2) (a) TMD, 51 (1) (b) CTMR); or
- if in consequence of the use by the proprietor or with his consent, the trade mark is liable to mislead the public (Articles 12 (2) (b) TMD, 51 (c) CTMR).

While the legal consequences of non-use are rather frequently addressed in case law (see above, section 4.4.3.2), the two other grounds for revocation only seldom become topical in decisions by Community Courts.

The requirements for assessing whether a trade mark has become generic were discussed in *Björnekulla* v. *Procordia*.[162] The case turned on the question of whether the term 'Bostongurka' had become a common name in Sweden for chopped pickled gherkins. Both parties had produced evidence sustaining their positions: while market research surveys among consumers appeared to support the contention that the term had become generic, surveys among leading operators in the grocery, mass catering and food stall sectors showed that the term was still perceived as a trade mark indicating products of a specific commercial origin. In response to the question which of the two circles was relevant for determining whether the mark is liable to revocation, the ECJ stated that, as usual, the answer had to be given in the light of the essential trade mark function:

> (23) If the function of the trade mark as an indication of origin is of primary importance to the consumer or end user, it is also relevant to intermediaries who deal with the product commercially . . . (24) In general, the perception of consumers or end users will play a decisive role. The whole aim of the commercialisation process is the purchase of the product by those persons . . . (25) Accordingly, the relevant classes of persons comprise principally consumers and end users. However, depending on the features of the product market concerned, the influence of intermediaries on decisions to purchase, and thus their perception of the trade mark, must also be taken into consideration. (26) The answer to the question referred must therefore be that Article 12 (2) (a) [TMD] should be interpreted as meaning that in cases where intermediaries participate in the distribution to the consumer or the end user of a product which is the subject of a registered trade mark, the relevant classes of persons whose views fall to be taken into account in determining whether that trade mark has become the common name in the trade for the product in question comprise all consumers and end users and, depending on the features of the market concerned, all those in the trade who deal with that product commercially.

Revocation of a trade mark on the grounds that it has become misleading due to the use made by the proprietor was addressed in *Emanuel* v. *Continental Shelf*.[163] As related above (p. 188), the ECJ had to consider whether a trade mark consisting of the personal name of a well-known designer of wedding dresses had become deceptive due to the fact that the designer herself no longer took part in the business. The question was denied, stating that the primary message conveyed by the mark – that the firm owning it was responsible for the quality of the products offered – remained unaffected,

---

162 ECJ Case C-371/02, *Björnekulla Fruktindustrier v. Procordia*, [2004] ECR I-5791.
163 ECJ Case C-259/04, *Emanuel v. Continental Shelf*, [2006] ECR I-3089.

and that, even if according to the findings of the national court the new proprietor should have acted fraudulently by making consumers believe that the designer was still involved in the production, those practices would not mean that the trade mark itself has become deceptive.[164]

Invalidation

Grounds for invalidation

The grounds for invalidity of trade marks are basically the same as the grounds forming – absolute or relative – grounds for refusal. In the TMD, those grounds are listed in Articles 3 and 4. In the CTMR, the pertinent provisions, Articles 52 and 53, also make reference primarily to the grounds for refusal set out in Articles 7 and 8. However, in addition to that, Article 52 CTMR lists application in bad faith as further ground for invalidity. Furthermore, Article 53 stipulates that in addition to the different categories of distinctive signs listed as relative grounds for refusal in Article 8 CTMR, claims for invalidation can also be based on the right to a name,[165] a personal portrayal, a copyright or an industrial property right.

'Curing' of initial invalidity for certain absolute grounds

Under the CTMR and the TMD alike, trade marks cannot be cancelled for the absolute grounds listed in Articles 7 (1) (b)–(d) CTMR or 3 (1) (b)–(d) TMD if they have *acquired distinctiveness* after registration by use in trade, in the meaning of Articles 7 (3) CTMR and 3 (3) TMD.

Bad faith

Bad faith as grounds for invalidation of a CTM was addressed in the 'Goldhase' decision (*Lindt & Sprüngli* v. *Hauswirth*).[166] The plaintiff in the main case had registered as a CTM the three-dimensional shape of a sitting chocolate Easter Bunny in golden wrapping. The defendant counter-claimed for invalidation, arguing that the plaintiff at the time of application had known that the defendant used, and held a valuable interest position ('wertvoller Besitzstand'), in a similar shape for his own products. The ECJ held that:

---

164 Ibid., Paragraph 50.
165 For a conflict between a CTM application and a personal name see ECJ Case C-263/09 P, *Edwin* v. *OHIM* ('Fiorucci'), [2011] ECR I-0000.
166 ECJ Case C-529/07, *Lindt & Sprüngli AG* v. *Hauswirth*, [2008] ECR I-08823.

(40) [T]he fact that the applicant knows or must know that a third party has long been using . . . an identical or similar sign for an identical or similar product capable of being confused with the sign for which registration is sought is not sufficient, in itself, to permit the conclusion that the applicant was acting in bad faith . . . [However] (43) the intention to prevent a third party from marketing a product may . . . be an element of bad faith on the part of the applicant. (44) That is in particular the case when it becomes apparent, subsequently, that the applicant applied for registration of a sign as a Community trade mark without intending to use it, his sole objective being to prevent a third party from entering the market. . . . [However, even if the applicant knows about use of the sign by others,] (48) . . . the applicant's registration of the sign may be in pursuit of a legitimate objective . . . [for instance if] . . . (49) the applicant knows . . . that a third party . . . is trying to take advantage of that sign by copying its presentation, and the applicant seeks to register the sign with a view to preventing use of that presentation. (50) Moreover . . . [i]n a case where the sign for which registration is sought consists of the entire shape and presentation of a product, the fact that the applicant is acting in bad faith might more readily be established where the competitors' freedom to choose the shape of a product and its presentation is restricted by technical or commercial factors, so that the trade mark proprietor is able to prevent his competitors not merely from using an identical or similar sign, but also from marketing comparable products. (51) Furthermore . . . consideration may be given to the extent of the reputation enjoyed by a sign at the time when the application for its registration as a Community trade mark is filed. (52) The extent of that reputation might justify the applicant's interest in ensuring a wider legal protection for his sign.

Procedural aspects of invalidation

Under the CTMR, claims for revocation or invalidity may be filed with OHIM (Article 56 CTMR) or, by way of counterclaim, in infringement proceedings before the Community courts (Article 96 (d) in conjunction with Article 100 TMD). Counterclaims filed in infringement proceedings have to be rejected if a decision taken by OHIM relating to the same subject matter and cause of action and involving the same parties has already become final (Article 100 (2) CTMR). Vice versa, an application for revocation or invalidity filed with OHIM shall be declared inadmissible if an application relating to the same subject matter and cause of action and involving the same parties has been adjudicated by a court in a Member State and has already become final (Article 56 (3) CTMR).

1 The 'Goldhase' decision concerned a special case of (potential) bad faith, when an applicant for a CTM (arguably) tries to oust competitors from a market where they have been active for a prolonged period. However, this is usually not considered as the main example for a situation when a registration is taken out in bad faith. Can you think of other constellations? How would they have to be solved?

2 Think back to the Opel case, where Opel tried to enjoin a maker of toy cars from using the Opel mark on the cars. Could there be a certain parallel with 'Goldhase'?

4.6 Trade marks as objects of property

While the provisions in the TMD and the CTMR are largely congruent with regard to requirements and scope of protection, the CTMR holds more extensive regulations with regard to trade marks as objects of property (Title II Section 4, Articles 16 to 23 CTMR).

The only common provisions in the CTMR and the TMD with regard to those aspects concern certain basic rules addressing licences, which are found in Articles 8 TMD and 22 CTMR respectively. According to those provisions, licenses can be exclusive or non-exclusive, and can be granted for all or part of the goods for which a mark is registered, and for the whole or part of the territory for which it is protected (Articles 8 (1) TMD, 22 (1) CTMR). Furthermore, it is regulated both with regard to national marks and CTMs that claims for infringement may be raised against a licensee who violates certain fundamental elements of the license contract, such as duration, form of use, territory, or quality of the goods or services (Articles 8 (2) TMD, 22 (2) CTMR).

In addition to that, the CTMR addresses the necessity for the licensee to obtain the consent of the proprietor to instigate infringement proceedings, as well as the exceptions from that rule (Article 22). Further provisions deal with transfer (Article 17), rights *in rem* (Article 19), and levy of execution regarding CTMs as well as their involvement in insolvency proceedings (Articles 20, 21). All acts involving the CTM as an object of property are recorded in the CTM register, if that is requested by one of the parties. While registration is only optional, it is important in practice because licenses, rights *in rem* and transfers are only effective against third parties if they have been recorded, unless the third party was aware of the disposition (Article 23). In the case of transfers, registration of the new owner is denied by OHIM if it is obvious from the documents that it leads to deception of the public (Article 17 (4) CTMR).

Case law dealing with those provisions is scarce.[167] However, some light is shed on the possibility to claim trade mark infringement by a licensee violating the stipulations of the contract with regard to the quality of goods. The issue was addressed in *Copad* v. *Dior*,[168] concerning a selective distribution network set up for luxury goods such as perfumes. According to the terms of the licence contract, it was agreed between the parties that the goods should be displayed in sales outlets in a manner that enhances their value and contributes to the reputation of the goods at issue, thereby sustaining the aura of luxury surrounding them. Under those circumstances, the ECJ found that:

> (30) . . . it is conceivable that the sale of luxury goods by the licensee to third parties that are not part of the selective distribution network might affect the quality itself of those goods, so that, in such circumstances, a contractual provision prohibiting such sale must be considered to be falling within the scope of Article 8 (2) [TMD] . . . (32) In this respect, it is important to take into consideration, in particular, first, the nature of the luxury goods bearing the trade mark, the volumes sold and whether the licensee sells the goods to discount stores that are not part of the selective distribution network regularly or only occasionally and, secondly, the nature of the goods normally marketed by those discount stores, and the marketing methods normally used in that sector of activity.

Consequently, the sales on the grey market were considered not only as violation of the license contract, but constituted trade mark infringement.

? QUESTIONS.

1 In contrast to the situation under previous law in some Member States, European trade mark legislation does not impose a general obligation on trade mark holders granting licenses to monitor the quality of the goods produced by the licensee lest the trade mark should become invalid ('abandonment' under US law). How do you evaluate the lack of a binding provision in that regard – does it create an actual risk for consumers?
2 Does the provision that a mark will be liable to invalidation if it becomes deceptive due to the way in which it is used by the proprietor or which his

---

167 See, however, on the question whether a trade mark has become deceptive in consequence of transfer ECJ Case C-259/04, *Emanuel* v. *Continental Shelf*, [2006] ECR I-3089 (this chapter, section 4.3.2.4.2).
168 ECJ Case C-59/08, *Copad* v. *Dior*, [2009] ECR I-3421.

consent constitutes a sufficient substitute for such a rule (if a substitute should be needed)?

3 Which other legal instruments could apply in order to safeguard the interests of consumers?

5

Copyright

5.1 Introduction

History and objectives

Out of all immaterial goods, copyright protects original works in the field of literature and the arts. Traditionally, these include writings, musical compositions and works of visual arts as well as other creations of the mind. In addition, performing artists and the investment of phonogram and film producers as well as broadcasting organisations are generally protected by so-called related or neighbouring rights. Together, copyright in the narrow sense and related rights form copyright in the broad sense (although it should be noted that not all national laws make a marked distinction in this respect). Moreover, it is worth noting that in later years some functional and investment intensive objects of protection such as computer programs and databases also have found their way into copyright. Contrary to protection under patent law and mostly under trade mark law, which require registration, copyright comes into existence without any formalities. Like the term of other IP rights, the term of copyright protection is also limited, but with an international minimum of life plus 50 years and in the EU 70 years after the death of the author, it is comparatively long. The terms of related rights are mostly shorter (70, 50 or 25 years) than the term of protection for copyright in the narrow sense, and they are mostly calculated from the date of first publication or public communication of the object protected.

Initially, the rationale for copyright protection consisted of protecting the investment made by publishers in the printing of books. Later, the focus shifted to the author. Somewhat simplified, one line of arguments sees the work as an emanation of the personality of its author, which justifies both moral and economic rights. Following the property justification of John Locke, another line of arguments regards the work as the fruit of the labour of its author, which justifies the adjudication of the proceeds generated by the exploitation of the work to its author. Although it is hard to separate both rationales underlying copyright protection, it can be said that the first rationale (the so-called *droit d'auteur* approach) prevails in most continental European countries, and in particular in France and Germany, whereas the second rationale (the so-called copyright approach) prevails in most countries which have a common law tradition, and in Europe in particular in the United Kingdom and Ireland. Of course, apart from the legal protection granted to performing artists, which also addresses both personal and economic concerns, the rationale for protection granted by related rights to the investment made against misappropriation is purely economic in nature. In view of the increasing importance of copyright in the marketplace and for the economy at large, copyright law is increasingly seen as a legal instrument to further innovation and to regulate competition.

In spite of the numerous differences that may exist amongst national copyright legislations in detail and which are deeply rooted in each country's legal system and historical development, today's national copyright laws are quite similar in structure. In general, they contain a definition of protected subject matter (works; related subject matter, such as performances, phonograms, broadcasts, films); the condition for protection (originality or the author's own intellectual creation); rules on first ownership (the author or the holder of a related right) and subsequent transfers of title; moral rights and exclusive economic rights as well as limitations and exceptions thereto; rules on copyright contracts which define the types of rights' transfers possible (assignment, transfer of either copyright as such or of use rights) and which eventually lay down certain rules for the interpretation of copyright contracts; provisions on the term of protection, and remedies against infringement, including anti-circumvention protection. Some national laws also contain rules regarding the protection of foreigners as well as transition provisions. However, due to the fact that copyright comes into existence merely by creating a copyrightable work (the same applies to related rights which come into existence with the fixation of a performance or the production of the object of related rights protection), copyright legislation generally does not contain any rules on registration and the administration of the registration process. It should be noted, however, that under some national laws, registration of contractual assignments or licenses may be required in order to make the assignment or licence effective not only against the assignee or licensee, but also against third parties.

Although all these features can be found in IP legislation in general, attention has to be drawn to two particularities of copyright laws. Firstly, it should be noted in this respect that the limitations/exceptions to the exclusive rights play a much greater role in copyright law than in any other IP law. In addition, some but not all countries have introduced claims for remuneration in cases in which no authorisation by the author is required but in which it seems justified that the author receives an adequate share of the proceeds of the exploitation of his work. Secondly, as answer to the numerous mass transactions by which copyright licensing is characterised and which makes individual licensing difficult if not impossible, collecting societies have formed in many countries (though not as regards all types of works). Typically, collecting societies grant users blanket licences for the repertoire of the works for which the authors have transferred their rights to the collecting societies. In addition, collecting societies are generally involved in collecting the remuneration paid in countries whose legislation provides for claims for remuneration.

Copyright law in Europe: overview

Similar to patent and trade mark law it took some time before copyright came into contact with the provisions of the EEC Treaty of 1957. The main reason why copyright, which protects literary and artistic works, came into the focus of EU law only at a relatively late stage probably is that due to language barriers and Member States' differing cultural traditions trans-border exploitation of copyrighted works was for a long time not of major economic importance. This, however, changed with the advent both of new subject matter such as computer programs and databases, which in general can be used irrespective of differences in language and culture on the one hand, and of new communication technologies such as cable, satellite and, most notably, the internet on the other.

Like patents and trade marks, copyright is firmly based on the principle of territoriality.[1] This means that national rules govern copyrighted subject matter within the territory of a given Member State. It also means that – absent a community-wide copyright – one and the same work is protected by different laws in each of the EU Member States. Consequently, quite like in patent and in trade mark law, the first conflict that had to be solved under the EEC Treaty was the dichotomy between the territoriality of national copyright and the principle of freedom of movement of goods (now Article 34 TFEU). The issue was whether or not the author or right-holder of a copyrighted work can invoke his national copyright law in one of the EU Member

---

1 For discussion see Chapter 1, section 1.3.2.1.

States in order to prevent copyrighted works that were legally put onto the market in another Member State from being re-imported or freely circulating within the EU. As already discussed in Chapter 2,[2] beginning in 1971 the ECJ held that the effects of the principle of territoriality should not enable the author or right-holder to partition the common market for copyrighted works. Technically speaking, in order to have the principle of free movement of goods prevail the ECJ developed the concept of *Community-wide exhaustion* of the national distribution rights. Exhaustion takes place if the original or a copy of a copyrighted work has been put onto the market within one of the Member States by the right-holder or with his consent.[3] However, the ECJ also held that exhaustion only applies to the distribution right and hence to physical copies of copyrighted works, whereas no exhaustion takes place as regards the non-physical public communication of copyrighted works.[4]

As already discussed in Chapter 2, in the late 1980s, however, the ECJ made clear that the freedom of movement of goods does *not* prevail in cases in which the importation of copyrighted goods was prevented on the basis of differences between Member States' national copyright legislation regarding the conditions, scope or duration of protection.[5] The effect of these decisions was that the Commission proposed and the Council and Parliament adopted a series of Directives[6] the purpose of which was exactly to harmonise differences that might exist or arise between Member States' national copyright legislation, and to avoid distortions of competition within the single market. It is this piecemeal harmonisation which distinguishes the harmonisation of copyright within the EU from the harmonisation of both patent and trade mark law.[7] In addition, since copyright does not require any formalities, contrary to patent and trade mark law, there is no need to create any mechanism for applications by foreign applicants nor for harmonising such procedures. As stated in the initial policy paper, the 1988 Green Paper on copyright and the challenge of technology, 'Community legislation should be restricted to what is needed to carry out the tasks of the Community. Many

---

2 Chapter 2, section 2.2.1 in general, and, as regards copyright in particular, section 2.2.1.3.2.
3 ECJ Case 78/70, *Deutsche Grammophon v. Metro SB*, [1971] ECR 487. See also ECJ Joined Cases C-55/80 and C-57/80, *Musik-Vertrieb Membran* and *K-Tel International v. GEMA*, [1981] ECR 147.
4 ECJ Case 62/79, *Coditel v. Ciné Vog Films*, [1980] ECR 881. For further development of case law regarding exhaustion in the field of copyright see in this chapter, section 5.3.2.6.
5 ECJ Cases C-158/86, *Warner Brothers v. Christiansen*, [1988] ECR 2605, and Case C-341/87, *EMI Electrola v. Patricia*, [1989] ECR 79. For the facts of these cases and additional discussion see Chapter 2, section 2.2.1.3.
6 For explanation of the instrument of the 'Directive' as opposed to a 'Regulation', see Chapter 2, sections 2.3.1.2 and 3.
7 See Chapter 3 section 3.1.2 and 3.4.1.2.

issues of copyright law do not need to be subject of action at Community level.'[8]

Consequently, the approach chosen in copyright within the EU so far did not lead to full harmonisation. Of course, to the extent an issue is covered by an existing Directive, it is to be regarded as an autonomous concept of European Union law, which must be interpreted in a uniform manner throughout the territory of the European Union. Likewise, unless the Directive expressly provides otherwise, harmonisation by way of a Directive both fixes a minimum and a maximum of protection. In other words, once a particular issue has been harmonised, Member States are no longer free to grant either less or more protection than the one defined in the Directive.

In spite of this, there is a lack of harmonisation in at least two respects. First, many areas – most notably moral rights, limitations and exceptions including private copying, certain related rights as well as copyright contract law – remain un-harmonised. Second, even as regards the areas that have been harmonised by the EU copyright Directives, national laws may differ from each other, either because Member States have made different use of implementation options provided for by the Directives themselves, or because the statutory language implementing the Directives varies depending on each Member States' national legislative language tradition.

Moreover, since harmonisation of national laws leaves untouched the principle of territoriality, clearance of rights by providers of transnational content services can be extremely difficult and costly. In some instances, the Commission tried to overcome this situation. Thus, Satellite Directive 93/83/EEC declared the law of only one Member State relevant regarding trans-border satellite broadcasting. With Recommendation 2005/737/EC the Commission directly addressed the market players in order to facilitate multi-territorial online music services over the internet by way of self-regulation of the parties involved. This problem has been addressed again by the Commission in 2012 in its proposal for a Directive on collective management of copyright and related rights and multi-territorial licensing of rights in musical works for online uses in the internal market (COM(2012) 372 final).

However, although the present number of 27 Member States makes it rather difficult to compromise for new legislative measures in the area of copyright

---

8 'Copyright and the challenge of technology – copyright issues requiring immediate action', COM/88/172 of 07.06.1988, Paragraph 1.4.9. See also COM/90/584 of 17.01.1991, 'Follow-up to the Green Paper 1991 – Working Programme of the Commission in the field of copyright and neighbouring rights'.

and although since Lisbon Article 118 TFEU expressly empowers the Council and the European Parliament to create community IP rights, so far no community copyright has been created on the basis of Article 118 TFEU. Contrary to the Community rights in existence (trade marks, designs, plant varieties, and, as planned, also patents), copyright within the EU still is not a unitary right, but only a bundle of national laws.

From this it follows that currently it is mostly the ECJ which contributes to the further harmonisation of Member States' national copyright laws within the EU by way of interpreting the existing Directives. However, the number of copyright cases decided by the ECJ does not reach in any way the number of trade mark cases. But the recent rise in the number of copyright cases referred to the ECJ by national courts can certainly be expected to continue in the years to come.

5.2 Harmonisation of national copyright laws

Harmonisation strategy

Internal market concerns

In its *Patricia* decision of 1989, the ECJ referred to '*the present state of Community law*, which is characterised by a lack of harmonisation or approximation of legislation governing the protection of literary and artistic property'.[9] This was interpreted as a hint to the Community legislature to change the present state of Community law by way of harmonisation of Member States' national copyright laws, to the extent the Community legislature wished to do away with the negative consequences disparities in national laws had on the free movement of goods and services. Indeed, following the *Warner Brother* and *Patricia* decisions of the ECJ, the Commission became active in the field of copyright. The process has been described by *Dreier/Hugenholtz*, Concise European Copyright Law, 2006, p. 2, as follows:

> *Harmonizing strategy.* On the basis of several policy papers (Green Paper on Copyright and the Challenge of Technology, 1988;[10] Working Programme of the Commission in the Field of Copyright and Neighbouring Rights, 1992; Green Paper on Copyright and Related Rights in the Information Society, 1995, and Follow-Up to the Green Paper on Copyright and Related Rights in the

---

9 ECJ Case C-341/87, *EMI Electrola* v. *Patricia*, [1989] ECR 79, Paragraph 11 (emphasis added). For more details on this case see Chapter 2, section 2.2.1.3.2.3.
10 Above, footnote 8.

Information Society, 1996), the EU has reacted to this line of case law and harmonised Member States' national copyright laws by way of several Directives. Apart from harmonising the protection for certain subject matter – notably computer programs and databases – the aim was to remove existing differences which adversely affected the functioning of the single market to a substantial degree, and to prevent new differences from arising. At the same time, a high level of protection should be maintained in order to protect investment and encourage innovation.

Existing copyright Directives. Up until now, the EU has enacted the following seven copyright Directives: Computer Programs Directive; Rental Right Directive; Term Directive; Satellite and Cable Directive; Database Directive; Information Society Directive; and Resale Right Directive. In addition, the Enforcement Directive, which deals with the enforcement of intellectual property rights in general, also covers the enforcement of copyrights.

Other economic and political concerns

Of course, the harmonising activity in the area of copyright was not only driven by mere internal market concerns. Several additional factors also played a role, both economic and political. First of all, in the mid-1980s, the growing economic importance of the copyright industries for national economies and hence growth, innovation and development was recognised. In 1994, this led to the adoption of the Agreement on Trade-Related Aspects of Intellectual Property Rights (TRIPS) as an integral part of the WTO Agreement. In 1996, the two WIPO Treaties (WIPO Copyright Treaty, WCT; WIPO Performances and Phonograms Treaty, WPPT) followed suit. In essence, developed countries undertook to effectively protect, on a worldwide scale, but also within the EU, their competitive industries against misappropriation and free-riding. This rationale is well formulated in Recital 4 of the Information Society Directive 2001/29/EC:

> A harmonised legal framework on copyright and related rights, through increased legal certainty and while providing for a high level of protection of intellectual property, will foster substantial investment in creativity and innovation, including network infrastructure, and lead in turn to growth and increased competitiveness of European industry, both in the area of content provision and information technology and more generally across a wide range of industrial and cultural sectors. This will safeguard employment and encourage new job creation.[11]

---

11 See also in greater detail the Report commissioned by the EU Commission 'The contribution of copyright and related rights to the European economy based on data from the year 2000' of 20 October 2003; ec.europa.eu/internal_market/copyright/docs/studies/etd2002b53001e34_en.pdf.

At the same time, this approach can be seen as the driving force behind the continuing trend towards ever stronger ('upward') protection. This trend was also supported by the fact that some Member States referred to the legal protection of copyright as 'property' under their national Constitution and made the argument that for constitutional reasons vested rights could not be reduced with retroactive effect.

In economic terms, however, this rationale seems highly questionable. If no protection allows for too much free-riding, total protection, inversely, stifles competition. By definition, the optimum of legal protection must lie somewhere in the middle. Nevertheless, more often than not effective lobbying for a particular group of right-holders' interests during the process of copyright harmonisation has resulted in an increase in the level of protection.

Copyright and culture

Moreover, the economic underpinning of the EU-harmonisation concept in the field of copyright has somewhat obscured the fact that copyrighted works are not merely 'goods', but that they – and the creativity which copyright is supposed to strengthen – likewise belong to the realm of culture. However, due to the mandate of the EEC as an economic institution, cultural concerns were – and could only be – indirectly addressed by way of economic legislation. As phrased in para 1.4.4 of the 1988 Green Paper on Copyright and the Challenge of Technology:

> Intellectual and artistic creativity is a precious asset, the source of Europe's cultural identity and of that of each individual State. It is a vital source of economic wealth and of European influence throughout the world. This creativity needs to be protected; it needs to be given a higher status and it needs to be stimulated.[12]

Accordingly, up until now, the main responsibility for copyright within the Commission has always remained with DG Internal Market.[13] This is irrespective of the fact that other DGs became involved as well, in particular DG Competition and – after the advent of the internet – the DG responsible for the information society.

This has not changed under the 'culture clause' of what is now Article 167 (1) TFEU, according to which:

---

12 Above, footnote 8.
13 See ec.europa.eu/internal_market/copyright/index_en.htm.

> [t]he Union shall contribute to the flowering of the cultures of the Member States, while respecting their national and regional diversity and at the same time bringing the common cultural heritage to the fore

nor after the EU has signed the UNESCO Universal Declaration on Cultural Diversity of November 2, 2001.[14] Rather, since the 'culture-clause' is not on equal footing with the competency norms of securing the internal market (Articles 4 (2) (a) and 26 TFEU), the creation of an internal market on the one hand, and the preservation of each Member State's cultural tradition on the other hand, may well conflict with each other. Also, harmonising the rules which govern a unified economic market often have as their effect to level off cultural differences. Up until now it seems rather unclear how the dual character of copyrighted works as both goods or services and cultural artefacts and practices and the two corresponding objectives can be reconciled.

 QUESTIONS

1　In your opinion, was the process of harmonising copyright within the EU driven more by internal market concerns or the general international trend of developed countries to grant strong IP protection for their IP industries?

2　Are you aware of any examples where the harmonisation process in copyright resulted in reducing legal protection that was granted before?

3　In your country, would the argument be valid that the vested scope of copyright once granted could not be reduced for constitutional reasons? In this regard, what is the effect of Article 17 (2) of the Charter of Fundamental Rights of the European Union, according to which '[i]ntellectual property shall be protected'?

4　The economic analysis of law has also focused on both the effects of existing and of ideal future IP legislation. In your opinion, what factors other than the economic value of IP rights for the right-holders would have to be taken into consideration? What about, e.g., transaction cost of licensing, or overall social welfare regarding both licensing revenue and access cost?

5　Can you think of a practical example, where the economic rationale of the functioning of the internal markets contradicts the cultural aim of preserving the Member States' national cultural diversity?

14　See portal.unesco.org/en/ev.php-URL_ID=13179&URL_DO=DO_TOPIC&URL_SECTION=201. html.

The existing copyright Directives

There follows a brief description of each of the seven Directives which have been adopted so far. Although some of the Directives have been republished in a consolidated form, taking into account the changes which subsequent Directives have brought about, the Directives are presented here in chronological order. Apart from the text cited, reading the full legislative text and having a look at the Recitals of each of the Directives provides additional information. Please note that the case law by which the ECJ has subsequently interpreted the existing copyright Directives will be treated in a separate section.[15]

Directive 2009/24/EC on the legal protection of computer programs (originally published as 91/250/EEC): Computer Programs Directive[16]

Aim

In the 1980s it became apparent that computer programs constituted a new object the intellectual creation of which necessitated considerable personal and financial resources, but which could easily be copied at relatively low cost. In spite of the fact that computer programs are mostly functional in nature, copyright finally emerged as the IP right under which computer programs were granted exclusive protection. There were several reasons for this development. First, patent protection was not available at that time for computer programs under either US and European law.[17] Second, plans to adopt a *sui generis* protection for computer programs at the international level within WIPO had been abandoned in 1985. Third, as an IP right which does not require any formalities, copyright can easily be obtained. Hence, copyright proved to be a suitable protection scheme in particular as regards the interests of software developers who needed quick, easy to prove and potentially far-reaching exclusive legal protection against one-to-one copying and adaptations which competitors develop on the basis of their programs. Of course, from a right-holder's perspective, copyright protection also has its shortcomings: it only protects the expression of a program, but not the ideas underlying a program. However, although it can be argued that the protec-

---

15 See this chapter, section 5.2.5.

16 Council Directive 91/250/EEC of 14 May 1991 on the legal protection of computer programs, [1991] OJ L 122/42; republished as Directive 2009/24/EC of the European Parliament and of the Council of 23 April 2009 on the legal protection of computer programs, [2009] OJ L/16.

17 According to Article 52 (2) (c) and (3) EPC. Regarding the patentability of software-related inventions, however, see Chapter 3, section 3.4.2.

tion of a program's expression extends to some of the program's internal structure, copyright does not protect a computer program's functionalities which more often than not are its essential and economically valuable features. Finally, from the point of view of competitors, copyright protection which covers the life of the author plus 70 years after his death lasts far too long, keeping competitors away from entering the market with incremental program improvements.

After the US had opted for copyright as the main scheme of protection of computer programs – a choice that was retained in several bilateral trade agreements of the US with developing countries – the EU felt compelled to harmonise the legal framework for computer programs by way of copyright. Before the Directive was initially adopted in 1991, it was not clear whether all Member States would protect computer programs by copyright at all and, if so, under what conditions they would do so. The gap was particularly wide between Germany and the UK. Whereas the German threshold for copyright protection required rather high level creativity on the part of the programmer in order for a program to be protected by copyright, under British law, all programs enjoyed protection which were not copied and not banal. The reasons for enacting the Computer Program Directive are summarised in Recitals (2)–(6) of the Directive's codified version of 2009 as follows:[18]

(2) The development of computer programs requires the investment of considerable human, technical and financial resources while computer programs can be copied at a fraction of the cost needed to develop them independently.

(3) Computer programs are playing an increasingly important role in a broad range of industries and computer program technology can accordingly be considered as being of fundamental importance for the Community's industrial development.

(4) Certain differences in the legal protection of computer programs offered by the laws of the Member States have direct and negative effects on the functioning of the internal market as regards computer programs.

(5) Existing differences having such effects need to be removed and new ones prevented from arising, while differences not adversely affecting the functioning of the internal market to a substantial degree need not be removed or prevented from arising.

(6) The Community's legal framework on the protection of computer programs can accordingly in the first instance be limited to establishing that Member States should accord protection to computer programs under copyright law as literary

---

18 See also already the 1985 White Paper 'Completing the internal market', COM (85) 310 final, and the 1988 Green Paper 'Copyright and the challenge of technology' (above, footnote 8).

works and, further, to establishing who and what should be protected, the exclusive rights on which protected persons should be able to rely in order to authorise or prohibit certain acts and for how long the protection should apply.

Scope

The Directive contains provisions on the object of protection (Article 1 (1), (2)) without, however, defining the term computer program. However, as rephrased in Recital 7, 'the term "computer program" shall include programs in any form, including those which are incorporated into hardware. This term also includes preparatory design work leading to the development of a computer program provided that the nature of the preparatory work is such that a computer program can result from it at a later stage.' The manual, however, is an independent object of legal protection. The originality criterion defined in Article 1 (3) as 'the author's own intellectual creation' was intended to bridge the gap that existed prior to the Directive between the high German threshold (according to the *Collection Programm* decision of the German Federal Supreme Court,[19] only programs of far-above average creativity enjoyed copyright protection) and the low British standard (copyrightability of anything not copied and not banal). Even if Article 2 does not really harmonise authorship, according to Article 2 (3), unless otherwise provided by contract, the employer exclusively shall be entitled to exercise all economic rights in the program created by an employee in the execution of his duties or following the instructions given by his employer. Article 4 (1) lists the exclusive rights (which, since 1993, also include the rental of computer programs), Article 4 (2) reiterates the Community-wide exhaustion of the distribution right. Limitations benefitting legitimate users ('lawful acquirer') including the right to make a backup copy where necessary are contained in Article 5 (1) and (2). Articles 5 (3) ('line-monitoring') and 6 ('decompilation') have been inserted in order to serve the need for interoperability of different – and even competing – programs and devices. With regard to this issue the most extensive lobbying took place, focusing particularly on the extent to which copyright protection of computer programs should be limited to enable access to and use of code for the purposes of enabling the creation of new programs that can be used with existing ones (so–called 'interoperability'). Finally, Article 7 obliges Member States to provide for certain remedies in infringement cases, including an early form of anti-circumvention protection (Article 7 (1) (c)). It should be noted that while the latter provision was drafted well before the Enforcement Directive,

---

19 German Federal Supreme Court, Case I ZR 52/83 of 9 September 1985, Collection Program, English translation in 17 IIC 681 (1986).

the Enforcement Directive has left it intact (see Recital 16 of Directive 2004/48/EC).

The Directive was subsequently amended by the Council's Term Directive which repealed Article 8, replacing the term of copyright with the 70-year post mortem auctoris period. Other later Directives, however, have purported to operate 'without prejudice' to the Computer Programs Directive.[20]

In April 2000, the Commission published a report on the implementation and effects of the Computer Programs Directive, thereby fulfilling a commitment it had made at the time of the adoption of the common position to report on the working of the Directive by the end of 1996.[21] However, this brief report was mostly concerned with the EU Member State's implementation activities and it did not contain an in-depth economic analysis of the effects of the Computer Program Directive on the software market.

QUESTIONS

1 In the evaluation report of 2000, the Commission did, however, conclude that '[t]he adoption of the Directive has promoted the computer programs industry in relation to four important points: A reduction in piracy . . ., an increase in employment . . ., a move towards open systems . . ., and harmonisation for employee-created computer programs'. What is your opinion about this conclusion?

2 In your opinion, how big was the harmonising effect of the Software Directive, in particular as regards the criterion of originality ('the author's own intellectual creation', Article 1 (3)) and authorship (Article 2 (1))?

3 Article 4 (1) lists as exclusive rights the reproduction, adaptation and distribution rights. Why is the right to public communication not mentioned?

4 So far, the ECJ only had to deal with three cases under the Software Directive. What could be the reasons for the relatively small number of cases decided on both the EU and the national level under the Software Directive?

5 In particular, the most controversial provisions on line-monitoring and decompilation (Articles 5 (3) and 6) were almost never applied. Does this mean that these provisions are perfect laws, that infringements are

---

20 See Article 3 Rental Right Directive (below, footnote 22), Article 2 (a) Database Directive (below, footnote 40) and Article 1 (2) (a) Information Society Directive (below, footnote 44).
21 See eur-lex.europa.eu/LexUriServ/LexUriServ.do?uri=CELEX:52000DC0199:EN:NOT , p. 17.

impossible to detect, or that the Software Directive has been overtaken by software developing technology and the rise of open source software?

6 In its Microsoft decision (T-204/04 of 17 September 2007) the Court of First Instance (now the General Court) only briefly mentioned the Software Directive, but mainly relied on competition law in ordering Microsoft to provide access to interface information to its competitor Sun Microsystems. Can you imagine why?

Directive 2006/115/EC on rental right and lending right and on certain rights related to copyright in the field of intellectual property (originally published as Directive 92/100/EEC): Rental and Lending Right Directive[22]

Aim

The second European directive in the field of copyright is the Rental and Lending Directive. On the one hand, this Directive is the Community legislature's reaction to case C-158/86 – *Christiansen*[23] in which the ECJ held that it was not in violation of the freedom of movement of goods if a rightholder prevents copies of his works which he had put into circulation in one Member State from being hired-out in another Member State on the basis of an exclusive rental right in that second Member State. On the other hand, the decision to adopt the Rental and Lending Directive was driven by certain considerations regarding piracy and new forms of distributing copyrighted works, as explained in detail in the European Commission's Green Paper on Copyright and the Challenge of Technology of 1988 (in particular its chapters 2 on piracy and 4 on the distribution right, exhaustion and rental right). As explained in Recitals 2–4 of the Rental Right Directive:

> (2) Rental and lending of copyright works and the subject matter of related rights protection is playing an increasingly important role in particular for authors, performers and producers of phonograms and films. Piracy is becoming an increasing threat.
>
> (3) The adequate protection of copyright works and subject matter of related rights protection by rental and lending rights as well as the protection of the subject matter of related rights protection by the fixation right, distribution right,

---

22 Directive 2006/115/EC of the European Parliament and of the Council of 12 December 2006 on rental right and lending right and on certain rights related to copyright in the field of intellectual property, [2006] OJ L 376/28, originally published as Council Directive 92/100/EEC of 19 November 1992 on rental right and lending right and on certain rights related to copyright in the field of intellectual property, [1992] OJ L 346/61. Note that in the process of consolidation, the numbering of the articles has partly changed and certain provisions that have become obsolete have been repealed.

23 For discussion see above in this chapter, section 5.1.2 and in Chapter 2, secrtion 2.2.1.3.2.3.

right to broadcast and communication to the public can accordingly be considered as being of fundamental importance for the economic and cultural development of the Community.

(4) Copyright and related rights protection must adapt to new economic developments such as new forms of exploitation.

Consequently, the Directive not only deals with rental and lending rights, as its informal title suggests, but it also harmonises neighbouring ('related') rights of performing artists, phonogram producers, film producers and broadcasting organisations. In this respect, it should be noted that the initial version of the Directive adopted in 1992 preceded both the TRIPS Agreement (see Article 14 TRIPS) of 1994 and the WIPO Performances and Phonograms Treaty (WPPT) of 1996. The purpose was to provide at least a harmonised minimum level of protection for the major groups of holders of related rights throughout the EU. Later on, the protection granted to holders of related rights provisions under the Rental and Lending Directive has been complemented by the provisions of the Information Society Directive, which otherwise leaves the Provisions of the Rental and Lending Directive intact (Art 2 (2) (b) of the Information Society Directive).

Scope

In line with its aim, the Rental and Lending Directive has two main chapters. Chapter I mandates Member States to grant to authors and holders of certain neighbouring rights (performers, phonogram producers and film producers, Article 3 (1)) an exclusive right to rental and lending (Article 1 (1)), with the exception of rental and lending rights in relation to buildings and to works of applied art (Article 3 (2)). Articles 2 (1) (a) and (b) define 'rental' as 'making available for use, for a limited period of time and for direct or indirect economic or commercial advantage', and 'lending' as 'making available for use, for a limited period of time and not for direct or indirect economic or commercial advantage, when it is made through establishments which are accessible to the public'. As regards lending, however, derogations are possible, provided that at least authors obtain remuneration for such lending. Moreover, Member States may exempt certain categories of establishments from the payment of the remuneration (Article 6 (1) and (3)). The exclusive rental and lending right is not exhausted by the fact that a copy which is later rented has initially been sold or otherwise distributed by the right-holder or with his consent (Article 1 (2)). In addition, a couple of provisions are addressing contracts related to rental and lending rights. On the one hand, when a contract concerning film production is concluded by performers with a film producer, subject to contractual clauses to the contrary, the performer is presumed to have transferred his rental right (Article 3 (4); the same is true as regards authors, Article 3 (5)). On the other hand, if Member States provide that the signing of a contract concluded between a performer and a film producer concerning the production of a film has the effect of authorising rental, the contract must provide for an equitable remuneration (Article 3 (6)). In addition, as regards rental, even after transferring or assigning his rental right concerning a phonogram or a film to a phonogram or film producer, that author or performer retains an unwaivable claim for equitable remuneration, which may be exercised by collecting societies (Article 6).

Chapter II of the Rental and Lending Directive grants to performers, phonogram and film producers as well as to broadcasting organisations related rights regarding the fixation, broadcasting and public communication and distribution of the related subject matter in question (Articles 7–9). It should be noted, however, that with regards to cases where the performance is itself already a broadcast performance or is made from a fixation, both performers and phonogram producers do not enjoy an exclusive right. Rather, if a phonogram published for commercial purposes, or a reproduction of such phonogram, is used for broadcasting by wireless means or for any communication to the public, their rights are limited to a single equitable remuneration to be paid by the user and to be shared between the relevant performers and phonogram producers (Article 8 (2)). Finally, Article 10 contains the corresponding limitations.

The implementation of the Rental and Lending Directive was evaluated in a report published by the Commission, as required by Article 5 (4) of the initial version of the Directive, in the course of 2002.[24]

? QUESTIONS

1 What is the economic rationale for a rental right? Why does Article 11 TRIPS prescribe a rental right only for computer programs and films (and here also only under certain circumstances), but not for sound recordings?

2 What is the rationale for the derogations from the exclusive public lending right in Article 6 (1)? What institutions would, in your opinion, qualify as 'certain categories of establishments'?

3 According to Article 3 (2), the Rental and Lending Directive does not

---

24 COM(2002) 502 final of 12.9.2002, eur-lex.europa.eu/LexUriServ/LexUriServ.do?uri=CELEX:52002D C0502:EN:NOT.

cover rental and lending rights 'in relation to buildings and to works of applied art'. What is meant by this and what is the reason?

4 Why are not all rights in Chapter II of the Rental and Lending Directive granted to all categories of holders of related rights (e.g., phonogram and film producers are not mentioned as regards the fixation right of Article 8)?

5 Why do performers and phonogram producers not enjoy an exclusive right, but only a claim for remuneration according to Article 8 (2)? Compare this with the relevant provisions of the Rome Agreement, TRIPS and the WIPO Performances and Phonograms Treaty! (WPPT).

Directive 93/83/EEC on the coordination of certain rules concerning copyright and rights related to copyright applicable to satellite broadcasting and cable retransmission: Satellite and Cable Directive[25]

Aim

Additional problems related to the exchange of copyrighted works within the EU were identified by the Commission with regard to multi-territory satellite programs on the one hand, and to trans-border cable retransmission of foreign radio and TV programs on the other. It was perceived that too little information in the form of broadcasting services travelled across the European borders. In order to enable fuller use of new trans-frontier communications technologies and to enhance cultural exchange within the EU, the Green Paper on Television without Frontiers published by the European Commission already in 1984[26] proposed to eliminate legal barriers to trans-frontier television services within the European Community, especially in the area of broadcasting regulation and copyright law. The Green Paper eventually led to the Television without Frontiers Directive of 1989[27] which, however, did not contain any rules on copyright. Copyright was subsequently regulated by the Satellite and Cable Directive.

The Satellite and Cable Directive sticks somewhat out from the other harmonising directives. The reason is that the obstacles to trans-border

---

25 Council Directive 93/83/EEC of 27 September 1993 on the coordination of certain rules concerning copyright and rights related to copyright applicable to satellite broadcasting and cable retransmission, [1993] OJ L 248/15.

26 Doc. COM(84) 300 final of 14 June 1984.

27 Council Directive 552/89/EEC of 3 October 1989 on the coordination of certain provisions laid down by Law, Regulation or Administrative Action in Member States concerning the pursuit of television broadcasting activities, [1989] OJ L 298/23 as later amended.

broadcasting services result less from differences in national copyright laws but rather from the multi-territoriality of the internal market. Exhaustion of the distribution right with regard to physical copies of copyrighted works as developed by the ECJ does not help here, since trans-border broadcasting does not involve physical copies but the public communication right which is not exhausted when it is first exercised.[28] Therefore, the emphasis of the Satellite and Cable Directive is less on harmonising diverging existing national rules regarding satellite transmission and cable retransmission of copyrighted subject matter. Rather, it tries to overcome a certain contractual market failure. It does so by introducing two legal instruments designed to facilitate the licensing of satellite broadcasting and cable retransmission of radio and television programs:

> Firstly, the Directive has established a Community-wide right of communication to the public by satellite, which is a restricted (protected) act only in the country of origin (uplink) of the satellite transmission. This instrument was felt necessary because in some Member States courts had determined that a satellite broadcast is a restricted act in all States within the footprint of the satellite, meaning that right holders in one Member State would be able to block a satellite broadcast intended for the whole of Europe. Second, the Directive has created a system of compulsory collective management of cable retransmission rights, in order to facilitate and promote collective licensing. This instrument was felt necessary because cable operators are unable to negotiate licenses with all right holders concerned prior to the broadcasting of the programme. It was feared that individual right holders might exercise their exclusive rights of retransmission, and thus create 'black–outs' in programmes retransmitted by cable operators.[29]

Scope

In line with this, the Satellite and Cable Directive has two distinctive parts, one dealing with satellite transmission, the other with simultaneous cable retransmission.

As regards the trans-border communication of copyrighted works and protected related subject matter, Chapter II of the Satellite and Cable Directive confirms the exclusive right to communicate protected subject matter to the public by satellite (Articles 2 and 4). Except for cinematographic works, collective agreements are allowed and can be extended to right-holders who are not represented by the collecting society which has concluded the agree-

---

28 See Chapter 2, section 2.2.1.
29 *Hugenholtz*, in: Dreier/Hugenholtz (eds.), Concise European Copyright Law, 2006, pp. 263–264.

ment (Article 3 (2)–(4)). The Directive applies to satellites the signals of which can be publicly received, irrespective on which frequency bands they are operating (Article 1 (1)), and also for encrypted programs, if the decoders have been provided to the public by the broadcaster or with his consent (Article 1 (2) (c)). The novelty introduced by the Directive is, however, hidden in the definitions contained in Article 1. According to Article 1 (2) (b):

> [t]he act of communication to the public by satellite occurs solely in the Member State where, under the control and responsibility of the broadcasting organization, the programme-carrying signals are introduced into an uninterrupted chain of communication leading to the satellite and down towards the earth.

In other words, trans-border communication via satellite only requires authorisation in the country of the uplink, not, however, in all other countries in which the signals can be received. It should be noted that this rule is not a conflicts of law rule, but rather a rule of substantive copyright law. Under certain circumstances, this rule also applies in cases in which the uplink as defined by the Directive takes place in a non-EU Member the copyright protection of which stays behind the EU level (technical uplink station and uplink-commissioning broadcasting station situated in a Member State as subsidiary points of attachment, Article 1 (2) (d) (i)–(ii)). Recital 17 makes clear that in calculating the remuneration to be paid, account should be taken of 'all aspects of the broadcast, such as the actual audience, the potential audience and the language version'. Again in other words, even if authorisation is only required as regards the rights in the country of uplink, the remuneration should also take into consideration the public in the countries of downlink. Correspondingly, collecting societies have to distribute the sums collected in the country of uplink to the collecting societies in the countries of downlink. According to Article 7 (2), from the beginning of the year 2000 the new regime also applies to older contracts. Finally, Article 7 (3) contains a special clause for co-production agreements that were concluded prior to 1 January 1995.

Chapter III lays down the rules for trans-border retransmission of programs by cable. It begins with providing for an exclusive right of simultaneous, unaltered and unabridged retransmission by cable or microwave system of an initial broadcast from another Member State by wire, or over the air (Articles 8 (1), 1 (3)). However, with the exception of rights of or transferred to broadcasting organisations (Article 10), this exclusive right can only be exercised by collecting societies (Article 9 (1)). Outsiders, i.e. right-holders not represented by collecting societies only retain a claim for remuneration against the collecting society in question (Article 9 (2)). To ensure that agreements concerning the trans-border cable retransmission are concluded, Articles 11 and 12 provide for mediation and mechanisms to prevent the abusive refusal to negotiate or the abusive withholding of consent.

Pursuant to Article 14 (3) an evaluation report was published by the European Commission in July 2002.[30]

QUESTIONS

1 When the Satellite and Cable Directive was enacted, the issue was hotly debated whether in the case of trans-border satellite transmission of protected works only the law of the uplink country applied, or whether, in addition, the laws of all the countries applied, in which the signals could be received (so-called Bogsch-theory, named after the then Director-General of WIPO). In this respect, what is the meaning of the above sentence 'It should be noted that this rule is not a conflicts of law rule, but rather a rule of substantive copyright law'?

2 In your opinion, what is the reason why Article 10 of the Satellite and Cable Directive exempts broadcasting organisations from exercising both their own retransmission rights and the retransmission rights transferred to them by the holders of the rights to the content of their broadcasts from being exercised only by a collecting society?

3 Article 1 (3) defines – and hence limits – the special regime of cable retransmission to retransmission 'by cable and microwave systems' (microwave systems being a special form of program transmission that was used at the time only in Ireland), and therefore does not extend to retransmission via satellite. In your opinion, does this technology-specific formulation make sense today, where broadcasters communicate their programmes both by traditional means of broadcasting and the internet?

4 In your opinion, would it make sense to apply the satellite part of the Satellite and Cable Directive to dissemination to works over the internet? What conditions would have to be fulfilled in order to do so?

---

30 COM(2002) 430 of 26.07.2002 final, eur-lex.europa.eu/LexUriServ/LexUriServ.do?uri=CELEX:52002 DC0430:EN:NOT.

Directive 2006/116/EC on the term of protection of copyright and certain related rights (originally published as Directive 93/98/EEC): Term Directive[31] and Directive 2011/77/EU amending Directive 2006/116/EC on the term of protection of copyright and certain related rights[32]

Aim

Before the adoption of the Term Directive, different terms of protection existed throughout the EU. In short, the differences can be summarised as follows:

> 2. Need for harmonization. . . . (b) Situation before the Directive. Before the adoption of the Directive different terms of protection existed in the EU. Most Member States provided a term of protection of fifty years after the death of the author (hereinafter: post mortem auctoris), following the Berne Convention minimum. The term of protection in Germany was seventy years post mortem auctoris, whereas in Spain the term was sixty years post mortem auctoris. In France the protection for musical works without words was seventy years post mortem auctoris, and for all other works it was fifty years post mortem auctoris. Several countries provided for extensions for copyright terms running during the world wars. In France, for example, the term of protection was (and still is) extended for a further term of thirty years if the author, the composer or the artist has died for France, as recorded in the death certificate.[33]

In the *Patricia* case,[34] the ECJ had held that it was not contrary to the principle of free movement of goods that the importation of records from Denmark into Germany which had been lawfully brought on the market in Denmark where the rights in the recordings had already expired could be prevented by the record producer on the basis of the longer term of protection for those records under German law. Since this situation negatively affected the trade in copyright protected goods and services in the internal market, the Community legislature felt compelled to harmonise the term of protection throughout the EU. The Directive harmonises the term of copyright at the

---

31 Directive 2006/116/EC of the European Parliament and of the Council of 12 December 2006 on the term of protection of copyright and certain related rights, [2006] OJ L 372/12; originally published as Council Directive 93/98/EEC of 29 October 1993 harmonising the term of protection of copyright and certain related rights, [1993] OJ L 290/9.

32 Directive 2011/77/EU of the European Parliament and of the Council of 27 September 2011 amending Directive 2006/116/EC on the term of protection of copyright and certain related rights, [2011] OJ L 265/1.

33 *Visser*, in: Dreier/Hugenholtz (eds.), *Concise European Copyright Law*, 2006, p. 287.

34 ECJ Case 341/87, *EMI Electrola v. Patricia*, [1989] ECR 79. For discussion see Chapter 2, sections 2.2.1.3.2.3 and in this chapter, section 5.2.1.1.

relatively high level of seventy years after the death of the author, while for related (related) rights the term is set at 50 years. As explained by *Visser*, the reason for harmonisation at 70 years post mortem auctoris was as follows:

> (c) . . . Several reasons were given for the decision to harmonize at seventy years rather than fifty years, which was the more common term in Europe. One was that harmonizing at fifty years would have led to lengthy transitional measures for those countries that had the longer term of seventy years if all existing rights had to be respected (see recital 9[35]). Another reason was that the term of protection should be sufficient to cover two generations and that the increasing average lifespan in the EU would require a longer term of protection. It was even suggested that lengthening the term of protection would strengthen the position of the author during his lifetime when negotiating the assignment of his rights.[36]

It should be noted that in order to have the desired harmonising effect, the Directive provides for minimum and maximum harmonisation. In other words, Member States are not allowed to provide either shorter or longer terms of protection than those prescribed by the Directive. In addition, the harmonising effect was further strengthened by the fact that all works benefitted from the extension that were still protected in at least one Member State on 1 July 1995, the implementation date of the Term Directive. In other words, in many States the term of protection for works that had already fallen into the public domain was revived. However, the Term Directive does not contain any rules as to who – initial author or producer, to whom the author had transferred his economic rights – benefits from the extension of the term. Moreover, the Directive expressly left it to the Member States to adopt provisions necessary to protect acquired rights of third parties, which had begun exploitation after the initial term of protection had expired. This lack of rules at the community level led to substantial differences amongst national legislations.

Scope

Article 1 (1) fixes the term of protection of works within the meaning of the Berne Convention to 70 years after the death of the author. This term, like any other term, is to be calculated from the beginning of the year following the death of the author (Article 8). Article 1 (2)–(6) regulates the running of the term for works of joint authorship, anonymous and pseu-

---

35 This reference goes to the version of the Directive as initially published. The recitals have been rewritten in the codified version.

36 *Visser*, in: Dreier/Hugenholtz (eds.), *Concise European Copyright Law*, 2006, pp. 287–288.

donymous works, collective works, works published in volumes etc., and for works for which the term of protection is not calculated from the death of the author. Concerning the calculation of the term of protection of cinemato-graphic and audiovisual works, Article 2 (2) limits the number of authors to be taken into consideration to the following four: the principal director, the author of the screenplay, the author of the dialogue, and the composer of the music.

Regarding the term of protection of related rights, Article 3 fixed the dura-tion to 50 years after the date of performance (for performers), fixation (for phonogram and film producers), and first transmission (for broadcasters). However, if during this time publication or first public communication took place, then the term was calculated from this date. Theoretically, this could lead to a maximum protection of 100 years after the said dates. Article 4 grants a 25-year related right to the editors of previously unpublished works which had already fallen into the public domain, and Article 5 makes it optional for Member States to also protect critical and scientific editions for a maximum of 30 years.

According to Article 9, this Directive does not affect national rules on the terms of moral rights. Article 7 lays down the protection vis-á-vis third countries and, most important, Article 10 lays down the transition rules: the Directive does not have the effect of shortening longer national terms which were already running (Article 10 (1)); the terms provided for in this Directive apply to all works that were still protected in at least one Member State on 1 July 1995 (Article 10 (2)), and, finally, the prolongation is without prejudice to any acts performed before 1 July 1995. However, Member States 'shall adopt the necessary provisions to protect . . . acquired rights of third parties' (Article 10 (3)). In this respect, it should be noted that the Directive did not regulate whether or not a copyright agreement concluded for the life of the copyright prior to the entering into force of the Directive also extended to the prolongation period. Moreover, due to the working together of Article 10 (1) and (2) of the Term Directive and the *Phil Collins* decision of the ECJ, which barred Member States from applying the comparison of terms (i.e. the option allowed for by Article 7 (8) of the Berne Convention to deviate from the national treatment principle and protect foreign nation-als only for a term as fixed in the country of origin of the work in question),[37] quite a substantial number of rights revived in many Member States, leading

---

37 ECJ Cases C-92/92 and C-326/92, *Phil Collins* v. *Imtrat* and *Patricia* v. *EMI Electrola*, [1993] ECR I-5145. For discussion of the scope of the *Phil Collins* decision and the principle of non-discrimination of Article 18 TFEU on the term of protection and the persons benefitting from the extension, see Chapter 2, section 2.2.2.

to the question whether a person who had already begun an exploitation and who was relying on the fact that copyright in his country had already expired could continue, and if so, whether an additional remuneration was due.

In addition, the Term Directive contains two provisions which harmonise substantive copyright law. First, according to Article 2 (1) the four persons who have to be taken into account in calculating the term of protection for cinematographic and audiovisual works likewise have to be regarded, as a minimum, as co-authors of the cinematographic or audiovisual work in national law (here, the Term Directive went beyond Article 2 (2) of the Rental and Lending Directive as initially published, which only had the principal director as mandatory author). Second, according to Article 6 photographs which are original in the sense that they constitute their author's own intellectual creation, have to be protected as copyrighted works.

Directive 2011/77/EU: prolongation of the term of protection of performers and producers of phonograms

In view of declining record sales and rampant peer-to-peer file-sharing over the internet, record producers and performing artists lobbied extensively with the Commission and the Member States to obtain a prolongation of their existing term of protection for performances fixed in a phonogram which was for 50 years after publication (or 50 years after the performance of making of the fixation).

The initial proposal[38] foresaw a term of 95 years after the respective dates. The proposal had been justified with the economic needs of performers. However, because contracts concluded before the entering into force of the proposed Directive were deemed to continue to produce effects and because the performer would not in all cases have received a share of any additional proceeds generated during the prolongation period, performers would have benefitted from the term extension much less than producers of phonograms. In view of this, both the extension and the provisions concerning the contractual arrangements attracted criticism. As expressed in an open letter signed by 17 law professors published in the London *Times*:

> The simple truth is that copyright extension benefits most those who already hold rights. It benefits incumbent holders of major back-catalogues, be they record

---

38 Proposal for a European Parliament and Council Directive amending Directive 2006/116/EC of the European Parliament and of the Council on the term of protection of copyright and certain related rights, COM(2008) 464/3, and the accompanying Commission Staff Working Document SEC(2008) 2287 of 16.7.2008, both available at ec.europa.eu/internal_market/copyright/term-protection/index_en.htm.

companies, ageing rock stars or, increasingly, artists' estates. It does nothing for innovation and creativity. The proposed Term Extension Directive undermines the credibility of the copyright system. It will further alienate a younger generation that, justifiably, fails to see a principled basis. . . . [M]easures to benefit performers would look rather different. They would target unreasonably exploitative contracts during the existing term, and evaluate remuneration during the performer's life-time, not 95 years.[39]

Although these arguments did not succeed in preventing the term extension Directive in its entirety, the version finally adopted after several amendments had been proposed by the European Parliament limited the extension to 70 years instead of the 95 years initially proposed. Also, contracts concluded before the entering into force of the Directive and in which a performer has transferred or assigned his rights in the fixation of his performance to a phonogram producer continue to produce their effects during the prolonga-tion period, unless there are clear contractual indications to the contrary. However, if such a contract gives the performer a right to claim a non-recurring remuneration, under the Directive the performer has an unwaiv-able right to receive an additional share of the proceeds generated during the prolongation period. The overall amount to be set aside by record produc-ers for such additional remuneration shall correspond to 20 per cent of the revenue which the phonogram producer has derived, during the year preced-ing that for which the said remuneration is paid, from the reproduction, dis-tribution and making available of the phonogram in question. The collection and distribution of these payments are to be administered by a collecting society. In addition, a performer may terminate the contract if during the period of prolongation, the phonogram producer ceases to offer copies of the phonogram for sale in sufficient quantity or to make it available online to the public, by wire or wireless means.

? QUESTIONS

1 What arguments are there for a longer and for a shorter term of protec-tion? In particular, should the term ideally be calculated upon the life of the author or rather according to economic considerations?
2 How exactly do the prolongation as provided for under the Term Directive, Article 10 (2) of the Directive, the principle of non-discrimination of Article 18 TFEU, and the comparison of terms according to Article 7 (8) Berne Convention 'work together' producing the result of a revival of certain terms of protection that had already expired in a Member State?

---

39 See www.timesonline.co.uk/tol/comment/letters/article4374115.ece?php.

3 Can you give a precise date which currently is the 'watershed' between works that are still protected in the EU and works that have already fallen in the public domain?

4 In the discussions revolving around user-generated content on the internet, it has been proposed, particularly in the US, but also by some academics in Europe, to get back to a shorter initial term, which could then be prolonged once upon registration. What is your opinion on this? Should the second term be linked to a payment into a general fund supporting artistic creation in general (so-called 'domaine public payant'), rather than being granted as a prolongation of the exclusive right?

5 Do you consider the criticism that was aimed at the prolongation of the term of protection of performers and producers of phonograms justified? In your opinion, does it also apply to the Directive as finally adopted? Can you describe the connection between the prolongation of terms and innovation? How would it improve protection for performing artists?

Directive 96/6/EC on the legal protection of databases: Database Directive[40]

Aim

In line with Article 2 (5) of the Berne Convention for the Protection of Literary and Artistic Works, most if not all Member States protected collections of literary works which, by reason of the selection and/or arrangement of their contents constitute intellectual creations as such as copyrighted works. The protection attaching to a particular collection is without prejudice to the copyright in each of the works that forms part of such collection. In the analogue world, classic examples were encyclopaedias and anthologies. In the digital world, databases are of central importance for the information economy. However, digital databases often don't qualify for copyright protection since neither the selection of the data contained in a database nor their arrangement show sufficient originality. Mere economic investment and intellectual effort are generally not sufficient for copyright protection. Of course, in some countries, protection of databases may be available against unauthorised misappropriation under a theory of protection against unfair competition or similar torts. But such protection was not available in all EU Member States.

In view of this, the EU legislature concluded that databases were not sufficiently protected in all Member States by existing legislation and that existing differences had direct negative effects on, and tended to distort, the func-

---

40 Directive 96/9/EC of the European Parliament and of the Council of 11 March 1996 on the legal protection of databases, [1996] OJ L 77/20.

tioning of the internal market. As stated in Recitals 5 and 6 of the Database Directive, although copyright was still considered 'an appropriate form of exclusive right for authors who have created databases'. It was also felt that:

> in the absence of a harmonized system of unfair-competition legislation or of case-law, other measures are required in addition to prevent the unauthorized extrac-tion and/or re-utilization of the contents of a database.

The reason is that the unauthorised extraction and/or re-utilisation of the contents of a database might have serious economic and technical conse-quences regarding future investment in this area. Consequently:

> . . . [t]he Database Directive has created a two–tier protection regime for elec-tronic and non–electronic databases. Member States are to protect databases by copyright as intellectual creations (Chapter 2), and provide for a sui generis right (database right) to protect the contents of a database in which the producer has substantially invested (Chapter 3). Both rights, however, may apply cumulatively if the prerequisites for both regimes are fulfilled.[41]

It should be noted, however, that up until now, the new *sui generis* database right created by the Database Directive still remains a particular European creation. Although an international database treaty had been proposed in 1996 when the two WIPO Treaties (WIPO Copyright Treaty, WCT; WIPO Performances and Phonograms Treaty, WPPT) were negotiated, it was not adopted mainly due to the reluctance of the US and the resistance of devel-oping countries. In particular, the US scientific community has so far suc-ceeded in defeating any attempt to enact similar legislation in the US.

Scope

Chapter I on the scope of the Database Directive in Article 1 (2) notably contains the definition of what is to be considered a database, namely 'a collection of independent works, data or other related materials arranged in a systematic or methodical way and individually accessible by electronic or other means'. Computer programs used in the making or operation of a database are not part of the database (Article 1 (3)), but rather enjoy a legal life of their own under the Software Directive. Likewise, the contents of a database (works, data or other related material) has to be distinguished from the 'database' as the object of legal protection (Article 3 (2)).

---

41 *Hugenholtz*, in: Dreier/Hugenholtz (eds.), *Concise European Copyright Law*, 2006, pp. 307–308.

Chapter II defines databases which are subject to copyright as those which 'by reason of the selection or arrangement of their contents, constitute the author's own intellectual creation' (Article 3 (1)). Article 4 determines authorship, Article 5 circumscribes the restricted acts and Article 6 defines the exceptions thereto.

Chapter III introduces the newly created *sui generis* right protecting databases which show 'qualitatively and/or quantitatively a substantial investment in either the obtaining, verification or presentation of the contents' against 'extraction and/or re-utilization of the whole or of a substantial part, evaluated qualitatively and/or quantitatively', of its contents (Article 7 (1), with definitions of 'extraction' and 're-utilization' in Article 7 (2)). As a right to protect investment, the *sui generis* right vests with the 'maker of the database', i.e. 'the person who takes the initiative and the risk of investing', not including subcontractors (Recital 41). In addition, the 'repeated and systematic extraction and/or re-utilization of insubstantial parts of the contents of the database' is also reserved to the owner of the database right, if it conflicts with the normal exploitation of the database or unreasonably prejudices against the legitimate interests (Article 7 (5)). Article 8 contains the limitations of the exclusive rights vis-à-vis lawful users (which cannot be signed away, Article 15), and Article 9 the exceptions vis-à-vis third parties. The term of protection of the *sui generis* rights is 15 years, calculated from the year of completion of the making of the database in question (Article 10 (1)). However, '[a]ny substantial change, evaluated qualitatively or qualitatively, to the contents of a database, . . . which would result in the database being considered to be a substantial new investment' qualifies the modified database for a term of protection of its own (Article 10 (3)). In practice, this means that *sui generis* protection lasts as long as a database is maintained by deploying substantial investment for its maintenance.

It should be noted that copyright and *sui generis* protection are not mutually exclusive (Article 7 (4)). Rather, a database can be protected by either copyright, or *sui generis* protection, or both copyright and *sui generis* protection, or not at all. Finally, due to the fact that the proposed international database treaty fell through in 1996, Article 11 contains a reciprocity clause according to which *sui generis* protection to nationals and firms from countries which do not provide for similar protection do not benefit from the EU *sui generis* protection.

Finally, it was hoped that the creation of the *sui generis* right would eliminate the gap that existed in the level of investment in the database sector between the Community and the world's largest database-producing countries. However, a report assessing the economic impact of the *sui generis* right published by the Commission in 2005[42] was sceptical about the beneficial effect the introduction of the *sui generis* right has had on the production of databases in the Community. Although several future policy options were outlined in the report, including repealing the Directive, after consultation with the parties concerned no legislative changes were made or proposed.

? QUESTIONS

1   How precise is the definition of a 'database'? In some Member States, the issue has arisen whether printed newspapers qualify as – and hence might benefit from *sui generis* protection for – databases. What do you think? In this respect, see also Recital 19, according to which 'as a rule, the compilation of several recordings of musical performances on a CD does not come within the scope of this Directive, both because as a compilation, it does not meet the conditions for copyright protection and because it does not represent a substantial enough investment to be eligible under the *sui generis* right'. Do you agree? Finally, in the digital age, where every work is digitised, couldn't any work be regarded as a 'database' of 0s and 1s?

2   It has been pointed out that under the Database Directive, there are fewer limitations to the *sui generis* rights than there are to the exclusive copyright in databases. How could this be justified?

3   If an existing database which qualifies for *sui generis* protection is updated by way of substantial investment, does the new term extend to the whole database or only to the part that was added?

4   The Report issued by the Commission in 2005 was talking about some 3,000 databases EU-wide. A German lower court, however, had qualified a list of 251 links as protected by the *sui generis* right of the Database Directive, which probably suggests a much higher number of databases protected by the *sui generis* right under the Directive. How can this difference be reconciled?

5   In your opinion, is the *sui generis* protection justified? What are the reasons of natural scientists to object? And which of the options proposed by the Report issued by the Commission in 2005 (repeal the whole Directive; withdraw the *sui generis* right; amend the *sui generis* provisions, or maintain the status quo) would you personally prefer, and why?

6   Does the reciprocity requirement as laid down in Article 11 – which was a retaliatory measure against the reciprocity requirement in the US Semiconductor Chip Protection Act of 1984[43] – really exclude US

---

42 DG Internal Market and Services Working Paper, ec.europa.eu/internal_market/copyright/docs/databases/evaluation_report_en.pdf.

43 For the protection of semiconductor chip topographies see Chapter 6, section 6.5.

companies from benefitting from the *sui generis* right? What about the validity of such a reciprocity requirement in the light of the national treatment principle of both the Paris Convention (PC) and TRIPS?

Directive 2001/29/EC on the harmonisation of certain aspects of copyright and related rights in the information society: Information Society (InfoSoc) Directive[44]

Aim

Up to 2001, harmonisation of copyright within the EU had indeed been rather piecemeal in that each Directive only dealt in a sectorial way with individual categories of works (computer programs, databases), individual rights (rental and lending; broadcasting by satellite and cable retransmission; related rights) or other individual issues (term of protection). However, subsequently, a more ambitious approach towards harmonisation was undertaken in the form of the Information Society Directive.

The Directive harmonises several essential rights (reproduction right, distribution right and the right of communication to the public of works as well as the right of making available to the public other subject matter) of authors and those of four related right-holders (performers, phonogram producers, film producers and broadcasting organisations) as well as limitations and exceptions to these rights. It also harmonises the protection of technological measures and of rights management information as well as – to a lesser extent – sanctions and remedies (later to be further harmonised in a horizontal way to include all IP rights by the Enforcement Directive[45]). At the same time, the Information Society Directive implements two international treaties (WCT and WPPT) which had been concluded in December 1996. It should be noted, however, that in many areas the Directive goes well beyond the international obligations of both treaties.

Scope

The ambitious, 'horizontal' Information Society Directive harmonises, in its Chapter II, for all works as well as to a large extent for performers, phonogram and film producers and broadcasting organisations the reproduction right (Article 2), the right of communication to the public of works and the right of making works available to the public (Article 3), the distribution right, including its exhaustion (Article 4) and the limitations and excep-

---

44 Directive 2001/29/EC of the European Parliament and of the Council of 22 May 2001 on the harmonization of certain aspects of copyright and related rights in the information society, [2011] OJ L 167/10.
45 See Chapter 8, section 8.2.1.

tions to the exclusive rights, including a reiteration of the three-step test (Article 5). Chapter III is devoted to the legal protection of technical protection measures (Article 6) and rights management information (Article 7). Finally, Chapter III contains, *inter alia*, some basic provisions on remedies, which have largely been supplanted by the Enforcement Directive 2004/48/EC and are also governed by the Electronic Commerce Directive 2001/31/EC.[46] It should be noted, however, that the Information Society Directive does not replace the Copyright Directives which had been enacted earlier.

At first sight, the harmonisation achieved looks substantial. But a closer look reveals that out of the 21 exceptions, only one (temporary acts of reproduction, Article 5 (1)) is mandatory, whereas the remaining 20 are optional. The reason is that Member States didn't want to give up the exceptions existing in their respective national laws prior to the enactment of the Directive and hence could not agree on a list binding for all Member States. Therefore, the list of Article 5 was drawn more or less on the basis of existing national exceptions. Moreover, like at various instances before, the Commission could not convince Member States to adopt a harmonised scheme as regards private copying. It was only laid down that if Member States chose to maintain or adopt the limitation for private copying and certain other limitations, then right-holders have to receive 'fair compensation'. Details are left to the Member States, but Recital 35 at least gives some guidelines in stating that:

> [w]hen determining the form, detailed arrangements and possible level of such fair compensation, account should be taken of the particular circumstances of each case. When evaluating these circumstances, a valuable criterion would be the possible harm to the rightholders resulting from the act in question. In cases where rightholders have already received payment in some other form, for instance as part of a licence fee, no specific or separate payment may be due. The level of fair compensation should take full account of the degree of use of technological protection measures referred to in this Directive. In certain situations where the prejudice to the rightholder would be minimal, no obligation for payment may arise.

In spite of all this, the harmonisation effect of the Directive in this respect is minimal. Moreover, the Directive is:

> without prejudice to the arrangements in the Member States concerning the management of rights such as extended collective licences. (Recital 18)

---

46 See Chapter 8, sections 8.2.1 and 8.2.2.1.

Finally, as regards the relationship between statutory limitations and technical protection devices, the Directive mandates Member States to take appropriate measures to ensure that right-holders make available to the beneficiary of certain limitations (not including private copying) the means of benefitting of that exception. However, if the protected content is made available online, technical protection measures always prevail (Article 6 (4) (1) and (4)).

For implementation of Directive 2001/29/EC in the different Member States see both the Commission's internal implementation report and the outside in-depth study commissioned by the Commission from the Dutch Instituut voor Informatierecht.[47]

? QUESTIONS

1 Article 1 (2) leaves, inter alia, the Computer Program Directive intact. Hence, different legal rules apply depending on whether a computer program or another copyrighted work are used in, let's say, a digital network. Does this make sense? How could possible differences in legal treatment be avoided?

2 Article 4 (2) reiterates the doctrine of EU-wide exhaustion. In this respect, according to Recital 29, '[t]he question of exhaustion does not arise in the case of services and on-line services in particular.' In your opinion, does this properly reflect the holding of the ECJ in case 62/79 of 18 March 1980 – *Coditel I*?

3 It has often been criticised that Article 5 (1)–(3) contains a closed list of exceptions. In your opinion, would it be useful to allow Member States to adopt additional limitations and exceptions, or at least to add a more flexible fair use-type exception to the list?

4 Article 5 (5) of the Directive reiterates the three-step test of Articles 13 TRIPS, 10 WCT and 16 (2) WPPT in its entirety. In other words, although Article 5 (1)–(3) already lists certain special cases, each of these cases has again to pass the first step ('certain special cases') of the three-step test. Does this make sense, or shouldn't there only be a two-step test? What difference would it make?

5 In implementing the anti-circumvention protection of Articles 10 WCT

---

47 For the Study concerning the implementation of the Information Society Directive see SEC(2007) 1556 of 30.11.2007, ec.europa.eu/internal_market/copyright/docs/copyright-infso/application-report_en.pdf. See also IVIR, Study on the implementation and effect in Member States' laws of Directive 2001/29/EC on the harmonization of certain aspects of copyright and related rights in the information society, February 2007; ec.europa.eu/internal_market/copyright/docs/studies/infosoc-study_en.pdf; and the executive summary at ec.europa.eu/internal_market/copyright/docs/studies/infosoc-exec-summary.pdf.

and 18 WPT, Article 6 of the Directive makes both the act of circumventing and of manufacturing and distributing anti-circumvention devices illegal. In your opinion, is this broadening of anti-circumvention protection justified? Also, the WIPO Treaties only provide for anti-circumvention protection to the extent that works are protected by copyright and not exempt by way of limitations and exceptions. Why does the Information Society Directive not contain such limitation of the anti-circumvention protection?

6 Directive 98/84/EC on the legal protection of services based on, or consisting of, conditional access (Conditional Access Directive) contains measures against illicit devices which give unauthorised access to protected services. What is the relationship between these provisions and Article 6 of the Information Society Directive?

Directive 2001/84/EC on the resale right for the benefit of the author of an original work of art: Resale Right Directive[48]

Aim

Contrary to the Information Society Directive, the Resale Right Directive is a Directive which addresses only a very particular issue. The Resale Royalty Right (or 'droit de suite') is the right of the author of a work of the visual arts to participate in the proceeds of the public resale of his works of art. This right forms an exception to the general rule that once the owner of a physical object has transferred ownership to someone else, he no longer holds any rights in the object sold. According to Recital 3 of the Directive, the reason which is usually given for the artist's resale royalty right, which is also foreseen in Article 14 *ter* of the Berne Convention as an optional right, is:

> to ensure that authors of graphic and plastic works of art share in the economic success of their original works of art. It helps to redress the balance between the economic situation of authors of graphic and plastic works of art and that of other creators who benefit from successive exploitations of their works.

In particular, many artists create and sell the works which make them famous at an early stage of their career in which prices for their works are still low. Moreover, the creative output of artists often is rather uneven over the years and, finally, artists often are in dire financial need when they are old. Critics, however, point out that collectors and gallery owners are largely responsible

---

48 Directive 2001/84/EC of the European Parliament and of the Council of 27 September 2001 on the resale right for the benefit of the author of an original work of art, [2001] OJ L 272/32.

for building up an artist's reputation and hence should be entitled to the full increase in the value of the works of art they trade and collect. Finally, it has been pointed out that successful artists whose works are expensive anyway and their heirs benefit most from the resale royalty right, whereas it hardly produces any meaningful income for those poorer artists who are most in need.

Since a resale right was known in about half of the EU Member States, but not in the others, the EU Commission felt compelled to harmonise this right as well. However, the Directive met with fierce opposition by those Member States that did not provide for a resale right prior to the Directive (such as the United Kingdom and the Netherlands). Although it was feared that the introduction of such a right might negatively affect national art markets, in particular vis-à-vis non-EU auction places such as Zurich and New York, the Directive was finally adopted, albeit with an unusually generous transposition period of over four years. Also, it should be noted:

> that the Directive does not harmonize every aspect of the resale right. Harmonisation is limited to . . . the scope of the resale right, the categories of works of art subject to the right, the persons entitled to receive royalties, the rates applied, the transactions subject to payment of a royalty and the debtor of the resale right. However, Member States remain free to provide domestic rules concerning the exercise of the resale right, particularly with regard to the way it is managed, and the collection and distribution of royalties.[49]

Scope

Chapter I of the Resale Royalty Directive defines the scope of the inalienable, unwaivable (Article 1 (1)) resale royalty right, which comes into being whenever art market professionals, such as salesrooms, art galleries and, in general, any dealers in works of art are involved as sellers, buyers or intermediaries (Article 1 (2)). The right attaches to works of art including photographs and multiples, which have been made in limited numbers by the artist himself or under his authority (Article 2). However, Member States can exempt acts of resale where the seller has acquired the work directly from the author less than three years before that resale and where the resale price does not exceed €10,000 (Article 1 (3)). The royalty due is, as a rule, is to be paid by the seller (Article 1 (4)).

---

49 *Vanhees*, in: Dreier/Hugenholtz (eds.), *Concise European Copyright Law*, 2006, pp. 405–406.

Chapter II fixes the minimum threshold at €3,000 (Article 3), and Article 4 sets the degressive rates to be calculated on the basis of the net sales price (Article 5): 4 per cent (alternatively: 5 per cent) for the first €50,000; 3 per cent for the portion of the sales price between €50,000 and €200,000; 1 per cent for the portion of the sales price from €200,000 to €350,000; 0.5 per cent between €350,000 and €500,000 and 0.25 per cent for the portion exceeding €500,000, with a cap at a total resale royalty of €12,500. If a Member State sets the threshold lower than at €3,000, the rate for this portion may not be lower than 4 per cent (Article 4 (3)). The royalty payments go to the author or to his heirs, and they can also be collectively exercised (Article 6 (1) and (2)). Persons or collecting societies entitled to receive payments also have, against the debtors, a claim for information necessary to secure payment of royalties in respect of the resale during three years after the sale took place (Article 9).

Since the resale royalty right is not mandatory under Article 14 *bis* of the Berne Convention, Article 7 of the Directive contains a reciprocity requirement. Article 8 (1) aligns the term of the resale royalty right to the general copyright term of the Term Directive. Articles 8 (1) and (2) contain transitional provisions, enabling Member States which did not provide for a resale royalty right in their national law prior to the entry into force of the Directive, to postpone implementation until the beginning of 2010 or, as the case may be, 2012.[50]

? QUESTIONS

1 The resale right is intended to ensure that authors of graphic and plastic works of art share in the economic success of their original works of art. Since these authors hardly benefit from the successive exploitation of their works by way of, e.g., publishing, film production or television broadcasting, the resale right is intended to create for them a similar economic result (see Recital 3). Do you agree with this rationale?

2 In what ways does the harmonisation and, in some Member States, mandatory introduction of the resale royalty right 'preserve the competitiveness of the European market' (Recital 8)?

3 What other legislative and non-legislative factors than the resale royalty right affect the competitiveness of the art market?

---

50 For the status of implementation as well as resulting changes in the art auction market see the Report published by the Commission, COM(2011) 878 final of 14 December 2011, ec.europa.eu/internal_market/copyright/docs/resale/report_en.pdf.

'Better regulation' approach: the Online-Music Recommendation 2005/737/EC

With the number of EU Member States increasing, the process of harmonisation by way of directives became increasingly burdensome, even if accession as such did not pose a major problem, since newly acceding Member States have to accept the 'acquis communautaire' that exists at the time of accession as part of the so-called 'Europe agreements'. On the one hand, the process of harmonisation by way of directives is in itself burdensome. Member States must first be convinced by the Commission to agree to a new Directive before they are under an obligation to amend their national laws correspondingly, which in turn has to be supervised by the Commission, and if a Member State does not meet its implementation duties the Commission has to seek recourse at the ECJ. On the other hand, in spite of Articles 114 (1), 26, 289, 294 TFEU, according to which harmonisation measures have to be adopted by the 'ordinary legislative procedure' and hence do not require unanimity, the adoption of legislative texts has become increasingly difficult after the enlargement of the Union.

In view of this, rather than merely harmonising Member States' national copyright laws by additional directives, the Commission adopted – under the so-called 'Better regulation' approach – for a brief period a strategy of advising private parties what to do rather than mandate Member States to change their national legislation. The aim was to directly influence markets and 'make markets work' by way of supervised self-regulation. Consequently, the instrument used was that of a recommendation rather than that of a directive.[51] At the same time, this approach was supposed to cut back economic regulation to the minimum necessary to have a functioning internal market.

In the area of copyright, the 'Better regulation' approach has been applied by the Commission in the area of trans-border licensing of music by way of the Online-Music Recommendation 2005/737/EC of 18 May 2005.[52] As explained by Tilman Lüder, then Head of the Copyright Unit, DG Internal Market and Services:[53]

> The copyright unit was previously concerned with substantive aspects of copyright, such as the scope of these rights, the introduction of related rights (such as

---

51 For an explanation of the instrument of a Recommendation, see Chapter 2, section 2.3.1.3.

52 Recommendation 2005/737/EC of 18 May 2005 on collective cross-border management of copyright and related rights for legitimate online music services, [2005] OJ EU L 276/54.

53 *Lüder*, Legislative and Policy Developments in the European Union, Speech given at the 13th Annual Conference on International Intellectual Property Law & Policy, Fordham, April 2005.

producers' or performers' rights) and the length of protection. We've . . . found that this has not brought about efficiency gains in how copyright is commercially exploited. . . . [H]armonisation at the rule-making level cannot overcome the fact that copyright still is administered on a national basis – and this has precluded the economies of scale usually associated with the Internal Market.

. . .

We went to stakeholders for their opinions . . . This exercise revealed that the current management of copyright [by collecting societies] – within defined territories that usually are national borders – is a source of considerable inefficiency. This is not least because digital technology is fast rendering the old system obsolete. . . . However, under the current system, content destined for the entire continent's consumption may be subjected to clearance 25 times through 25 different national authorities. For online operators this constitutes a considerable administrative burden and in some Member States online licences are not even available.

Commenting upon the Online-Music Recommendation, in 2007 Mr Lüder further explained:[54]

Online retailers . . . require cross-border or trans-national copyright clearance in line with their international reach and clearance services. These services cannot be provided effectively or efficiently when copyright clearing services remain mostly national in scope. . . . Simple and efficient rights clearance not only enables online service providers to achieve economies and efficiencies of scale, but it also leads to market entry by innovators, the development of new online services and, most importantly, has the potential to increase the revenue stream that flows back to the right-holders. . . . Instead of twenty-seven local licenses, the Recommendation seeks to foster a single package comprising access to attractive repertoire at little overhead.

It should be noted that prior to the Recommendation, the European collecting societies had established a system of pan-European licensing, but which – because such a license could only be obtained from the collecting society in the country in which the commercial user had its principal place of business – violated European competition law.[55] Apart from creating a single source for obtaining pan-European rights, the Commission wanted to incite competition amongst national European collecting societies. It was hoped that, as a result, licensing would become more transparent and less costly, also

---

54 *Lüder*, Making markets work – The case for EU-wide online licensing, speech given at the 15th Annual Conference on International Intellectual Property Law & Policy; iplj.net/blog/wp-content/uploads/2009/09/Article-THE-NEXT-TEN-YEARS-IN-EU-COPYRIGHT-MAKING-MARKETS-WORK.pdf--

55 For further discussion see Chapter 7, section 7.2.3.2.3.

lowering the cost for platform providers and ultimately the consumers. It was also hoped that efficient and low-cost licensing of music for trans-border online music services would lead to more attractive platforms as well as an increase in music consumption, and that right-holders might ultimately also benefit from the new system. Moreover, authors and right-holders should have the option 'of either mandating one society with the EU-wide management of their works or giving a mandate to several societies who again compete to license the entrusted repertoire to commercial users'.[56]

The Online-Music Recommendation has indeed led to the formation of a few joint ventures amongst European collecting societies, such as CELAS.[57] However, not least in view of the complicated split of rights in the musical sector, the initiative of the Commission proved not to be very successful. In particular, it didn't lead to the enhancement of competition amongst collecting societies servicing the same repertoire at the European level, but had the inherent danger to further increase the number of portals. Also, it remains unclear whether authors and right-holders can in fact increase their revenue if licensing tariffs are lowered. In order to help the development of a Single Market for cultural content online, in its proposal for a Directive on collective management of copyright and related rights and multi-territorial licensing of rights in musical works for online uses in the internal market,[58] the Commission has in the meantime proposed a series of additional measures in order to overcome the difficulties which service providers still face in acquiring licences with an aggregated repertoire for the territory of more than one Member State.

? QUESTIONS

1 What do you think of the 'Better regulation' approach? Shouldn't all legislation be subject to an economic impact assessment?

2 What about the legislative focus on 'making markets work': should legislation in the area of copyright always be 'market' oriented? What about protecting the interests of participants, in particular those of authors, or even those of end-users? Does a market-oriented approach always favour commercial users, such as online music stores? Who benefits in the end?

3 In your opinion, are Member States happy with the Commission using the instrument of a recommendation rather than that of a directive? What might be their reasons?

---

56 *Lüder* (above, footnote 54).
57 See www.celas.eu.
58 See in this chapter, section 5.2.4.3.

Possible future directives

The 'Better regulation' approach did not exclude, however, additional harmonising efforts by the Commission. Again, however, the issues currently
under discussion are of a piecemeal nature and do not reflect an all englobing
vision of a harmonised EU copyright. At the time of publication, the following initiatives were under discussion.

Consolidation of existing Directives

To begin with, it has long been suggested that the Commission should make
an attempt to abolish existing inconsistencies amongst the directives already
adopted by way of a so-called 'clean-up' or 'umbrella' directive.[59] These
inconsistencies range from minor ones (e.g., Article 4 (a) of the Computer
Program Directive defines reproduction as 'the permanent or temporary
reproduction of a computer program by any means and in any form, in part
or in whole', whereas Article 5 (a) of the Database Directive is phrased 'temporary or permanent reproduction by any means and in any form, in whole
or in part', thus using a slightly different word order), to major ones (e.g.,
Article 5 (1) Computer Program Directive describes the use acts exempt
from the exclusive reproduction right as those that 'are necessary for the
use of the computer program by the lawful acquirer in accordance with its
intended purpose', whereas Article 6 (1) of the Database Directive speaks
of 'acts which are necessary for the purposes of access to the contents of the
databases and normal use of the contents by the lawful user'). This piecemeal
approach to legislation has also produced seemingly arbitrary inconsistencies in levels of protection between different subject matters, with practical
implications where various subject matters are combined in the same artefact
(such as a computer video game, comprising software and artistic works).
Eventually, such a clean-up Directive might also fill some of the gaps which
still exist in the harmonisation, but which are not too controversial in nature.

However, up until now the Commission has contented itself with republish-
ing the following three Directives in a consolidated version which now incorporates subsequent changes made to the initial text by later Directives: the
Computer Program Directive (initially 91/250/EEC, now 2009/24/EC),
the Rental and Lending Directive (initially 92/100/EEC, now 2006/115/
EC) and the Term Directive (initially 93/98/EEC, now 2006/116/EC).

---

59 See Commission Staff Working Paper on the Review of the EC legal framework in the field of copyright
and related rights, SEC(2004) 995, Brussels, 19 July 2004, www.aepo-artis.org/usr/docs review acquis com/
Commission staff working paper.pdf.

QUESTIONS

1 Do you think that such a consolidation directive might be useful?
2 Which inconsistencies can you spot and how do you think they should be solved?

Orphan works legislation

After Google had started digitising books in the US and offering access to these scans via the internet for free, either in the form of so-called snippets or in the form of full text, Europe reacted by setting up the project of 'Europeana', an online service that would bring together Europe's cultural heritage.[60] As explained on the official website:

> [in] 2005 the European Commission published the initiative 'i2010: communication on digital libraries', where it announced its strategy to promote and support the creation of a European digital library, as a strategic goal within the European Information Society i2010 Initiative, which aims to foster growth and jobs in the information society and media industries. The European Commission's goal for Europeana is to make European information resources easier to use in an online environment. It will build on Europe's rich heritage, combining multicultural and multilingual environments with technological advances and new business models.
>
> . . .
>
> Europeana is a Thematic Network funded by the European Commission under the eContentplus programme, as part of the i2010 policy. . . . Overseeing the project is the EDL Foundation, which includes key European cultural heritage associations from the four domains. . . . Europeana.eu is about ideas and inspiration. It links you to 6 million digital items: Images (paintings, drawings, maps, photos and pictures of museum objects); texts (books, newspapers, letters, diaries and archival papers); sounds (music and spoken word from cylinders, tapes, discs and radio broadcasts) and videos (films, newsreels and TV broadcasts). Some of these are world famous, others are hidden treasures from Europe's museums and galleries, archives, libraries and audio-visual collections.

It should be noted that the project is largely confined to materials in the public domain. However, in order to make the scanning of documents possible without infringing existing copyrights in works still protected, the problem of 'orphan works' has to be solved. As explained in the Communication from

---

60 See www.europeana.eu/portal/. See also the Commission's Digital Libraries initiative, ec.europa.eu/information_society/activities/digital_libraries/index_en.htm.

the Commission 'Copyright in the Knowledge Economy' of 10 October 2009,[61]

> Orphan works are works that are in copyright but whose right holders cannot be identified or located. Protected works can become orphaned if data on the author and/or other relevant right holders (such as publishers, photographers or film producers) is missing or outdated.
>
> A work can only be exploited after obtaining prior permission from the right holders. In the case of orphan works, granting such authorisation is not possible. This leads to a situation where millions of works cannot be copied or otherwise used e.g. a photograph cannot be used to illustrate an article in the press, a book cannot be digitised or a film restored for public viewing. There is also a risk that a significant proportion of orphan works cannot be incorporated into mass-scale digitisation and heritage preservation efforts such as *Europeana* or similar projects.
>
> . . .
>
> For publishers, collecting societies and other right holders, orphan works are a rights-clearance issue. They are sceptical about introducing a blanket exception to use orphan works. For them, the crucial issue is to ensure that a good faith due diligence search to identify and locate the right holders is carried out, using existing databases.

Earlier initiatives, notably such as the Commission Recommendation 2006/585/EC[62] and the 2008 Memorandum of Understanding on Diligent Search Guidelines for Orphan Works,[63] are not legally binding acts and therefore do not provide sufficient legal certainty nor solve the fact that using orphan works constitutes a copyright infringement. Therefore, a legislative approach at the European level was called for to allow different uses of orphan works. In May 2011 the Commission proposed a Directive the main element of which is the cross-border mutual recognition of orphan works.[64] This means that once a diligent search carried out in accordance with Article 3 of the proposed Directive has not led to the identification and location of the author, and the work in question has subsequently been declared an 'orphan work' according to the definition contained in Article 2 of the proposed Directive in one Member State, this work shall be considered an

---

61 Doc. COM(2009) 532 final, Paragraph 3.2, http://eur-lex.europa.eu/LexUriServ/LexUriServ.do?uri=COM:2009:0532:FIN:EN:PDF
62 Commission Recommendation 2006/585/EC on the digitisation and online accessibility of cultural material and digital preservation.
63 See ec.europa.eu/information_society/activities/digital_libraries/doc/hleg/orphan/mou.pdf.
64 Proposal for a Directive of the European Parliament and of the Council on certain permitted uses of orphan works, COM(2011) 289 final. In June 2012, after informal trilogues a slightly modified version was prepared for adoption by the Permanent Representatives Committee. Discussion is based on this later draft.

orphan work in all other Member States (Article 4). It should be noted that the proposal does not open up the market for any sort of use of orphan works. Rather, it only privileges publicly accessible libraries, educational establishments or museums as well as archives, film and audio heritage institutions and public service broadcasting organisations. Uses that can be undertaken by these institutions include reproduction for the purposes of digitisation, making available, indexing, cataloguing, preservation and restoration as well as making the works publicly available online, to the extent this is in line with the privileged institutions' public interest missions, notably preservation, restoration and the provision of cultural and educational access to works contained in their collections. In order to achieve this, Member States shall provide for an additional new exception or limitation beyond the closed catalogue of exceptions provided for in Art. 5 (1)–(3) of Directive 2001/29/EC. The privileged institutions may generate revenues in the course of such uses only for the purpose of covering their costs of digitising and making available orphan works. Fair remuneration to authors of orphan works is only due once they have put an end to the orphan status of their works and other protected subject matter. In this respect, Member States shall be free to determine the circumstances under which the payment of such compensation may be organised (Article 6). It remains to be seen to what extent this legislative measure – which has now been adopted as Directive 2012/28/EU – can solve the problem posed by orphan works for memory institutions. The danger that a work might be qualified as 'orphan' in one Member State, although its author is known in another, may serve as an incentive to authors to invest in, and provide information to databases which contain author and work-related information.

A related issue is how to deal with out-of-print works.[65] Here, the author or at least the right-holder is known, but for commercial reasons, the publisher, who has initially published the works no longer keeps them in his backlist and does not plan to make a reprint or new edition either. In view of the fact that this type of market failure could be more easily corrected, the Commission left it to the parties concerned to sign a common Memorandum of Understanding.[66] In this memorandum, although it was recognised by the parties that:

---

65 For a comprehensive overview of the issues see the High Level Expert Group, Copyright Subgroup Final Report on Digital Preservation, Orphan Works, and Out-of-Print Works of 4 June 2008, ec.europa.eu/information_society/activities/digital_libraries/doc/hleg/reports/copyright/copyright_subgroup_final_report_26508-clean171.pdf.
66 Memorandum of Understanding – Key Principles on the Digitisation and Making Available of Out-of-Commerce Works of 20 September 2011, ec.europa.eu/internal_market/copyright/docs/copyright-infso/20110920-mou_en.pdf.

the large-scale digitisation and making available of Europe's cultural heritage contained in the collections of publicly accessible cultural institutions is in the public interest as well as in the interest of the cultural and creative sector

the principle of voluntary agreements on out-of-commerce works was reiterated and the role which collecting societies could play defined.

? QUESTIONS

1 In your opinion, does the issue of orphan works really play a major role with regard to the building up of Europeana?
2 Do you think the mutual recognition approach taken in the proposed Directive on orphan works is superior to full harmonisation? Or is it just the result because full harmonisation could not be agreed upon amongst all the Member States? What are the advantages/disadvantages of the mutual recognition approach?
3 Should the uses allowed under the proposed orphan works Directive be subject to remuneration?
4 Some have criticised the proposed orphan works Directive as being limited to certain public interest institutions, rather than paving the way for competition as regards the exploitation of orphan works by third parties in general. Do you agree?
5 In your opinion, should there also be a legally binding instrument on out-of-print works?

Harmonising the framework for collecting societies

Finally, after years of hesitation, in July 2012 the Commission tabled a proposal to regulate the governance of collective rights management in the EU. There may be several reasons for this past hesitation to tackle the issue of collecting societies. Firstly, not all Member States are equally in favour of having collecting societies involved in dealings with copyright. Member States such as, for example, the UK have traditionally preferred strong exclusive rights in the hands of individual right-holders over collective non-exclusive licensing, even in areas such as non-commercial reproduction. Secondly, in Member States in which the collective management of rights has traditionally been strong, collecting societies do not want to see the rules on transparency and supervision become stricter than they presently are. Thirdly, within the Commission there is a difference in opinion as regards the justification and usefulness of collecting societies between the copyright unit, which forms part of the Internal Market and Services Directorate General of the Commission on the one hand, and the unit responsible within the

Directorate General for Competition on the other. Whereas the former is not fundamentally opposed to creating a legal framework, the latter has traditionally taken a rather critical view of collecting societies' activities.[67] In its agenda for the hearing in April 2010, the copyright unit of the Commission expressed a rather strong concern in favour of the role of collecting societies:[68]

> Effective relationships between the owners of copyright, the collective managers of copyright and the commercial users of copyright-protected products and services are crucial for the development of artistic creativity. The aim . . . is to explore . . . what efforts might be needed to further develop the benefits of the collective management of copyright and related rights.
>
> With this overall goal in mind, . . . the standards of governance and transparency underpinning the relationships (a) between collective rights managers and their members (b) of collective rights managers among themselves and (c) between collective rights managers and those parties that license copyright or related rights [will be looked at].

The proposal that was finally made by the Commission not only contains rules on the collective management of copyright and related rights, but likewise contains a chapter on multi-territorial licensing of rights in musical works for online uses in the internal market (COM(2012) 372 final). Compared with the text of earlier copyright Directives, the text of the proposed Directive on collective management and multi-territorial licensing is rather detailed. This is probably due to the fact that the instrument undertakes to establish – and hence to define – organisational and transparency rules which apply to all types of collecting societies. As summarised in the Explanatory Memorandum of the Directive:

> Chapter 1 [of Title II] provides for rules governing the membership organisation of collecting societies. Article 4 lays down certain requirements which should apply to the relations between collecting societies and rightholders. Article 5 ensures that rightholders can authorise the collecting society of their choice to manage rights and to withdraw such authorisation partially or completely. Societies should base their rules on membership and participation in the internal decision-making on objective criteria (Article 6). Article 7 sets out the minimum powers of the general meeting of the members. Article 8 requires collecting societies to establish a supervisory function enabling their members to monitor and exercise control over their management, while respecting the different institutional arrangements in the

---

67 For discussion see Chapter 7, section 7.2.3.2.3.
68 The agenda and the presentations by the representatives of collecting societies can be accessed at ec.europa.eu/internal_market/copyright/management/index_en.htm.

Member States. Article 9 establishes certain obligations to ensure that societies are managed in a prudent and sound manner.

The following chapters set out rules on collecting societies' financial management (Chapter 2), establish the non-discrimination requirement for the management by a collecting society of rights on behalf of another society pursuant to a representation agreement (Chapter 3), lay down the requirement for collecting societies and users to conduct negotiations in good faith and call for tariffs to be based on objective criteria and to reflect the value of the rights in trade as well as of the actual service provided by the society (Chapter 4). Finally, the levels of disclosure by collecting societies as regards transparency and reporting are defined (Chapter 5).

Title III of the proposed Directive establishes a number of conditions that an author's collecting society must respect when providing multi-territorial licensing services for online rights in musical works. Although a collecting society may decide not to grant multi-territorial licences for online rights in musical works, a number of specific safeguards shall ensure that the repertoire of all societies have access to multi-territorial licensing, so that 'repertoires can be easily aggregated for the benefit of music service providers who want to offer a service as complete as possible across Europe and for the benefit of cultural diversity and consumers at large.' These measures include that a collecting society may request another society granting multi-territorial multirepertoire licences to have its repertoire represented on a non-discriminatory and non-exclusive basis for the purpose of multi-territorial licensing. The society receiving the request may not refuse if it is already representing (or if it offers to represent) the repertoire of one or more collecting societies for the same purpose. Moreover, following a transitional period, right-holders shall be able to grant licences (either directly or through another intermediary) for their own online rights if their collecting society does not grant multi-territorial licences. However, these provisions do not apply if a collecting society grants multiterritorial licences to broadcasters for the online use of their radio or television programmes containing musical works.

Finally, in order to enforce compliance with all these duties, collecting societies are required to make available to their members and right-holders complaint and dispute resolution procedures. Mechanisms should also be available to settle disputes on licensing conditions between users and collecting societies. Finally, certain types of disputes, in relation to multi-territorial licensing, between collecting societies and users, right-holders or other societies could be submitted to an independent and impartial alternative dispute resolution system. However, Member States are not obliged to set up independent supervisors specifically dedicated to the oversight of collecting societies.

? QUESTIONS

1 In your opinion, what are the advantages of the involvement of collecting societies in dealings in copyright, and what are possible disadvantages?
2 Do you think the role of collecting societies has changed with digitisation and the internet? If so, for what reasons? How, in your opinion might collecting societies develop in the future, in particular in view of an increasing amount of individual transactions between media enterprises and end-users (such as Apple i-tunes, pay-per-view newspaper subscriptions and other information value-added services)?
3 Do you think the proposed harmonising measure regarding collecting societies will serve its purpose? Which of the measures proposed seem superfluous, non-realistic or irrelevant, and which additional measures might prove useful? Do you think the measures to supervise the activities of collecting societies as prescribed in the proposed Directive are strong enough?
4 In your opinion, will the new rules on multi-territorial licensing of rights in musical works for online uses in the internal market have the positive effect desired? Could they be extended to trans-border exploitation of works other than musical works?

Policy papers

During the last few years, the Commission has formulated its future policy with regard to copyright in the EU in a series of policy papers. However, rather than expressing a sustainable agenda, these policy papers seem to reflect the political thinking of the day. Hence only some of them merit being briefly mentioned here.

Green Paper on 'Copyright in the knowledge economy'

In 2008 in its Green Paper on 'Copyright in the knowledge economy'[69] the Commission focused on the issue of how research, science and educational materials are disseminated to the public and whether knowledge is freely circulating in the internal market. The Green Paper was not limited to scientific and educational material in the narrow sense, but rather included any mat-

---

69 Green Paper of the Commission 'Copyright in the knowledge economy', COM(2008) 466 final, ec.europa. eu/internal_market/copyright/docs/copyright-infso/greenpaper_en.pdf.

erial which has value in enhancing knowledge. In particular, the following question was raised:[70]

> The combined operation of broad exclusive rights with specific and limited excep-tions highlights the question of whether the exhaustive list of exceptions under the Directive achieves 'a fair balance of rights and interests between [. . .] the differ-ent categories of rightholders and users'.
> . . . Technologies and social and cultural practices are constantly challenging the balance achieved in the law, while new market players, such as search engines, seek to apply these changes to new business models. Such developments also have the potential to shift value between the different entities active in the online environ-ment and affect the balance between those who own rights in digital content and those who provide technologies to navigate the Internet.

In particular, the Green Paper discussed exceptions for libraries and archives (digitisation/preservation; the making available of digitised works; orphan works), the exception for the benefit of people with a disability, the dis-semination of works for teaching and research purposes and user-created content.

Following, a Communication on 'Copyright in the knowledge economy'[71] was issued in which the Commission – apart from orphan works – discussed possible measures with regard to libraries and archives in order to secure 'simple and cost efficient rights clearance systems covering digitisation and online dissemination'; with regard to teaching and research, in order to 'open access to publicly-funded research results', to 'reduce . . . the licensing burden encountered by European universities', and to 'monitor the evolu-tion of an integrated European space for cross-border distance learning;' with regard to persons with disabilities, in order to 'encourage publishers to make more works in accessible formats available to disabled persons. TPM should not prevent the conversion of legally acquired works into accessible formats;' and with regard to user-generated content, in order to provide for 'solutions for easier, more affordable and user-friendly rights clearance for amateur users.' However, the Commission concluded that:

> [i]n the immediate future, the preferred tool for many of the issues raised . . . is a structured dialogue between relevant stakeholders, facilitated by services of the

---

70 Ibid., p. 20.
71 Communication from the Commission 'Copyright in the knowledge economy' of 10 October 2009, Doc. COM(2009) 532 final, ec.europa.eu/internal_market/copyright/docs/copyright-infso/20091019_532_en.pdf.

European Commission. In particular, the dialogue on creating information products, publications and cultural material in formats accessible for persons with disabilities should be taken forward as a priority. Another priority should be finding appropriate licensing solutions for mass-scale digitisation in a European context.[72]

Reflection Paper 'Creative content in a single European market: Challenges for the future'

Another reflection document published in autumn 2009 jointly by DG InfoSoc and DG Market,[73] however, addressed the issues of consumer access, commercial users' access and protection of right-holders as 'main challenges'. Although a broad range of legal measures was discussed, such as extended collective licensing, further harmonisation of limitations and exceptions, streamlining of the pan-European and/or multi-territory licensing process, the consolidation of fragmented rights in musical works, accessibility of ownership and licensing information, alternative forms of remuneration, governance of collecting societies, collaboration with ISPs and, last but not least, the possibility to create a Community copyright, the conclusions of this paper remained rather vague:

> The Commission intends to continue to take a pro-active role in order to ensure a culturally diverse and rich online content market for consumers, while creating adequate possibilities for remuneration and improved conditions in the digital environment for rightholders. The Commission will strive to put in place balanced and durable foundations for an innovative and competitive market place across Europe, upon which market players can construct sustainable online service offerings. Stakeholders can expect the European Digital Agenda to be inspired by these overall objectives.
>
> All interested parties are invited to comment on the ideas raised in this reflection paper . . . [74]

Communication 'A single market for intellectual property rights'

Copyright issues were also addressed, in 2011, in the general IP-related Communication 'A single market for intellectual property rights'.[75] Although

---

72 Ibid., Paragraph 4.

73 See ec.europa.eu/avpolicy/docs/other_actions/col_2009/reflection_paper.pdf. For the comments received see ec.europa.eu/avpolicy/other_actions/content_online/consultation_2009/index_en.htm.

74 Ibid., p. 20.

75 COM(2011) 287 of 24.05.2011, 'A single market for intellectual property rights boosting creativity and innovation to provide economic growth, high quality jobs and first class products and services in Europe', ec.europa.eu/internal_market/copyright/docs/ipr_strategy/COM_2011_287_en.pdf. See also DG Information Society's 'Digital Agenda for Europe – Annual Progress Report 2011', Paragraph 2.1, p. 2,

the Communication purported to aim at the 'Creation of a comprehensive framework for copyright in the digital single Market', yet again it singled out a number of individual issues (European copyright governance and management; technology and database management; user-generated content; private copying levies; access to Europe's cultural heritage and fostering media plurality; performers' rights; audiovisual works and artists' resale right).

Although the conclusion once more remains extremely vague in stating that:

> [a]s new challenges and new priorities emerge in the light of experience and of rapid changes in technology and society, the Commission is committed to review this strategy and draw the appropriate conclusions in close cooperation with stakeholders[76]

the Commission established a rather ambitious list of issues it intends to deal with in the area of copyright, some of which have already been addressed in the meantime:

- orphan works: proposal for a Directive, now adopted;[77]
- multi-territorial collective management of copyright: proposal for a legal instrument;
- audiovisual works: Green Paper on various issues relating to the online distribution of audiovisual works;[78]
- further measures in the area of copyright: assessing the need for further measures to allow EU citizens, online content services providers and right-holders to benefit from the full potential of the digital internal market;
- private copying levies: appointment of a mediator;[79]
- user-generated content: stakeholder consultation.

The Commission has also announced its intention to assess and discuss with stakeholders the possibilities of a European Copyright Code.[80]

---

ec.europa.eu/digital-agenda/sites/digital-agenda/files/dae_annual_report_2011.pdf.

76 Ibid., at p. 22.

77 See above, in this chapter, section 5.2.4.3.

78 See now the 'Green paper on the online distribution of audiovisual works in the European Union – opportunities and challenges towards a digital single market', COM(2011) 427 final of 13 July 2011; ec.europa.eu/internal_market/consultations/docs/2011/audiovisual/green_paper_COM2011_427_en.pdf. For discussion of the policy approaches towards a unified copyright regime in the EU see in this chapter, section 5.4.2.

79 For information see ec.europa.eu/internal_market/copyright/levy_reform/index_en.htm.

80 For discussion see below in this chapter, section 5.4.3.

? QUESTIONS

1 In your opinion, should the EU legislate in the field of research and education? If so, what rules should be adopted?
2 What might be the explanation for the shift of focus from the protection of authors and right-holders to facilitating access by users?
3 If you were responsible within the Commission, which further harmonising measures would you propose?
4 Do you have an explanation for the preference of a stakeholder dialogue over harmonising legislative acts?
5 In your opinion, is there still room for useful harmonisation of Member States' copyright, provided the speed of technological development and, following, of business models in the digital and networked environment?

5.3 Harmonisation by interpretation: the role of the ECJ

General trends

If the law-making process has slowed down in the last years as regards copyright in the EU, the number of cases handed down by the ECJ interpreting the existing Directives has seen a sudden and considerable rise since the middle of the 2000s. Of course, compared to the caseload the ECJ has to face in the area of trade mark, the increase from one or two copyright cases per year to now some 10 or more cases looks relatively modest. However, many of these cases are not limited to some minor detail, but affect certain fundamental notions of copyright law. The rise in the number of copyright cases can most likely be explained by the fact that the broad scope of the Information Society Directive gives rise to a number of questions as regards the compatibility of national law with the provisions of this Directive. Moreover, the willingness of national courts to refer issues to the ECJ seems to have increased during the last years. Issues are not only referred to the ECJ from courts in Member States which traditionally have done so (such as, for example Germany), but also from courts in states which have had a long-standing reluctance to look for guidance outside of their own jurisdiction (as in the example of the UK) or which have only recently adhered to the EU. Last but not least, in copyright litigation where major business interests are at stake, the willingness of the parties involved to 'fight it to the end' seems to be on the rise. This is all the more true if the answer given by the ECJ to the issue in question has a bearing on the use of copyrighted works in several Member States or even throughout the EU.

Most interestingly, particularly in recent cases, rather than limiting itself to interpreting existing Directives the ECJ seems to have succumbed to the temptation to fill certain gaps that still exist in the harmonised EU copyright landscape. In particular, in *Infopaq*[81] the ECJ considered the criterion of an 'author's own intellectual creation' as the general criterion of originality for all works, although the Community legislature had expressly limited this criterion to computer programs, databases or photographs.[82] In spite of certain criticism, the ECJ has reiterated this view in a number of subsequent cases.[83] Moreover, in a series of cases the ECJ developed its own rather elaborate definition of what constitutes 'public communication' rather than staying within the limits of what is commonly understood by this notion in most of the Member States. It will be interesting to see whether these cases were mere 'accidents', attributable to the fact that the ECJ lacks the expertise of a specialised court, or whether this can be taken as a sign of the ECJ's intention to play a more active role in the process of EU copyright harmonisation. Of course, by definition, the possibility of the ECJ to intervene is limited by the cases and questions referred to it by the national courts.

 QUESTIONS

1 Do you agree with the reasons given for the rise in the number of copyright cases referred to the ECJ in recent years?
2 Do you think the ECJ was justified in its *Infopaq* and subsequent decisions in harmonising the criterion of originality and applying it even in cases in which the existing Directives have not expressly prescribed the 'author's own intellectual creation'?
3 In studying the copyright case law of the ECJ, do you find other instances where the ECJ has 'filled existing gaps in the present copyright harmonisation'?
4 In your opinion, to what extent can or should the ECJ contribute to the harmonisation of copyright within the EU?

---

81 ECJ Case C-5/08, *Infopaq International* v. *Danske Dagblades Forening*, [2009] ECR I-6569, Paragraph 37, without any further discussion.
82 Arts. 1 (3) of Directive 2009/22, 3 (1) of Directive 96/9 and Article 6 of Directive 2006/116. For the latter see ECJ Case C-145/10, *Painer* v. *Standard VerlagsGmbH and others*, [2011] ECR I-0000, Paragraph 87.
83 ECJ Cases C-393/09, *Bezpečnostní softwarová asociace* v. *Ministerstvo kultury*, [2010] ECR I-13971, Paragraph 45; Joined Cases C-403/08 and C-429/08, *Football Association Premier League* v. *QC Leisure and Karen Murphy* v. *Media Protection Services*, [2011] ECR I-10909, Paragraph 97.

Issues addressed

Without going into detail, the copyright cases so far decided by the ECJ can be summarised as follows. Although each case only covers a limited set of individual issues, read together these cases nevertheless contribute to the emergence of what ultimately might lead to a uniform European Copyright law. Hence, the cases are not presented here in a chronological order, nor in the order of the Directives which they interpret, but in the order in which the different copyright issues are usually dealt with in a legislative instrument.

Subject matter

In *BSA*,[84] the first case under the Software Directive upon referral by a Czech court, the ECJ had to speak up on the definition of what constitutes a computer program. It held that a graphic user interface is not an expression in any form of a computer program, but rather is entitled to copyright protection as a work of its own within the meaning of Article 2 (a) of the Information Society Directive. In *SAS Institute*,[85] the ECJ had the chance to clarify that under Article 1 (2) of the Software Directive neither the functionality of a computer program nor the programming language and the format of data files used in a computer program in order to exploit certain of its functions constitute a form of expression of that program and, as such, are protected by copyright in computer programs. To decide otherwise would make it possible to monopolise ideas, to the detriment of technological progress and industrial development.

Moreover, in an obiter, in *Football Association Premier League*[86] the ECJ held that sporting events, and soccer matches in particular, cannot be classified as works that can enjoy copyright protection, because they are subject to rules of the game, leaving no room for creative freedom for the purposes of copyright. Finally, in *Flos*, a case concerning design protection, the ECJ also held with regard to copyright that both registered and unregistered designs may enjoy copyright protection, provided they meet the conditions required for protection under Directive 2001/29/EC.[87]

---

84 ECJ Case C-393/09, *Bezpečnostní softwarová asociace v. Ministerstvo kultury*, [2010] ECR I-13971.
85 ECJ Case C-406/10, *SAS Institute v. World Programming*, [2012] ECR I-0000, Paragraphs 39 *et seq.*
86 ECJ Joined Cases C-403/08 and C-429/08, *Football Association Premier League v. QC Leisure* and *Karen Murphy v. Media Protection Services*, [2011] ECR I-0000, Paragraphs 96 and 98.
87 ECJ Case C-168/09, *Flos SpA v. Semeraro Casa e Famiglia SpA*, [2011] ECR I-181, Paragraphs 34 and 41.

Conditions of protection

As already stated above, in *Infopaq*, *BSA* and *Football Association Premier League*[88] the ECJ expressed the opinion that the criterion of 'the author's own intellectual creation' is the yardstick for all works protected by copyright under the Information Society Directive, irrespective of the fact that until now this criterion has expressly been formulated by the EU legislature only with regard to computer programs, original databases and photographic works. Following, as regards photographic works, in *Painer*[89] the ECJ specified that whereas it is for the national court to determine in each case whether or not such photograph is an intellectual creation of the author, relevant criteria are whether the work reflects the author's personality and expresses his free and creative choices in the production of the work. Moreover, in *Football Dataco and others*,[90] a case concerning the fixture lists of the English and Scottish football leagues and the originality of databases, the ECJ first held that the mere intellectual effort and skill of creating the data as such are not relevant in order to assess the copyrightability of the database (likewise, it is irrelevant whether or not the selection or arrangement of the data includes the addition of important significance to the data). Most important, in this case the ECJ held that the significant labour and skill required for setting up a database cannot as such justify copyright protection for a database if they do not express any originality in the selection or arrangement of the data which that database contains. In view of the harmonising effect of the Directive, national legislation is precluded from granting copyright protection under conditions which are different from those set out in the Directive. This came as somewhat of a shock to the UK, where so far the courts did consider labour and skill when ascertaining a work's originality.

With regard to the conditions and the scope of the *sui generis* database right granted by the Database Directive, in a series of four cases handed down under the names of *British Horseracing* and *Fixtures Marketing*,[91] the ECJ had the chance to interpret the condition of protection of 'substantial investment' laid down in Article 7 (1) of Directive 96/9/EC. *British Horseracing* concerned the use of a database containing horseracing data (information

88 ECJ Cases C-5/08, *Infopaq International v. Danske Dagblades Forening*, [2009] ECR I-6569; C-393/09, *Bezpečnostní softwarová asociace v. Ministerstvo kultury*, [2010] ECR I-13971; C-403/08 and C-429/08, *Football Association Premier League* v. *QC Leisure* and *Karen Murphy v. Media Protection Services*, [2011] ECR I-0000.
89 ECJ Case 145/10, *Painer v. Standard VerlagsGmBH and others*, [2011] ECR I-0000, Paragraphs 88 *et seq.*
90 ECJ Case C-604/10, *Football Dataco and others v. Yahoo! UK*, [2012] ECR I-0000.
91 ECJ Cases C-203/02, *British Horseracing Board v. William Hill Organization*, [2004] ECR I-10415; C-46/02, *Fixtures Marketing v. Oy Veikkaus*, [2004] ECR I-10365; C-338/02, *Fixtures Marketing v. Svenska Spel AB*, [2004] ECR I-10497; and C-444/02, *Fixtures Marketing v. OPAP*, [2004] ECR I-10549.

supplied by horse owners, trainers, horse race organisers and others involved in the racing industry) for betting services that was not authorised by the maker of the database in question. The *Fixtures Marketing* cases concerned a database which contained English and Scottish league football data (data concerning the date, the time and the identity of the teams in a particular match) which were used, again without authorisation, by a number of foreign operators of gambling services. In particular, the ECJ held that in order to determine whether or not the database in question required 'substantial investment' to be made, the investment to be considered is limited to:

> (34) . . . the resources used, with a view to ensuring the reliability of the information contained in that database, to monitor the accuracy of the materials collected when the database was created and during its operation

thus excluding all:

> resources used for verification during the stage of creation of materials which are subsequently collected in a database.

Therefore, in the *Horseracing* case, the investment made in order 'to draw up a list of horses in a race and to carry out checks in that connection' did not constitute investment in the obtaining and verification of the contents of the database in which that list appears. In the *Fixtures Marketing* cases, the ECJ came to the same conclusion with regard to 'the resources used to establish the dates, times and the team pairings for the various matches in the league.' In other words, only the investment incurred in seeking out, collecting and storing in a database of *existing* materials can be factored into the 'investment' necessary in order to obtain *sui generis* protection, but not the investment made in order to create the respective data.

Ownership of rights

In *Salvador Dalí*[92] the ECJ interpreted Article 6 (1) of the Resale Royalty Directive:

> (24) . . . as not precluding a provision of national law . . . which reserves the benefit of the resale right to the artist's heirs at law alone, to the exclusion of testamentary legatees.

---

92 ECJ Case C-518/08, *Fundación Gala-Salvador Dalí and VEGAP v. ADAGP*, [2010] ECR I-3091.

In addition:

> (35) ... it is for the referring court, for the purposes of applying the national provision transposing Article 6 (1) of Directive 2001/84/EC, to take due account of all the relevant rules for the resolution of conflicts of laws relating to the transfer on succession of the resale right.

In *Luksan*,[93] upon referral by an Austrian Court, the ECJ clarified that both under the Satellite and Cable Directive 93/83/EEC and the Infosoc Directive 2001/29/EC as well as under the Rental and Lending Directive 2006/115/EC and the Term Directive 2006/116/EC the rights to exploit a cinematographic work (reproduction right, satellite broadcasting right and any other right of communication to the public through the making available to the public) vest by operation of law, directly and originally, in the principal director. Consequently, national provisions which allocate those exploitation rights by operation of law exclusively to the producer of the work in question are incompatible with European copyright law. However, Member States are free to introduce a presumption of transfer, in favour of the producer of a cinematographic work, of rights to exploit the cinematographic work, provided that such a presumption is not an irrebuttable one precluding the principal director of that work from agreeing otherwise.

Also, in the same case the ECJ made clear that as the author of a cinematographic work, the principal director thereof must be entitled, by operation of law, directly and originally, as regards claims for remuneration under a national private copying exception. In this respect, however, Member States may not provide neither for a rebuttable nor irrebuttable presumption of transfer of the claim for remuneration in favour of the producer of a cinematographic work.

Exclusive rights

Reproduction right

In the *Infopaq* decision[94] mentioned above, the ECJ also had to deal with the infringement of the *reproduction right* of Article 2 (a) of the Information Society Directive. The case was about a digitised news extracting service which made reproductions of newspaper articles using an automated process that consisted in the scanning and subsequent conversion of the articles into

---

93 ECJ Case C-277/10, *Martin Luksan v. Petrus van der Let*, [2012] ECR I-0000.
94 ECJ Case C-5/08, *Infopaq International v. Danske Dagblades Forening*, [2009] ECR I-6569.

digital files followed by electronic processing of that file. In arriving at its conclusion, the ECJ examined each sub-part of the whole process in view of its copyright relevance and then held that:

> (51) . . . [a]n act occurring during a data capture process, which consists of storing an extract of a protected work comprising 11 words and printing out that extract, is such as to come within the concept of reproduction in part within the meaning of Article 2 of [the] Directive

but left it to the national court to make this determination. Similarly, in *Football Association Premier League*,[95] the ECJ held that the reproduction right of Article 2 (a) of the Information Society Directive:

> (159) . . . extends to transient fragments of the works within the memory of a satellite decoder and on a television screen, provided that those fragments contain elements which are the expression of the authors' own intellectual creation, and the unit composed of the fragments reproduced simultaneously must be examined in order to determine whether it contains such elements.

In *SAS Institute*,[96] as regards computer programs the ECJ stated that – in spite of the general non-copyrightability of both the programming language and the data format used in a computer program – it has to be considered an infringement, if a third party were to procure the part of the source code or the object code relating to the programming language or to the format of data files used in a computer program, and if that party were to create, with the aid of that code, similar elements in its own computer program. Moreover, it has to be considered a reproduction if copyrighted elements described in a user manual for a computer program are found in a computer program or a user manual for another program. Whether or not such elements are as such protected is, of course, a matter for national courts to decide.

Distribution right

In *Peek & Cloppenburg*,[97] for the ECJ the issue was whether it constitutes a *distribution* within the meaning of Article 4 (1) if copyrighted chairs can be used by third parties to sit on or can be seen in display windows. The ECJ concluded that:

95 ECJ Joined Cases C-403/08 and C-429/08, *Football Association Premier League* v. *QC Leisure* and *Karen Murphy* v. *Media Protection Services*, [2011] ECR I-0000.
96 ECJ Case C-406/10, *SAS Institute* v. *World Programming*, [2012] ECR I-0000, Paragraph 43.
97 ECJ Case C-456/06, *Peek & Cloppenburg* v. *Cassina*, [2008] ECR I-2731.

(41) . . . [t]he concept of distribution to the public, otherwise than through sale, of the original of a work or a copy thereof . . . applies only where there is a transfer of the ownership of that object. As a result, neither granting to the public the right to use reproductions of a work protected by copyright nor exhibiting to the public those reproductions without actually granting a right to use them can constitute such a form of distribution.

The outcome of the case may not be surprising. However, it should be noted that in order to arrive at this result, the ECJ solely relied on the similar wording of the WIPO Treaties, without taking into consideration the fact that the WIPO Treaties only define minimum rights, whereas the purpose of the Information Society Directive is to harmonise copyright amongst Member States.

Moreover, in *Donner*,[98] which concerned cross-border distribution, the ECJ concluded that it amounts to an act of distribution within the meaning of Article 4 (1) of Directive 2001/29/EC in the country in which the final delivery of goods takes place, if a foreign trader directs his advertising at members of the public residing in the Member State in which later on the delivery takes place and creates or makes available to them a specific delivery system and payment method, or allows a third party to do so.

Communication to the public

In a series of cases the ECJ had to clarify under what circumstances a 'communication to the public' was to be found under the different Directives by which this right is granted. First, in *Egeda*[99] the ECJ held that the question of whether the reception by a hotel establishment of satellite or terrestrial television signals and their distribution by cable to the various rooms of that hotel is an 'act of communication to the public' or 'reception by the public' had not yet been harmonised under the Satellite and Cable Directive and therefore must consequently be decided in accordance with national law. However, in a subsequent decision dealing with broadcasting law, the ECJ held that reception of broadcasting signals by the public requires, under Community law, 'an indeterminate number of potential television viewers, to whom the same images are transmitted simultaneously'.[100] Also, in *SGAE*[101] the ECJ interpreted the notion of 'communication to the public' under the Information Society Directive as meaning that:

---

98 ECJ Case C-5/11, *Donner*, [2012] ECR I-0000.
99 ECJ Case C-293/98, *EGEDA v. Magnatrading*, [2000] ECR I-629.
100 ECJ Case C-89/04, *Mediakabel v. Commissariaat voor de Media*, [2005] ECR I-4891, Paragraph 30.
101 ECJ Case C-306/05, *SGAE v. Rafael Hoteles*, [2006] ECR I-11519.

(47) . . . while the mere provision of physical facilities does not as such amount to communication . . ., the distribution of a signal by means of television sets by a hotel to customers staying in its rooms, whatever technique is used to transmit the signal, constitutes communication to the public within the meaning of Article 3(1) of that directive.

In particular:

(54) . . . [t]he private nature of hotel rooms does not preclude the communication of a work by means of television sets from constituting communication to the public within the meaning of Article 3(1).

However, in *Football Association Premier League*[102] the ECJ held that the picking up of the broadcasts and their visual display in private circles as such does not reveal an act restricted by EU legislation.

Similarly to *SGAE*, in *OSDDTOE*[103] the ECJ concluded that the hotel owner who installs TV-sets in the hotel rooms that are connected to a central antenna undertakes an act of communication to the public within the meaning of Article 3 (1) of the Information Society Directive. According to *Phonographic Performance (Ireland)*[104] the same applies under Art. 8 (2) of the Rental and Lending Directive 2006/115/EC to a hotel operator which provides in guest bedrooms televisions and/or radios to which it distributes a broadcast signal or other apparatus and phonograms in physical or digital form which may be played on or heard from such apparatus. Also, Member States may not exempt such hotel operators from payment of the remuneration prescribed by Article 10 (1) (a) of that Directive.

In *Football Association Premier League*[105] it was also held that the transmission of the broadcast works, via a television screen and speakers, to the customers present in a public house, is covered by the notion of 'communication to the public'. But in *SCF Consorzio Fonografici*[106] the ECJ held that the broadcasting, free of charge, of phonograms within private dental practices engaged

---

102 ECJ Joined Cases C-403/08 and C-429/08, *Football Association Premier League* v. *QC Leisure* and *Karen Murphy* v. *Media Protection Services*, [2011] ECR I-0000, Paragraph 196.
103 ECJ Case C-136/09, *Organismos Sillogikis Diacheirisis Dimiourgon Theatrikon kai Optikoakoustikon Ergon* v. *Divani Acropolis Hotel and Tourism AE*, [2010] ECR I-37.
104 ECJ Case C-162/10, *Phonographic Performance (Ireland)* v. *Ireland*, [2012] ECR I-0000.
105 ECJ Joined Cases C-403/08 and C-429/08, *Football Association Premier League* v. *QC Leisure* and *Karen Murphy* v. *Media Protection Services*, [2011] ECR I-0000, Paragraph 171.
106 ECJ Case C-135/10, *Società Consortile Fonografici (SCF)* v. *Marco Del Corso*, [2012] ECR I-0000, Paragraphs 90 *et seq.*

in professional economic activity does not fall under the definition of 'communication to the public' under the Information Society Directive, since the number of persons is small, the music is not part of the dental service, the music is enjoyed by the patients without any active choice on their part and, in a dental practice, the clients are not receptive to the music in question.

In *Circul Globus București*,[107] upon referral by a Romanian Court the ECJ concluded that the right to public communication provided for by Article 3 (1) of the Information Society only refers to communication to a public which is not present at the place where the communication originates. Hence, the right to communicate a work directly in a place open to the public by way of public performance or direct presentation of the work, does not fall under the Information Society Directive and hence remains unharmonised within the EU.

It should be noted in this respect that in order to ascertain a communication to the public, the ECJ requires an indeterminate number of potential listeners, and, in addition, implies a fairly large number of persons. Moreover, the profit-making nature of the communication plays a role in that it must constitute an additional service performed with the aim of obtaining some benefit and not merely be caught by chance by the end-users. In some of the decisions cited, the ECJ in addition required that a 'new public' be reached by the communication in question, although the Court did not have a problem in finding such a 'new public' as regards the guests of a hotel to which protected works were communicated to their private rooms as well as regards the customers of a sports bar.[108] However, since it is rather unclear how all these different criteria newly formulated by the ECJ relate to each other, the ECJ has not created much legal security in this area. In the subsequent case *ITV-Broadcasting*,[109] the referring UK court wanted to know whether it also constitutes an act of communication to the public if a company provides an internet stream of a terrestrial free-to-air television broadcast to individual subscribers within the intended area of reception of the broadcast who could lawfully receive the broadcast on a television receiver in their own homes, and to what extent the answer depends on the technical set-up and advertising model used.

---

107 ECJ Case C-283/10, *Circul Globus București* v. *UCMR - ADA*, [2011] ECR I-0000.
108 See, in particular, ECJ Joined Cases C-403/08 and C-429/08, *Football Association Premier League* v. *QC Leisure* and *Karen Murphy* v. *Media Protection Services*, [2011] ECR I-0000, Paragraph 189 *et seq.* and Case C-135/10, *Società Consortile Fonografici (SCF)* v. *Marco Del Corso*, [2012] ECR I-0000, Paragraphs 83 *et seq.*
109 ECJ Case C-607/11, *ITV Broadcasting Ltd. and others* v. *TV Catch up Ltd.*, pending at the time of printing.

The right of communication was also further interpreted as regards the Satellite and Cable Directive. In *Airfield and Canal Digitaal*[110] emanating from Belgium, the ECJ clarified the meaning and scope of the right to broadcast copyrighted works via satellite under the Satellite and Cable Directive in situations in which the supplier of a digital satellite television service does not transmit his own program, but, rather, either receives the program-carrying signals from a broadcasting station, or instructs a broadcaster to transmit program-carrying signals to a satellite from which they are beamed down to subscribers of the digital satellite television service. The ECJ strengthened the position of the right-holders in deciding that even indirect transmission requires authorisation, unless the right-holders have agreed with the broadcasting organisation concerned that the protected works will also be communicated to the public through that provider, on condition, in the latter situation, that the provider's intervention does not make those works accessible to a new public.

Finally, in *BSA*[111] mentioned above, the ECJ arrived at the correct conclusion that television broadcasting of a graphic user interface does not constitute communication to the public. Although the reasoning of the ECJ is somewhat obscure in this respect, the reason is that because the viewers only receive a communication in a passive manner and do not have the possibility of intervening, they do not have access to interactivity which forms the essential element characterising the interface.

Sui generis *database right*

With regard to the scope of the *sui generis* database right, if the decisions in *British Horseracing* and *Fixtures Marketing*[112] mentioned above limit the number of cases in which the *sui generis* right attaches, the ECJ further held that that the prohibition laid down by Article 7(5) of the Database Directive against insubstantial taking only applies if the unauthorised acts of extraction or re-utilisation have the cumulative effect of reconstituting and/or making available to the public the entire or a substantial part of the contents of that database and thereby seriously prejudice the investment of the maker. This likewise severely limits the scope of *sui generis* protection provided to investment intensive databases, and hence opens up downstream competition for

---

110 ECJ Joined Cases C-431/09 and C-432/09, *Airfield and Canal Digitaal* v. *Sabam* and *Airfield NV* v. *Agicoa Belgium BVBA*, [2011] ECR I-0000.

111 ECJ Case C-393/09, *Bezpečnostní softwarová asociace* v. *Ministerstvo kultury*, [2010] ECR I-13971.

112 ECJ Cases C-203/02, *British Horseracing Board* v. *William Hill Organization*, [2004] ECR I-10415; C-46/02, *Fixtures Marketing* v. *Oy Veikkaus*, [2004] ECR I-10365; C-338/02, *Fixtures Marketing* v. *Svenska Spel AB*, [2004] ECR I-10497; and C-444/02, *Fixtures Marketing* v. *OPAP*, [2004] ECR I-10549.

value-added information products that are in part, or even in whole, based on pre-existing databases. The ECJ has cut back what many commentators in legal literature had already criticised as being an overly broad scope of legal protection.

Moreover, in *Directmedia Publishing,*[113] the ECJ held that an 'extraction' (Article 7 (1), (2) (a)) of the contents of a database did not require the act of physical copying. Rather, 'extraction' could be found in:

> (60) . . . [t]he transfer of material from a protected database to another database following an on screen consultation of the first database and an individual assessment of the material contained in that first database.

Moreover, *Apis-Hristovich*[114] dealt with the issue of what serves as the object of comparison when it comes to evaluating the substantiality of a taking from a database protected by the *sui generis* right. According to the ECJ, the answer depends on the fact whether the database protected is composed of separate modules or not. In the first case:

> (74) . . . the volume of the materials allegedly extracted and/or re-utilised from one of those modules must . . . be compared with the total contents of that module, if the latter constitutes, in itself, a database which fulfils the conditions for protection by the sui generis right. . . . Otherwise, . . . the comparison must be made between the volume of the materials allegedly extracted and/or re-utilised from the various modules of that database and its total contents.

Also:

> [t]he fact that the materials allegedly extracted and/or re utilised from a database protected by the sui generis right were obtained by the maker of that database from sources not accessible to the public may, according to the amount of human, technical and/or financial resources deployed by the maker to collect the materials at issue from those sources, affect the classification of those materials as a substantial part . . . within the meaning of Article 7 of Directive 96/9.

Moreover, regarding the issue of proof whether or not extraction has taken place, the ECJ held that:

> (55) . . . [t]he fact that the physical and technical characteristics present in the contents of a protected database made by a particular person also appear in the

---

113 ECJ Case C-304/07, *Directmedia Publishing v. Albert-Ludwigs-Universität Freiburg,* [2008] ECR I-7565.
114 ECJ Case C-545/07, *Apis-Hristovich v. Lakorda,* [2009] ECR I-1627.

contents of a database made by another person may be interpreted as evidence of extraction within the meaning of Article 7 of Directive 96/9, unless that coincidence can be explained by factors other than a transfer between the two databases concerned. The fact that materials obtained by the maker of a database from sources not accessible to the public also appear in a database made by another person is not sufficient, in itself, to prove the existence of such extraction but can constitute circumstantial evidence thereof.

Finally, in a second case involving *Football Dataco*,[115] the ECJ held that it constitutes an act of 're-utilisation' within the meaning of Article 7 (2) (b) of Directive 96/9/EC if a party uploads data from a protected database onto that party's web server and, in response to requests from a user the web server sends such data to the user's computer so that the data is stored in the memory of that computer and displayed on its screen. Moreover, in case of transborder transmission the act of re-utilisation takes place at least in the receiving State if users in that State have been targeted by the sender. Further clarification on the meaning of both substantial and insubstantial taking according to Art. 7 (1) and (5) of the Database Directive is also sought in the case *Innoweb*[116] in view of screen-scraping software, by which a third party makes it possible for the public to search the whole contents of someone else's protected database or a substantial part thereof in real time with the aid of a dedicated meta search engine.

Exceptions

Scope

First, it should be pointed out that the ECJ has repeatedly taken the position that exceptions and limitations must be 'interpreted strictly', because it regards the exceptions circumscribed in the Directives as 'a derogation from the general rule' of the exclusive rights.[117] The ECJ thus does not follow the more modern view which understands limitations and exceptions as fine-tuning the scope of the exclusivity granted to right-holders vis-à-vis the freedom to act for third parties.

---

115 ECJ Case C-173/11, *Football Dataco et al. v. Sportradar GmbH and Sportradar AG*, [2012] ECR I-0000.
116 ECJ Case C-202/12, *Innoweb B.V. v. Wegener ICT Media B.V.*, likewise still pending at the time of printing.
117 See for the reproduction right of the Information Society Directive ECJ Case C-5/08, *Infopaq International v. Danske Dagblades Forening*, [2009] ECR I-6569, Paragraphs 56 and 57, and Joined Cases C-403/08 and C-429/08, *Football Association Premier League v. QC Leisure* and *Karen Murphy v. Media Protection Services*, [2011] ECR I-0000, Paragraph 162.

In particular, in *Infopaq*,[118] a case which involved a media monitoring and analysis business which consisted in drawing up summaries of articles selected on the basis of certain subject criteria chosen by its customers from Danish daily newspapers and other periodicals, and which was carried out by a technical data capture process before being sent to the customers by email, the ECJ had to speak out on the exception for transient copying under Article 5 (1) of the Information Society Directive. The ECJ gave it a narrow interpretation by holding:

> (74) . . . [t]he act of printing out an extract of 11 words, during a data capture process . . . does not fulfil the condition of being transient in nature as required by Article 5 (1) . . . and, therefore, that process cannot be carried out without the consent of the relevant rightholders.

In the subsequent *Infopaq II* decision[119] on the same facts, the ECJ further specified the conditions of the exception of Article 5 (1) by stating, *inter alia*, that in order to apply the act of reproduction must pursue the lawful use of a protected work as sole purpose and that it may not enable the generation of an additional profit going beyond that derived from the lawful use of the protected work. Also, the acts of temporary reproduction must not lead to a modification of the work in question.

In addition, according to the ECJ's decision in *Football Association Premier League*,[120] mentioned above, acts of reproduction which are performed within the memory of a satellite decoder and on a television screen, fulfil the conditions of the exception laid down in Article 5 (1) of the Information Society Directive and may therefore be carried out without the authorisation of the copyright holders concerned.

Clarifying the exception of ephemeral recordings of works made by broadcasting organisations by means of their own facilities and for their own broadcasts contained in Article 5 (2) (d) of the Information Society Directive, the ECJ in *DR and TV2 Danmark*[121] held that a broadcasting organisation's own facilities include the facilities of any third party acting on behalf of or under the responsibility of that organisation, which is for the national courts to assess. However, as regards whether the third party may be regarded as acting 'under the responsibility' of the broadcasting organisation, the ECJ proved

118 ECJ Case C-5/08, *Infopaq International v. Danske Dagblades Forening*, [2009] ECR I-6569.
119 ECJ Case C-302/10, *Infopaq International v. Danske Dagblades Forening*, [2012] ECR I-0000.
120 ECJ Joined Cases C-403/08 and C-429/08, *Football Association Premier League* v. *QC Leisure* and *Karen Murphy* v. *Media Protection Services*, [2011] ECR I-0000.
121 ECJ Case C-510/10, *DR and TV2 Danmark* v. *Nordisk Copyright Bureau*, [2012] ECR I-0000.

rather creative by considering it essential that the broadcasting organisation is required to pay compensation for any adverse effects of acts and omissions by the third party vis-à-vis, in particular, the authors who may be harmed by an unlawful recording of their works.

In *Painer*[122] the ECJ had the chance to make certain clarifications regarding the exception of Article 5 (3) (d) and (e) of the Information Society Directive concerning the use of copyrighted photographs in the press for purposes of public security. As regards Article 5 (3) (d), the ECJ held that the citation right also applies to works other than literary works. In addition, interpreting Article 5 (3) (e) strictly, the ECJ held that the media may not use, of their own volition, a work protected by copyright by invoking an objective of public security. Rather, in specific cases, a newspaper publisher might publish a photograph of a person for whom a search has been launched, provided, however, that this is done on the initiative of, and in coordination with the competent national authorities (although no express appeal for publication of a photograph for the purposes of an investigation is necessary on the part of the security authorities). Moreover, Article 5 (3) (d) requires the indication of the source, including the name of the author, whereas under Article 5 (3) (e) naming only the source is sufficient.

Other cases concern the scope of limitations provided for by the Software Directive. Thus, in *SAS Institute*,[123] mentioned above, the ECJ could clarify the scope of the use acts permitted under Article 5 (1) and the scope of the provision on line-monitoring, Article 5 (3) of the Software Directive. As regards Article 5 (1), the ECJ held that the owner of the copyright in a computer program may not prevent, by relying on the licensing agreement, the licensee from determining the ideas and principles which underlie all the elements of that program, provided the licensee carries out acts which the licence permits him to perform. Similarly, as regards Article 5 (3) a person who has obtained a copy of a computer program under a licence is entitled, without the authorisation of the owner of the copyright, to observe, study or test the functioning of that program so as to determine the ideas and principles which underlie any element of the program, provided this person carries out acts which are either covered by the licence or acts of loading and running necessary for the use of the computer program. Also, the person may not otherwise infringe the exclusive rights of the owner of the copyright in that program.

---

122 ECJ Case C-145/10, *Painer v. Standard Verlags GmbH and others*, [2011] ECR I-0000.
123 Case C-406/10, *SAS Institute v. World Programming*, [2012] ECR I-0000, Paragraphs 47 *et seq.*

Moreover, in *UsedSoft*[124] the ECJ held that a person who can invoke the exhaustion of the distribution right has to be regarded as 'lawful acquirer' within the meaning of Article 5 (1) of the Software Directive and therefore is not required to obtain the consent of the right-holder to any acts necessary for the use of the computer program.

Adequate/equitable remuneration

A series of cases had to deal with the issue of what constitutes an 'equitable' or 'adequate remuneration'.

Although this issue is mainly discussed under Article 5 (2) of the Information Society Directive, the first case, *SENA*,[125] of February 2003 concerned the notion of 'equitable remuneration' under the Rental and Lending Directive. In this case, the ECJ held that although the notion of 'equitable remuneration' to be paid by a broadcaster of commercial phonograms to both performing artists and phonogram producers under Article 8 (2) of the Rental and Lending Directive 92/100/EEC must be interpreted uniformly in all the Member States, it is nevertheless:

> (38) . . . for each Member State to determine, in its own territory, the most appropriate criteria for assuring . . . adherence to that Community concept.

In particular, according to the ECJ, this:

> (46) . . . does not preclude a model for calculating what constitutes equitable remuneration for performing artists and phonogram producers that operates by reference to variable and fixed factors, . . . provided that that model is such as to enable a proper balance to be achieved between the interests of performing artists and producers in obtaining remuneration for the broadcast of a particular phonogram, and the interests of third parties in being able to broadcast the phonogram on terms that are reasonable.

Also, concerning Article 5 (1) of the Rental and Lending Directive, in *VEWA*,[126] the ECJ concluded that a national rule which fixes the remuneration payable to authors in the event of public lending exclusively according to the number of borrowers registered with public establishments, on the basis of a flat-rate amount fixed per borrower and per year is not permissible.

---

124 Case C-128/11, *UsedSoft* v. *Oracle International*, [2012] ECR I-0000.
125 ECJ Case C-245/00, *SENA* v. *NOS*, [2003] ECR I-1251.
126 ECJ Case C-271/10, *VEWA* v. *Belgische Staat*, [2011] ECR I-0000.

As was to be expected, the national remuneration schemes for copyright exceptions also came under scrutiny by the ECJ. In *Padawan*,[127] the ECJ was faced with the Spanish private copying regime. The ECJ first held that although the:

> (37) . . . concept of 'fair compensation', within the meaning of Article 5 (2) (b) . . . is an autonomous concept of European Union law which must be interpreted uniformly in all the Member States that have introduced a private copying exception

Member States are free to determine:

> the form, detailed arrangements for financing and collection, and the level of . . . fair compensation.

However, since Article 5 (2) (b):

> (50) . . . must be interpreted as meaning that the 'fair balance' between the persons concerned . . . fair compensation must be calculated on the basis of the criterion of the harm caused to authors of protected works by the introduction of the private copying exception.

Concluding, the ECJ upheld national legislation which:

> provide[s] that persons who have digital reproduction equipment, devices and media and who on that basis, in law or in fact, make that equipment available to private users or provide them with copying services are the persons liable to finance the fair compensation, inasmuch as they are able to pass on to private users the actual burden of financing it.

But also, for the very same reason, it held that:

> (59) . . . the indiscriminate application of the private copying levy, in particular with respect to digital reproduction equipment, devices and media not made available to private users and clearly reserved for uses other than private copying, is incompatible with [the Information Society] Directive.

It should be noted that in spite of its inherent logic, the decision poses substantial problems in cases in which copying equipment is both used for commercial and private use, and for national levy systems which, based on Article

---

127 ECJ Case C-467/08, *Padawan v. SGAE*, [2010] ECR I-10055.

5 (2) (a) of the Information Society Directive, levy both private and commercial copying activities.

Following, in *Stichting de Thuiskopie*[128] emanating from the Netherlands, the ECJ reiterated its view already expressed in *Padawan* that although the private user who makes the reproduction of a protected work must, in principle, be regarded as the person responsible for paying the fair compensation provided for in Article 5 (2) (b), Member States are free to opt for a private copy levying scheme under which the persons who make reproduction equipment, devices and media available to the end-user have to pay the remuneration due. The reason is that the latter persons are able to pass on the amount of that levy in the price paid by the final user for that service. Moreover, in order to ensure that the authors actually receive the fair compensation intended to compensate them for the harm caused by private copying, the remuneration also has to be paid if the commercial distance seller is established in a Member State other than that in which the purchasers reside.

However, this is not the end of clarification sought by national courts on the notion of 'fair compensation' as referred to in Articles 5 (2) (a) and (b) of the Information Society Directive. First, in a series of referrals[129] the German Federal Supreme Court sought clarification as to whether digital printers have to be considered as devices using 'any kind of photographic technique or by some other process having similar effects' within the meaning of Article 5 (2) (a) and hence give rise to remuneration; whether a remuneration is due if another device in the chain of devices capable of making the relevant reproductions is already subject to the payment of a levy; whether the possibility of applying technological measures under Article 6 of the Directive abrogates the condition relating to fair compensation within the meaning of Article 5 (2) (b); and, finally, whether fair compensation has to be paid if the right-holders have expressly or implicitly authorised reproduction of their works. Second, the Austrian Supreme Court seeks clarification of whether or not its national compensation scheme for private copying is in line with EU law as regards, *inter alia*, the remuneration to be paid to collecting societies on media capable of reproducing the works of the right-holders irrespective of whether the media are marketed to intermediaries, to natural or legal

---

128 ECJ Case C-462/09, *Stichting de Thuiskopie v. Opus Supplies Deutschland GmbH and Others*, [2011] ECR I-0000.
129 Cases C-457/11 and C-458/11, *VG Wort v. Kyocera Mita Deutschland GmbH and Others* and *VG Wort v. Canon Deutschland GmbH*; Case C-459/11, *Fujitsu Technology Solutions v. VG Wort*; and Case C-460/11, *Hewlett-Packard v. VG Wort*, all pending at the time of publication.

persons for use other than for private purposes or to natural persons for use for private purposes. Also, the referring court wants to know whether a person who uses the media for reproduction with the authorisation of the right-holder or who prior to its sale to the final consumer re-exports the media has an enforceable right against the collecting society to obtain reimbursement of the remuneration.[130]

Three-step test

Although in some cases the ECJ also had to deal with the application of the three-step test contained in Article 5 (5) of the Information Society Directive. According to this test – which has been borrowed from Articles 9 (2) BC, 13 TRIPS, 10 (2) WCT and 16 (2) WPPT – the exceptions and limitations provided for in Article 5 (1)–(4) 'shall only be applied in certain special cases which do not conflict with a normal exploitation of the work or other subject-matter and do not unreasonably prejudice the legitimate interests of the rightholder.' However, the language of the ECJ shows some ambiguity in this respect. Whereas in *Football Premier League Association*[131] the ECJ stated that:

(181) . . . in order for the exception [of Article 5 (1)] . . . to be capable of being relied upon, those acts must also fulfil the conditions of Article 5 (5) of the Copyright Directive. In this regard, suffice it to state that, in view of the considerations set out in paragraphs 163 to 179 of the present judgment, the acts also satisfy those conditions.

In the subsequent *Infopaq II* decision[132] the ECJ referred to this earlier holding by stating that:

(56) . . . if [the] acts of reproduction fulfil all the conditions of Article 5 (1) of Directive 2001/29, . . . it must be held that they do not conflict with the normal exploitation of the work or unreasonably prejudice the legitimate interests of the rightholder.

This language seems to insinuate that an act which fulfils any of the specific limitations of Article 5 (1)–(4) invariably also passes the three-step test.

---

130 Case C-521/11, *Amazon.com International Sales and others* v. *Austro-Mechana Gesellschaft zur Wahrnehmung mechanisch-musikalischer Urheberrechte Gesellschaft m.b.H.*, pending at the time of publication.
131 ECJ Joined Cases C-403/08 and C-429/08, *Football Association Premier League* v. *QC Leisure* and *Karen Murphy* v. *Media Protection Services*, [2011] ECR I-0000.
132 ECJ Case C-302/10, *Infopaq International* v. *Danske Dagblades Forening*, [2012] ECR I-000.

Even if, as a rule, this may well be so, understood in this way the three-step test would be depleted of any normative content.

Exhaustion

In one of the earliest cases dealing with the interpretation of the Directives, the ECJ in *Laserdisken*[133] clarified that a first rental of a copy of protected subject matter does not exhaust the rental right (neither before nor after the adoption of the Directive).

In *Laserdisken II*,[134] the first case referred to the ECJ under the Information Society Directive, the ECJ both upheld the European legislature's decision against international exhaustion formulated in Article 4(2) of this Directive, and it also held that Member States are precluded from adopting national laws that provide to the contrary.

In *UsedSoft*,[135] mentioned above, the ECJ had to answer the question whether or not the distribution right of a computer program was exhausted according to Article 4 (2), if the buyer has himself made the copy after having downloaded the program via the internet. Focusing on the material copy that resulted after the download rather than on the act of offering the program for downloading, the ECJ held that the distribution right with regard to that particular copy is indeed exhausted, provided, however, that the copyright holder had conferred a right to use that copy for an unlimited period of time. The main reason is that in such circumstances the copyright holder may obtain a remuneration corresponding to the economic value of the copy of the software in question. In addition, the same result applies if a maintenance agreement which provided for regular updates was concluded for the program in question. However, since exhaustion requires that the copy of the reseller be made unusable at the time of its resale, the initial acquirer of a licence which allows him to use the program for a certain number of users may not – without the authorisation of the right-holder – 'resell' the number of user rights he doesn't need for himself. Finally, it is worth noting that the ECJ limited its holding to the Software Directive, thus leaving open the question whether the same result applies to works protected under Directive 2001/29/EC, such as for example E-Books.

---

133 ECJ Case C-61/97, *Foreningen af danske Videogramdistributører, acting on behalf of Egmont Film and others v. Laserdisken*, [1998] ECR I-5171.
134 ECJ Case C-479/04, *Laserdisken v. Kulturministeriet*, [2006] ECR I-8089.
135 ECJ Case C-128/11, *UsedSoft v. Oracle International*, [2012] ECR I-0000.

A cross-border issue of the exhaustion of the distribution right was raised in *Donner*,[136] mentioned above, a case concerning the distribution of a work that was copyright-protected in Germany but not in Italy. According to the ECJ, under these circumstances Member States are not precluded from bringing a prosecution under national criminal law for the offence of aiding and abetting the prohibited distribution of copyright-protected works.

Term of protection

The Term Directive leaves open certain issues regarding both the scope of its application in particular as regards the terms of protection of authors of newly acceding EU Member States and the rules which Member States may adopt in order to protect acquired rights of third parties.

In *Butterfly*,[137] the ECJ in interpreting Article 10 (2) of the Term Directive confirmed that because of the harmonisation which the Directive intended to achieve as rapidly as possible the Directive may indeed lead to a revival of rights that had already expired in a Member State. Moreover, the ECJ concluded that Member States are obliged to protect acquired rights of third parties, but that the detail of such measures is left to the discretion of the Member States. The Court thus upheld the Italian legislation which provided for a limited time in which sound recording media may be distributed by persons who, by reason of the expiry of the rights relating to those media under the previous legislation, had been able to reproduce and market them before the revival took effect. The same reasoning was applied by the ECJ to the revival of copyright protection for designs which were previously protected by another intellectual property right and the protection for which had already expired.[138]

In *Ricordi*,[139] the ECJ had to rule on the effects of the principle of non-discrimination[140] on the term of protection. The Court concluded that a Member State could not grant to foreign authors which had already died before the EC Treaty entered into force in the Member State of which he was a national, a shorter term than the term granted to the works of its own nationals.

136 ECJ Case C-5/11, *Donner*, [2012] ECR I-0000.
137 ECJ Case C-60/98, *Butterfly Music v. Carosello Edizioni Musicali e Discografiche*, [1999] ECR I-3939.
138 ECJ Case C-168/09, *Flos v. Semeraro*, [2011] ECR I-181, Paragraph 43.
139 ECJ Case C-360/00, *Land Hessen v. G. Ricordi & Co. Bühnen- und Musikverlag GmbH*, [2002] I-5089.
140 For discussion see Chapter 2, section 2.2.2.

In *Sony Music Entertainment*,[141] the ECJ held with regard to Article 10 (2) of the Term Directive that the life-plus-70-year term of protection is also applicable, pursuant to Article 10 (2) of the Directive where the subject matter at issue has at no time been protected in the Member State in which the protection is sought. The case was about the distribution in Germany of discs with songs by Bob Dylan which had initially been released on albums in the USA before 1 January 1966. According to the Geneva Convention for the Protection of Producers of Phonograms against Unauthorised Duplication of their Phonograms, in force both in Germany and the United States, such producers of phonograms are entitled to copyright protection in Germany only in relation to activities which took place after 1 January 1966. However, due to the aim of the Directive as a harmonising instrument, the ECJ concluded that Article 10 (2) of the Term Directive, according to which all subject matter benefits from the longer term which on 1 July 1995 were protected in at least one Member State, does not require that Member State to be the state in which the protection provided for by the Directive is sought.

Related rights

Interestingly, up until now no questions have been referred to the ECJ seeking clarification on the notion, status and rights of neighbouring right-holders.

Contracts

Since so far, there is little EU law concerning copyright contracts, the number of ECJ cases addressing this issue is also rather limited.

However, in *Uradex*,[142] interpreting Article 9 (2) of the Cable and Satellite Directive the ECJ held that the mandate of a collecting society active in the area of cable retransmission rights is not limited to the management of the pecuniary aspects of those rights but that the society also has the power to exercise the right-holders' rights to grant or refuse authorisation to a cable operator for cable retransmission. In addition, the ECJ clarified that the Directive does not prevent a provision in national copyright law, according to which performers assign to producers the exclusive right of audiovisual exploitation of their performances unless otherwise agreed.

---

141 ECJ Case C-240/07, *Sony Music Entertainment v. Falcon Neue Medien Vertrieb GmbH*, [2009] ECR I-263.
142 ECJ Case C-169/05, *Uradex v. RTD and BRUTELE*, [2006] ECR I-4973.

Also, in *Luksan*[143] mentioned above with regard to authorship of cinematographic works, the ECJ held that while national law may provide for a rebuttable presumption of transfer, in favour of the producer of a cinematographic work, of rights to exploit the cinematographic work, which allows the principal director of the cinematographic work to agree otherwise, Member States may not have, in their national laws, a comparable presumption regarding the principal director's right to fair compensation under a national private copying scheme.

Remedies

Although the EU has enacted a separate Enforcement Directive, and the issue of liability if internet service providers is dealt with by the E-Commerce Directive,[144] issues of remedies also arise with regard to the Information Society Directive. In particular, the question is how the requirement of 'effective' remedies under Article 8 of the Information Society Directive can be reconciled with the protection of personal data according to the EU's data protection laws.[145] So far, the ECJ has had to deal with this problem in several cases, without, however, having been able to come up with a clear-cut solution. The cases *Promusicae*,[146] *LSG*,[147] *Scarlet Extended*,[148] *SABAM*[149] and *Bonnier Audio et al*[150] are discussed in Chapter 8.[151]

Technological protection measures

It should be noted that although the case *Football Association Premier League*[152] dealt with the issue of partitioning the Internal Market by way of technical decoders that were only sold in one Member State and not in others, it only touched upon the legal protection of technological protection measures under the Conditional Access Directive 98/84/EC (the ECJ considering the use of any copyrighted works exempt under Article 5 (1) of

---

143 ECJ Case C-277/10, *Martin Luksan* v. *Petrus van der Let*, [2012] ECR I-0000.

144 See Chapter 8, section 8.2.1 for the Enforcement Directive, and Chapter 8, section 8.2.2 for the E-Commerce Directive.

145 For additional discussion of this issue, see Chapter 8, section 8.2.2.2.

146 ECJ Case C-275/06, *Promusicae* v. *Telefonica*, [2008] ECR I-271.

147 ECJ Case C-557/07, *LSG-Gesellschaft zur Wahrnehmung von Leistungsschutzrechten* v. *Tele2 Telecommunication GmbH*, [2009] I-1227.

148 ECJ Case C-70/10, *Scarlet Extended* v. *SABAM*, [2011] I-0000.

149 ECJ Case C-360/10, *SABAM* v. *Netlog*, [2012] ECR I-0000.

150 ECJ Case C-461/10, *Bonnier Audio* v. *Perfect Communication*, [2012] ECR I-0000.

151 See Chapter 8, section 8.2.2.1.2.

152 ECJ Joined Cases C-403/08 and C-429/08, *Football Association Premier League* v. *QC Leisure* and *Karen Murphy* v. *Media Protection Services*, [2011] ECR I-0000, Paragraphs 96 and 98.

the Information Society Directive 2001/29/EC). In view of this, the subsequent *UEFA and British Sky Broadcasting*,[153] which would have brought clarification regarding the issue to what extent territorially split licensing can be secured by the legal anti-circumvention protection granted to technological protection measures according to Article 6 of the Information and Society Directive, had been withdrawn.

Territoriality

A clarification to the new regime for trans-border satellite transmission was brought about by the decision in the case *Lagardère*.[154] Here, the ECJ held that the somewhat exceptional program carrying trans-border signal transport from France first to a foreign transmitting station and from there back to parts of the French audience, did not fall under the definition of the 'uninterrupted chain of communication leading to the satellite and towards the earth.' Consequently, the Court held, the fee for phonogram use to be paid according to Article 8 (2) of the Public Rental and Lending Directive as implemented in national law, can be governed not only by the law of the Member State in whose territory the broadcasting company is established, but also by the legislation of the Member State in which, for technical reasons, the terrestrial transmitter broadcasting to the first State is located. At the same time, the ECJ restated the fundamental principle of European copyright law that the:

> (46) . . . rights are . . . of a territorial nature and, moreover, domestic law can only penalise conduct engaged in within national territory.

However, it should be noted that in *Football Association Premier League* [155] mentioned above, upon referral by the English High Court of Justice the ECJ held that it was not compatible with the freedom of services laid down in Article 56 TFEU that national legislation of a Member State makes it unlawful to import into, sell and use in that state foreign decoding devices which give access to an encrypted satellite broadcasting service from another Member State that includes subject matter protected by the legislation of that first state. In this case English pub owners had used foreign decoding devices to access Premier League matches that were broadcast in another Member State the subscription to which was less expensive than BSkyB's subscription

---

153 ECJ Case C-228/10, *UEFA and British Sky Broadcasting*.
154 ECJ Case C-192/04, *Lagardère Active Broadcast v. SPRE*, [2005] I-7199.
155 ECJ Joined Cases C-403/08 and C-429/08, *Football Association Premier League v. QC Leisure* and *Karen Murphy v. Media Protection Services*, [2011] ECR I-0000, Paragraphs 96 and 98.

in the UK. The decoder cards had been manufactured and marketed with the authorisation of the service provider, but their use outside of the national territory concerned had been prohibited. From this decision, which according to the ECJ is not altered by any of the provisions of the Satellite and Cable Directive nor of the Conditional Access Directive,[156] it seems to follow that the internal market can no longer be divided by the program producers at least for TV-subscription programs. In this respect, territoriality has been overcome within the EU. However, it remains unclear what effects this decision has for the territoriality of copyright, in particular for rights regarding the content of the broadcasts are concerned or the broadcasters' fixation right under Article 7 (2) of the Rental and Lending Directive as well as their right of communication of their broadcasts to the public which is laid down in Article 8 (3) of that Directive, or the right to reproduce fixations of their broadcasts according to Article 2 (e) of the Information Society Directive.

? QUESTIONS

1 Having read this overview of the cases decided by the ECJ in the area of copyright, do you think that the ECJ follows a coherent line? Or does it decide more on a case-to-case basis?

2 To name just one example: in cases C-403/08 and C-429/08 of 4 October 2011 – *Football Association Premier League et al*, the ECJ stated that '[i]n order to be appropriate, such remuneration must be reasonable in relation to the economic value of the service provided. In particular, it must be reasonable in relation to the actual or potential number of persons who enjoy or wish to enjoy the service' (para. 109). What might be the bearing of this as regards the other instances in which Directives refer to 'equitable' or 'adequate' remuneration?

3 Do you think a specialised Court might come up with better solutions?

4 In order to answer the following question, you might wish to consider the opinions handed down by the ECJ's Advocate General in each individual case with the actual outcome of the decision by the ECJ. In general, does the Court follow the opinion given by the Advocate General?

5 In your opinion, will copyright be further harmonised within the EU by the cases decided by the ECJ, and if so, to what extent can harmonisation be achieved by way of court decisions? Are there any political constraints?

6 As regards territoriality, what, in your opinion, are the effects of the decision in cases C-403/08 and C-429/08 – *Football Association Premier League et al* as regards the territoriality of copyright within the EU? Note

---

156 Directive 98/84/EC of the European Parliament and of the Council of 20 November 1998 on the legal protection of services based on, or consisting of, conditional access, [1998] OJ L 320/54.

also that in this case the ECJ held that acts of reproduction of the copyrighted contents of a satellite program taking place both during the transmission stage and at the reception end are exempt from copyright under the exception of transient copying in Article 5 (1) of the Information Society.

5.4   Towards a Community Copyright?

Shortcomings of piecemeal harmonisation

True, the concept of harmonisation has resulted in a rather impressive harmonisation work. Eliminating certain inconsistencies, bringing national copyright laws closer and making them much more similar to each other than ever before removed many differences in Member States' national copyright laws, which in former days posed barriers to the free movement of goods and services and which distorted competition within the EU.

However, the process also has severe shortcomings, in particular with regard to its future development. As already stated above, the piecemeal approach adopted by the Commission and the Member States in the harmonisation process has not led to complete harmonisation. As can be seen from the list of directives adopted so far, a certain number of even major copyright issues which have a bearing on commerce amongst Member States are still unregulated. In particular, these unregulated issues comprise:

- the criterion of originality, which so far has only been expressly harmonised with regard to computer programs, databases and photographic works;[157]
- moral rights;
- the issue of levies;
- copyright contracts and
- the law of collecting societies.

Indeed, several attempts by the Commission to harmonise the private copying regime have failed. Consequently, Article 5 (2) (a) and (b) of the Information Society Directive leaves it to the Member States' discretion whether they want to replace the exclusive reproduction right by a claim for remuneration against the manufacturers, importers and dealers of recording machinery and blank recording media to be collected and distributed by

---

157 For the harmonising effect of the cases decided by the ECJ on the notion of originality see, however, above footnotes 81–83.

collecting societies, or stick to the exclusive right.[158] As regards other limitations and exceptions to the exclusive rights the list of 20 optional limitations and exceptions in Article 5 (2) and (3) of the Information Society Directive was all that Member States could agree upon. In other areas, such as copyright contracts, the Commission didn't even attempt to come up with a proposal, knowing that no agreement could be reached amongst Member States in view of too great differences in their respective copyright laws. In general, there seems to be a lack of political will to further harmonisation and to abandon long-standing national copyright traditions in favour of a future Community copyright.

Moreover, the harmonisation process itself creates a burden of transaction cost at the procedural level: national legislatures have to try to 'sell' their national solutions to both the Commission and other Member States, or 'defend' their national solutions in Brussels as the case may be. Negotiating and agreeing on the final text of a Directive became more burdensome with each increase in the number of EU Member States, irrespective of the fact that unanimity is not required for a Directive to be adopted (Articles 238, 294 TFEU). Once a Directive has been adopted, Member States have to engage in the process of 'implementing' the solution adopted at EU level in their domestic legislation, i.e. to make the changes necessary where they hadn't been able to successfully 'sell' or 'defend' their own existing national solution.

Most important, however, the harmonisation strategy leaves intact the principle of territoriality. This was expressly recognised by the ECJ in its *Lagardère* decision.[159] EU copyright is still a bundle of 27 national copyrights which operate independently of each other. To ascertain their exact scope and determine the outcome of their application in a given situation is not always an easy task, not least due to language barriers and diverging national legal traditions both at the level of statutory interpretation and of procedural law. Differences in interpretation of national norms which have their origin or legal basis in a Directive can only be clarified by the ECJ, which already suffers from an ever increasing caseload. Finally, as regards trans-border transactions, licensing tends to become more burdensome the more national copyright regimes are involved. Finally, in case of trans-border infringements, the principle of territoriality gives rise to intricate issues of jurisdiction and applicable law.[160]

---

158 See the information at the website of the Intellectual Property Unit of the EC, ec.europa.eu/internal_market/copyright/levy_reform/index_en.htm.
159 ECJ Case C-192/04, *Lagardère Active Broadcast* v. *SPRE*, [2005] I-7199.
160 For discussion of the issues of jurisdiction and applicable law see Chapter 9.

1 Discussing the harmonisation/unification process of copyright law in the EU, Professor Hugenholtz has claimed that '[b]asing its harmonization agenda primarily on disparities between national laws, the European legislature has been aiming, as it would seem, at the wrong target'.[161] Do you agree?

2 If a film producer wants to license the rights, let's say, to turn a novel into a movie, all that is required is one contract, in which the author of the novel authorises the film producer to make the movie and exploit it within the EU. In which situations does the territoriality of copyright within the EU then make trans-border licensing more difficult in the EU?

3 If the territoriality principle means that trans-border online-dissemination of works touches upon as many Member States' national copyright laws as from which the work made available online can be accessed, what is the explanation for the comparably small number of court decisions concerning making works available across borders over the internet?

Attempts to overcome territoriality

Of course, several attempts can be discerned that were made in order to overcome the problems which the territoriality of copyright presented to effective trans-border licensing within the single market.

First of all, the exhaustion principle developed by the ECJ beginning with *Deutsche Grammophon*,[162] and later codified in Article 4 (2) of the Information Society Directive has cleared much of the way for physical goods to freely move across borders within the EU. However, due to the *Coditel I* decision,[163] trans-border content-related services still remain vulnerable to limited territorial licensing and hence a partitioning of the Internal Market that can, in addition, most likely be secured by technical protection devices.[164]

Second, as regards trans-border satellite transmission, under the Satellite and Cable Directive only the uplink-country (or home country) of the satellite

---

161 *Hugenholtz*, Copyright without frontiers, in: Derclaye (ed.), *Research Handbook on the Future of EU Copyright*, Elgar, 2009, p. 18.

162 ECJ Case 78/70, *Deutsche Grammophon v. Metro SB*, [1971] ECR 487. For discussion see Chapter 2, section 2.2.1.

163 ECJ Case 62/79, *Coditel v. Ciné Vog Films*, [1980] ECR 881.

164 See, however, ECJ Joined Cases C-403/08 and C-429/08, *Football Association Premier League v. QC Leisure* and *Karen Murphy v. Media Protection Services*, [2011] ECR I-0000, above in this chapter, section 5.3.2.1.

program-carrying signals is considered as relevant for purposes of copyright. It follows that for one work to be transmitted only one authorisation for only one country is necessary, even if the signals transmitted via the satellite can be received in other countries as well (payment should, of course, take into consideration the whole reception area and thus be distributed amongst the right-holders concerned in all reception countries).[165] However, as the Commission had to admit in its review of the Satellite and Cable Directive, in spite of this approach, market fragmentation continued to exist within the EU in the sector of satellite transmission of TV programs.

Third, under the Online-Music Recommendation[166] the Commission tried to incite collecting societies to grant community-wide licenses to online-music platforms. The aim was to enable these platforms to operate on a pan-European basis rather than via a multitude of national portals. However, by its very nature the Recommendation was not binding. Also, it operates in an area in which there exists a high degree of exclusive rights being split in a rather complex way. Moreover, the Recommendation was limited to musical works only. Reflections of the Commission to extend the scheme to other works as well were no longer pursued, mainly in view of the relative lack of success of the Online-Music Recommendation.

In all, it has to be concluded that until now the EU legislature has not followed a coherent strategy aiming at overcoming the effects of territoriality for copyright in the EU. However, in its Green Paper on the online distribution of audiovisual works in the European Union of July 2011,[167] the Commission outlined several policy approaches and options which might overcome the effects of a strictly applied territoriality principle within the Single Market. One such option would be to extend the 'country of origin' principle set out in the Satellite and Cable Directive and which underpins acts of broadcasting by satellite to the delivery of programming online. Another approach suggested is to make available, on a voluntary basis, an optional title which could coexist with national titles, giving authors or producers of audiovisual works the option to register their works and then obtain a single title that would be valid throughout the EU. Finally, in legal literature, it is proposed to have basic copyright principles on which agreement could be achieved to be covered by a Regulation. This

---

165 For discussion see above in this chapter, section 5.2.2.3.
166 For discussion see above in this chapter, section 5.2.3.1.
167 Green Paper on the online distribution of audiovisual works in the European Union: opportunities and challenges towards a digital single market, Doc. COM(2011) 427 final of 13 July 2011, part 3, p. 12 *et seq.*; ec.europa.eu/internal_market/consultations/docs/2011/audiovisual/green_paper_COM2011_427_en.pdf.

Regulation would both replace harmonising measures and pre-empt the different, heterogeneous national laws. In all other areas, in which the Regulation remained silent, the issues would continue to be regulated by the Member States' individual – and more or less harmonised – national laws.

1 Can you explain why the EU legislature only attempted to overcome the effects of the principle of territoriality in these isolated instances, but not in others?
2 Could there be any reasons other than legal ones that in spite of the solution retained for trans-border satellite television in the Satellite and Cable Directive, no flourishing market has developed for pan-European TV-programs?
3 What are the respective advantages and disadvantages of the different policy options discussed by the Commission in its Green Paper on audio-visual services? In particular, would the creation of a second title conditional upon registration be compatible with the prohibition on formalities contained in Article 5 (2) of the Berne Convention?

The Community Copyright as a solution?

Even if total harmonisation of national laws could be achieved, there will be no complete internal market, as long as there are territorially-defined national copyrights and related rights. This raises the issue of whether – beyond any means of overcoming the effects of territoriality as just described – the solution to the problem of territoriality is to be found in the creation of a unitary Community Copyright along the lines of the Community Trade mark and Community Design. In this respect, Article 118 (1) TFEU now expressly contains the legal competency for the EU. Other than in these latter cases, where Community rights and national rights can coexist in the form of cumulative protection, it would, however be mandatory that a future Community Copyright pre-empt national rules. In view of the fact that because of the prohibition of formalities in Article 5 (2) of the Berne Convention, copyright comes into existence immediately upon creation of a work, national copyright laws would in all likelihood have to be abolished once a Community Copyright comes into existence. This is so because otherwise a national rule providing for stronger protection – and hence more restrictive access possibilities – than the Community copyright would always prevail, thus undermining the object of unification. In creating a Community Copyright, the EU would follow the tradition of most federal states (such as the USA, but also Belgium and Germany), in which copyright legislation is a federal matter.

The main advantage of a Community Copyright would, of course, be that enacted as a Regulation, it would be directly binding in all 27 Member States and have EU-wide effect, thus avoiding lengthy implementation processes and the risk of belated and defective implementation which in many cases can only be corrected – if at all – by way of judicial action taken by the Commission at the ECJ. A Community Copyright would replace the subdivided territoriality by a unique territory for a truly single Internal Market for both goods and services. Moreover, it would invariably lead to further consolidation of the EU *acquis*, increase transparency and legal certainty. Also, it would clarify which use acts are exempt by law, rather than permitting Member States which limitations and exceptions are permitted. Perhaps it might lead to a recalibration of the balance between exclusive rights and limitations.

Of course, creating an EU-wide, unitary Community Copyright also has certain disadvantages. In abolishing national copyright laws, Member States will lose some of their competency to pursue their own cultural policy for their own territory. Also, it would end the possibility of trying and testing diverging solutions within the EU ('competition of systems'). Also, a unitary Community Copyright might have negative effects on the cultural diversity within the EU, contributing to the flowering of which the EU legislature is also under a legal obligation (Article 167 TFEU). In particular, authors from smaller countries might find it more difficult to compete in a bigger market, and collecting societies might no longer be in a position to support national, regional or even local creativity. Similarly, as long as the consumers' personal income varies within the EU from Member State to Member State, there might be a certain need for, and economic efficiency gains in, setting different prices for identical products and services (so-called price-discrimination) and hence for territorial segmentation of the Internal Market. Moreover, it is not to be overlooked that in spite of globalisation and intra-European trade, dealings in copyright are still to a large extent national in nature, mostly because of differences in languages and cultural preferences within the EU.

Yet another question is what the substantive rules of a future Community Copyright should or might look like. In this respect, there is a danger that a Community Copyright might not reflect a proper balance between proprietary rights on the one hand, and access rights on the other. It is at least an open issue whether a Community Copyright would continue the trend of ever increasing and ever longer exclusive protection which the EU legislature has pursued for such a long time. Of course, the torso developed by the academic Wittem project could well serve as a nucleus of a future European Copyright Code.[168] However, it is one thing for a limited number of copyright scholars to agree upon what ideal copyright legislation should look like. It is yet another for interested parties, politicians and legislatures to agree upon a unitary solution. In view of past experience which demonstrated that Member States could only agree on one limitation, but not on 20 others, there is no reason to be optimistic and believe that the very same Member States might agree on one single solution which suits and fits the needs of all of them.

Perhaps rather than creating a full-fledged Community Copyright all in one go, the proper solution may indeed be found in some form of hybrid system as described above, in which only the basic principles in respect of establishing the Internal Market will be laid down and which would pre-empt the different, heterogeneous national laws only to the extent such common rules have been formulated. In all other areas in which Community copyright law remained silent, the national laws would govern. Hence, one could start with unifying, for example, originality, first ownership and perhaps even exclusive rights and limitations and exceptions. Later on, step by step, more and more issues could be codified in European copyright law until in the end a fully developed Community Copyright might have come to being. If this approach is chosen, then the Wittem Code's main defect, i.e. that it is only a torso, may indeed be its main advantage.

However, at least for the time being there seems to be a lack of political will to abandon long-standing national copyright traditions in favour of a future Community copyright, irrespective of which formal approach is chosen.

? QUESTIONS

1 According to Article 118 TFEU, '[i]n the context of the establishment and functioning of the internal market, the European Parliament and the Council ... shall establish measures for the creation of European intellectual property rights to provide uniform protection of intellectual property rights throughout the Union and for the setting up of centralised Union-wide authorisation, coordination and supervision arrangements.' Although, contrary to Article 36 TFEU, which only speaks of industrial property, Article 118 TFEU speaks of 'intellectual property', some commentators have raised doubts whether Article 118 TFEU provides

---

168 See www.copyrightcode.eu.

a competency base for the creation not only of Community industrial property rights, but also for a Community Copyright. What might be the reasons for this conclusion? Do you think these reasons are convincing?

2 Would you prefer a Community-wide copyright over harmonised national laws, if you were (a) a US film producer, (b) a European musical composer, (c) a Slovenian novelist, (d) a pan-European online music store, (e) a national broadcaster, or (f) the owner of a local discotheque?

3 Which of the legislative approaches presented – further harmonisation by way of Directives, the creation of a full-fledged Community Copyright, or the transformation of the existing *Acquis* into a European unitary framework copyright to be filled in by national laws which subsequently will be replaced step-by-step – would you prefer?

4 What is your opinion on the substance of the Wittem Code, in particular on its – controversial – limitations and exceptions? In your country, would the Wittem Code stand a chance of being accepted as binding European law, pre-empting, as far as it regulates, the national copyright legislation of your country?

6

Other intellectual property rights: plant varieties, geographical indications, industrial designs, semiconductor topographies

6.1 Introduction

The areas addressed in this chapter are not as much in the spotlight of legal discussions as patents, trade marks and copyright. With the exception of semiconductor topographies,[1] those rights, however, are of strong and growing relevance in practice. As in the other areas of IP, they concern intangible goods capable of creating positive externalities. By allocating the right of commercial exploitation to the persons providing crucial input to the achievement, further investment will be encouraged and market failure shall be prevented.

The creation of special types of IP in the areas concerned proved necessary because for various reasons, the subject matter did not fit into the scheme provided by the 'classical' IP rights. For instance, while designing the appearance of utility objects regularly involves technical skills and creative activity, it is seldom regarded as 'innovative' in the meaning of patent law, and does not count as a true 'work of art' either. As to geographical indications, they are, like trade marks, signs conveying information about the specific properties of products; however, they do not relate to commercial origin and are not ascribable to one specific, identifiable owner. Finally, although successful plant breeding requires a high level of skill and experience, the subject matter cannot be qualified as 'industrial' in the meaning of industrial

---

1 See in this chapter, section 6.5: contrary to initial expectations, *sui generis* protection for semiconductor topographies has proven to be of very little significance in practice.

property (quite apart from the fact that it has no relationship with copyright). Indeed, integrating plant varieties into the framework of international IP protection proved to be quite difficult: whereas industrial design and geographical indications are listed in the Paris Convention as areas falling into the ambit of industrial property, a special convention had to be created for plant varieties, in order to adjoin it to the overall network of international IP protection (UPOV; see below).

At the time of their conception, plant varieties, geographical indications and (to a lesser extent) industrial designs were fairly distinct from other fields of IP. This has changed quite profoundly in recent times. Remarkable changes occurred not least in the relationship between plant variety protection and patent law: due to the growing importance and sophistication of biotechnological engineering, a significant area of potential overlap has emerged. In a somewhat different way, this also applies to geographical indications vis-à-vis trade mark law, as the tendency to grant broader and stronger protection for both types of rights entails a higher risk of conflict between them. And regarding industrial designs, they have always been so closely related to copyright that occasional overlaps were unavoidable. This is even more so under contemporary conditions, as product design is increasingly acknowledged as a category of art which is hardly inferior to other forms of creative expression, and as further potential overlaps result from the possibility to obtain trade mark protection for the shape of products.

This chapter gives an overview on the legal bases and the contours of protection in the three areas mentioned, including the interfaces and overlaps with the adjacent fields of IP. The order of presentation follows the pattern in which the 'classical' fields to which the respective rights are most closely related were addressed in the previous chapters.

6.2 Plant varieties

Background and legal bases

Already before the laws of genetic inheritance were detected and described by the Austrian scientist and friar Gregor Mendel (1822–1884), farmers and other breeders of plants had gained experience in the modification and improvement of crops. However, only after understanding and consciously applying the underlying hereditary pattern could the results be optimised. It took even longer before the commercial potential of professional plant breeding was realised, and before that led to enactment of the first legal instruments aimed at protecting the results of such activities. The dilemma that such regulations must try to solve is that plants have a natural capacity to propagate, meaning that sales made of new varieties will inevitably enable the buyer to grow more of the same. Other than in case of trademarked products or patented devices, there is no need for the customer to repeat purchases from which a constant source of income for the breeder would result. Interfering with that natural scheme is not only practically difficult, but it also raises general concerns that plant breeders might obtain the right to control and even monopolise the production of food crops and other vitally relevant plants. Addressing the issue of permissible propagation in a fair and feasible manner (typically in the form of the so-called farmers' privilege, see below) is therefore a crucial element of every plant variety protection system.

Legislation on plant variety protection was first enacted in the USA (1930). Most European countries only followed suit in the second half of the last century. Forerunners were the Netherlands with the Breeders' Ordinance (1941) and Germany with the Law on the Protection of Varieties and the Seeds of Cultivated Plants (1953). Protection in Europe and elsewhere became more widespread after plant breeders' rights had received international recognition in the UPOV Convention, which was first adopted in 1961.[2] In 2005, the European Union acceded to the most recent version of the convention (UPOV 1991). Unlike other international treaties in the area of IP, UPOV is not administered by WIPO, but has its own, independent organisation, which is however closely linked with WIPO when it comes to practical matters.

The TRIPS Agreement does not contain any specific regulations about plant variety protection. However, TRIPS Members are requested to provide for protection of plant varieties either by way of patents or *sui generis* regimes or a combination of both (Article 27 (3) (b) 2nd sentence TRIPS). As protection of plant varieties produced by essentially biological processes is excluded from patentability under Article 53 (b) EPC, it was considered necessary for ensuring compatibility with TRIPS that a regime for protection of plant varieties be established on the Community level.

The Regulation on Community Plant Variety Rights (CPVR Reg.) entered into force in 1994, shortly after the TRIPS Agreement.[3] Contrary to the scheme followed with regard to trade marks and industrial designs, no

---

2 International Convention for the Protection of New Varieties of Plants. For additional information see www. upov.org.
3 Council Regulation 2100/94 on Community plant variety rights, [1994] OJ L 227/1.

simultaneous harmonisation of national laws occurred. Instead, the national regimes stay in force, and plant breeders can choose between the systems. However, again in contrast to trade mark and design legislation, it is not possible to cumulate protection on the national and the Community level. Where national rights are granted in contradiction to that rule, they are considered as ineffective (Article 92 (1) CPVR Reg.). However, this only applies during the existence of the respective CPVR, so that national protection can be 'revived' after the lapse of the protection term on the Community level.

Even without formal harmonisation on the national level, many or most national regimes are very similar in substance to the CPVR Reg. That effect ('cold harmonisation') was first observed in patent law, where promulgation of the (failed) Community Patent Convention (CPC) in the 1970s also entailed a fairly high degree of *de facto* harmonisation of national patent laws.[4]

The CPVR Reg. interacts with other Community legislation, *inter alia* regarding the marketing of seeds.[5] Of interest also is the interface between PVR protection and patent law, as patent protection for genetically engineered plants increasingly tends to overlap with plant breeders' rights. This creates political tensions on the European level, but also worldwide: while plant breeder's rights are traditionally tailored with a view also towards the interests of farmers using the protected material for their own purposes ('farmers' privilege'), patent law is more right-holder oriented and rather tends to foreclose any kind of utilisation of the invention which results in a diminution of the premium paid to the proprietor. The issue becomes topical on the international level when, typically in the framework of bilateral trade agreements, countries are moved to forsake the choice given by Article 27 (3) (b) 2nd sentence TRIPS, and to offer protection under patent law instead of, or in addition to, *sui generis* PVR protection.

Protection under the CPVR Regulation

Protection requirements

The object of CPVR protection is defined in Article 5 (1) CPVR Reg. as:

---

4 See Chapter 3, section 3.1.2.
5 European legislation governing the marketing of seeds and plant propagating material within the European Union currently comprises 12 directives. More information is available at ec.europa.eu/food/plant/propagation/evaluation/index_en.htm.

varieties of all botanical genera and species, including, *inter alia*, hybrids between genera or species.

The term 'variety' is further defined in Article 5 (2) as referring to:

a plant grouping within a single botanical taxon of the lowest known rank, which grouping, irrespective of whether the conditions for the grant of a plant variety right are fully met, can be:
- defined by the expression of the characteristics that results from a given genotype or combination of genotypes,
- distinguished from any other plant grouping by the expression of at least one of the said characteristics, and
- considered as a unit with regard to its suitability for being propagated unchanged.

As protection requirements, Article 6 sets out that the variety must be:

- distinct,
- uniform,
- stable[6] and
- new.

The same criteria are also enshrined in Article 5 of the UPOV Convention (1991); hence they reflect an internationally accepted standard. It is the aim of those criteria that only such varieties shall be protected which are clearly discernible in their specificities from plant varieties which are already known, and which can be reproduced without losing the characteristics that make them so specific.

In accordance with those aims, the protection requirements are more closely defined in Articles 7 to 10. Article 7 (1) stipulates that a variety shall be deemed as distinct if:

... it is clearly distinguishable by reference to the expression of the characteristics that results from a particular genotype or combination of genotypes, from any other variety whose existence is a matter of common knowledge on the date of application ...

Article 7 (2) specifies that a plant variety is deemed to be a matter of common knowledge in particular if the same variety had been filed for registration, or

---

6 The three first requirements are often referred to in abbreviated form as DUS criteria.

had been registered, in a register of plant varieties on the national level or at an international organisation (UPOV).

Concerning uniformity, Article 8 sets forth that:

> A variety shall be deemed to be uniform if, subject to the variation that may be expected from the particular features of its propagation, it is sufficiently uniform in the expression of those characteristics which are included in the examination for distinctness, as well as any others used for the variety description.

Stability will be found pursuant to Article 9:

> if the expression of the characteristics which are included in the examination for distinctness as well as any others used for the variety description, remain unchanged after repeated propagation or, in the case of a particular cycle of propagation, at the end of each such cycle.

And finally, Article 10 declares that a variety is novel:

> if, at the date of application . . ., variety constituents or harvested material of the variety have not been sold or otherwise disposed of to others, by or with the consent of the breeder . . ., for purposes of exploitation of the variety:
> (a) earlier than one year before the abovementioned date, within the territory of the Community;
> (b) earlier than four years or, in the case of trees or of vines, earlier than six years before the said date, outside the territory of the Community.

Registration and examination procedures

In order to obtain protection under the CPVR Reg., an application for registration must be filed with the Community Plant Variety Office (CPVO) which has its seat in Angers (France).[7] Applications can be filed directly at the CPVO or at a sub-office or national agency, a list of which is published in the CPVO gazette, Part B (Article 49). The CPVO performs an examination of the formalities (Article 53), and it also examines whether the variety meets the definition under Article 5 and is new in the meaning of Article 10 (substantive examination; Article 54). If no obstacles for protection are found, the CPVO arranges for the so-called technical examination, i.e. for assessment of the distinctness, uniformity and stability of the variety under Articles

---

7 For more detailed information on the Office see www.cpvo.europa.eu/.

7 to 9, which is carried out by the national office or offices entrusted with that responsibility by the Administrative Council (examination office; Article 55 (1)). The routines followed in that regard are described in the Final Report (April 2011) on the Evaluation of the Community Plant Variety Right *Acquis* (in the following: CPV *Acquis* Report)[8] as follows:

> Technical examinations for CPVR applications are conducted through national testing centres entrusted by the CPVO Administrative Council. For certain species, particularly ornamentals, there is only one entrusted examination centre (i.e. 'centralised testing'). Conversely, agricultural species have several competent examination offices. If more than one examination office is entrusted for the same species, CPVO may consider criteria such as the climate, the breeder's domicile and breeder requests to determine the testing centre. When CPVO receives an application for a variety for which there is no entrusted testing centre, CPVO will make a call for tender. If none of the entrusted offices makes an offer, the CPVO may request an examination office outside the EU to conduct the test.

As a result of its evaluations, the examining office issues a technical examination report which is communicated, through the CPVO, to the applicant, who must be given an opportunity to comment (Article 57). Depending on the examination report and the reactions of the applicant, e.g. by amending deficiencies that have been identified by the examining office, the CPVO decides whether to refuse the application or to grant the CPVR (Articles 61, 62).

Pursuant to Article 87, the CPVO keeps two registers: one for applications and another one for rights that have been granted. New entries into both registers are published at periodic intervals (at least every two months; Article 89). Any time after the application and prior to a decision on grant or refusal, third parties can object to the grant of a CPVR on the ground that it does not meet the requirements under Article 7 to 10, or that the person in whose name the application has been filed is not entitled to become the right-holder pursuant to Article 11 (Article 59 (1), (3) (a)). Special rules apply to objections against the denomination of the variety (see below).

After the grant of protection, the continuing, unaltered existence of the protected variety is monitored by the CPVO, with the assistance of an examining office which is entrusted with the task of technical verification (Articles 64, 65).

---

8 Available at ec.europa.eu/food/plant/propertyrights/docs/cpvr_evaluation_final_report.pdf.

The CPVO is also competent for declaring the nullity of a CPVR if the variety did not comply with the protection requirements at the time of grant, or if it has been granted to a person who is not entitled to it (Article 20). Also, the right may be cancelled with effect for the future *inter alia* if it is established that the conditions laid down in Article 8 and 9 – uniformity and stability – are no longer complied with (Article 21 (1)). Decisions taken by the CPVO can be appealed to the Appeal Boards within the Office, and further on to the General Court.

Denominations

Every plant variety must be identified by its proper denomination. For that purpose, a designation must be proposed in the application (Article 50 (3)). The suitability of the proposed denomination is assessed by the CPVO under the criteria listed in Article 63 (3) and (4). Pursuant to Paragraph 3, an impediment for the designation of a plant variety denomination exists where:

(a) its use in the territory of the Community is precluded by the prior right of a third party;

(b) it may commonly cause its users difficulties as regards recognition or reproduction;

(c) it is identical or may be confused with a variety denomination under which another variety of the same or of a closely related species is entered in an official register of plant varieties or under which material of another variety has been marketed in a Member State or in a Member of the [UPOV Convention], unless the other variety no longer remains in existence and its denomination has acquired no special significance;

(d) it is identical or may be confused with other designations which are commonly used for the marketing of goods or which have to be kept free under other legislation;

(e) it is liable to give offence in one of the Member States or is contrary to public policy;

(f) it is liable to mislead or to cause confusion concerning the characteristics, the value or the identity of the variety, or the identity of the breeder or any other party to proceedings.

The same applies pursuant to Paragraph 4:

where, in case of a variety which has already been entered
(a) in one of the Member States; or

(b) in a Member of the International Union for the Protection of New Varieties of Plants; or

(c) in another State for which it has been established in a Community act that varieties are evaluated there under rules which are equivalent to those laid down in the Directives on common catalogues; in an official register of plant varieties or material thereof and has been marketed there for commercial purposes, and the proposed variety denomination differs from that which has been registered or used there, unless the latter one is the object of an impediment pursuant to Paragraph 3.

Objections against proposed denominations for the reasons set out in Article 63 (3) and (4) can be filed within three months after the publication in the Official Gazette of the CPVO in accordance with Article 89. If no impediments exist, the denomination is published together with the specifications of the plant variety right when it is granted.

Use of the denomination is obligatory whenever the plant variety is offered for sale or is otherwise used for commercial purposes. If a trade mark or trade name is used in addition to the denomination, the denomination must be clearly recognisable as such. This obligation persists even after the termination of the plant variety right (Article 17 (1), (3)). In order to ensure full compliance with that obligation, it is stipulated in Article 18 (1) and (2) that rights acquired in regard of a designation which is identical to the denomination of a protected plant variety may not be invoked in order to hamper the use of the denomination in connection with the plant variety, unless the right to that designation was granted before the denomination was designated pursuant to Article 63. That rule also applies after the termination of the plant variety right. Finally, in accordance with the identification purposes intended to be served by the denomination, it is prohibited under Article 18 (3) to use a denomination designating a plant variety which is protected under the CPVR Reg. or a national protection regime within the EU or in a Member State of the UPOV Convention for another variety of the same species, either in an identical or a confusingly similar form.

Rights conferred and limitations

Prohibited acts

Article 13 (2) CPVR Reg. stipulates that the following acts require authorisation by the right-holder, if they are undertaken in respect of protected material:

(a) production or reproduction (multiplication);
(b) conditioning for the purpose of propagation;

(c) offering for sale;
(d) selling or other marketing;
(e) exporting from the Community;
(f) importing to the Community;
(g) stocking for any of the purposes mentioned in (a) to (f).

The same applies with regard to varieties which are essentially derived from the protected variety, or which are not distinct from it, or the production of which requires the repeated use of the protected variety (Article 13 (5)).

The term 'protected material' in Article 13 (2) refers to constituents of the variety or harvested material. However, acts undertaken with respect to harvested material are only covered by the provision if the material was obtained through the unauthorised use of variety constituents of the protected variety, and unless the holder had a reasonable opportunity to exercise his rights with regard to the use of those constituents (Article 13 (3)). Hence, the right-holder must act at an early stage by exercising his rights and terminating the infringement; he cannot simply wait until the adverse party has used the variety constituents for planting, growing, and finally harvesting, in order to save his own labour while reaping the benefits.

Agricultural exception (farmers' privilege)

Notwithstanding the prohibitions under Article 13 (2), Article 14 (1) stipulates that:

> farmers are authorized to use for propagating purposes in the field, on their own holding the product of the harvest which they have obtained by planting, on their own holding, propagating material of a variety other than a hybrid or synthetic variety, which is covered by a Community plant variety right.

In accordance with the aim of the provision to safeguard agricultural production, the right to use such farm-saved seeds (FSS) is restricted to agricultural plant species of fodder plants, cereals, potatoes, and oil and fibre plants, all of which are further specified in Article 14 (2) (a) to (d).

The conditions for giving effect to the derogation contained in Article 14 (1) are set out in Article 14 (3). Most importantly, with the exception of small farmers,[9] equitable remuneration for the use must be paid by the farmers

---

9 For the definition of 'small farmers', Article 14 (3) 4th indent refers to Regulation 1765/92 establishing a support system for producers of certain arable crops.

making use of the agricultural exemption. As is specified in Article 14 (3), 6th indent, that amount shall be sensibly lower than what is charged for the licensed production of propagating material of the same variety in the same area. More detailed provisions are found in Regulation (EC) No 1768/95, which was enacted as an implementing regulation on the basis of Article 114.[10] As a rule, and unless guidelines exist in the form of voluntary agreements between stakeholder organisations, equitable remuneration should be set at 50 per cent of usual license fees. With reference to that rule, the ECJ has held in Joined Cases *Saatgut* v. *Deppe* that a standard rate of 80 per cent of the usual license fee does not satisfy the condition that the remuneration has to be 'sensibly lower' than the amount charged for the licensed production of propagating material.[11]

The CPVR does not establish a uniform system for collecting the remuneration; it is left to the stakeholders in each Member State to develop their own royalty collecting schemes. It appears that the issue is not solved satisfactorily in practice. The CPV *Acquis* Report notes that:

> [r]ights' holders in each Member State are free under the CPVR legislation to develop their own royalty collection systems for farm saved seed. Most commonly this takes the form of self-declaration by the farmer, whereby the farmer indicates the level and types of farm saved seed used. Breeders charge a levy on this use, which serves as remuneration to the breeder for the farmer's use of a protected variety. Regulation (EC) No 2100/94 states that monitoring compliance for the above processes is the exclusive responsibility of the rights holders and there are no provisions for assistance from official bodies. . . . The biggest problem cited with this approach is the high level of false or undeclared FSS use . . .

The problems are said to be enhanced by the fact that the ECJ has imposed rather strict standards for obliging farmers to provide information to plant breeders about the use of farm-saved seeds falling under Article 14. According to the CPV *Acquis* Report:[12]

> [c]omplaints are linked to three decisions by the European Court of Justice, which have restricted breeders' ability to collect information regarding FSS:

---

10 See Commission Regulation (EC) No 1768/95 of 24 July 1995 implementing rules on the agricultural exemption provided for in Article 14 (3) of Council Regulation (EC) No 2100/94 on Community plant variety rights (OJ L 173 25 July 1995 p.14), amended by Regulation 2605/98 (OJ L 328 4 December 1998 p.6). An unofficial codified version including the amendments is available on the CPVO's website, at www.cpvo.europa.eu/documents/lex/consolidated/EN1768consolide.pdf.

11 ECJ Joined Cases C-7/05 to 9/05, *Saatgut Treuhandsverwaltung GmbH* v. *Deppe*, [2006] ECR I- 5045.

12 CPV Acquis Report, above footnote 8, at 4.2.4.3; footnotes added.

– *Schulin* v. *Saatgut* (C-305/00, 2003) established that a breeder could not request information from a farmer regarding FSS use without prior evidence of such use;
– *Schulin* v. *Jäger* (C-182/01, 2004) confirmed the 2003 ruling; and
– *Saatgut* v. *Brangewitz* (C-336/02, 2004) established that, similar to the *Schulin* ruling, information could not be obtained from a registered seed processor regarding a farmer's use of protected varieties without prior evidence that the contractor had processed protected varieties.

In *Geistbeck and Geistbeck*, the ECJ clarified, however, that if the farmer violates his duty to report, he can no longer rely on the reduced fee payable under Article 14 as equitable remuneration and is liable to pay the full market price usually required for a license.[13]

The CVP *Acquis* Report further notes that in response to the difficulties, voluntary declaration systems have been established in several Member States which oblige farmers to provide information without prior evidence of use. However, such systems do not operate everywhere, and where they do, they often do not cover all kinds of crops. As a result, the question is still open whether the system should be complemented by an element of public supervision.

Other limitations: compulsory licenses

Further limitations are set out in Article 15. Use for private, non-commercial purposes, experimental use, and acts done for the purpose of breeding, or discovering and developing other varieties, as well as certain other modes of use addressed in Article 15 (d) and (e) are permitted without the right-holder's authorisation, and without an obligation to pay remuneration for the use. In particular the use for breeding of new varieties is considered to be a cornerstone of the system, which is designed to provide incentives for such activities. A mandatory limitation exempting the utilisation of the variety as an initial source of variation for the purpose of creating other varieties or for the marketing of such varieties is also set out in Article 5 (3) 1st sentence UPOV 1991. This does not apply, however, if repeated use of the variety is necessary for the commercial production of another variety, Article 5 (3) 2nd sentence UPOV 1991. That provision is mirrored in Article 13 (5) (c) CPVR Reg.

---

13 ECJ Case C-509/10, *Geistbeck and Geistbeck* v. *Saatgut Treuhandverwaltung*, [2012] I-ECR I-0000. In ECJ Case C-56/11, *Raiffeisen Waren Zentrale Rhein Main* (pending at the time of publication), Advocate General Jääskinen has declared that the evidence standard required for showing that reporting obligations have been neglected should not be set too high.

Article 29 provides for compulsory licenses being granted to one or more persons by the CPVO. Such licenses may only be granted on grounds of public interest, and after consulting the Administrative Council of the Office. However, as in other fields of intellectual property law, compulsory licenses are an instrument that is rarely, if ever, used in practice.

Exhaustion

As in other fields of European intellectual property, CPVRs are subject to the principle of regional exhaustion, i.e. the right-holder cannot interfere with acts concerning material which has been disposed of to others by the right-holder or with his consent in any part of the EU, and the same applies to material which is derived from such material (Article 16). However, in order to safeguard justified interests of the right-holder vis-à-vis an uncontrollable proliferation of the protected variety, Article 16 further provides that exhaustion does not apply with regard to acts which:

(a) involve further propagation of the variety in question, except where such propagation was intended when the material was disposed of; or

(b) involve an export of variety constituents into a third country which does not protect varieties of the plant genus or species to which the variety belongs, except where the exported materials is for final consumption purposes.

Duration

Pursuant to Article 19 (1), the regular term of CPV protection is 25 years, or, in the case of vines and trees, 30 years. Those protection periods are considerably longer than the minimum duration of protection set out in UPOV 1991, which is 15 years in general and 18 years for vines and trees (Article 8 UPOV 1991). The protection period ends at the end of the calendar year and is calculated from the year following the grant.

With respect to specific genera or species, the EU Council may, by qualified majority, extend the protection terms set out in Article 19 (1) by a further five years. So far, use of that option has been made with regard to potatoes (Regulation No 2470/96).[14] However, the marketing periods are often much shorter than that. As the CPVR *Acquis* Report notes:

Many CPVRs are terminated by the rights holder long before the end of the legal protection provided to them by the legislation. Many are terminated after only a

---

14 Regulation 2470/96 providing for an extension of the terms of a Community plant variety right in respect of potatoes, [1996] OJ L 335/10.

few years. On the basis of experience to date, around 75% of CPVRs for fruit varieties are still maintained after 10 years but only about 40% of CPVRs granted for ornamental and agricultural crops . . . Terminated CPVRs to date have been, on average, between three and five years old when discontinued.[15]

Interface with patent law

Article 53 (b) EPC excludes from protection plant or animal varieties or essentially biological processes for the production of plants or animals; however, the provision does not apply to microbiological processes or the products thereof. Although no direct overlap exists therefore with regard to plant varieties, the areas of protection are not clearly separated either. This is particularly acute in the area of biotechnological inventions. As is explained in Recital 29 of the Preamble to the Biotech Directive (98/44/EC),[16] biotechnological inventions are not excluded from protection where the application of the invention is not technically confined to a single plant (or animal) variety. If, therefore, an invention covers a trait which occurs in multiple plant groupings forming individual varieties in the sense of Article 5 (2) CPVR Reg., a patent can be granted, although it will cover (a number of) plant varieties as well.

The borderline between patents and plant variety protection has become topical in a number of decisions by the EPO Appeal Boards.[17] Further decisions have investigated the difference between 'technical' and 'essentially biological' processes for the production of plants (and animals). This concerns in particular the decisions by the Enlarged Board of Appeal in the tomato and broccoli cases[18] that were addressed in Chapter 3, section 3.4.1.3.2.5.

Apart from patentability, the most sensitive and practically important issue resulting from potential overlaps concerns the agricultural exemption under Article 14 (3) CPVR Reg. which allows farmers to use farm-saved seeds on their own holdings for propagating purposes. In order to synchronise the systems in that regard, Article 11 (1) of the Biotech Directive transposes a corresponding provision into patent law. However, discrepancies

---

15 CPV Acquis Report, above footnote 8, at 4.2.2.2.

16 Directive 98/44/EC of the European Parliament and of the Council on the legal protection of biotechnological inventions, [1998] OJ L 21313. See Chapter 4 for more specific information.

17 The parallel issue concerning 'animal varieties' (as opposed to genetically modified traits applying to a higher taxonomic unit) was of relevance in the Oncomouse case which is addressed in Chapter 3, section 3.5.1.3.2.1.

18 EPO Enlarged Board of Appeals, G 2/07 *Broccoli/PLANT BIOSCIENCE*, [2012] OJ EPO 230 and G 1/08, *Tomatoes/STATE OF ISRAEL*, OJ EPO 206.

between the two regimes are not thus completely ruled out. For instance, the Biotech Directive does not contain a provision directly corresponding to the breeder's right, which allows using protected varieties in order to bring forth new ones. While the concept underlying that exception is similar to use for experimental purposes which is admissible under the patent laws of most EU Member States,[19] this is not considered as rendering a reliable basis for the relevant activities. According to the CPVR *Acquis* Report:

> Member States implement this right [i.e., the experimental use exception] incon-sistently: the distinction between permissible and non-permissible acts varies by Member State (though all commercial acts are seen to be infringing[20]). This creates a high degree of uncertainty for the users of protected material as to the activities that may be considered infringing in this regard.[21]

Relief could be offered by Article 12 of the Biotech Directive, which provides for the possibility to apply for a compulsory license if a plant breeder cannot acquire or exploit a plant variety right without infringing a prior patent. In such cases, the patent holder would be entitled to receive a cross license from the plant breeder. However, the requirements for obtaining a compulsory license are rather demanding; in particular, it must be demonstrated that the plant variety constitutes significant technical progress of considerable eco-nomic interest compared with the invention (and vice versa). As the Report on the CPV *Acquis* notes, there are no known cases of compulsory (cross-) licenses being sought to date.[22]

? QUESTIONS

1 Contrary to trade marks and designs, protection of plant varieties on the national and the Community level cannot be cumulated. What could be the reason for that? Can you imagine why national protection systems were left in place at all, if accumulation is to be avoided?
2 As set out in Article 10 CPVR Reg. (above), a distinction is made with regard to the novelty requirement between publications that were made in the EU and in non-EU countries, and also with regard to the kind of plants concerned. Can you give an explanation for that?
3 Why are plant breeders under an obligation to indicate a denomination

---

19 Chapter 3, section 3.3.5.3.
20 This statement must be qualified to some extent insofar as the commercial character of experimentation does not necessarily lead to inadmissibility; see the reference to the German Federal Supreme Court's deci-sion, Chapter 3, section 3.3.5.3.
21 CPV Acquis Report, above footnote 8, at 4.5.3.1.
22 CPV Acquis Report, above footnote 8, at 4.5.3.2.

for the variety? Should it not be left to their own discretion whether or not they want to market the new variety under a specific designation?

4 The two 'classical' exceptions from plant variety rights – the breeders' exception and the agricultural exception ('farmers' privilege') are difficult to implement – the farmers' privilege because of difficulties in collecting royalties, and the breeders' exception – in certain fields – because of potential overlaps with patent law. How could the system be amended so as to function satisfactorily in the interest of all parties involved?

6.3 Geographical indications

Background and legal bases

Objectives and forms of protection

There is no doubt in principle that indications of the geographical origin of goods (and to a lesser extent also of services) regularly provide valuable input to decision-making processes. This applies in particular where the provenance of the product bears a direct influence on the objective quality – the taste and other properties – of the varieties offered. It is therefore a given task of the law to provide protection against illicit use of designations of geographic origin, where they might cause confusion, or create false impressions among the relevant public.

However, it is less clear which form the protection should take, and whether it should extend beyond the baseline described. More fundamentally, the question can be raised whether protection of geographical indications finds its sole objective in the protection of the public against misleading labelling of products, or whether in addition to that, the efforts of those who bring forth the local or regional product varieties should receive positive recognition by according them a special kind of property right. In the latter case, protection does not necessarily depend on the actual perception of the public and their risk of being misled, but it also seeks to honour and preserve the traditional ways and means of production, processing, and preparation of local specialties.

The attitude prevailing in different countries with regard to those objectives depends not least on the strength of local and regional traditions, in particular in agriculture, and on the value attributed to those traditions. Furthermore, a 'cultural gap' separates societies with long-standing histories in agriculture and craftsmanship from immigrant nations, where newcomers were highly appreciated who imported and practised their home-bred skills in the new environment. Not uncommonly, the goods produced in such circumstances were named after the town or region where the skills had been acquired, as homage to the place of origin and as an appeal to those who craved the old places and specialties. Out of that resolved a more 'relaxed' attitude towards the use of traditional designations of geographical origin, which is characteristic for 'new world' countries such as the USA and Australia. By contrast to that, the EU has become a promoter of strong protection, in particular in the area of agricultural production.

Protection in the EU

EU-wide protection for geographical indications for foodstuff and agricultural products was first established on the basis of Regulation No 2081/92. In addition to consumer protection, legislation was motivated by agricultural policy concerns, as pointed out in the Preamble:

> . . . as part of the adjustment of the common agricultural policy the diversification of agricultural production should be encouraged so as to achieve a better balance between supply and demand on the markets; . . . the promotion of products having certain characteristics could be of considerable benefit to the rural economy, in particular to less-favoured or remote areas, by improving the incomes of farmers and by retaining the rural population in these areas . . . [23]

In 2006, Regulation No 2081/92 was repealed and replaced by the current Regulation No 2006/510 (in the following: Foodstuff Regulation).[24] A separate EU Regulation (No 110/2008) applies to wines and spirits.[25] Of further interest in the area of labelling is also Regulation No 1234/2007.[26]

Due to the restricted ambit of the Foodstuff Regulation, geographical indications for other than agricultural products, be they of natural or industrial origin – for instance, Carrara marble or Brussels lace – can currently only obtain protection under national regulations.

No harmonisation directive concerning protection of geographical indications has been passed so far. However, national law of all EU Member States

---

23 Preamble of Regulation 2081/92, Recital no. 7.
24 Council Regulation No 2006/510 of 20 March 2006 on the Protection of Geographical Indications and Designations of Origin for Agricultural Products and Foodstuffs, [2008] OJ L 335M/213.
25 Regulation (EC) No 110/2008 of the European Parliament and of the Council of 15 January 2008 on the Definition, Description, Presentation, Labeling and the Protection of Geographical Indications of Spirit Drinks, [2008] OJ L 39/16.
26 Council Regulation No 1234/2007 of 22 October 2007 Establishing a Common Organization of Agricultural Markets and on Specific Provisions for Certain Agricultural Products, [2007] OJ L 299/1.

must comply with Articles 22 to 24 TRIPS, which impose a certain minimum level of protection: protection must be granted against misleading use of such indications, and applications of trade marks bearing a misleading indication of origin must be rejected or cancelled (Article 22). Furthermore, designations of wines and spirits must be granted absolute protection to the effect that they cannot be used or registered for products of different origin, irrespective of whether this would cause a risk of confusion or consumer deception (Article 23). Exceptions from that rule are regulated in Article 24: Member States may permit further use of designations of which long-term good faith use has been made prior to the entry into force of the TRIPS Agreement.

In addition to observing the minimum rules enshrined in TRIPS, EU Member States have developed different national regimes for protection of geographical indications. Countries with strong agricultural traditions, such as France, Italy and Spain have long since regarded geographical indications – in particular in the qualified form of 'appellations of origin' – as an important branch of intellectual property, and have established specific protection regimes based on registration. In others, such as the UK, Germany and the Nordic countries, protection of geographical indications is rather considered as a task to be covered by the laws against misleading marketing measures, without specific regulations being called for.

The diversity of attitudes is also mirrored on the international level by the manner in which protection for geographical indications was addressed prior to TRIPS. The Paris Convention lists geographical indications in Article 2 as object of intellectual property, without imposing any specific form of protection apart from an obligation of Member States to provide for the possibility to seize imported goods bearing a false indication of origin (Article 10 Paris Convention). That provision provided the basis for the Madrid Agreement for the Repression of False or Deceptive Indications of Source on Goods (1891).[27] More ambitious in its substance is the Lisbon Agreement for the Protection of Appellations of Origin and their International Registration (1951).[28] Members of that Agreement commit themselves to protecting 'appellations of origin' (defined in Article 2 as the geographical denomination of a country, region, or locality, which serves to designate a product originating therein, the quality or characteristics of which are due exclusively or essentially to the geographical environment, including natural and human factors) that have been registered under the terms of the Agreement, irrespective of a likelihood of confusion or deception arising in their own

---

27 See www.wipo.int/treaties/en/ip/madrid/.
28 See www.wipo.int/treaties/en/registration/lisbon/.

country. Neither the Madrid nor the Lisbon Agreement have attracted many members; the number of contracting states stagnates at 35 (11 EU Member States) and 27 (7 EU Member States) respectively.

The interplay of national, regional and international regulations that is characteristic for this field is further complicated by the fact that many EU Member States have concluded bilateral agreements ensuring, usually on the basis of reciprocity, that certain geographical indications of particular value from a national viewpoint are protected in the other contracting state, and vice versa. All of this results in a dense and highly complex web of obligations and privileges, which makes it very difficult to deal with. The following section will therefore only give a brief glimpse of the area, with the focus being laid on the Foodstuff Regulation.

The Foodstuff Regulation (No. 510/2006)

Definitions

Geographical indications for which protection can be obtained are defined in Article 2 of the Foodstuff Regulation. A distinction is made therein between 'Designations of origin' and 'geographical indications'. Both apply to the 'name of a region, a specific place or, in exceptional cases, a country used to describe the geographic origin of an agricultural product or a foodstuff'. However, the notion of 'designation of origin' is stricter, insofar as it requires that the quality or characteristics of the product so designated are essentially or exclusively due to a particular geographical environment with its inherent natural and human factors, and that the production, processing and preparation take place in that area. By contrast, it suffices for a geographical indication if (in addition or instead of the quality or characteristics of the product) its *reputation* is attributable to the geographic origin. This allows taking into account subjective elements, such as consumer appreciation, which are not necessarily founded on verifiable facts, and may therefore be easier to establish and maintain. Also, it suffices for production *and/or* processing *and/or* preparation of the product to take place in the designated area.

As a third category to which protection under the Foodstuff Regulation may also pertain, Article 2 (2) lists 'traditional geographical or non-geographical names designating an agricultural product or a foodstuff'. Other than the two other forms of indications mentioned above, such traditional names do not necessarily relate to a geographic region or place, but have become associated with a specific origin, and are therefore protected under the same conditions and in the same way as designations of origin or geographical indications.

Irrespective of those differences, designations of origin, geographical indications and traditional names are regularly referred to under the common acronym of 'GIs', which is also used in the following text.

Procedure

Simplified procedure

For a period of six months after enactment of Regulation No 2081/72, Member States were provided with the opportunity to draw up lists of all GIs protected under their national law and submit those lists to the Commission. The Commission then examined those lists, and, if satisfied that the requirements were fulfilled, registration was carried out in a so-called simplified procedure (Article 17 Regulation No 2081/92). Many of the GIs currently protected were registered in that way.

Regular procedure: indications relating to Member States

For regular proceedings, the Regulation provides as follows: an application must be filed by a 'group', i.e. an association of producers or processors working with the same agricultural product or foodstuff (Article 5 (1)). Where the application concerns a geographical area in a Member State, the application must be addressed to that Member State. Each Member State must designate a competent authority which shall scrutinise the application by appropriate means to check that it is justified and meets the conditions of the Regulation. As a step within that procedure, the application must be published in an adequate manner and a reasonable period must be foreseen within which any natural or legal person having a legitimate interest and is established or resident on its territory may lodge an objection to the application (Article 5). If no obstacles are found, a favourable decision is taken, and is again published with a possibility for appeal being granted. Thereafter, the application is forwarded to the Commission, together with the relevant documents. The Commission performs another scrutiny of the application, to be concluded within 12 months (Article 6). A positive decision is published as a single document in the Official Journal of the EU, with an opportunity being given for third parties to appeal against the decision in the course of six months. After that, the geographical indication is finally registered or rejected (Article 7).[29]

---

29 The register of GIs protected under the Foodstuff Regulation including pending applications can be accessed under ec.europa.eu/agriculture/quality/door/list.html.

Indications relating to non-EU States

Under Regulation No 2081/82 it was foreseen that indications relating to geographical areas outside the EU could only be registered if they were protected, or had been found protectable, under a comparable legal regime in their country of origin. This meant in particular that the initial scrutiny of applications as to the fulfillment of the conditions for protection had to be performed by an authority in the country of origin before the GI could be forwarded to the Commission. In practice, this amounted to an exclusion from protection of designations from countries such as the USA, where protection for geographical indications is solely obtained through registration of collective marks, without any substantive examination as to the link between the natural or human factors in the relevant region and the specifics or reputation of the products designated by the collective mark.

A complaint was therefore brought by the USA and Australia before the WTO, based *inter alia* on the argument of non-compliance with Article 3 TRIPS (national treatment). In a report issued on 20 April 2005[30] a WTO Dispute Settlement Panel found that certain international norms had indeed been violated. In the summary of the report to be found on the WTO website,[31] it is stated that:

> the Panel agreed with the United States and Australia that the EC's GI Regulation does not provide national treatment to other WTO Members' right holders and products, because: (i) registration of a GI from a country outside the European Union is contingent upon the government of that country adopting a system of GI protection equivalent to the EC's system and offering reciprocal protection to EC GIs; and (ii) the Regulation's procedures require applications and objections from other WTO Members to be examined and transmitted by the governments of those Members, and require those governments to operate systems of product inspection like EC member States. Therefore, foreign nationals do not have guaranteed access to the EC's system for their GIs, unlike EC nationals.

In reaction to the Panel report, the legislation in the EU was amended so as to provide equal treatment to geographical indications from non-EU countries. Under Regulation No 2006/510, applications from such countries are submitted, either directly or through an authority in the country of origin, to the Commission, which will perform the entire scrutiny.

---

30 DS290 European Communities – Protection of Trademarks and Geographical Indications for Agricultural Products and Foodstuffs (EU – GIs).

31 See www.wto.org/english/tratop_e/dispu_e/cases_e/ds290_e.htm.

Specification, monitoring

A very important element of GI protection is the so-called product specification. Pursuant to Article 4 (2) the product specification to be filed with the
application for protection must comprise at least the following elements:

(a) the name of the agricultural product or foodstuff comprising the designation of
origin or the geographical indication;

(b) a description of the agricultural product or foodstuff, including the raw materials, if appropriate, and principal physical, chemical, microbiological or organolep-
tic characteristics of the product or the foodstuff;

(c) the definition of the geographical area and, where appropriate, details indicating compliance with the requirements of Article 2 (3);

(d) evidence that the agricultural product or the foodstuff originates in the defined
geographical area referred to in Article 2 (1) (a) or (b), as the case may be;

(e) a description of the method of obtaining the agricultural product or foodstuff
and, if appropriate, the authentic and unvarying local methods as well as information concerning packaging, if the applicant group within the meaning of Article
5 (1) so determines and gives reasons why the packaging must take place in the
defined geographical area to safeguard quality or ensure the origin or ensure
control;

(f) details bearing out the following:

(i) the link between the quality or characteristics of the agricultural product or
foodstuff and the geographical environment referred to in Article 2 (1) (a) or,
as the case may be,

(ii) the link between a specific quality, the reputation or other characteristic of
the agricultural product or foodstuff and the geographical origin referred to in
Article 2 (1) (b);

(g) the name and address of the authorities or bodies verifying compliance with
the provisions of the specification and their specific tasks;

(h) any specific labeling rule for the agricultural product or foodstuff in question;

(i) any requirements laid down by Community or national provisions.

Those indications form the basis for Member States' and the Commission's
scrutiny of whether the conditions for protection are fulfilled. Furthermore,
compliance with the specification is checked by controls to be performed by
authorities designated by the relevant Member States (or in case of non-EU
GIs, by an authority designated by the relevant country) prior to marketing
of the product. The specification may only be changed after registration if
a legitimate interest can be shown, in particular to take account of developments in scientific and technical knowledge or to redefine the geographical
area referred to (Articles 9 to 11).

If the Commission comes to the conclusion that a GI no longer meets the conditions for protection as set out in the specification, it will initiate cancellation proceedings. A reasoned request for cancellation can also be filed by any legal or natural person having a legitimate interest. Cancellation proceedings follow the same pattern as registration; the relevant provisions apply *mutatis mutandis* (Article 12).

Effects of registration

Registration of a GI under the Foodstuff Regulation allows (and obliges!) persons marketing agricultural products or foodstuff and originating in the EU which conform to the specification to include the indications 'protected designation of origin' (PDO) or 'protected geographical indication' (PGI) or the respective community symbols in the labeling. For non-EU GIs, such labeling is optional (Article 8).

Pursuant to Article 13, GIs are protected against:

(a) any direct or indirect commercial use of a registered name in respect of products not covered by the registration in so far as those products are comparable to the products registered under that name or in so far as using the name exploits the reputation of the protected name;

(b) any misuse, imitation or evocation, even if the true origin of the product is indicated or if the protected name is translated or accompanied by an expression such as 'style', 'type', 'method', 'as produced in', 'imitation' or similar;

(c) any other false or misleading indication as to the provenance, origin, nature or essential qualities of the product, on the inner or outer packaging, advertising material or documents relating to the product concerned, and the packing of the product in a container liable to convey a false impression as to its origin;

(d) any other practice liable to mislead the consumer as to the true origin of the product.

GIs and generic names

A recurring issue in the context of GI protection concerns the fact that, especially in countries and regions where no strong tradition exists in that regard, names and designations that were originally linked to specific places of origin for the products so designated may 'degenerate' in the course of time, that is, develop into mere indications of kind or quality. In order to exclude such developments at least for the future, Article 13 (2) of the Foodstuff Regulation stipulates that once they have been registered, GIs cannot become generic.

However, if an originally geographical name has already become generic before the application for registration was filed, the result cannot be undone. Article 3 of the Foodstuff Regulation therefore excludes from protection names which have developed into the common name of an agricultural product or a foodstuff in the Community (generic names). In order to decide whether a name has become generic, all relevant factors must be taken into account, including 'the existing situation in the Member States and in areas of consumption' and 'the relevant national or Community laws' (Article 3 (1) (a), (b)).

The provision lay at the centre of a long-standing dispute concerning the protection of 'Feta' for cheese. Protection under Regulation No. 2081/92 was claimed for cheese made of ewes' milk and produced on the Greek territory, with only few parts being excluded from the geographical area allegedly designated by the name (excluded were the island of Crete and the Sporades, the Cyclades, and the Dodecanese and Ionian Islands). Registration was granted by the Commission, but was later annulled upon a decision by the ECJ[32] for failure to consider evidence submitted to the effect that 'Feta' had been used for a considerable time in some Member States to designate cheese not originating from Greece. After renewed examination by the Commission, this time taking the evidence into account, protection for Feta as a designation of origin relating to (most parts of) Greece was re-installed. An appeal was filed against that decision by Germany and Denmark, arguing that:

- the word 'feta', is not a geographical name, but comes from Italian and means 'slice'. It is used not only in Greece but also in other countries in the Balkans and the Middle East, to refer to a cheese in brine;
- considerable quantities of cheese under the name of Feta were lawfully produced in other countries than Greece prior to enactment of the regulation by which use of the name was reserved to Greece.

However, the ECJ rejected the appeal,[33] based *inter alia* on the arguments that:

- although the name feta as a word did not relate to a specific place or region, it could be protected as a 'traditional non-geographical name' which can also obtain protection pursuant to Article 3 (3) if it designates

---

32 ECJ Joined Cases C-289/96, C-293/96 and C-299/96, *Denmark and others v. Commission*, [1999] ECR I-1541.
33 ECJ Joined Cases C-465/02 and C-466/02, *Germany and Denmark v. Commission*, [2005] ECR I-9115.

an agricultural product or a foodstuff which fulfils the conditions under Article 3 (1);

- although Feta is produced in sizeable quantities outside Greece, 85% of the production still originates there; furthermore, on packages of Feta cheese produced in other countries, allusion is often made to Greece by using typical colours (white and blue) and motives,
- whereas the majority of consumers in Denmark consider that Feta is a generic term and has no geographic connotation, the majority of Greek consumers still believe that Feta indicates geographic origin.

As a result, the designation 'Feta' may currently only be used for cheese of Greek origin.

In other cases, the protection of GIs under the Foodstuff Regulation has led to the banning of similar designations that were previously used in a generic sense. Thus, the word 'Parmesan', which was widely understood in Germany as a generic term designating grated hard cheese of any origin, was found to conflict with the protected GI 'Parmigiano Reggiano', and was consequently prohibited.[34]

GIs and trade marks

The legal provisions

Article 14 stipulates that if use of a trade mark would give rise to a situation addressed in Article 13, the application shall be rejected, or, if already registered, the registration of the mark must be cancelled. An exception is made for trade marks which were registered, applied for, or established by use in good faith in the Community prior to the date of protection of the GI in the country of origin or before 1 January 1996.

On the other hand, when a new GI for which protection is sought under the Regulation is identical with or similar to an existing trade mark, registration of the GI is only excluded if in view of the trade mark's reputation and renown and the length of time it has been used, registration is liable to mislead the consumer as to the true identity of the product (Article 4 (3)). Otherwise, the GI can be registered, and the prior trade mark will have to coexist with it.

That latter effect of the Regulation was criticised by the USA as clashing with Article 16 TRIPS, and was therefore also considered in the Panel Report

---

34 ECJ Case C-132/05, *Commission v. Republic of Germany*, [2008] ECR I-957.

rendered on 20 April 2005 (DS290).[35] In this aspect, the Panel agreed with the EC 'that, although its GI Regulation allows it to register GIs even when they conflict with a prior trade mark, the Regulation, as written, is sufficiently constrained to qualify as a 'limited exception to trade mark rights' in the meaning of Article 17 TRIPS'. However, the Panel also emphasised that this did not allow unqualified coexistence of trade marks and GIs, for instance by allowing to broaden the scope of protection actually granted to a GI by using translations that are not covered by the registration as entered into the Commission's registry.

Case law

Many decisions made by the ECJ have elaborated on the trade mark/GI interface. The following are only examples of a broad array of relevant cases.

- In *Consorzio per la tutela del formaggio Gorgonzola*[36] it was found that the artifical term Cambozola 'evoked' the GI Gorgonzola, in the sense that when the consumer is confronted with the name of the product, the image triggered in his mind is that of the product whose designation is protected, all the more because the actual product was a soft blue cheese which is not dissimilar in appearance to Gorgonzola. The ECJ therefore concluded that use of the name might infringe Article 13, irrespective of the fact that the packaging indicated the product's true origin.
- In *Consorzio per la tutela del formaggio Grana Padano*[37] a request for invalidation of the CTM GRANA BIRAGHI was filed by the consorzio per la tutela del formaggio Grana Padano, in whose name the designation 'Grana Padano' had been registered as GI. The owner of the CTM argued that the GI had only been registered for the complex designation 'Grana Padano', the only genuine geographical part of which lay in the word 'Padano' (referring to the valley of the river Po), whereas 'Grana' was commonly understood as a generic term referring to grated cheese. The Board of Appeal at OHIM had sustained the argument, based *inter alia* on findings in specialised dictionaries for cheese referring to 'grana' as a special type of Italian cheeses. Contrary to that, the General Court found that although the term 'grana' had been used in Italy as the common term for cheeses produced in different geographical areas, all those areas were situated in the same region, namely in the Po valley.

---

35 Above, footnote 30.
36 ECJ Case C-87/97, *Consorzio per la tutela del formaggio Gorgonzola v. Käserei Champignon Hofmeister* (Cambozola), [1999] ECR I-1301.
37 General Court Case T-291/03, *Consorzio per la tutela del formaggio Grana Padano v. OHIM* (GRANA BIRAGHI), [2007] ECR II-3081.

Therefore, it was concluded that the term 'grana' itself had become a substantial part of the GI, and had been infringed by the contested CTM.

Relationship with national protection systems

The Foodstuff Regulation does not expand on the relationship between Community GIs and national protection systems, in particular whether parallel protection can be granted under both kinds of regimes. It is clear, however, that a possible exclusion of double protection could only apply to products and designations falling into the ambit of the Foodstuff Regulation. Protection on the basis of national law is therefore always possible for signs indicating the geographical origin of other products than foodstuff or agricultural products.[38] Furthermore, designations referring to particular types of landscapes without thereby indicating a specific region – such as 'montagne' for a mountainous area – are not protectable under the Foodstuff Regulation and are therefore only subject to national regulations on misleading marketing measures, without being exclusively reserved for products originating from individual Member States.

More problematic is the relationship between the Foodstuff Regulation and national law where the former is basically applicable. The issue was addressed in a somewhat indirect manner in the context of the simplified procedure applying under Regulation 2081/72 (see above). During the period when applications were considered under that procedure, Member States were entitled to grant transitional protection for the designation, but such protection ceased after the decision on the registration as a Community GI was made. This allows concluding that, apart from the situation covered by the provision, protection for the same type of product under the Foodstuff Regulation is meant to be exclusive. This was confirmed by the ECJ in a case brought against producers of cheese, who had used the term 'Époisses' for cheese which did not fulfil the relevant specification in the national registration. However, the designation protected on the Community level was not 'Époisses' but 'Époisses de Bourgogne'. The national registration had been changed to 'Époisses' after 'Époisses de Bourgogne' had been filed for registration as a Community GI under the simplified procedure. According to the defence, the change in the national registration could not alter the scope of protection of the GI, which was solely determined by the registration on the Community level. The ECJ agreed with that reasoning:[39]

---

38 See this chapter, Introduction to section 6.3.
39 ECJ Joined Cases C-129 and 130/97, *Chiciak* and *Fol*, [1998] ECR I-3315.

(29) It is implicit in the uniform protection of designations of origin which was introduced by the 1992 regulation that a Member State which considers it appropriate for an alteration to be made to the designation of origin for which registration has been requested in accordance with the regulation should comply with the procedures established for that purpose. (30) Any alteration of an element of the product specification, such as the name of the product, that is to say the registered designation of origin, can therefore be procured only within the framework of the Community arrangements and procedures laid down by the 1992 regulation . . . (33) [Therefore], the 1992 regulation must be interpreted as meaning that, since its entry into force, a Member State may not, by adopting provisions of national law, alter a designation of origin for which it has requested registration in accordance with Article 17 and protect that designation at national level.

Similarly, it was held in one of the many cases dealing with the right to use the designation 'Bud' for beer that no protection on the basis of a bilateral agreement can be claimed for a geographical indication in case that the opportunity has been missed during the available time period to apply for protection under the GI Regulation, although the designation would have qualified for such protection.[40]

The impact of the Foodstuff Regulation on protection of 'simple' GIs – designations which do relate to the geographical origin of foodstuff or agricultural products and thus fall into the ambit of the Regulation, without fulfilling the specific requirements for protection – remained unclear for some time. The issue became topical in a dispute concerning beer marketed under the designation 'Warsteiner'.[41] The designation relates to a place in Germany, but it is hardly recognised as such by the German public; also, no objective and verifiable connection exists between the place of origin and the quality or reputation of the product so designated. The question was posed to the ECJ whether in such a case the provisions anchored in German trade mark on the protection of simple geographical indications could be applied, or whether this was precluded by the Foodstuff Regulation. The ECJ answered that:

(44) It is common ground that simple geographical indications of source, in the case of which . . . there is no link between the characteristics of the product and its geographical provenance, do not fall within [the ambit of] Regulation No 2081/92. (45) However, there is nothing in Regulation No 2081/92 to indicate that such geographical indications of source cannot be protected under the

---

40 ECJ Case C-478/08, *Budějovický Budvar* v. *Ammersin*, [2009] ECR I-7721.
41 ECJ Case C- 312/98, *Schutzverband gegen Unwesen in der Wirtschaft* v. *Warsteiner Brauerei*, [2000] ECR I-9187.

national legislation of a Member State. . . .(54) . . . the answer to be given to the question referred to the Court must be that Regulation No 2081/92 does not preclude the application of national legislation which prohibits the potentially mis-leading use of a geographical indication of source in the case of which there is no link between the characteristics of the product and its geographical provenance.

GIs and primary EU law

Similar to trade marks and other intellectual property rights, GIs can form an obstacle against the free movement of goods over borders, thereby causing disruptions of intra-Community trade. The first ECJ case[42] addressing the issue concerned the designation 'Touron de Alicante', a special kind of nougat made on the Costa Blanca, which is protected in Spain and also in France, by virtue of a bilateral agreement concluded between the two coun-tries. Import into France of nougat under the designation, but not produced in the region, was prohibited on the basis of the Franco-Spanish agreement. The importers challenged the decision on the argument it impeded the free movement of goods (Article 34 TFEU; then: Article 30 EC). With the support of the Commission, they argued that GIs only merit legal protection in the meaning of Article 36 TFEU if they are 'qualified' in the sense that the product to which the protected name applies possesses qualities and charac-teristics which are due to its geographical place of origin and are such as to give it its individual character. However, the ECJ declared that protection should extend also to 'simple' GIs:

[i]t would have the effect of depriving of all protection geographical names used for products which cannot be shown to derive a particular flavour from the land and which have not been produced in accordance with quality requirements and manufacturing standards laid down by an act of public authority . . . Such names may nevertheless enjoy a high reputation amongst consumers and constitute for producers established in the places to which they refer an essential means of attracting custom. They are therefore entitled to protection.

Regarding the justifiability under Article 36 of the objectives pursued by the Franco-Spanish agreement and the consequences ensuing therefrom for the free movement of goods, the ECJ concluded that:

[t]he aim of the Convention is to prevent the producers of a Contracting State from using the geographical names of another State, thereby taking advantage of the reputation attaching to the products of the undertakings established in the

---

42 ECJ Case C-3/91, *Exportur SA v. LOR SA and Confiserie du Tech SA*, [1992] ECR I-05529.

regions or places indicated by those names. Such an objective, intended to ensure fair competition, may be regarded as falling within the sphere of the protection of industrial and commercial property within the meaning of Article 36, provided that the names in question have not, either at the time of the entry into force of that Convention or subsequently, become generic in the country of origin.

The export of products bearing a GI was at stake in a case concerning the well-known denomination 'Parma Ham' (Prosciutto di Parma). It had been registered with the 'first wave' of GIs filed on the basis of the 'simplified procedure' under Article 17 Regulation No 2081/92 (see this chapter, section 6.3.2.2.1). The specifications included not only the 'method of obtaining' the product, i.e. the raising of cattle and curing the ham, but they also related to the slicing and packaging of the finalised product. A dispute arose when entire hams that had been imported to the UK were sliced and packed there, i.e. outside the area to which the GI related. The association representing the authorised makers of Parma filed suit in the UK against such practices, but failed in the first instance and the court of appeal. The House of Lords then referred to the ECJ the question whether to prohibit slicing and packaging of genuine products designated by a GI was legitimately covered by Regulation No 2081/92, or whether it constituted an impediment to export which was not appropriately justified by the objective it was intended to serve.

The ECJ[43] started by elaborating on the objective of GIs, which:

> (64) . . . fall within the scope of commercial and industrial property rights. The applicable rules protect those who are entitled to use them against improper use by third parties seeking to profit from the reputation they have acquired. They are intended to guarantee that the product bearing them comes from an specified geographical area and displays certain characteristics. They may enjoy a high reputation amongst consumers and constitute for producers who are entitled to using them an essential means of attracting custom. The reputation of designations of origin depends on their image in the mind of consumers. That image in turn depends essentially on the characteristics and the quality of the product . . . (65) The specification of the PDO 'Prosciutto di Parma', by requiring the slicing and packaging to be carried out in the region of production, is intended to allow the persons entitled to use the PDO to keep under their control one of the ways in which the product appears on the market. The condition it lays down aims better to safeguard the quality and authenticity of the product and consequently the reputation of the PDO . . . (66) Against that background, a condition such as at

---

43 ECJ Case C-108/01, *Consorzio di Prosciutto di Parma v. Asda Stores*, [2003] ECR I-5121.

issue must be regarded as compatible with Community law despite its restrictive effects on trade . . .

The importers had argued that even if the method of slicing and packaging was important for safeguarding the specific quality of Parma Ham, a less restrictive means than prohibiting any such processing abroad would be to give instructions, and monitor the performance, of slicing and packaging in other countries. However, the ECJ did not agree:

> (75) . . . it must be accepted that checks performed outside the region of produc-
> tion would provide fewer guarantees of the quality and authenticity of the product
> . . . (C)hecks carried out in accordance with (the procedure as it is carried out in
> the region of production) are thorough and systematic in nature, and are done by
> experts who have specialized knowledge of the characteristics of Parma ham . . .
> (I)t is hardly conceivable that representatives of persons entitled to use the PDO
> could effectively introduce such checks in other Member States . . .

Parallel proceedings with a similar outcome related to the grating of 'Grana Padano' cheese outside the area of production.[44]

? QUESTIONS

1 The EU Commission is currently considering plans to introduce specific legislation on the Community level for protection of GIs designating other commodities than foodstuff or agricultural products. How would you evaluate such a novel regime? What are its advantages over the current minimum protection available in all Member States (in accordance with TRIPS) against misleading use of such designations? What are the downsides, if any?

2 In addition to specific protection of GIs, most Member States allow for associations representing the authorised producers of relevant products to register the designation as a collective or certification mark. In other legal systems outside the EU, in particular the US, registration of such marks is considered as the most or only suitable way of acquiring and granting protection for GIs. Do you agree? Please compare the two forms of protection.

3 The ECJ has been criticised for granting overly strong protection for GIs. In particular the 'Feta' judgment and by 'Parma ham' and 'Grana Padano' decisions (concerning the slicing and ham and grating of cheese) have been targets of criticism. What is your opinion about those decisions?

---

44 ECJ Case C-469/00, *Ravil v. Bellon*, [2003] ECR I-5053.

4 Pursuant to Article 6 (1) (b) TMD and Article 12 (b) CTMR, protected marks may be used by a competitor in order to describe the quality or characteristics of his own product. By contrast to that, GIs may not be used in relation to products not originating in the relevant region, even if 'disclaimers' (such as 'style', 'type', 'method', 'as produced in', 'imitation' or similar) are added. What are the reasons for the different regulations? Are they justified?

6.4 Industrial designs

Background and legal bases

The appreciation of product design – understood in a broad sense, as referring to the shape and/or ornamentation of commodities – as an object of intellectual property protection has changed considerably since the early days of industrialisation. From an additive of generally low esteem, mainly intended to mask the function-related sobriety of industrial utility objects (machines, etc.), design has developed into an important and omnipresent form of cultural expression, quite apart from the fact that it also constitutes an eminent marketing tool: as the objective utility of products tends to converge and the number of available alternatives is very high, choices are frequently based mainly on the visual appeal of the product appearance.

The recognition of design as an important sector of cultural achievement as well as its strong commercial impact have led to a certain proliferation of legal tools that are available for protection. First is the specific legislation in the EU for protection of industrial designs, established by the Design Directive 71/1998/EC,[45] and the Community Design Regulation (CDR).[46] In its two-tiered scheme – a harmonisation directive being complemented by the overarching structure of a unitary Community right – EU industrial design legislation follows the pattern of EU trade mark law. The commonalities between both areas are further marked by the fact that design registrations on the Community level are administered by the OHIM in Alicante. As a novel feature in EU legislation, the Community Design Regulation further provides for short-term Community-wide protection of unregistered designs.

---

45 Directive 98/71/EC of the European Parliament and of the Council on the legal protection of designs, [1998] OJ L 289/28.
46 Council Regulation 6/2002 on Community Designs; [2002] OJ L 3/1; consolidated version with subsequent amendments available at the OHIM website, at http://oami.europa.eu/ows/rw/resource/documents/RCD/regulations/62002_en_cv.pdf.

In addition, product appearances can attract protection under other legal titles, such as copyright, trade mark or unfair competition law. Whereas some legal regimes were traditionally reluctant to grant protection on such other grounds, in particular under copyright, the Design Directive stipulates that such protection should remain possible, or is even mandatory pursuant to Article 17 DD:

[a] design protected by a design right registered in or in respect of a Member State in accordance with this Directive shall also be eligible for protection under the law of copyright of that State as from the date on which the design was created or fixed in any form

However:

the extent to which, and the conditions under which, such a protection is conferred, including the level of originality required, shall be determined by each Member State.

As a matter of principle, product appearances can also obtain (indirect) protection on the basis of patent or utility model law, in particular where the product design results from an optimal blending of form and function. However, differently from the other legal bases mentioned, patent or utility model protection will not entail protection of the product appearance as such.

In the following section, a brief account will be given of specific EU design legislation; thereafter, some remarks will follow on protection of product appearances under copyright and unfair competition law, whereas trade mark protection for product appearances is addressed in Chapter 4.

Specific industrial design legislation

Outlines of design legislation (Design Directive and Community Design Regulation)

As was set forth in the introduction, the situation in industrial design legislation is similar to that in trade mark law: the national laws were harmonised on the basis of Directive 98/71/EC (DD), and a unitary Community right was created by the Community Design Regulation (CDR). As a consequence, the substantive provisions on specific design protection on the national as well as on the Community level are fully congruent.

A broad definition of designs that are eligible for protection is contained in Article 1 DD and Article 3 CDR. Protection pertains to the appearance of products or parts of products resulting from the features of, in particular, the lines, contours, colours, shape, texture and/or materials of the product itself and/or its ornamentation. 'Product' means any type of product, including parts of complex products, graphic symbols and typographic typefaces.

Designs are excluded from protection if they are contrary to public order or morality. Furthermore, design rights do not subsist in features of a product which are solely dictated by its technical function. The same applies to 'must-fit' features of parts of complex products which are technically necessary for assembling the part with the product in which or in connection with which it shall operate (Article 7 and 8 DD; Article 8 and 9 CDR). Moreover, parts of complex products must fulfil the protection requirements in themselves, and they only attract protection to the extent that they remain visible during the regular use of the complex product.

The requirements for protection are novelty and individuality (Articles 3 to 5 DD, Articles 4 to 6 CDR). Novelty refers to the identity or quasi-identity of the design with what is already available to the public, whereas individual character denotes a qualitative step, i.e. the design must also differ to some extent from the available wealth of forms, with the relevant perspective for the assessment being that of an 'informed user' (see below). As a further guideline for the assessment, it is stipulated that the degree of freedom of the designer in developing the design shall be taken into consideration.

Novelty and individual character must be assessed as of the relevant date, which is the date on which the application was filed, or, if priority is claimed in accordance with Article 4 Paris Convention, the date of priority. As a matter of principle, the assessment is subject to an absolute standard, meaning that novelty and individual character are challenged by all designs that were made available to the public prior to the relevant date. This principle is qualified in two respects. First, prior publications are not detrimental if they were made by the designer or his successor in title within the 12 months preceding the filing date; the same applies if the design was published by a third party without the designer's consent (Article 6 (2) DD; Article 7 (2) CDR). Second, publications are not taken into consideration if they could not 'reasonably have become known in the normal course of business to the circles specialised in the sector concerned' (Article 6 (1) DD; Article 7 (1) CDR).

Following registration, designs are protected for five years with the possibility of prolongation up to a maximum period of 25 years. The registered design right confers on its holder protection against commercial exploitation of the same or a similar design by a third party (Article 12 DD; Article 19 CDR). Whether a later design is infringing is decided according to the same standards that apply to the assessment of the requirements for protection: the crucial factor is again the perspective of an informed user of products of the type in question, with the degree of freedom of the designer having to be taken into consideration (Article 9 DD; Article 10 CDR). Acts done in private are excluded from protection; furthermore, use of design is also permissible if it is for teaching or experimental purposes, or if parts protected by a design right are necessary to repair ships or aircraft that are only temporarily in the country covered by the protection (Article 12 DD; Article 20 CDR). The right to oppose further circulation of articles incorporating the design is exhausted if the goods were put on the market in the Community (including the EEA) by the holder of the right or with his consent (Article 15 DD; Article 21 CDR).

Specific features of the Community Design Regulation

Registered Community Designs[47]

Registration of Community designs is administered by the OHIM. The application must contain particulars of the applicant's identity as well as a reproducible representation of the form for which protection is sought. The OHIM determines whether the object of the application is eligible for protection according to Article 4 CDR, and whether it is contrary to morality (Article 9 CDR); otherwise, examination is limited to the formal requirements (meaning that novelty and individual character are *not* examined *ex officio*). When protection is sought for several designs, costs can be saved by combining them in a multiple application, on condition that the products in which the designs shall be incorporated belong to the same class of the international classification system which is used by the OHIM (Article 37 CDR).

The applicant can request that the publication of the design be deferred for a period of up to 30 months. In that case, the initial fees to be paid at the date of application are reduced accordingly. At the expiry of the deferment period the publication fees must be paid in order to maintain the right, otherwise it lapses (Article 50 CDR).

After registration, Community designs are published in the Official Gazette of the OHIM; in case of deferment, publication is limited to information

---

47 Most of those features are also found in the national design systems, without being mandatory.

identifying the applicant (Article 49; Article 50 (3) CDR). Registration establishes a presumption of validity of the Community design (Article 85 (1) CDR). Third parties who wish to raise objections to validity may apply to the Invalidity Division of OHIM (Article 52 CDR); this can be pursued in an appeal to the Boards of Appeal of the OHIM, as well as to the General Court, and where appropriate to the Court of Justice of the EU (Article 55 *et seq.*). Invalidity can also be invoked in the form of a counterclaim within the framework of infringement proceedings before Community design courts (Arts. 80, 81 CDR).

In the case where a registered design allegedly infringes another, prior design, it had been contentious in some Member States whether the design must first be declared invalid before infringement proceedings can be brought against the owner. The ECJ decided in *Celaya*[48] that this is not necessary, but that infringement proceedings can be initiated in spite of the fact that the allegedly infringing design is covered by a registration.[49]

Similar to patents and trade marks, industrial designs can also be registered internationally. The relevant instrument is provided by the Hague Agreement Concerning the International Registration of Industrial Designs in its most recent version, the Geneva Act (1999),[50] to which the EU acceded on 1 January 2008.

The protection conferred by a registered Community design has a barring effect, meaning that it applies irrespective of whether the maker of a subsequent design was familiar with the protected product appearance (Article 10 CDR). There are two exceptions to this principle. First, as long as publication of the design is deferred, protection is limited to imitations (Article 19 (3) CDR). Second, any third party, who at the date when the application for the Community design was filed (or, if priority was claimed, at the relevant priority date) had commenced use of a corresponding design in good faith or had made substantial preparations to do so, is also entitled to continue to use the design to the same extent as before (prior user's right, Article 22 CDR).

Community designs can be the subject of simple or exclusive licences; furthermore, they can be given as security or be the subject of rights *in rem* (Arts. 29, 32 CDR). In the case of assignment of a registered Community

---

48 ECJ Case C-488/10, *Celaya Emparanza y Galdos International* v. *Proyectos Integrales de Balizamiento SL*, [2012] ECJ I-0000.
49 The ruling applies to Community designs as well as to registered national designs.
50 See www.wipo.int/hague/en/legal_texts/wo_haa_t.htm.

design, the transfer of rights to third parties does not take effect until a corresponding recordal has been made in the Community design register (Article 28 (b) CDR). The same applies to licences and other *in rem* rights related to registered Community designs, to the extent that the third party did not know of the act at the date on which the rights were acquired (Article 33 (2) CDR).

Unregistered Community Designs

Apart from registration at the OHIM, a design right at Community level can also be acquired by use or other means of making the design available to the public (Unregistered Community Design, UCD). In order to be protected, the design must meet the general requirements of novelty and individuality; furthermore, the design must have been used or made available to the public *within the territory of the Community* (Article 11 in combination with Article: 110a (5) CDR).[51] The term of protection is three years with no possibility of extension; the right-holder is protected against imitations, that is, the infringer must have been provably familiar with the design (Article 19 (2) CDR).

Summary: options for protection under design legislation

European design legislation allows the designer to choose among several options to obtain and secure protection for different periods of time. In summary, those alternatives can be listed out as follows:

1. *Immediate registration*: Full protection is obtained for a maximum of 25 years (5 years plus 4 consecutive prolongations of five years each).
2. *Registration after grace period*: The design is first used without registration during a maximum period of 12 months; after that, an application for registration is filed. Full protection for a maximum period of 25 years is acquired through registration (as under (1)). During the preceding 12 months, protection against copying is granted on the basis of the UCD acquired by virtue of the publication (provided it was made available in the Community).
3. *Protection without registration*: If the design is not registered upon lapse of the grace period, it will continue to be protected against copying for another two years on the basis of the UCD. Thereafter, design protection lapses.
4. *Registration with deferred publication*: Protection against copying is

---

51 Consolidated version, see above, note 46.

acquired upon registration. If the publication fee is paid after 30 months (maximum), full protection is acquired for the remaining duration of the design right, that is, for up to 22 years and six months. If no payment is made, the design lapses.

Relevant legal issues

Individual character: 'informed user' and 'freedom of designer'

The most relevant issues in practice for design protection evolve around the assessment of novelty and individual character of a design. This concerns in particular the yardstick to be applied for appreciating individual character, which informs not only the assessment of protectability, but also that of infringement: as noted above, the criteria to be employed on both levels are worded exactly the same.

The 'informed user'
The relevant perspective is that of an 'informed user'. This is a novel concept – situated halfway between the 'person skilled in the art' (as in patent law) and the 'average consumer' (as in trade mark law). The ECJ explained in *Pepsico*[52] that the concept:

> (53) . . . must be understood as lying somewhere between that of the average consumer, applicable in trade mark matters, who need not have any specific knowledge and who, as a rule, makes no direct comparison between the trade marks in conflict, and the sectoral expert, who is an expert with detailed technical expertise. Thus, the concept of the informed user may be understood as referring, not to a user of average attention, but to a particularly observant one, either because of his personal experience or his extensive knowledge of the sector in question.

Freedom of the designer
As the informed user is supposed to be knowledgeable about the sector concerned, it is generally submitted that her attention usually lies on those details which are not entirely determined by technical constraints. This was pointed out in the first decision of the Cancellation Division at OHIM, concerning the form of a bar stool:

> (16) The degree of freedom of a designer is limited by the fact that stools of the type to which the CD relates necessarily comprise a base, a central column and

---

52 ECJ Case C-281/10 P, *PepsiCo* v. *OHIM* (Grupo Promer), [2011] ECR I-0000; see further on this case below.

a seat in order that the stool fulfils its function. (17) The informed user is familiar with the basic features of stools. When assessing the overall impression of the design he/she takes into consideration the limitations to the freedom of the designer and weighs the various features consequently. He/she will pay more attention to similarities of non necessary features and dissimilarities of necessary ones.[53]

The principle is confirmed by Article 6 (2) CDR,[54] which stipulates that account must be taken of the freedom of the designer for the assessment of individual character. The issue was of relevance in *PepsiCo*, which resulted in the first design appeal decision by the ECJ.[55] The impugned design concerns products known as 'pogs', 'rappers' or 'tazos', which are usually given away as promotional items together with e.g. chips, fruit juice or other beverages, and are used for different kinds of games. Usually, the surface of the item is painted, but the contested registration and the prior design on the basis of which it was challenged relate only to the shape: a rounded form being raised in the middle by concentric circles of different width. The outcome of the dispute depended *inter alia* on the degree of freedom enjoyed by the designer for the making of rappers which are supposed to fulfil their purpose, i.e. to be used for promotion and in games. In the decision under appeal before the ECJ, the General Court[56] had noted a number of similarities between the two designs, for instance:

> (79) [t]he designs at issue both contain a concentric circle approximately one third of the way from the edge to the centre . . . The Court finds that that central part could have been delineated by a shape other than a circle. (T)hat finding cannot be called into question by the argument . . . that the shape had to be elementary in order not to distort the image which may cover the disc, since a triangular, hexagonal, or even a square or oval shape instead of circular one would not have distorted the image any more. . . . (82) In the absence of any specific constraint imposed on the designer, the similarities [noted by the Court in the previous Paragraphs] relate to elements in respect of which the designer was free to develop the contested design. It follows that those similarities will attract the

53 OHIM Decision of 24.4.2004, *Eredu* v. *Armet*, ICD000000024, [2004] ECDR 24.
54 Also: Article 5 (2) DDir. For infringement see Article 10 (2) CDR; Article 9 (2) DDir.
55 ECJ Case C-281/10 P, *PepsiCo* v. *OHIM* (Grupo Promer) [2011] ECR I-0000. For similar reasoning, see also the case law of the General Court, cases T-9/07, *PepsiCo* v. *OHIM* (Grupo Promer) [2010] ECR II-981; T-11/08, T-148/08, *Beifa* v. *OHIM* (Schwan Stabilo), [2010] ECR II-1681; T-513/09, *Shenzen Taiden* v. *OHIM* (Bosch), [2010] ECR II-0000; T-11/08, *Kwang Yang Motors* v. *OHIM* (Honda), [2011] ECR II-0000; T-68/10, *Sphere Time* v. *OHIM* (Punch), [2011] ECR II-0000; T-53/10, *Reisenthel* v. *OHIM* (Dynamic Promotion), [2011] ECR II-0000; T-246/10, *Industrias Francisco Ivars* v. *OHIM* (Motive Srl), [2011] II-0000.
56 General Court Case T-9/07, *Grupo Promer Mon Graphic* v. *OHIM* (PepsiCo), [2010] ECR II-00981.

informed user's attention, all the more so because . . . the upper surfaces are, in the present case, the most visible surfaces for that user. (83) As regards the differences between the designs at issue . . . when viewed from above, . . . the contested design has two additional circles compared with the prior design. In profile, the two designs differ in that the contested design is more curved. However, it must be found that since the degree of curvature is slight, and the discs are thin, that curvature will not be easily perceived by the informed user, in particular when viewed from above . . . (84) In the light of the similarities noted it must be held that the differences . . . are insufficient for the contested design to produce a different overall impression on the informed user from that produced by the prior design.

The ECJ found no reason to reverse the decision and did not even comment on the matter, as these were considered to be factual evaluations that could not be called in question in ECJ proceedings.

Disclosure and destruction of novelty

Another issue of practical concern in design matters is the derogation from a strict novelty assessment in case that a prior design could not reasonably have come to the attention of the circles active in the field concerned in Europe (Article 6 DD; Article 7 CDR, see above). Among the few (national) decisions addressing the issue is a judgement by the German Federal Supreme Court. The unregistered Community design claimed by the plaintiff in the shape of a utensil for pressing dough (Gebäckpresse) was challenged by the defendant on the basis that the same product had been filed by the plaintiff for design registration in China, and was subsequently published in the official Chinese Design Gazette prior to first marketing in Europe. The Federal Supreme Court held that the publication was indeed sufficient to destroy novelty: as had been pointed out by the appeal court in this case, the Chinese market is an important market place for kitchen utensils, and it is therefore submitted that new designs, including those published in consequence of design registrations, are within the area screened by European designer circles.[57]

Prior publications and their impact on novelty are also at stake in a case pending before the General Court.[58] The dispute concerns rubber shoes (clogs), which are widely known under the trade mark 'Crocs'. A Community design for the shoe filed on 22 November 2004 and claiming priority for 28

---

57 German Federal Supreme Court Case, *Gebäckpresse*, [2008] I 126/06 (no English translation available).
58 OHIM Appeal Board decision of 26 March 2010, R 9/2008-3, appeal pending as T-302/10, *Crocs* v. *OHIM* (Holey Soles and Partenaire Hospitalier International).

April 2004 was challenged by a competitor on the basis that 'Crocs' had been shown at a Boat Show in Fort Lauderdale in October and November 2002 and had been for sale on a website set up under www.crocs.com prior to 23 April 2003. The holder of the design contested that the events could be novelty-destructive, because the stand at the Boat Show was 'small, in a remote corner of the hall and not terribly well attended', and the website was 'unsophisticated and practically impossible to access'. Counterevidence procured by the challenger included screenshots of the website as it looked in 2003, and the fact that 10,000 pairs of clogs had been sold after the launch of the product at the Boat Show. Concerning the fact that the clogs had been launched at a Boat Show (instead of a shoe fair), the Third Board of Appeal at OHIM observed that:

> [t]he 'circles specialised in the sector concerned, operating within the Community' are represented, in the present context, by footwear designers, footwear industry and footwear trade, who operate in the Community. The 'sector concerned' is the one concerned by the Challenged Design, i.e. footwear, and particularly boat or beach footwear or, more generally, leisure footwear. Even though the Holder identified the product as 'footwear', not 'boat footwear' or 'beach footwear' or 'clogs', the design represents doubtlessly a boat or leisure clog . . .

Concerning the volume of sales, it was held that:

> 10,000 pairs of shoes . . . by no means represent a symbolic act but a fully-fledged commercial activity . . . shoes are design items, which fashion-conscious people immediately start to wear and proudly show around rather than storing them away far from public sight. It is likely that the 10,000 pairs of clogs have therefore been seen by tens of thousands of people in the US and beyond.

Finally, regarding the website, which appeared to be active already in early 2003, the Board of Appeal remarked:

> 'Crocs' clogs are described in full detail and represented in colours . . . And . . . the website was configured to function . . . as a sales channel. The Board considers that a website which, before the relevant date, featured products made according to the Challenged Design and which could be ordered online, manifestly amounts to a disclosure that destroys novelty.

Novelty was also at issue in *Sphere Time*,[59] concerning the shape of a watch attached to a lanyard. The design was challenged on the argument that very

---

59 General Court Case T-68/10, *Sphere Time v. OHIM* (Punch), [2011] ECR II-0000.

similar watches had been manufactured in China and were marketed in Europe before the relevant priority date. *Inter alia*, evidence was provided by a catalogue showing two watch designs made by a Chinese firm as well as by a certificate from that company stating that those designs had been marketed in Europe since 2004. Those documents were accompanied by a shipping invoice and a certificate of origin relating to the delivery of 2000 samples of one of the two designs to a customer situated in the Netherlands. The owner of the contested design argued that the documents might be unreliable, as the party procuring them had a personal interest in having the design declared invalid. However, the General Court, in accordance with the Board of Appeal, found that the shipment documents provided sufficient evidence for the fact that the articles had been disclosed before the relevant date, and that the doubts articulated by the design owner were not such as to discredit their probative value.[60]

Designs made in the course of employments and other contracts

Designs are often made on commission, or in the course of employment contracts. With regard to the latter, the CDR stipulates in Article 14 (3) that if the design was created in the execution of the employee's duties or following the instructions given by his employer, the right to the Community design shall vest in the employer, with deference to national rules specifying otherwise, or having been agreed upon by the parties. The provision became topical in a dispute between the Spanish Foundation for the Progress of Arts (FEIA) and a firm marketing, without authorisation by FEIA, a series of cuckoo clocks which had been designed in the framework of a contract with FEIA. No registration of the design had been effected.

Spanish design law includes a provision according to which the right in the design is vested not only in the employer under the conditions set out in Article 14 (3) CDR, but also in a person who has commissioned the creation of a design outside an employment contract. As, however, the provision only relates to registered designs, the decisive question was whether Article 14 (3) CDR could be interpreted broadly so as to include also commission or service contracts, or whether a person creating a design on commission could be considered, under Spanish law, as having transferred the right to the commissioner as his 'successor in title' (Article 14 (1) CDR). The ECJ did not give an explicit answer to the question regarding Article 14 (3), but made it clear that the only possibility for FEIA to claim a right in the design was to

---

60 Ibid., Paragraph 31 *et seq.*

establish that under Spanish law, the design right had been transferred by way of contract, i.e. not merely by operation of law.[61]

The spare parts debate

Whereas DD and CDR jointly have achieved a rather high degree of harmonisation in the field of industrial design protection, a wide gap remains with regard to protection of spare parts. As pointed out above, parts of complex products are eligible for protection, provided that the usual requirements for protection are fulfilled and the parts remain to be visible during normal use.[62] This leaves the possibility of claiming protection for the outer, visible parts of a complex product – in particular: the so called 'crash parts' (the wings, door, and bonnet) of automobiles, with the exception of the so-called 'must-fit' elements of the shape (see above). It is feared that by excluding independent manufacturers from the making or selling of such parts for repair purposes, the right-holder is granted a full monopoly on the secondary market for spare parts. In order to avoid distortions of competition resulting therefrom, the proposal was made to allow the unauthorised reproduction of parts where that is necessary to restore the original appearance of a complex product by way of repair ('repairs clause'). Against that, it was argued by the car industry and other interested circles that the monopoly ensuing from design protection of parts was nothing but the usual effect of an exclusive right, and that to include a repairs clause would lead to a dangerous erosion of the very tenets of the intellectual property system. Since no agreement could be reached, the DD was enacted without a harmonising provision. Instead, it includes a so-called freeze-plus clause (Article 14 DD), pursuant to which the rules on spare parts that were in effect at the time the DD entered into force may be retained, and amendments are only permissible to the extent that they lead to a liberalisation of the spare parts market.

Whereas the solution on the national level is thus largely left to the individual legislatures, Article 110 CDR provides that, until entry into force of a final Community-wide solution, parts of complex products cannot be prevented from being manufactured and distributed for repair purposes, to the extent that the parts must necessarily be exactly replicated in order to restore the appearance of the original product.

---

61 ECJ Case C-32/08, *FEIA v. Cul de Sac*, [2009] ECR I-05611.
62 For an interpretation of that requirement with regard to the shape of a combustion engine for lawn mowers see General Court Case T-11/08, *Kwang Yang Motors v. OHIM* (Honda), [2011] ECR II-0000.

An attempt to end the stalemate was undertaken by the Commission in 2004, submitting a legislative proposal including a repairs clause into the DD. The proposal found consent in the European Parliament in December 2007. However, since then the issue has been stalled. Although the proposal was not been formally rejected until now, it is unlikely that it will ever succeed, due to the resistance put up in the Council by Member States with strong car industries.

? QUESTIONS

1 Recital 14 to the CDR states that in order for a design to have individual character, the overall impression produced on an informed user must 'clearly differ' from that produced on him by the existing design corpus. By contrast to that, Article 6 (1) only requires that the overall impression must be 'different'. It has been argued with a view to that discrepancy that the threshold for granting design protection should be high (the design must 'clearly differ'), whereas its scope of protection should be narrow (no infringement is found if the designs are 'different'). Do you agree? Does the approach comply with established rules of legal interpretation?

2 In *PepsiCo v. Grupo Promer*, it was contentious *inter alia* which type of 'informed user' should be governing the assessment – a sales manager intending to use the pogs as promotional items, or a five-year-old child using them for games? The General Court considered the issue but arrived at the conclusion that it did not make a difference for the decision. Do you agree?

3 The proposals for the DD and CDR drew criticism during the legislative process because novelty and individual character were to be assessed through 'European lenses' (only publications which were or could become known to European designers should be taken into account for the assessment). It was feared that this would encourage 'stealing' of designs in non-European countries (in other industrialised countries but also misappropriation of valuable indigenous designs). The European legislature reacted by applying a basically absolute notion of novelty and individual character, and shifting the burden to establish that the design could not 'reasonably have become known' to the right-owner. Do you think this is sufficient to disperse the misgivings raised? Would an absolute notion of novelty and individual character provide a better solution? What, if any, would be the downsides of such an approach?

4 The Unregistered Community Design only comes into existence if the design has been published 'in the territory' of the EU. Thus, imitation of an unregistered design which was first published outside the EU cannot

be prohibited on the basis of the UCD by the creator. A wise regulation or not? Please consider for your response that a different yardstick applies for the assessment of whether publications occurring abroad are detrimental to novelty, as is demonstrated by the German Federal Supreme Court's decision 'Gebäckpresse'.

Protection of product appearances under copyright and unfair competition law

Copyright

Notion and protection threshold for works of applied art

Copyright law protects the appearance of useful articles, in particular the shape of three-dimensional objects, as 'works of applied art' or, under British law, as 'works of artistic craftsmanship'. As such, works of applied art form part of the mandatory catalogue of works eligible for copyright protection in Article 2 of the Berne Convention. However, Article 2 Berne Convention does not specify the criteria determining the protectability of such works, in particular the threshold which must be overcome in order to be recognised as a work of (applied) art.

In the course of their history, EU Member States have developed widely differing attitudes towards copyright protection for product appearances. The following account mentions some typical examples.

The most generous approach is traditionally endorsed by *French* copyright law, which adheres to the principle of 'unity of art' (*unité de l'art*), meaning that for all work categories alike, the only requirement is that work must be the author's own creation. No creative achievement is too 'humble' to attract copyright protection, unless it is of such a technical nature that it could be patented. In practice, this attitude leads to a total overlap (*cumul total*) between copyright and industrial design protection.

By contrast to that, the *German* approach governing the assessment of copyright protection for works of applied art is known as the 'theory of tiers' (Stufentheorie): in essence, it is required that works of applied art must surpass a higher threshold of artistic character than other work categories, so as to leave a meaningful margin of protection which is solely covered by industrial design protection. The principle was reiterated by the German Federal Supreme Court in a decision concerning copyright protection for a brooch and ear-clips in the shape of a plant (silver thistle):

[C]ase law in the field of musical and literary creations acknowledges the so-called 'small change' that covers simple creations that are only barely susceptible to protection . . . In contrast, however, the case law on applied art, to the extent that it is entitled to design protection, has always applied stricter criteria . . . Since even a design that is susceptible to design protection must stand out from unprotected average designs, against what is merely workmanlike and everyday, an even greater difference must apply for copyright protection, i.e., the work must clearly surpass works of average design. Hence *a greater degree of creative individuality* is to be required for copyright protection than for objects entitled only to design protection, whereby the cross-over point between the two should not be set too low.[63] (References to previous German case law omitted; emphasis added)

While the German approach still results in a certain area of overlap between copyright and industrial designs, a strict distinction between both fields previously applied in Italian law, due to the criterion of separability (*scindibilità*): only if the artistic elements of an article could be separated – physically or conceptually – from the functional elements, could copyright protection be granted. In practice, this meant that the design of primarily functional articles such as furniture, for example, remained excluded from protection.

In the course of implementing the Design Directive, the Italian legislature decided to abolish the criterion of *scindibilità* so as not to clash with Article 17 DD: as explained in the introduction, the provision makes it mandatory to grant copyright protection for product appearances qualifying as industrial designs, with only the fixing of the threshold being left to national law. After the amendment, the approach adopted by Italian law is similar to the one observed in Germany. The question remained, however, whether copyright protection could be claimed for articles which had been ineligible for protection when they were first made, and had fallen into the public domain after the lapse of design protection that had been acquired instead. Italian law included a provision pursuant to which the copyright subsisting in such designs could not be enforced vis-à-vis third parties who had commenced good-faith use of the design before the new legislation entered into force. In its first version, the regulation was subject to a 10-year transition period; afterwards, any time limits were deleted.

The issue was referred to the ECJ in a lawsuit concerning the importation and marketing in Italy of a lamp which, pursuant to previous Italian copyright legislation, had fallen into the public domain before the entry into force

---

63 German Federal Supreme Court Case I ZR 119/93, '*Silver Thistle*', English translation in [1997] 38 IIC 141.

of the new legislation. The ECJ held that Italian regulation in both versions (with and without the 10-year time limit initially foreseen) was incompatible with Article 17 DD:[64]

> (65) ... Article 17 ... must be interpreted as precluding legislation of a Member State which – either for a substantial period of 10 years or completely – excludes from copyright protection designs which, although they meet all the requirements for copyright protection, entered into the public domain before the date of entry into force of that legislation, that being the case with regard to any third party who has manufactured or marketed articles based on that design in that State – irrespective of the date on which such activities were performed.

Substantive restrictions of copyright protection (UK law)

Specific rules on copyright protection for product design have applied until now in the United Kingdom.[65] First, Sec. 51 CDPA 1988 excludes from the scope of copyright protection for drawings the making of three-dimensional articles according to the drawing (other than artistic works). That way, the result ensuing from previous legislation shall be avoided, which allowed claiming copyright infringement if technical shapes constructed on the basis of a drawing were reproduced (e.g. spare parts used for repair purposes). Second, pursuant to Sec. 52 CDPA 1988, copyright protection against reproduction of articles is limited to 25 years if the article has been reproduced by industrial process and is commercially exploited (i.e., if more than 50 copies have been made).

Both provisions became topical in a dispute between Lucasfilm, the holder of copyright in the 'Star Wars' film series and related artefacts, and Mr Ainsworth, who had manufactured – though not designed – the so-called 'Stormtrooper helmet', worn in the film by an army of clone warriors.[66] Mr Ainsworth was sued by Lucasfilm after having made and sold merchandising articles representing the helmet. Pursuant to Sec. 51 CDPA 1988, no copyright protection was available for the making of the article according to the drawing which had been used by Mr Ainsworth as the basis for making the prototype, unless the helmet was to be considered an artistic work. Furthermore, as more than 25 years had passed from the first making, no copyright protection could be asserted in the helmet itself, unless it fell

---

64 ECJ Case C-168/09, *Flos v. Semeraro*, [2011] ECR I-181; see also ECJ case C-198/10, *Cassina S.p.A v. Alivar Alivar Srl, Galliani Host Arredamenti Srl*, [2011] ECR I-0000 (decided by way of order).

65 Legislative reform is pending, which may lead to abolishment of the time limits set out in Sec. 52 CDPA 1988.

66 UK Supreme Court, [2011] UKSC 39, *Lucasfilm v. Ainsworth*.

into the category of 'sculpture', which is exempted from the curtailment of protection. In line with the previous instances, and after an instructive recount of case law distinguishing between 'sculptures' and other artefacts, the Supreme Court of the UK came to the conclusion that the Stormtrooper helmet, for all the fantasy elements involved, was not a sculpture, but a utilitarian object deserving only limited (in time) protection:

> (45) It would not accord with the normal use of language to apply the term 'sculpture' to a 20th century military helmet used in the making of a film . . . however great its contribution to the artistic effect of the finished film. The argument for applying the term to an Imperial Stormtrooper helmet is stronger, because of the imagination that went into the concept of the sinister cloned soldiers dressed in uniform white armour. But it was the Star Wars film that was the work of art that Mr Lucas and his companies created. The helmet was utilitarian in the sense that it was an element in the process of production of the film.

❓ QUESTIONS

1 In ECJ case C-5/08 – *Infopaq International* v. *Danske Dagbladets Forening* as well as in subsequent decisions, the Court declared that the notion of a work 'in the meaning of Article 2 (a) of Directive 2001/29 is liable to apply only in relation to a subject-matter which is original in the sense that it is its author's own intellectual creation' (see Chapter 5). Under that definition, any additional threshold requirement such as 'artistic character' would be excluded. Before that backdrop, how do you assess the compatibility with European law of legal systems applying a 'theory of tiers' such as in German law? (Don't forget to take Article 17 DD into account!)

2 Article 7 (4) Berne Convention allows to limit the duration of protection for works of applied art (and photographic works) to 25 years, whereas all other works enjoy a minimum protection period of life plus 50 years. However, in the copyright term Directive (2006/116/EC; see Chapter 5), no exceptions were made for such works. What is your opinion? Which policy objectives may have played a role, and how do you evaluate them?

3 As related above, Sec. 52 UK CDPA 1988 prescribes in its current form that copyright cannot be enforced against reproduction of the work after the lapse of 25 years from its industrial reproduction and commercial exploitation by the right-holder or a licensee. A provision which is similar in its effects is anchored in Polish copyright law: protection against reproduction of a work of applied art is not available after the lapse of industrial design protection which was acquired for the same article. How do

you evaluate the compatibility of those provisions with the Copyright Term Directive (Chapter 5, section 5.2.2.4), and the Infosoc Directive (29/2001/EC), *inter alia* Article 5? What about Article 17 DD and the way in which it was interpreted in C-168/09 – *Flos* v. *Semeraro*? (Please note that amendment of Sec. 52 UK CDPA 1988 is pending, see above, footnote 65.)

Unfair competition law

General concept

There is no common European understanding of what 'unfair competition' means. Particularly for British lawyers, 'unfairness' is inappropriate as a legal concept informing a special kind of tort. And even in continental Europe, where long-standing legal traditions exist in the area, the notion of unfair competition and its place in the system remain somewhat enigmatic, not least under a comparative perspective.

It is a reflection of that diversity that no attempt has been made so far in European law to harmonise the area other than in regards of marketing activities directed at consumers (see Chapter 7). Imitations of product appearances are of primary concern for business-to-business relations, and are thus not directly comprised by the harmonisation measures. Although a certain overlap does exist with provisions addressing misleading marketing practices, the primary focus in this area lies on rules dealing with practices often labelled as 'slavish imitation' or 'parasitic behaviour' etc. The area is therefore still largely governed by concepts developed under national law. Although this means that the details as well as the terminology may vary between the systems, it is submitted that the following brief account gives a fairly appropriate picture of the basic features characterising protection under unfair competition law in most (continental) EU Member States.

Requirements for finding of unfair conduct

Legal systems granting unfair competition protection against product imitation regularly adhere to the general rule that outside the area of exclusive intellectual property protection, achievements conferring competitive advantages on those who make use of them should in principle be free for everyone to enjoy. Hence, court decisions addressing the issue usually start by reiterating the statement that 'imitation as such' is permissible. Indeed, the basic axiom is that unfair competition does not provide any basis for protecting valuable achievements, i.e., it is not object-oriented, but only concerns the evaluation of *conduct*. Such conduct will only be found inadmissible if it is rendered unfair by aggravating circumstances.

The following observations take *German law* as their point for departure, submitting that it is to a certain extent representative for other legal regimes that basically acknowledge and apply a concept of unfair competition. As a minimum condition for finding of 'aggravating circumstances', courts in Germany regularly require that the imitated item owns so called competitive individuality (*wettbewerbliche Eigenart*). That notion combines elements of 'individual character' (as in design law) with some (usually modest) degree of market recognition. In addition, the conduct must either have a certain potential to cause confusion, or it must be likely to exploit or deteriorate the reputation enjoyed by the product. The potential for confusion and thus for a finding of unfair conduct rises in proportion with the closeness of the imitation. Furthermore, the imitation must be 'avoidable', meaning that the reproduction of the relevant features is not necessary for technical reasons.

It transpires from this rough sketch that what is considered by the jurisprudence as 'aggravating circumstances' rendering a basically legitimate imitation 'unfair' closely resembles the systemic structure underlying intellectual property protection, under a combined approach based on elements from industrial design (or copyright) law on the one hand and trade mark law on the other. In the light of this, the distinction between intellectual property and unfair competition law sometimes appears more like a theoretical construct than a valid rule impacting actual practice. In many cases, courts will find sufficient reason in the arsenal of arguments available under the relevant scheme to prohibit at least very close imitations of product appearances irrespective of the fact that the object of imitation is not, or no longer, protected by an intellectual property right. Exceptions from that scheme only apply if shapes are imitated which are of a purely technical nature, in particular when a patent previously granted for the article has expired.

For other than technical shapes, claiming protection on the basis of unfair competition after expiry of regular intellectual property protection is less problematic. This is of particular relevance for the protection of shapes after the expiry of the three-year period set out in the CDR for protection of unregistered Community designs. The issue was addressed in a lawsuit filed in Germany on account of the close imitation of a pair of jeans. *Inter alia*, the defendant had argued that the shape was neither registered as a trade mark nor as industrial design, and that, as more than three years had passed since first marketing, the regular protection period provided by the European legislature for protectable but unregistered shapes had lapsed. The German

Federal Supreme Court found, however, that the imitation might cause a certain risk for consumer confusion (without being actually misleading in a strict sense), and concluded that:

> (The) objective of the Act Against Unfair Competition can be distinguished from that of the Community Design Regulation, which protects a specific achievement in the form of a Community design. The time-limited protection for an unregistered Community design accordingly does not affect the claim . . . based on supplementary protection of achievement under competition law on the grounds of an avoidable deception as to origin.[67]

Accordingly, it was found that the jeans could be protected against imitation beyond a period of three years.

Primary Community law

To prohibit the marketing of particular product appearances based on rules of unfair competition may pose an obstacle to the free movement of goods (Article 34 TFEU, see Chapter 2). As Article 36 TFEU offers a justification only for measures safeguarding the specific subject matter of intellectual property, impediments resulting from laws against unfair competition must be weighed in light of the limitations inherent in Article 34 TFEU itself.

The issue was brought to the fore in the *Beele* case.[68] The dispute concerned the importation into the Netherlands of a specific type of cable duct previously protected by a patent, by the (ex) patent holder's German competitor. The Dutch Courts of first and second instance concurred in finding that the cable ducts could have been made differently without impairing their function, and concluded that the defendant was needlessly offering a nearly precise imitation of the plaintiff's products. However, being aware of the effect the ruling would have on the free movement of goods on the Common Market, the appeal court referred to the ECJ the question whether to prohibit importation was compatible with primary law. For an answer, the ECJ referred *inter alia* to the principles developed in its earlier decision *Cassis de Dijon*,[69] stating that:

> disparities between national legislation must be accepted in so far as legislation . . . may be justified as being necessary in order to satisfy mandatory requirements

---

67 German Federal Supreme Court Case I ZR 151/02, '*Jeans*', English translation in 48 IIC 130, (2007).
68 ECJ Case 6/81, *Industrie Diensten Groep v. Beele*, [1982] ECR 707.
69 ECJ Case 120/78, *Rewe v. Bundesmonopolverwaltung für Branntwein*, [1979] ECR 649; further on that case see Chapter 7, section 7.3.2.1.

relating in particular to the protection of consumers and fairness in commercial transactions.

Regarding the case at stake, the Court continued that:

national case-law prohibiting the precise imitation of someone else's products that is likely to cause confusion may indeed protect consumers and promote fair trading . . .

? **QUESTIONS**

1 In the 'Jeans' decision by the German Federal Supreme Court, the court emphasised the potential of the product appearance to indicate commercial origin, and the risk for consumer deception ensuing from the imitation. However, this was the same pair of jeans that was the object of ECJ decision C-371/06 – Benetton/G-Star, where it was found that the shape of the jeans gave substantial value to the product and hence remained excluded from trade mark protection (see Chapter 4). In your opinion, would the same argument be relevant in the framework of unfair competition law?

2 The 'Beele' judgment (above) was handed down by the ECJ in 1982. Today, it is still considered as giving 'carte blanche' to national laws prohibiting product imitation irrespective of the (non)availability or previous expiry of intellectual property protection. Do you consent to that? What, if anything, may have changed in the meantime so as to mandate a more critical look? Are the premises on which the Dutch court based its request for a preliminary ruling – that the public was actually at risk to be deceived, and that the cable ducts could have been made differently – precise enough? If a court were in a similar situation today, which additional guidelines might it want to receive from the ECJ for the interpretation of those criteria?

6.5 Semiconductor topographies

Background and legal basis

Finally, the legal protection of semiconductor topographies is another IP right granted at the level of the EU. In view of its rather limited practical importance this IP right needs only a brief mention here.

This relatively recent IP right goes back to the attempts of the US semiconductor chip manufacturing industry to secure exclusive legal protection against the unauthorised copying of the layout of circuitry elements on the different layers which compose a semiconductor computer chip (so-called 'topographies'). The development of such topographies requires considerable investment of human, technical and financial resources, while topographies of such products can be copied at a fraction of the cost needed to develop them independently. The protection was granted, for the first time, in 1984 by the US Semiconductor Chip Protection Act (SCPA).[70] The approach taken was that of a *sui generis* law, combining copyright-style conditions for protection with a registration requirement and a term of protection of ten years from the date of registration. Protection only relates to the 'mask work', i.e. the topographic creation embodied in the masks and chips, but not the functionality of the chip's electrical circuitry itself. The exclusive rights are limited to a reproduction and distribution right. Reverse engineering, however, was permitted. Other exceptions concern the exhaustion of the distribution right after first sale and acts of distribution by innocent infringers. In order to encourage other states to adopt similar legislation the SCPA contained a reciprocity clause.

Consequently, following Japan, the EU hardly had an alternative but to adopt a Directive on the legal protection of topographies of semiconductor products, the first harmonisation directive adopted by the Community in the field of intellectual property.[71] Under the Directive, Member States were obliged to adopt national legislation providing for legal protection of semiconductor topographies in accordance with the provisions of the Directive.

An international treaty in intellectual property in respect of integrated circuits was negotiated at an international conference in Washington in 1989 (so-called Washington Treaty[72]), but never entered into force due to the fact that both the US and Japan considered the provisions on compulsory licensing and the exoneration of innocent infringers from the duty to pay remuneration too far-reaching. However, in 1994, a section on 'Layout-Designs (Topographies) of Integrated Circuits' was inserted in the TRIPS Agreement (Part II.6), making this IP right a part of the international standard.

Details

According to Article 2 (2), a topography of a semiconductor product is protected in so far as it is the 'result of its creator's own intellectual effort and is

---

70 17 U.S.C. §§ 901–914.

71 Council Directive 87/54/EC of 16 December 1986 on the legal protection of topographies of semiconductor products, [1987] OJ L 24/36.

72 See www.wipo.int/export/sites/www/treaties/en/ip/washington/pdf/trtdocs_wo011.pdf.

not commonplace in the semiconductor industry', or if the combination of commonplace elements fulfils this condition. The object of protection is the 'three-dimensional pattern of the layers of which a semiconductor product is composed; and . . . in which series, each image has the pattern or part of the pattern of a surface of the semiconductor product at any stage of its manufacture' (Article 1 (1) (b)), not, however, any concept, process, system, technique or encoded information embodied in the topography other than the topography itself (Article 8).

The right to protection initially vests in the creator of the topography, but Member States are free to decide that if a topography has been created in the course of the creator's employment or under a commissioning contract, the right to protection applies in favour of the creator's employer or the commissioning party, unless the terms of employment or commissioning contract provide to the contrary (Article 3 (1), (2)).

According to Article 4, Member States may make – but are not under an obligation to do so – the coming into existence or the continuation of the exclusive rights dependent upon registration within two years of the topography's first commercial exploitation. If material identifying or exemplifying the topography is required to be deposited with a public authority, Member States must make sure that trade secrets are properly protected.

The exclusive rights cover the reproduction of a topography as well as its commercial exploitation or the importation for the purpose of exploitation of a topography or of a semiconductor product manufactured by using the topography. As regards the exceptions, according to Article 5 (2)–(7) of the Directive, Member States have to provide for the exhaustion of the importation and distribution right within the EU and for the freedom to reverse engineer, i.e. to commit the protected acts for the purpose of analyzing, evaluating or teaching the concepts, processes, systems or techniques embodied in the topography, and of creating another topography on the basis of such an analysis and evaluation. The additional exception of private reproduction for non-commercial aims is optional. Innocent infringers who did not know, or did not have reasonable grounds to believe, that the product they deal with is protected, may continue to commercially exploit that product in question. However, an innocent infringer has to pay an adequate remuneration to the right-holder, for any acts of exploitation committed after that person knows, or has reasonable grounds to believe, that the semiconductor product is so protected.

Like its US counterpart, Article 7 (3) of the EU Directive provides for a term of protection of ten years after the earlier of the protected topographies' first commercial exploitation or filing for registration (with a maximum delay between a topography's fixation or encoding and its first commercial exploitation of 15 years).

Similar to the US SCPA, Article 3 (3)–(8) of the EU Directive subject the benefit of the legal protection granted to semiconductor topographies to other persons and companies than EU nationals, residents and companies or other legal persons which have a real and effective industrial or commercial establishment on the territory of a Member State to a reciprocity clause. It should be noted, however, that after the legal protection of topographies of semiconductor products was extended to natural persons, companies and other legal persons first from the United States and Canada, and then to Members of the WTO (and finally the Isle of Man),[73] this reciprocity clause has lost most of its importance.

 QUESTIONS

1 In view of the fact that semiconductor chip topographies arguably are 'industrial property' within the meaning of, and covered by Article 1 (1) of the Paris Convention, and in view of the fact that according to Article 2 of the Paris Convention nationals of Member States to the Paris Convention enjoy national treatment, do you think that the US legislature was entitled to make protection under the SCPA for foreign nationals dependent on the requirement of reciprocity?

2 Comparing the text of the Washington Treaty and the corresponding provisions of the TRIPS Agreement, what exactly are the differences? In your opinion, are these differences big enough to explain or even justify the rejection of the Washington Treaty by the US and Japan?

3 If you compare the reverse engineering provisions of Article 5 (3) and (4) of Directive 87/54/EEC for topographies with the similar provisions contained in Articles 5 (3) and 6 of Directive 2009/24/EC (formerly 91/250/EEC) for computer programs, do you spot any differences?

4 Although after the Directive on the legal protection of of topographies of semiconductor products was implemented in the Member States, in some of these Member States a substantial number of registrations were applied for. In spite of this, almost no dispute made it to the courts. Do you have an explanation?

---

73 Council Decisions 93/16/EEC of 21 December 1992, [1993] OJ L 11/16; 94/700/EC of 24 October 1994, [1994] OJ L 284/61; 94/824/EC of 22 December 1994, [1994] OJ L 349/201, and 96/644/EC of 11 November 1996, [1996] OJ L 293/18.

7

IPRs and competition law

7.1 Introduction

IPRs confer on their holders exclusive rights with regard to the use of IP. Whereas the aim of providing for IPRs is usually to provide for incentives and thus *further* innovation and competition, the exclusivity of IPRs may, however, also be used by the holder of the IPR to *hinder* competition, thus preventing new and innovative products and services from being developed, marketed and used. Such restrictions may result from a refusal to license, the use of restrictive licensing conditions or even the exclusive exercise of an IPR with regard to a particular good which cannot be substituted and which hence enables the right-holder to obtain so-called monopoly rents. From a European perspective, such effects of the exclusivity granted by IPRs are problematic in respect of the Union's competition policy (Articles 101 *et seq.* TFEU; ex Articles 81 and 82), and they likewise threaten to conflict with the free movement of goods and services (Articles 34, 36 TFEU). This gives rise to the question regarding the relationship between IPRs and competition law on the one hand, and the repercussions of the free movement of goods and services on the exercise of IPRs on the other. Whereas the latter issue has been addressed by the ECJ under the heading of the 'exhaustion' of national distribution rights, which takes place whenever the first sale or other transfer of ownership of goods protected by an IPR is made in the Community by the right-holder or with his consent,[1] the application of competition law to dealings in IPRs shall be discussed in the first part of this chapter.

Moreover, competition also is regulated by rules combating *unfair trade practices*. Whereas competition law (in the narrow sense) has the purpose of creating and preserving the structural framework for undistorted competition, unfair competition law is designed to combat unfair business practices. Although rules combating unfair competition only declare certain actions as inadmissible and are not providing for exclusive IPRs as such, they are

---

1 See the discussion in Chapter 2, section 2.2.1.

traditionally considered as forming part of industrial property legislation (see Article 10 *bis* of the Paris Convention and the at least partial reference to this provision in Articles 22 (2) (b) and 39 (1) TRIPS with regard to geographical indications and undisclosed information). Moreover, in particular as regards issues such as slavish imitation of someone else's products or comparative advertising, there is a certain overlap of IP protection and protection against unfair competition. It should be noted that national law of the Member States does provide for protection against unfair competition by different means. Some Member States (such as Germany) have adopted special legislation, whereas others (such as the UK) offer a number of discrete actions covering defined sub-classes of unfair competition but no action for unfair competition *per se*. Moreover, in some Member States the focus is on private enforcement, whereas some states oversee the behaviour of market participants by administrative bodies. However, uninterested in these differences and the rather fragmented nature of rules concerning unfair competition (which ranges from misleading advertising to the protection of trade secrets), the EU has already for some time been rather active in this area. In doing so, the EU has not targeted unfair competition as such, but has rather acted on the basis of its consumer protection policy (see Articles 4 (2) (f), 12 and 169 TFEU). Hence the activities of the EU in the area of unfair competition will be discussed in the second part of this chapter.

7.2 Competition law

EU and competition law

Competition and the TFEU

In line with the general goal of the EU to create a single market in which the fundamental economic freedoms (movement of goods, services, persons and capital) are secured and in which there is no distortion of competition amongst Member States, one of the major policies of the EU is the competition policy (Articles 101 to 109 TFEU). The two major provisions of this section which are of concern for IPRs are the prohibition on cartels (Article 101 TFEU) and on the abuse of a dominant position (Article 102 TFEU):

Article 101

1. The following shall be prohibited as incompatible with the internal market: all agreements between undertakings, decisions by associations of undertakings and concerted practices which may affect trade between Member States and which have as their object or effect the prevention, restriction or distortion of competition within the internal market, and in particular those which:

(a) directly or indirectly fix purchase or selling prices or any other trading conditions;

(b) limit or control production, markets, technical development, or investment;

(c) share markets or sources of supply;

(d) apply dissimilar conditions to equivalent transactions with other trading parties, thereby placing them at a competitive disadvantage;

(e) make the conclusion of contracts subject to acceptance by the other parties of supplementary obligations which, by their nature or according to commercial usage, have no connection with the subject of such contracts.

2. Any agreements or decisions prohibited pursuant to this Article shall be automatically void.

3. The provisions of paragraph 1 may, however, be declared inapplicable in the case of:

- any agreement or category of agreements between undertakings,
- any decision or category of decisions by associations of undertakings,
- any concerted practice or category of concerted practices,

which contributes to improving the production or distribution of goods or to promoting technical or economic progress, while allowing consumers a fair share of the resulting benefit, and which does not:

(a) impose on the undertakings concerned restrictions which are not indispensable to the attainment of these objectives;

(b) afford such undertakings the possibility of eliminating competition in respect of a substantial part of the products in question.

Article 102

Any abuse by one or more undertakings of a dominant position within the internal market or in a substantial part of it shall be prohibited as incompatible with the internal market in so far as it may affect trade between Member States.

Such abuse may, in particular, consist in:

(a) directly or indirectly imposing unfair purchase or selling prices or other unfair trading conditions;

(b) limiting production, markets or technical development to the prejudice of consumers;

(c) applying dissimilar conditions to equivalent transactions with other trading parties, thereby placing them at a competitive disadvantage;

(d) making the conclusion of contracts subject to acceptance by the other parties of supplementary obligations which, by their nature or according to commercial usage, have no connection with the subject of such contracts.

In this book, these provisions are only examined as regards their bearing on exclusive IPRs. Hence, a few general comments will have to suffice.

First, as regards Article 101 TFEU, it should be noted that the prohibition on anti-competitive agreements concerns both horizontal (agreements between competitors on the same level) and vertical (agreements between competitors on different levels) undertakings.[2]

Second, Article 101 (3) TFEU provides for an exemption of agreements which are in general pro-competitive, but which contain certain provisions restrictive of competition. In certain areas, Article 101 (3) TFEU has been concretised by so-called block exemption regulations such as the technology transfer block exemption regulation (TTBER, see below). The legal basis for the Commission to act is contained in Regulation 19/65, as amended by Regulation (EC) No 1/2003.[3] Where such regulations are lacking, the compatibility of agreements with Article 101 (3) must be appraised through an individual analysis.

Third, according to Article 1 of Regulation (EC) No. 1/2003, the earlier possibility of individual exemption and of notification of individual agreements has been abolished. Since then a prior decision of the Commission is no longer necessary as a condition for agreements, decisions and concerted practices to be allowed under Articles 101 (1), (3) and 102 TFEU. In other words, Regulation (EC) No 1/2003 introduced a paradigm shift from the principle of a general prohibition with certain exceptions to the principle of general permission with certain prohibitions. In order to alleviate the effects of the new system on market participants, the burden of proving an infringement of Article 101 (1) or of Article 102 TFEU in any national or Community proceedings rests on the party or the authority alleging the infringement. If, however, the undertaking or association of undertakings claims the benefit of Article 101 (3) TFEU, it then bears the burden of proving that the conditions of that paragraph are fulfilled (Article 2 of Regulation (EC) No. 1/2003).

Fourth, as regards IPRs, currently several areas of particular activity can be witnessed. One area concerns licensing practices in the pharmaceutical sector.[4] Another area concerns collecting societies which constitute legally

---

2 ECJ Joined Cases 56/64 and 58/64, *Établissements Consten* and *Grundig* v. *Commission*, [1966] ECR 299.
3 Council Regulation 1/2003 on the implementation of the rules on competition laid down in Articles 81 and 82 of the Treaty, [2003] OJ L 1/1, complemented by Commission Regulation 773/2004 relating to the conduct of proceedings by the Commission pursuant to Articles 81 and 82 of the EC Treaty, [2004] OJ L 123/18. See also Commission Notice on cooperation within the Network of Competition Authorities, [2004] OJ L 101/43, and Commission Notice on the co-operation between the Commission and the courts of the EU Member States in the application of Articles 81 and 82 EC, [2004] OJ L 101/54.
4 See in this chapter, section 7.2.3.2.2.

recognised monopolies and which have established a licensing system that contains certain clauses restricting competition amongst collecting societies from different Member States. Here, the main question is to what extent competition law can be used to force collecting societies to open up the possibility for pan-European licensing.[5] Finally, if an IPR holder refuses to license his or her IPR to competitors, the issue is under what circumstances a dominant position of the IPR holder can be found, and under what conditions such a dominant position has been abused within the sense of Article 102 TFEU.[6]

Enforcing competition law in the EU

Regulations or Directives which give effect to the principles of Article 101 and 102 are adopted by the Council, on a proposal from the Commission and after consulting the European Parliament (Article 103 (1) TFEU). Otherwise, enforcement of Articles 101 and 102 TFEU is in the hands of the Commission, the powers of which as administrative competition authority are defined by Regulation (EC) No. 1/2003 already cited and which is based on Article 103 (2) (d) TFEU. These powers include not only the right, *inter alia*, to examination and inspection, but also to impose fines on those undertakings which have been found in violation of EU competition law.

In addition to the supervision and enforcement measures exercised by the Commission, private parties who have suffered harm on account of restrictions of competition violating the TFEU are entitled to claim damages in national court proceedings.[7] However, the efficiency of that remedy differs from jurisdiction to jurisdiction. Some national regimes have tried to enhance the prospects of victims to claim damages. The improvement of the legal framework on an EU-wide basis has been on the agenda of the Commission for several years, without so far leading to tangible results.[8]

Within the Commission, DG Competition[9] is responsible both for defining the goals and, in particular, to act as administrative body administering the competition law rules of the TFEU. Decisions of the Commission can be

---

5 See in this chapter, section 7.2.3.2.3.2.

6 See in this chapter, section 7.2.3.3.

7 This principle was confirmed by the ECJ in Case C-453/99, *Courage v. Bernard Crehan* and *Bernard Crehan v. Courage and Others*, [2001] ECR I-6297, and in Joined Cases C-295/04, C-296/04, C-297/04 and C-298/04, *Manfredi*, [2006] ECR I-6619.

8 For details and documents addressing the issue see ec.europa.eu/competition/antitrust/actionsdamages/documents.html.

9 See the information on the website of DG Competition ec.europa.eu/dgs/competition/index_en.htm.

reviewed by the General Court and subsequently an appeal to the ECJ is possible on a point of law (Articles 263, 256 (1) TFEU). In addition, the ECJ has unlimited jurisdiction to review decisions whereby the Commission has fixed a fine or periodic penalty payment. It may cancel, reduce or increase the fine or periodic penalty payment imposed (Article 31 of Regulation (EC) No. 1/2003).

As regards the relationship between EU and national competition law, Regulation (EC) No. 1/2003 has created a system of parallel competences. This means that the Commission and the Member States' competition authorities can both apply Articles 101 and 102 TFEU and EU competition law does not exclude per se the application of national competition law. However, it has to be kept in mind that as far as cases are covered by EU law, EU law has to be applied, and because of the general principle of primacy of EU law[10] the parallel application of national competition law to agreements may not lead to a different outcome from that which would result from the application of EU competition law. In other words, in cases in which agreements, decisions or practices may affect trade between EU countries within the meaning of Article 101 (1) TFEU or which concern an abuse prohibited by Article 102 TFEU, national courts have to – at least also – apply EU competition rules. If in such cases no infringement is found under Article 101 (1) and 102 TFEU, or if the conditions of Article 101 (3) TFEU are fulfilled, the agreement, decision or practice cannot be prohibited under national competition law (Article 3 (2) of Regulation (EC) No. 1/2003). Similarly, if an agreement, decision or practice violates Article 101 (1) TFEU and does not fulfil the conditions of Article 101 (3) TFEU, it cannot be upheld under national law. As regards Article 102 TFEU, the principle of primacy of EU law also applies, even though Article 3 of the Regulation (EC) No 1/2003 does not expressly provide for a similar convergence obligation, so that in the event of conflicting provisions, national courts here also have to not apply any provision of national law which contravenes an EU rule, regardless of whether that national law provision was adopted before or after the EU rule.

In purely national cases, however, i.e. in cases which do not affect trade between Member States, national courts can, but are under no obligation to, apply Articles 101 and 102 TFEU without it being necessary to apply national competition law in parallel. Also, they can apply national competition law rules which are stricter than the rules laid down in Articles 101, 102 TFEU.

---

10 See Chapter 2, section 2.3.3.

? **QUESTIONS**

1 How do you evaluate the possibility for private parties to claim damages in case of anticompetitive conduct? Can you explain the reason why the remedy has not been employed very frequently in practice until now?

2 If you consult the website of the EU Commission's DG Competition (ec. europa.eu/competition/index_en.html) you find it structured according to 'policy areas' on the one hand, and 'sectors' on the other hand. The application of competition law in the area of IP law does not appear as a separate and prominent topic. Do you have any idea what might be the reason for this?

Technology Transfer Block Exemption Regulation (TTBER) and Block Exemption on R&D Agreements (R&DBER)

Technology transfer and research and development agreements contain in many, if not all, cases restrictions with regard to the use of the IP in question. Such restrictions may well have anti-competitive effects. However, both technology and research and development agreements usually improve economic efficiency (see below, Recital 5 TTBER).

Consequently, making use of the instrument of a block exemption according to Article 101 (3) TFEU, and on the basis of Regulation No 19/65/EEC as amended by Regulation (EU) No 1/2003,[11] the Commission has issued the Technology Transfer Block Exemption Regulation (TTBER),[12] which replaces the older technology block exemption Regulation (EC) No 240/96. This block exemption is of great importance as regards IP licensing of technology-related IP (patents, know-how and software copyright). In addition, on the basis of Regulation (EEC) No 2821/71,[13] with Regulation No 1217/2010 the Commission has, amongst others,[14] issued another block

---

11 [1965] OJ 36/533, as last amended by Regulation 1/2003, [2003] OJ L 1/1. In the case at stake, an exclusive license had been granted to an enterprise which was later acquired by a business having a strongly dominant position on the relevant market. Although the exclusive license had been covered by a group exemption when it was granted, the fact that the acquisition by the market leader considerably strengthened its already dominant position and substantially increased the hurdles for market entrance by newcomers was considered as abusive. On this case see also below, section 7.2.4.3.1.

12 Commission Regulation 772/2004 on the application of Article 81 (3) of the Treaty to categories of technology transfer agreements, [2004] OJ L 123/11. See also the accompanying Commission Notice 'Guidelines on the application of Article 81 of the EC Treaty to technology transfer agreements', [2004] OJ C 101/2. On the relevance of the Guidelines with regard to patent pools see in this chapter, section 7.2.2.3.

13 Council Regulation 2821/71 on application of Article 85 (3) of the Treaty to categories of agreements, decisions and concerted practices, [1971] OJ L 285/46.

14 See Commission Regulation 2790/1999 on the application of Article 81 (3) to categories of vertical agree-

exemption regarding categories of research and development agreements (R&D Agreements)[15] which replaced Commission Regulation (EC) No 2659/2000 and which also has a bearing on the licensing of IPRs.

TTBER

According to Article 1 (1) (b) TTBER:

> 'technology transfer agreement' means a patent licensing agreement, a know-how licensing agreement, a software copyright licensing agreement or a mixed patent, know-how or software copyright licensing agreement, including any such agreement containing provisions which relate to the sale and purchase of products or which relate to the licensing of other intellectual property rights or the assignment of intellectual property rights, provided that those provisions do not constitute the primary object of the agreement and are directly related to the production of the contract products; assignments of patents, know-how, software copyright or a combination thereof where part of the risk associated with the exploitation of the technology remains with the assignor, in particular where the sum payable in consideration of the assignment is dependent on the turnover obtained by the assignee in respect of products produced with the assigned technology, the quantity of such products produced or the number of operations carried out employing the technology, shall also be deemed to be technology transfer agreements

As stated in Recital 5 TTBER:

> [t]echnology transfer agreements concern the licensing of technology. Such agreements will usually improve economic efficiency and be pro-competitive as they can reduce duplication of research and development, strengthen the incentive for the initial research and development, spur incremental innovation, facilitate diffusion and generate product market competition.

Whereas under the previous block exemption (No 240/96), all exempted clauses were listed in a limited way, so that no other clauses were allowed, the TTBER has decided to:

---

ments and concerted practices, [1999] OJ L 366/21; Commission Regulation 2658/2000 on the application of Article 81 (3) to categories of specialization agreements, [2000] OJ L 304/3.

15 Commission Regulation 1217/2010 on the application of Article 101 (3) of the Treaty on the functioning of the European Union to categories of research and development agreements, [2010] OJ L 335/36. See also Communication from the Commission 'Guidelines on the applicability of Article 101 of the Treaty on the Functioning of the European Union to horizontal co-operation agreements', [2011] OJ C 11/1. For the relevance of those Guidelines with regard to standardisation agreements see in this chapter, section 7.2.2.3.

place greater emphasis on defining the categories of agreements which are exempted up to a certain level of market power and on specifying the restrictions or clauses which are not to be contained in such agreements. This is consistent with an economics-based approach which assesses the impact of agreements on the relevant market. It is also consistent with such an approach to make a distinction between agreements between competitors and agreements between non-competitors.[16]

In line with this, the TTBER firstly defines certain market thresholds for agreements to which Article 101 (1) TFEU shall, according to Article 2 TTBER, not apply. These thresholds are defined in Article 3 TTBER as follows:

> (1) Where the undertakings party to the agreement are competing undertakings, the exemption provided for in Article 2 shall apply on condition that the combined market share of the parties does not exceed 20 % on the affected relevant technology and product market.
> (2) Where the undertakings party to the agreement are not competing undertakings, the exemption provided for in Article 2 shall apply on condition that the market share of each of the parties does not exceed 30 % on the affected relevant technology and product market.
> (3) For the purposes of paragraphs 1 and 2, the market share of a party on the relevant technology market(s) is defined in terms of the presence of the licensed technology on the relevant product market(s). A licensor's market share on the relevant technology market shall be the combined market share on the relevant product market of the contract products produced by the licensor and its licensees.

Article 4 (1) and (2) TTBER then describes a number of clauses which directly or indirectly, in isolation or in combination with other factors under the control of the parties, have strong anti-competitive effects so that the exemption provided for in Article 2 TTBER shall not apply (so-called hardcore restrictions). These restrictions include, *inter alia*, the restriction of a party's ability to determine its prices when selling products to third parties; certain allocations of markets or customers; and the restriction of the licensee's ability to exploit its own technology (in detail, the restrictions vary according to whether the parties are competing enterprises or not). Additional restrictions are contained in Article 5 TTBER concerning obligations on the licensee to grant an exclusive license or assign rights to the licensor or to a third party designated by the licensor in respect of its own

---

16 TTBER, Recital 4.

severable improvements to, or its own new applications of, the licensed technology; as well as obligations on the licensee not to challenge the validity of intellectual property rights which the licensor holds in the common market (it is, however possible, to provide for termination of the technology transfer agreement in the event that the licensee challenges the validity of one or more of the licensed intellectual property rights).

According to Article 6 TTBER, the Commission may withdraw the benefit of the TTBER where it finds in any particular case that a technology transfer agreement to which the exemption provided for in Article 2 applies nevertheless has effects which are incompatible with Article 101 (3) TFEU. Moreover, it should be noted that Article 102 TFEU (abuse of a dominant market position) can apply to license agreements, even if the latter are covered by the TTBER or otherwise are covered by Article 101 (3) TFEU.[17]

This leaves the question of how agreements outside of the scope of the TTBER are to be treated. According to Recital 12 TTBER:

> [t]here can be no presumption that above these market share thresholds technology transfer agreements do fall within the scope of Article 101 (1) TFEU. For instance, an exclusive licensing agreement between non-competing undertakings does often not fall within the scope of Article 101 (1) TFEU. There can also be no presumption that – above these market-share thresholds – technology transfer agreements falling within the scope of Article 101 (1) TFEU will not satisfy the conditions for exemption. However, it can also not be presumed that they will usually give rise to objective advantages of such a character and size as to compensate for the disadvantages which they create for competition.

In other words, outside the scope of the TTBER, parties must assess whether their individual case falls under Article 101 (1) TFEU and, if so, whether the conditions of Article 101 (3) TFEU are satisfied.

R&DBER

Agreements which have as their object the research and development of products, technologies or processes up to the stage of industrial application, and exploitation of the results, including provisions regarding intellectual property rights, may in certain cases fall within the scope of Article 101 (1) TFEU. However, according to Article 179 (2) TFEU the EU is called upon

---

17 General Court (then: Court of First Instance) Case T-51/89, *Tetra Pak v. Commission*, [1990] ECR II-309.

to encourage undertakings, including small and medium-sized undertakings, in their research and technological development activities of high quality, and to support their efforts to cooperate with one another. Moreover, the joint exploitation of results, including the exploitation of intellectual property rights that substantially contribute to technical or economic progress, are to be considered as the natural consequence of joint research and development. In order to facilitate research and development while at the same time effectively protecting competition, the Commission has therefore issued Regulation No 1217/2010 on the application of Article 101 (3) TFEU to categories of research and development agreements (R&DBER).[18] Similar to the TTBER, this Regulation also defines certain categories of research and development agreements which the Commission regards as normally satisfying the conditions laid down in Article 101 (3) TFEU.

In particular, are covered by this legislation:

> all intellectual property rights, including industrial property rights, copyright and neighbouring rights. (Article 1 (1) (h) R&DBER)

According to Article 2 (2) R&DBER:

> [t]he exemption . . . shall apply to research and development agreements containing provisions which relate to the assignment or licensing of intellectual property rights to one or more of the parties or to an entity the parties establish to carry out the joint research and development, paid-for research and development or joint exploitation, provided that those provisions do not constitute the primary object of such agreements, but are directly related to and necessary for their implementation.

The exemption granted by the R&DBER applies, provided, *inter alia*, the following conditions are met (Article 3 (2)–(5) R&DBER):

> (2) The research and development agreement must stipulate that all the parties have full access to the final results of the joint research and development or paid-for research and development, including any resulting intellectual property rights and know-how, for the purposes of further research and development and exploitation, as soon as they become available. Where the parties limit their rights of exploitation in accordance with this Regulation, in particular where they specialise in the context of exploitation, access to the results for the purposes of exploita-

---

18 Commission Regulation 1217/2010 on the application of Article 101 (3) of the Treaty on the functioning of the European Union to categories of research and development agreements, [2010] OJ L 335/36.

tion may be limited accordingly. Moreover, research institutes, academic bodies, or undertakings which supply research and development as a commercial service without normally being active in the exploitation of results may agree to confine their use of the results for the purposes of further research. The research and development agreement may foresee that the parties compensate each other for giving access to the results for the purposes of further research or exploitation, but the compensation must not be so high as to effectively impede such access.

(3) Without prejudice to paragraph 2, where the research and development agreement provides only for joint research and development or paid-for research and development, the research and development agreement must stipulate that each party must be granted access to any pre-existing know-how of the other parties, if this know-how is indispensable for the purposes of its exploitation of the results. The research and development agreement may foresee that the parties compensate each other for giving access to their pre-existing know-how, but the compensation must not be so high as to effectively impede such access.

(4) Any joint exploitation may only pertain to results which are protected by intellectual property rights or constitute know- how and which are indispensable for the manufacture of the contract products or the application of the contract technologies.

However, as summarised in Recital 15, according to Article 5 and 6 R&DBER, the Regulation does:

> not exempt agreements containing restrictions which are not indispensable to the attainment of the positive effects generated by a research and development agreement.

Therefore:

> agreements containing certain types of severe restrictions of competition such as limitations on the freedom of parties to carry out research and development in a field unconnected to the agreement, the fixing of prices charged to third parties, limitations on output or sales, and limitations on effecting passive sales for the contract products or contract technologies in territories or to customers reserved for other parties [are] excluded from the benefit of the exemption established by this Regulation irrespective of the market share of the parties.

In particular, as regards IPRs, according to Article 6 (a) R&DBER, in order to benefit from the exemption, an agreement may not provide for:

> the obligation not to challenge after completion of the research and development the validity of intellectual property rights which the parties hold in the internal

market and which are relevant to the research and development or, after the expiry of the research and development agreement, the validity of intellectual property rights which the parties hold in the internal market and which protect the results of the research and development, without prejudice to the possibility to provide for termination of the research and development agreement in the event of one of the parties challenging the validity of such intellectual property rights.

Finally, as regards the market threshold and the duration of the exemption, Article 4 (1) and (2) R&DBER differentiates between agreements entered into by non-competing and by competing undertakings. In the first case, the exemption applies, irrespectively of any market threshold, for the duration of the research and development. Moreover, if the results are jointly exploited, the exemption applies for 7 years from the time the contract products or contract technologies are first put on the market within the internal market. In the second case, the exemption and its duration is made dependent of a market threshold: if the combined market share of competing parties to a research and development agreement does not exceed 25 per cent on the relevant product and technology markets, the same rules apply as regards agreements made by non-competing undertakings, and, according to Article 4 (3) R&DBER the exemption continues to apply as long as the combined market share of the parties does not exceed 25 per cent on the relevant product and technology markets. If, however, the combined market share does exceed 25 per cent, then, in line with the philosophy of the exemptions granted under Article 101 (3) TFEU:

> there is no presumption that research and development agreements are either caught by Article 101 (1) of the Treaty or that they fail to satisfy the conditions of Article 101 (3) of the Treaty once the market share threshold set out in this Regulation is exceeded or other conditions of this Regulation are not met.

Rather:

> [i]n such cases, an individual assessment of the research and development agreement needs to be conducted under Article 101 of the Treaty. (Recital 13)

Patent pools and standardisation agreements

Both the TTBER and the R&DBER are only concerned with bilateral agreements. They do not apply to agreements between multiple partners, such as agreements between several firms cooperating in research and development of new technologies, and engaging in common licensing schemes (usually referred to as 'patent pools').[19] Such arrangements have become very frequent and practically important not least in the sector of information and communication technology (ICT), where the high number of existing patents combined with the fact that the development of new products requires the acquisition of a large portfolio of patents pertaining to practically all of the necessary components would result, unless access to bundled and facilitated licensing schemes were granted, in prohibitive transaction costs.

Regarding the competition aspects of patent pools, a distinction must be made between the pooling arrangement on the one hand and the license agreements concluded between members of the pools and individual contract partners on the other. Whereas the latter would be covered by the TTBER or R&DBER just as any other license agreement, no corresponding regulation exists with regard to the preceding agreement establishing the pool. However, the legal framework for assessing the compatibility of patent pools with Article 101 (1) and (3) TFEU is addressed in the Commission's Guidelines on the application of Article 81 of the EC Treaty to technology transfer agreements (Technology Transfer Guidelines).[20] Although the compatibility of the individual agreement concerned depends on a number of factors and must be assessed on a case-by-case basis, it is generally held that no restriction of competition will result from the formation of a pool if the patents included are essential and complementary,[21] and if licenses are granted under fair, reasonable and non-discriminatory terms ('FRAND').

Similarly, risks for competition, but also benefits for technological progress may result from the establishment of industry standards. For the same reasons as patent pools, standardisation agreements between multiple participants are not covered by the Block Exemption Regulations, but they have been addressed in the Commission's Guidelines on the applicability of Article 101 TFEU to horizontal co-operation agreements.[22] Without going into detail, one important aspect in that regard as well concerns the willingness of those

---

19 See also Recital 7 of the TTBER: 'This Regulation . . . should . . . not deal with licensing agreements to set up technology pools, that is to say, agreements for the pooling of technologies with the purpose of licensing the created package of intellectual property rights to third parties.'

20 Guidelines on the application of Article 81 of the EC Treaty to technology transfer agreements, [2004] OJ C 101/2, Paragraph 210 *et seq.* ('technology pools'). Further of interest are the more recent Guidelines on the applicability of Article 101 of the Treaty on the Functioning of the European Union to horizontal co-operation agreements, OJ C 2011/11; see also below, footnote 22.

21 For explanations see Paragraphs 215 to 222 of the Guidelines on the application of Article 81 of the EC Treaty to technology transfer agreements, [2004] OJ C 101/2.

22 Guidelines on the applicability of Article 101 of the Treaty on the Functioning of the European Union to horizontal co-operation agreements, [2011] OJ C 211/1, Paragraphs 257 *et seq.*

who own rights to essential elements of the standard technology to grant licenses under FRAND terms.[23]

If the relevant technology is used without a license, the user would be infringing the patents covered by the standard. However, it is unclear whether the patent holder would abuse a dominant position if the patent is enforced without a FRAND license being offered. Courts in Europe have taken differing views on the issue: the German Federal Supreme Court has argued in *Orange Book* that if the infringer himself offers a reasonable license fee and fulfills other obligations usually incumbent on a licensee, a 'competition defense' may apply, meaning that upholding the infringement claim may amount to abuse.[24] A different result was reached by the District Court in The Hague in the *Philips* case: as long as no license agreement has actually been concluded, the patent holder is not hindered from enforcing the patent against infringement.[25]

? QUESTIONS

1 Recital 4 of the TTBER states that it 'is appropriate to move away from the approach of listing exempted clauses and to place greater emphasis on defining the categories of agreements which are exempted up to a certain level of market power and on specifying the restrictions or clauses which are not to be contained in such agreements'. Can you give reasons for this conclusion arrived at by the EU legislature?

2 Note that if holders of IPRs exceed the thresholds provided for by the TTBER, this does not necessarily entail the prohibition of the respective technology transfer agreement. Rather, it is now the responsibility of the parties to the agreement to assess themselves whether or not the agreement is prohibited under Article 101 (1) TFEU or not. What are the advantages and disadvantages of this system as opposed to the prior existing individual exemptions and notifications, which are no longer possible under Regulation (EU) No 1/2003?

3 Can you explain why, as a rule, the patents included in a patent pool must be complementary and essential?

---

23 Ibid., Paragraphs 278 and 280–286.

24 German Federal Supreme Court, Case KZR 39/06 of 6 May 2009, *Orange book standard*, English translation in 41 IIC, 396 (2010).

25 District Court of The Hague, 17 March 2010, Cases No. 316533/HA ZA 08-2522 and 31635/HA ZA 082524, *Philips v. SK Kassetten GmbH*.

The IP and competition law overlap

General

As stated above, both IPR legislation and the provisions were intended to prevent anti-competitive behaviour aim at furthering competition. However, the means employed are radically different. IPRs further competition by creating exclusive positions, whereas competition law directly aims at preventing behaviour which is restrictive of competition. At an abstract level, this gives rise to the question how these two areas of law can or should be reconciled. Concretely speaking, the issue has to be solved which use restrictions initiated by an IPR holder on the basis of his or her exclusive right have to be regarded as an undue restraint of competition and hence be considered illegal from the perspective of competition law.

In the beginning, the view prevailed that abstractly speaking both sets of rules were independent from each other, since both had been enacted by the legislature and the legislature, aware of possible anti-competitive effects of IPRs had, after all, granted them (theory of immunity of IPRs from competition law). The opposing view would subject all IPRs to control by competition law, since the overall aim is to secure competition (theory of superiority of competition law). The now prevailing opinion works on the assumption that on the one hand, IPRs and their effects on competition should be generally accepted as defined by the legislature. On the other hand, this does not exclude dealings in IPRs from control by competition law.

The issue then is how to draw the line, i.e., how to define under what circumstances the exercise of IPRs is barred by way of competition law. In the beginning, the ECJ took over the distinction between the mere 'existence' and the 'exercise' of an intellectual property right,[26] if the exercise manifests itself 'as the subject, the means or the consequence of an agreement'.[27] According to this distinction, whereas the mere use of an intellectual property right as granted by the legislature does as such not conflict with competition law, certain ways of using intellectual property rights can indeed violate competition law both as regards anti-competitive restrictions and abuses

---

26 See, in particular, ECJ Joined Cases 56/64 and 58/64, *Établissements Consten* and *Grundig v. Commission*, [1966] ECR 299; ECJ Case 24/67, *Parke Davis v. Centrafarm*, [1968] ECR 55; ECJ Case 40/70, *Sirena v. Eda*, [1971] ECR 69; ECJ Case 258/78, *Nungesser v. Commission*, [1982] ECR 2015, p. 2061.

27 ECJ Case 258/78, *Nungesser v. Commission*, [1982] ECR 2015, p. 2061; ECJ Case 144/81, *Keurkoop v. Nancy Kean Gifts*, [1982] ECR 2853, 2873; ECJ Case 262/81, *Coditel v. Ciné-Vog Films* (Coditel II), [1982] ECR 3381, p. 3401.

of a dominant market position. For example, in the early copyright case of *Coditel II*,[28] the ECJ stated that:

> (17) [a]lthough copyright in a film and the right deriving from it, namely that of exhibiting the film, are not, therefore, as such subject to the prohibitions contained in Article 85 [now: Article 101 TFEU], the exercise of those rights may, nonetheless, come within the said prohibitions where there are economic or legal circumstances the effect of which is to restrict film distribution to an appreciable degree or to distort competition on the cinematographic market, regard being had to the specific characteristics of that market.

Consequently, the ECJ has held that, as a rule, the exercise of an IPR as such is not in violation of competition law. Nor does the mere existence of an IPR necessarily place the right-holder into a dominant position, especially if there are possibilities to substitute the product or service protected by an IPR. However, the problem with the distinction between 'existence' and 'exercise' is that both uses of an existing IPR which do and which do not restrict competition are likewise ways of 'exercising' the existing right. Even if it were possible to define the scope of the 'existence', it still has to be ascertained which manner of exercising an existing IPR constitutes behaviour restrictive of competition and which does not. Consequently, an additional element has to be ascertained in order to find anti-competitive behaviour.

Article 101 TFEU: agreements and concerted practices

Assignments and licensing agreements

Since assigning and, in particular, licensing IPRs is part of the exclusive rights granted by law to the IPR holder, both assignment and licensing agreements that fall under Article 101 (1) TFEU almost invariably concern special factual situations. However, one recurring feature of these cases is that the IPR intends to eliminate the effects of exhaustion of the distribution right[29] by way of contractual clauses which aim at restricting parallel import and creating territorially limited exclusivity for the distributers of his products. Since assessing the anti-competitive effects of such and other agreements also requires a careful analysis in each individual case of any positive effects which the restrictions in question may eventually have, these cannot be discussed here in detail. Rather, a brief mentioning of the most prominent cases that have been decided by the ECJ will have to suffice.

---

28 ECJ Case 262/81, *Coditel v. Ciné-Vog Films* (Coditel II), [1982] ECR 3381.
29 See Chapter 2, section 2.2.1.

Thus, for example, in the early case *Grundig and Consten* v. *Commission*, the fact that the German firm Grundig had consented to its sole distributor in France obtaining a registration in his own name of the additional trade mark 'GINT' in order to enable the distributor to block entry of legitimate goods from other Member States, thus undermining the effect of EU exhaustion, was held to be in violation of Article 101 (1) TFEU (then: Article 85 TEEC), since it restored the national divisions in trade between Member States which the TEEC intended to abolish.[30]

Other than that, an agreement by which the owner of a trade mark protected in several Member States transfers the mark for one or more of those Member States to an independent company, with the consequence that the former owner has no influence on the use of that mark and the goods sold under it in the Member State(s) for which the transfer has been effected, does not violate Article 101, unless the transfer is part of an agreement on market sharing. As stated by the ECJ in *Ideal Standard*:[31]

> (59) [w]here undertakings independent of each other make trade-mark assignments following a market-sharing agreement, the prohibition of anti-competitive agreements under Article 85 of the Treaty [now Article 101 TFEU] applies and assignments which give effect to such an agreement are consequently void. However, . . . a trade-mark assignment can be treated as giving effect to an agreement prohibited by Article 85 [now Article 101 TFEU] only after an analysis of the context, the commitments underlying the assignment, the intention of the parties and the consideration for the assignment.

In addition, the ECJ held in *Nungesser* that an open exclusive license to the benefit of a national distributor in one Member State which obliges the licensor to refrain from producing or selling, or having the relevant goods protected by an IPR produced or sold by other licensees in the state for which the exclusive license has been granted, thus eliminating direct competition by the licensor, does not violate Article 101 (1) TFEU, provided the restriction can be justified. In the particular case, the justification was found in the fact that in the special case of a cost-intensive new product (maize seeds) the absence of an exclusive license 'would be damaging to the dissemination

---

30 ECJ Case 56/64, *Établissements Consten and Grundig* v. *Commission*, [1966] ECR 299. The case was the first ECJ decision dealing with the interface between IP rights and the principle of free movement of goods; it was decided several years before the ECJ developed its doctrine of regional exhaustion in Case 78/70, *Deutsche Grammophon* v. *Metro SB*, see Chapter 2, section 2.2.1.2.

31 ECJ Case C-9/93, *IHT Internationale Heiztechnik* v. *Ideal Standard*, [1994] ECR 2789; see also the earlier Cases 51/75, *EMI Records* v. *CBS*, [1976] ECR 1976, 811 and 40/70, *Sirena* v. *Eda*, [1971] ECR 69.

of a new technology and would prejudice competition in the Community between the new product and similar existing products.'[32]

However, in *Windsurfing International* where the holder of a patent for a rig used on a sailboard had drafted various contractual restrictions in order to secure product differentiation amongst his licensees' sailboards to cover the widest possible spectrum of market demand and to exercise far-reaching control as to how the patented rigs should be used, the ECJ declared inadmissible a number of clauses which went beyond the scope of the IPR, including non-challenging clauses concerning the licensor's patent as well as his trade mark rights.[33]

Moreover, the ECJ established the principle that if an IPR has been acquired by an agreement in violation of competition law, both the agreement and the subsequent exercise of the IPR on the basis of that agreement are in violation of Article 101 (1) TFEU.[34] This is of importance, if the underlying agreement has already expired or otherwise ceased to be in force at the time of the alleged anti-competitive conduct.[35]

In particular: the pharmaceutical sector

As already discussed with regard to the principle of exhaustion, behaviour which limits parallel importation within the EU not only partitions the internal market, but it also has as its effect that different prices can be asked for identical goods.[36] These price differences usually tend to be just monopoly rents achieved by the IPR holder which ultimately have to be borne by the consumers. However, in exceptional cases, in particular as regards pharmaceuticals, they can be justified due to the fact that in the pharmaceutical sector prices often are not market prices but are fixed as maximum prices by national health services.

Consequently, producers of pharmaceutical products face the problem that wholesalers in a low price country (such as, for example, Spain) tend to sell into high price countries (such as, for example, the UK) where they undercut the higher sales price by the local distributor. Reacting to this, producers of pharmaceuticals try to prevent parallel importation by way of

---

32 ECJ Case 258/78, *Nungesser v. Commission*, [1982] ECR 2015, 2069. See also ECJ Case 28/77, *Tepea v. Commission*, [1978] ECR 1391.

33 ECJ Case 193/83, *Windsurfing International v. Commission*, [1986] ECR 611.

34 ECJ Case 144/81, *Keurkoop v. Nancy Kean Gifts*, [1982] ECR 2853.

35 ECJ Case 51/75, *EMI Records v. CBS*, [1976] ECR 811.

36 See Chapter 2, section 2.2.1.1.

contractual agreements that restrict parallel trade either through the imposition of a Supply Quota System (SQS) or by means of dual pricing. The issue then arises whether, and if so, to what extent and under what circumstances such agreements have to be regarded as void under Article 101 and/or Article 102 TFEU. On the one hand, it may be argued that they undermine the freedom of movement of goods, lead to a segmentation of markets and apply dissimilar conditions to equivalent transactions with other trading parties, thereby placing them at a competitive disadvantage. On the other hand, it may be argued that if parallel trade could not be stopped and dual pricing not be maintained, then the artificially low prices in some of the Member States would set the level of income of pharmaceutical companies, thus depriving them from the funds necessary to conduct research for the development of future drugs. Also, it may be argued that because the price differences in the different Member States do not reflect market realities, maintaining sales quota[37] and dual pricing is not hindering competition *per se*.

The ECJ and the General Court have been rather friendly towards the pharmaceutical industry, holding that such restrictions to parallel trade are not per se anti-competitive, but only if it can be presumed that their effect is to deprive consumers of the advantages of competition. If, on the other hand, such an agreement objectively contributes to improving the production or distribution of goods or to promoting technical or economic progress, and if such objective advantages offset the resulting disadvantages for competition, then such an agreement is capable of being exempted under Article 101 (3) TFEU. In view mainly of the fact that wholesalers which engage in parallel trade tend to undercut prices on other Member States only marginally and no more than necessary in order to attract buyers, agreements providing for supply quota and dual pricing agreement have been upheld in view of Article 101 TFEU.[38] As regards Article 102 TFEU, the ECJ has summarised both the problem and its solution as follows:

---

37 It should be noted, however, that Directive 2001/83 on the Community code relating to medicinal products for human use, [2001] OJ L 311/67, as amended by Directive 2004/27, [2004] OJ L 136/34, although explicitly not affecting the powers of the Member States' authorities to set of prices for medicinal products, now requires holders of a marketing authorisation for and the distributors of a medicinal product that was placed on the market in a Member State to 'ensure appropriate and continued supplies'.

38 See General Court (then: Court of First Instance) Case T-168/01, *GlaxoSmithKline v. Commission*, [2006] ECR II-2969; see also the opinion of the Advocate General in case C-53/03, *SYFAIT v. GlaxoSmithKline*, [2005] ECR 4609 (the ECJ, however, declined jurisdiction since the Greek antitrust authority was not entitled to ask for a preliminary ruling). It should be noted that the unilateral reduction of sales quota does not fall under Article 101 TFEU; ECJ Joined Cases C-2/01 P and C-3/01 P, *BAI and Commission v. Bayer*, [2004] ECR 23, but can, of course constitute an abuse of a dominant position according to Article 102 TFEU.

(67)... [I]t cannot be ignored that... a system of price regulation in the pharmaceuticals sector... is one of the factors liable to create opportunities for parallel trade. (68) Furthermore, in the light of the Treaty objectives to protect consumers by means of undistorted competition and the integration of national markets, the rules on competition... [cannot be]... interpreted in such a way that, in order to defend its own commercial interests, the only choice left for a pharmaceuticals company in a dominant position is not to place its medicines on the market at all in a Member State where the prices of those products are set at a relatively low level.... (71) [A]lthough such a company, in a Member State where prices are relatively low, cannot be allowed to cease to honour the ordinary orders of an existing customer for the sole reason that that customer, in addition to supplying the market in that Member State, exports part of the quantities ordered to other Member States with higher prices, it is none the less permissible for that company to counter in a reasonable and proportionate way the threat to its own commercial interests... (77) Article 82 EC [now Article 102 TFEU] must therefore be interpreted as meaning that an undertaking occupying a dominant position on the relevant market for medicinal products which, in order to put a stop to parallel exports carried out by certain wholesalers from one Member State to other Member States, refuses to meet ordinary orders from those wholesalers, is abusing its dominant position. It is for the national court to ascertain whether the orders are ordinary in the light of both the size of those orders in relation to the requirements of the market in the first Member State and the previous business relations between that undertaking and the wholesalers concerned.[39]

Another problem besides supply quota and dual pricing are attempts by pharmaceutical companies to delay or hamper the introduction of generic medicines or of new, innovative drugs that may compete with their products already on the market.[40] In order to uncover the causes of the apparent low levels of competition in the pharmaceutical sector, beginning in 2008 the Commission has conducted a sector inquiry.[41] In its final Report, the Commission concluded to 'a decline of novel medicines reaching the market', pointing 'to certain company practices that might contribute to this phenomenon.' Also, as regards delays of generic drugs after the expiry of patent protection for the original drugs:

---

39 ECJ Joined Cases C-468/06 to 478/06, *Sot. Lélos kai Sia et al v. GlaxoSmithKline*, [2008] ECR I-7139.

40 See the fine imposed in case COMP A.37.507/F3, *AstraZeneca*, where a pharmaceutical company had blocked or at least delayed market access for generic versions of its drug even after the patent had expired (so-called 'evergreening').

41 See ec.europa.eu/competition/sectors/pharmaceuticals/inquiry/index.html.

[t]he inquiry showed that originator companies use a variety of instruments to extend the commercial life of their products without generic entry for as long as possible.

As a consequence, the Commission has indicated that it:

will apply increased scrutiny under . . . antitrust law to the sector and bring specific cases where appropriate

both as regards the delay of generic entry and defensive patenting strategies that mainly focus on excluding competitors without pursuing innovative efforts. In addition:

[t]o reduce the risk that settlements between originator and generic companies are concluded at the expense of consumers, the Commission undertakes to carry out further focused monitoring of settlements that limit or delay the market entry of generic drugs.[42]

The effects of this new attempt by the Commission to enhance competition in the pharmaceutical sector still remain to be seen.

In particular: collecting societies and competition law

A series of cases decided by the ECJ concerns various aspects of the dealings of copyright collecting societies. Collecting societies are more prone to behaviour restricting competition both as regards licensing practices and abuses of their dominant position, since they often enjoy a factual, if not outright legal monopoly with regard to the rights in copyrighted works and related subject matter.

One of the problems with collecting societies in the trans-border community context was that initially, some national societies refused to accept nationals from other EU Member States as members. This is, of course, inadmissible under the non-discrimination principle of Article 18 TFEU (ex Article 12 EC).[43]

Additional problems arise from the way in which national collecting societies have organised the representation of the repertoire of their sister societies

---

42 Press release IP/09/1098 of 8 July 2009. For the full report and the 2nd Report on the monitoring of patent settlements of July 2011, see ec.europa.eu/competition/sectors/pharmaceuticals/inquiry/index.html.
43 See ECJ Case 7/82, *GVL v. Commission*, [1983] ECR 383.

located in other EU countries. In general, national authors tend to entrust their respective national collecting society with the representation of world-wide rights in their works. Whereas, for example, the German collecting society (GEMA) represents the German musical repertoire, SACEM, its French counterpart, represents the French musical repertoire. GEMA and SACEM have subsequently entered into a mutual agreement (so-called sister agreement) by which GEMA has mandated SACEM to represent GEMA's repertoire in France and, vice versa, SACEM has mandated GEMA to represent its repertoire in Germany. Since virtually all national musical collecting societies have entered into such sister-agreements, any national musical collecting society holds the rights not only to the national, but, as a matter of fact, to the worldwide musical repertoire. Collecting societies thus form a one-stop shop (i.e., one entity from which all the rights with regard to the worldwide repertoire can be acquired), much to the benefit to the users whose licensing transaction cost are thus reduced. However, the sister-agreements also contain a clause according to which the national collecting societies refrain from marketing their own repertoire in the other party's national territory. Clearly, this agreement has the effect of partitioning the internal market and it likewise restricts competition within the EU, since users in any one Member State can only acquire the rights to use protected works from the collecting society located in this particular Member State. Moreover, if a user wants to acquire the exploitation rights for more than one state or even EU-wide, then this user needs to contract with as many national collecting societies as the number of states his exploitation touches upon. This has proven to be particularly burdensome for users who want to offer trans-border online-music services. Collecting societies have argued that these restrictions can be explained by the necessity to provide for costly supervision of infringement activities (which would lead to increased cost, if any national society would have to set up such a supervision system all over Europe), and does not aim at charging the users monopolistic prices. The question therefore is whether such restrictions are justified in view of the benefits such a system brings to both authors and perhaps also to consumers.

National dealings of collecting societies
Anti-competitive behaviour of collecting societies can not only occur vis-à-vis users, but also vis-à-vis authors, as well as in dealings with other collecting societies. Indeed, at several instances, the ECJ had to examine all three of these relationships. Although it did not regard collecting societies as 'undertakings entrusted with the operation of services of general economic interest' which would have benefited from the special regime laid down in what is now Article 106 (2)

TFEU,[44] the ECJ has so far been rather sympathetic to the essential elements of collective management of rights by collecting societies. However, the ECJ has corrected – or at least left it to national authorities to correct – some unjustified anomalies arising from collecting society's factual and legal monopoly situation. Thus, as regards the issue whether charging a 'mechanical reproduction fee' under French law in addition to the fee for the public performance of phonograms in discothèques, for records which were put onto the market in another Member State where no such 'mechanical reproduction fee' had to be paid, the ECJ concluded that this did not constitute an abuse within what is now Article 102 TFEU.[45] Similarly, although reiterating that a collecting society which occupies a dominant position may not impose upon its members obligations which are not absolutely necessary for the attainment of its object and which thus encroach unfairly upon the members' freedom to exercise their copyrights, in the *SABAM II* decision, the ECJ held that it was up to the national courts to ascertain whether in the concrete case the mandatory assignment of global rights, past and future of the members to the collecting society constituted an abuse of a dominant position.[46] Similarly, the ECJ referred to national authorities the case to decide whether or not the fact that a national collecting society granted only the full repertoire and refused to license foreign repertoire with a foreign collecting society constitutes an abuse.[47] And in yet another case, the ECJ concluded:

> (33) . . . that a national copyright-management society holding a dominant position in a substantial part of the common market imposes unfair trading conditions where the royalties which it charges to discothèques are appreciably higher than those charged in other Member States, the rates being compared on a consistent basis

unless the collecting society in question is:

> able to justify such a difference by reference to objective and relevant dissimilarities between copyright management in the Member State concerned and copyright management in the other Member States.[48]

---

44 See ECJ Case 127/73, *BRT* v. *SABAM II*, [1973] ECR 313; Case 7/82, *GVL* v. *Commission*, [1983] ECR 483.

45 ECJ Case 402/85, *Basset* v. *SACEM*, [1987] ECR 1747.

46 ECJ Case 127/73, *BRT* v. *SABAM II*, [1973] ECR 313, Paragraphs 12 and 13.

47 ECJ Case C-395/87, *Ministère Public* v. *Tournier*, [1989] ECR 2521.

48 Joined Cases C-110/88, C-241/88 and C-242/88, *Lucazeau* v. *SACEM*, [1989] ECR 2811. For further development of the situation in France see T-5/93, *Tremblay* v. *Commission*, [1995] ECR II-185.

It should be noted, however, that the ECJ has so far taken a more cautious approach vis-à-vis the well-established system of collective rights management in the EU than the Commission which wishes to break up the existing system of trans-border rights management in the field of online music licensing, if not for all trans-border collective licensing within Europe.

Europe-wide online music

As a response to meet the demand for trans-border, pan-European licences concerning the use of copyrighted musical works in online-music services, collecting societies initially had set up a system for pan-European and world-wide licensing, which enabled each national collecting society to grant a license not only – as was the case before – for its own national territory, but for making available the works Europe- or even worldwide (so-called Barcelona and Santiago/BIEM Agreements). However, these contracts contained a residency clause which stipulated that each collecting society could only grant an EU-wide license to internet broadcasters established in, and operating from within, the national territory of the respective collecting society. Although generally in favour of pan-European licensing, the Commission, in April 2004 declared a 'statement of objection' to the so-called 'Santiago Agreement', because it was of the opinion that the residency clause was in violation of EU competition law (consequently, the collecting societies also abandoned the similar BIEM/Barcelona Agreement), and in 2008 the Commission adopted an antitrust decision prohibiting 24 European collecting societies from restricting competition by limiting their ability to offer their services to authors and commercial users outside their domestic territory.[49] In October 2005, the Commission then communicated its own ideas in a Recommendation on collective cross-border management of copyright and related rights for legitimate online music services.[50] Similar

---

49 COMP/C2/38.698 of 16 July 2008, requiring collecting societies no longer to apply membership clauses which prevent authors from choosing or moving to another collecting society as well as territorial restrictions which prevent a collecting society from offering licences to commercial users outside their domestic territory and to authorize another collecting society to administer its repertoire on a given territory on an exclusive basis. The decision has been appealed by the collecting societies see General Court, Case T-425/08 – *KODA* v. *Commission*, still pending at the time of printing. It can only be noted here that, in contrast, the Commission was more favorable towards the IFPI simulcast agreement, see Decision 2003/300 of 8 October 2002, [2003] OJ L 107/56. The (no longer available) clearance was initially limited until the end of 2004; later on, upon request of the Commission, the national territory clause was removed, so that any simulcaster located within the EU and the EEA could seek a multi-territorial license from any of the national collecting societies. Moreover, the record companies covered agreed to provide for transparency regarding the apportioning of administrative fees and royalties in their overall license fee.

50 Recommendation 2005/737/EC of 18 May 2005 on collective cross-border management of copyright and related rights for legitimate online music services, [2005] OJ L 276/54. For discussion see Chapter 5, section 5.2.4.3.

plans were announced, but so far have not been followed up, for all content online.[51] Whereas the collecting societies, in particular the bigger ones, have reacted by creating common licensing structures such as CELAS (a joint venture of the German GEMA and the UK MCPS-PRS),[52] in legal literature, the proposal has mostly met with criticism. It is an open question whether the system proposed by the Commission will indeed lead to more competition and ultimately a better consumer satisfaction, or whether, to the contrary, it will lead to a concentration of collective management structures at the detriment of authors, performing artists and cultural variety in Europe, together with an increase in licensing cost to the disadvantage of consumers.[53] For additional measures designed to break up monopolies by collecting societies and to facilitate trans-border exploitation of online-music, see also the proposal for a Directive concerning collecting societies tabled by the Commission in July 2012 (see Chapter 5, section 5.2.4.3).

? QUESTIONS

1 In your opinion, is the system of sister-agreements amongst collecting societies, and in particular the clause which limits the activity of a national collecting society with regard to a foreign territory, justified?
2 Also in your opinion, does the idea of competition amongst collecting societies within Europe make sense? What will be the effects of the model proposed by the Commission on authors, trans-border users and consumers? To what extent could a Directive on transparency of dealings by collecting societies provide a solution?

Article 102 TFEU: abuse of a dominant market position

Abuse of a dominant market position granted by an IPR

There is, of course, a great variety of possible abuses of a dominant market position. Such abuses can take place either on the market on which the dominant position is held, or on another market, where the dominant position on the first market is used in order to gain an undue, anti-competitive advantage on a second market. For a general overview and extensive citations to case

---

51 Communication from the Commission to the European Parliament, the Council, the European Economic and Social Committee and the Committee of the Regions on Creative Content Online in the Single Market, COM(2007) 836 final, 3 January 2008, www.eur-lex.europa.eu/LexUriServ/LexUriServ.do?uri=COM:2007: 0836:FIN:EN:PDF.

52 For details see the website of CELAS at www.celas.eu.

53 Defending the proposal, however, *Lüder*, 'The Next Ten Years in E.U. Copyright, Making Markets Work', Fordham Intell. Prop. Media & Ent. L.J., Vol. 18, iplj.net/blog/wp-content/uploads/2009/09/Article-THE-NEXT-TEN-YEARS-IN-EU-COPYRIGHT-MAKING-MARKETS-WORK.pdf.

law see the 'Guidance on its enforcement priorities in applying Article 82 (EC) to abusive exclusionary conduct by dominant undertakings' issued by DG Competition at the end of 2008 within the so-called Article 82 review, in which the Commission announces its intention to primarily focus on those types of conduct that are most harmful to consumers.[54]

As far as IPRs are concerned, in the light of what has been said above with regard to the IPR competition law overlap, the mere existence of an IPR does not necessarily place its holder in a dominant position, nor is, even if a dominant position is to be ascertained, the exclusion of third parties which results from exercising an IPR necessarily an abuse of that dominant position. Rather, an individual assessment of the facts of a given case is called for. As far as IPRs are concerned, the abuse can come in the form of overly restrictive licensing conditions as well as of an outright refusal to license.[55]

With regard to licensing conditions, the ECJ has in several decisions held, for example, that a higher sale price for goods protected by an IPR as compared with unpatented products is not necessarily improper on the one hand, but that it could indicate an abuse of a dominant position, in particular, if it is exceptionally high and not justified, on the other hand.[56] However, it remains rather unclear where exactly the boundary runs. In another case, the Court concluded that it constitutes an abuse to needlessly protract negotiations for a compulsory license by charging, in the meantime, exorbitantly high prices.[57] Moreover, an abuse may be found if an undertaking in a dominant market position acquires another company which holds an exclusive patent licence to the competing product, thus 'strengthening its already dominant position, further weakening existing competition and rendering even more difficult the entry of any new competition'.[58]

---

54 Communication from the Commission – Guidance on the Commission's enforcement priorities in applying Article 82 of the EC Treaty to abusive exclusionary conduct by dominant undertakings, [2009] OJ C 47/7. See in general, ec.europa.eu/competition/antitrust/art82/index.html and for the preparatory Discussion paper, ec.europa.eu/comm/competition/antitrust/art82/discpaper2005.pdf.

55 For discussion of the latter, see in this chapter, section 7.2.3.3.2, for the particular problems of the pharmaceutical sector, see above also in this chapter, section 7.2.3.2.2.

56 ECJ Case 24/67, *Parke, Davis* v. *Centrafarm*, [1968] ECR 85; Case 53/87, *CICRA et al.* v. *Renault*, [1988] ECR 6039; Case 238/87, *Volvo* v. *Veng*, [1988] ECR 6211.

57 General Court (then: Court of First Instance) Case T-30/89, *Hilti* v. *Commission*, [1991] ECR II-1439, 1483, appeal dismissed by ECJ case 53/92 [1994] ECR I-667.

58 General Court (then: Court of First Instance) Case T-51/89, *Tetra Pak* v. *Commission*, [1990] ECR II-309.

In particular: refusal to license IPRs

If the distinction between 'subject matter' and 'exercise' of an IPR may give some guidance in cases where restrictive licensing conditions are at issue, it certainly is of not much help in cases in which an IPR holder refuses to license, since refusing a license appears as the very essence of the exclusive right. Thus, in *Volvo v. Veng*,[59] the ECJ had stated that:

> (8) . . . the right of a proprietor of a protected design to prevent third parties from manufacturing and selling or importing, without his consent, products incorporating the design constitutes the very subject-matter of his exclusive right

and that, consequently:

> an obligation imposed upon the proprietor of a protected design to grant to third parties, even in return for a reasonable royalty, a license for the supply of products incorporating the design would lead to the proprietor thereof being deprived of the substance of his exclusive right, and that a refusal to grant such a license cannot in itself constitute an abuse of a dominant position.

However, already in this case, the ECJ had pointed out that:

> (9) . . . the exercise of an exclusive right by the proprietor of a registered design in respect of car body panels [might] be prohibited by Article [now 102 TFEU] if it involve[d], on the part of an undertaking holding a dominant position, certain abusive conduct such as the arbitrary refusal to supply spare parts to independent repairers, the fixing of prices for spare parts at an unfair level or a decision no longer to produce spare parts for a particular model even though many cars of that model [were] still in circulation, provided that such conduct [was] liable to affect trade between Member States.

Following, there is indeed – an albeit small – number of yet rather important cases, in which both the ECJ and the Court of First Instance (now: General Court) found an abuse of a dominant position by a right-holder who refused to license his protected IP. In these cases, the Court restricted the IPR holder's freedom to license or not to license, and rather imposed on him an obligation to contract. Of course, all those cases related to rather special facts, where doubts may have existed whether the IP protection granted by law wasn't too broad or far-reaching in the first place, thus requiring some

---

59 ECJ Case 238/87, *Volvo v. Veng*, [1988] ECR 6211. See also Case 53/87, *CICRA et al. v. Renault*, [1988] ECR 6039.

ex-post correction by way of competition law. Moreover, the ECJ has been careful in limiting each of the compulsory licenses to a particular set of limiting conditions. In doing so, the ECJ keeps the exclusivity of IPRs intact as a rule, but at the same time limits the scope of an IPR holder's rights by subjecting him, under particular circumstances to a duty to contract. However, the relationship between the individual conditions which have to be fulfilled before a duty to contract exists still remains somewhat unclear.

Magill[60]

In *Magill*, Irish and British TV-stations published their own weekly program previews and allowed newspapers to reprint the daily program. However, they refused to license Magill TV Guide Ltd, which attempted to publish a comprehensive weekly television guide but was prevented from doing so by the TV stations which claimed copyright in their program listings. At that time, no comprehensive weekly television guide was available on the market in Ireland or in Northern Ireland.

The ECJ held that:

- broadcasting companies are in a dominant position when, by reason of their de facto monopoly over the information relating to the listings of their programs they are in a position to prevent effective competition on the market in weekly television magazines in the areas concerned;
- the conduct of an undertaking in a dominant position, consisting of the exercise of a right classified by national law as copyright, cannot, by virtue of that fact alone, be exempt from review in relation to Article 82 of the Treaty [now Article 102 TFEU];
- in the absence of Community standardization or harmonization of laws, determination of the conditions and procedures for granting protection of an intellectual property right is admittedly a matter for national rules and the exclusive right of reproduction forms part of the author's rights, with the result that refusal to grant a license, even if it is the act of an undertaking holding a dominant position, cannot in itself constitute abuse of a dominant position;
- however, the exercise of an exclusive right by a proprietor may, in exceptional circumstances, involve abusive conduct. Such will be the case when broadcasting companies rely on copyright conferred by national legislation to prevent another undertaking from publishing on a weekly basis information (channel, day, time and title of programs) together with commentaries and pictures obtained independently of those companies, where, in the first place, that conduct prevents the appearance of a new product, a comprehensive weekly

---

60 ECJ Joined Cases C-241/91 and C-242/91, *RTE and ITP v. Commission* (Magill), [1995] ECR I-743.

guide to television programs, which the companies concerned do not offer and for which there is a potential consumer demand; where, second, there is no justification for that refusal either in the activity of television broadcasting or in that of publishing television magazines; and where, third, the companies concerned, by their conduct, reserve to themselves the secondary market of weekly television guides by excluding all competition from the market through denial of access to the basic information which is the raw material indispensable for the compilation of such a guide; and that

- in order to satisfy the condition that trade between Member States must be affected within the meaning of Article 82 of the Treaty [now Article 102 TFEU], it is not necessary that the conduct in question should in fact have substantially affected that trade. It is sufficient to establish that the conduct is capable of having such an effect. This will be the case where an undertaking excludes all potential competitors on the geographical market consisting of one Member State and part of another Member State and thus modifies the structure of competition on that market, thereby affecting potential commercial exchanges between those Member States.

IMS Health[61]

In *IMS Health*, two companies, IMS and NDC, were engaged in tracking sales of pharmaceutical and healthcare products. IMS had developed a 'brick structure' for the provision of German regional sales data on pharmaceutical products (the structure consisted of 1,860 bricks, each corresponding to a designated geographic area and taking account of various criteria, such as the boundaries of municipalities, postcodes, population density, transport connections and the geographical distribution of pharmacies and doctors' surgeries). IMS provides data on regional sales of pharmaceutical products in Germany to pharmaceutical laboratories formatted according to the brick structure. IMS not only marketed its brick structures, but also distributed them free of charge to pharmacies and doctors' surgeries. This practice helped those structures to become the normal industry standard to which its clients adapted their information and distribution systems. NDC also wanted to market similar data, but on account of reticence manifested by potential clients, who were accustomed to structures consisting of 1,860 bricks, NDC decided to use structures of 1,860 bricks very similar to those used by IMS. IMS invoked its database copyright on the brick structure and refused to license NDC.

Here, the ECJ held that:

---

61 ECJ Case C-418/01, *IMS Health v. Commission*, [2004] ECR I-5039.

(52) . . . [t]he refusal by an undertaking which holds a dominant position and owns an intellectual property right in a brick structure indispensable to the presentation of regional sales data on pharmaceutical products in a Member State to grant a license to use that structure to another undertaking which also wishes to provide such data in the same Member State, constitutes an abuse of a dominant position within the meaning of Article 82 EC [now Article 102 TFEU] where the following conditions are fulfilled:

- the undertaking which requested the license intends to offer, on the market for the supply of the data in question, new products or services not offered by the owner of the intellectual property right and for which there is a potential consumer demand;
- the refusal is not justified by objective considerations;
- the refusal is such as to reserve to the owner of the intellectual property right the market for the supply of data on sales of pharmaceutical products in the Member State concerned by eliminating all competition on that market.

Microsoft[62]

Finally, in *Microsoft*, the company had not made publicly available certain interface information of its client PC operating system software that was needed in order to create competing software products on the server market. Thus Microsoft had secured itself an advantage on that market over its competitor Sun. Moreover, Microsoft had integrated its Windows Media Player into its Windows operating system, thus affecting if not eliminating competition in the market for player software. Microsoft was therefore ordered to lay open interface information and to offer its Windows Operating System also without an integrated player.

The General Court in following the prior case law by the ECJ concludes that:

(331) It follows from the case-law cited above that the refusal by an undertaking holding a dominant position to license a third party to use a product covered by an intellectual property right cannot in itself constitute an abuse of a dominant position within the meaning of Article 82 EC [now Article 102 TFEU]. It is only in exceptional circumstances that the exercise of the exclusive right by the owner of the intellectual property right may give rise to such an abuse.

(332) It also follows from that case-law that the following circumstances, in particular, must be considered to be exceptional:

---

62 General Court Case T-201/04, *Microsoft* v. *Commission*, [2007] ECR II-3601. See earlier for a similar case regarding information held back by IBM Joined Cases 60/81 and 190/81 R, *IBM* v. *Commission*, [1981] ECR 2639.

- in the first place, the refusal relates to a product or service indispensable to the exercise of a particular activity on a neighbouring market;
- in the second place, the refusal is of such a kind as to exclude any effective competition on that neighbouring market;
- in the third place, the refusal prevents the appearance of a new product for which there is potential consumer demand.

(333) Once it is established that such circumstances are present, the refusal by the holder of a dominant position to grant a license may infringe Article 82 EC [now Article 102 TFEU] unless the refusal is objectively justified.

Finding that all those elements had been present and not finding any grounds for justification of Microsoft's behaviour, the General Court upheld the fine imposed upon Microsoft by the Commission in the amount of a record €497 million.

Discussion
In sum, it may be concluded that:

- firstly, IPRs are not totally immune from review by competition law;
- secondly, ownership of an IPR does not necessarily confer a dominant position; rather, in order to find a dominant position, a definition of the relevant market has to be undertaken beforehand;
- thirdly, the refusal to license as such does not yet constitute an abuse of a dominant position; rather, a refusal to license is only to be considered abusive, if exceptionally there are additional circumstances;
- fourthly, as such exceptional circumstances, the ECJ and the General Court have identified that (a) the refusal prevents the appearance of a new product or service (or a product or service which is indispensable to the exercise of a particular activity on a neighbouring market) for which there is potential consumer demand; (b) the exclusion of effective competition on that neighbouring market, and (c) that the right-holder wants to reserve the neighbouring market for himself;
- fifthly, however, the relationship between these circumstances is still not quite clear. In particular, it is open to discussion whether the prevention of a new product and the control of a secondary market must be found cumulatively (this seems to be required in *IMS Health*), or in the alternative (this seems to be insinuated in *Magill* and perhaps also *Microsoft*);
- sixthly, if the exceptional circumstances are given, it is up to the IPR holder to prove the existence of circumstances which exceptionally justify what absent such justifying circumstances would qualify as an abuse of a dominant market position within the meaning of Article 102 TFEU. At that stage, however, the mere fact that the IPR holder wants

to make use of the exclusivity of his IPR, cannot be considered a valid justification.

Finally, it should be noted that in its Guidance on the Commission's enforcement priorities in applying Article 102 TFEU to abusive exclusionary conduct by dominant undertakings already cited above,[63] the Commission declared that it:

> does not regard it as necessary for the refused product to have been already traded.

Rather:

> it is sufficient that there is demand from potential purchasers and that a potential market for the input at stake can be identified. Likewise, it is not necessary for there to be actual refusal on the part of a dominant undertaking; 'constructive refusal' is sufficient. Constructive refusal could, for example, take the form of unduly delaying or otherwise degrading the supply of the product or involve the imposition of unreasonable conditions in return for the supply.

Other constellations: the 'green dot'

According to an Ordinance on waste reduction established under German law, companies were obliged to take back and recover all used packages from consumers; however, they could escape that obligation by participating in self-managed recycling schemes. The only nationwide scheme established for the purpose was the Duales System Deutschland (DSD), which used as its identifying logo the so-called 'green dot'.[64] Companies participating in the system obtained licenses for using the sign on their packages and were obliged to pay license fees measured in proportion to the amount of packages on which the sign appeared. Complaints were raised when parallel systems to DSD were established on a regional basis and companies wanted to make use of them, but became wary of the fact that this would mean having to pay license fees twice, unless they renounced using the green dot on the packages for which the alternative schemes were to be used. Refraining from using the green dot on those packages, however, appeared as unfeasible for economic and practical reasons, *inter alia* because the decision as to whether

---

63 Communication from the Commission – Guidance on the Commission's enforcement priorities in applying Article 82 of the EC Treaty to abusive exclusionary conduct by dominant undertakings, [2009] OJ C 47/7, Paragraph 79.

64 General Court Case T-151/01, *Duales System Deutschland v. Commission*, [2007] ECR II-1607. For procedural issues see the decision by the ECJ upon Appeal Case C-385/07 P, *Der Grüne Punkt - Duales System Deutschland GmbH v. Commission*, [2009] ECR I-6155.

DSD or the alternative system would be used was ultimately made by consumers after the purchase. It was therefore argued that the fees collected by DSD should be calculated on the basis of the packages actually submitted to DSD's recycling system, and not rely on the number of packages bearing the green dot. The Commission shared the view and issued an order against DSD, which was principally affirmed by the General Court. It was held that under the special circumstances of the case, with DSD being the only nationwide system established in accordance with the Ordinance on waste reduction and thus having a dominant position, to insist on full payment of license fees per use of the green dot, even where other recycling systems had been used, would constitute abuse. However, contrary to the Commission's order, the General Court found that the possibility should not be excluded for DSD to levy an adequate (lower) fee for merely using the mark:

> (194) . . . even if that packaging is not actually brought to the DSD system and it is shown that its equivalent in material has been collected or recovered by a competitor system, it is none the less the case that the mark leaves it open to the consumer to dispose of that packaging through the DSD system. Such a possibility offered to the consumer for all the packaging put into circulation with the [green dot], whether part of the DSD system or not, after checking the quantities collected, is likely to have a price which, even if it cannot represent the actual price of the collection and recovery service, as could be the case under the provisions in dispute of the Trade Mark Agreement, should be able to be paid to DSD in consideration for the service offered in the present case, namely the making available of its system.

? QUESTIONS

1 What is your opinion of the different conditions that must be met, according to the ECJ, in order to conclude a duty to contract?

2 Article 6 of the Software Directive 91/250/EEC (republished in a consolidate version as Directive 2009/24/EC) contains a special provision dealing with the scope of permitted reverse engineering in order 'to obtain the information necessary to achieve the interoperability of an independently created computer program with other programs.' In the case T-201/04, Microsoft argued that Article 6 of this Directive strikes a 'careful balance between copyright and competition policies'. The Court, however, referred to what is now Recital 17 (ex-Recital 26), which states that '[t]he provisions of this Directive are without prejudice to the application of the competition rules under Articles [101 and 102 TFEU] if a dominant supplier refuses to make information available which is necessary for interoperability as defined in this Directive' and dismissed

Microsoft's argument that Article 6 should prevail as a special competition law norm (see para 1337). Do you agree?

3 In their proposal for a 'European Copyright Code' (see www.copyright-code.eu), the academic drafters included a newly crafted exception for 'uses for the purpose of enhancing competition' (Article 5.4 of the Code), which in its paragraph 2 incorporates competition law elements into copyright. What are the advantages and the disadvantages of such an ex ante-control of anti-competitive practices as opposed to the ex-post control traditionally exercised by competition law?

7.3 Regulating unfair competition

Background

The term 'unfair competition' has no distinct meaning in European law. While it derives from Article 10 *bis* Paris Convention – and thereby from an international norm which must be implemented in all Member States – that common basis has not resulted in a uniform approach being taken towards the issue. The differences are anchored in a divide concerning the understanding of the objectives on which legislation aimed at regulating unfair practices are based. Some countries, such as Germany, Austria, and Belgium, follow an integrated approach, meaning that the relevant legislation is aimed at protecting the interests of consumers and entrepreneurs by the same set of rules. Others separate between legislation in the field of consumer protection, and the protection of commercial actors against unfair conduct of competitors. In civil law jurisdictions, such as France, the rules addressing the latter field may be cast in the form of general tort clauses with a broad range of application. Different from that, common law systems only recognise specific torts such as passing off or libel and slander as a basis for claiming inadmissibility of competitive conduct.

Apart from the conceptual differences, Member States also diverge with regard to the procedural mechanisms installed for the monitoring of unfair competition. In states following the integrated approach, the regular way to pursue claims is by private litigation brought before the civil courts. In practice, this means that most of the monitoring is done by private parties or by associations representing certain groups of stakeholders. In addition, a right to sue is typically given to consumer associations, and, depending on the legal system and the claims that shall be brought, even to individual consumers. Other systems, in particular in the Nordic countries, rely on a bifurcated structure, allowing civil claims to be brought before the (specialised) courts, whereas a special agency – the consumer bureau or consumer ombudsman – is empowered to monitor commercial practices which are contrary to consumer interests, and to issue injunctions against them. Some countries, in particular the Accession States, have entrusted the same agency with the competence to monitor unfair competition as well as anti-competitive practices; a similar structure also exists in Italy in the form of the 'autorità garante'. In France, surveillance of marketing rules is largely effected through the means of criminal proceedings. Certain States put much emphasis on statutes and bodies of self-control; in others, the role played by such institutions is rather marginal.

So far, legal harmonisation in the area has taken a fragmented approach. Attempts undertaken in the 1970s for a comprehensive harmonisation basically reflecting the German model of an integrated approach, including as its characteristic feature a wide general clause against any acts of unfair competition, were unsuccessful. One major reason for that is seen in the fact that a regulation of unfair competition based on a general clause appeared as an unacceptably vague concept for common law jurisdiction, meaning that the harmonisation project became politically unfeasible after the accession of the UK and Ireland to the EEC in 1978. Instead, a directive on deceptive and misleading advertisement was passed in 1984,[65] and was complemented in 1997[66] with provisions harmonising the conditions for admissibility of comparative advertisement. A codified version of the ensuing directive has been enacted as Directive 2006/114/EC.[67]

Whereas the misleading advertising directive and its successors were still based on an integrated approach – although the accent obviously lay on consumer protection – that concept was abandoned by the Directive on Unfair Commercial Practices (2005/29/EC; UCP Directive).[68] Pursuant to the preamble, the Directive only aims at marketing measures directed towards consumers (B2C), and does not purport to regulate matters of fair conduct between entrepreneurs (B2B). Apart from questioning

---

65 Council Directive 84/450/EEC of 10 September 1984 relating to the approximation of the laws, regulations and administrative proceedings of the Member States concerning misleading advertisement, [1984] OJ L 250/17.

66 Directive 97/55/EC of the European Parliament and the Council of 6 October 1997 amending Directive 84/450/EEC concerning misleading advertising so as to include comparative advertising, [1997] OJ L 290/10.

67 Directive 2006/114/EC of the European Parliament and of the Council of 12 December 2006 concerning misleading and comparative advertising (codified version), [2006] OJ L 376/21.

68 Directive 2005/29/EC of the European Parliament and of the Council of 11 May 2005 concerning unfair business-to-consumer commercial practices in the internal market and amending Council Directive 84/450/EEC, Directives 97/7/EC, 98/27/EC and 2002/65/EC of the European Parliament and of the Council and Regulation 2006/2004 of the European Parliament and of the Council, [2005] OJ L 149/22.

the wisdom of that distinction, it is frequently pointed out that it creates problems and might lead to inconsistencies where those two areas overlap.

In addition to misleading and comparative advertising as well as unfair commercial practices, a number of more specific directives addresses advertisement and other marketing measures in specific fields, such as pharmaceuticals[69] or foodstuffs,[70] or by specific media, such as television and radio broadcasting.[71] For commercial communications over the internet, the E-Commerce Directive (2000/31/EC) is of interest, in particular as it establishes the rule that commercial messages complying with the relevant regulations in the Member State from which it is communicated cannot be prohibited under the rules applying in the State where it is received (Article 3 (2) E-Commerce Directive; 'country of origin principle'). In addition, the Directive sets out certain substantive requirements, in particular concerning the transparency of messages containing unsolicited offers (Article 7) and information to be provided in the context of marketing measures such as promotional offers, premiums and gifts (Article 6).

Harmonising activities were also directed at the related field of consumer contracts. The most important piece of legislation in that regard is the Unfair Contract Terms Directive.[72] More specific directives concern consumer credit, distance sales and contracts negotiated away from business premises, real property used on a timeshare basis, and others.[73]

Finally, while the procedural aspects of monitoring and pursuing claims relating to misleading or unfair commercial conduct have not been harmonised to any larger extent, a minimum amount of coordination has been achieved by the Consumer Injunctions Directive,[74] which ensures that consumer organisations fulfilling certain requirements are granted *locus standi*

---

69 Directive 2001/83/EC of the European Parliament and of the Council of 6 November 2001 on the Community code relating to medicinal products for human use, [2004] OJ L 311/67.

70 Directive 2000/13/EC of the European Parliament and of the Council of 20 March 2000 on the approximation of the laws of the Member States relating to the labelling, presentation and advertising of foodstuffs, [2000] OJ L 109/29.

71 Directive 97/36/EC of the European Parliament and of the Council of 30 June 1997 amending Council Directive 89/552/EEC on the coordination of certain provisions laid down by law, regulation or administrative action in Member States concerning the pursuit of television broadcasting activities, [1997] OJ L 202/60.

72 Council Directive 93/13 of 5 April 1993 on unfair terms in consumer contracts, [1993] OJ L 95/29.

73 For more specific information, consult www.europa.eu/legislation_summaries/consumers/protection_of_consumers/index_en.htm.

74 Directive 2009/22/EC of the European Parliament and of the Council of 23 April 2009 on injunctions for the protection of consumers' interests (Codified version), [2009] OJ L 110/30.

in all Member States for bringing claims concerning cross-border marketing measures affecting consumers in the territory where the association is based. Apart from that, the pertinent directives basically confine themselves to stipulating that persons or organisations who are regarded under national law as having a legitimate interest in the combating of unfair conduct must have access to efficient remedies, which must include the right to claim preliminary or permanent injunctions against unfair conduct occurring or threatening within the jurisdiction.

Of immediate interest for this volume are only acts of unfair competition in the relationship between commercial actors, i.e. B2B measures which until now have not been harmonised. The most relevant segment within that area concerns imitation of goods and services, which was addressed in the previous chapter. In this chapter, the remaining areas of unfair competition will be covered briefly, to the extent that they are at least of an indirect interest for intellectual property. This concerns in particular the directive on comparative and misleading advertising, where a broad area of overlap exists with trade mark law. Some remarks will also address the structure and contents of the UCP directive. Prior to that, an account is given on the development of principles governing the relationship between measures against unfair competition and primary community law in the jurisprudence of the ECJ.

? **QUESTIONS**

1 How is the law against marketing practices and other forms of unfair conduct organised in your country? Does a separation apply between legal rules addressing B2C and B2B-related measures respectively?
2 How do you assess the advantages and disadvantages of the different models?
3 Why, in your opinion, is the European legislature so reluctant when it comes to harmonising the structures and procedures for monitoring and seeking redress against unfair commercial practices?

Measures against unfair competition in the light of primary Community law

Impediments for free movement of goods

While import bans based on the diversity of national intellectual property rights caught the attention of the ECJ in the 1960s, the first case when the free movement of goods was allegedly impeded by measures under marketing rules was brought and decided in 1974 (*Dassonville*).[75] It concerned the import into Belgium of products labelled as Scottish whisky, which had been brought into the Community (which at that time did not extend to the UK) under the French customs regulations. Other than in Belgium, an accompanying document certifying the authenticity of the geographical origin of the product was not required in France. As the import did not satisfy the respective requirements under Belgian law, the Public Prosecutor instituted proceedings against the importers. The deciding court referred to the ECJ the question whether the Belgian regulations and the way they were employed in this case were compatible with primary EU law. Concerning the applicability of the provision on free movement of goods (at that time: Article 30 TEEC) the ECJ endorsed a broad interpretation, declaring that:

> (5) [a]ll trading rules enacted by Member States which are capable of hindering, *directly or indirectly, actually or potentially*, intra-Community trade are to be considered as measures having an effect equivalent to quantitative restrictions. (Emphasis added)

It was further emphasised that Member States are entitled to take measures to prevent unfair practices, under the conditions that they are reasonable and do not act as a hindrance of intra-Community trade, as in the case at stake.[76]

The conditions under which measures allegedly serving to prevent unfair competition can be considered as admissible under primary EU law were further elaborated in a decision concerning the prohibition of import into Germany of the liqueur 'Cassis de Dijon'.[77] The argument was made by the agency supervising the import of spirits that according to German law, only potable spirits containing a wine-spirit content of at least 32 per cent could be marketed, whereas Cassis de Dijon contained between 15 and 20 per cent of wine spirit. The ECJ confirmed that this doubtless was a 'measure having equivalent effect' to quantitative restrictions, and continued that:

> (8) Obstacles to movement of goods within the Community resulting from disparities between the national laws relating to the marketing of the products in question must be accepted in so far as those provisions may be recognized as being *necessary* in order to satisfy *mandatory requirements* relating in particular to . . . the protection of public health, the fairness of commercial transactions and the defence of the consumer. (Emphasis added)

---

75 ECJ Case 8/74, *Procureur du Roi v. B. and G. Dassonville*, [1974] ECR 837.
76 Ibid., Paragraphs 6–9.
77 ECJ Case 120/1978, *Rewe v. Bundesmonopolverwaltung für Branntwein* (Cassis de Dijon), [1979] ECR 6349.

Quite obviously, in the case at stake, those conditions did not apply, and the measure was therefore considered as incompatible with primary law.

Together, the two ECJ decisions formed the basis for a large and growing number of requests for preliminary decisions, whenever a rule affecting marketing activities in a Member State appeared to be more restrictive than those in other Member States, thereby arguably having at least an indirect or potential effect on intra-Community trade in the meaning of *Dassonville*, which might fall short of the grounds for justification established in *Cassis de Dijon*. In a case dealing with the prohibition under French law to offer goods at a price undercutting the actual purchase price (*Keck & Mithouard*),[78] the ECJ finally called for a halt, stating that:

> (14) [i]n view of the increasing tendency of traders to invoke [ex-]Article 30 of the Treaty as a means of challenging any rules whose effect is to limit their commercial freedom even where such rules are not aimed at products from other Member States, the Court considers it necessary to re-examine and clarify its previous test … (16) … [C]ontrary to what has previously been decided, the application to products from other Member States of national provisions restricting or prohibiting certain selling arrangements is not such as to hinder directly or indirectly, actually or potentially, trade between Member States within the meaning of the *Dassonville* judgment … so long as those provisions apply [without discriminating against traders or products from other Member States].

Ever since that decision, the distinction between product-related measures and mere selling arrangements has become the litmus test for the possibility to request a preliminary decision from the ECJ on the compatibility of marketing rules with primary EU law.

The 'average consumer'

In comparison with other Member States, German judicial practice used to be deemed as markedly paternalistic, in the sense that judges tended to assume that advertising was misleading even when the probability of actual deception was very low. This was blamed on the 'consumer image' (Verbraucherleitbild) employed by the German courts, which, according to critical voices, pictured the relevant circles as near-imbeciles, incapable of exercising even a minimum degree of attention and discrimination.

---

78 ECJ Joined Cases C-267/91 and C-268/91, *Keck and Mithouard*, [1993] ECR I-6097.

The issue was referred to the ECJ in a lawsuit concerning the sales of eggs in packages labelled as '6 grains – fresh eggs' (C-210/96 – *Gut Springenheide & Tusky*).[79] In a note inserted in the packages, the beneficial effect of the grain feed on the quality of the eggs was extolled. The Office for the Supervision of Foodstuffs initiated proceedings against the producer, arguing that the label and the insert were likely to mislead a significant proportion of consumers in that they implied falsely that the feed given to the hens is made up exclusively of the six cereals indicated, thereby giving the eggs particular characteristics, whereas in reality, only 60 per cent of the mix given to the hens consisted of those grains. In the revision procedure before the Federal Administrative Court, several questions were referred to the ECJ, *inter alia* whether the view of the informed average consumer or that of the casual consumer formed the correct test for assessing the actual expectations of consumers. The ECJ answered that:

> (37) [i]n order to determine whether a statement or description . . . is liable to mislead the purchaser, in breach of Article 10 (2) (e) of Regulation No 1907/90, the national court must take into account the presumed expectations which it evokes in an average consumer who is reasonably well-informed and reasonably observant and circumspect.

Based on that test, it was found unlikely that consumers could actually be deceived by the label and the insert. In a similar vein, it was held in other decisions, that:

- the name 'Clinique' does not mislead consumers into thinking that a cosmetic product sold under the name had medicinal properties (*Clinique*);[80]
- the indication '+ 10' on a candy bar during a short marketing campaign (a) does not give rise to the mistaken belief that the bar is sold at the same price as previously, and (b) does not convey a misleading impression of the increase in size and volume (though the brightly coloured part of the package on which the indication appeared covered more than 10 per cent of the article) (*Mars*).[81]
- national legislation must not prohibit reference to expert medical opinions in the marketing of cosmetic products - in particular, the use of the statement 'dermatologically tested' – if that reference does not include information relating to the contents and outcome of those assessments (*Linhart*).[82]

---

79 ECJ Case C-210/96, *Gut Springenheide und Rudolf Tusky v. Amt für Lebensmittelüberwachung*, [1998] ECR I-4657.
80 ECJ Case C-315/92, *VSW v. Clinique and Estée Lauder*, [1994] ECR I-317.
81 ECJ Case C-370/93, *Verein gegen Unwesen in Handel und Gewerbe v. Mars*, [1995] ECR I-1923.
82 ECJ Case C-99/01, *Gottfried Linhart v. Hans Biffl*, [2002] ECR I-9375.

The formula referring to the 'average consumer who is reasonably well-informed and reasonably observant and circumspect' has been repeated in many other decisions as the standard test for assessing risks of consumer deception. Also in trade mark law, the test is employed for the evaluation of likelihood of confusion.[83]

? QUESTIONS

1 The distinction established by the ECJ in *Keck & Mitouard* between product-related measures and mere selling arrangements was only made with regard to Article 34 TFEU, i.e. free movement of goods, and does therefore not apply – or at least not explicitly – to free movement of services. Do you consider that as a mere oversight, or could there be an explanation for the different treatment?

2 The ECJ has instituted the 'average' – as opposed to the 'casual' – consumer as the standard test in unfair competition law and adjacent areas, including trade mark law. Do you consider that as justified? Is the same test applicable in all situations, or should there be more room for differentiations? If so, which scheme should be governing the differentiation?

Misleading and comparative advertising

Contents of the Directive: overview

The legal objectives of the Directive concerning Misleading and Comparative Advertising (2006/114/EC) are set out in Recitals 5 and 6:

(5) The differences between the laws of the Member States on advertising which misleads business hinder the execution of advertising campaigns beyond national boundaries and thus affect the free circulation of goods and provision of services.

(6) The completion of the internal market means a wide range of choice. Given that consumers and traders can and must make the best possible use of the internal market, and that advertising is a very important means of creating genuine outlets for all goods and services throughout the Community, the basic provisions governing the form and content of comparative advertising should be uniform and the conditions of the use of comparative advertising in the Member States should be harmonised. If these conditions are met, this will help demonstrate objectively the merits of the various comparable products. Comparative advertising can also stimulate competition between suppliers of goods and services to the consumer's advantage.

---

83 ECJ Case C-342/97, *Lloyd Schuhfabrik Meyer v. Klijsen Handel*, [1999] ECR I-3819. For discussion see Chapter 4, section 4.4.1.3.2.3.

Article 2 defines *inter alia* the central notions of 'advertising', 'misleading advertising' and 'comparative advertising':

> (a) 'advertising' means the making of a representation in any form in connection with a trade, business, craft or profession in order to promote the supply of goods or services, including immovable property, rights and obligations;
>
> (b) 'misleading advertising' means any advertising which in any way, including its presentation, deceives or is likely to deceive the persons to whom it is addressed or whom it reaches and which, by reason of its deceptive nature, is likely to affect their economic behaviour or which, for those reasons, injures or is likely to injure a competitor;
>
> (c) 'comparative advertising' means any advertising which explicitly or by implication identifies a competitor or goods or services offered by a competitor.

Article 3 sets out the factors which are to be taken into account for assessing whether an advertisement is misleading, namely:

> (a) the characteristics of goods or services, such as their availability, nature, execution, composition, method and date of manufacture or provision, fitness for purpose, uses, quantity, specification, geographical or commercial origin or the results to be expected from their use, or the results and material features of tests or checks carried out on the goods or services;
>
> (b) the price or the manner in which the price is calculated, and the conditions on which the goods are supplied or the services provided;
>
> (c) the nature, attributes and rights of the advertiser, such as his identity and assets, his qualifications and ownership of industrial, commercial or intellectual property rights or his awards and distinctions.

Article 4 stipulates that comparative advertising must be permitted if:

> (a) it is not misleading within the meaning of Articles 2 (b), 3 and 8 (1) of this Directive or Articles 6 and 7 of [the UCP Directive];
>
> (b) it compares goods or services meeting the same needs or intended for the same purpose;
>
> (c) it objectively compares one or more material, relevant, verifiable and representative features of those goods and services, which may include price;
>
> (d) it does not discredit or denigrate the trade marks, trade names, other distinguishing marks, goods, services, activities or circumstances of a competitor;
>
> (e) for products with designation of origin, it relates in each case to products with the same designation;
>
> (f) it does not take unfair advantage of the reputation of a trade mark, trade name or other distinguishing marks of a competitor or of the designation of origin of competing products;

(g) it does not present goods or services as imitations or replicas of goods or services bearing a protected trade mark or trade name;

(h) it does not create confusion among traders, between the advertiser and a competitor or between the advertiser's trade marks, trade names, other distinguishing marks, goods or services and those of a competitor.

Articles 5 *et seq.* concern procedures and sanctions, leaving Member States a choice between civil and administrative institutions and remedies.

Case law (comparative advertisement)

The notion of 'comparison'

The term 'comparative advertising' as defined in Article 2 determines the scope of application of Directive 2006/114/EC. Its ambit was tested in *Toshiba*,[84] the first case referred to the ECJ under the predecessor of the current legislation, Directive 97/55/EC. It concerned the sales of spare parts and consumable items to be used for photocopiers distributed by Toshiba Europe. In the defendant's catalogues the articles were set out in categories listing the products specific to a group of particular models of Toshiba photocopiers, e.g. by referring to 'products for Toshiba photocopiers 1340/1350'. Each list consisted of four columns with the first one, headed 'OEM product number', showing Toshiba Europe's order number for the corresponding product sold by it. According to the national court, 'OEM' is understood in the relevant business sector as meaning 'Original Equipment Manufacturer'. The second column headed 'Katun product number', contained the defendant's order number. The third column contained a description of the product. The fourth column referred to the number of the particular model or models for which the product was intended. As the catalogue did not contain an explicit comparison of the products, the question was referred to the ECJ whether advertisement for spare parts listing the respective OEM product numbers fell into the ambit of the Directive. The Court answered in the affirmative, endorsing a broad interpretation:

(31) In order for there to be comparative advertising within the meaning of Article 2 (2a) of Directive 84/450 as amended, it is . . . sufficient for a representation to be made in any form which refers, even by implication, to a competitor or to the goods or services which he offers. It does not matter [whether] there is a comparison between the goods and services offered by the advertiser and those of a competitor.

---

84 ECJ Case C-112/99, *Toshiba Europe* v. *Katun Germany*, [2001] ECR I-7945.

Although a strictly literal reading of the directive might lead to the result that comparative advertising is only admissible if it actually compares goods or services in an objective manner, it was found that the same must apply to a case like this, when only the respective product numbers are listed, because:

> (38) . . . specification of the product numbers of the equipment manufacturer alongside a competing supplier's product numbers enables the public to identify precisely the products of the equipment manufacturer to which that supplier's products correspond. (39) Such an indication does . . . constitute a positive statement that the two products have equivalent technical features, that is to say, a comparison of material, relevant, verifiable and representative features of the products within the meaning of [the relevant provision in the directive].

Price comparisons

Price comparisons are of particular interest for consumers. The ECJ has specified the conditions for such comparisons in the following decisions.

In *Pippig* v. *Hartlauer*,[85] it had been argued that the objects of comparison had been chosen selectively so as to render an unfavourable impression of the plaintiff's average price level, and that the result amounted to discrediting. The Court responded that:

> (81) [t]he choice as to the number of comparisons which the advertiser wishes to make between the products which he is offering and those offered by his competitors falls within the exercise of his economic freedom. Any obligation to restrict each price comparison to the average prices of the products offered by the advertiser and those of rival products would be contrary to the objectives of the Community legislature. (82) In the words of the second recital in the preamble to Directive 97/55, comparative advertising must help demonstrate objectively the merits of the various comparable products. Such objectivity implies that the persons to whom the advertising is addressed are capable of knowing the actual price differences between the products compared and not merely the average difference between the advertiser's prices and those of its competitors . . . (84) [Therefore] a price comparison does not entail the discrediting of a competitor, within the meaning of Article 3a (1) (e) of Directive 84/450 either on the grounds that the difference in price between the products compared is greater than the average price difference or by reason of the number of comparisons made.

---

85 ECJ Case C-44/01, *Pippig* v. *Hartlauer*, [2003] ECR I-3095.

The ECJ further clarified that it also does not amount to discrediting if, in addition to citing the competitor's name, its logo and a picture of its shop front are reproduced in the advertisement, if the advertising otherwise complies with the conditions for lawfulness laid down by Community law.[86]

In *Lidl v. Colruyt*,[87] the ECJ (Grand Chamber) further specified with regard to comparisons of the general price level of two competing chains of supermarkets that advertisements claiming, on the basis of a sample of products, that the advertiser's general price level is lower than his main competitors' are misleading when the advertisement does not reveal that the comparison:

- is related only to such a sample and not to all the advertiser's products;
- does not identify the details of the comparison made or inform the persons to whom it is addressed of the information source where such identification is possible;
- or contains a collective reference to a range of amounts that may be saved by consumers who make their purchases from the advertiser rather than from his competitors without specifying individually the general level of the prices charged, respectively, by each of those competitors and the amount that consumers are liable to save by making their purchases from the advertiser rather than from each of the competitors.[88]

'Generic' comparisons

A special issue was presented in C-381/05 (*De Landtsheer*).[89] The defendant, a Belgian Brewery, had advertised its beer as being made according to the method used to produce sparkling wine. *Inter alia*, he had referred to the beer as 'the first BRUT beer in the world', and as 'champagne beer'. The *comité interprofessionel du vin de champagne*, whose aim it is to protect the denomination 'champagne' for sparkling wines, filed suit against him, arguing *inter alia* that the marketing violated the clause in the Comparative Advertising Directive which restricts the possibility to compare products with designation of origin to products with the same designation (Article 4 (e) of the current directive, Article 3a (1) (f) of the previous text). The ECJ found, firstly, that:

---

86 Ibid., Paragraph 84.
87 ECJ Case C-356/04, *Lidl Belgium v. Etablissementen Franz Colruyt*, [2006] ECR I-08501.
88 Ibid., Paragraph 85.
89 ECJ Case C-381/05, *De Landtsheer Emmanuel SA v. Comité interprofessionel du vin de Champagne*, [2006] ECR I-3115.

(56) advertising which refers to a type of product without thereby identifying a competitor or the goods which it offers is not impermissible with regard to Article 3a (1) of the directive, [and] that the conditions governing whether such advertising is permissible must be assessed in the light of other provisions of national law or, where appropriate, of Community law, irrespective of the fact that that could mean a lower level of protection for consumers or competing undertakings.

Furthermore, regarding the question whether (ex) Article 3a (1) (f) imposes an absolute ban against any comparison with products bearing a protected designation of origin with other kinds of products, the Court pointed out that:

(63) It is settled case-law that the conditions required of comparative advertising must be interpreted in the sense most favourable to it . . . (64) Secondly, Article 3a (1) (f) of the directive must be read in conjunction with Article 3a (1) (g) of the same directive. (65) Under the latter provision, comparative advertising is to be permitted provided that it does not take unfair advantage of the reputation of a trade mark, trade name or other distinguishing marks of a competitor or of the designation of origin of competing products. (66) The effectiveness of that requirement would be partly compromised if products without designation of origin were prevented from being compared to those with designation of origin . . . (70) Where all the other conditions governing whether such advertising is permissible are met, protection of designation of origin which would have the effect of prohibiting absolutely comparisons between products without designation of origin and others with designation of origin would be unwarranted and could not be justified under the provisions of Article 3a (1) (f) of the directive.

Protection of trade marks and other signs

Trade marks

The relationship between the Comparative Advertisement Directive and trade mark law has long been unclear. In particular, different positions were endorsed with regard to the question whether use of a competitor's trade mark in comparative advertising constitutes use 'as a mark' in the meaning of trade mark law, or whether the Comparative Advertisement Directive – more precisely: the national regulations implementing that directive – should take precedence.[90] The issue has been clarified by the ECJ in cases *O2 Holdings*[91]

---

90 On the requirements for a mark being used 'as a mark' and the relevant ECJ case law see Chapter 4, section 4.4.1.2.

91 ECJ Case C-533/06, *O2 Holdings v. Hutchinson*, [2008] ECR 2008 I-04231.

and *L'Oréal* v. *Bellure*,[92] in the sense that trade mark law applies when another person's trade mark is referred to, with the reservation, however, that the use of a mark which complies with the legal conditions set out in the comparative advertising directive is not to be considered as infringing.[93]

Whereas in the first of the two cases – which concerned the question of whether the advertisement created a likelihood of confusion[94] – the advertisement was considered to be compatible with the rules on comparative advertising, a different result was endorsed in *L'Oréal* v. *Bellure*. The dispute concerned the marketing of 'smell-alikes' in bottles and get-ups which, although not being similar in a manner creating confusion, evoked the image of the prestigious brands which they tried to emulate. For instance, the fragrance (allegedly) smelling like 'Trésor' by Lancôme was designated as 'Value', with a treasure chest depicted on the package. In addition, charts juxtaposing the precious brand's name and that of the cheap smell-alike were distributed to retailers. The issue arose therefore whether those practices amounted to presenting the smell-alike as an 'imitation or replica' in the meaning of Article 4 (g) (at the relevant time: Article 3a (1) (h) Directive 84/450/EEC). The ECJ declared that:

> (76) It is not in dispute that the object and effect of the comparison lists at issue in the main proceedings are to draw the attention of the relevant public to the original fragrance of which the perfumes marketed by [the defendants] are purportedly an imitation. Those lists thus attest to the fact that those perfumes are imitations of the fragrances marketed under certain marks belonging to L'Oréal and Others, and they consequently present the goods marketed by the advertiser as being imitations of goods bearing a protected trade mark within the meaning of Article 3a (1) (h) of Directive 84/450. . . . [I]t is irrelevant in that regard whether the advertisement indicates that it relates to an imitation of the product bearing a protected mark as a whole or merely the imitation of an essential characteristic of that product such as, in the present case, the smell of the goods in question.

In addition, the ECJ found that the link created with the precious brands by the various elements of the packages and get-ups which alluded to the original perfumes amounted to taking advantage of the original brands' reputation, and therefore conflicted with Article 4 (f) (then: Article 3a (1) (g) Directive 84/450/EEC).

---

92 ECJ Case C-487/07, *L'Oréal* v. *Bellure*, [2009] ECR I-05185.
93 Chapter 4, section 4.4.1.2.3.2.4.2 and section 4.2.1.1.
94 See Article 4 (h) of Directive 2006/114/EEC. At the relevant time, the same rule was enshrined in Article 3a (1) (d) of Directive 84/450/EEC.

Other signs

In addition to its relevance for trade marks falling under the TMD or CTMR, the Comparative Advertising Directive also regulates the admissibility of comparisons where a competitor is identified by other means, for instance by using his trade name or other kinds of designations.

An example for such a situation was provided in *Siemens v. VIPA*.[95] The defendant manufactured and sold component parts matching programmable controllers made and sold by Siemens. It had adopted a product identification system consisting of letters and numerals that was virtually identical to that used by Siemens; however, by placing its own acronym 'VIPA' at the beginning of each number, it was obvious for the customers that the component part originated from the defendant. The referring court posed the question whether, by using a quasi-identical identification system, the defendant took unfair advantage of the reputation of 'another distinguishing mark' in the meaning of Article 4 (f). The ECJ emphasised the importance of comparative advertisements for the information of consumers and concluded that:

> (26) [i]n the present case, if a different core element were to be used for the order numbers of goods distributed by VIPA and intended for use with Siemens controllers as add-on components, the users concerned would be required to look in comparative listings for the order numbers corresponding with the goods sold by Siemens. That would be disadvantageous, as the national court pointed out, to consumers and to VIPA. The possibility that there would be restrictive effects on competition in the market for add-on components to the controllers manufactured by Siemens cannot therefore be excluded. (27) [The Directive] must [therefore] be interpreted as meaning that, in circumstances such as those in the main proceedings, by using in its catalogues the core element of a manufacturer's distinguishing mark which is known in specialist circles, a competing supplier does not take unfair advantage of the reputation of that distinguishing mark.

? QUESTIONS

1 As is apparent from case law cited above, ECJ jurisprudence is usually rather generous towards comparative advertising. Please compare that attitude with the *L'Oréal* v. *Bellure* decision!

2 Article 4 (e) prohibits any comparison of products with a protected designation with products of other designations. Do you agree with the ECJ that the rule was not applicable in De Landtsheer? Does it make sense

---

95 ECJ Case C-59/05, *Siemens AG v. VIPA Gesellschaft für Visualisierung und Prozeßautomatisierung mbH*, [2006] ECR I-02147.

within its proper scope of application, or is it merely a token of successful lobbying by the relevant industries?

3 In consequence of the ECJ rulings in *O2 Holdings* and *L'Oréal* v. *Bellure*, a major part of comparative advertising – where the trade mark is mentioned – fall into the purview of trade mark law. What are the practical consequences, if any? Do you consider the discrimination between trade marks on the one hand and trade names and other distinguishing marks on the other implied therein as justified?

The Unfair Commercial Practices Directive (UCP)

The aims and limits of the UCP Directive as well as its relations with existing legislation in the field are set out in Recital 6 of the Preamble:

> (6) This Directive . . . approximates the laws of the Member States on unfair commercial practices, including unfair advertising, which directly harm consumers' economic interests and thereby indirectly harm the economic interests of legitimate competitors. In line with the principle of proportionality, this Directive protects consumers from the consequences of such unfair commercial practices where they are material but recognises that in some cases the impact on consumers may be negligible. It neither covers nor affects the national laws on unfair commercial practices which harm only competitors' economic interests or which relate to a transaction between traders; taking full account of the principle of subsidiarity, Member States will continue to be able to regulate such practices, in conformity with Community law, if they choose to do so. Nor does this Directive cover or affect the provisions of Directive 84/450/EEC on advertising which misleads business but which is not misleading for consumers and on comparative advertising. Further, this Directive does not affect accepted advertising and marketing practices, such as legitimate product placement, brand differentiation or the offering of incentives which may legitimately affect consumers' perceptions of products and influence their behaviour without impairing the consumer's ability to make an informed decision.

The purpose and aims of the directive as well as the definitions employed are further detailed in Articles 1-4. Article 5 (1) contains a general clause prohibiting unfair commercial practices ('Unfair commercial practices shall be prohibited'). Article 5 (2)–(5) specify the contents of that notion as follows:

> 2. A commercial practice shall be unfair if:
>   (a) it is contrary to the requirements of professional diligence, and
>   (b) it materially distorts or is likely to materially distort the economic

behaviour with regard to the product of the average consumer whom it reaches or to whom it is addressed, or of the average member of the group when a commercial practice is directed to a particular group of consumers.

3. Commercial practices which are likely to materially distort the economic behaviour only of a clearly identifiable group of consumers who are particularly vulnerable to the practice or the underlying product because of their mental or physical infirmity, age or credulity in a way which the trader could reasonably be expected to foresee, shall be assessed from the perspective of the average member of that group. This is without prejudice to the common and legitimate advertising practice of making exaggerated statements or statements which are not meant to be taken literally.

4. In particular, commercial practices shall be unfair which:

(a) are misleading as set out in Articles 6 and 7,

or

(b) are aggressive as set out in Articles 8 and 9.

5. Annex I contains the list of those commercial practices which shall in all circumstances be regarded as unfair. The same single list shall apply in all Member States and may only be modified by revision of this Directive.

The rules on misleading advertisement in Article 6 are more comprehensive than what can be found in Directive 2006/114, but in general, the outcome reached on the basis of both legal instruments should not be different. However, as a novel feature, Article 7 addresses omissions which are regarded as misleading if:

(1) ... in its factual context, taking account of all its features and circumstances and the limitations of the communication medium, it omits material information that the average consumer needs, according to the context, to take an informed transactional decision and thereby causes or is likely to cause the average consumer to take a transactional decision that he would not have taken otherwise.

(2) It shall also be regarded as a misleading omission when, taking account of the matters described in paragraph 1, a trader hides or provides in an unclear, unintelligible, ambiguous or untimely manner such material information as referred to in that paragraph or fails to identify the commercial intent of the commercial practice if not already apparent from the context, and where, in either case, this causes or is likely to cause the average consumer to take a transactional decision that he would not have taken otherwise.

Article 8 relates to aggressive practices:

A commercial practice shall be regarded as aggressive if, in its factual context, taking account of all its features and circumstances, by harassment, coercion, including the use of physical force, or undue influence, it significantly impairs or is likely to significantly impair the average consumer's freedom of choice or conduct with regard to the product and thereby causes him or is likely to cause him to take a transactional decision that he would not have taken otherwise.

The terms harassment, coercion and undue influence are further defined in Article 9:

In determining whether a commercial practice uses harassment, coercion, including the use of physical force, or undue influence, account shall be taken of:

(a) its timing, location, nature or persistence;

(b) the use of threatening or abusive language or behaviour;

(c) the exploitation by the trader of any specific misfortune or circumstance of such gravity as to impair the consumer's judgement, of which the trader is aware, to influence the consumer's decision with regard to the product;

(d) any onerous or disproportionate non-contractual barriers imposed by the trader where a consumer wishes to exercise rights under the contract, including rights to terminate a contract or to switch to another product or another trader;

(e) any threat to take any action that cannot legally be taken.

Article 10 addresses codes of conduct the use of which is encouraged, while the provision emphasises the primate of judicial and administrative control. Articles 11 to 13 concern enforcement which must be provided by adequate and efficient means, without imposing substantial restrictions on Member States' freedom to choose the kind of procedures that they consider as appropriate.

Of interest – and a novelty so far in the field of unfair competition law – is the 'black list' in the Annex, declaring a number of commercial statements as per se illegal. The list is made up of 31 items:

1. Claiming to be a signatory to a code of conduct when the trader is not.

2. Displaying a trust mark, quality mark or equivalent without having obtained the necessary authorisation.

3. Claiming that a code of conduct has an endorsement from a public or other body which it does not have.

4. Claiming that a trader (including his commercial practices) or a product has been approved, endorsed or authorised by a public or private body when he/it has not or making such a claim without complying with the terms of the approval, endorsement or authorisation.

5. Making an invitation to purchase products at a specified price without disclosing the existence of any reasonable grounds the trader may have for believing that

he will not be able to offer for supply or to procure another trader to supply, those products or equivalent products at that price for a period that is, and in quantities that are, reasonable having regard to the product, the scale of advertising of the product and the price offered (bait advertising).

6. Making an invitation to purchase products at a specified price and then:

(a) refusing to show the advertised item to consumers;

or

(b) refusing to take orders for it or deliver it within a reasonable time;

or

(c) demonstrating a defective sample of it,

with the intention of promoting a different product (bait and switch).

7. Falsely stating that a product will only be available for a very limited time, or that it will only be available on particular terms for a very limited time, in order to elicit an immediate decision and deprive consumers of sufficient opportunity or time to make an informed choice.

8. Undertaking to provide after-sales service to consumers with whom the trader has communicated prior to a transaction in a language which is not an official language of the Member State where the trader is located and then making such service available only in another language without clearly disclosing this to the consumer before the consumer is committed to the transaction.

9. Stating or otherwise creating the impression that a product can legally be sold when it cannot.

10. Presenting rights given to consumers in law as a distinctive feature of the trader's offer.

11. Using editorial content in the media to promote a product where a trader has paid for the promotion without making that clear in the content or by images or sounds clearly identifiable by the consumer (advertorial). This is without prejudice to Council Directive 89/552/EEC [1].

12. Making a materially inaccurate claim concerning the nature and extent of the risk to the personal security of the consumer or his family if the consumer does not purchase the product.

13. Promoting a product similar to a product made by a particular manufacturer in such a manner as deliberately to mislead the consumer into believing that the product is made by that same manufacturer when it is not.

14. Establishing, operating or promoting a pyramid promotional scheme where a consumer gives consideration for the opportunity to receive compensation that is derived primarily from the introduction of other consumers into the scheme rather than from the sale or consumption of products.

15. Claiming that the trader is about to cease trading or move premises when he is not.

16. Claiming that products are able to facilitate winning in games of chance.

17. Falsely claiming that a product is able to cure illnesses, dysfunction or malformations.

18. Passing on materially inaccurate information on market conditions or on the possibility of finding the product with the intention of inducing the consumer to acquire the product at conditions less favourable than normal market conditions.

19. Claiming in a commercial practice to offer a competition or prize promotion without awarding the prizes described or a reasonable equivalent.

20. Describing a product as 'gratis', 'free', 'without charge' or similar if the consumer has to pay anything other than the unavoidable cost of responding to the commercial practice and collecting or paying for delivery of the item.

21. Including in marketing material an invoice or similar document seeking payment which gives the consumer the impression that he has already ordered the marketed product when he has not.

22. Falsely claiming or creating the impression that the trader is not acting for purposes relating to his trade, business, craft or profession, or falsely representing oneself as a consumer.

23. Creating the false impression that after-sales service in relation to a product is available in a Member State other than the one in which the product is sold.

Aggressive commercial practices

24. Creating the impression that the consumer cannot leave the premises until a contract is formed.

25. Conducting personal visits to the consumer's home ignoring the consumer's request to leave or not to return except in circumstances and to the extent justified, under national law, to enforce a contractual obligation.

26. Making persistent and unwanted solicitations by telephone, fax, e-mail or other remote media except in circumstances and to the extent justified under national law to enforce a contractual obligation. This is without prejudice to Article 10 of Directive 97/7/EC and Directives 95/46/EC [2] and 2002/58/EC.

27. Requiring a consumer who wishes to claim on an insurance policy to produce documents which could not reasonably be considered relevant as to whether the claim was valid, or failing systematically to respond to pertinent correspondence, in order to dissuade a consumer from exercising his contractual rights.

28. Including in an advertisement a direct exhortation to children to buy advertised products or persuade their parents or other adults to buy advertised products for them. This provision is without prejudice to Article 16 of Directive 89/552/EEC on television broadcasting.

29. Demanding immediate or deferred payment for or the return or safekeeping of products supplied by the trader, but not solicited by the consumer except where the product is a substitute supplied in conformity with Article 7 (3) of Directive 97/7/EC (inertia selling).

30. Explicitly informing a consumer that if he does not buy the product or service, the trader's job or livelihood will be in jeopardy.

31. Creating the false impression that the consumer has already won, will win, or will on doing a particular act win, a prize or other equivalent benefit, when in fact either:

- there is no prize or other equivalent benefit,

or

- taking any action in relation to claiming the prize or other equivalent benefit is subject to the consumer paying money or incurring a cost.

Case law concerning the UCP directive has repeatedly held that beyond the black list, *per se* prohibitions of commercial practices which do not take into account the specific circumstances of the case are incompatible with the directive; see Joined Cases *VTB-VAB* and *Sanoma*[96] as well as *Telecomunikacja Polska*[97] (concerning an absolute prohibition to make combined offers, except for certain specified cases, which applied in Belgian respective Polish law); *Wettbewerbszentrale* v. *Plus*[98] (concerning an absolute prohibition anchored in German law to make participation in a prize competition or lottery dependent on the purchase of an article); see also *Mediaprint*,[99] where it was held that the possibility of participating in a prize competition, linked to the purchase of a newspaper, does not constitute an unfair commercial practice simply on the ground that, for at least some of the consumers concerned, that possibility of participating in a competition represents the factor which determines them to buy that newspaper.

The only decision so far expanding on other parts of the UCP directive concerned internet advertising for travels (*Ving*[100]). *Inter alia*, it was specified that:

- an invitation to purchase exists as soon as the information on the product advertised and its price is sufficient for the consumer to be able to make a transactional decision, without it being necessary for the commercial communication also to offer an actual opportunity to purchase the product;

---

96 Joined Cases C-261/07 and C-299/07, *VTB-VAB* v. *Total Belgium* and *Galatea* v. *Sanoma magazines*, [2009] ECR I-2949.

97 ECJ Case C-522/08, *Telecomunikacja Polska* v. *Prezes Urzędu Komunikacji Elektronicznej*, [2010] ECR I-2079.

98 ECJ Case C-304/08, *Zentrale zur Bekämpfung unlauteren Wettbewerbs eV* v. *Plus Handelsgesellschaft mbH*, [2010] ECR I-217.

99 ECJ Case C-540/08, *Mediaprint Zeitungs- und Zeitschriftenverlag* v. *Österreich Zeitschriftenverlag*, [2010] ECR I-0000.

100 ECJ Case C-122710, *Konsumentombudsmannen* v. *Ving Sverige*, 2011 ECR I-0000.

- the requirement relating to the indication of the price of the product may be met if the commercial communication contains an entry-level price, that is to say the lowest price for which the advertised product or category of products can be bought. Such indication of an entry-level price does not constitute a misleading omission in the meaning of Article 7 (4);
- it may be sufficient for only certain of a product's main characteristics to be given and for the trader to refer in addition to its website, on the condition that on that site there is essential information on the product's main characteristics, price and other terms in accordance with the requirements in Article 7.

? QUESTIONS

1 Articles 8 and 9 UCP prohibit 'aggressive practices'. Can you think of concrete examples? What about such practices as doorstep sales, sales promotion via telephone, telefax or email; or soliciting business in public places – are they prohibited or subject to specific preconditions in your country?

2 Pursuant to Article 7 UCP, also omissions can be regarded as misleading. To what extent does that clash, in your opinion, with an entrepreneur's basically legitimate interest to present his offers in a positive light? Is Article 7 formulated clearly enough to offer a reliable basis for drawing the borderline?

3 Do you think it makes sense to draw up a 'black list' of marketing measures which are considered unlawful under any circumstances? What are the advantages and disadvantages of such an approach?

8

Remedies in cases of infringement

8.1 Introduction

Infringement, counterfeiting and piracy

It is one thing to provide for exclusive rights, it is yet another thing to make sure that the rights granted are respected and, if they are not, can be enforced against infringers in practice. Providing for appropriate remedies and an efficient judicial system in the framework of which infringements can be prosecuted and adjudicated is therefore of the essence for a well-functioning IP system.

However, while it is a truism that law is not worth much if it remains in the book, it is also true that infringement, when it occurs in normal business, is 'part of the game', and to some extent may even be inevitable. For instance, if a product is launched under a new trade mark, the mark can easily be found (too) similar to a prior right and hence be considered as infringing. Especially in areas with a high density of marks such as pharmaceuticals or household goods, it is hardly possible for commercial actors to avoid any such risks. Infringement based on likelihood of confusion can hardly be assessed in a strictly objective manner, but always involves a good portion of subjective evaluation, making it virtually impossible to predict the outcome with sufficient certainty. Similar to that, it can be difficult for a competitor to appraise the exact scope of technological solutions covered by a patent, and also in copyright, grey zones remain between what is permissible or not when it comes to adaptations or other uses eventually covered by limitations and exceptions. In all those cases, the resulting infringements can hardly be considered as particularly grave; in any case, they do not pose a more serious threat than the opposite constellation, also occurring quite frequently, when a right-holder overestimates the scope of his right and files infringement claims which, in the end, are rejected as unfounded.

In the political discourse, however, infringements are seldom addressed as the inevitable downside of the legal uncertainty caused by the fuzzy boundaries of IP rights, resulting in transgressions from both sides. They are rather conceived of as a form of serious economic crime, as is reflected in statements such as 'the constant rise of infringements of intellectual property rights constitutes a genuine threat not only to the Union economy, but also to the health and safety of Union consumers'.[1] In that context, 'infringement' is understood in the narrower sense of 'counterfeiting and piracy', which typically concerns 1:1 imitations or copies of protected items that are produced and sold within organisational structures resembling, or being linked to, organised crime.[2]

It is indeed a basic dilemma of enforcement policy and legislation in Europe that the notions of 'infringement' on the one hand and 'counterfeiting and piracy' on the other are not clearly separated from each other. Health- and security-related concerns are regularly invoked for the purpose of bolstering political demands for stronger IP protection, whereas the rules ensuing from such demands are meant to apply horizontally to all kinds of infringements.[3] Such divergences between the political motivation proffered for new legislation and the actual scope of the law can easily lead to imbalances, as the strong political focus on counterfeiting and piracy tends to distract the attention of the legislature from the fact that overprotection can be as detrimental to economy as insufficient protection, and that it might seriously harm the legitimate interests of persons accused of infringement.

---

1 Regulation (EU) No 386/2012 of the European Parliament and of the Council of 19 April 2012 entrusting the Office for Harmonisation in the Internal Market (Trade Marks and Designs) with certain tasks related to the protection of intellectual property rights, including the assembling of public and private sector representatives as a European Observatory on Counterfeiting and Piracy, [2012] OJ L 129/1, Recital 4. See also the Global Europe strategy (regarding the enforcement of 'European' IPR worldwide), trade.ec.europa.eu/doclib/docs/2006/october/tradoc_130376.pdf.

2 Definitions of the terms 'counterfeit trade mark goods' and 'pirated copyright goods' are contained in footnote 14 to Article 51 TRIPS:

> For the purposes of this Agreement:
> (a) 'counterfeit trade mark goods' shall mean any goods, including packaging, bearing without authorization a trade mark which is identical to the trade mark validly registered in respect of such goods, or which cannot be distinguished in its essential aspects from such a trade mark, and which thereby infringes the rights of the owner of the trade mark in question under the law of the country of importation;
> (b) 'pirated copyright goods' shall mean any goods which are copies made without the consent of the right holder or person duly authorised by the right holder in the country of production and which are made directly or indirectly from an article where the making of that copy would have constituted an infringement of a copyright or a related right under the law of the country of importation.

3 For a critical view on that tendency see the MPI Statement on the proposed Regulation entrusting the OHIM with the tasks of the European Observatory on Counterfeiting and Piracy, www.ip.mpg.de/files/pdf2/Observatory_statement_MPIIP1.pdf.

Another problem to be observed in the context results from the difficulties to make an exact and objective appraisal of the dimensions and economic consequences of the problem.[4] High and rising figures of counterfeit goods distorting trade flows and disrupting honest business are regularly announced by stakeholder organisations and customs authorities. For example, in the 2009 update to the 2008 OECD study on the economic impact of counterfeiting and piracy it was pointed out that:[5]

> [t]he OECD (2008) study concluded that international trade in counterfeit
> and pirated goods could have accounted for up to USD 200 billion in 2005. The
> updated estimates, based on the growth and changing composition of trade
> between 2005 and 2007, suggest that counterfeit and pirated goods in interna-
> tional trade grew steadily over the period 2000–2007 and could amount to up to
> USD 250 billion in 2007. The share of counterfeit and pirated goods in world trade
> is also estimated to have increased from 1.85% in 2000 to 1.95% in 2007.[6]

On the other hand, the actual basis for such estimations often remains somewhat obscure. In particular, it is unclear to what extent they are based on hard and fast data, or rather on subjective assessments by the affected firms and industries.[7] Also, it remains open whether the figures concern 'counterfeits' in a narrow definition or include every kind of trade mark use or other IP infringement that is considered as infringing. Reservations also result from the aspect that some particularly partisan business organisations tend to ground their estimates about economic damage and job loss on the assumption that the number of counterfeit products equates to that of non-effected legitimate purchases, despite the fact that such computation is utterly unrealistic, in particular where it concerns cheap copies of high-end luxury goods.

Arriving at objective estimations is even more difficult in the contested area of online distribution of protected content, such as films and music.

---

4 For an excellent discussion of the problem see Digital Opportunity – A Review of Intellectual property and Growth, an Independent Report by Professor Ian Hargreaves (Hargreaves Report), www.ipo.gov.uk/ipreview-finalreport.pdf, Chapter 8.

5 See www.oecd.org/industry/industryandglobalisation/44088872.pdf. For the original study see www.oecd.org/sti/industryandglobalisation/theeconomicimpactofcounterfeitingandpiracy.htm.

6 For further reports on the magnitude of counterfeiting and piracy from a business perspective see: TERA Consultants, 'Building a Digital Economy: March 2010'; OECD, Magnitude of counterfeiting and piracy of tangible products – November 2009 update, www.oecd.org/sti/industryandglobalisation/44088872.pdf; Technopolis (2007), 'Effects of counterfeiting on EU SMEs', ec.europa.eu/enterprise/newsroom/cf/_getdocument.cfm?doc_id=4506; Frontier Economics, (May 2009), 'The impact of counterfeiting on Governments and Consumers', www.icc.se/policy/statements/2009/BASCAP.pdf, and UNICRI, 'Counterfeiting – a global spread', 2008, counterfeiting.unicri.it/report2008.php.

7 A critical view on the data is taken in the report by the US Accountability Office, GAO 10-423, Intellectual Property – Observations on Efforts to Quantify the Economic Effects of Counterfeiting and Pirated Goods.

According to a study carried out on behalf of the Business Action to Stop Counterfeiting and Piracy (BASCAP),[8] 'EUR 10 billion and more than 185,000 jobs were lost due to piracy in the music, movie, TV, and software industries in the EU in 2008'. By contrast to that, studies commissioned by the Dutch[9] and the Swiss governments[10] arrived at the conclusion that online piracy remains economically neutral *per saldo*. In view of those uncertainties, it is little wonder that views differ widely as regards the appropriate legal reactions to the phenomenon.

Legal developments

While sanctions and enforcement measures have always formed part of national IP laws, they were usually not addressed on the international level. A fundamental shift occurred in that regard in the TRIPS Agreement which contains in its Part III, for the first time in the history of international intellectual property conventions, a comprehensive set of rules regarding enforcement measures. The purpose of these provisions is set out in Article 41 (1) and (2) TRIPS as follows:

> (1) Members shall ensure that enforcement procedures as specified in this Part are available under their law so as to permit effective action against any act of infringement of intellectual property rights covered by this Agreement, including expeditious remedies to prevent infringements and remedies which constitute a deterrent to further infringements. These procedures shall be applied in such a manner as to avoid the creation of barriers to legitimate trade and to provide for safeguards against their abuse.
> (2) Procedures concerning the enforcement of intellectual property rights shall be fair and equitable. They shall not be unnecessarily complicated or costly, or entail unreasonable time-limits or unwarranted delays.

In particular, the TRIPS Agreement provides rather detailed rules on civil and administrative procedures and remedies, provisional measures, special requirements related to border measures and criminal procedures, which more or less mirrored the *acquis* as regards enforcement legislation of industrialised states at the beginning of the last decade of the 20th century.

---

8 BASCAP is a right-holder organization founded on an initiative of the International Chamber of Commerce (ICC).

9 Ups and downs – Economische en culturele gevolgen van file sharing voor muziek, film en games, www.tno.nl/content.cfm?context=thema&content=inno_publicatie&laag1=897&laag2=918&item_id=473.

10 See www.ejpd.admin.ch/content/ejpd/de/home/dokumentation/mi/2011/2011-11-30.html.

In the EU, enforcement was for a long time considered to fall into the sole competence of Member States, due to the fact that it did not affect the functioning of the internal market as directly as divergences in substantive law. However, already shortly before the adoption of the TRIPS Agreement, the EU had created a mechanism for the seizure of infringing goods at its outer borders in the form of the Border Measures Regulation, which was revised and expanded in 2003.[11] Following the TRIPS Agreement, the EU, in 2004, then harmonised the remedies for IPR infringements by way of a Directive,[12] obliging Member States to adopt common legal standards *inter alia* with regard to injunctive relief (including preliminary injunctive relief), damages, claims for information and claims for preserving of evidence.

In addition to civil remedies, all national IP laws also provide for criminal sanctions for the infringement of IPRs. A harmonising Directive was proposed in 2005/6; however, it was halted by the European Parliament due to concerns regarding the legal basis of the proposal as well as certain elements of its contents.[13]

Regarding the sensitive area of enforcement measures on the internet, another piece of Community legislation comes into the picture: in that regard, the E-Commerce Directive is of special relevance as it contains certain rules limiting the legal responsibility of Internet Service Providers.[14]

Furthermore, in an effort to gain reliable data and as a measure supporting private actors in their fight against infringement, the Commission established in 2009 the so-called European Observatory on Counterfeiting and Piracy.[15] According to the Commission, the Observatory shall be 'the

---

11 Council Regulation (EC) No 1383/2003 of 22 July 2003 concerning customs action against goods suspected of infringing certain intellectual property rights and the measures to be taken against goods found to have infringed such rights, [2003] OJ L 196/7 (Border Measures Regulation). The initial Council Regulation (EC) No 3295/94 of 22 December 1994 which only dealt with border measures regarding trade marks and copyright, was subsequently amended so as to also cover patents and other IPRs; see Article 2 (1) of Regulation (EC) No 1383/2003.

12 Directive 2004/48/EC of the European Parliament and of the Council of 29 April 2004 on the enforcement of intellectual property rights, [2004] OJ L 195/16 (IP Enforcement Directive, IPRED).

13 Proposal for a European Parliament and Council Directive on criminal measures aimed at ensuring the enforcement of intellectual property rights of 12 July 2005, COM(2005) 276 final, and, subsequently, Amended proposal for a Directive of the European Parliament and of the Council on criminal measures aimed at ensuring the enforcement of intellectual property rights of 26 April 2006, COM(2006) 168 final.

14 Directive 2000/31/EC of the European Parliament and of the Council of 8 June 2000 on certain legal aspects of information society services, in particular electronic commerce, in the Internal Market, [2000] OJ L 178/1 (E-Commerce Directive).

15 See Communication from the Commission to the Council, the European Parliament and the European

central resource for gathering, monitoring and reporting information and data related to all IPR infringements'; and it shall 'be used as a platform for cooperation between representatives from national authorities and stakeholders to exchange ideas and expertise on best practices, to develop joint enforcement strategies and to make recommendations to policy-makers.'[16] From 2012, the tasks of the Observatory have been entrusted to OHIM.[17]

Finally, considering that the adoption and basically worldwide implementation of the TRIPS Agreement had not provided the expected relief against the rising surge of trade in counterfeit and pirated goods the EU[18] and a number of other WTO members[19] negotiated the Anti Counterfeiting Trade Agreement (ACTA),[20] which was finalised on 3 December 2010. The Agreement contains provisions on civil enforcement (availability of civil procedures, injunctions, damages, other remedies, information related to infringement, provisional measures), on border measures, and on criminal enforcement, as well as special rules on the enforcement of IP rights in the digital environment. ACTA was supposed to be ratified by the EU and all Member States in 2012. However, it appears that the Agreement has become the ultimate bone of contention for those opposing any further strengthening of enforcement measures, in particular with regard to the digital environment. Due to the misgivings caused thereby, the European Parliament in July 2012 denied its consent to the ratification of ACTA. This has brought the process to a halt within Europe,[21] with potential repercussions worldwide.

Economic and Social Committee – Enhancing the enforcement of intellectual property rights in the internal market, COM(2009) 467 final.

16 For further information on the Observatory and its activities, see ec.europa.eu/internal_market/iprenforcement/observatory/index_en.htm.

17 Regulation (EU) No 386/2012 of the European Parliament and of the Council of 19 April 2012 entrusting the Office for Harmonisation in the Internal Market (Trade Marks and Designs) with certain tasks related to the protection of intellectual property rights, including the assembling of public and private sector representatives as a European Observatory on Counterfeiting and Piracy, [2012] OJ L 129/1.

18 See Council Resolution of 25 September 2008 on a comprehensive European anti-counterfeiting and anti-piracy plan, [2008] OJ C 253/1, and also Council Resolution of 1 March 2010 on the enforcement of intellectual property rights in the internal market, ec.europa.eu/internal_market/iprenforcement/docs/council/20100401_resolution_ipr_enforcement_en.pdf.

19 The negotiating parties of ACTA were a mix of developed and emerging economies: Australia, Canada, the European Union, Japan, Korea, Mexico, Morocco, New Zealand, Singapore, Switzerland and the United States.

20 For the European Website see http://ec.europa.eu/trade/tackling-unfair-trade/acta.

21 Prior to the rejection of ACTA by the European Parliament, the question whether ACTA is compatible with European law, in particular the Charter of Fundamental Rights, was referred to the ECJ, where it is still pending at the time of publication.

? **QUESTIONS**

1 In your opinion, to what extent is there a plausible link between IP infringements on the one hand, and negative effects to economic growth, job losses and safety for consumers? If so, are there any differences regarding the different IP rights?

2 As pointed out above, the terms 'infringement' and 'counterfeiting and piracy' are often not clearly distinguished and are even used as synonyms. Which reasons account for that (apart from political convenience)? Is it possible at all to draw a clear line between the notions (e.g. based on the definition of counterfeit and pirated goods in footnote 14 to Article 51 TRIPS)?

3 In your opinion, is it justified to enforce IP rights in the same way in both industrialised and developing countries? For your answer, please consider also Article 41 (5) TRIPS.

8.2 Civil remedies

Enforcement Directive 2004/48/EC

Overview

Whereas the early IP Directives mostly contained, if at all, only a mere standard reference to the effect that 'Member States shall provide appropriate remedies in respect of infringements of the rights provided for in this Directive',[22] the EU in 2004 – following Articles 41 *et seq.* TRIPS – harmonised its Member States' remedies with regard to the infringement of IPRs by way of the Enforcement Directive 2004/48/EC.[23] This Directive is a 'horizontal' one, since it does not only harmonise a particular aspect of a particular IPR, but rather affects all IPRs alike. Indeed, in a Communication to Article 2 (1) according to which the Directive applies to 'any infringement of intellectual property rights as provided for by Community law and/or by the national law of the Member State concerned', the Commission has stated[24] that it considers at least the following intellectual property rights as covered by the Directive: copyright, rights related to copyright, *sui generis* right of a database maker, rights of the creator of the topographies of a semi-

---

22 E.g., Article 12 of the Database Directive 96/9/EC.

23 Directive 2004/48/EC of the European Parliament and of the Council of 29 April 2004 on the enforcement of intellectual property rights, [2004] OJ L 195/16 (Enforcement Directive).

24 Statement by the Commission concerning Article 2 of Directive 2004/48/EC of the European Parliament and of the Council on the enforcement of intellectual property rights (2005/295/EC), [2005] OJ L 94/37.

conductor product, trade mark rights, design rights, patent rights, including rights derived from supplementary protection certificates, geographical indications, utility model rights, plant variety rights, and trade names, in so far as these are protected as exclusive property rights in the national law concerned. It should be noted that there was little discussion regarding the question whether such a 'one-size-fits-all' solution really is appropriate, and has the same effects, with regard to all IPRs.

In particular, the Directive contains rules regarding:

- access to evidence which is in the hands of the infringer (Article 6);
- preservation of evidence (Article 7);
- right of information of the infringed person against third parties (Article 8);
- provisional and precautionary measures (Article 9);
- corrective measures, i.e., recall, removal and destruction of infringing goods (Article 10);
- injunctions (Article 11);
- alternative measures, i.e. pecuniary payments in case of unintentional and non-negligent infringements (Article 12);
- damages (Article 13);
- legal costs (Article 14);
- publication of judgments (Article 15).

The harmonisation thus achieved is a minimum harmonisation. According to Article 2 (1), Member States may apply other appropriate sanctions in cases where intellectual property rights have been infringed, provided that they are more favourable to the right-holder. Moreover, the Commission has proposed to complement these civil sanctions by mandatory criminal sanctions.[25]

In 2010, the Commission evaluated the implementation and the practical application and effect of the Enforcement Directive,[26] and has thus started a consultation process with the parties concerned. It is proposed to supplement the regulatory framework with complementary non-legislative measures. Developing such measures and guidelines in cooperation with the

---

25 See in this chapter, section 8.3.3.
26 See the Report from the Commission to the Council, the European Parliament and the European Social Committee on the application of Directive 2004/48/EC, COM(2010) 779 final, and, accompanying, Commission Staff Working Document 'Analysis of the application of Directive 2004/48/EC in the Member States', SEC(2010) 1589 final.

interested circles is also among the tasks to be carried out by the European Observatory on Counterfeiting and Piracy.[27]

Details

General principles

Article 3 (1) and (2) of the Enforcement Directive sets out the general principles according to which:

> measures, procedures and remedies shall be fair and equitable and shall not be unnecessarily complicated or costly, or entail unreasonable time-limits or unwarranted delays.

In addition:

> [t]hose measures, procedures and remedies shall also be effective, proportionate and dissuasive and shall be applied in such a manner as to avoid the creation of barriers to legitimate trade and to provide for safeguards against their abuse.

Article 4 defines the persons who are entitled to apply for the application of the measures, procedures and remedies. In addition to right-holders and other persons having a direct interest in the enforcement, such as licensees, this includes also collecting societies and similar organisations ('intellectual property collective rights management bodies'), provided that they are entitled under national law to represent right-holders.

Article 5 contains a legal presumption in favour of authors of copyrighted works and of holders of related rights whose name appears on the work or the respective subject matter. This shall ensure that efficient enforcement is not hampered by the adverse party demanding that the plaintiff produce full and exhaustive evidence of ownership, which is sometimes difficult to manage.

Procurement of evidence

Article 6 deals with access to evidence which is in the hands of the infringer. If the right-holder has presented reasonably accessible evidence sufficient

---

27 See above, text accompanying footnote 15. For current information see the Commission Website at http://ec.europa.eu/internal_market/iprenforcement/directive/index_en.htm as well as the website of the Observatory, at ec.europa.eu/internal_market/iprenforcement/observatory/index_en.htm.

to support his claims and has, in substantiating those claims, specified evidence which lies in the control of the opposing party, the competent judicial authority may order that the opposing party produce the evidence under its control. In particular, the provision enables Member States to provide that courts may consider a sample of copies to constitute sufficient evidence for the entire infringement. This possibility was new for some Member States and has reportedly improved enforcement especially of copyright.

In case the infringement was committed on a 'commercial scale', Member States may even enable the national courts to order, upon request of one party and under appropriate circumstances, the communication of banking, financial or commercial documents under the control of the opposing party, subject to the protection of confidential information. The crucial term 'acts committed on a commercial scale' is defined in Recital 14 of the Preamble as relating to:

> [a]cts . . . carried out for direct or indirect economic or commercial advantage; this would normally exclude acts carried out by end-consumers acting in good faith.

In spite of this attempt at a definition, it appears that the term has been interpreted differently by the courts in different Member States.

Article 7 on the preservation of evidence, as summarised in the Commission's Staff Working Document:

> requires that Member States shall, even before the commencement of proceedings on the merits of the case, order prompt and effective provisional measures to preserve relevant evidence, subject to the protection of confidential information. Such measures may include the detailed description (search), with or without the taking of samples, the physical seizure of the infringing goods and, in appropriate cases, of materials and implements used in the production and/or distribution of these goods and the documents relating thereto. Where necessary, these measures shall be taken without the other party having been heard. They shall be revoked or cease to have effect if the applicant does not initiate, within a period specified by the Directive, proceedings leading to a decision on the merits of the case before the competent judicial authority. In that case or where the infringement of the intellectual property right was not established in the judicial proceeding, the judicial authorities shall have the power to order the applicant to provide the defendant with an appropriate compensation for any injury caused by those measures.[28]

---

28 Commission Staff Working Document 'Analysis of the application of Directive 2004/48/EC in the Member States', SEC(2010) 1589 final, p. 8.

It should be noted that in harmonising the rules on the preservation and the duty of the alleged infringer to make evidence available to the presumably infringed plaintiff, the Directive heavily draws on the models established in French law under the name of 'saisie contrefaçon' and under British case law as 'Anton Pillar order' and 'Mareva injunction', whereas such procedural measures were lacking (or not as strong) in other states. In this aspect, harmonisation therefore led to a substantial strengthening of the position of IPR holders. Nevertheless, according to the Commission practical difficulties can still be observed, notably in the area of cross-border collection of evidence as well as in internet cases.

Right to information

Article 8 contains one of the central and most disputed elements in the Enforcement Directive. Giving infringed persons a right of information against third parties on the origin and distribution networks of infringing goods goes well beyond the traditional claim which is only directed at the infringer, and was as such new for some Member States. Consequently, this has led to an increase in requests for information, but has also raised issues of balancing the right to information with opposing rights of privacy. The clash of interests is particularly acute with regards to right-holders' requests for information concerning data relevant to infringements over the internet, in particular dynamic IP addresses. Often such data have not been stored, or may not be stored, or, if stored, may not be communicated in view of data protection laws. Indeed, a conflict seems to exist between, on the one hand, Article 8 (and Article 11) of the Enforcement Directive as well as Article 8 (3) of the Information Society Directive, which all tend to favour the interests of right-holders, and, on the other hand, the E-Commerce Directive and the Data Protection Directives, which rather restrain the options for enforcement in the digital environment.[29]

Apart from those specific issues that will be considered in more detail below, protection of privacy and confidentiality also pose a general concern with regard to the measures taken under Articles 6 to 8. It is remarkable that neither the Enforcement Directive nor – as far as can be seen – other legal instruments on the EU level undertake to circumscribe in more detail the requirements for protection of confidentiality that Member States must ensure in order to guarantee the necessary balance between the interests involved, thereby inviting legal uncertainty and divergent practices.

---

29 For more detailed discussion and ECJ case law see in this chapter, section 8.2.2.2.2.

Injunctions

Injunctions in the form of provisional and precautionary measures (inter-locutory injunctions) and in the form of permanent prohibitive orders are addressed in Articles 9 and 11 respectively. In both cases, Member States must ensure that injunctions may be directed against intermediaries whose services have been used for committing an infringement.[30] Regarding inter-locutory injunctions, Article 9 largely echoes the requirements and obliga-tions set out in Article 50 TRIPS, in particular that a possibility must exist to issue, in case of urgency, an interlocutory injunction without the adverse party having been heard (ex-parte injunctions),[31] but also that preliminary injunctions must be confirmed in ordinary proceedings to be installed shortly after the order has been issued, by default of which it will cease to have effect,[32] and that courts may order payment of compensation to the adverse party in case that an interlocutory injunction lapses or is held to have been unfounded.[33] As a TRIPS-Plus element, Article 9 (2) Enforcement Directive stipulates that if infringements are carried out on a commercial scale, and if the infringed party demonstrates by circumstantial evidence that payment of damages is likely to be endangered, the court can even order the precautionary seizure of the movable and immovable property of the alleged infringer, including the blocking of his bank accounts and other assets.

In its assessment of the actual impact of the Enforcement Directive on the law and practice of the Member States, the Commission concluded in respect of Articles 9 and 11 that:

> [d]espite the general positive assessment of the interlocutory injunctions, the information at hand suggests that the level of evidence required by the courts to grant an injunction differs significantly between Member States and, in general, is rather high.[34]

Also, there still seem to be:

---

30 With regards to intermediaries whose services have been used for infringement of copyright and related rights, the grant of injunctions is, however, subject to the criteria set out in the Infosoc Directive 29/2001/EC.

31 Article 9 (4) Enforcement Directive; Article 50 (2) TRIPS.

32 Article 9 (5) Enforcement Directive; Article 50 (6) TRIPS.

33 Article 9 (7) Enforcement Directive; Article 50 (7) TRIPS.

34 Commission Staff Working Document 'Analysis of the application of Directive 2004/48/EC in the Member States', SEC(2010) 1589 final, p. 14.

uncertainties as to which kind of intermediaries, regardless of their liability, may be subject to a specific measure when contributing to or facilitating an infringement.[35]

Corrective measures

Article 10 lists as corrective measures that can be ordered in addition to payment of damages:

(a) recall from the channels of commerce,
(b) definitive removal from the channels of commerce, or
(c) destruction.

Those measures shall apply to goods that were found to be infringing, and, in appropriate cases, to materials and implements principally used in the creation or manufacture of those goods.

Whereas destruction of infringing goods was already anchored in most Member States' legislation prior to implementing the Enforcement Directive,[36] recall and removal of infringing goods from the channels of commerce have been new to most of them. Perhaps consequently, or because they are difficult to enforce once the infringing goods are no longer in the possession of the infringer, right-holders seem to make only limited use of these corrective measures. In practice, therefore, the destruction of goods still seems to be the preferred method.

Article 12 provides an option for Member States to allow that instead of imposing injunctions or corrective measures, the competent judicial authorities may order pecuniary compensation to be paid to the injured party. However, this shall only apply where the infringer has acted without intent or negligence, and where the sanctions available under Articles 10 and 11 would cause him disproportionate harm, whereas pecuniary compensation appears reasonably satisfactory. According to the Commission's assessment report, such alternative measures have been introduced only in less than half of the Member States.

Damages; conclusions

As regards the determination by the judicial authorities of damages to be paid by the infringer who knowingly, or with reasonable grounds to know, engaged in an infringing activity, Article 13 provides for two possibilities.

---

35 Cross-border injunctions are discussed in Chapter 9 on jurisdiction and applicable law.
36 A corresponding obligation is also anchored in Article 46 TRIPS.

Courts can either base the amount on the actual prejudice (e.g. the right-holder's lost profits, the infringer's unfair profits, moral prejudice and other negative economic consequences), or they can award lump sum damages based on at least the (single) amount of royalties which would have been due if the infringer had requested authorisation to use the intellectual property right(s) in question (e.g. if an infringer had concluded a licensing agreement with a right-holder). This leaves a relatively great freedom for national traditions of assessing damages to be continued even after implementation of the Enforcement Directive into the national law of Member States. Moreover, as summarised by the Commission:

> in respect of specific infringements (mostly infringements of copyright and rights related to copyright), a significant number of Member States[37] appear to have gone beyond the minimum rules set out by the Directive by introducing lump sum damages set as multiple (mostly double) amounts of royalties (licensing fees) due. Furthermore, at least one Member State reports to provide for punitive damages[38].[39]

Summing up the results of its assessment, the Commission arrived at the conclusion:

> that the Directive has provided a solid basis for the enforcement of intellectual property rights in the internal market and led to considerable improvements of the legal frameworks in place in the Member States. However, the analysis shows that some of the provisions of the Directive have led to diverging interpretations by the Member States and by the courts, and some of these provisions have not fully reached the objectives pursued by the Directive. At the same time, infringements of intellectual property rights have reached a significant level. The provisions concerned could therefore be clarified. Clarification could also be necessary in order to reinforce the dissuasive effect of the Directive and therefore its effectiveness.[40]

ECJ case law

Until now, the provisions of the Enforcement Directive were only addressed once in a decision by the ECJ (*L'Oréal* v. *eBay*).[41] The dispute concerned the

---

37 E.g. Austria, Belgium, Czech Republic, Germany, Greece, Lithuania, Poland, Romania and Slovenia.
38 Slovenia.
39 Commission Staff Working Document 'Analysis of the application of Directive 2004/48/EC in the Member States', SEC(2010) 1589 final, p. 24.
40 Ibid., p. 26. For current information see ec.europa.eu/internal_market/iprenforcement/index_en.htm.
41 ECJ Case C-324/09, *L'Oréal et al* v. *eBay*, [2011] ECR I-0000. The case also concerned the interpretation of the E-Commerce Directive with regard to ISPs; see in this chapter, section 8.2.2.1.

sale of goods alleged to be counterfeits via an intermediary who is an online marketplace. In such situations, the problem arises that while it is obvious that removal of the infringing offer from the website can be ordered once the intermediary has obtained knowledge of the infringing character of the content stored, it is less clear whether and to what extent that also leads to an obligation for the future to monitor the content stored on the website so as to prevent the same content being displayed again.[42] The referring UK High Court of Justice therefore asked the ECJ whether the injunction as prescribed in Article 11 of the Enforcement Directive should have been interpreted as requiring Member States to ensure that the trade mark proprietor could obtain an injunction against an intermediary to prevent further infringements of the said trade mark, in addition to discontinuation of that specific act of infringement, and if so, what the scope of the injunction would be.

The ECJ did not give a concrete and exhaustive answer, but declared in a general manner that:

> (144) . . . the third sentence of Article 11 of Directive 2004/48 must be interpreted as requiring the Member States to ensure that the national courts with jurisdiction in relation to the protection of intellectual property rights are able to order the operator of an online marketplace to take measures which contribute, not only to bringing to an end infringements of those rights by users of that marketplace, but also to preventing further infringements of that kind. Those injunctions must be effective, proportionate, dissuasive and must not create barriers to legitimate trade.

 QUESTIONS

1 Do you think the horizontal approach to harmonise civil remedies for infringements of IP rights is appropriate? Why does patent law not receive a special regime as regards civil law sanctions, as in Article 61 TRIPS?
2 Why do you think unfair competition has not been included?
3 According to its Recital 10, the Enforcement Directive intends 'to ensure a high, equivalent and homogeneous level of protection'. Shouldn't the issue of possible overprotection by too strong remedies have been discussed which might deter market participants from fully exercising the freedom to act as granted by substantive IP law?
4 According to what you hear, have the civil law remedies granted under the

---

42 The same problem is discussed with regard to the E-Commerce-Directive which will be considered in more detail in this chapter, section 8.2.2.2.2.

Enforcement Directive been effective in your country? Have they unduly burdened non-right-holders?

5 In your opinion, which of the remedies would most deserve 'clarification'?

6 In what ways can clarification 'reinforce the dissuasive effect of the Directive and therefore its effectiveness' as stated by the Commission?

Enforcing IPRs on the internet

A particular problem exists with regard to enforcing IPRs on the internet. The problem has several facets. First, due to the multitude of possible infringers, it might not always be easy to detect infringement of IPRs on the internet. Second, because the internet eliminates physical distance, the act responsible for the infringement of domestic IPRs might be undertaken abroad, and indeed often is undertaken in faraway countries, where the infringer has little or no legal prosecution to fear. Third, even if an infringement is detected, it is not always easy for the holder of the infringed IPR to find out the identity of the infringer. Due to the possibilities to remain anonymous on the internet, all the IPR holder might have is an IP address of the infringer. This is particularly true regarding P2P file-sharing where IP addresses are often dynamic rather than static. Finally, the sheer mass of (infringing) transactions done over the internet pose a serious problem for law enforcement, not only for IPRs themselves, but likewise and in particular at the administrative level (courts; prosecutors' offices).

Hence, apart from issues of international jurisdiction and the law applicable to trans-border dissemination of copyrighted works, which will be discussed in Chapter 9,[43] effective enforcement of IPRs on the internet depends, on the one hand, on the extent to which internet service providers can be held liable for the acts committed by infringers of IPRs using the services offered by the ISPs. On the other hand, the need of the IPR holder to identify the infringer might collide with the latter's legitimate concern to see his personal data protected under existing data protection legislation.

Liability of ISPs

Regulation in the E-Commerce Directive

ISPs can be defined as all those persons who provide technical support and services in and around the internet. 'Classical' functions are providing access

---

43 See Chapter 9, sections 9.2 and 9.3.

and connectivity to the net, providing transmission lines, managing domain names and providing email facilities, storing material and hosting websites of those who use the internet. However, activities of ISPs do not stop there. In a broad sense, they go beyond providing services necessary to get connected to and make use of the internet, and can be understood as any service offered via the internet which may be used by third parties in order to create, store and communicate their own content. Examples are offerings of platforms, chat rooms, search engines, browsers, P2P software, computing power etc. Thus, in Article 2 (a) and (b) of EU Directive 2000/31/EC on electronic commerce[44] (E-Commerce Directive) the term 'service provider' is defined as 'any natural or legal person providing an information society service', the latter in turn already being defined in Article 1 (2) of Directive 98/34/EC of 22 June 1998 laying down a procedure for the provision of information in the field of technical standards and regulations and of rules on information society services as amended by Directive 98/48/EC.[45] This definition covers 'any service normally provided for remuneration, at a distance, by means of electronic equipment for the processing (including digital compression) and storage of data, and at the individual request of a recipient of a service.'[46]

Of the provisions of the E-Commerce Directive (which also deals with establishment and information requirements, commercial communication, contracts concluded by electronic means), only the ones regarding the legal liability of ISPs are of interest here (Articles 14 to 15).

In this respect, it should first be noted that in many cases, ISPs will not themselves undertake acts which infringe someone else's copyright (although, depending of the facts of the case at bar, and of the national IP law rules, national courts might find otherwise in certain cases). Rather, ISPs typically provide the means, enable or make it easier for those who use the internet infrastructure to commit infringements of someone else's IPRs. Therefore, the issue of ISP liability is generally one of secondary infringement. Second, it should be noted that apart from some isolated instances (such as Article 7 of the Computer Program Directive with regard to computer programs), and apart from the E-Commerce Directive, the law of secondary infringe-

---

44 Directive 2000/31/EC of the European Parliament and of the Council of 8 June 2000 on certain legal aspects of information society services, in particular electronic commerce, in the Internal Market, [2000] OJ L 178/1 (E-Commerce Directive).

45 [1998] OJ L 204/37, p. 37; for the amendment see [1998] OJ L 217/18. See also Directive 98/84/EC of 20 November 1998 on the legal protection of services based on, or consisting of, conditional access, [1998] OJ L 320/54.

46 For detail see the two Directives and Recitals 17 and 18 of Directive 2000/31/EC.

ment has not been harmonised within the EU. Rather, it is still regulated, to a large extent, by Member States' diverging national laws. One of the reasons for this is that the rules of secondary infringement more often than not form part of the Member States' general law of torts or of civil procedure, which as such is not subject to harmonisation by the EU.

This notwithstanding, in its E-commerce Directive the EU has laid down certain rules which are intended to harmonise legal liability of ISPs, at least partly. However, rather than describing in a positive way under what circumstances ISPs should be held liable, the Directive follows the approach of defining when ISPs should *not* be held liable, thus carving out certain exemptions from liability that might otherwise exist under national law. In a certain way, this follows the approach taken when the WIPO Copyright Treaty (WCT) was negotiated in 1996. Here, the parties negotiating the Treaty had agreed that 'the mere provision of physical facilities for enabling or making a communication does not in itself amount to communication within the meaning of this Treaty or the Berne Convention'.[47] But more important, this approach was the result of the intention of the EU legislature to develop electronic commerce in view of its significant employment opportunities, and to enable European citizens and operators to take full advantage of the potential of e-commerce.[48] Hence liability of ISPs was reduced rather than enlarged, even if this meant a weakening of enforceability of IPRs, in particular copyright and trade marks, over the internet. As explained in Recital 42 of Directive 31/2000/EC:

> [t]he exemptions from liability established in this Directive cover only cases where the activity of the information society service provider is limited to the technical process of operating and giving access to a communication network over which information made available by third parties is transmitted or temporarily stored, for the sole purpose of making the transmission more efficient; this activity is of a mere technical, automatic and passive nature, which implies that the information society service provider has neither knowledge of nor control over the information which is transmitted or stored.

Articles 12 to 15 distinguish the scope of the exemption from liability according to the different activities undertaken by IPSs. The following activities are defined: mere conduit (Article 12), caching (Article 13), and hosting

---

47 Agreed statement to Article 8 WCT.
48 Also, in accordance with the principle of proportionality, the measures provided for in this Directive must be limited to the minimum needed to achieve the objective of the proper functioning of the internal market; Directive 31/2001/EC, Recital 10.

(Article 14), as well as a prohibition of a general obligation to monitor (Article 15). According to these rules:

- an ISP who merely transmits someone else's information, or provides access to a communication network, is not liable as long as he does not initiate the transmission, does not select the receiver of the transmission, and does not select or modify the information contained in the transmission. This includes the automatic, intermediate and transient storage of the information transmitted in so far as this takes place for the sole purpose of carrying out the transmission in the communication network, and provided that the information is not stored for any period longer than is reasonably necessary for the transmission (Article 12);
- similarly, activities of caching (defined as 'the automatic, intermediate and temporary storage of that information, performed for the sole purpose of making more efficient the information's onward transmission to other recipients of the service upon their request') are not subject to liability, as long as the ISP, amongst other duties, does not modify the information and, in particular, acts expeditiously to remove or to disable access to the information it has stored upon obtaining actual knowledge of the fact that the information at the initial source of the transmission has been removed from the network, or access to it has been disabled, or that a court or an administrative authority has ordered such removal or disablement (Article 13);
- where the ISP stores content of a third party, he shall not be liable, provided he does not have actual knowledge of illegal activity or information and, as regards claims for damages, is not aware of facts or circumstances from which the illegal activity or information is apparent, and if he, upon obtaining such knowledge or awareness, acts expeditiously to remove or to disable access to the information. However, this does not affect the possibility for a court or administrative authority in a Member State of requiring the ISP to terminate or prevent an infringement, nor does it affect the possibility for Member States of establishing procedures governing the removal or disabling of access to information (Article 14);
- finally, Member States may not impose a general obligation on ISPs to monitor the information which they transmit or store, nor a general obligation actively to seek facts or circumstances indicating illegal activity (Article 15).

This regulation of ISP's liability gives rise to at least three remarks. First, it should be noted that these provisions do not cover all activities of ISPs. In particular, the E-commerce Directive is explicitly silent on the issue of liability for linking (see Article 21 (2)). Second, contrary to, for example, the U.S. Digital Copyright Millennium Act (DCMA),[49] the E-commerce Directive does not define a particular notice-and-take-down procedure to be followed once allegedly infringing material has been spotted. Rather, as stated in Recital 40:

> this Directive should constitute the appropriate basis for the development of rapid and reliable procedures for removing and disabling access to illegal information; such mechanisms should be developed on the basis of voluntary agreements between all parties concerned.

However, absent such clear provisions, it remains unclear what right-holders have to do in order to have the ISP remove a particular item from being accessible via the service, at what point ISPs have to react (in particular, what constitutes 'actual knowledge'), and – quite to the contrary – under what circumstances removing would infringe upon the rights of the party which makes the allegedly infringing material accessible via the ISPs information society service. Third, since injunctive relief is not *per se* excluded and, in particular, an obligation to remove exists after the ISP has obtained actual knowledge of a particular infringement, and since Article 15 only bars Member States from placing a *general* obligation to monitor, there might be room for *special* monitoring duties. Indeed, some national courts have concluded that there exists a duty, e.g., to monitor content in a reasonable way for similar infringements once a particular infringement has been ascertained (to this effect, see also Recital 47). In sum, the application of these provisions has given rise to rather diverging national court judgments, both as regards the issue who can be liable for injunctive relief as an ISP, and under what conditions.

ECJ case law

Surprisingly, in spite of its practical importance and the great number of cases at the national level, up until now there have been few referrals by the national courts asking the ECJ for clarification on the exact scope of the exemptions from ISP liability under the E-commerce Directive. However, in two recent cases, at least some clarification was brought about.

In the *Google* judgment[50] concerning the liability of Google for providing to its customers the possibility to use others' trade marks for triggering

---

49 § 512 (g) (2) (C) DCMA.
50 ECJ Joined Cases C-236/08 to C-238/08, *Google France and Google v. Louis Vuitton*, [2010] ECR I-2417.

advertisements (keyword advertisements, or 'adwords'),[51] the question was whether the activity of an internet referencing service qualifies as 'hosting' under Article 14 of the E-commerce Directive so that the referencing service provider cannot be held liable unless, having obtained knowledge of the unlawful nature of those data or of that advertiser's activities, it failed to act expeditiously to remove or to disable access to the data concerned. Pointing to Recital 42 of the E-Commerce Directive, the ECJ concluded that:

> (114) in order to establish whether the liability of a referencing service provider may be limited under Article 14 of Directive 2000/31, it is necessary to examine whether the role played by that service provider is neutral, in the sense that its conduct is merely technical, automatic and passive, pointing to a lack of knowledge or control of the data which it stores.

In the cases at bar, the ECJ thought it to be relevant that Google processes the data entered by advertisers and that the resulting display of the ads is made under conditions which Google controls; however, the mere facts that the referencing service is subject to payment, and that Google sets the payment terms or that it provides general information to its clients cannot have the effect of depriving Google of the exemptions from liability; and, likewise, concordance between the keyword selected and the search term entered by an internet user is not sufficient of itself to justify the view that Google has knowledge of, or control over, the data entered into its system by advertisers and stored in memory on its server. Ultimately, it is a question to be ascertained by the national courts, whether the service provider has not played an active role of such a kind as to give it knowledge of, or control over, the data stored.

In *L'Oréal* v. *eBay*[52] the operator of an electronic marketplace stored on its website on behalf of its clients offers for sale of counterfeit products.[53] The referring UK court asked the ECJ whether – apart from, and in case of, trade mark infringement[54] – such use consists of or includes 'the storage of information provided by a recipient of the service' within the meaning of Article 14 (1) of the E-Commerce Directive, and, if so, whether there is also exemption from liability if the use does not entirely fall under Article 14 (1). With regard to those questions the ECJ answered that storage of data will

---

51 For a discussion of the trade mark aspects involved in the case see already above, Chapter 4, section 4.4.1.2.4.2.

52 ECJ Case C-324/09, *L'Oréal et al v. eBay*, [2011] ECR I-0000; see already above in this Chapter, B 1.).

53 The case also concerned a number of other trade mark-related issues some of which are addressed in Chapter 4.

54 For discussion of the trade mark issues involved, see Chapter 4, section 4.4.1.2.4.2.

not as such result in liability under Article 14. On the other hand, it is only exempted if it does not occur under circumstances that result in the provider having control over, or actual knowledge of, the data stored; and again, it is for the national court to decide on the issue.[55] Furthermore, the referring court sought clarification on whether it constitutes 'actual knowledge' or 'awareness' within the meaning of said Article, if the operator of the online marketplace has knowledge that goods have been advertised, offered for sale and sold on its website in infringement of registered trade marks, and that infringements of such registered trade marks are likely to continue to occur by the same or different users of the website. The ECJ answered that:

> (122) The situations . . . covered include . . . that in which the operator of an online marketplace uncovers, as the result of an investigation undertaken on its own initiative, an illegal activity or illegal information, as well as a situation in which the operator is notified of the existence of such an activity or such information. In the second case, although such a notification admittedly cannot automatically preclude the exemption from liability provided for in Article 14 of Directive 2000/31, given that notifications of allegedly illegal activities or information may turn out to be insufficiently precise or inadequately substantiated, the fact remains that such notification represents, as a general rule, a factor of which the national court must take account when determining, in the light of the information so transmitted to the operator, whether the latter was actually aware of facts or circumstances on the basis of which a diligent economic operator should have identified the illegality.

In *Scarlet Extended*,[56] the referring Cour d'appel de Bruxelles asked the ECJ whether national courts may order an ISP to introduce, for all its customers and as a preventive measure, at the cost of that ISP, a system for filtering all electronic communications, both incoming and outgoing, that pass via its services, in particular those involving the use of peer-to-peer software, in order to identify on its network the sharing of electronic files containing copyrighted works. The ECJ answered that the obligation to impose such a filtering system would not respect the need to strike a fair balance between the interests to protect IPR on the one hand and the fundamental rights of users, data protection, and the freedom to impart or receive information on the other, and that accordingly, injunctions such as the one at stake would be irreconcilable with European law.

---

55 ECJ Case C-324/09, *L'Oréal et al* v. *eBay*, [2011] ECR I-0000, Paragraphs 111–117.
56 ECJ Case C-70/10, *Scarlet Extended* v. *SABAM*, [2011] ECR I-0000.

Monitoring and subsequent developments

According to Article 21 of the E-Commerce Directive, the Commission shall monitor the application of the Directive. Although the two-year monitoring interval prescribed was missed by far, the Commission commissioned two studies delivered in 2007, one on the economic impact[57] and another one on the application of the provisions on the liability of internet intermediaries[58] under the E-Commerce Directive. The latter identifies and describes in great detail the issues which might be in need of clarification, in particular the criterion of 'actual knowledge' and possible notice and take-down procedures, but also issues of hyperlinks, search engines and technical filtering options. The report, which is well worth studying, describes the wide spectrum of possible solutions.

One such solution favoured in particular by proponents of strong and un-curtailed protection concerns the so-called 'graduate response'-approach (or 'three strikes and you are out') as initially developed in France. As an alternative to notice and take-down procedures, this model would end an infringer's account or even cut his internet access if the infringer didn't stop the infringing activity after the third unsuccessful warning. This approach requires the cooperation of the ISPs and, most likely, the involvement of some independent supervision body, such as the French HADOPI (Haute Autorité pour la diffusion des oeuvres et la protection des droits sur Internet), which would ascertain the infringing nature of the incriminated acts as well as obtain the contact details of the user of a particular IP address. Similarly, with Sec. 3–18 of the Digital Economy Act 2010 the UK as complemented by a code of the Office of Communications (Ofcom) has opted for a comparable system which aims to increase the ease of tracking down and suing persistent infringers, and after a certain time permits the Secretary of State to lay down an order for ISPs to impose 'technical measures' reducing the quality of, or potentially terminate, targeted infringers' internet connections. At the European level, the 'Report on enforcement of intellectual property rights in the internal market' by the European Parliament's Committee on Legal Affairs (Gallo Report), published in June 2010, proposed the introduction of a similar system on the EU level.[59] However, given the strong resistance by interested circles against any mention of such a solution in a draft text of

---

57 See ec.europa.eu/internal_market/e-commerce/docs/study/ecd/%20final%20report_070907.pdf.
58 See ec.europa.eu/internal_market/e-commerce/docs/study/liability/final_report_en.pdf.
59 Doc. A7-0175/2010 of 3 June 2010, Paragraph 27, www.europarl.europa.eu/sides/getDoc.do?pubRef=-//EP//NONSGML+REPORT+A7-2010-0175+0+DOC+PDF+V0//EN. For further information see ec.europa.eu/internal_market/e-commerce/directive_en.htm#consultation.

ACTA,[60] it is rather unlikely that the 'three strikes' approach has a chance of being implemented at EU level.

On the other side of the spectrum, the model of a so-called culture flat-rate is promoted by proponents of unimpeded internet communication. Under such a scheme, internet users and/or ISPs would be obliged to pay a certain fee to collective management organisations or similar organisations that would then distribute the money to authors and other right-holders, while peer-to-peer file-sharing or similar modes of use of protected content would be permitted. Such proposals appear appealing to those who contend that the pronounced leverage of right-holders on the dissuasive power of sanctions has not achieved the desired results so far, and is unlikely to do so in the future, in particular as the quest for more deterring sanctions and the perfection of surveillance mechanisms are likely to generate clashes with fundamental rights, such as the right to information and to privacy. However, even if it should be possible to find agreement about the basic tenets of such an alternative system, it would still be a long way until the many legal and practical problems connected with the issue are resolved and practically feasible solutions can be implemented.

 QUESTIONS

1 In your opinion, do the categories of activities as defined in Articles 12 to 14 of the E-Commerce Directive still properly reflect today's activities of ISPs?

2 In your country, who is responsible as intermediary? For what acts and under what circumstances? Under what legal theory is liability found?

3 In your opinion, according to the ECJ decisions Google France and Google and L'Oréal et al v. eBay will information service providers always be exempt from liability because of the fact that their service is fully automated?

4 What steps should an appropriate notice-and-take-down procedure contain?

5 If you were to redraft Articles 12 *et seq.* of the E-commerce Directive, how would you redraft them? In particular, how should ISPs cooperate in preventing infringing activities by the users of the services offered by the ISPs? What about incentives to improve the technical monitoring of infringements? Would you favour a 'graduated response', perhaps even in the form of a 'three-strikes-and-you-are-out'?

6 How do you evaluate the alternative system of a culture flat-rate? In

---

60 Anti-Counterfeiting Trade Agreement, see in this chapter, section 8.5.

particular, what are the problems that need to be solved in connection with the introduction of such a system?

Enforcement of IPRs versus data protection

Relevant legislation

If IPR holders want to enforce their IPRs on the internet, another difficulty arises. Once IP right-holders, and copyright holders in particular, have discovered an infringing act on the internet, in most cases they only know the dynamic IP address which has at one point in time been attributed by the ISP to the infringer in an automated process. However, they do not know either name or address of the infringer. This gives rise to the question whether IPR holders have a claim for information against the ISP to disclose the name and address which corresponds to a given dynamic IP address, and if so, under what conditions such a claim might exist (e.g., proof of protectability of subject matter, of ownership of exclusive rights and of infringement; requirement of prior notice given by the IPR holder to the ISP or even requirement of a court order). Or does legislation protecting personal data prevent the ISP from communicating such information to IPR holders?

In view of the harmonisation of both IP enforcement and personal data protection by way of EU Directives, the issue is not merely a national one. Rather, any national legislation has to be in conformity with EU legislation both as regards the enforcement of IP rights and the protection of personal data. However, the Directives are in conflict with each other. On the one hand, according to Article 8 (1) of the Information Society Directive 2001/29/EC and Article 3 (2) of the Enforcement Directive 2004/48/EC, Member States have to provide sanctions in cases of IP infringements, which shall be 'effective, proportionate and dissuasive'. More precisely, Article 8 (1) (c) of Directive 2004/48/EC obliges Member States to provide for a claim for information – in response to a justified and proportionate request of the person claiming to be an infringed IPR holder and as ordered by judicial authorities, against infringers and all those persons who have provided 'on a commercial scale services used in infringing activities'. On the other hand, according to Article 7 (f) of Directive 95/46/EC on the protection of individuals with regard to the processing of personal data and on the free movement of such data,[61] personal data – defined in Article 2 (a) Directive

---

61 [1995] OJ L 281/31.

95/46/EC as 'any information relating to an identified or identifiable natural person ("data subject")' – may be processed

> only if: . . . processing is necessary for the purposes of the legitimate interests pursued by the controller or by the third party . . . to whom the data are disclosed, except where such interests are overridden by the interests or fundamental rights and freedoms of the data subject which require protection.

In addition, according to Article 6 (1) and (2) of Directive 2002/58/EC on privacy and electronic communications,[62] traffic data relating to subscribers and users processed and stored by the provider of a public communications network or publicly available electronic communications service must be erased or made anonymous when it is no longer needed for the purpose of the transmission of a communication'. The

> [t]raffic data necessary for the purposes of subscriber billing and interconnection payments may be processed, [but s]uch processing is permissible only up to the end of the period during which the bill may lawfully be challenged or payment pursued.' However, according to Article 15 (1) of that Directive, Member States may restrict the data protection to the extent this is 'a necessary, appropriate and proportionate measure within a democratic society to safeguard national security (i.e. State security), defence, public security, and the prevention, investigation, detection and prosecution of criminal offences or of unauthorized use of the electronic communication system.

ECJ case law

The ECJ has had several occasions of clarifying the relationship between the antagonistic goals of data protection on the one hand and efficient IP enforcement on the other, upon requests by Member States' national courts to assess whether a particular national legislation was in conformity with EU law.

In *Promusicae*,[63] a case which opposed the Spanish collecting society Promusicae and the service provider Telefonica over data identifying users who had used the KaZaA P2P file-sharing program, Spanish national law obliged operators of electronic communications networks and services, providers of access to telecommunications networks and providers of data storage services to retain for a maximum of 12 months the connection

---

62 [2002] OJ L 201/37.
63 ECJ Case C-275/06, *Promusicae v. Telefonica*, [2008] I-271.

and traffic data generated by the communications. The ECJ first found that:

> (45) [i]t is not disputed that the communication sought by Promusicae of the names and addresses of certain users of KaZaA involves the making available of personal data, that is, information relating to identified or identifiable natural persons, in accordance with the definition in Article 2(a) of Directive 95/46 [and t]hat communication of information . . . is stored by Telefonica constitutes the processing of personal data within the meaning of the first paragraph of Article 2 of Directive 2002/58, read in conjunction with Article 2(b) of Directive 95/46.

The ECJ then examined the relationship between data protection on the one hand, and effective enforcement of IP rights on the other hand, concluding that the directives in question, including the E-Commerce Directive:

> (41) . . . *do not require* the Member States to lay down . . . an obligation to communicate personal data in order to ensure effective protection of copyright in the context of civil proceedings.

However, Community law requires that:

> (68) . . . when transposing those directives, the Member States take care to rely on an interpretation of them which allows *a fair balance to be struck* between the various fundamental rights protected by the Community legal order. Further, when implementing the measures transposing those directives, the authorities and courts of the Member States must . . . make sure that they do not rely on an interpretation of them which would be in conflict with those fundamental rights or with the other general principles of Community law, such as the principle of proportionality. (Emphases added)

Clarification to this rather sibylline judgement was brought about in *LSG-Gesellschaft zur Wahrnehmung von Leistungsschutzrechten,*[64] which was on comparable facts. Here, in view of Austrian legislation, according to which '[i]ntermediaries . . . shall give the person whose rights have been infringed information as to the identity of the infringer (name and address) or the information necessary to identify the infringer', the ECJ concluded that existing Community law:

---

64 ECJ Case C-557/07, *LSG-Gesellschaft zur Wahrnehmung von Leistungsschutzrechten* v. *Tele2 Telecommunication GmbH,* [2009] ECR I-01227 (decided by way of order).

(29) . . . does not preclude Member States from imposing an obligation to disclose to private third parties personal data relating to Internet traffic in order to enable them to bring civil proceedings for copyright infringements.

In *Scarlet Extended*,[65] the ECJ has further clarified after reading all relevant Directives together in the light also of fundamental rights that internet service providers cannot be required to install, as a preventive measure, at its own expense and for an unlimited period of time, a system for filtering all electronic communications passing via its services, in particular those involving the use of peer-to-peer software, which applies indiscriminately to all its customers, in order to indentify copyrighted content that has been illegally file-shared.

Similarly, in *SABAM*[66] the ECJ held that national courts must not require a host provider to install, as a preventative measure, exclusively at its expense and for an unlimited period of time, a system for indiscriminately filtering information which is stored on its servers by its users to the benefit of right-holders who want to identify infringing electronic files containing musical, cinematographic or audiovisual with a view to preventing those works from being made available to the public in breach of copyright.

In *Bonnier Audio*[67] a Swedish court sought clarification about the compatibility with EU law of a national provision 'which permits an internet service provider in civil proceedings, in order to identify a particular subscriber, to be ordered to give a copyright holder or its representative information on the subscriber to whom the internet service provider provided a specific IP address, which address, it is claimed, was used in the infringement.' The ECJ responded that the provision is in conformity with EU law, including the data protection directives, provided that the court or authority applying the provision has the possibility to balance the interests involved on both sides on a case by case basis taking due account of the requirements of the principle of proportionality.

? QUESTIONS

1 What is the legislation in place in your country regarding the storage and divulgation of information relating to an internet user's name and address to a person whom the right-holder claims to infringe his IP right? Does

---

65 ECJ Case C-70/10, *Scarlet Extended* v. *SABAM*, [2011] I-0000.
66 ECJ Case C-360/10, *SABAM* v. *Netlog*, [2012] ECR I-0000.
67 ECJ Case C-461/10, *Bonnier Audio* v. *Perfect Communication* [2012] ECR I-0000.

legislation and/or case law in your country differentiate between different IP rights?

2 In your opinion, should ISPs be under an obligation to store and make available the names and addresses of their internet users?

3 How can IP rights be effectively protected on the internet and, at the same time, the protection of personal data be safeguarded?

8.3 Border measures

Regulation 1383/2003

Background and relevant provisions

Once goods have entered the EU, it will be difficult to control their further dissemination due to the fact that border controls between Member States have been abolished. Therefore, and because the bulk of infringing goods is manufactured outside of the EU, it is the most efficient solution to provide for the possibility of seizure of infringing goods at the outer borders of the EU, in order to protect the interests of right-holders as well as the general economic and social interests of the EU and its consumers. Hence, the EU has created a special procedure that facilitates the seizure and disposal of IP-infringing products, before they enter the channels of commerce within the EU. The Regulation has repeatedly been amended; its current version is Council Regulation (EC) 1383/2003 of 22 July 2003 concerning customs action against goods suspected of infringing certain intellectual property rights and the measures to be taken against goods found to have infringed such rights.[68] The EU border measures complement national rules which govern importation into national territories of the EU Member States.

In order to have a practical, speedy and effective procedure, the seizure by customs authorities can take place upon application by the right-holder who has reasons to believe that goods imported infringe his IPRs without the need to first obtain a court order to this effect (Arts. 5–9 and 13–14 of the Regulation). In addition, even where no application has yet been lodged, Member States are authorised to detain the goods for a certain period to

---

68 [2003] OJ L 196/7. For additional details see Commission Regulation (EC) No 1891/2004 of 21 October 2004 laying down provisions for the implementation of Council Regulation (EC) No. 1383/2003 concerning customs action against goods suspected of infringing certain intellectual property rights and the measures to be taken against goods found to have infringed such rights, [2004] OJ L 328/16, as last amended by Regulation (EC) No 1172/2007 of 5 October 2007, [2007] OJ L 261/12.

allow right-holders to lodge an application for action with the customs authorities (Article 4). Moreover, the EU Regulation provides for a simplified procedure allowing the destruction of seized infringing goods, without there being any obligation to initiate proceedings to establish whether an intellectual property right has been infringed, if such a procedure has been implemented in national law (Article 11 of the Regulation). It should be noted that the question of whether or not an IPR is infringed is determined according to the national law of the Member State within the territory of which the goods are placed (Article 10 (1) of the Regulation).

Only the following details of the procedure can be pointed out here:

- Article 1 of the Regulation defines when the border measures can take place. This definition covers both import and export.
- Article 2 defines the terms 'counterfeit goods' and 'pirated goods' in a similar manner as footnote 14 to Article 51 TRIPS, meaning in particular that products are only considered as 'counterfeit goods' if they bear a mark which is identical with or indistinguishable from a protected trade mark, or goods which are exact copies of material protected by copyright; furthermore, Article 2 lists the IPRs covered by the Regulation.
- Article 3 makes clear that the Regulation does not apply to parallel imports, even where the right to distribution within the Community has not been exhausted;[69] the reason is that the Regulation has the purpose of keeping only non-original goods out of the EU. Also, non-commercial counterfeit or pirated goods found in travellers' personal luggage are not subject to the Regulation.
- Article 4 allows *ex officio* measures: customs authorities, if they have sufficient grounds for suspecting that goods infringe an IPR, may detain them for up to three working days from the moment the right-holder is notified, who can then submit an application.
- Articles 5 to 9 and 13 to 14, the core of the Regulation, contain the rules for the procedure of seizure. It usually starts with an application by the holder of an IPR with the competent customs authorities on a particular form to be processed by the customs authorities within 30 working days after its receipt (Article 5). The application has to be accompanied by a declaration of liability of the IPR-holder vis-à-vis third parties in cases

---

69 According to ECJ Case C-355/96, *Silhouette International v. Hartlauer*, [1998] ECR I-4799, no exhaustion of distribution rights within the EU takes place even if the right-holder has put the goods covered by an IPR either himself or with his consent into the market *outside* of the EU (principle of no international exhaustion). For discussion see Chapter 2, section 2.2.1.

where the procedure is discontinued, including administrative costs of the customs authorities (Article 6). The application remains valid for a maximum of one year (Article 8 (1)). If then customs offices suspect particular goods to infringe applicant's IPRs, they suspend the release of the goods or detain them, notify the applicant and give him the opportunity to inspect the goods (for details of the information communicated see Article 9 (2) and (3)). The applicant has then 10 working days (which can be extended by another 10 days, but only non-extendable three days in the case of perishable goods) to initiate court proceedings to determine whether his IPRs have been violated. If no such action is commenced, the customs offices shall release the goods (Article 13). In the case of alleged infringement of a design right, patent, supplementary protection certificate or plant variety right, the declarant, importer, holder or consignee of the goods can obtain release of the goods against provision of security (Article 14).

Where Member States so provide in their national laws, goods detained or not released by customs authorities can be destroyed if the declarant, holder or owner of the goods either consents or does not respond within the periods set forth in Article 11 of the Regulation (so-called simplified procedure). This does not only solve the storage problem, but it helps to stop infringing goods even without any judicial procedure in cases where the infringer gives up, once his attempt to illegally import infringing goods has been discovered. As decided by the ECJ in *Schenker*,[70] the administrative authorities in the country concerned may, even if goods are destroyed under the simplified procedure upon consent by the parties, impose an administrative fine on the party whom they deem to have infringed the IP right.

Goods in transit

Particular issues arise if goods enter the territory of the EU while they are in transit. As the term 'transit' is not defined in the legislation, uncertainties have arisen as to the scope of the application of the Border Measures Regulation to such goods. According to one possible interpretation, seizure and detention of goods are possible if, had they been manufactured in the EU, they would be found infringing ('manufacturing fiction'). Proponents of that position relied *inter alia* on ECJ judgments[71] in which it had been held that the Regulation is 'designed to apply' to goods in transit, because 'there is

---

70 ECJ Case C-93/08, *Schenker v. Latvian Customs Authorities*, [2009] ECR I-903.
71 ECJ Case C-383/98, *The Polo/Lauren Company v. PT. Dwidua Langgeng Pratama International Freight Forwarders*, [2000] ECR I-2519 and Case C-60/02, *Rolex and others v. X*, 2004] ECR I-665.

a risk that counterfeit goods placed under the external transit procedure may be fraudulently brought on to the Community market'.[72]

Based on that approach, Dutch authorities in 2008 intercepted several shipments of generic drugs transiting EU ports for suspected patent infringements. Most of the shipments originated in India and were destined for developing countries such as Brazil and other South American or African countries. The drugs at issue were protected in the EU, but apparently not in the countries of origin or destination. Following the seizures, both India and Brazil filed a complaint with the WTO, requesting consultations under the Dispute Settlement Procedure with the European Union and the Netherlands.[73] According to the two countries, the measures at issue were inconsistent with *inter alia* Article V GATT, which guarantees the freedom of international trade.[74] Finding itself in the defensive position, the EU contended that the measures had been due to a misinterpretation of the legal provisions and that such interceptions will not occur in the future.

In Joined Cases *Nokia* and *Philips*[75] the ECJ clarified its position concerning the seizure by customs authorities of counterfeit goods arriving from, and being destined for, non-EU countries. It was first pointed out that, in accordance with previous case law interpreting Article 5 of the Trade Mark Directive, infringement must be denied unless a pertinent risk of diversion of transit goods to the European Union consumers can be demonstrated.[76] The ECJ then went on to clarify that such a risk can be established for instance by the following factors:

> (61) . . . the destination of the goods is not declared whereas the suspensive procedure requested requires such a declaration, the lack of precise or reliable information as to the identity or address of the manufacturer or consignor of the goods, a lack of cooperation with the customs authorities or the discovery of documents or correspondence concerning the goods in question suggesting that there is liable to be a diversion of those goods to European Union consumers.

---

72 ECJ Case C-383/98, *The Polo/Lauren Company* v. *PT. Dwidua Langgeng Pratama International Freight Forwarders*, [2000] ECR I-2519, Paragraph 34.

73 DS 408 and DS 409, *EU – Seizure of generic drugs in transit*.

74 For a summary account of the dispute see www.wto.org/english/tratop_e/dispu_e/cases_e/ds409_e.htm.

75 ECJ Joined Cases C-446/09 and 495/09, *Philips* v. *Lucheng Meijing* and *Nokia* v. *HMRC*, [2011] ECR I-0000; see already above, Chapter 4, section 4.4.1.2.2.2b.

76 See ECJ Case C-115/02, *Administration des douanes et droits indirects* v. *Rioglass and Transremar*, [2003] ECR I-12705, Paragraph 27; Case C-281/05, *Montex* v. *Diesel*, [2006] ECR I-10881, Paragraph 34.

Furthermore – probably with a view to the political quarrels arising from the seizure of generics by the Dutch customs authorities – the Court emphasised that:

> (63) It should be borne in mind . . . that imitations and copies coming from a non-member State and transported to another non-member State may comply with the intellectual property provisions in force in each of those States. In the light of the common commercial policy's main objective . . . consisting in the development of world trade through the progressive abolition of restrictions on trade between States, it is essential that those goods be able to pass in transit, via the European Union, from one non-member State to another without that operation being hindered, even by a temporary detention, by Member States' customs authorities. Precisely such hindrance would be created if [the Border Measures Regulation] were interpreted as permitting the detention of goods in transit without the slightest indication suggesting that they could be fraudulently diverted to European Union consumers.

Practical effects

In practice, the EU border measures have gained significant importance and seem to work quite well.[77] As summarised in the 'Report on EU customs enforcement of IP rights – Results at the EU border' for 2010:[78]

> Over the years, the number of applications recorded in the annual reports on EU customs enforcement of intellectual property rights has steadily increased. In 2000, there were less than 1,000 applications submitted by right-holders; in 2005, the number had increased to over 5,000. However, in 2010, the number of applications across the EU has risen to over 18,000.
>
> . . .
>
> In 2010 the majority of articles detained by customs were suspected of infringing a Community or national trade mark and covered a wide variety of goods across all product sectors. With regard to suspicion of patent infringements, the main categories of products detained were electronic devices working with MP3/DVD technology, unrecorded CD/DVD and medicines. With regard to copyright infringements, CD/DVD were the products most affected, though a wide variety of other products were also detained. For design and model rights, there was a single detention involving a large amount of tobacco products other than ciga-

---

77 For current information see ec.europa.eu/taxation_customs/customs/customs_controls/counterfeit_piracy/index_en.htm.

78 ec.europa.eu/taxation_customs/resources/documents/customs/customs_controls/counterfeit_piracy/statistics/statistics_2010.pdf, pp. 6 and 20.

rettes, though a wide variety of other products were also concerned, such as shoes, medicines and toys.

In more than 90% of all cases, customs action was started whilst the goods concerned were under an import procedure. In 6% of the cases, goods were discovered whilst being in transit with destination the EU and 1% in transit with destination a country outside the EU.

Statistically:

[o]verall, China continued to be the main source country from where goods suspected of infringing an IPR were sent to the EU (85% of the total amount of articles). However, in certain product categories, other countries were the main source, notably Turkey for foodstuffs, Thailand for beverages other than alcoholic beverages, Hong Kong for memory cards and India for medicines. On EU export controls we find Italy as the main country of provenance for foodstuffs and Bulgaria for packaging materials.

. . .

The top categories of articles detained were cigarettes which accounted for 34% of the overall amount, followed by office stationery (9%), other tobacco products (8%), labels, tags and emblems (8%), clothing (7%) and toys (7%).

. . .

The increase in the number of cases related mostly to postal traffic and principally concerned clothing, shoes and electrical goods. In terms of number of articles detained in postal traffic, nearly 69% were medicines.

. . .

Products for daily use and products that would be potentially dangerous to the health and safety of consumers (i.e. suspected trade mark infringements concerning food and beverages, body care articles, medicines, electrical household goods and toys) accounted for a total of 14.5% of the total amount of detained articles (compared to 18% in 2009).

. . .

In 90% of the cases of detentions by customs, the goods were either destroyed after the holder of the goods and the right-holder agreed on destruction, or the right-holder initiated a court case to establish an IPR infringement. In only 7% of the cases, goods were released because they were either non-infringing original goods (2.5%) or the right-holder did not react to the notification by customs (4.5%).[79]

Two additional remarks should be made. First, with 90.05 per cent trade marks are the IP rights which give rise to the vast majority of retention of

---

79 Ibid., p. 2.

infringing goods, followed by a mere 4.99 per cent for patent, 3.57 per cent of copyright and related rights infringements as well as only 1.32 per cent of design rights. Second, in view of 2 per cent of the world trade in goods which being believed to be counterfeit and pirated goods (estimated by the OECD), and a very roughly estimated 18 million TEU (20-foot equivalent units) containers of imports of goods from third countries into the Community carried by sea already in 2006, there still seems to be much room to increase the number of customs interceptions in Europe.

Following Council Resolution of 25 September 2008 on a comprehensive European anti-counterfeiting and anti-piracy plan,[80] Regulation 1383/2003 is currently under review,[81] in particular with regards to the following points: clarification of the situations in which customs may take action; the provisions concerning small consignments involving goods suspected of infringing IPR; the implementation of a simplified procedure, enabling customs authorities to have infringing goods abandoned for destruction under customs control, without there being any need to determine whether an intellectual property right has been infringed; and with regards to the costs of storage and destruction of goods and the concerns raised by right-holders regarding their financial responsibilities under the current regulation.

? QUESTIONS

1 The position of the ECJ in the *Nokia* and *Philips* decisions that goods in transit can only be the subject of detention and other measures if a concrete risk of diversion on the internal market can be demonstrated has given rise to concern among the proprietors of trade mark rights who fear that it will be too difficult to prove such risks, and that a chance will be lost to take an efficient stand against trade in counterfeit goods. Do you agree to that criticism or do you find the considerations of the ECJ convincing? How else could the right balance be struck between freedom of international trade and protection against counterfeiting?

2 How do you explain the fact that trade mark rights make up the vast majority of border seizures by customs authorities?

3 Increasingly, right-holders use technological measures in order to either prevent piracy altogether or at least make its detection easier. Do you know how these measures work? In your opinion, how successful can they be in the future?

---

80 [2008] OJ C 253/1.
81 See ec.europa.eu/taxation_customs/common/consultations/customs/ipr_2010_03_en.htm.

8.4   Criminal sanctions

Introduction

As a matter of principle, enforcement of IPRs is much stronger if it is not only achieved by civil but also by criminal sanctions. Indeed, from the perspective of right-holders, criminal sanctions have several advantages. First, they are administered by the public prosecutor's office rather than by private action. In general, the public prosecutor has greater powers regarding inspection and seizure of infringing materials and documents relating thereto than private parties. Second, to a much greater extent than civil law damages, the main purpose of which is to make the infringed party whole, criminal law monetary fines may annihilate any profits which the infringer has made by the infringement. Indeed, criminal sanctions may even impose a payment which goes beyond the profits made, thus punishing the infringer and acting as an effective deterrent against future infringements. Needless to say that other sanctions existing in some Member States such as confiscation of business equipment or even the closing down of the infringer's whole business, not to speak of personal imprisonment of the infringer, may also may be a strong deterrence.

However, it should also be noted that criminal sanctions only seem to be appropriate in cases of wilful and large-scale infringement, such as is often undertaken by organised crime, whereas criminal sanctions would seem too harsh if applied on the occasional and often only negligent infringer. Also, if criminal sanctions may seem justified in cases of blatant, obvious 1:1 infringement, it appears to be more problematic and hence more difficult to justify in the area of 'normal' infringement, i.e. equivalent solutions (patents), likelihood of confusion (trade mark) and adaptations (copyright). Economically speaking, too harsh sanctions might lead to overdeterrence and hence to underproduction and underuse of protected IP goods, in much the same way as too strong protection. Moreover, in modern democracies, criminal sanctions are generally seen as *ultima ratio*, i.e. as last resort in cases where the application of civil law sanctions does not seem to produce the desired effect of correcting the wrong that has been done.

At the international level, whereas both the Paris and the Berne Conventions were silent in this respect, criminal sanctions were first addressed in the TRIPS Agreement (Article 61). In the EU, criminal sanctions were initially proposed as part of the Enforcement Directive, but were dropped in the course of deliberations. Rather, following the adoption of the Enforcement Directive in 2004 the Commission in 2005 tabled a proposal for a Directive which shall exclusively deal with criminal matters. After controversial discussion in the European Parliament, the proposal was amended by the Commission which again made the European Parliament vote for substantial amendments. However, so far no further action has been taken in this matter. Rather, the Commission seems to have concentrated its efforts on introducing a section on criminal enforcement into the Anti-Counterfeiting Trade Agreement (ACTA).

? QUESTIONS

1 In your opinion, is there a need to provide for criminal sanctions in cases of infringement of IP rights in addition to civil law remedies? What possible advantages would criminal sanctions have?
2 What is meant by the sentence '[e]conomically speaking, too harsh sanctions might lead to overdeterrence and hence to underproduction and underuse of protected IP goods, in as much the same way as too strong protection'? Can you give examples?
3 In your country, what is the relationship between civil and criminal sanctions with regard to infringements of IP rights? Is it any different from the sanctions of other torts?
4 Also, in your country, to what extent are criminal sanctions applied in practice in cases of IP violations? Have infringers been sent to jail or have they just been fined? What is the average amount of such fines? Are there any statistics?

TRIPS

Whereas prior to TRIPS, all international Conventions were silent on criminal sanctions in the case of a violation of IPRs, in its Part III Sec. 5, the TRIPS Agreement for the first time contains a provision on criminal sanctions. According to Article 61 TRIPS:

> Members shall provide for criminal procedures and penalties to be applied at least in cases of willful trade mark counterfeiting or copyright piracy on a commercial scale. Remedies available shall include imprisonment and/or monetary fines sufficient to provide a deterrent, consistently with the level of penalties applied for crimes of a corresponding gravity. In appropriate cases, remedies available shall also include the seizure, forfeiture and destruction of the infringing goods and of any materials and implements the predominant use of which has been in the commission of the offence. Members may provide for criminal procedures and penalties to be applied in other cases of infringement of intellectual property rights, in particular where they are committed wilfully and on a commercial scale.

It should be noted that this provision dedicated to criminal procedures and remedies is considerably briefer and less detailed than the other TRIPS provisions on enforcement. Moreover, brief as it is, Article 61 TRIPS also contains significant limitations and flexibilities. To begin with, as all other provisions of TRIPS, Article 61 is not self-executing, but only puts an obligation on TRIPS Members ('shall') to have their domestic legislation in line with the requirements of the first two sentences of this provision. The requirements of the rest of the provision are either subject to certain flexibility ('[i]n appropriate cases'), or optional ('may provide'). In particular, Article 61 does not require Members to criminalise all copyright and trade mark infringements, but only those which have been committed wilfully and, moreover, 'on a commercial scale', without a definition of that notion being given in the text of the Agreement.

The issue was addressed in a complaint of the US against China's criminal measures which exclude some copyright and trade mark infringements from criminal liability where the infringement falls below numerical thresholds fixed in terms of the amount of turnover, profit, sales or copies of infringing goods. The Panel found that the term 'commercial scale' meant 'the magnitude or extent of typical or usual commercial activity with respect to a given product in a given market'.[82] Although the Panel did not endorse China's thresholds, it concluded that the factual evidence presented by the United States was inadequate to show whether or not the cases excluded from criminal liability met the TRIPS standard of 'commercial scale' when that standard is applied to China's marketplace.

Finally, it should be noted that by confining the obligation to provide for criminal sanctions to (certain cases of) trade mark and copyright infringements, TRIPS does not require Member States to criminalize patent infringements and infringements of the other IP rights covered by the Agreement (industrial designs, geographical indications, semiconductor topographies).

? **QUESTIONS**

1 As stated above, in the WTO Dispute Settlement Report WT/DS362/R mentioned above the Panel found that the term 'commercial scale' meant 'the magnitude or extent of typical or usual commercial activity with respect to a given product in a given market'. How would you define this notion? What criteria should be taken into account?

---

82 WTO Dispute Settlement Panel Report WT/DS362/R of 20 March 2009, docsonline.wto.org/ DDFDocuments/t/IP/d/26A1.doc, Paragraphs 7.501 *et seq.*

2 In your opinion, what are 'crimes of corresponding gravity'? How, in your opinion, should the level of penalties for IP infringements be fixed?

Proposed Directive on criminal sanctions

As already stated, other than initially planned, Directive 2004/48/EC does not contain any provisions dealing with criminal sanctions.[83] However, Recital 28 of that Directive stated that 'in addition to the civil and administrative measures, procedures and remedies provided for under this Directive, criminal sanctions also constitute, in appropriate cases, a means of ensuring the enforcement of intellectual property rights.' Consequently, in 2005 the Commission came up with an additional proposal for introducing criminal sanctions within the EU.[84] For competency reasons, the proposal for a Directive was initially accompanied by a proposed Framework Decision on the level of penalties. The Framework Decision was, however, subsequently abandoned and, in 2006, an amended proposal of the Directive[85] was tabled, after the ECJ had clarified, in a case concerning criminal sanctions for environmental offences, that although:

> (47) . . . as a general rule, neither criminal law nor the rules of criminal procedure fall within the Community's competence . . . (48) . . . [this] does not prevent the Community legislature, when the application of effective, proportionate and dissuasive criminal penalties by the competent national authorities is an essential measure for combating serious . . . offences, from taking measures which relate to the criminal law of the Member States as long as it considers such action necessary in order to ensure that [protective Community legislation is] fully effective.[86]

The Commission interpreted this decision to the effect that the provisions of criminal law required for the effective implementation of Community law are a matter for the EC Treaty,[87] and hence felt entitled to regulate both the offences and their details. The Commission admitted, however, that

---

83 See Recital 28 and Article 2 (3) (b) of Directive 2004/48/EC.

84 Proposal for a European Parliament and Council Directive on criminal measures aimed at ensuring the enforcement of intellectual property rights of 12 July 2005, COM(2005) 276 final.

85 Amended proposal for a Directive of the European Parliament and of the Council on criminal measures aimed at ensuring the enforcement of intellectual property rights of 26 April 2006, COM(2006) 168 final. The only provisions not incorporated in the amended proposal were those relating to jurisdiction and the cooperation of proceedings; in this respect, see also COM(2005) 696 final.

86 Case C-176/03, *Commission v. Council*, [2005] ECR I-7879, Paragraph 48.

87 Communication from the Commission to the European Parliament and the Council on the implications of the Court's judgment of 13 September 2005 (Case C 176/03 *Commission v Council*), COM(2005) 0583 final, Paragraph 11.

the necessity of a particular measure has to be ascertained 'on a case by case basis'.

The Commission justified its proposal as follows:

> Counterfeiting and piracy, and infringements of intellectual property in general, are a constantly growing phenomenon which nowadays have an international dimension, since they are a serious threat to national economies and governments. The disparities between the national systems of penalties, apart from hampering the proper functioning of the internal market, make it difficult to combat counterfeiting and piracy effectively. In addition to the economic and social consequences, counterfeiting and piracy also pose problems for consumer protection, particularly when health and safety are at stake. Increasing use of the Internet enables pirated products to be distributed instantly around the globe. Finally, this phenomenon appears to be increasingly linked to organised crime. Combating this phenomenon is therefore of vital importance for the Community. Counterfeiting and pirating have become lucrative activities in the same way as other large-scale criminal activities such as drug trafficking. There are high potential profits to be made without risk of serious legal penalties. Additional provisions to strengthen and improve the fight against counterfeiting and piracy are therefore necessary to supplement Directive 2004/48/EC of 29 April 2004 on the enforcement of intellectual property rights. In addition to the civil and administrative measures, procedures and remedies provided for in Directive 2004/48/EC, criminal penalties also constitute, in appropriate cases, a means of enforcing intellectual property rights.[88]

Under the proposal, Member States were obliged to ensure that all intentional infringements of an intellectual property right on a commercial scale, and attempting, aiding or abetting and inciting such infringements, are treated as criminal offences (Article 3). The obligation should cover all IP rights, both rights granted under national law and as Community rights, also including, in particular, patent rights. Penalties to be provided for concerned custodial sentences (for natural persons) and fines, confiscation of the object, instruments and products stemming from infringements or of goods whose value corresponds to those products (for natural and legal persons) (Article 4 (1) (a) and (b)). In appropriate cases, Member States should also provide for the following penalties: (a) destruction of the goods infringing an intellectual property right; (b) total or partial closure, on a permanent or

---

88 Amended proposal for a Directive of the European Parliament and of the Council on criminal measures aimed at ensuring the enforcement of intellectual property rights of 26 April 2006, COM(2006) 168 final.

temporary basis, of the establishment used primarily to commit the offence; (c) a permanent or temporary ban on engaging in commercial activities; (d) placing under judicial supervision; (e) judicial winding-up; (f) a ban on access to public assistance or subsidies; (g) publication of judicial decisions (Article 4 (2)). In Article 5, the level of criminal penalties was fixed at a maximum term of at least four years' imprisonment when they are committed under the aegis of a criminal organisation, or where they carry a health or safety risk.[89] For natural persons or legal entities who commit the offences listed in Article 5, the penalties included criminal and non-criminal fines to a maximum of at least €100,000 for cases other than the most serious cases and to a maximum of at least €300,000 for offences carried out under the aegis of a criminal organisation or which carry a health or safety risk, even where the dangerous product has not yet caused any damage. In addition, according to Article 6 of the Amended Proposal, in cases of organised crime or where the counterfeit goods carry a health or safety risk, Member States should provide for extended powers of confiscation, i.e., to allow the total or partial confiscation of goods belonging to convicted natural or legal persons. Finally, Article 7 allowed right-holders and their experts to assist in investigations by joint investigation teams.

The proposal met with severe criticism both as regards the need to regulate and the contents of the regulation.[90] With regard to contents, crucial points of criticism concerned the involvement of private parties in criminal investigations, the lack of procedural safeguards regarding the interests of the accused party, lack of precision *inter alia* regarding notions such as 'aiding and abetting', and the breadth of the proposal, which appeared to extend even to parallel imports of genuine goods. The criticism was shared by the European Parliament[91] and the Draft Directive was only approved in April 2007 with major amendments.[92] In particular, the Parliament opted for

---

89 The threshold of four years' imprisonment was chosen because it broadly corresponds to the criterion used to identify a serious offence. It is the threshold selected in Joint Action 98/733/JHA and in the proposal for a Council Framework Decision on the fight against organized crime (COM(2005) 6 final) and in the United Nations Convention against Organized Transnational Crime; Amended Proposal, op. cit., Explanatory Memorandum to Article 5.

90 See *inter alia* the statement by the Max Planck Institute, *Hilty/Kur/Peukert*, Max Planck Institute for Intellectual Property, Competition and Tax Law on the Proposal for a Directive of the European Parliament and of the Council on Criminal Measures Aimed at Ensuring the Enforcement of Intellectual Property Rights, www.ip.mpg.de/files/pdf2/Comments-Enforcement OfIP-Rights.pdf which articulates the most important points of criticism and proved to be quite influential in the legislative process.

91 See European Parliament, Committee on Legal Affairs, Report on the amended proposal for a directive of the European Parliament and of the Council on criminal measures aimed at ensuring the enforcement of intellectual property rights (27 March 2007) A6-0073/2007.

92 European Parliament, Amendments to the Draft Directive: Enforcement of intellectual property rights (criminal measures) (25 April 2007) P6_TA(2007)0145.

'patent rights, utility models and plant variety rights, including rights derived from supplementary protection certificates' to be excluded from the scope of the Directive, as well as for exclusion of 'parallel imports of original goods from a third country which have been allowed by the rightholder'. It further defined 'infringements on a commercial scale' in the same sense as in Recital 14 of the Enforcement Directive,[93] thereby excluding 'acts carried out by private users for personal and not-for-profit purposes'. The term 'intentional infringements of an intellectual property right' was defined as 'any deliberate and conscious infringement of the right concerned for the purpose of obtaining an economic advantage on a commercial scale', meaning that a criminal offense should not result in case that an infringer simply underestimated the scope of a right, or acted in the belief that the use was covered by limitations and exceptions.

Further amendments proposed by the European Parliament concerned the notion of 'serious crime'[94] as well as provisions counterbalancing the involvement of private parties in criminal investigations and safeguarding the rights of the accused party.

In view of the discrepancies between the original proposal made by the Commission and the text as amended by the European Parliament,[95] until the time of printing and apart from an announcement now and then to the contrary, the Commission has not pursued the Draft Directive any further.

? QUESTIONS

1 The amendments proposed by the European Parliament do not per se exclude threats of criminal proceedings, nor that criminal measures are employed for the enforcement of the requirements of civil law, but rather only obliges Member States to prevent misuse in this respect. In your opinion, what could be regarded as 'misuse'?

2 Would you personally favour the introduction of harmonised criminal sanctions for IP infringements?

---

93 Directive 2004/48/EC of the European Parliament and of the Council of 29 April 2004 on the enforcement of intellectual property rights, [2004] OJ L 195/16.

94 Reference was made in that regard to Article 3 (5) of Directive 2005/60/EC on the prevention of the use of the financial system for the purpose of money laundering and terrorist financing , [2005] OJ L 309/15.

95 See, however, the more positive approach towards criminal sanctions in the 'Report on enforcement of intellectual property rights in the internal market' by the European Parliament's Committee on Legal Affairs (Gallo Report), Doc. A7-0175/2010 of 3 June 2010, Paragraph 6, www.europarl.europa.eu/sides/getDoc. do?pubRef=-//EP//NONSGML+REPORT+A7-2010-0175+0+DOC+PDF+V0//EN.

8.5 The Anti-Counterfeiting Trade Agreement (ACTA)

Background and political concerns

As was stated in the introduction to this chapter, together with several other states the EU concluded the Anti-Counterfeiting Trade Agreement (ACTA).[96] Apart from provisions on enhancing international cooperation, the Agreement aims at a 'more effective international enforcement'. Hence, in its substantive provisions, ACTA addresses border measures, civil sanctions and criminal sanctions. In doing so, it goes beyond simply rephrasing the existing *acquis* under TRIPS, not only adding more details, but also enhancing the level of sanctions. Regarding the established enforcement standards within the EU, in particular the rules set out in EU Regulation 1383/2003 and Directive 2004/48/EC, the divergences are less obvious. Nevertheless, ACTA has provoked strong misgivings in the civil society and also in academic circles, which have caused the European Parliament to refuse to give consent to the ratification. Before that, the Commission, at Parliament's request, had submitted to the ECJ the question of whether ACTA clashes with Community law, in particular with the Charter of Fundamental Rights. The issue is still pending at the time of printing. It remains unclear whether, if ACTA should be found compatible with EU law after all, renewed efforts will be made by the Commission to continue and conclude the ratification process, or whether for political reasons, ACTA is 'dead' anyhow.

General standards and civil remedies

The text of ACTA sets out a number of provisions defining the aims and intentions of the Contracting Parties, and the spirit in which the obligations resulting from it should be implemented. Having already been confronted during the (initially suspiciously secretive) negotiation process with protests and negative reactions, it is pointed out in the initial part what ACTA shall *not* be or do: in particular, it shall not introduce new standards under the substantive law governing the availability and scope of rights (Article 3), it shall not oblige Parties to disclose information that is confidential under its legislation (Article 4), and parties shall not be under an obligation to re-distribute resources with the aim of creating a more efficient enforcement

---

96 Until now, ACTA has been signed by the EU, Japan, Australia, Canada, Morocco, New Zealand, Singapore, South Korea and the United States. The agreement will enter into force after having been ratified by six states. At the time of publication, Japan is the only state so far where the internal ratification process has been concluded. For more information on the contents and background of ACTA (from the perspective of the EU Commission) see ec.europa.eu/trade/creating-opportunities/trade-topics/intellectual-property/anti-counterfeiting.

system (Article 1 (2)). Furthermore, reference is made in Article 2 (3) to the Principles in Part I of TRIPS, in particular Articles 7 and 8 TRIPS.[97] Lastly, Article 6 (General Obligations) sets forth that enforcement procedures shall be fair and equitable, and that they shall provide for the rights of all participants subject to those proceedings to be appropriately protected, and that each Contracting Party 'shall take into account the need for proportionality between the seriousness of the infringement, the interests of third parties, and the applicable measures, remedies and penalties'.

In spite of such soothing statements, observers have strongly criticised the fact that language relating to the need of taking proportionality aspects into account, and to protect the interests of third parties, is not reiterated in the black letter text of provisions setting out the individual means and remedies.[98] Also, where the wording of ACTA leaves room for interpretation, critical commentators tend to assume that if ACTA becomes the governing standard, it will be applied in the strictest possible manner.

For instance, Article 8 (injunctions) stipulates that:

> Each Party shall provide that . . . its judicial authorities have the authority to issue [an injunction] against a party to desist from an infringement . . .

In a statement of Opinion by European Academics on ACTA,[99] it is contended that this might mean that the option granted under Article 12 of the Enforcement Directive is 'lost or at least called into question', namely that under appropriate circumstances (if the infringer acted unintentionally and without negligence, and if the measure would cause 'disproportionate harm'), the court may order the infringer to pay pecuniary compensation instead of issuing the measure requested by the right-holder. That interpretation would ignore, however, that it is generally accepted that in the context of international agreements, the wording 'courts shall have the authority . . .' only means that courts must be *entitled* to issue a particular measure, without being obliged to do so.

Similarly, with regard to damages, where Article 9 (1) ACTA sets out that:

---

97 Article 7 TRIPS enshrines the principle of balance of rights and obligations, and Article 8 allows TRIPS Members to adopt measures necessary to pursue policies of vital importance, in particular related to health concerns and nutrition.

98 For a pointedly critical view on ACTA see the Opinion by European Academics, www.iri.uni-hannover.de/acta-1668.html and at www.jipitec.eu/issues/jipitec-2-1-2011/2965/JIPITEC_ACTA.pdf.

99 Ibid.

> [i]n determining the amount of damages for infringement of intellectual property rights, a Party's judicial authorities shall have the authority to consider, *inter alia,* any legitimate measure of value the right holder submits, which may include lost profits, the value of the infringed goods or services measured by the market price, or the suggested retail price

the concern is expressed that this may mean that even in cases when cheap copies are sold of high-priced articles, the damage will be calculated on the basis of the retail price for the original goods as multiplied with the number of counterfeits sold.

Although some of those fears appear exaggerated, ACTA certainly does have a certain potential, depending on its interpretation, to induce a tightening of the current enforcement regime. Regarding damages, that potential is primarily reflected in Article 9 (3) ACTA, according to which one or more of the following types of damages must be available in cases of trade mark counterfeiting or infringement of copyright and related rights:

(a) pre-established damages; or
(b) presumptions for determining the amount of damages sufficient to compensate the right holder for the harm caused by the infringement; or
(c) at least for copyright, additional damages.

Considering that under US law, pre-established damages can be very high, the formulation does evoke misgivings, in particular with regards to the effect it may have in the case of copyright infringements.

Border measures

Border measures are addressed in Articles 15 *et seq.* ACTA. Those provisions are particularly strict and offer the clearest example for regulations arguably going beyond current EU legislation. Thus, ACTA does not adopt the same scope of application as Article 2 (1) of the EU Border Measures Regulation which applies for trade mark infringements to 'counterfeit goods' only. Instead, Article 13 ACTA requires border measures being set in place 'in a manner that does not discriminate unjustifiably between intellectual property rights . . .'. The wording is explained by the fact that the EU originally tried to oblige the other Contracting Parties to extend border measures also to protected geographical indications. As that attempt was unsuccessful, it was decided to add wording which would at least clarify that geographical indications, where they are protected as intellectual property rights, should not get less protection at the borders than other IPRs. However, as a side-effect of that political bargaining, it may result that border measures must also be available against all kinds of trade mark infringements, even based on mere similarity of signs, instead of being confined to the narrower case of 'counterfeits'. On the other hand, by only banning *unjustified* discrimination', Article 13 does not prevent justified differentiation between, on the one hand, counterfeit goods which are easy to detect by the customs authorities and which call for immediate action, and on the other hand, other kinds of trade mark infringement that should rather remain a matter for ordinary court proceedings.

ISP liability

The strongest political reactions were triggered by the consequences ACTA might have on enforcement measures in the digital environment. In particular, fears were voiced that ISPs will be forced to disclose all user-related data to right-holders for the purpose of enforcement, that ISPs themselves will be held liable for IP violations under criminal law for any infringements committed through the service provided, and that ACTA will ultimately establish the 'three strikes and you're out' solution (graduated response), already adopted in France, throughout Europe and the world.

However, similar to other provisions of ACTA that are in the focus of critique, the black letter text of the Agreement does not fully sustain such misgivings. In particular, contrary to earlier versions, the internet chapter[100] no longer contains provisions regarding the graduated response or similar solutions. Instead the desire is expressed in the Preamble 'to promote cooperation between service providers and right-holders to address relevant infringements in the digital environment'.[101] Regarding in particular the information obligations of ISPs, it is set forth in Article 27(4) that:

> A Party may provide, in accordance with its laws and regulations, its competent authorities with the authority to order an online service provider to disclose expeditiously to a right holder information sufficient to identify a subscriber whose account was allegedly used for infringement, where that right holder has filed a legally sufficient claim of trade mark or copyright or related rights infringement, and where such information is being sought for the purpose of protecting or enforcing those rights. These procedures shall be implemented in a manner that avoids the creation of barriers to legitimate activity, including electronic

---

100 Chapter II, Section 5, Article 27.
101 ACTA, Recital 7.

commerce, and, consistent with that Party's law, preserves fundamental principles such as freedom of expression, fair process, and privacy.

Whereas that provision goes beyond TRIPS (where the right to information is only a non-mandatory option), it does not appear to be broader than the current obligation under the pertinent law in the EU, and it also leaves sufficient room for taking account of countervailing interests and values. Rather than being founded on the text as such, the virulent protests provoked by the rule seem to express a general distrust regarding the intentions underlying the Agreement, and the anticipation that the standards enshrined in the black letter are only a first step in a development ultimately leading to substantial curtailment of user rights and civil freedoms.

In the same context and for similar reasons, it is criticised that Article 27 (5), (6) and (8) provide rather strong protection of technical protection measures, *inter alia* by prohibiting both acts of circumvention and preparatory acts, and by covering technological measures having dual (both legal and illegal) functions. And although Article 27 (8) allows preservation of exceptions and limitations, it is critically remarked that the text does not provide any mechanisms to ensure their exercise and enforcement.[102]

Criminal sanctions

In view of the fact that so far criminal sanctions for infringement of IP rights have not been harmonised within the EU, the EU also voted in favour of having a section on criminal sanctions included in ACTA.[103] On the other hand, this has invited the protest of those who see this as a strategic manoeuvre to circumvent, by way of 'forum shifting', the resistance put up by the European Parliament against previous attempts to legislate in the area.

Section 4 of ACTA defines in Article 23 the infringing acts for which Member States shall provide criminal procedures and penalties. These are:

- 'at least . . . cases of wilful trade mark counterfeiting or copyright or related rights piracy on a commercial scale' (Article 23 (1)), and
- cases of 'wilful importation and domestic use, in the course of trade and on a commercial scale, of labels or packaging: (a) to which a mark has

---

102 Opinion of European Academics on ACTA, above footnote 98.
103 For objectives and history see, e.g., the information on the Commission's website ec.europa.eu/trade/creating-opportunities/trade-topics/intellectual-property/anti-counterfeiting.

been applied without authorization which is identical to, or cannot be distinguished from, a trade mark registered in its territory; and (b) which are intended to be used in the course of trade on goods or in relation to services which are identical to goods or services for which such trade mark is registered.' (Article 23 (2)).

- Criminal procedures and penalties regarding the unauthorised copying of cinematographic works from a performance in a motion picture exhibition facility generally open to the public, however, are optional (Article 23 (3)).
- Criminal liability for aiding and abetting also has to be provided for (Article 23 (4)).

The obligation to provide for criminal measures also extends 'to establish the liability, which may be criminal, of legal persons for the offences specified', without prejudice to the criminal liability of the natural persons who have committed the criminal offences, but only to the extent this is 'consistent with its legal principles' (Article 23 (5)).

Moreover, Article 23 (1) defines 'acts carried out on a commercial scale' as 'includ[ing] at least those carried out as commercial activities for direct or indirect economic or commercial advantage'. Penalties for mandatory criminal offences shall include 'imprisonment as well as monetary fines sufficiently high to provide a deterrent to future acts of infringement, consistently with the level of penalties applied for crimes of a corresponding gravity' (Article 24).

Article 25 contains detailed obligations regarding seizure, forfeiture and destruction.

Finally, Article 26 states that Member States shall see to the fact that 'in appropriate cases, its competent authorities may act upon their own initiative (ex officio) to initiate investigation or legal action' with respect to the mandatory criminal offences specified in Article 23.

Although it was stated by ACTA's negotiating parties that ACTA provided 'state-of-the-art provisions on the enforcement of intellectual property rights',[104] it should be noted that in several respects the criminal law provisions of ACTA clearly go beyond the *acquis* of the EU, at least as long as the

---

104 See Joint statement on the Anti-Counterfeiting Trade Agreement (ACTA) from all the negotiating partners of the agreement of 15 November 2010, trade.ec.europa.eu/doclib/press/index.cfm?id=659&serie=384&langId=en.

proposed EU Directive on criminal sanctions has not been adopted. It therefore is hardly surprising that the criminal provisions of ACTA also attracted much criticism. Indeed, ACTA contains some of the elements that have motivated the European Parliament to withhold their support for the proposed criminal enforcement Directive. *Inter alia*, this concerns the definition of 'commercial scale', which determines the scope of mandatory application of criminal sanctions. As pointed out in the pre-cited Opinion of European Academics on ACTA:[105]

> *7. Scope*: Article 23.1 ACTA provides for a broad definition of 'commercial scale' covering all acts carried out on a commercial scale including at least those carried out as commercial activities for direct or indirect economic or commercial advantage. By contrast, in its Position of 25 April 2007, the European Parliament (EP) expressly excluded acts 'carried out by private users for personal and not-for-profit purposes'[106]. The EP also declared that 'the fair use of a protected work, including such use by reproduction in copies or audio or by any other means, for purposes such as criticism, comment, news reporting, teaching (including multiple copies for classroom use), scholarship or research, does not constitute a criminal offence'. ACTA does not reaffirm these safeguards for private users and for limitations and exceptions.

Furthermore, regarding parallel imports:

> Article 23.2 ACTA prescribes criminal procedures and penalties on the wilful importation and domestic use on a commercial scale of goods infringing trade mark rights. The vague language of the article could seem to cover importation and domestic use of products which, although lawfully marketed in the exporting country, have not been authorised in the importing country. Such interpretation would hinder parallel imports in the EU. The EP in Article 1 of its Position suggested that parallel imports should be specifically excluded from the scope of criminal offences. Such exclusion is not reflected in ACTA.

? QUESTIONS

1 In general, what is your opinion on the necessity of concluding ACTA in addition to the already existing TRIPS Agreement? Is it an instrument 'merely preaching to the already convicted', as one commentator suggested, or will it be used as a leverage tool in order to increase the level

---

105 Above, footnote 98.

106 Position of the European Parliament adopted at first reading on 25 April 2007 with a view to the adoption of Directive 2007/. . ./EC of the European Parliament and of the Council on criminal measures aimed at ensuring the enforcement of intellectual property rights (EP-PE_TC1-COD(2005)0127).

of enforcement on a worldwide basis? If so, how do you think will this be achieved?

2 Do you think that in negotiating and signing ACTA, the EU has enlarged its legal competency as regards the harmonization of criminal sanctions existing in its Member States' national laws, or even the basis for creating community-wide sanctions?

3 In what ways does ACTA deviate from existing EU legislation? The Commission repeatedly has stated that ACTA merely reflects the EU standard. What differences can you spot?

4 Do you agree with the criticism of ACTA? If so, for what reasons?

9

Jurisdiction and applicable law

9.1 Introduction

As explained in Chapter 8, enforcement is a vital part of intellectual property protection. The attribution of such rights is not worth much if they are not respected by others, and if violations cannot be pursued in court proceedings leading to appropriate and efficient sanctions. Whereas central aspects of sanctions and proceedings have been harmonised by the Enforcement Directive (48/2004/EC), it remains for the national legislatures to determine the venue before which such proceedings can be brought. Furthermore, as long as the matter concerns an infringement occurring within the Member State where the court is located, the matter will regularly be solved under domestic law.

It is more complicated if the dispute concerns the alleged infringement of one or several rights existing abroad, or if claims are derived from contracts to which a foreign law applies or may apply. In that case, it needs to be determined whether the court seized with the proceedings is actually competent to hear and decide the case, and which law is to be applied in the proceedings. Whereas formerly, such issues were only rarely raised in proceedings dealing with intellectual property matters, the size and frequency of litigation extending beyond the borders of one single territory have increased, due to the expansion of cross-border trade and communication. Also, the creation of Community-wide titles with unitary effect, such as the Community trade mark and the Community design, has necessitated specific rules determining the competent venue for cross-border claims.

Jurisdiction in civil litigation over intellectual property matters as well as the law applying with regard to contractual and non-contractual matters involving intellectual property are regulated by the Brussels I Regulation[1] and the

---

1 Council Regulation No 44/2001 on the Recognition and Enforcement of Foreign Judgments in Civil and Commercial Matters ('Brussels I'), [2001] OJ L 12/1.

Rome I and Rome II Regulations.[2] Special rules concerning jurisdiction and applicable law in proceedings involving Community trade marks and Community designs are set out in the CTMR and CDR respectively.

Prior to the enactment of the Brussels I and Rome I Regulations, common rules on jurisdiction and the law applicable to contractual obligations ensued from international conventions concluded between the Member States, namely the Brussels Convention (1968) concerning jurisdiction and the Rome Convention (1980) concerning the law applicable to contractual obligations. Most of the structure and wording of those earlier conventions was taken over into the current Brussels I and Rome I Regulations. Previous ECJ case law interpreting the two conventions has therefore retained its relevance. Most of the decisions to which reference is made in the following date from that period.

After having been in operation for somewhat less than 10 years, the Brussels I Regulation is currently under consideration for reform. Only few of the issues addressed in the Commission's reform proposal[3] are of direct interest for intellectual property matters. Where that is the case, the text will refer to it.

The following will first elaborate on jurisdiction as determined by the Brussels I Regulation and, for Community rights, by the CTMR and CDR, with some remarks also being made on European patents and the envisaged Agreement on the Unified Patent Court. Then a brief account will be given on the provisions in the Rome I and II Regulations on the law applicable to contractual and non-contractual obligations to the extent they are of relevance for intellectual property matters.

9.2 Jurisdiction

Scope of application

The Brussels I Regulation applies in all EU Member States with the exception of Denmark, where the Brussels Convention still applies. A parallel regime to the Brussels Convention was established by the Lugano Convention (1988).

---

2 Regulation No 593/2008 of the European Parliament and of the Council on the Law Applicable to Contractual Obligations ('Rome I') [2008] OJ L 177/6; Regulation No 864/2007 of the European Parliament and of the Council on the Law Applicable to Non-Contractual Obligations, ('Rome II'), [2007] OJ L 199/40.
3 COM(2010) 748 final.

An amended version of the Lugano Convention dating from 2007 is in force with regard to Switzerland, Norway and Iceland.

The Brussels I Regulation determines the competence of courts in the Member States to exercise international jurisdiction in civil and commercial matters, including matters concerning national intellectual property rights. The details concerning the local or subject-matter competence of courts within the domestic court system are, as a matter of principle, not concerned thereby.[4] Hence, the Brussels I Regulation does not impact issues of judicial competence in regard of purely internal matters.

The Brussels I Regulation applies when the defendant is domiciled in the EU, irrespective of nationality (Article 2). For legal persons, the meaning of 'domicile' is explained in Article 60: a company is domiciled where it has its statutory seat, or its central administration, or its principal place of business. If the defendant is domiciled in a non-EU State, the court seized with the claim applies its own procedural law, in the same manner as against defendants who are domiciled in the state where the court is located (Article 4). This includes the possibility of the plaintiff availing himself of 'exorbitant' grounds of jurisdiction anchored in national law (listed in Annex I of the Brussels I Regulation). On the contrary, if the defendant is domiciled in another Member State, and the Brussels I Regulation is thus applicable, the court seized with the matter is prohibited from employing the exorbitant grounds for jurisdiction listed in the Annex (Article 3 (2)).

Structure and contents of the Brussels I Regulation: overview

Heads of jurisdiction

Where the Brussels I Regulation applies, the permissible grounds for jurisdiction are organised according to the following scheme:

- *General jurisdiction* is vested in the courts in the state where the defendant is habitually resident (Article 2). As a matter of principle, all claims against the defendant may be brought there, with the sole exception of claims for which another court is exclusively competent on the basis of Article 22 Brussels I Regulation, or in case of an exclusive choice of court agreement (Article 23).

---

4 However, some provisions in the Brussels I Regulation also determine the local competence of national courts, see in particular ECJ Case C -386/05, *Color Drack v. Lexx International,* [2007] ECR I-3699, Paragraph 30.

- Courts having *special jurisdiction* pursuant to Articles 5 to 21 are competent to hear particular claims specified in the provisions. Of relevance for intellectual property matters are Article 5 (1) (matters relating to contract), Article 5 (3) (matters relating to torts, delicts, or quasi-delicts) and Article 6 (1) (claims filed against multiple defendants). In case that courts having special jurisdiction are located outside the Member State where the defendant is domiciled, the plaintiff has an option to choose among the competent venues ('forum shopping').
- If a court has *exclusive jurisdiction* over a certain subject matter, pertinent claims must be raised in that court, irrespective of where the defendant is domiciled. Courts seized with claims for which another court has exclusive jurisdiction must, of their own motion, decline jurisdiction (Article 25). Of relevance for intellectual property matters is Article 22 (4) pursuant to which the courts in the country of registration are exclusively competent to hear claims concerned with the registration or validity of patents, trade marks, industrial designs or other rights which must be registered or deposited.

With the exception of courts having exclusive competence pursuant to Article 22, the parties may also *choose the court* that shall settle the dispute between them (prorogation; Article 23). Unless specified otherwise, the competence of such courts is deemed to be exclusive. Prorogation also results if the defendant appears in the venue chosen by the plaintiff, unless this is to contest jurisdiction (Article 24).

Whereas the jurisdiction provisions are mandatory for main proceedings, Article 31 permits to apply for *provisional and preliminary measures* in any court that is competent under the law of the state where it is located, even if the courts in another country have jurisdiction over the substance of the matter.

Where two (or more) courts are seized with the *same cause of action*, the court second seized must stay the proceedings until the court first seized has established its jurisdiction. If the court first seized decides that it has competence to hear the claim, the court second seized must decline jurisdiction; otherwise, proceedings are resumed in the court second seized (*lis pendens*; Article 27). Where the actions pending in different courts are merely *related*, the court second seized may likewise stay the proceedings, without being obliged to do so (Article 28).

Recognition and enforcement

In addition to determining the venue for proceedings in a secure and predictable manner, the Brussels I Regulation aims to facilitate and render more efficient the recognition and enforcement of judgments within the EU. For that purpose, the rule is established that judgments rendered by courts in other Member States must be recognised without any special proceedings being necessary. The mechanism is founded on the principle of mutual trust, which is set out in the Preamble as follows:

> (16) Mutual trust in the administration of justice in the Community justifies judgments given in a Member State being recognised automatically without the need for any procedure except in cases of dispute.
>
> (17) By virtue of the same principle of mutual trust, the procedure for making enforceable in one Member State a judgment given in another must be efficient and rapid. To that end, the declaration that a judgment is enforceable should be issued virtually automatically after purely formal checks of the documents supplied, without there being any possibility for the court to raise of its own motion any of the grounds for non-enforcement provided for by this Regulation.

Exceptions from that rule only apply where recognition would be manifestly contrary to public policy in the Member State in which recognition is sought, or if fundamental procedural rules have been neglected (such as failure to serve the defendant with the document instituting the proceedings), or if it is irreconcilable with another judgment which is to be given priority (Article 33). Similar rules apply to enforcement (Art. 38 *et seq.*).

Obligation of competent courts to hear claims

Recital 11 of the Preamble to the Brussels I Regulation sets forth that:

> [t]he rules of jurisdiction must be highly predictable and founded on the principle that jurisdiction is generally based on the defendant's domicile and jurisdiction must always be available on this ground save in a few well-defined situations in which the subject-matter of the litigation or the autonomy of the parties warrants a different linking factor.

Consequently, where the Brussels I Regulation is applicable and confers jurisdiction on a court in a Member State seized with proceedings, that court is obliged to hear and decide the case. Most importantly, this means that under the Brussels I Regulation (as well as under its predecessor, the Brussels Convention), there is no room for applying the doctrine of *forum non conven-*

iens, which forms part of the legal traditions in particular of common law countries. Under that doctrine a court seized with proceedings may decline jurisdiction of its own discretion if it finds that another court is better placed to decide the case.

The non-applicability of *forum non conveniens* in the framework of the Brussels Convention was confirmed by the ECJ in a case concerning an accident suffered by a British citizen during his vacation in Jamaica. The plaintiff sued another British resident – the owner of the holiday villa on the beach where the accident happened – as well as several other persons who were all resident in Jamaica. The claims against all defendants were basically the same: liability for failure to warn against a dangerous sandbank below the waterline. The UK court seized with the claim against the British resident found that for reasons of procedural efficiency, it would be more appropriate to bring the claims against all defendants in Jamaica. The question was therefore referred to the ECJ whether it was compatible with EU law to apply the doctrine of *forum non conveniens* in a case when, as in the actual dispute, jurisdiction of the British resident was clearly established under Article 2 of the Brussels Convention.[5] The ECJ responded that:

> (37) It must be observed, first, that Article 2 of the Brussels Convention is mandatory in nature and that, according to its terms, there can be no derogation from the principle it lays down except in the cases expressly provided for by the Convention . . . It is common ground that no exception on the basis of the *forum non conveniens* doctrine was provided for by the authors of the Convention, although the question was discussed when the Convention of 9 October 1978 on the Accession of Denmark, Ireland and the United Kingdom was drawn up . . .

Making reference to the Preamble of the Brussels Regulation, which was intended to 'strengthen in the Community the legal protection of persons established therein, by laying down common rules on jurisdiction to guarantee certainty as to the allocation of jurisdiction among the various national courts before which proceedings in a particular case may be brought',[6] the ECJ further observed that:

> (38) Respect for the principle of legal certainty, which is one of the objectives of the Brussels Convention . . ., would not be fully guaranteed if the court having jurisdiction under the Convention had to be allowed to apply the *forum non conveniens* doctrine . . . (41) Application of the *forum non conveniens* doctrine, which

---

5 ECJ Case C-281/02, *Owusu v. Jackson*, [2005] ECR I-1383.
6 Ibid., Paragraph 39.

allows the court seised a wide discretion as regards the question whether a foreign court would be a more appropriate forum for the trial of an action, is liable to undermine the predictability of the rules of jurisdiction laid down by the Brussels Convention, in particular that of Article 2 . . . (43) Moreover, allowing *forum non conveniens* in the context of the Brussels Convention would be likely to affect the uniform application of the rules of jurisdiction contained therein in so far as that doctrine is recognised only in a limited number of Contracting States, whereas the objective of the Brussels Convention is precisely to lay down common rules to the exclusion of derogating national rules.

? QUESTIONS

1 Do you agree that to exclude any application of the *forum non conveniens* doctrine in such cases is necessary to preserve the predictability of the forum and to ensure harmonised practice?

2 In the scheme underlying the Brussels I Regulation, the courts at the place of the defendant's domicile are regarded as providing (with few exceptions) the most appropriate venue to decide claims raised against him/her. Do you agree? What are the underlying policy reasons for that scheme?

Issues of particular relevance for intellectual property matters

Article 5 (1): contractual matters

As a general rule, Article 5 (1) (a) establishes the principle that in matters relating to a contract, the courts at the place of performance of the obligation in question have jurisdiction. In Article 5 (1) (b), more specified rules are given for contracts concerning the sales of goods and the provision of services. No specific mention is made of contracts involving the licensing or transfer of intellectual property rights; for such cases, Article 5 (1) (c) refers back to the general rule in Article 5 (1) (a).

The ECJ was asked to consider the provision in a dispute concerning *inter alia* a claim for royalty payments launched on behalf of the successors in title to the late Austrian singer Falco, against a defendant, resident in Germany, to whom licenses had been granted for the marketing of video recordings of a concert given by the singer.[7] As jurisdiction had been contested by the defendant, the Austrian Supreme Court referred to the ECJ the following question:

---

7 ECJ Case C-533/07, *Falco Privatstiftung v. Weller-Lindhorst*, [2009] ECR I-3327.

Is a contract under which the owner of an intellectual property right grants the other contracting party the right to use that right (a licence agreement) a contract regarding 'the provision of services' within the meaning of Article 5(1)(b) [of the Brussels I Regulation]?

The ECJ denied that question, pointing out that:

(31) [b]y [a license] contract, the only obligation which the owner of the right granted undertakes with regard to its contractual partner is not to challenge the use of that right by the latter.... [T]he owner of an intellectual property right does not perform any service in granting a right to use that property and undertakes merely to permit the licensee to exploit that right freely.... (37) The broad logic and scheme of the rules governing jurisdiction laid down by Regulation No 44/2001 require, on the contrary, a narrow interpretation of the rules on special jurisdiction, including the rule contained, in matters relating to a contract, in Article 5(1) of that Regulation, which derogate from the general principle that jurisdiction is based on the defendant's domicile.

 QUESTIONS

1 How would you define the 'place of performance' of an IP license or a transfer? Do you think that it would be possible to formulate a rule which fits to all kinds of IP contracts? (see also this chapter, section 9.3.2.2).

2 Do you agree with the ECJ that IP licenses cannot be classified as 'service' in the meaning of Article 5 (1) b?

Article 5 (3): infringement jurisdiction

General remarks

Article 5 (3) reflects the practically universally accepted principle that jurisdiction for claims arising from tortuous conduct should be vested, in addition to and apart from the courts at the defendant's place of domicile, in the courts at the place where the harmful event occurs. Not only do those courts typically have the best access to witnesses, factual evidence and other circumstances of relevance for the decision, due to the equally broadly accepted principle of *lex loci delicti commissi* (or *lex protectionis*) with regard to intellectual property infringement (see below), they will also regularly be in the position to apply domestic law when assessing the merits of the case.

Article 5 (3) refers to 'torts, delicts and quasi-delicts'. It is undisputed that this involves claims for intellectual property infringement, irrespective of whether the actual claim filed is based on the infringement provisions anchored in intellectual property law proper or on general doctrines of civil law, such as unjust enrichment or *negotiorum gestio*.

Jurisdiction for such claims is vested in the courts of the country 'where the harmful event occurs or may occur'. The previous version of Article 5 (3) in the Brussels Convention of 1968 did not contain the word '*may*' occur, thereby raising doubts as to whether claims for *threatening* infringement could be brought in the courts of the State where the infringement was imminent. That gap was closed in the course of transposing the Brussels Convention into the Brussels I Regulation, which leaves no doubt about the admissibility of claims in the country where the infringement is threatening.

Article 5 (3) as a basis for cross-border litigation

General principles
If torts committed in one country take effect in another one, jurisdiction exists in both States. This was confirmed by the ECJ in an early case (*Bier v. Mines de Potasse d'Alsace*)[8] concerning the pollution of Rhine water in France by the defendant, which caused damage to the plaintiff's crops in the Netherlands. As the Court pointed out, the wording of the Brussels Convention was not unambiguous:

> (14) The form of the words 'place where the harmful event occurs' . . . leaves open the question whether, in the situation prescribed, it is necessary to choose as the connecting factor the place of the event giving rise to the damage, or the place where the harmful event or the place where the damage occurred, or to accept that the plaintiff has an option between the one or the other of the two options . . .

The Court then chose the last option, which was motivated *inter alia* as follows:

> (17) Taking into account the close connexion between the component parts of every sort of liability, it does not appear appropriate to opt for one of the two connecting factors mentioned to the exclusion of the other, since each of them can, depending on the circumstances, be particularly helpful from the point of view of the evidence and of the conduct of proceedings. . . . (19) Thus the meaning of the expression 'place where the harmful event occurred' in Article 5 (3) must be established in such a way as to acknowledge that the plaintiff has an option to com-

---

8 ECJ Case 21/76, *Bier v. Mines de Potasse d'Alsace*, [1976] ECR 1735.

mence proceedings either at the place where the damage occurred or the place of the event giving rise to it. (20) This conclusion is supported by the consideration ... that to decide in favour only of the place of the event giving rise to the damage would, in an appreciable number of cases, cause confusion between the heads of jurisdiction laid down by Articles 2 and 5 (3) of the Convention, so that the latter provision would, to that extent, lose its effectiveness.

That having been settled, two issues remained to be clarified with regard to cases when the results of the harmful event are 'dispersed' in the sense that they occur simultaneously in several countries rather than in one single Member State. First, it is of interest with regard to such situations whether claims can be brought in *all* the Member States where part of the damage occurs, and second, whether a forum exists (in addition to the courts in the infringer's country of domicile) where the damages can be awarded *in their entirety*.

The leading decision on those issues, *Shevill*,[9] concerned a case of libel. The plaintiff, Miss Fiona Shevill, claimed that she had suffered injury by a French press report insinuating that she had been involved in money-laundering while she was employed by a French bank. A number of copies of the magazine in which the report appeared had been delivered to the UK, where she was currently domiciled. In a lawsuit filed by her against the publisher of the magazine, the question arose and was referred to the ECJ whether British courts had jurisdiction over the claim, and if so, whether it was possible for Miss Shevill to seek redress for the alleged tort in its entirety. The ECJ declared that:

> (32) ... [t]he plaintiff always has the option of bringing his entire claim before the courts *either* of the defendant's domicile *or* of the place where the publisher of the defamatory publication is established. (Emphasis added)

Apart from that, a choice is granted between the courts having competence to decide on remedies for the claim in its entirety, and courts with territorially limited competence:

> (33) [T]he victim of a libel by a newspaper article distributed in several Contracting States may bring an action for damages against the publisher either before the courts of the Contracting State of the place where the publisher of the defamatory publication is established, which have jurisdiction to award damages

---

9 ECJ Case C-68/93, *Fiona Shevill v. Presse Alliance*, [1995] ECR I-415.

for all the harm caused by the defamation, or before the courts of each Contracting State in which the publication was distributed and where the victim claims to have suffered injury to his reputation, which have jurisdiction to rule solely in respect of the harm caused in the State of the court seised.

By allowing the claim of remedies for a tort in its entirety at the defendant's place of domicile *or* at the place of publication (in addition to claiming territorially limited damages in each country where the publication is distributed), *Shevill* has somewhat enlarged the options available for the victim of defamation to engage in 'forum shopping'. However, in practice the places of publication and of the defendant's domicile will often coincide, so that the enlargement of options remains rather theoretical.

A more robust step towards promoting the victim's interests was taken with regard to infringements of personality rights occurring on the internet: in Joined Cases *eDate* and *Martinez*[10] the ECJ held that in view of ubiquity of communication over the internet, and also regarding the specific vulnerability of natural persons against the wide distribution of content attacking their integrity, it should also be possible to establish a venue for claiming the entire damage at the place where the injured party's centre of interest lies.[11] In practice this means that consolidated claims for infringement of personality rights occurring on the internet can regularly be brought at the *plaintiff's* place of domicile.

Application of Article 5 (3) in case of IP infringement on the internet
Whereas identifying the place where intellectual property rights are infringed is not difficult as long as the making, selling and uses made of physical items or use by analogue means are concerned, the issue becomes problematic when infringing goods are offered, or use is made of protected content, on the internet or through other ubiquitous media. To determine whether such use infringes intellectual property rights existing in the state where the messages are received is primarily a task for substantive law.[12] However, it is also closely linked with the question of whether courts should establish or decline jurisdiction in such cases. A certain dilemma is presented by the fact that on the one hand, right-holders have an interest in bringing proceedings for damages or injunctions regarding the infringement in its entirety not only

---

10 ECJ Joined Cases C-509/09 and C-161/10, *eDate* v. *X* and C 161/10, *Martinez* v. *MGN*, [2011] ECR I-0000.
11 Ibid., Paragraph 48.
12 The following remarks only concern Article 5 (3), meaning that they solely address *jurisdiction* in case of ubiquitous infringement. For a discussion of the equally problematic issues of determining the applicable law see this chapter, section 9.4.

at the defendant's place of domicile, but at any (other) venue which may be convenient to them. On the other hand, if jurisdiction can be established in any country where content is technically accessible, this results in a high risk for persons using trade marks or other potentially protected content on the internet without being aware that they may be infringing another person's IP right. The topic is widely debated in the literature and on the international level. Without a harmonised solution having been anchored in any binding text, the discussions basically reflect general agreement on the fact that communication over the internet should not automatically lead to infringement wherever it can be received, but only where it has a certain effect in the territory where the allegedly infringed content is, or can be accessed (see also this chapter, section 9.4).

In line with those considerations, courts in some EU Member States tend to decline jurisdiction where the allegedly infringing conduct does not appear to have a commercial effect in the forum state, whereas others are more generous in accepting jurisdiction, and consider the presence and degree of commercial effect only at the subsequent stage when the merits of the case are considered. The issue was addressed in passing in *eDate* and *Martinez*,[13] where the ECJ stated that (in case of infringement of personality rights) jurisdiction under Article 5 (3) is conferred on the 'courts in each Member State in the territory of which content placed online *is or has been accessible*'. (Emphasis added)[14]

Understood literally, this appears to mean that jurisdiction under Article 5 (3) is vested in the courts of any country in the EU where content is or has been *technically* accessible, with no attention being paid to the potential effect on commerce.[15]

However, with *eDate* and *Martinez* only being concerned with infringement of personality rights, the situation regarding IP remained unclear. More clarification was expected from *Wintersteiger*,[16] which concerned a dispute about trade mark infringement allegedly caused by the use of 'adwords'. The Austrian Supreme Court had asked whether the infringement occurs, in the meaning of Article 5 (3), only in the state indicated by the top level domain of the search engine where the advertisements triggered by the adword are

---

13 ECJ Joined Cases C-509/09 and C-161/10, *eDate* v. *X* and *Martinez* v. *MGN*, [2011] ECR I-0000.

14 Ibid., Paragraph 51.

15 That understanding seems to have been excluded by Advocate General Cruz Villalón's opinion of 16 February 2012 in *Wintersteiger*; however, the decision of the ECJ is less clear in that regard; see the text below.

16 ECJ Case C-523/10, *Wintersteiger* v. *Products 4U*, [2012] ECR I-0000.

shown (in the concrete case: '.de'), or also in other states from which the services of the search engine can be used, and if so, whether and which additional factors must be taken into account for the decision.

The ECJ took the opportunity to clarify that, due to the principle of territoriality that distinguishes intellectual property from personality rights, *eDate* and *Martinez* does *not* apply insofar as the additional venue at the place of the alleged victim's centre of interest is concerned.[17] Apart from that, it is only stated that in the case at stake, jurisdiction under Article 5 (3) can be established both at the place where the allegedly infringed right is registered (in Austria)[18] and at the place where the advertiser is established (Germany), the main argument being that this is a 'definite and identifiable place', and that the decision to activate the display process, and hence the action eventually leading to the harm occurring in Austria, was taken there.[19] No further comment is offered with regard to the specific requirements for establishing jurisdiction in case of internet infringement.[20] The question of how to determine the place where the harmful event occurs in case of internet infringement was therefore referred again to the ECJ in *Pinckney*, this time concerning copyright-infringing content offered online.[21] As the case is still pending at the time of printing, no conclusion can be drawn so far.

Negative declaratory actions

An issue which was not decided until recently concerns the question of whether Article 5 (3) provides a venue for negative declaratory actions. Such actions are frequently filed by persons who are confronted with a warning letter by the holder of an allegedly infringed intellectual property right; in order to defend themselves proactively, such persons may bring suit against the right-holder, seeking a declaration that the contested conduct is non-infringing. Such actions may become relevant in the context of so-called torpedo litigation, which is considered below. Regarding judicial competence, a problem arises from the fact that a strict reading of Article 5 (3) appears to render the provision inapplicable, because unlike what is set out

---

17 Ibid., Paragraph 24.
18 Ibid., Paragraph 29.
19 Ibid., Paragraphs 37, 38.
20 In contrast to the remarkable silence observed by the ECJ, Advocate General Cruz Villalón declared in his opinion of 16.02.2012 (without mentioning the ECJ's dictum in *eDate*) that mere accessibility of content is not sufficient to establish jurisdiction, but that there must be a certain, sizeable effect in the territory where the message is received.
21 ECJ Case C-170/12, *Pieter Pinckney v. KDG mediatech AG* (pending).

in Article 5 (3), it is regularly asserted in negative declaratory actions that *no* harmful event occurs or may occur in the respective state.

Clarification on this point was brought by the ECJ in a pending case concerning claims for non-violation of antitrust law, which was referred for a preliminary decision by the German Federal Supreme Court.[22] The Court held that the wording of Article 5(3) does not exclude that claims for declaration of non-infringement are brought in the same venue as claims for positive remedies.

? **QUESTIONS**

1 In the case *Bier* v. *Mines de Potasse d'Alsace*, the ECJ stated that at least as a theoretical option, Article 5 (3) might restrict jurisdiction in disputes falling under the provision to either the courts at the place where the event giving rise to the damage, or the damage itself, occurred. Does that distinction make sense at all with regard to intellectual property infringements (try to think of practical examples)?

2 In *Wintersteiger*, the ECJ declared that the option granted in eDate and Martinez to claim remedies for the infringement of personality rights in their entirety at the place of the victim's centre of interest in case of torts committed over the internet is not applicable in regards of IP infringement. Do you agree? Try to find arguments in favour of, and against a parallel being drawn in this regard! What are the commonalities and the differences between infringements of personal rights on the one hand and intellectual property infringements on the other?

3 Which criteria should, in your opinion, determine whether a court has jurisdiction over content placed on the internet? For your considerations, please consult the WIPO Joint Recommendation concerning provisions on the protection of marks, and other industrial property rights in signs, on the internet, at http://www.wipo.int/about-http://www.wipo.int/about-ip/en/development_iplaw/pub845.htm.

Article 6 (1): multiple defendants

Prerequisites; existence of a close connection

Where several defendants are joined in a claim, suit may be filed against them in the courts of the state where one of them is domiciled, provided that the claims are so closely connected that it is expedient to hear and determine

---

22 ECJ Case C-133/11, *Folien Fischer* v. *Ritrama* (ECR [2012] I-0000).

them together to avoid the risk of irreconcilable judgments resulting from separate proceedings (Article 6 (1) Brussels I).

The corresponding provision in the Brussels Convention did not contain the qualification of a 'close connection' having to exist between the claims. Instead, the requirement was first established by case law.[23] Pointing out that Article 6 (1) constitutes an exception from the general rule that proceedings are to be brought in the courts of the defendant's country of domicile, the ECJ concluded that the provision must be interpreted narrowly, so as not to call in question the very existence of that fundamental principle.[24] And the Court continued:

> (9) That possibility might arise if a plaintiff were at liberty to make a claim against a number of defendants with the sole object of ousting the jurisdiction of the courts of the State where one of the defendants is domiciled . . . For that purpose, there must be a connection between the claims made against each of the defendants.

In the course of transposition of the Brussels Convention into the Brussels I Regulation, the requirement was spelled out expressly in the provision, and it was further specified that the connection between the claims must be such that litigation in different courts would evoke the risk that the resulting judgments are 'irreconcilable'.[25]

ECJ case law

The conditions for applying Article 6 (1) in cases regarding parallel patent infringements occurring in several Member States were addressed by the ECJ in a dispute involving as defendants the Dutch head office and several affiliates of the pharmaceutical company Roche. The plaintiffs, domiciled in the USA, held patents in seven European countries (EU Member States and Switzerland), which they claimed to be infringed by concerted actions committed by Roche and its affiliates. The question referred to the ECJ sought to establish whether the infringement claims against all defendants could be consolidated in the Netherlands.[26]

---

23 ECJ Case C-189/87, *Anastasios Kalfelis v. Bankhaus Schröder, Hengstmeier, Münch & Co*, [1988] ECR 5565.
24 Ibid., Paragraph 8.
25 Appeal Court The Hague, *Expandable Grafts v. Boston Scientific*, decision of 23 April 1998 Nr. 97/1296.
26 ECJ Case C-539/03, *Roche Nederland v. Primus and Goldenberg*, [2006] ECR 6535.

Elaborating on the notion of 'irreconcilable judgments' in Article 6 (1), the ECJ specified that such a risk only exists if the divergence resulting from separate litigation arises 'in the context of the same situation of law and fact' (paragraph 26). With regard to the situation at stake, i.e. European patent infringement proceedings involving a number of companies established in various Contracting States, each acting in one or more of those states, it is found that the judgments rendered would in any case not be irreconcilable in that sense, because:

> (29) . . . although the [EPC] lays down common rules on the grant of European patents, it is clear from Articles 2 (2) and 64 (1) of that convention that such a patent continues to be governed by the national law of each of the Contracting States for which it has been granted. . . . (31) It follows that, where infringement proceedings are brought before a number of courts in different Contracting States in respect of a European patent granted in each of those States, against defendants domiciled in those States in respect of acts allegedly committed in their territory, any divergences between the decisions given by the courts concerned would not arise in the context of the same legal situation.

A somewhat different opinion was endorsed in *Painer*.[27] The dispute concerned the unauthorised publication in several newspapers and magazines of a photograph taken by the plaintiff. The publisher of one of the papers sued is established in Austria, whereas the other defendants are seated in Germany. The plaintiff filed suit against all of them in Austria, joining the German defendants in the claim. The German defendants objected, and the issue was referred to the ECJ. Concerning the application of Article 6 (1), it was held that:

> (79) . . . the Court has stated that, in order for judgments to be regarded as irreconcilable within the meaning of Article 6 (1) . . ., it is not sufficient that there be a divergence in the outcome of the dispute, but that divergence must also arise in the same situation of fact and law. (80) However, in assessing whether there is a connection between different claims, that is to say a risk of irreconcilable judgments . . . the identical legal bases of the actions brought is only one relevant factor among others. It is *not an indispensable requirement* for the application of Article 6 (1) . . . (81) Thus, a difference in legal basis between the actions brought against the various defendants, does not, in itself, preclude the application of Article 6 (1) of Regulation No 44/2001, provided however that it was foreseeable by the defendants that they might be sued in the Member State where at least one of

---

27 ECJ Case C-145/10, *Painer v. Standard VerlagsGmbH and Others*, [2011] ECR I-0000.

them is domiciled. (82) That reasoning is stronger if, as in the main proceedings, the national laws on which the actions against the various defendants are based are, in the referring court's view, substantially identical. (Emphasis added; citations omitted[28])

The ECJ has further distanced itself from a strict reading of *Roche* by holding in *Solvay v. Honeywell* that irrespective of the fact that multistate infringement proceedings regarding European bundle patents involve different national laws, a risk for irreconcilable judgments and hence a reason for applying Article 6 (1) may exist in the situation at stake in the actual dispute, which concerned the infringement of parallel patents by several defendants.[29] Different from *Roche*, the defendants are claimed to have acted together with regard to each of the infringements occurring in the Member States involved, i.e. they have not acted separately in the Member State where they are domiciled.

 QUESTIONS

1 From your knowledge (Chapter 3) of the EPC and how it impacts the legal assessment of infringements of European bundle patents, granted for several Contracting States, do you find the reasoning by the ECJ convincing, that there is no risk that the outcome of lawsuits involving concerted actions allegedly violating bundle patents in several Member States might be 'contradictory'?

2 How is the situation in *Painer* distinguished from Roche? Are the findings consistent?

Exclusive jurisdiction: the limits of cross-border litigation

General rule and exception: the relationship between Article 2 and Article 22 (4)

As Article 2 allows bringing any claims against a defendant in the courts of the Member State where he or she is domiciled, the provision appears to offer a secure basis for adjudication of claims concerning infringement of intellectual property rights occurring abroad, and for granting remedies against such infringements in the form of cross-border injunctions or (aggregated) damages. That potential of Article 2 was realised rather late in practice: the first case was brought in the Netherlands twenty years after the Brussels

---

28 Quite remarkably, there is no reference at all to Roche in the entire Painer judgment; reference is only (and frequently) made to ECJ Case C-98/06, *Freeport v. Arnoldsson*, [2007] ECR I-8340, which concerns contractual matters.

29 ECJ Case C-616/10, *Solvay v. Honeywell*, [2012] ECJ I-0000.

Convention had been concluded. Thereafter, consolidation of infringement proceedings in the state of the defendant's domicile (or, in case of multiple defendants being involved, in the State where one of the defendants is domiciled, see above) became primarily relevant in patent infringement cases. In particular in the Netherlands and in Germany, cross-border injunctions in patent infringement cases were generally accepted by the courts as constituting a viable option for the plaintiff, if the defendant was domiciled in the forum state.

In other countries, in particular in the UK, the notion of cross-border injunctions involving patents and other registered rights was firmly rejected. It was pointed out that general jurisdiction of the courts in the defendant's place of domicile only prevails if no other court has exclusive competence pursuant to Article 22 (4) Brussels I Regulation (previously: Article 16 (4) Brussels Convention). Under that provision, exclusive jurisdiction:

> in proceedings concerned with the registration or validity of patents, trade marks, designs, or other similar rights required to be deposited or registered, [is vested in] the courts of the Member State in which the deposit or registration has been applied for, has taken place or is under the terms of a Community instrument or an international convention deemed to have taken place.

As proceedings dealing with the infringement of patents regularly involve a judgment on validity – either implicitly, when validity is taken for granted, or by explicit reasoning, when the defendant raises invalidity of the patent as a plea in objection – the argument was made that courts other than those located in the state of registration were barred from adjudicating upon infringement claims relating to foreign patents and other registered rights.

Against that, proponents of the option to file claims for cross-border injunctions raised the counterargument that according to established case law, the general rule embedded in Article 2 reflects a fundamental principle that must prevail over all exceptions from that rule, so that, as a consequence, exceptions such as those enshrined in Article 22 (4) must be interpreted narrowly. That principle had indeed been confirmed by the ECJ in a case concerning the entitlement of a former employee of an insolvent firm to keep the patents that had been registered in his name (*Duijnstee*[30]). Having been asked whether the courts in the country of registration had exclusive competence, the ECJ responded that:

---

30 ECJ Case C-288/82, *Duijnstee* v. *Goderbauer*, [1983] ECR 3663; see also C-144/10, *BVG* v. *JP Morgan Chase Bank*, [2011] ECR I-0000.

(25) [i]f... the dispute does not itself concern the validity of the patent or the existence of the deposit or registration, there is no special reason to confer exclusive jurisdiction on the courts of the Contracting State in which the patent was applied for or granted, and consequently such a dispute is not covered by Article 16 (4).

Invalidity as an incidental issue: GAT v. LuK

Based on the concept that Article 16 (4) Brussels Convention (now Article 22 (4) Brussels I Regulation) must be interpreted narrowly and only applies where the proceedings would directly affect the registration or validity of the right, German courts regularly affirmed their jurisdiction in patent infringement cases, even if the defendant invoked invalidity of the right as a defense. As a further detail, it must be noted in this context that the English and the German (as well as the French, Italian and Dutch) versions of the Brussels Convention were not congruent: whereas in the original text of the Convention dating from 1968, Article 16 (4) referred, in the languages of all Contracting States, to proceedings 'which *have as their object*' the registration or validity of a registered right, the English text which was promulgated when the UK joined the EEC in 1973 refers to 'proceedings *concerned with*' registration or validity. The original wording found in the 1968 text appeared to underpin the restrictive attitude reflected in *Duijnstee* (above), and to confer exclusive jurisdiction on courts in the State of registration only where invalidity or registration are the object of the principal claim, with the effect that the decision would become effective as against third parties (*erga omnes*).

In view of the pronounced diversities existing in the court practice of different Member States regarding adjudication of invalidity as an incidental matter, the Dusseldorf Court of Appeal referred the issue to the ECJ. The case concerned a dispute between two German companies over the alleged infringement of a French patent. The plaintiff had filed a claim for declaration of non-infringement against the defendant, arguing that the defendant's patent was invalid.

In its decision of 13 July 2006[31] the ECJ first declared that the divergences in the different language versions of the provision were without relevance for the decision. Instead of embarking on a similarly narrow interpretation as in *Duijnstee*, the Court then pointed out that:

---

31 ECJ Case C-4/03, *GAT v. LuK*, [2006] ECR I-6509.

(22) ... [t]he courts of the Contracting State on whose territory the registers are kept may rule, applying their own national law, on the validity and effects of the patents which have been issued in that State. This concern for the sound administration of justice becomes all the more important in the field of patents since, given the specialised nature of this area, a number of Contracting States have set up a system of specific judicial protection, to ensure that these types of cases are dealt with by specialised courts. (23) That exclusive jurisdiction is also justified by the fact that the issue of patents necessitates the involvement of the national administrative authorities ...

As a result, the ECJ contends that exclusive jurisdiction applies whenever validity issues are brought up in the proceedings, whether by principal claim or as an incidental matter.

Consequences

The *GAT* v. *LuK* judgment has drawn nearly unanimous critique in the literature. However, as long as it remains to be the only authoritative statement addressing the issue, the findings constitute a mandatory guideline for judicial practice. One practically relevant issue arising in this situation is to know how a court must react when it is seized with infringement proceedings concerning a patent (or a trade mark or design right) which is registered abroad, and the defendant raises the invalidity defense in the course of the proceedings.

The most radical consequence to be drawn from *GAT* v. *LuK* would be to decline any infringement jurisdiction over foreign registered intellectual property rights, as the possibility always exists that the defense is raised, rendering another court exclusively competent. On the other hand, as was pointed out in *Owusu*, a court cannot deny its competence under Article 2 in favour of another court which it deems better placed to decide the case. Hence, the only possible result appears to be that courts which are fully competent to decide an infringement claim at the time when the proceedings are brought lose that competence subsequently, when the validity defense is raised. That, however, clashes with the principle of *perpetuatio fori* (perpetuation of forum), which is otherwise considered to form an important feature of international procedural law: once a court has validly established its jurisdiction, this will not be changed by subsequent events, e.g. by the defendant moving his/her domicile into another country.

A third possibility would be to allow a court first seized with an infringement claim to stay the proceedings until the validity issue has been decided by the competent court in the country of registration. That solution was chosen in a decision by the Zurich Commercial Court in the aftermath of *GAT* v. *LuK*. The invalidity defense was raised in a lawsuit filed against a Swiss resident for infringement of a Community trade mark. The court granted the defendant a period of six weeks within which to file invalidation proceedings at the OHIM, indicating that in case of failure to act within that period, the proceedings would be resumed and the defense ignored.[32]

Reform proposals

The results of *GAT* v. *LuK* and their repercussions for cross-border infringement proceedings in the EU are also under debate in the current efforts to reform the Brussels I Regulation. According to the Commission's proposal,[33] the restrictive approach adopted by the ECJ shall be expressly anchored in the wording of Article 22 (4), by inserting the phrase 'irrespective of whether the issue is raised by way of an action or as a defence'. The same changes were already introduced into the Lugano Convention when it was amended in 2007.

Quite to the opposite, proposals have been made to change Article 22 (4) in a manner which would provide for a better chance to consolidate infringement proceedings before one single competent court and thereby facilitate the enforcement of intellectual property rights in Europe. According to the International Max Planck Group on Conflict of Laws in Intellectual Property (CLIP), a strict implementation of *GAT* v. *LuK* in the legal provision would have serious detrimental effects, because it would encumber the efficient enforcement of patent rights in Europe.[34] It is therefore proposed to insert into Article 22 (4) a subparagraph stating that exclusive jurisdiction does not apply:

> where validity or registration arises in a context other than by principal claim or counterclaim. The decisions resulting from such proceedings do not affect the validity or registration of those rights as against third parties.[35]

---

32 Commercial Court (Handelsgericht) Zurich, judgment of 23 October 2006, HG 050410, *Eurojobs Personaldienstleistungen SA* v. *Eurojob AG*, [sic!] 2006, 854; confirmed by the Swiss Federal Court, judgment of 4 April 2007, I. Zivilabteilung 4C.439/2006). The conditions under which a court seized with cross-border infringement claims must decline jurisdiction, or may stay the proceedings in favour of another court adjudicating on validity was also among those referred to the ECJ in Case C-616/10 – *Solvay* v. *Honeywell*. However, the ECJ did not address the matter, as it was held that Article 22 (4) is not applicable in the actual dispute which had been brought in the form of specific summary proceedings available under Dutch law (so-called *kort geding*); see also below, on Article 31.
33 COM (2010) 748 final.
34 See the critical comments at http://www.cl-ip.eu/files/pdf2/clip_brussels_i_dec_06_final4.pdf.
35 The CLIP proposal is available at www.cl-ip.eu/files/pdf2/Final_Text_1_December_2011.pdf. The provision quoted above forms part of Article 2:401 of the CLIP proposal.

The CLIP proposal was endorsed, albeit as only one among several alternatives, in a Report conducted on behalf of the Commission on the functioning of the Brussels Regulation by a number of academic experts.[36] As another alternative, it was proposed:

> (822) . . . to vest the courts seised with infringement proceedings with proper power to monitor the interdependence of infringement proceedings and proceedings aimed at the declaration of invalidity of intellectual property rights. . . .In substance the idea is the following: The court seised with infringement proceedings must not take into account objections based on invalidity attacks which in the court's mind have little prospect of success. Should they have substantial prospect of success the court may suspend its proceedings for a limited period of time for the defendant to obtain a judgment on the invalidity issue . . . (823) The proposal that the infringement proceedings will be reopened should the defendant not institute invalidation proceedings within the deadline fixed by the court, corresponds to the solution found by the *Handelsgericht Zürich* under the Judgment Convention [see above].

On the other hand, if – and provided that – the unitary patent system is finally established including the creation of the Unified Patent Court, the problems will be solved in practice at least inasfar as unitary patents as well as European patents validated in the EU Member States participating in the system are concerned.

Unregistered rights (copyright)

Article 22 (4) only applies to 'patents, trade marks, designs, or other similar rights required to be deposited or registered'. Hence it does not apply to copyright, unregistered design rights or unregistered trade marks (where available under national law), meaning that infringement proceedings can be brought, without any restrictions, at the defendant's place of domicile. That was even accepted in the UK, where traditionally, adjudication of claims for infringement of foreign intellectual property rights was not found acceptable. In a lawsuit concerning the alleged breach of copyright in an architectural work which had been copied in the Netherlands (*inter alia*) by a British resident.[37]

A different result was endorsed by the Appeal Court in a lawsuit between Lucasfilm and Mr Ainsworth. The dispute concerned the making and selling

---

36 Report on the application of Regulation Brussels I (Hess Report), ec.europa.eu/civiljustice/news/docs/study_application_brussels_1_en.pdf.
37 High Court, Chancery Division, *Pearce v. Ove Arup Partnership*, [2001] EWHC Ch B9.

copies, as merchandising articles, of the 'Stormtrooper helmet' known from the 'Star Wars' film series. A prototype of that helmet had been made, but was not designed, by Mr Ainsworth.[38] In addition to the (unsuccessful) claim for violation of copyright under UK law, Lucasfilm also sought to establish claims for infringement of the copyright pertaining to the helmet in the USA, where a few articles had been sold. The claim was rejected on the argument that, under established rules of procedural law applying in the UK, English courts had no jurisdiction over foreign intellectual property rights. It was further held that the result was not changed by the Brussels Regulation, as according to the judge, it did not imply rules on 'extra-EU jurisdiction'.[39]

The decision was reversed by the UK Supreme Court,[40] *inter alia* for the following reasons:

> (105) We have come to the firm conclusion that, in the case of a claim for infringement of copyright of the present kind, the claim is one over which the English court has jurisdiction, provided that there is a basis for in personam jurisdiction over the defendant, or, to put it differently, the claim is justiciable . . . (107) There is no doubt that the modern trend is in favour of the enforcement of foreign intellectual property rights. First, Article 22 (4) of the Brussels I Regulation only assigns exclusive jurisdiction to the country where the right originates in cases which are concerned with registration or validity of rights which are 'required to be deposited or registered' and does not apply to infringement actions in which there is no issue as to validity. This can rarely, if ever, apply to copyright. Second, the Rome II Regulation [on the law applicable to non-contractual obligations] also plainly envisages the litigation of foreign intellectual property rights and, third, the professional and academic bodies which have considered the issue, the American Law Institute and the Max Planck Institute, clearly favour them, at any rate where issues of validity are not engaged. (109) There are no issues of policy which militate against the enforcement of foreign copyright . . .

Remarkably, however, the Supreme Court came to its conclusions by referring to doctrines and precedents established under English law, and avoided taking a position on the question whether Article 2 of the Brussels I Regulation leaves a choice at all for a different result to be reached.

---

38 On the design aspects of the dispute see Chapter 6, section 6.4.3.1.2.
39 Court of Appeal (Jacob LJ), *Lucasfilm v. Ainsworth*, [2009] EWCA Civ 1328.
40 UK Supreme Court, [2011] UKSC 39.

? **QUESTIONS**

1 One central argument of the ECJ in *GAT* v. *LuK* has been that the courts in the state where the patent is registered are 'best placed' to adjudicate the infringement. Please compare that argument with the choice of court regularly granted to a plaintiff between general jurisdiction under Article 2 and special jurisdiction under Article 5 (3).

2 What are the commonalities between e.g. a tort committed through damage done to a person's property abroad, and a patent (or trade mark) infringement? What are the differences? Do you agree with the ECJ's finding that it makes no difference whether the text of Article 22 (4) refers to 'proceedings having as their object' and 'proceedings concerned with'?

3 How can *GAT* v. *LuK* be distinguished from *Duijnstee* v. *Goderbauer*? Or are the two judgments irreconcilable? Consider also C-144/10, *BVG* v. *JP Morgan Chase Bank*, [2011] ECR I-0000.

4 Why does the Brussels Regulation impose no restrictions with regard to proceedings concerned with the validity of unregistered rights?

Torpedoes

Where courts in different Member States are seized with proceedings involving the same subject-matter and pending between the same parties, the court second seized must stay the proceedings until the court first seized decides on its jurisdiction, and, if jurisdiction has been established, jurisdiction of the court second seized must be declined (Article 27).

It is generally accepted that the objective underlying that rule is sound, as it enhances the predictability of jurisdiction. However, the provision may also be misused so as to sabotage an efficient enforcement. The issue has become topical in patent litigation, where it gave rise to the phenomenon commonly referred to as 'torpedo'. In the Hess Report evaluating the application of the Brussels I Regulation,[41] the problem is described as follows:

> (804) The tactical device, called 'torpedo action', is in essence the following: The alleged infringer of an intellectual property right himself sues the alleged victim requesting a negative declaration either of noninfringement or, even, of the patent's invalidity. Since, under the Court of Justice's rulings, the objective of a request for negative declaration is the same as of an action for damages or for

---

41 Report on the application of Regulation Brussels I (Hess Report), ec.europa.eu/civiljustice/news/docs/study_application_brussels_1_en.pdf.

refraining from continuing the incriminated activity[42] the consequent infringement proceedings are stayed under Article 27 [Brussels I Regulation]. The
torpedo action aims just at this effect. The risk that finally the torpedo action will
fail is well calculated, because it is more than outweighed by the time to be gained.
Indeed, in intellectual property matters, time gained is of a much higher value than
in other kinds of litigation. Therefore, torpedo claims are sometimes deliberately
instituted in jurisdiction known for their time-consuming proceedings. Hence, the
term 'Italian' or 'Belgian' torpedo. The device is successful even if it is quite evident
that the court seised is lacking jurisdiction.

The Report then reviews case law in the EU dealing with torpedo actions,
and notes that:

> (807) Some courts did their best to overcome such an abuse. The *Rechtsbank
> Den Haag* (DSM./.NOVO *Nordisk*, IER 2000, 39) the *Landgericht Düsseldorf*
> (12/19/2002, InstGE 3, 8) and the *Tribunal de Grande Instance Paris (Schaerer,
> Schweiter./.Fadis*, IIC 2002, 325).997 as well as the *Tribunal de Bruxelles* (GRUR
> Int 2001, 170 – *Röhm-Enzyme*) stated directly that they deliberately disregarded
> abusive torpedo actions. . . The Italian *Corte di Cassazzione* made the point that
> in infringement proceedings instituted on the basis of Article 5 (3) JR and nega-
> tive declaration or annulment proceedings have distinct objects (*BL Machine
> Automatiche Windmöller./.Hölscher*, No. 19550, GRUR Int 2005, 264). The
> *Tribunal de grande instance* of Paris (04/28/2001, GRUR Int 2001, 173) had
> adopted the same view. It is reported that the English courts disregarded an
> Italian torpedo where the Italian court was lacking jurisdiction. (808) All these
> approaches, however, do not comply with the case law of the Court of Justice . . .

No ECJ decision so far has addressed the issue directly. However, as is
also noted in the Report, it seems rather unlikely that the ECJ would look
favourably on attempts made by national courts to disregard Article 27 and
assume jurisdiction on the ground that they consider the filing of a declaratory action in the court of another Member State as abusive or vexatious.
This was affirmed at least indirectly in a case concerning an 'anti-suit injunction' filed with the High Court in London:[43] the plaintiff, a British resident,
sought to prohibit a group of firms by whom he had been formerly employed
from filing suit against him in Spain. According to the plaintiff, with whom
the English court agreed, the Spanish courts had no competence to hear the
claim, and instigating proceedings in Spain therefore amounted to mere harassment. However, the ECJ pointed out that:

---

42 ECJ Case C-144/86, *Gubisch v. Palumbo*, [1987] ECR 4861.
43 ECJ Case C-159/02, *Turner v. Grovit*, [2004] ECR I-3565.

(28) [the interference resulting from an anti-suit injunction] cannot be justified by the fact that it is . . . intended to prevent an abuse of process by the defendant in the proceedings in the forum State. In so far as the conduct for which the defendant is criticised consists in recourse to the jurisdiction of the court of another Member State, the judgment made as to the abusive nature of that conduct implies an assessment of the appropriateness of bringing proceedings before a court of another Member State. Such an assessment runs counter to the principle of mutual trust . . .

As the current wording and structure of the Brussels I Regulation do not appear to yield efficient remedies against torpedo litigation, the topic is also among those debated in the framework of the pending Brussels I reform. According to the Commission's 2012 proposal the court first seized must establish its jurisdiction within six months, unless exceptional circumstances make this impossible. The latter alternative is reflected in the Commission proposal of 2010:[44] the draft provision contains an obligation for the court first seized to establish its jurisdiction within six months, unless exceptional circumstances make this impossible. However, the legal consequences ensuing from failure to meet the deadline are not specified.

? QUESTIONS

1 It has been argued that the *GAT* v. *LuK* decision for all its problematic aspects at least provides an efficient way to 'dismantle' torpedo litigation. Do you agree?
2 One possibility to overcome the torpedo problem would be to give claims for positive remedies precedence over negative declaratory actions. That option was discussed, but ultimately rejected in the course of transposition of the Brussels Convention into the Brussels I Regulation. What is your opinion about the option?

Provisional and protective measures

Article 31 contains a dispensation from the obligation to observe the Brussels I jurisdiction provisions when an application is filed for provisional, including protective measures: such measures can be issued by the court seized even if the courts in another Member State are competent to adjudicate on the substance of the claims. This raises the question of whether Article 31 grants a basis for issuing cross-border injunctions for which no competence could be established if the claims were filed in main proceedings.

---

44 COM(2010) 748 final.

As a matter of principle, it is held by majority opinion that the only require-ment for a court to assume jurisdiction on the basis of Article 31 is that such competence exists under national law. Although the scope of jurisdic-tion with regard to provisional and protective measures may therefore be rather broad, it must be noted that according to established ECJ case law, such measures cannot be enforced abroad if they were issued *ex parte*, i.e. without the defendant being heard.[45] Therefore, unless the adverse party appears in court to answer the claim (and thereby accepts jurisdiction pur-suant to Article 24), the effects of cross-border injunctions issued on the basis of Article 31 are rather limited. In the context of the pending reform of the Brussels I Regulation, it is therefore debated whether provision should be made for granting, under certain circumstances, extraterritorial effect to *ex parte* measures issued by a court whose competence is merely based on Article 31.

In *Solvay v. Honeywell*, the ECJ further confirmed that as long as measures sought under Article 31 are of a preliminary character and do not purport to a full examination of the merits, Article 22 (4) does not take precedence.[46] The issue is of particular relevance for lawsuits filed in the Netherlands, as the particular kind of summary proceedings (*kort geding*) available under Dutch procedural law is frequently employed and has acquired a certain reputation for offering a speedy and relatively 'cheap' way to obtain a deci-sion in patent litigation, which, in most cases, even settles the dispute for good. Hence, a defendant may be inclined to appear and answer the claim in court, thereby accepting jurisdiction (prorogation by appearance, Article 24).

? QUESTIONS

1 What is your opinion about the proposals made to allow enforcement abroad of preliminary injunctions and other provisional measures which have been handed down in ex parte proceedings? Is there a practical need for cross-border enforcement of such measures? Try to think of practical examples.

2 In your opinion, what could be the reason why it is possible under Article 31 to apply for provisional and preliminary measures in other courts than those which are competent to adjudicate on the merits?

---

45 ECJ Case 125/79, *Denilauler v. SNC Couchet Frères*, [1980] ECR 1553.
46 ECJ Case C-616/10, *Solvay v. Honeywell*, Paragraphs 49 to 51.

Specific regulations concerning IP litigation

Community trade marks and Community designs

The Community Trade Mark Regulation (CTMR) and Community Design Regulation (CDR) each contain specific provisions on jurisdiction and procedures in legal actions concerning CTMs and CDs. The rules are congruent in their contents; references made in the following to the CTMR therefore apply, *mutatis mutandis*, to the CDR.

Pursuant to Article 95 CTMR, Member States must designate a number 'as limited as possible' of national courts that shall serve as Community trade mark courts (likewise: Community design courts). A list of those courts can be found on the website of the OHIM.[47] Whereas most Member States have designated only one Community trade mark court for each instance, others have designated several (Germany: 16!) such courts.[48]

The Community trade mark courts have exclusive competence for actions seeking to establish the infringement and, if permitted under national law, the threatened infringement or a declaration of non-infringement, of a CTM; furthermore, they are also exclusively competent to hear counterclaims for invalidity or revocation raised in defense to an infringement action (Article 96).

Regarding the scope of jurisdiction exercised by Community trade mark courts, a distinction applies between courts of central and restricted competence. Central competence is vested in the courts located in the Member State of the defendant's domicile, or, if the defendant is not domiciled in the EU, where he has a business establishment; if he has none of those, the courts in the Member State of the plaintiff's domicile – or, if he is not domiciled in the EU, where he has his business establishment – have central competence. If neither party is domiciled or has a business establishment in the EU, central competence is vested in the courts of the State where the Office has its seat, i.e. in Spain (Article 97 (1)–(3) in conjunction with Article 98 (1)). Central competence of the Community trade mark courts in any Member State can also be established by way of prorogation (Article 97 (4)). Lastly, claims for infringement, with the exception of actions for a declaration of non-infringement of a Community trade mark, may also be brought in the

---

47 See oami.europa.eu/pdf/mark/ctmcourts.pdf.

48 The number of designated Community design courts is even higher in Germany: currently, 20 courts are competent to exercise that function.

courts of the Member State where the infringement has been committed or threatened (Article 97 (5)). In that case, however, a court whose competence is solely based on Article 97 (5) has jurisdiction only in respect of acts committed or threatened within the territory of the forum state, whereas the scope of jurisdiction exercised by courts of central competence extends to the entire territory of the EU.

Patents

The EPC and the Protocol on Recognition

With a common judiciary still lacking, litigation involving European patents granted on the basis of the EPC are subject to the rules of the Brussels I Regulation, or the Lugano Convention in the case of non-EU Contracting Members that are bound to the latter (Switzerland, Norway, and Iceland). In addition, provisions concerning lawsuits dealing with the grant of European patents are set out in the Protocol on Jurisdiction and Recognition of Decisions in Respect of the Right to the Grant of a European Patent ('Protocol on Recognition'). The Protocol applies in case of disagreement between parties about who among them owns the right to claim a patent. It is important that the competence of courts[49] to decide such lawsuits is fully recognised in all Contracting States, whether they are members of the Brussels Regulation, the Lugano Convention, or neither of both.[50] For that aim, the Protocol sets out that:

- if the applicant against whom a claim concerning the right to the patent is raised has his domicile or principal place of business in one of the Contracting States of the EPC, the proceedings must be brought before the courts in that State (Article 2);
- if the applicant resides outside the EPC Contracting States and only the person claiming the right resides in one of the EPC countries, the courts in the latter state shall have exclusive jurisdiction (Article 3);
- if none of the parties resides within the purview of the EPC, German courts (being the courts in the country where the EPO has its seat) have exclusive jurisdiction (Article 6[51]).

---

49 In the context of the Protocol, the term 'court' includes also authorities which, according to the national law in the Contracting State, have competence to decide on claims to the right to be granted a patent, Article 1 (2).

50 It must be noted, however, that Article 167 EPC allows Member States to file a reservation against the applicability of the Recognition Protocol.

51 Article 6 also applies as a default clause if jurisdiction cannot be determined on the basis of Article 4 (employee's invention) or Article 5 (choice of court agreements).

Disputes concerning the right to claim a patent frequently arise in the context of inventions made by an employee. In that regard, Article 4 provides for a link between jurisdiction and applicable law by allocating exclusive competence to the courts in the Contracting State whose law applies to the dispute in accordance with Article 60 EPC.[52] This means that in the first place, the courts in the country in which the employee is mainly employed, or, if that cannot be determined, the country in which the employer has the place of business to which the employee is attached are exclusively competent for the decision.

Finally, Article 5 allows parties to choose, with exclusive effect, the court that shall decide on the dispute. Such choice of court agreements override the exclusive competence of courts otherwise established on the basis of the Protocol, with the sole exception of Article 5: For employee's inventions, the competence of the courts determined by Article 4 cannot be abrogated.

The Unified Patent Court

In the context of establishing the unitary patent system based on enhanced cooperation, it is envisaged to establish a common court that is competent to hear claims for infringement and invalidity. The legal basis is set out in the (Draft) Agreement on a Unified Patent Court (dUPCA).[53]

Pursuant to Article 3 dUPCA, the Agreement shall apply to unitary patents, Supplementary Protection Certificates, and European (EPC) patents. The Unified Patent Court (UPC) to be established shall comprise a Court of First Instance, a Court of Appeal and a Registry (Article 4). The Court of First Instance comprises a central division as well as local and regional divisions. Local divisions are set up in Contracting Member States upon their request; where the number of patent cases filed annually exceeds 100, an additional local division can be established there. Regional divisions are established upon request by two or more Member States; this being primarily an option for Member States with a rather low level of litigation. In case of issues regarding the interpretation of the Basic Treaties, decisions by the ECJ are to be requested in accordance with Article 267 TFEU.

Further parts of the dUPCA deal with institutional matters such as the composition of the Court of First Instance and the Appeal Court as well as with the eligibility criteria and appointment of judges. Most remarkably, Chapter

---

52 See Chapter 3, section 3.3.6.1.

53 Consolidated version dated 12 October 2012, Council Document 14750/12 PI 127 Cour 67, register. consilium.europa.eu/pdf/en/12/st14/st14750.en12.pdf.

IIIB (Articles 14e to 14i) contains rules on substantive law which would largely synchronise the scope and limitations of protection of European patents with that of unitary patents, as set out in the draft Regulation on the implementation of enhanced cooperation in the area of the creation of unitary patent protection (draft Unitary Patent Regulation, see Chapter 3, sections 3.3.1. and 3.3.5.3[54]).

Regarding jurisdiction, the issues currently arising under the Brussels Regulation would be reduced to matters concerning the internal distribution of competences between the different regional or national divisions of which the Court of First Instance is composed. As a general rule, actions for infringement and provisional measures are to be brought before the local division located in the Member State[55] where the infringement occurs. If the defendant is established in one of the Contracting States,[56] lawsuits can also be brought in that State[57] (Article 15a (1) dUPCA).

When infringement litigation has been established, counterclaims for revocation of the patent can be filed in the same court. In that case, the court, after hearing the parties, may either:

- continue with the case in its entirety and ask for assistance by a technically qualified judge from the pool of judges to be established under the UPCA, or
- refer the validity issue to the central division and continue to hear, or suspend, the infringement action, or,
- with the agreement of both parties send the entire case to the central division, (Article 15a (2) dUPCA).

'Isolated' actions for revocation as well as actions for declaration of non-infringement and actions regarding remuneration for so-called licenses of right based on Article 11 of the Unitary Patent Regulation have to be brought before the central division. If an action for revocation is pending, infringement actions can still be brought at any local or regional division which is competent in accordance with Paragraph 1 (i.e., where the

---

54 In the draft version of the UPCA, these provisions are: Article 14f (direct infringement); Article 14g (indirect infringement); Article 14h (limitations and exceptions) and Article 14i (safeguarding the privilege granted under national law to persons entitled to claim a prior user's right).

55 If no local division is established in that State the claim has to be filed instead before the regional division in which the Member State participates.

56 If the defendant is not domiciled in one of the Contracting States, claims can be brought either at the place where the infringement occurs or at the place of the central division.

57 Or the respective regional division, see the previous footnote.

infringement occurs or at the defendant's domicile), with the same options being available to the local division as are set out in Paragraph 2 (Article 15a (4) dUPCA). If a claim for declaration of non-infringement action is pending before the central division, it can be stayed if an infringement action concerning the same patent between the same parties[58] is filed within three months from filing the negative declaratory action (Article 15a (5) dUPCA).

In case of unitary patents, decisions by the UPC have effect throughout the territories of the Member States participating in the enhanced cooperation on the establishment of the unitary patent system. Decisions concerning European patents take effect in the Contracting States where the European patent has been validated. In consequence of the ECJ opinion 1/09 declaring previous plans as incompatible with EU law that would have established, on the basis of an international convention, a common judiciary in which all Members of the EPC participate,[59] only EU Members can accede to the UPCA, meaning that the territorial effect of UPC judgments is confined to the EU. In relation to EU Member States that do not participate in enhanced cooperation (Spain and Italy), and that are therefore unlikely to accede to the UPCA, jurisdiction and the effect of UPC judgments are regulated by the Brussels Regulation. The relationship with Switzerland, Norway and Iceland is governed by the Lugano Convention.

? QUESTIONS

1 As pointed out in Chapter 3, the creation of a Community patent is closely linked with the establishment of a patent judiciary, in the sense that one has become a *conditio sine qua non* for the other. For Community trade marks and design, however, the Community legislature was much less ambitious. Why?

2 Article 16 UPCA stipulates that decisions handed down by the UPC take effect in all Member States participating in the system, irrespective of whether the defendant is domiciled or has an establishment in the forum state. Contrary to that, decisions by a Community trade mark court only have Community-wide effect if the court has central competence under Article 97 in conjunction with Article 98 CTMR. What is the reason for that distinction?

---

58 The same applies if the infringement action is brought between an exclusive licensee and the party requesting a declaration of non-infringement, Article 15a (5) UPCA.
59 See Chapter 3, section 3.6.2.1.

9.3 Applicable law

Universal application of the Regulations

The Rome I and Rome II Regulations determine the law which must be applied in proceedings conducted before courts located in EU Member States, whenever a conflict of laws arises. That principle is not qualified in any manner; neither the nationality or residence of any party nor the fact that the law designated by the provisions may be the law of a non-Member State allow to derogate from the Regulations.

The law applicable to contractual obligations: Rome I

The basic rule: freedom of choice

The Rome I Regulation applies to contractual obligations in civil and commercial matters, with few exceptions being specified in Article 2. It is undisputed that the ambit of Rome I comprises contracts concerning intellectual property rights, in particular licensing agreements and assignments.

As a general rule, the parties are free to choose the law that shall govern the contract between them (Article 3). Pursuant to Article 3 (1), the choice can be made expressly or implicitly. In the latter case, the choice must be 'clearly demonstrated by the terms of the contract or the circumstances of the case'. Rules under which the formal and substantive validity of such contracts is assessed are set out in Articles 10, 11 and 13. If the case is manifestly more closely connected with another country than the country whose law has been chosen, the choice of the parties does not exclude the application of mandatory rules of that other country. Likewise, if all the elements of the case are located in one or several Member States, and the chosen law is the law of a non-Member State, the choice made by the parties does not exclude the application of mandatory Community law which has been implemented in the respective Member States (Article 3 (4), (5)).

As contracts involving intellectual property rights such as licences and assignments are usually concluded between persons engaged in commercial activities, they do not fall within the categories of contracts for which the possibility to choose the applicable law has been restricted, such as for consumer contracts (Article 6), insurance contracts (Article 7) and individual employment contracts (Article 8).

Determination of the law applying in absence of choice

While a deliberate choice of the applicable law is the preferable option, the parties of a contract frequently forget or ignore the issue at the time when the contract is concluded. When difficulties arise and the parties cannot agree on an *ex post* choice of law, the deciding court has to determine the applicable law under the rules set out in Article 4 Rome I. For that purpose, Article 4 (1) sets out a catalogue of different default rules for specified types of contracts, including sales, franchise, and distribution contracts, but not listing contracts concerning intellectual property rights. The applicable law must therefore be determined in accordance with the general rule set forth in Article 4 (2), stipulating that:

> Where the contract is not covered by paragraph 1 . . ., the contract shall be governed by the law of the country where the party required to effect the *characteristic performance* of the contract has his habitual residence. (Emphasis added)

In contrast to the current text, the Commission's proposal for the Rome I Regulation had included a specific default rule for intellectual property matters, which referred to the law of the country where the person who transfers or assigns an intellectual property right has his habitual residence. However, in a statement launched by the CLIP Group (see above), the approach was criticised as too inflexible:

> The wide variety of contracts relating to intellectual property rights . . . calls for a differentiated solution instead of one strict, clear-cut rule. Even though the application of the law of the assignor or transferor of the intellectual property right might be appropriate in simple contracts which resemble an outright sale – such as an assignment or license for consideration in the form of a lump sum payment – this does not hold true as a general rule. More complex intellectual property transactions often include an explicit or implicit duty of the licensee to exploit the intellectual property right, sometimes supplemented by clauses indicating quantities of production or modalities of use, while the licensor does not accept any commitment beyond the toleration of use of his rights. This casts doubt on the proposition that it is the licensor who effects the performance characteristic of the contract (as it is the licensee who accepts the commercial risks linked to the exploitation). It may also be the case that the intellectual property rights licensed or assigned are mainly exercised in the country of the licensee's or transferee's habitual residence or principal place of business . . . [60]

---

60 CLIP Statement on Rome I proposal, http://www.ip.mpg.de/shared/data/pdf/clip-rome-i-comment-04-01-20062.pdf.

Instead, the proposal sets out a list of factors on the basis of which it shall be decided which state is most closely connected with the contract. In Article 3:502 (2) of the CLIP Principles[61] those factors are listed as follows:

(a) . . . factors tending to the law of the State in which the transferee or licensee has its habitual residence at the time of conclusion of the contract:

- the transfer or license concerns intellectual property rights granted for the State of the transferee's or licensee's habitual residence or place of business;
- the transferee or licensee has the explicit or implicit duty to exploit the right;
- the royalties or other form of money consideration is expressed as a percentage of the sales price;
- the licensee or transferee has a duty to report about her/his efforts to exploit the rights;

(b) . . . factors tending to the law of the State in which the creator, transferor or licensor has its habitual residence at the time of conclusion of the contract:

- the transfer or license concerns intellectual property rights granted for the State of the transferor's or licensor's habitual residence or place of business;
- the transferee or licensee has no other explicit or implicit duty but to pay a flat sum as money consideration;
- the license is for a single use;
- the creator of the protectable subject matter has the duty to create that matter.

Furthermore, if no clear decision can be made under those factors and the transfer or license concerns intellectual property rights for only one state, it shall be presumed under the CLIP Principles that the contract is most closely connected with that state. If the transfer or license concerns intellectual property rights for multiple states, it shall be presumed that the state with which the contract is most closely connected shall be the state in which the creator, transferor or licensor has its habitual residence at the time of conclusion of the contract.

Without such a list having been included in the text of the Rome I Regulation, courts have to embark on their own assessment of the circumstances characterising the mutual obligations of the parties in order to determine the applicable law. In such situation, the CLIP Principles or similar proposals may serve as a guideline.

It has also been suggested that license contracts concerning an IP right may fall under Article 4(1)(b) (contract for the provision of services), meaning

---

61 The final text of the CLIP Principles is available at www.cl-ip.eu/files/pdf2/Final_Text_1_ December_2011.pdf.

that absent a choice of law made by the parties, the applicable law would be the law of the country where the service provider has his habitual residence. However, after the ECJ decided in case C-533/07 – *Falco Privatstiftung* v. *Weller-Lindhorst*[62] that license contracts over intellectual property rights cannot be qualified as service contracts for the purpose of establishing jurisdiction, the issue has become moot.

? QUESTIONS

1 Do you agree to the statement that the law applicable to intellectual property contracts in absence of choice cannot be brought under one single rule?
2 Would any more clarity have resulted for intellectual property contracts if the ECJ had held that they can be considered as a type of service contract? Who would be the provider, and who the recipient of services?

The law applicable to non-contractual obligations: Rome II

Lex protectionis *as the basic rule*

As a general rule applying to non-contractual obligations arising out of torts, Article 4 (1) Rome II establishes that the applicable law:

> shall be the law of the country in which the damage occurs irrespective of the country in which the event giving rise to the damage occurred and irrespective of the country or countries in which the indirect consequences of that event occur.

More specific rules applying to particular types of torts are set out in Articles 5, 6 and 7 (product liability; unfair competition and acts restricting free competition; environmental damage) as well as in Article 9 (industrial action).

Intellectual property rights are addressed in Article 8. The term 'intellectual property rights' is specified in the Preamble (Recital 26) 'as meaning, for instance, copyright, related rights, the sui generis right for the protection of databases and industrial property rights.' Pursuant to the basic rule enshrined in Article 8 (1), the law applicable to obligations resulting from an infringement of an intellectual property right is the law of the country for which protection is claimed (*lex loci protectionis*, or *lex protectionis* for short). As likewise set out in Recital 26, the legislative intention is that 'the universally acknowledged principle of the lex loci protectionis should be preserved'.

---

62 ECJ Case C-533/07, *Falco Privatstiftung* v. *Weller-Lindhorst*, [2009] ECR I-3327; (see above, section 9.2.3.1).

A long-standing academic debate has evolved about the question of whether the principle of *lex protectionis* already follows from the territoriality of intellectual property right, or whether it is a mandatory feature under the international intellectual property conventions, being derived either from the principle of national treatment[63] or, more specifically, from Article 5 (2) 2nd sentence of the Berne Convention, which stipulates that:

> the extent of protection, as well as the means of redress afforded to the author to protect his rights, shall be governed exclusively by the laws of the country where protection is claimed.

At least according to the ECJ, however, the Berne Convention does not aspire to determine the applicable law. Instead:

> [a]s is apparent from Article 5 (1) of the Berne Convention, the purpose of that convention is not to determine the applicable law on the protection of literary and artistic works, but to establish, as a general rule, a system of national treatment of the rights appertaining to such works.[64]

In spite of diverging opinions on this point, it is uncontested in principle that the spirit and purpose of fundamental principles governing intellectual property law such as territoriality and national treatment are best served by applying the *lex protectionis* at least with regard to 'existence and remedies', thus covering the infringement of intellectual property rights and the consequences ensuing from it.

Even before the Rome II Regulation went into force, the large majority of EU Member States followed the rule of *lex protectionis* (which was sometimes also understood as a consequence of the more general rule of *lex loci delicti*). Exceptions from that rule were only found in Greece, Portugal and Rumania, where according to domestic private international law the law of the country of origin (*lex originis*) was designated as the law applicable to copyright, thereby also extending to infringement of rights. In consequence of such rules, the national judge was forced to apply foreign law whenever an infringement of a work first published abroad was claimed. After enactment of the Rome II Regulation, such rules are no longer compatible with EU law.

As a consequence of the application of *lex protectionis*, conduct extending over national borders must be adjudicated under the different laws apply-

---

63 Article 2 Paris Convention, Article 5 (1) Berne Convention and Article 3 TRIPS.
64 ECJ Case C-28/04, *Tod's SpA and Tod's France SARL v. Heyraud*, [2005] ECR I-5781, Paragraph 32.

ing in each of the countries where it results, or may result, in an infringement. For instance, if machines are produced in Member State A and sold in Member State B, it must be assessed whether the acts undertaken in A and in B respectively fulfil the conditions for patent (or trade mark) infringement under the national law of each country separately. With regard to copyright, the same approach was confirmed by the ECJ in *Lagardère*, which concerned the broadcasting of protected content to France via a transmitter located in Germany. The fact that the application of *lex protectionis* resulted in the application of both German and French copyright law and hence to remuneration owed to the collecting societies in both countries was held to follow necessarily from the territoriality of the right.[65]

It must be noted, however, that the application of *lex protectionis* becomes unfeasible where the number of countries where an infringement occurs becomes too high. Hence it is clearly impossible to resolve on that basis disputes involving ubiquitous infringements in the sense that the infringement is held to occur in all countries where content spread over the internet is technically accessible. Those cases are addressed below.

Scope of application

Article 15 Rome II

The scope of the rules determining the law applicable to non-contractual obligations is defined in Article 15 Rome II. Most importantly, the law determined by those rules applies to 'the basis and extent of liability, including the determination of persons who may be held liable for acts performed by them', as well as to the limitations and exceptions from liability (Article 15 (1) (a), (b)). While that definitely covers the violation of the right as such as well as the remedies, it has been contended by some that it also covers existence and, in particular, ownership of the right. However, a clear majority opinion holds that Article 8 in conjunction with Article 15 does not determine the law applicable to first ownership, meaning that EU Member States are free to maintain in their national law provisions or doctrines that designate another law than *lex protectionis* as the law governing ownership.

---

65 ECJ Case C-192/04, *Lagardère Active Broadcast v. SPRE*, [2005] I-7199. A detailed discussion of this somewhat atypical case is found in Chapter 5, section 5.3.2.1. For direct broadcast to the public via satellite, the cable and satellite directive provides a different solution which leads to the application of one law only, see this chapter, section 9.5.1 and Chapter 5, section 5.2.2.3.

First (copyright) ownership

The issue is of interest primarily with regard to the law applicable to the first ownership of copyright in a work.[66] In that regard, the attitude between Member States shows strong divergences: whereas some apply *lex protectionis* also to ownership, others emphasise that in view of the universal nature of copyright, and also for reasons of practical convenience, it is preferable to subject the question as to who has acquired authorship in a work to one single law, namely the law of the country of origin.

The difference becomes particularly relevant in relation to countries where, in contrast to most EU Member States, copyright in a 'work made for hire', i.e. a work made in the course of employment, is vested in the employer. Other than in (continental) Europe, this means that the 'author' of a work, in a legal sense, is not necessarily the personal creator, but it can also be a company financing and organising the work, e.g. a film producing company. Accordingly, if *lex originis* is applied as the law determining first ownership, a court adjudicating on infringement of a work created in a country where the work made for hire doctrine applies will be forced to deny the right to claim authorship to the person by whom the work was actually created, even though under domestic law, the principle of personal authorship would be governing.

In practice, however, the conflict is rarely as acute as the theory might suggest. In most cases, what is at stake in infringement cases are the economic rights of exploitation, and those rights are regularly transferred by the personal author to the company commissioning the work, so that as a result, the differences between the systems will not be of practical relevance. However, the issue may become topical when the 'moral rights' of authors are at stake, such as the right to be named, or to oppose the distortion, mutilation or similar modification of the work (*droit moral*, Article 6 *bis* Berne Convention). Under the law of EU Member States applying *lex protectionis* to first ownership, such rights would not be denied to the personal creators of works originating from countries where the work made for hire doctrine

---

66 Regarding registered industrial property rights, the issue regularly does not pose a problem, because ownership is determined anyhow by the registration. It is a different issue whether another person than the registered owner has a right to claim the right. The law applicable to such disputes is determined according to the relationship between the parties, for instance, if the right has arisen out of a pre-existing contractual relationship, by the law determined under the Rome I Regulation. Regarding claims to a European patent by an employee, Article 60 EPC stipulates that the applicable law is the law of the country where the employee is mainly employed, or, if that cannot be determined, the country where the employer has the place of business to which the employee is attached; see this chapter, section 9.2.4.2.1 and Chapter 3, section 3.3.6.1.

applies, whereas a different result would ensue in principle from the application of *lex originis*. On the other hand, even Member States applying *lex originis* as the general rule with regard to ownership may be inclined to grant at least some protection to personal authors in such cases, based on considerations of public policy.

An example of such a situation is offered by the *John Huston* case, concerning the film 'Asphalt Jungle'. A claim was raised by John Huston's heirs in France for violation of *droit moral* by the broadcasting on French TV of a colour version of the film, which had been deliberately produced by John Huston in black and white. The colourisation had been commissioned by the defendant who had acquired the rights in the film by the American producer. In its decision of 6 July 1989 the Appeal Court in Paris held that according to US law, the rights had been validly transferred and thus no *droit moral* could be invoked on John Huston's behalf by his heirs. The court then examined whether French *ordre public* nevertheless compelled the droit moral to be respected. After weighing the mutual interests, the conclusion was drawn that whereas *ordre public* did not furnish sufficient reason to prohibit the broadcasting, the heirs should at least be entitled to demand that a disclaimer be added to the film so as to let the public know that they, in the name of John Huston, disapproved of the changes.

Upon appeal to the Supreme Court (cour de cassation), the decision was reversed. Without going into any detail about the applicable law, the Supreme Court held that:

> [a]ccording to Art. 1 (2) of Act No. 64-689 of July 8, 1964, the integrity of a literary or artistic work in France must not be impaired; this applies independently of the state in which the work was first published. On the basis of Art. 6 of the Copyright Act of March 11, 1957, the person who is the author of the work is entitled to claim droit moral merely due to the actual creation of the work; this right was specifically provided for in this Article in order to benefit authors. The provisions are to be strictly applied. . . . The court of appeals rejected the plaintiff's claim with the argument that the facts described and the legal merits of the case 'forbade the supplantation of U.S. law and the disregard of the contracts' – contracts concluded between the producer and the director, which denied the latter the status as author of the film 'Asphalt Jungle'. By deciding on these grounds, the court of appeal has misinterpreted the abovenamed provisions by non-application . . . [and is therefore] declared null and void.[67]

---

67 French Supreme Court (cour de cassation), 28 May1991, English translation in 23 IIC 702 (1992).

Unitary Community rights

Article 8 (2) Rome II stipulates that:

> for non-contractual obligations arising from an infringement of a unitary
> Community intellectual property right, the law applicable shall, for any question
> that is not governed by the relevant Community instrument, be the law of the
> country in which the act of infringement was committed.

The purpose of the rule is twofold: first, it is intended to clarify that the legal
rules enshrined in the respective Community instruments are applicable in
all aspects covered by them, and second, it shall determine the law applying
in case that no such rules are contained in the respective instruments.

The second scenario is of practical relevance particularly with regard to the
sanctions for infringement of Community rights such as Community trade
marks and Community designs:[68] apart from prohibitive injunctions and
other sanctions of minor interest, neither the CTMR nor the CDR contain
any provisions dealing with remedies, such as damages, right to information, publication of judgments and other corrective measures. And although
the catalogue of available sanctions has been harmonised under Directive
48/2004, the laws of Member States by which the gap must be filled are quite
diverse.

Although the aims pursued by Article 8 (2) Rome II are rather obvious, the
solutions are less clear. First, it has been pointed out that a problem might
result from Article 27 Rome II, which stipulates that the application of provisions of Community law which contain specific conflict-of-law rules shall
not be prejudiced. Reference is made in that context to Article 101 CTMR
(correspondingly: Article 88 CDR), pursuant to which Community trade
mark courts shall apply, in matters that are not governed by the CTMR, their
own national law, 'including their private international law'. The argument
could therefore be made that the national law of Member States, including the domestic conflict of law rules, takes precedence over Article 8 (2)
Rome II. On the other hand, the risk for serious problems caused by such
an interpretation is minimised if it is acknowledged that Member States'
'national' private international law has now been replaced by the Rome II
Regulation.

---

68 The same applies to geographical indications that are registered on the Community level, Community
plant variety rights, and Supplementary Protection Certificates. For patents having unitary effect see the text
below.

More serious is the fact that Article 8 (2) Rome II fails to provide for a well-defined solution when the infringement of a Community right extends over several Member States. In particular, it is unclear whether it leads to the application of one single law – the law of the Member State where the infringement was essentially committed – or whether it rather compels the application of a 'mosaic approach' consisting of the laws in all Member States where the infringement takes effect. The matter calls for clarification by the ECJ. At present, however, no decisions addressing the issue have been handed down, nor are such cases pending.

Regarding European patents falling within the purview of the envisaged unified patent court, the issue is less acute. Although the draft Regulation implementing the unitary patent protection, like the CTMR and the CDR, does not contain a catalogue of sanctions, sanctions and procedural measures to be applied in case of patent infringement litigation modelled on the Enforcement Directive are regulated comprehensively in the draft UPCA. In addition, Article 14e of the draft UPCA enumerates the sources of law to be applied by the UPC where the relevant rules are not found in the UPCA, or if the UPCA is not applicable with regard to an issue of national law.

Exclusion of choice

The problems caused by the ambiguity of Article 8 (2) Rome II in case of Community right infringement extending over several Member States could be alleviated in practice if the parties were granted the option to choose the law applicable to the remedies. However, pursuant to Article 8 (3), such choices are strictly forbidden. In that regard, Article 8 constitutes an exception within the framework of the Rome II Regulation. Regarding other types of torts, including product liability and environmental damage, the parties are free to choose the applicable law in accordance with Article 14. Such agreements can be concluded either after the damage arose, or, if all the parties pursue commercial activities, by way of freely negotiated *ex ante* agreements.

The only other restriction for choice of law applying under the Rome II Regulation concerns non-contractual obligations arising from acts of unfair competition or restrictions of free competition (Article 6). However, also with regard to those torts the rule is not as strict as for intellectual property infringement. If competition-restricting behaviour results, or is likely to result, in damage affecting the national markets of several Member States, the person seeking compensation for such damage may choose to base the claim on the law of the court seized (*lex fori*). The option is qualified in order to ensure that the law applied has a substantial connection with the damage done: the market in the Member State where the court is located must be among those directly and substantially affected by the restriction of competition. If several defendants are joined in the claim (based on Article 6 (1) Brussels I Regulation, see above), the option to choose the law of the forum state only exists if the competition-restricting measures taken by each one of them have a direct and substantial effect on that market.

? QUESTIONS

1 In your opinion, what are the advantages and disadvantages of applying *lex protectionis* – as compared to *lex originis* – to (a) infringement and (b) first ownership?

2 The wording of Article 8 (1) Rome II is closely modelled on Article 5 (2) 2nd sentence Berne Convention. However, it deviates from the wording of the Berne Convention in one particular aspect. Which one? What is the relevance, if any, of the different wording?

3 As pointed out above, the Rome II Regulation forbids any choice of the law applying to intellectual property infringements, in contrast to all other kinds of torts. What could be the reason for that? Do you agree that a choice must be excluded? Which risks would ensue if a choice were permitted?

9.4 Ubiquitous infringements: towards an internationally harmonised approach?

Challenges

As pointed out above with regard to jurisdiction, the traditional scheme of private international law is challenged when content is spread over the internet with the result that infringements occur or may occur simultaneously in a multitude of countries, or even on a global scale. Due to the principles of territoriality and *lex protectionis*, such situations might lead to parallel litigation being conducted in a (large) number of countries, and to the application of many – in extreme cases 180-plus – different national laws. It hardly needs to be emphasised that such consequences would lead to severe detriments for the parties involved, and to an obstruction of justice. Nevertheless, current law – in Europe and elsewhere – does not provide for specific rules addressing multi-state or ubiquitous IP infringements.

When similar issues arose in the context of satellite broadcasting, the apparent tension between potentially diverging national laws and the supranational character of communication techniques was resolved in the Satellite and Cable Directive (93/83/EEC) by defining 'communication to the public by satellite' as an act occurring solely in the country from which the programme-bearing signals are uploaded.[69] However, although similar in its effects to a conflicts rule, the solution operates on the level of substantive law: if protection is claimed expressly for a state which is at the receiving end of the transmission chain, the court seized with the claim would not be hindered to apply the national law of the state for which protection is sought; only the claim would have to be denied due to the fact that the infringing action, by definition, only occurs in the State where the upload takes place.

Another example from EU law addressing the difficulties potentially resulting from a multitude of substantive laws applying to a single act of communication concerns the 'country-of-origin principle' in Article 3 (2) of the E-Commerce Directive (2000/31/EC), establishing the rule that information society services rendered within the harmonised area should only be subject to substantive control in the Member State from which they emanate, and should not be prohibited on the basis of national provisions in other Member States. However, as resolves from Article 1 (4) of Directive 2000/31/EC, that rule is not intended to interfere with established rules of private international law or jurisdiction.[70] Furthermore, intellectual property is explicitly excluded from the operation of Article 3 (2), so as not to interfere with the territoriality principle.

In spite of a positive regulation of the issue lacking, it is trite to state that in practice, judgements prohibiting or otherwise regulating conduct on the internet more often than not entail global effects, even where they only purport to pertain to the national territory. For instance, if a person is enjoined from using a domain name under a particular top level domain, or is ordered to transfer the domain name to the adverse party in the proceedings, the effect will be global insofar as that domain name under the top level domain cannot be acquired or used by the same person in any other country. Worldwide effects will also accrue in practice when a person is ordered to shut down a website as a result of alleged trade mark or copyright infringement: such measures do not only affect traffic from within the country for which the judgment was handed down, but also from other countries where the website can be accessed. Nevertheless, judgments in such cases are usually based on the application of domestic law alone. And also with regard

---

69 Article 1 (2) Directive 93/83/EEC; see Chapter 5, section 5.2.2.3.
70 This was confirmed in ECJ Joined Cases C-509/09, *eDate* v. *X* and *Martinez* v. *MGN* [2011] ECR I-0000, Paragraph 68.

to damages, courts frequently do not confine their decisions to computing the losses sustained in a single territory; however, they hardly ever examine the issue under the laws applying in all the countries where infringements have arguably taken place.

Whereas the problems are not acutely felt in practice, the situation remains unsatisfactory. It is therefore strongly advisable to develop a solid and transparent framework of rules for adjudication of disputes relating to ubiquitous infringements. As such disputes are *global* in the sense that they cannot be confined to a specific region or continent, such efforts should not be focused on Europe alone, but they should try to aim at an international understanding about the essential principles governing the legal assessment.

Initiatives and proposed solutions

The hazards of litigation for alleged violation of IP rights on the internet, and the need to devise rules limiting the risks, were first put on the international agenda by the WIPO Standing Committee on the Law of Trademarks, Industrial Designs and Geographical Indications (SCT). The efforts resulted in the promulgation of the Joint Recommendation Concerning Provisions on the Protection of Marks, and Other Industrial Property Rights in Signs, on the Internet (2001).[71] In its core provision (Article 2) the Joint Recommendation stipulates that a sign which is used on the Internet shall only be considered as being used in a specific country if it has *commercial effect* there. A comprehensive list of factors is set forth as a basis for the assessment, relating to various factors indicating whether the user is doing or seriously intends to do business in the respective territory. Such factors are *inter alia* the language, the top level domain under which the website is operated, the currency indicated, and actual business conducted in the territory; furthermore, the principle is established that remedies for trade mark infringement and unfair competition shall only apply if the user has been notified of the conflict and failed to react in an adequate manner, for instance by adding a disclaimer or otherwise taking reasonable steps to avoid creating commercial effects in the state where the conflict exists (Article 9). While the Joint Recommendation is primarily aimed at the level of substantive law, it echoes considerations which in some jurisdictions, in particular in the USA, are taken into account for limiting the competence of courts to hear claims concerning internet-related infringements,[72] and which are also applied,

---

71 See www.wipo.int/about-ip/en/development_iplaw/pub845.htm.
72 *Zippo Manufacturing Company v Zippo Dot Com* [1997] U.S.D.C. W.D. Pennsylvania 952 F.Supp. 1119; *Panavision International v Toeppen* [1998] 9th Cir 141 F.3d 1316.

albeit on insecure ground, by certain courts in Europe.[73] In addition, several academic initiatives were formed with the aim of promulgating catalogues of principles governing jurisdiction, applicable law, and enforcement in cross-border IP cases. In the USA, the American Law Institute (ALI) launched a project under the title 'Intellectual Property: Principles Governing Principles Governing Jurisdiction, Choice of Law, and Judgments in Transnational Disputes'.[74] A parallel project was conducted in Europe by the European Max-Planck Group on Conflict of Laws in Intellectual Property (CLIP),[75] and finally, the Japanese Transparency project[76] as well as a Japanese–Korean Group organised by the Global Centre of Excellence at Waseda University, Tokyo, added their contributions from a Japanese/Asian perspective.

Although all projects deal with jurisdiction and applicable law in its entirety including contractual matters and other more traditional issues arising in the analogue world, their special focus lies on infringements occurring on the internet. And whereas the proposals adopted by each group differ in their details, they show rather far-reaching commonalities with regards to the basic structure. Concerning jurisdiction, all projects emphasise the necessity of restricting the establishment of a competent venue where allegedly infringing content is technically accessible on the internet, without being directed to, or having an effect in, the forum state. The restrictions are particularly severe where the decision rendered by the court seized would have extraterritorial or even global effect. Regarding applicable law, all proposals stipulate that (at least[77]) in the case of ubiquitous infringement, courts may deviate from *lex protectionis* and apply a single law, which should be the law having the closest connection with the infringement in its entirety. For determining that law, all projects have promulgated a list of relevant factors that must be taken into account. Furthermore, and most importantly, all proposals provide that either party has the right to establish that the applicable law in a country involved in the claims differs from the law identified by the court as the law having the closest connection in an aspect which is relevant for the decision, with the consequence that the court must apply both laws, or, where that is not possible, that the court must take both laws into account when fashioning the remedies.

---

73 See ECJ Case C-523/10, *Wintersteiger v. Products 4U*, [2012] ECR I-0000.

74 For information see www.ali.org/index.cfm?fuseaction=projects.members&projectid=1.

75 See www.cl-ip.eu/en/pub/home.cfm.

76 See www.tomeika.jur.kyushu-u.ac.jp/intl/private/.

77 Differences in that regard apply insofar as the ALI proposal as well as the two Japanese proposals allow the application of a single law when the infringement occurs in multiple countries, whereas the CLIP project applies a stricter concept of ubiquity.

It is unclear whether the proposals will find acceptance in practice, if and to the extent that current law leaves sufficient leeway for the adoption of such flexible solutions. Also, only the future will show whether the different approaches reflected in the proposals can be merged into one common, truly global solution.

? QUESTIONS

1 What is your opinion about the solution proposed with regard to the law applicable to ubiquitous infringements? Would it be practically feasible? How would you evaluate potential alternatives, such as application of the law of the country where the act giving rise to the infringement was carried out, or, instead of applying one particular law, giving courts freedom to promulgate their own 'supra-territorial rules', taking account of all the circumstances of the case?

2 The CLIP project has proposed a special rule for ISPs, stipulating that the law applicable to their activities is the law of the country where the center of the ISP's activities lie, without the possibility being given to the infringed party to plead a different law. Contrary to that, pursuant to the other proposals the law applicable to indirect infringement (including ISPs) is the same law as the law applicable to the main infringement. Can you imagine the reasons for the CLIP proposal?

3 Rules on applicable law are of relevance in particular where law is not harmonised, so that the application of one or another law can be decisive for the outcome of a dispute. Consequently, an alternative to aiming at an international consensus with regard to the rules determining the applicable law could be to embark on substantive harmonisation. How would you evaluate that option?

Recommended literature

IP, IPRs and the international context

Correa, Carlos: Intellectual property rights, the WTO and developing countries: The TRIPS agreement and policy options, Edward Elgar, Cheltenham, 2000

Correa, Carlos (ed.): Research Handbook on the protection of intellectual property under WTO rules, Edward Elgar, Cheltenham, 2010

Dinwoodie, Graeme & Dreyfus, Rochelle: A neofederalist vision of TRIPS, Oxford University Press, Oxford, 2012

Gervais, Daniel: Intellectual property, trade and development: strategies to optimize economic development in a TRIPS plus era, Oxford University Press, Oxford, 2007

Gervais, Daniel: The TRIPS Agreement: drafting history and analysis, 3nd ed., Sweet & Maxwell, London, 2008

Goldstein, Paul & Hugenholtz, P. Bernt: International copyright. Principles, law, and practice, 2nd ed., Oxford University Press, Oxford, 2010

Goldstein, Paul & Trimble, Marketa: International legal materials on intellectual property, Foundation Press, New York, 2011

Kur, Annette with Levin, Marianne (eds): Intellectual property rights in a fair world trade system, Edward Elgar, Cheltenham, 2011

Kur, Annette & Mizaras, Vytautas (eds): The structure of intellectual property law – can one size fit all? Edward Elgar, Cheltenham, 2011

v. Lewinski, Silke: International copyright law and policy, Oxford University Press, Oxford, 2008

Maskus, Keith E. & Reichman, Jerome H.: International public goods and transfer of technology under a globalized intellectual property regime, 2005

Ricketson, Sam & Ginsburg, Jane C.: International copyright and neighbouring rights, 2nd ed., Oxford University Press, Oxford, 2005

Senftleben, Martin: Copyright, limitations and the three-step test. An analysis of the three-step test in international and EC copyright law, Kluwer Law International, The Hague, 2004

Sherman, Brad & Bently, Lionel: The making of modern intellectual property law, Cambridge University Press, Cambridge, 2008

Torremans, Paul (ed.): Intellectual property and human rights, Wolters Kluwer Law & Business, Austin, 2008

UNCTAD/ICTSD Resource book on TRIPS and sustainable development, Cambridge University Press, Cambridge, 2005

WIPO Intellectual property handbook – policy, law and use, 2nd ed., Geneva, 2004

European (and international) IP law (overviews and treatises)

Aplin, Tanya & Davis, Jennifer: Intellectual Property. Text, cases and materials. Oxford University Press, Oxford, 2009

Bently, Lionel & Sherman, Brad: Intellectual property law, 3rd ed., Oxford University Press, Oxford, 2009

Cook, Trevor M.: EU intellectual property law, Oxford University Press, Oxford, 2010

Cornish, William R.; Llewelyn, David & Aplin, Tanya, Intellectual property – patents, copyright, trade marks and allied rights, 7th ed., Sweet & Maxwell, London, 2010

Dimancescu, Katherine: Intellectual property law in the European community: Country by country review, 2nd ed., WorldTrade Executive, Concorde, 2007

Harris, Bryan: Intellectual Property law in the European Union, Hein, Buffalo, 2005

Seville, Catherine: EU Intellectual property law and policy, Edward Elgar, Cheltenham, 2009

Straus, Joseph & Xiaoguang, Shan: Leading court cases on European intellectual property, European Patent Office, Munich, 2011

Torremans, Paul & Holyoak, Jon: Intellectual property law, 6th ed., Oxford University Press, Online Resource Center, Oxford, 2010

Tritton, Guy: Intellectual property in Europe, 3rd ed., Sweet & Maxwell, 2007 (4th ed., 2012 forthcoming)

IP in the European legal context (special topics)

Barnard, Catherine: The substantive law of the EU. The four freedoms, 3rd ed., Oxford University Press, Oxford, 2010

Derclaye, Estelle & Leistner, Matthias: Intellectual property overlaps. A European perspective, Hart Publishers, Oxford, 2011

Mylly, Tuomas: Intellectual property and the European economic constitutional law; IPR University Center, Helsinki, 2009

Ohly, Ansgar (ed.): Common principles of European intellectual property law, Mohr Siebeck, Tübingen, 2012

Ward, David (ed.): The European Union and the culture industries: Regulation and the public interest, Ashgate, Hampshire, 2008

Patent law

Hacon, Richard & Pagenberg, Jochen (eds): Concise European Patent Law, 2nd ed., Kluwer Law International, Alphen aan den Rijn, 2008

Luginbühl, Stefan: European Patent Law. Towards a Uniform Interpretation, Edward Elgar, Cheltenham, 2011

Trade mark law

Cohen Jehoram, Tobias; van Nispen, Constant & Huydecoper, Tony: European Trademark Law. Community Trademark Law and Harmonized National Trademark Law, Kluwer Law international, Alphen aan den Rijn, 2010

Dinwoodie, Graeme B. & Janis Mark D.: Trademark Law and Theory. A Handbook of Contemporary Research, Edward Elgar, Cheltenham, 2008

Gielen, Charles & von Bomhard, Verena (eds):, Concise European trade mark and design law, Kluwer Law International, Alphen aan den Rijn, 2011

Griffiths, Andrew: An economic perspective on Trade mark law, Edward Elgar, Cheltenham, 2011

Maniatis, Spyros & Botis, Dimitris, Trade marks in Europe, 2nd ed., Sweet & Maxwell, London, 2009

Phillips, Jeremy (ed.): Trade marks at the limit, Edward Elgar, Cheltenham, 2006

Phillips, Jeremy & Simon, Ilanah: Trade mark use, Oxford University Press, Oxford, 2005

Sakulin, Wolfgang: Trademark protection and freedom of expression. Kluwer Law, Alphen aan den Rijn, 2011

Copyright law

Derclaye, Estelle (ed.): Research Handbook on the Future of EU Copyright, Edward Elgar, Cheltenham, 2009

Dreier, Thomas & Hugenholtz, P. Bernt (eds): Concise European Copyright Law, Kluwer Law International, Alphen aan den Rijn, 2006

Eechoud, Mireille; Hugenholtz, P. Bernt; van Gompel, Stefan J.; Guibault. Lucie & Helberger. Natali: Harmonizing European Copyright Law – The Challenges of Better Lawmaking, Walters Kluwer, Alphen aan den Rijn, 2009

Mazziotti, Giuseppe: EU digital copyright law and the end-user, Springer, Berlin, 2008

Walter, Michel & v.Lewinski, Silke (eds): European Copyright Law – A Commentary, Oxford University Press, Oxford, 2010

Other IP laws

Llewelyn, Margaret & Adcock, Mike: European plant intellectual property, Hart Publishers, Oxford, 2006

Musker, David: Community design law. Principles and practice, Sweet & Maxwell, London, 2002

Gangjee, Dev: Relocating the law of geographical indications, Cambridge University Press, Cambridge, 2012

Competition law (antitrust)

Anderman, Steven D.: EU Competition Law and intellectual property rights. The regulation of innovation, 2nd ed., Oxford University Press, Oxford, 2011

Anderman, Steven D. & Kallaugher, John J.: Technology transfer and the new EU competition rules. Intellectual Property licensing after modernization, Oxford University Press, Oxford, 2006

Anvret, Maria & Granieri, Massimiliano: A new approach to innovation policy and the European Union. Innovation Policy: Boosting EU competitiveness in a global economy, Centre for European Policy Studies, Brussels, 2010

Carrier, Michael A. (ed.): Intellectual Property and Competition, Edward Elgar, Cheltenham, 2011

Govaere, Inge & Ullrich, Hanns (eds): Intellectual property, market power and the public interest, P.I.E. Peter Lang, Brussels, 2008

Keeling, David T.: Intellectual property rights in EU law. Free movement and competition law, Oxford University Press, Oxford, 2004

Koch, Claudia: Incentives to innovate in the conflicting area between the EU competition law and intellectual property protection, Institute of Economic Law, Halle (Saale), 2011

Korah, Valentine: Intellectual Property rights and the EC competition rules, Hart Publishers, Oxford, 2006

Maggiolino, Mariateresa: Intellectual property and antitrust - a comparative economic analysis of US and EU law, Edward Elgar, Cheltenham, 2011

Turner, Jonathan: Intellectual property and EU competition law, Oxford University Press, Oxford, 2010

Unfair competition law

Henning-Bodewig, Frauke: Unfair Competition Law – European Union and member states, Kluwer Law International, The Hague, 2006

Hilty, Reto M. & Henning-Bodewig, Frauke: Law against unfair competition – Towards a new paradigm in Europe? Springer, Berlin, 2007

Ohly, Ansgar & Spence, Michael: Comparative advertising. Hart, Oxford, 2000.

Enforcement

Cottier, Thomas & Véron, Pierre: Concise International and European IP Law, Kluwer Law International, Alphen aan den Rijn, 2008

Geiger, Christophe (ed.): Constructing European IP: Achievements and News Perspectives Edward Elgar, Cheltenham, 2012

Jurisdiction and applicable law

Basedow, Jürgen, Drexl, Josef, Kur, Annette & Metzger, Axel (eds): Intellectual property in the conflict of laws, Mohr Siebeck, Tübingen, 2005

Leible, Stefan & Ohly, Ansgar (eds): Intellectual Property and Private International Law, Mohr Siebeck, Tübingen, 2009

Fawcett, James & Torremans, Paul: Intellectual Property and Private International Law, Oxford University Press, Oxford, 1998, 2nd ed. forthcoming in 2012

Important websites[1]

EU institutions

- DG Agriculture and Rural Development – Quality Policy: ec.europa.eu/agriculture/quality/index_en.htm
- DG Communications Networks, Content and Technology: ec.europa.eu/dgs/connect/index_en.htm
- DG Competition: ec.europa.eu/dgs/competition/index_en.htm
- DG Health and Consumers – Consumer Affairs: ec.europa.eu/consumers/index_en.htm
- DG Internal Market and Services – Copyright and Neighboring Rights: ec.europa.eu/internal_market/copyright/index_en.htm
- DG Internal Market and Services – Industrial Property: ec.europa.eu/internal_market/indprop/index_en.htm
- DG Justice – European Judicial Network in civil and commercial matters: ec.europa.eu/civiljustice/index_en.htm
- DG Taxation and Customs Union – Counterfeit, Piracy and other IPR violations: ec.europa.eu/taxation_customs/customs/customs_controls/counterfeit_piracy/index_en.htm
- Court of Justice of the European Union; General Court: curia.europa.eu
- European Parliament: europarl.europa.eu

---

1 All websites last accessed 6 November 2012; to avoid lengthy repetition (both here and in the text) where a website address is not prefixed with 'www' the default prefix is 'http://' or 'https://'.

EU legislation

Regulations

- Council Regulation (EC) No 2100/94 of 27 July 1994 on Community plant variety rights: eur-lex.europa.eu/LexUriServ/LexUriServ.do?uri=OJ:L:1994:227:0001:0030:EN:PDF
- Regulation (EC) No 1610/96 of the European Parliament and of the Council of 23 July 1996 concerning the creation of a supplementary protection certificate for plant protection products: eur-lex.europa.eu/LexUriServ/LexUriServ.do?uri=OJ:L:1996:198:0030:0035:EN:PDF
- Council Regulation 44/2001 of 22 December 2000 on the Recognition and Enforcement of Foreign Judgments in Civil and Commercial Matters ('Brussels I'): eur-lex.europa.eu/LexUriServ/LexUriServ.do?uri=OJ:L:2001:012:0001:0023:EN:PDF
- Council Regulation (EC) No 6/2002 of 12 December 2001 on Community designs: eur-lex.europa.eu/LexUriServ/LexUriServ.do?uri=OJ:L:2002:003:0001:0024:en:PDF
- Council Regulation (EC) No 1383/2003 of 22 July 2003 concerning customs action against goods suspected of infringing certain intellectual property rights and the measures to be taken against goods found to have infringed such rights: eur-lex.europa.eu/LexUriServ/LexUriServ.do?uri=OJ:L:2003:196:0007:0014:EN:PDF
- Council Regulation (EC) No 2006/510 of 20 March 2006 on the Protection of Geographical Indications and Designations of Origin for Agricultural Products and Foodstuffs: eur-lex.europa.eu/LexUriServ/LexUriServ.do?uri=OJ:L:2006:093:0012:0025:EN:PDF
- Regulation (EC) No 864/2007 of the European Parliament and of the Council of 11 July 2007 on the law applicable to non-contractual obligations (Rome II): eur-lex.europa.eu/LexUriServ/LexUriServ.do?uri=OJ:L:2007:199:0040:0049:EN:PDF
- Regulation 593/2008 of the European Parliament and of the Council of 17 June 2008 on the Law Applicable to Contractual Obligations ('Rome I'): eur-lex.europa.eu/LexUriServ/LexUriServ.do?uri=OJ:L:2008:177:0006:0016:EN:PDF
- Council Regulation (EC) No 207/2009 of 26 February 2009 on the Community trade mark (Codified version): eur-lex.europa.eu/LexUriServ/LexUriServ.do?uri=OJ:L:2009:078:0001:0042:en:PDF
- Regulation (EC) No 469/2009 of the European Parliament and of the Council of 6 May 2009 concerning the creation of a supplementary protection certificate for medicinal products (Codified version): eur-lex.europa.eu/LexUriServ/LexUriServ.do?uri=OJ:L:2009:152:0001:0010:en:PDF

Directives

- Council Directive 93/83/EEC of the European Parliament and of the Council of 27 September 1993 on the coordination of certain rules concerning copyright and rights related to copyright applicable to satellite broadcasting and cable retransmission: eur-lex.europa.eu/LexUriServ/LexUriServ.do?uri=OJ:L:1993:248:0015:0021:EN:PDF
- Directive 96/9/EC of the European Parliament and of the Council of 11 March 1996 on the legal protection of databases: eur-lex.europa.eu/LexUriServ/LexUriServ.do?uri=OJ:L:1996:077:0020:0028:EN:PDF
- Directive 98/44/EC of the European Parliament and of the Council of 6 July 1998 on the legal protection of biotechnological inventions: eur-lex.europa.eu/LexUriServ/LexUriServ.do?uri=OJ:L:1998:213:0013:0021:EN:PDF
- Directive 98/71/EC of 13 October 1998 of the European Parliament and of the

Council on the legal protection of designs: eur-lex.europa.eu/LexUriServ/LexUriServ.do?uri=CELEX:31998L0071:EN:HTML

- Directive 2000/31/EC of the European Parliament and of the Council 8 June 2000 on certain legal aspects of information society services, in particular electronic commerce, in the Internal Market ('Directive on Electronic Commerce'): eur-lex.europa.eu/LexUriServ/LexUriServ.do?uri=OJ:L:2000:178:0001:0001:EN:PDF
- Directive 2001/29/EC of the European Parliament and of the Council of 22 May 2001 on the harmonisation of certain aspects of copyright and related rights in the information society: eur-lex.europa.eu/LexUriServ/LexUriServ.do?uri=OJ:L:2001:167:0010:0019:EN:PDF
- Directive 2001/84/EC of the European Parliament and of the Council of 27 September 2001 on the resale right for the benefit of the author of an original work of art: eur-lex.europa.eu/LexUriServ/LexUriServ.do?uri=OJ:L:2001:272:0032:0036:EN:PDF
- Directive 2004/48/EC of the European Parliament and of the Council of 29 April 2004 on the enforcement of intellectual property rights: eur-lex.europa.eu/LexUriServ/LexUriServ.do?uri=OJ:L:2004:195:0016:0025:EN:PDF
- Directive 2005/29/EC of the European Parliament and of the Council of 11 May 2005 concerning unfair business-to-consumer commercial practices in the internal market and amending Council Directive 84/450/EEC, Directives 97/7/EC, 98/27/EC and 2002/65/EC of the European Parliament and of the Council and Regulation (EC) No 2006/2004 of the European Parliament and of the Council: eur-lex.europa.eu/LexUriServ/LexUriServ.do?uri=OJ:L:2005:149:0022:0039:EN:PDF
- Directive 2006/114/EC of the European Parliament and of the Council 12 December 2006 concerning misleading and comparative advertising (Codified version): eur-lex.europa.eu/LexUriServ/LexUriServ.do?uri=OJ:L:2006:376:0021:0027:EN:PDF
- Directive 2006/115/EC of the European Parliament and of the Council of 12 December 2006 on rental right and lending right and on certain rights related to copyright in the field of intellectual property (Codified version): eur-lex.europa.eu/LexUriServ/LexUriServ.do?uri=OJ:L:2006:376:0028:0035:EN:PDF
- Directive 2008/95/EC of the European Parliament and of the Council of 22 October 2008 to approximate the laws of the Member States relating to trade marks (Codified version): eur-lex.europa.eu/LexUriServ/LexUriServ.do?uri=OJ:L:2008:299:0025:0033:en:PDF
- Directive 2009/24/EC of the European Parliament and of the Council of 23 April 2009 on the legal protection of computer programs (Codified version): eur-lex.europa.eu/LexUriServ/LexUriServ.do?uri=OJ:L:2009:111:0016:0022:EN:PDF
- Directive 2011/77/EU of the European Parliament and of the Council of 27 September 2011 amending Directive 2006/116/EC 2006 on the term of protection of copyright and certain related rights: eur-lex.europa.eu/LexUriServ/LexUriServ.do?uri=OJ:L:2011:265:0001:0005:EN:PDF
- Directive 2012/28/EU of the European Parliament and of the Council of 25 October 2012 on certain permitted uses of orphan works: eur-lex.europa.eu/LexUriServ/LexUriServ.do?uri=OJ:L:2012:299:0005:0012:EN:PDF

Offices, organisations and institutions

Association of European Performers' Organisations: bie-paris.org
American Law Institute: ali.org
CLIP (International Max-Planck Group on Conflicts of Law in Intellectual Property): cl-ip.eu

CELAS: celas.eu
Community Plant Variety Office: cpvo.eu
Council of Europe: coe.int
Eidgenössisches Justiz- und Polizeidepartement (Switzerland): ejpd.admin.ch
Electronic Frontier Foundation: w2.eff.org/patent/wp.php
European Court of Human Rights: echr.coe.int
European Patent Office: epo.org
International Chamber of Commerce: iccwbo.org
International Union for the Protection of New Varieties of Plants (UPOV): upov.org
Internet Corporation for Assigned Names and Numbers: icann.org
Office for Harmonization in the Internal Market (OHIM; Spanish: OAMI): oami.europa.eu
Organisation for Economic Cooperation and Development (OECD): oecd.org
World Intellectual Property Organization (WIPO): wipo.org
World Trade Organization (WTO): wto.org

Texts of international conventions and declarations (selected)

Agreement on Trade Related Aspects of Intellectual Property Rights (TRIPS): wto.org/english/docs_e/legal_e/27-trips.pdf
Berne Convention for the Protection of Literary and Artistic Works: wipo.int/treaties/en/ip/berne/trtdocs_wo001.html
Convention on Biological Diversity: cbd.int/convention/text
(European) Convention for the Protection of Human Rights and Fundamental Freedoms: conventions.coe.int/Treaty/en/Treaties/Html/005.htm
London Agreement (translation arrangements for European Patents): epo.org/law-practice/legal-Protexts/london-agreement.html
Madrid Agreement: see Protocol Relating to the Madrid Agreement
Paris Convention on the Protection of Industrial Property: wipo.int/treaties/en/ip/paris/trtdocs_wo020.html
Patent Cooperation Treaty: www.wipo.int/treaties/en/registration/pct/
Protocol Relating to the Madrid Agreement Concerning the International Registration of Marks: wipo.int/treaties/en/registration/madrid_protocol/
UNESCO Universal Declaration on Cultural Diversity: portal.unesco.org/en/ev.php-URL_ID=13179&URL_DO=DO_TOPIC&URL_SECTION=20 1.html
UN Framework Convention on Climate Change: unfccc.int/2860.php
Universal Declaration of Human Rights: un.org/en/documents/udhr
Vienna Convention on the Law of Treaties (VCLT): untreaty.un.org/ilc/texts/instruments/english/conventions/1_1_1969.pdf
WIPO Copyright Treaty (WCT): wipo.int/treaties/en/ip/wct/trtdocs_wo033.html
7WIPO Performances and Phonograms Treaty (WPPT): wipo.int/treaties/en/ip/wppt/
(Other international IP treaties administered by WIPO to be found at wipo.int/treaties/en/)

Miscellaneous

European Copyright Code: copyrightcode.eu
Fordham University (Law) Publications: law.fordham.edu/publications
Frank Schechter, The Rational Basis of Trademark Law: 40 Harv. L Rev. 813 (1926–27).
Hargreaves Report: ipo.gov.uk/ipreview-finalreport

MPI – Statements of the Institute regarding (diverse) legislative proposals: ip.mpg.de/en/pub/publications/opinions.cfm

MPI – Study on the Overall Functioning of the European Trade Mark System: ec.europa.eu/internal_market/indprop/docs/tm/20110308_allensbach-study_en.pdf

Opinion of European Academics on ACTA: iri.uni-hannover.de/acta-1668.html
jipitec.eu/issues/jipitec-2-1-2011/2965/JIPITEC_ACTA.pdf

Washington Declaration on Intellectual Property and the Public Interest:
infojustice.org/washington-declaration

Index